# TITLE 11—APPENDIX

# FEDERAL RULES OF BANKRUPTCY PROCEDURE AND OFFICIAL BANKRUPTCY FORMS

*(Effective August 1, 1983, as amended to February 1, 2010)*

HISTORICAL NOTE

The Federal Rules of Bankruptcy Procedure were adopted by order of the Supreme Court on Apr. 25, 1983, transmitted to Congress by the Chief Justice on the same day, and became effective Aug. 1, 1983.

The Rules have been amended Aug. 30, 1983, Pub. L. 98–91, §2(a), 97 Stat. 607, eff. Aug. 1, 1983; July 10, 1984, Pub. L. 98–353, title III, §321, 98 Stat. 357; Apr. 29, 1985, eff. Aug. 1, 1985; Mar. 30, 1987, eff. Aug. 1, 1987; Apr. 25, 1989, eff. Aug. 1, 1989; Apr. 30, 1991, eff. Aug. 1, 1991; Apr. 22, 1993, eff. Aug. 1, 1993; Apr. 29, 1994, eff. Aug. 1, 1994; Oct. 22, 1994, Pub. L. 103–394, title I, §114, 108 Stat. 4118; Apr. 27, 1995, eff. Dec. 1, 1995; Apr. 23, 1996, eff. Dec. 1, 1996; Apr. 11, 1997, eff. Dec. 1, 1997; Apr. 26, 1999, eff. Dec. 1, 1999; Apr. 17, 2000, eff. Dec. 1, 2000; Apr. 23, 2001, eff. Dec. 1, 2001; Apr. 29, 2002, eff. Dec. 1, 2002; Mar. 27, 2003, eff. Dec. 1, 2003; Apr. 26, 2004, eff. Dec. 1, 2004; Apr. 25, 2005, eff. Dec. 1, 2005; Apr. 12, 2006, eff. Dec. 1, 2006; Apr. 30, 2007, eff. Dec. 1, 2007; Apr. 23, 2008, eff. Dec. 1, 2008; Mar. 26, 2009, eff. Dec. 1, 2009.



BANKRUPTCY RULES

# Title 11A, United States Code

## Federal Rules

Plus

## Bankruptcy Procedure

with

## Official Bankruptcy Forms

Iron Press Publishing

| Form | |
|---|---|
| 13. | Order Approving Disclosure Statement and Fixing Time for Filing Acceptances or Rejections of Plan, Combined with Notice Thereof. |
| 14. | Class *[ ]* Ballot for Accepting or Rejecting Plan of Reorganization. |
| 15. | Order Confirming Plan. |
| 16A. | Caption (Full). |
| 16B. | Caption (Short Title). |
| 16C. | Caption of Complaint in Adversary Proceeding Filed by a Debtor. [Abrogated] |
| 16D. | Caption for Use in Adversary Proceeding. |
| 17. | Notice of Appeal. |
| 18. | Discharge of Debtor. |
| 19. | Declaration and Signature of Non-Attorney Bankruptcy Petition Preparer (*See* 11 U.S.C. §110). |
| [19A. | Abrogated.] |
| [19B. | Abrogated.] |
| 20A. | Notice of [Motion to ] [Objection to ]. |
| 20B. | Notice of Objection to Claim. |
| 21. | Statement of Social Security Number. |
| 22A. | Chapter 7 Statement of Current Monthly Income and Means-Test Calculation. |
| 22B. | Chapter 11 Statement of Current Monthly Income. |
| 22C. | Chapter 13 Statement of Current Monthly Income and Calculation of Commitment Period and Disposable Income. |
| 23. | Debtor's Certification of Completion of Postpetition Instructional Course Concerning Personal Financial Management. |
| 24. | Certification to Court of Appeals by All Parties. |
| 25A. | Plan of Reorganization in Small Business Case under Chapter 11. |
| 25B. | Disclosure Statement in Small Business Case under Chapter 11. |
| 25C. | Small Business Monthly Operating Report. |
| 26. | Periodic Report Regarding Value, Operations and Profitability of Entities in Which the Debtor's Estate Holds a Substantial or Controlling Interest. |
| 27. | Reaffirmation Agreement Cover Sheet. |

## BANKRUPTCY RULES

EFFECTIVE DATE; APPLICATION; SUPERSEDURE OF PRIOR RULES; TRANSMISSION TO CONGRESS

Sections 2 to 4 of the Order of the Supreme Court, dated Apr. 25, 1983, provided:

"2. That the aforementioned Bankruptcy Rules shall take effect on August 1, 1983, and shall be applicable to proceedings then pending, except to the extent that in the opinion of the court their application in a pending proceeding would not be feasible or would work injustice, in which event the former procedure applies.

"3. That the Bankruptcy Rules, heretofore prescribed by this Court, be, and they hereby are, superseded by the new rules, effective August 1, 1983.

"4. That the Chief Justice be, and he hereby is, authorized to transmit these new Bankruptcy Rules to the Congress in accordance with the provisions of Section 2075 of Title 28, United States Code."

### Rule 1001. Scope of Rules and Forms; Short Title

The Bankruptcy Rules and Forms govern procedure in cases under title 11 of the United States Code. The rules shall be cited as the Federal Rules of Bankruptcy Procedure and the forms as the Official Bankruptcy Forms. These rules shall be construed to secure the just, speedy, and inexpensive determination of every case and proceeding.

(As amended Mar. 30, 1987, eff. Aug. 1, 1987; Apr. 30, 1991, eff. Aug. 1, 1991.)

NOTES OF ADVISORY COMMITTEE ON RULES—1983

Section 247 of Public Law 95–598, 92 Stat. 2549 amended 28 U.S.C. §2075 by omitting the last sentence. The effect of the amendment is to require that procedural rules promulgated pursuant to 28 U.S.C. §2075 be consistent with the bankruptcy statute, both titles 11 and 28 U.S.C. Thus, although Rule 1001 sets forth the scope of the bankruptcy rules and forms, any procedural matters contained in title 11 or 28 U.S.C. with respect to cases filed under 11 U.S.C. would control. See 1 Collier, *Bankruptcy* ¶3.04 [2][c] (15th ed. 1980).

28 U.S.C. §151 establishes a United States Bankruptcy Court in each district as an adjunct to the district court. This provision does not, however, become effective until April 1, 1984. Public Law 95–598, §402(b). From October 1, 1979 through March 31, 1984, the courts of bankruptcy as defined in §1(10) of the Bankruptcy Act, and created in §2a of that Act continue to be the courts of bankruptcy. Public Law 95–598, §404(a). From their effective date these rules and forms are to be applicable in cases filed under chapters 7, 9, 11 and 13 of title 11 regardless of whether the court is established by the Bankruptcy Act or by 28 U.S.C. §151. Rule 9001 contains a broad and general definition of "bankruptcy court," "court" and "United States Bankruptcy Court" for this purpose.

"Bankruptcy Code" or "Code" as used in these rules means title 11 of the United States Code, the codification of the bankruptcy law. Public Law 95–598, §101. See Rule 9001.

"Bankruptcy Act" as used in the notes to these rules means the Bankruptcy Act of 1898 as amended which was repealed by §401(a) of Public Law 95–598.

These rules apply to all cases filed under the Code except as otherwise specifically stated.

The final sentence of the rule is derived from former Bankruptcy Rule 903. The objective of "expeditious and economical administration" of cases under the Code has frequently been recognized by the courts to be "a chief purpose of the bankruptcy laws." See *Katchen v. Landy*, 382 U.S. 323, 328 (1966); *Bailey v. Glover*, 88 U.S. (21 Wall.) 342, 346–47 (1874); *Ex parte Christy*, 44 U.S. (3 How.) 292, 312–14, 320–22 (1845). The rule also incorporates the wholesome mandate of the last sentence of Rule 1 of the Federal Rules of Civil Procedure. 2 Moore, *Federal Practice* ¶1.13 (2d ed. 1980); 4 Wright & Miller, *Federal Practice and Procedure-Civil* §1029 (1969).

NOTES OF ADVISORY COMMITTEE ON RULES—1987 AMENDMENT

Title I of the Bankruptcy Amendments and Federal Judgeship Act of 1984, Pub. L. No. 98-353, 98 Stat. 333 (hereinafter the 1984 amendments), created a new bankruptcy judicial system in which the role of the district court was substantially increased. 28 U.S.C. §1334 confers on the United States district courts original and exclusive jurisdiction over all cases under title 11 of the United States Code and original but not exclusive jurisdiction over civil proceedings arising under title 11 and civil proceedings arising in or related to a case under title 11.

Pursuant to 28 U.S.C. §157(a) the district court may but need not refer cases and proceedings within the district court's jurisdiction to the bankruptcy judges for the district. Judgments or orders of the bankruptcy judges entered pursuant to 28 U.S.C. §157(b)(1) and (c)(2) are subject to appellate review by the district courts or bankruptcy appellate panels under 28 U.S.C. §158(a).

Rule 81(a)(1) F.R.Civ.P. provides that the civil rules do not apply to proceedings in bankruptcy, except as they may be made applicable by rules promulgated by the Supreme Court, *e.g.*, Part VII of these rules. This amended Bankruptcy Rule 1001 makes the Bankruptcy Rules applicable to cases and proceedings under title 11, whether before the district judges or the bankruptcy judges of the district.

NOTES OF ADVISORY COMMITTEE ON RULES—1991 AMENDMENT

The citation to these rules is amended to conform to the citation form of the Federal Rules of Civil Procedure, Federal Rules of Appellate Procedure, and Federal Rules of Criminal Procedure.

## PART I—COMMENCEMENT OF CASE; PROCEEDINGS RELATING TO PETITION AND ORDER FOR RELIEF

### Rule 1002. Commencement of Case

(a) PETITION. A petition commencing a case under the Code shall be filed with the clerk.

(b) TRANSMISSION TO UNITED STATES TRUSTEE. The clerk shall forthwith transmit to the United States trustee a copy of the petition filed pursuant to subdivision (a) of this rule.

(As amended Mar. 30, 1987, eff. Aug. 1, 1987; Apr. 30, 1991, eff. Aug. 1, 1991.)

NOTES OF ADVISORY COMMITTEE ON RULES—1983

Under §§301–303 of the Code, a voluntary or involuntary case is commenced by filing a petition with the bankruptcy court. The voluntary petition may request relief under chapter 7, 9, 11, or 13 whereas an involuntary petition may be filed only under chapter 7 or 11. Section 109 of the Code specifies the types of debtors for whom the different forms of relief are available and §303(a) indicates the persons against whom involuntary petitions may be filed.

The rule in subdivision (a) is in harmony with the Code in that it requires the filing to be with the bankruptcy court.

The number of copies of the petition to be filed is specified in this rule but a local rule may require additional copies. This rule provides for filing sufficient copies for the court's files and for the trustee in a chapter 7 or 13 case.

Official Form No. 1 may be used to seek relief voluntarily under any of the chapters. Only the original need be signed and verified, but the copies must be conformed to the original. See Rules 1008 and 9011(c). As provided in §362(a) of the Code, the filing of a petition acts as a stay of certain acts and proceedings against the debtor, property of the debtor, and property of the estate.

NOTES OF ADVISORY COMMITTEE ON RULES—1987 AMENDMENT

Rules 1002(a), governing a voluntary petition, 1003(a), governing an involuntary petition, and 1003(e), governing a petition in a case ancillary to a foreign proceeding, are combined into this Rule 1002. If a bankruptcy clerk has been appointed for the district, the petition is filed with the bankruptcy clerk. Otherwise, the petition is filed with the clerk of the district court.

The elimination of the reference to the Official Forms of the petition is not intended to change the practice. Rule 9009 provides that the Official Forms "shall be observed and used" in cases and proceedings under the Code.

*Subdivision (b)* which provided for the distribution of copies of the petition to agencies of the United States has been deleted. Some of these agencies no longer wish to receive copies of the petition, while others not included in subdivision (b) have now requested copies. The Director of the Administrative Office will determine on an ongoing basis which government agencies will be provided a copy of the petition.

The number of copies of a petition that must be filed is a matter for local rule.

NOTES OF ADVISORY COMMITTEE ON RULES—1991 AMENDMENT

*Subdivision (b)* is derived from Rule X-1002(a). The duties of the United States trustee pursuant to the Code and 28 U.S.C. §586(a) require that the United States trustee be apprised of the commencement of every case under chapters 7, 11, 12 and 13 and this is most easily accomplished by providing that office with a copy of the petition. Although 28 U.S.C. §586(a) does not give the United States trustee an administrative role in chapter 9 cases, §1102 of the Code requires the United States trustee to appoint committees and that section is applicable in chapter 9 cases pursuant to §901(a). It is therefore appropriate that the United States trustee receive a copy of every chapter 9 petition.

Notwithstanding subdivision (b), pursuant to Rule 5005(b)(3), the clerk is not required to transmit a copy of the petition to the United States trustee if the United States trustee requests that it not be transmitted. Many rules require the clerk to transmit a certain document to the United States trustee, but Rule 5005(b)(3) relieves the clerk of that duty under this or any other rule if the United States trustee requests that such document not be transmitted.

### Rule 1003. Involuntary Petition

(a) TRANSFEROR OR TRANSFEREE OF CLAIM. A transferor or transferee of a claim shall annex to the original and each copy of the petition a copy of all documents evidencing the transfer, whether transferred unconditionally, for security, or otherwise, and a signed statement that the claim was not transferred for the purpose of commencing the case and setting forth the consideration for and terms of the transfer. An entity that has transferred or acquired a claim for the purpose of commencing a case for liquidation under chapter 7 or for reorganization under chapter 11 shall not be a qualified petitioner.

(b) JOINDER OF PETITIONERS AFTER FILING. If the answer to an involuntary petition filed by fewer than three creditors avers the existence of 12 or more creditors, the debtor shall file with the answer a list of all creditors with their addresses, a brief statement of the nature of their claims, and the amounts thereof. If it appears that there are 12 or more creditors as provided in §303(b) of the Code, the court shall afford a reasonable opportunity for other creditors to join in the petition before a hearing is held thereon.

(As amended Mar. 30, 1987, eff. Aug. 1, 1987.)

NOTES OF ADVISORY COMMITTEE ON RULES

*Subdivision (a).* Official Form No. 11 (Involuntary Case: Creditors' Petition), is prescribed for use by petitioning creditors to have a debtor's assets liquidated under chapter 7 of the Code or the business reorganized under chapter 11. It contains the required allegations as specified in §303(b) of the Code. Official Form 12 is prescribed for use by fewer than all the general partners to obtain relief for the partnership as governed by §303(b)(3) of the Code and Rule 1004(b).

Although the number of copies to be filed is specified in Rule 1002, a local rule may require additional copies.

Only the original need be signed and verified, but the copies must be conformed to the original. See Rules 1008 and 9011(c). The petition must be filed with the bankruptcy court. This provision implements §303(b) which provides that an involuntary case is commenced by filing the petition with the court.

As provided in §362 of the Code, the filing of the petition acts as a stay of certain acts and proceedings against the debtor, the debtor's property and property of the estate.

*Subdivision (c)* retains the explicitness of former Bankruptcy Rule 104(d) that a transfer of a claim for the purpose of commencing a case under the Code is a ground for disqualification of a party to the transfer as a petitioner.

Section 303(b) "is not intended to overrule Bankruptcy Rule 104(d), which places certain restrictions on the transfer of claims for the purpose of commencing an involuntary case." House Report No. 95–595, 95th Cong., 1st Sess. (1977) 322; Senate Report No. 95–989, 95th Cong., 2d Sess. (1978) 33.

The subdivision requires disclosure of any transfer of the petitioner's claim as well as a transfer to the petitioner and applies to transfers for security as well as unconditional transfers, *Cf. In re 69th & Crandon Bldg. Corp.*, 97 F.2d 392, 395 (7th Cir.), cert. denied, 305 U.S. 629 (1938), recognizing the right of a creditor to sign a bankruptcy petition notwithstanding a prior assignment of his claim for the purpose of security. This rule does not, however, qualify the requirement of §303(b)(1) that a petitioning creditor must have a claim not contingent as to liability.

*Subdivision (d).* Section 303(c) of the Code permits a creditor to join in the petition at any time before the case is dismissed or relief is ordered. While this rule does not require the court to give all creditors notice of the petition, the list of creditors filed by the debtor affords a petitioner the information needed to enable him to give notice for the purpose of obtaining the copetitioners required to make the petition sufficient. After a reasonable opportunity has been afforded other creditors to join in an involuntary petition, the hearing on the petition should be held without further delay.

*Subdivision (e).* This subdivision implements §304. A petition for relief under §304 may only be filed by a foreign representative who is defined in §101(20) generally as a representative of an estate in a foreign proceeding. The term "foreign proceeding" is defined in §101(19).

Section 304(b) permits a petition filed thereunder to be contested by a party in interest. Subdivision (e)(2) therefore requires that the summons and petition be served on any person against whom the relief permitted by §304(b) is sought as well as on any other party the court may direct.

The rules applicable to the procedure when an involuntary petition is filed are made applicable generally when a case ancillary to a foreign proceeding is commenced. These rules include Rule 1010 with respect to issuance and service of a summons, Rule 1011 concerning responsive pleadings and motions, and Rule 1018 which makes various rules in Part VII applicable in proceedings on contested petitions.

The venue for a case ancillary to a foreign proceeding is provided in 28 U.S.C. §1474.

NOTES OF ADVISORY COMMITTEE ON RULES—1987 AMENDMENT

The subject matter of subdivisions (a), (b), and (e) has been incorporated in Rules 1002, 1010, 1011, and 1018.

## Rule 1004. Involuntary Petition Against a Partnership

After filing of an involuntary petition under §303(b)(3) of the Code, (1) the petitioning partners or other petitioners shall promptly send to or serve on each general partner who is not a petitioner a copy of the petition; and (2) the clerk shall promptly issue a summons for service on each general partner who is not a petitioner. Rule 1010 applies to the form and service of the summons.

(As amended Apr. 29, 2002, eff. Dec. 1, 2002.)

NOTES OF ADVISORY COMMITTEE ON RULES—1983

This rule is adapted from former Bankruptcy Rule 105 and complements §§301 and 303(b)(3) of the Code.

*Subdivision (a)* specifies that while all general partners must consent to the filing of a voluntary petition, it is not necessary that they all execute the petition. It may be executed and filed on behalf of the partnership by fewer than all.

*Subdivision (b)* implements §303(b)(3) of the Code which provides that an involuntary petition may be filed by fewer than all the general partners or, when all the general partners are debtors, by a general partner, trustee of the partner or creditors of the partnership. Rule 1010, which governs service of a petition and summons in an involuntary case, specifies the time and mode of service on the partnership. When a petition is filed against a partnership under §303(b)(3), this rule requires an additional service on the nonfiling general partners. It is the purpose of this subdivision to protect the interests of the nonpetitioning partners and the partnership.

COMMITTEE NOTES ON RULES—2002 AMENDMENT

Section 303(b)(3)(A) of the Code provides that fewer than all of the general partners in a partnership may commence an involuntary case against the partnership. There is no counterpart provision in the Code setting out the manner in which a partnership commences a voluntary case. The Supreme Court has held in the corporate context that applicable nonbankruptcy law determines whether authority exists for a particular debtor to commence a bankruptcy case. *See Price v. Gurney*, 324 U.S. 100 (1945). The lower courts have followed this rule in the partnership context as well. *See, e.g., Jolly v. Pittore*, 170 B.R. 793 (S.D.N.Y. 1994); *Union Planters National Bank v. Hunters Horn Associates*, 158 B.R. 729 (Bankr. M.D. Tenn. 1993); *In re Channel 64 Joint Venture*, 61 B.R. 255 (Bankr. S.D. Oh. 1986). Rule 1004(a) could be construed as requiring the consent of all of the general partners to the filing of a voluntary petition, even if fewer than all of the general partners would have the authority under applicable nonbankruptcy law to commence a bankruptcy case for the partnership. Since this is a matter of substantive law beyond the scope of these rules, Rule 1004(a) is deleted as is the designation of subdivision (b).

The rule is retitled to reflect that it applies only to involuntary petitions filed against partnerships.

*Changes Made After Publication and Comments.* No changes since publication.

## Rule 1004.1. Petition for an Infant or Incompetent Person

If an infant or incompetent person has a representative, including a general guardian, committee, conservator, or similar fiduciary, the representative may file a voluntary petition on behalf of the infant or incompetent person. An infant or incompetent person who does not have a duly appointed representative may file a voluntary petition by next friend or guardian ad litem. The court shall appoint a guardian ad litem for an infant or incompetent person who is a debtor and is not otherwise represented or shall make any other order to protect the infant or incompetent debtor.

(Added Apr. 29, 2002, eff. Dec. 1, 2002.)

COMMITTEE NOTES ON RULES—2002

This rule is derived from Rule 17(c) F.R. Civ. P. It does not address the commencement of a case filed on behalf of a missing person. *See, e.g., In re King*, 234 B.R. 515 (Bankr. D.N.M. 1999)

*Changes Made After Publication and Comments* changes were made.

## Rule 1005. Caption of Petition

The caption of a petition commencing a case under the Code shall contain the name of the court, the title of the case, and the docket number. The title of the case shall include the following information about the debtor: name, employer identification number, last four digits of the social-security number or individual debtor's taxpayer-identification number, any other federal taxpayer-identification number, and all other names used within eight years before filing the petition. If the petition is not filed by the debtor, it shall include all names used by the debtor which are known to the petitioners.

(As amended Mar. 30, 1987, eff. Aug. 1, 1987; Mar. 27, 2003, eff. Dec. 1, 2003; Apr. 23, 2008, eff. Dec. 1, 2008.)

NOTES OF ADVISORY COMMITTEE ON RULES—1983

The title of the case should include all names used by the debtor, such as trade names, former married names and maiden name. See also Official Form No. 1 and the Advisory Committee Note to that Form. Additional names of the debtor are also required to appear in the caption of each notice to creditors. See Rule 2002(m).

COMMITTEE NOTES ON RULES—2003 AMENDMENT

The rule is amended to implement the Judicial Conference policy to limit the disclosure of a party's social security number and similar identifiers. Under the rule, as amended, only the last four digits of the debtor's social security number need be disclosed. Publication of the employer identification number does not present the same identity theft or privacy protection issues. Therefore, the caption must include the full employer identification number.

Debtors must submit with the petition a statement setting out their social security numbers. This enables the clerk to include the full social security number on the notice of the section 341 meeting of creditors, but the statement itself is not submitted in the case or maintained in the case file.

*Changes Made After Publication and Comments.* The rule was changed only slightly after publication. The rule was changed to make clear that only the debtor's social security number is truncated to the final four digits, but other numerical identifiers must be set out in full. The rule also was amended to include a requirement that a debtor list other federal taxpayer identification numbers that may be in use.

COMMITTEE NOTES ON RULES—2008 AMENDMENT

The rule is amended to require the disclosure of all names used by the debtor in the past eight years. Section 727(a)(8) was amended in 2005 to extend the time between chapter 7 discharges from six to eight years, and the rule is amended to implement that change. The rule also is amended to require the disclosure of the last four digits of an individual debtor's taxpayer-identification number. This truncation of the number applies only to individual debtors. This is consistent with the requirements of Rule 9037.

*Changes Made After Publication.* No changes were made after publication.

## Rule 1006. Filing Fee

(a) GENERAL REQUIREMENT. Every petition shall be accompanied by the filing fee except as provided in subdivisions (b) and (c) of this rule. For the purpose of this rule, "filing fee" means the filing fee prescribed by 28 U.S.C. §1930(a)(1)–(a)(5) and any other fee prescribed by the Judicial Conference of the United States under 28 U.S.C. §1930(b) that is payable to the clerk upon the commencement of a case under the Code.

(b) PAYMENT OF FILING FEE IN INSTALLMENTS.

(1) *Application to Pay Filing Fee in Installments.* A voluntary petition by an individual shall be accepted for filing if accompanied by the debtor's signed application, prepared as prescribed by the appropriate Official Form, stating that the debtor is unable to pay the filing fee except in installments.

(2) *Action on Application.* Prior to the meeting of creditors, the court may order the filing fee paid to the clerk or grant leave to pay in installments and fix the number, amount and dates of payment. The number of installments shall not exceed four, and the final installment shall be payable not later than 120 days after filing the petition. For cause shown, the court may extend the time of any installment, provided the last installment is paid not later than 180 days after filing the petition.

(3) *Postponement of Attorney's Fees.* All installments of the filing fee must be paid in full before the debtor or chapter 13 trustee may make further payments to an attorney or any other person who renders services to the debtor in connection with the case.

(c) WAIVER OF FILING FEE. A voluntary chapter 7 petition filed by an individual shall be accepted for filing if accompanied by the debtor's application requesting a waiver under 28 U.S.C. §1930(f), prepared as prescribed by the appropriate Official Form.

(As amended Mar. 30, 1987, eff. Aug. 1, 1987; Apr. 23, 1996, eff. Dec. 1, 1996; Apr. 23, 2008, eff. Dec. 1, 2008.)

NOTES OF ADVISORY COMMITTEE ON RULES—1983

28 U.S.C. §1930 specifies the filing fees for petitions under chapters 7, 9, 11 and 13 of the Code. It also permits the payment in installments by individual debtors.

*Subdivision (b)* is adapted from former Bankruptcy Rule 107. The administrative cost of installments in excess of four is disproportionate to the benefits conferred. Prolonging the period beyond 180 days after the commencement of the case causes undesirable delays in administration. Paragraph (2) accordingly continues the imposition of a maximum of four on the number of installments and retains the maximum period of installment payments allowable on an original application at 120 days. Only in extraordinary cases should it be necessary to give an applicant an extension beyond the four months. The requirement of paragraph (3) that filing fees be paid in full before the debtor may pay an attorney for services in connection with the case codifies the rule declared in *In re Latham*, 271 Fed. 538 (N.D.N.Y. 1921), and *In re Darr*, 232 Fed. 415 (N.D. Cal. 1916).

NOTES OF ADVISORY COMMITTEE ON RULES AMENDMENT

*Subdivision (b)(3)* is expanded to prohibit payments by the debtor or the chapter 13 trustee not only to attorneys but to any person who renders services to the debtor in connection with the case.

NOTES OF ADVISORY COMMITTEE ON RULES AMENDMENT

The Judicial Conference prescribes miscellaneous fees pursuant to 28 U.S.C. §1930(b). In 1992, a $30 miscellaneous administrative fee was prescribed for all chapter 7 and chapter 13 cases. The Judicial Conference fee schedule was amended in 1993 to provide that an individual debtor may pay this fee in installments.

*Subdivision (a)* of this rule is amended to clarify that every petition must be accompanied by any fee prescribed under 28 U.S.C. §1930(b) that is required to be paid when a petition is filed, as well as the filing fee prescribed by 28 U.S.C. §1930(a). By defining "filing fee" to include Judicial Conference fees, the procedures set forth in subdivision (b) for paying the filing fee in installments will also apply with respect to any Judicial Conference fee required to be paid at the commencement of the case.

*GAP Report on Rule 1006.* No changes since publication, except for a stylistic change in subdivision (a).

COMMITTEE NOTES ON RULES—2008 AMENDMENT

Subdivision (a) is amended to include a reference to new subdivision (c), which deals with fee waivers under 28 U.S.C. §1930(f), which was added in 2005.

Subdivision (b)(1) is amended to delete the sentence requiring a disclosure that the debtor has not paid an attorney or other person in connection with the case. Inability to pay the filing fee in installments is one of the requirements for a fee waiver under the 2005 revisions to 28 U.S.C. §1930(f). If the attorney payment prohibition were retained, payment of an attorney's fee would render many debtors ineligible for installment payments and thus enhance their eligibility for the fee waiver. The deletion of this prohibition from the rule, which was not statutorily required, ensures that debtors who have the financial ability to pay the fee in installments will do so rather than request a waiver.

Subdivision (b)(3) is amended in conformance with the changes to subdivision (b)(1) to reflect the 2005 amendments. The change is meant to clarify that subdivision (b)(3) refers to payments made after the debtor has filed the bankruptcy case and after the debtor has received permission to pay the fee in installments. Otherwise, the subdivision may conflict with the intent and effect of the amendments to subdivision (b)(1).

*Changes Made After Publication.* No changes were made after publication.

## Rule 1007. Lists, Schedules, Statements, and Other Documents; Time Limits

(a) CORPORATE OWNERSHIP STATEMENT, LIST OF CREDITORS AND EQUITY SECURITY HOLDERS, AND OTHER LISTS.

(1) *Voluntary Case.* In a voluntary case, the debtor shall file with the petition a list containing the name and address of each entity included or to be included on Schedules D, E, F, G, and H as prescribed by the Official Forms. If the debtor is a corporation, other than a governmental unit, the debtor shall file with the petition a corporate ownership statement containing the information described in Rule 7007.1. The debtor shall file a supplemental statement promptly upon any change in circumstances that renders the corporate ownership statement inaccurate.

(2) *Involuntary Case.* In an involuntary case, the debtor shall file within 14 days after entry of the order for relief, a list containing the name and address of each entity included or to be included on Schedules D, E, F, G, and H as prescribed by the Official Forms.

(3) *Equity Security Holders.* In a chapter 11 reorganization case, unless the court orders otherwise, the debtor shall file within 14 days after entry of the order for relief a list of the debtor's equity security holders of each class showing the number and kind of interests registered in the name of each holder, and the last known address or place of business of each holder.

(4) *Chapter 15 Case.* In addition to the documents required under §1515 of the Code, a foreign representative filing a petition for recognition under chapter 15 shall file with the petition: (A) a corporate ownership statement containing the information described in Rule 7007.1; and (B) unless the court orders otherwise, a list containing the names and addresses of all persons or bodies authorized to administer foreign proceedings of the debtor, all parties to litigation pending in the United States in which the debtor is a party at the time of the filing of the petition, and all entities against whom provisional relief is being sought under §1519 of the Code.

(5) *Extension of Time.* Any extension of time for the filing of the lists required by this subdivision may be granted only on motion for cause shown and on notice to the United States trustee and to any trustee, committee elected under §705 or appointed under §1102 of the Code, or other party as the court may direct.

(b) SCHEDULES, STATEMENTS, AND OTHER DOCUMENTS REQUIRED.

(1) Except in a chapter 9 municipality case, the debtor, unless the court orders otherwise, shall file the following schedules, statements, and other documents, prepared as prescribed by the appropriate Official Forms, if any:

(A) schedules of assets and liabilities;

(B) a schedule of current income and expenditures;

(C) a schedule of executory contracts and unexpired leases;

(D) a statement of financial affairs;

(E) copies of all payment advices or other evidence of payment, if any, received by the debtor from an employer within 60 days before the filing of the petition, with redaction of all but the last four digits of the debtor's social-security number or individual taxpayer-identification number; and

(F) a record of any interest that the debtor has in an account or program of the type specified in §521(c) of the Code.

(2) An individual debtor in a chapter 7 case shall file a statement of intention as required by §521(a) of the Code, prepared as prescribed by the appropriate Official Form. A copy of the statement of intention shall be served on the trustee and the creditors named in the statement on or before the filing of the statement.

(3) Unless the United States trustee has determined that the credit counseling requirement of §109(h) does not apply in the district, an individual debtor must file a statement of compliance with the credit counseling requirement, prepared as prescribed by the appropriate Official Form which must include one of the following:

(A) an attached certificate and debt repayment plan, if any, required by §521(b);

(B) a statement that the debtor has received the credit counseling briefing required by §109(h)(1) but does not have the certificate required by §521(b);

(C) a certification under §109(h)(3); or

(D) a request for a determination by the court under §109(h)(4).

(4) Unless §707(b)(2)(D) applies, an individual debtor in a chapter 7 case shall file a statement of current monthly income prepared as prescribed by the appropriate Official Form, and, if the current monthly income exceeds the median family income for the applicable state and household size, the information, including calculations, required by §707(b), prepared as prescribed by the appropriate Official Form.

(5) An individual debtor in a chapter 11 case shall file a statement of current monthly in-

come, prepared as prescribed by the appropriate Official Form.

(6) A debtor in a chapter 13 case shall file a statement of current monthly income, prepared as prescribed by the appropriate Official Form, and, if the current monthly income exceeds the median family income for the applicable state and household size, a calculation of disposable income made in accordance with §1325(b)(3), prepared as prescribed by the appropriate Official Form.

(7) An individual debtor in a chapter 7 or chapter 13 case shall file a statement of completion of a course concerning personal financial management, prepared as prescribed by the appropriate Official Form. An individual debtor shall file the statement in a chapter 11 case in which §1141(d)(3) applies.

(8) If an individual debtor in a chapter 11, 12, or 13 case has claimed an exemption under §522(b)(3)(A) in property of the kind described in §522(p)(1) with a value in excess of the amount set out in §522(q)(1), the debtor shall file a statement as to whether there is any proceeding pending in which the debtor may be found guilty of a felony of a kind described in §522(q)(1)(A) or found liable for a debt of the kind described in §522(q)(1)(B).

(c) TIME LIMITS. In a voluntary case, the schedules, statements, and other documents required by subdivision (b)(1), (4), (5), and (6) shall be filed with the petition or within 14 days thereafter, except as otherwise provided in subdivisions (d), (e), (f), and (h) of this rule. In an involuntary case, the list in subdivision (a)(2), and the schedules, statements, and other documents required by subdivision (b)(1) shall be filed by the debtor within 14 days of the entry of the order for relief. In a voluntary case, the documents required by paragraphs (A), (C), and (D) of subdivision (b)(3) shall be filed with the petition. Unless the court orders otherwise, a debtor who has filed a statement under subdivision (b)(3)(B), shall file the documents required by subdivision (b)(3)(A) within 14 days of the order for relief. In a chapter 7 case, the debtor shall file the statement required by subdivision (b)(7) within 45 days after the first date set for the meeting of creditors under §341 of the Code, and in a chapter 11 or 13 case no later than the date when the last payment was made by the debtor as required by the plan or the filing of a motion for a discharge under §1141(d)(5)(B) or §1328(b) of the Code. The court may, at any time and in its discretion, enlarge the time to file the statement required by subdivision (b)(7). The debtor shall file the statement required by subdivision (b)(8) no earlier than the date of the last payment made under the plan or the date of the filing of a motion for a discharge under §§1141(d)(5)(B),[1] 1228(b), or 1328(b) of the Code. Lists, schedules, statements, and other documents filed prior to the conversion of a case to another chapter shall be deemed filed in the converted case unless the court directs otherwise. Except as provided in §1116(3), any extension of time to file schedules, statements, and other documents required under this rule may be granted only on motion for cause shown and on notice to the United States trustee, any committee elected under §705 or appointed under §1102 of the Code, trustee, examiner, or other party as the court may direct. Notice of an extension shall be given to the United States trustee and to any committee, trustee, or other party as the court may direct.

(d) LIST OF 20 LARGEST CREDITORS IN CHAPTER 9 MUNICIPALITY CASE OR CHAPTER 11 REORGANIZATION CASE. In addition to the list required by subdivision (a) of this rule, a debtor in a chapter 9 municipality case or a debtor in a voluntary chapter 11 reorganization case shall file with the petition a list containing the name, address and claim of the creditors that hold the 20 largest unsecured claims, excluding insiders, as prescribed by the appropriate Official Form. In an involuntary chapter 11 reorganization case, such list shall be filed by the debtor within 2 days after entry of the order for relief under §303(h) of the Code.

(e) LIST IN CHAPTER 9 MUNICIPALITY CASES. The list required by subdivision (a) of this rule shall be filed by the debtor in a chapter 9 municipality case within such time as the court shall fix. If a proposed plan requires a revision of assessments so that the proportion of special assessments or special taxes to be assessed against some real property will be different from the proportion in effect at the date the petition is filed, the debtor shall also file a list showing the name and address of each known holder of title, legal or equitable, to real property adversely affected. On motion for cause shown, the court may modify the requirements of this subdivision and subdivision (a) of this rule.

(f) STATEMENT OF SOCIAL SECURITY NUMBER. An individual debtor shall submit a verified statement that sets out the debtor's social security number, or states that the debtor does not have a social security number. In a voluntary case, the debtor shall submit the statement with the petition. In an involuntary case, the debtor shall submit the statement within 14 days after the entry of the order for relief.

(g) PARTNERSHIP AND PARTNERS. The general partners of a debtor partnership shall prepare and file the list required under subdivision (a), schedules of the assets and liabilities, schedule of current income and expenditures, schedule of executory contracts and unexpired leases, and statement of financial affairs of the partnership. The court may order any general partner to file a statement of personal assets and liabilities within such time as the court may fix.

(h) INTERESTS ACQUIRED OR ARISING A TITION. If, as provided by §541(a)(5) of the Code, the debtor acquires or becomes entitled to acquire any interest in property, the debtor shall within 14 days after the information comes to the debtor's knowledge or within such further time the court may allow, file a supplemental schedule in the chapter 7 liquidation case, chapter 11 reorganization case, chapter 12 family farmer's debt adjustment case, or chapter 13 individual debt adjustment case. If any of the property required to be reported under this subdivision is claimed by the debtor as exempt, the debtor shall claim the exemptions in the supplemental schedule. The duty to file a supple-

[1] So in original. Probably should be only one section symbol.

mental schedule in accordance with this subdivision continues notwithstanding the closing of the case, except that the schedule need not be filed in a chapter 11, chapter 12, or chapter 13 case with respect to property acquired after entry of the order confirming a chapter 11 plan or discharging the debtor in a chapter 12 or chapter 13 case.

(i) DISCLOSURE OF LIST OF SECURITY HOLDERS. After notice and hearing and for cause shown, the court may direct an entity other than the debtor or trustee to disclose any list of security holders of the debtor in its possession or under its control, indicating the name, address and security held by any of them. The entity possessing this list may be required either to produce the list or a true copy thereof, or permit inspection or copying, or otherwise disclose the information contained on the list.

(j) IMPOUNDING OF LISTS. On motion of a party in interest and for cause shown the court may direct the impounding of the lists filed under this rule, and may refuse to permit inspection by any entity. The court may permit inspection or use of the lists, however, by any party in interest on terms prescribed by the court.

(k) PREPARATION OF LIST, SCHEDULES, OR STATEMENTS ON DEFAULT OF DEBTOR. If a list, schedule, or statement, other than a statement of intention, is not prepared and filed as required by this rule, the court may order the trustee, a petitioning creditor, committee, or other party to prepare and file any of these papers within a time fixed by the court. The court may approve reimbursement of the cost incurred in complying with such an order as an administrative expense.

(*l*) TRANSMISSION TO UNITED STATES TRUSTEE. The clerk shall forthwith transmit to the United States trustee a copy of every list, schedule, and statement filed pursuant to subdivision (a)(1), (a)(2), (b), (d), or (h) of this rule.

(m) INFANTS AND INCOMPETENT PERSONS. If the debtor knows that a person on the list of creditors or schedules is an infant or incompetent person, the debtor also shall include the name, address, and legal relationship of any person upon whom process would be served in an adversary proceeding against the infant or incompetent person in accordance with Rule 7004(b)(2).

(As amended Mar. 30, 1987, eff. Aug. 1, 1987; Apr. 30, 1991, eff. Aug. 1, 1991; Apr. 23, 1996, eff. Dec. 1, 1996; Apr. 23, 2001, eff. Dec. 1, 2001; Mar. 27, 2003, eff. Dec. 1, 2003; Apr. 25, 2005, eff. Dec. 1, 2005; Apr. 23, 2008, eff. Dec. 1, 2008; Mar. 26, 2009, eff. Dec. 1, 2009.)

NOTES OF ADVISORY COMMITTEE ON RULES—1983

This rule is an adaptation of former Rules 108, 8-106, 10-108 and 11-11. As specified in the rule, it is applicable in all types of cases filed under the Code.

*Subdivision (a)* requires at least a list of creditors with their names and addresses to be filed with the petition. This list is needed for notice of the meeting of creditors (Rule 2002) and notice of the order for relief (§342 of the Code). The list will also serve to meet the requirements of §521(1) of the Code. Subdivision (a) recognizes that it may be impossible to file the schedules required by §521(1) and subdivision (b) of the rule at the time the petition is filed but in order for the case to proceed expeditiously and efficiently it is necessary that the clerk have the names and addresses of creditors. It should be noted that subdivision (d) of the rule requires a special list of the 20 largest unsecured creditors in chapter 9 and 11 cases. That list is for the purpose of selecting a committee of unsecured creditors.

*Subdivision (b)* is derived from former Rule 11-11 and conforms with §521. This subdivision indicates the forms to be used. The court may dispense with the filing of schedules and the statement of affairs pursuant to §521.

*Subdivisions (c) and (f)* specify the time periods for filing the papers required by the rule as well as the number of copies. The provisions dealing with an involuntary case are derived from former Bankruptcy Rule 108. Under the Code, a chapter 11 case may be commenced by an involuntary petition (§303(a)), whereas under the Act, a Chapter XI case could have been commenced only by a voluntary petition. A motion for an extension of time to file the schedules and statements is required to be made on notice to parties, as the court may direct, including a creditors' committee if one has been appointed under §1102 of the Code and a trustee or examiner if one has been appointed pursuant to §1104 of the Code. Although written notice is preferable, it is not required by the rule; in proper circumstances the notice may be by telephone or otherwise.

*Subdivision (d)* is new and requires that a list of the 20 largest unsecured creditors, excluding insiders as defined in §101(25) of the Code, be filed with the petition. The court, pursuant to §1102 of the Code, is required to appoint a committee of unsecured creditors as soon as practicable after the order for relief. That committee generally is to consist of the seven largest unsecured creditors who are willing to serve. The list should, as indicated on Official Form No. 9, specify the nature and amount of the claim. It is important for the court to be aware of the different types of claims existing in the case and this form should supply such information.

*Subdivision (e)* applies only in chapter 9 municipality cases. It gives greater discretion to the court to determine the time for filing a list of creditors and any other matter related to the list. A list of creditors must at some point be filed since one is required by §924 of the Code. When the plan affects special assessments, the definitions in §902(2) and (3) for "special tax payer" and "special tax payer affected by the plan" become relevant.

*Subdivision (g)* is derived from former Rules 108(c) and 11-11. Nondebtor general partners are liable to the partnership's trustee for any deficiency in the partnership's estate to pay creditors in full as provided by §723 of the Code. Subdivision (g) authorizes the court to require a partner to file a statement of personal assets and liabilities to provide the trustee with the relevant information.

*Subdivision (h)* is derived from former Bankruptcy Rule 108(e) for chapter 7, 11 and 13 purposes. It implements the provisions in and language of §541(a)(5) of the Code.

*Subdivisions (i) and (j)* are adapted from §§165 and 166 of the Act and former Rule 10-108(b) and (c) without change in substance. The term "party in interest" is not defined in the Code or the rules, but reference may be made to §1109(b) of the Code. In the context of this subdivision, the term would include the debtor, the trustee, any indenture trustee, creditor, equity security holder or committee appointed pursuant to §1102 of the Code.

*Subdivision (k)* is derived from former Rules 108(d) and 10-108(a).

NOTES OF ADVISORY COMMITTEE ON RULES—1987 AMENDMENT

*Subdivisions (b), (c), and (g)* are amended to provide for the filing of a schedule of current income and current expenditures and the individual debtor's statement of intention. These documents are required by the 1984 amendments to §521 of the Code. Official Form No. 6A is prescribed for use by an individual debtor for filing a schedule of current income and current expenditures in a chapter 7 or chapter 11 case. Although a partnership or corporation is also required by §521(1) to file a schedule of current income and current expenditures, no Official Form is prescribed therefor.

The time for filing the statement of intention is governed by §521(2)(A). A copy of the statement of intention must be served on the trustee and the creditors named in the statement within the same time. The provisions of subdivision (c) governing the time for filing when a chapter 11 or chapter 13 case is converted to a chapter 7 case have been omitted from subdivision (c) as amended. Filing after conversion is now governed exclusively by Rule 1019.

*Subdivision (f)* has been abrogated. The number of copies of the documents required by this rule will be determined by local rule.

*Subdivision (h)* is amended to include a direct reference to §541(a)(5).

*Subdivision (k)* provides that the court may not order an entity other than the debtor to prepare and file the statement of intention.

NOTES OF ADVISORY COMMITTEE ON RULES—1991 AMENDMENT

References to Official Form numbers and to the Chapter 13 Statement are deleted and subdivision (b) is amended in anticipation of future revision and renumbering of the Official Forms. The debtor in a chapter 12 or chapter 13 case shall file the list, schedules and statements required in subdivisions (a)(1), (b)(1), and (h). It is expected that the information currently provided in the Chapter 13 Statement will be included in the schedules and statements as revised not later than the effective date of these rule amendments.

*Subdivisions (a)(4) and (c)* are amended to provide the United States trustee with notice of any motion to extend the time for the filing of any lists, schedules, or statements. Such notice enables the United States trustee to take appropriate steps to avoid undue delay in the administration of the case. See 28 U.S.C. §586(a)(3)(G). Subdivisions (a)(4) and (c) are amended further to provide notice to committees elected under §705 or appointed pursuant to §1102 of the Code. Committees of retired employees appointed pursuant to §1114 are not included.

The additions of references to unexpired leases in subdivisions (b)(1) and (g) indicate that the schedule requires the inclusion of unexpired leases as well as other executory contracts.

The words "with the court" in subdivisions (b)(1), (e), and (g) are deleted as unnecessary. See Rules 5005(a) and 9001(3).

*Subdivision (l)*, which is derived from Rule X–1002(a), provides the United States trustee with the information required to perform certain administrative duties such as the appointment of a committee of unsecured creditors. In a chapter 7 case, the United States trustee should be aware of the debtor's intention with respect to collateral that secures a consumer debt so that the United States trustee may monitor the progress of the case. Pursuant to §307 of the Code, the United States trustee has standing to raise, appear and be heard on issues and the lists, schedules and statements contain information that, when provided to the United States trustee, enable that office to participate effectively in the case. The United States trustee has standing to move to dismiss a chapter 7 or 13 case for failure to file timely the list, schedules or statement required by §521(1) of the Code. See §§707(a)(3) and 1307(c)(9). It is therefore necessary for the United States trustee to receive notice of any extension of time to file such documents. Upon request, the United States trustee also may receive from the trustee or debtor in possession a list of equity security holders.

NOTES OF ADVISORY COMMITTEE ON RULES—1996 AMENDMENT

*Subdivision (c)* is amended to provide that schedules and statements filed prior to the conversion of a case to another chapter shall be deemed filed in the converted case, whether or not the case was a chapter 7 case prior to conversion. This amendment is in recognition of the 1991 amendments to the Official Forms that abrogated the Chapter 13 Statement and made the same forms for schedules and statements applicable in all cases.

This subdivision also contains a technical correction. The phrase "superseded case" creates the erroneous impression that conversion of a case results in a new case that is distinct from the original case. The effect of conversion of a case is governed by §348 of the Code.

*GAP Report on Rule 1007(c).* No changes since publication, except for stylistic changes.

COMMITTEE NOTES ON RULES—2001 AMENDMENT

*Subdivision (m)* is added to enable the person required to mail notices under Rule 2002 to mail them to the appropriate guardian or other representative when the debtor knows that a creditor or other person listed is an infant or incompetent person.

The proper mailing address of the representative is determined in accordance with Rule 7004(b)(2), which requires mailing to the person's dwelling house or usual place of abode or at the place where the person regularly conducts a business or profession.

*Changes Made After Publication and Comments.* No changes were made.

COMMITTEE NOTES ON RULES—2003 AMENDMENT

[*Subdivision (a).*] This rule is amended to require the debtor to file a corporate ownership statement setting out the information described in Rule 7007.1. Requiring debtors to file the statement provides the court with an opportunity to make judicial disqualification determinations at the outset of the case. This could reduce problems later in the case by preventing the initial assignment of the case to a judge who holds a financial interest in a parent company of the debtor or some other entity that holds a significant ownership interest in the debtor. Moreover, by including the disclosure statement filing requirement at the commencement of the case, the debtor does not have to make the same disclosure filing each time it is involved in an adversary proceeding throughout the case. The debtor also must file supplemental statements as changes in ownership might arise.

*Changes Made After Publication and Comments.* No changes since publication.

[*Subdivisions (c) and (f).*] The rule is amended to add a requirement that a debtor submit a statement setting out the debtor's social security number. The addition is necessary because of the corresponding amendment to Rule 1005 which now provides that the caption of the petition includes only the final four digits of the debtor's social security number. The debtor submits the statement, but it is not filed, nor is it included in the case file. The statement provides the information necessary to include on the service copy of the notice required under Rule 2002(a)(1). It will also provide the information to facilitate the ability of creditors to search the court record by a search of a social security number already in the creditor's possession.

*Changes Made After Publication and Comments* rule amendment is made in response to the extensive commentary that urged the Advisory Committee to continue the obligation contained in current Rule 1005 that a debtor must include his or her social security number on the caption of the bankruptcy petition. Rule 1005 is amended to limit that disclosure to the final four digits of the social security number, and Rule 1007 is amended to reinstate the obligation in a manner that will provide more protection of the debtor's privacy while continuing access to the information to those persons with legitimate need for that data. The debtor must disclose the information, but the method of disclosure is by a verified statement that is submitted to the clerk. The statement is not filed in the case and does not become a part of the court record. Therefore, it enables the clerk to deliver that information to the creditors and the trustee in the case, but it does not become a part of the court record governed by § 107 of the Bankruptcy Code and is not available to the public.

COMMITTEE NOTES ON RULES—2005 AMENDMENT

Notice to creditors and other parties in interest is essential to the operation of the bankruptcy system. Sending notice requires a convenient listing of the names and addresses of the entities to whom notice must be sent, and virtually all of the bankruptcy courts have adopted a local rule requiring the submission of a list of these entities with the petition and in a particular format. These lists are commonly called the "mailing matrix."

Given the universal adoption of these local rules, the need for such lists in all cases is apparent. Consequently, the rule is amended to require the debtor to submit such a list at the commencement of the case. This list may be amended when necessary. *See* Rule 1009(a).

The content of the list is described by reference to Schedules D through H of the Official Forms rather than by reference to creditors or persons holding claims. The cross reference to the Schedules as the source of the names for inclusion in the list ensures that persons such as codebtors or nondebtor parties to executory contracts and unexpired leases will receive appropriate notices in the case.

While this rule renders unnecessary, in part, local rules on the subject, this rule does not direct any particular format or form for the list to take. Local rules still may govern those particulars of the list.

Subdivision (c) is amended to reflect that subdivision (a)(1) no longer requires the debtor to file a schedule of liabilities with the petition in lieu of a list of creditors. The filing of the list is mandatory, and subdivision (b) of the rule requires the filing of schedules. Thus, subdivision (c) no longer needs to account for the possibility that the debtor can delay filing a schedule of liabilities when the petition is accompanied by a list of creditors. Subdivision (c) simply addresses the situation in which the debtor does not file schedules or statements with the petition, and the procedure for seeking an extension of time for filing.

Other changes are stylistic.

*Changes Made After Publication and Comment.* No changes since publication.

COMMITTEE NOTES ON RULES—2008 AMENDMENT

The title of this rule is expanded to refer to "documents" in conformity with the 2005 amendments to § 521 and related provisions of the Bankruptcy Code that include a wider range of documentary requirements.

Subdivision (a) is amended to require that any foreign representative filing a petition for recognition to commence a case under chapter 15, which was added to the Code in 2005, file a list of entities with whom the debtor is engaged in litigation in the United States. The foreign representative filing the petition for recognition must also list any entities against whom provisional relief is being sought as well as all persons or bodies authorized to administer foreign proceedings of the debtor. This should ensure that entities most interested in the case, or their representatives, will receive notice of the petition under Rule 2002(q).

Subdivision (a)(4) is amended to require the foreign representative who files a petition for recognition under chapter 15 to file the documents described in § 1515 of the Code as well as a corporate ownership statement. The subdivision is also amended to identify the foreign representative in language that more closely follows the text of the Code. Former subdivision (a)(4) is renumbered as subdivision (a)(5) and stylistic changes were made to the subdivision.

Subdivision (b)(1) addresses schedules, statements, and other documents that the debtor must file unless the court orders otherwise and other than in a case under chapter 9. This subdivision is amended to include documentary requirements added by the 2005 amendments to § 521 that apply to the same group of debtors and have the same time limits as the existing requirements of (b)(1). Consistent with the E-Government Act of 2002, Pub. L. No. 107–347, the payment advices should be redacted before they are filed.

Subdivision (b)(2) is amended to conform to the renumbering of the subsections of § 521.

Subdivisions (b)(3) through (b)(8) are new and implement the 2005 amendments to the Code. Subdivision (b)(3) provides for the filing of a document relating to the credit counseling requirement provided by the 2005 amendments to § 109 in the context of an Official Form that warns the debtor of the consequences of failing to comply with the credit counseling requirement.

Subdivision (b)(4) addresses the filing of information about current monthly income, as defined in § 101, for certain chapter 7 debtors and, if required, additional calculations of expenses required by the 2005 amendments to § 707(b).

Subdivision (b)(5) addresses the filing of information about current monthly income, as defined in § 101, for individual chapter 11 debtors. The 2005 amendments to § 1129(a)(15) condition plan confirmation for individual debtors on the commitment of disposable income, as defined in § 1325(b)(2), which is based on current monthly income.

Subdivision (b)(6) addresses the filing of information about current monthly income, as defined in § 101, for chapter 13 debtors and, if required, additional calculations of expenses. These changes are necessary because the 2005 amendments to § 1325 require that the determination of disposable income begin with current monthly income.

Subdivision (b)(7) reflects the 2005 amendments to §§ 727 and 1328 of the Code that condition the receipt of a discharge on the completion of a personal financial management course, with certain exceptions. Certain individual chapter 11 debtors may also be required to complete a personal financial management course under § 727(a)(11) as incorporated by § 1141(d)(3)(C). To evidence compliance with that requirement, the subdivision requires the debtor to file the appropriate Official Form certifying that the debtor has completed the personal financial management course.

Subdivision (b)(8) requires an individual debtor in a case under chapter 11, 12, or 13 to file a statement that there are no reasonable grounds to believe that the restrictions on a homestead exemption as set out in § 522(q) of the Code are applicable. Sections 1141(d)(5)(C), 1228(f), and 1328(h) each provide that the court shall not enter a discharge order unless it finds that there is no reasonable cause to believe that § 522(q) applies. Requiring the debtor to submit a statement to that effect in cases under chapters 11, 12, and 13 in which an exemption is claimed in excess of the amount allowed under § 522(q)(1) provides the court with a basis to conclude, in the absence of any contrary information, that § 522(q) does not apply. Creditors receive notice under Rule 2002(f)(11) of the time to request postponement of the entry of the discharge to permit an opportunity to challenge the debtor's assertions in the Rule 1007(b)(8) statement in appropriate cases.

Subdivision (c) is amended to include time limits for the filing requirements added to subdivision (b) due to the 2005 amendments to the Code, and to make conforming amendments. Separate time limits are provided for the documentation of credit counseling and for the statement of the completion of the financial management course. While most documents relating to credit counseling must be filed with the voluntary petition, the credit counseling certificate and debt repayment plan can be filed within 15 days of the filing of a voluntary petition if the debtor files a statement under subdivision (b)(3)(B) with the petition. Sections 727(a)(11), 1141(d)(3), and 1328(g) of the Code require individual debtors to complete a personal financial management course prior to the entry of a discharge. The amendment allows the court to enlarge the deadline for the debtor to file the statement of completion. Because no party is harmed by the enlargement, no specific restriction is placed on the court's discretion to enlarge the deadline, even after its expiration.

Subdivision (c) of the rule is also amended to recognize the limitation on the extension of time to file schedules and statements when the debtor is a small business debtor. Section 1116(3), added to the Code in 2005, establishes a specific standard for courts to apply in the event that the debtor in possession or the trustee seeks an extension for filing these forms for a period beyond 30 days after the order for relief.

*Changes Made After Publication.* Subdivision (a)(4) was amended to insert the requirement that the foreign representative who files the chapter 15 petition must file the corporate ownership statement. Subdivision (b)(4) was amended to provide that all individual debtors rather than just those whose debts are primarily consumer debts must file the statement of current monthly income. Subdivisions (b)(7) and (c) were amended to make the obligation to file a statement of the completion of a personal financial management course applicable to certain individual chapter 11 debtors as well as to individual debtors in chapters 7 and 13. Subdivision (c) is also amended to provide the court with broad discretion to enlarge the time to file the statement of completion of a personal financial management course. The Committee Note was amended to explain these changes.

COMMITTEE NOTES ON RULES—2009 AMENDMENT

The rule is amended to implement changes in connection with the amendment to Rule 9006(a) and the manner by which time is computed under the rules. Each deadline in the rule of fewer than 30 days is amended to substitute a deadline that is a multiple of seven days. Throughout the rules, deadlines are amended in the following manner:

- 5-day periods become 7-day periods
- 10-day periods become 14-day periods
- 15-day periods become 14-day periods
- 20-day periods become 21-day periods
- 25-day periods become 28-day periods

## Rule 1008. Verification of Petitions and Accompanying Papers

All petitions, lists, schedules, statements and amendments thereto shall be verified or contain an unsworn declaration as provided in 28 U.S.C. §1746.

(As amended Apr. 30, 1991, eff. Aug. 1, 1991.)

NOTES OF ADVISORY COMMITTEE ON RULES—1983

This rule retains the requirement under the Bankruptcy Act and rules that petitions and accompanying papers must be verified. Only the original need be signed and verified, but the copies must be conformed to the original. See Rule 9011(c).

The verification may be replaced by an unsworn declaration as provided in 28 U.S.C. §1746. See also, Official Form No. 1 and Advisory Committee Note.

NOTES OF ADVISORY COMMITTEE ON RULES—1991 AMENDMENT

The amendments to this rule are stylistic.

## Rule 1009. Amendments of Voluntary Petitions, Lists, Schedules and Statements

(a) GENERAL RIGHT TO AMEND. A voluntary petition, list, schedule, or statement may be amended by the debtor as a matter of course at any time before the case is closed. The debtor shall give notice of the amendment to the trustee and to any entity affected thereby. On motion of a party in interest, after notice and a hearing, the court may order any voluntary petition, list, schedule, or statement to be amended and the clerk shall give notice of the amendment to entities designated by the court.

(b) STATEMENT OF INTENTION. The statement of intention may be amended by the debtor at any time before the expiration of the period provided in §521(a) of the Code. The debtor shall give notice of the amendment to the trustee and to any entity affected thereby.

(c) STATEMENT OF SOCIAL SECURITY NUMBER. If a debtor becomes aware that the statement of social security number submitted under Rule 1007(f) is incorrect, the debtor shall promptly submit an amended verified statement setting forth the correct social security number. The debtor shall give notice of the amendment to all of the entities required to be included on the list filed under Rule 1007(a)(1) or (a)(2).

(d) TRANSMISSION TO UNITED STATES TRUSTEE. The clerk shall promptly transmit to the United States trustee a copy of every amendment filed or submitted under subdivision (a), (b), or (c) of this rule.

(As amended Mar. 30, 1987, eff. Aug. 1, 1987; Apr. 30, 1991, eff. Aug. 1, 1991; Apr. 12, 2006, eff. Dec. 1, 2006; Apr. 23, 2008, eff. Dec. 1, 2008.)

NOTES OF ADVISORY COMMITTEE ON RULES—1983

This rule continues the permissive approach adopted by former Bankruptcy Rule 110 to amendments of voluntary petitions and accompanying papers. Notice of any amendment is required to be given to the trustee. This is particularly important with respect to any amendment of the schedule of property affecting the debtor's claim of exemptions. Notice of any amendment of the schedule of liabilities is to be given to any creditor whose claim is changed or newly listed.

The rule does not continue the provision permitting the court to order an amendment on its own initiative. Absent a request in some form by a party in interest, the court should not be involved in administrative matters affecting the estate.

If a list or schedule is amended to include an additional creditor, the effect on the dischargeability of the creditor's claim is governed by the provisions of §523(a)(3) of the Code.

NOTES OF ADVISORY COMMITTEE ON RULES AMENDMENT

*Subdivision (a)* is amended to require notice and a hearing in the event a party in interest other than the debtor seeks to amend. The number of copies of the amendment will be determined by local rule of court.

*Subdivision (b)* is added to treat amendments of the statement of intention separately from other amendments. The intention of the individual debtor must be performed within 45 days of the filing of the statement, unless the court extends the period. Subdivision (b) limits the time for amendment to the time for performance under §521(2)(B) of the Code or any extension granted by the court.

NOTES OF ADVISORY COMMITTEE ON RULES AMENDMENT

The amendments to subdivision (a) are stylistic.

*Subdivision (c)* is derived from Rule X–1002(a) and is designed to provide the United States trustee with current information to enable that office to participate effectively in the case.

COMMITTEE NOTES ON RULES—2006 AMENDMENT

*Subdivision (c).* Rule 2002(a)(1) provides that the notice of the §341 meeting of creditors include the debtor's social security number. It provides creditors with the full number while limiting publication of the social security number otherwise to the final four digits of the number to protect the debtor's identity from others who do not have the same need for that information. If, however, the social security number that the debtor submitted under Rule 1007(f) is incorrect, then the only notice to the entities contained on the list filed under Rule 1007(a)(1) or (a)(2) would be incorrect. This amendment adds a new subdivision (c) that directs the debtor to submit a verified amended statement of social security number and to give notice of the new statement to all entities in the case who received the notice containing the erroneous social security number.

*Subdivision (d).* Former subdivision (c) becomes subdivision (d) and is amended to include new subdivision (c) amendments in the list of documents that the clerk must transmit to the United States trustee.

Other amendments are stylistic.

*Changes Made After Publication.* No changes since publication.

COMMITTEE NOTES ON RULES—2008 AMENDMENT

Subdivision (b) is amended to conform to the 2005 amendments to §521 of the Code.

*Changes Made After Publication.* No changes were made after publication.

### Rule 1010. Service of Involuntary Petition and Summons; Petition For Recognition of a Foreign Nonmain Proceeding

(a) SERVICE OF INVOLUNTARY PETITION AND SUMMONS; SERVICE OF PETITION FOR RECOGNITION OF FOREIGN NONMAIN PROCEEDING. On the filing of an involuntary petition or a petition for recognition of a foreign nonmain proceeding, the clerk shall forthwith issue a summons for service. When an involuntary petition is filed, service shall be made on the debtor. When a petition for recognition of a foreign nonmain proceeding is filed, service shall be made on the debtor, any entity against whom provisional relief is sought under §1519 of the Code, and on any other party as the court may direct. The summons shall be served with a copy of the petition in the manner provided for service of a summons and complaint by Rule 7004(a) or (b). If service cannot be so made, the court may order that the summons and petition be served by mailing copies to the party's last known address, and by at least one publication in a manner and form directed by the court. The summons and petition may be served on the party anywhere. Rule 7004(e) and Rule 4(*l*) F.R.Civ.P. apply when service is made or attempted under this rule.

(b) CORPORATE OWNERSHIP STATEMENT. Each petitioner that is a corporation shall file with the involuntary petition a corporate ownership statement containing the information described in Rule 7007.1.

(As amended Mar. 30, 1987, eff. Aug. 1, 1987; Apr. 30, 1991, eff. Aug. 1, 1991; Apr. 22, 1993, eff. Aug. 1, 1993; Apr. 11, 1997, eff. Dec. 1, 1997; Apr. 23, 2008, eff. Dec. 1, 2008.)

NOTES OF ADVISORY COMMITTEE ON RULES—1983

This rule provides the procedure for service of the involuntary petition and summons. It does not deal with service of a summons and complaint instituting an adversary proceeding pursuant to Part VII.

While this rule is similar to former Bankruptcy Rule 111, it substitutes the clerk of the bankruptcy court for the clerk of the district court as the person who is to issue the summons.

The modes of service prescribed by the rule are personal or by mail, when service can be effected in one of these ways in the United States. Such service is to be made in the manner prescribed in adversary proceedings by Rule 7004(a) and (b). If service must be made in a foreign country, the mode of service is one of that set forth in Rule 4(i) F.R.Civ.P.

When the methods set out in Rule 7004(a) and (b) cannot be utilized, service by publication coupled with mailing to the last known address is authorized. *Cf.* Rule 7004(c). The court determines the form and manner of publication as provided in Rule 9007. The publication need not set out the petition or the order directing service by publication. In order to apprise the debtor fairly, however, the publication should include all the information required to be in the summons by Official Form No. 13 and a notice indicating how service is being effected and how a copy of the petition may be obtained.

There are no territorial limits on the service authorized by this rule, which continues the practice under the former rules and Act. There must, however, be a basis for jurisdiction pursuant to §109(a) of the Code for the court to order relief. Venue provisions are set forth in 28 U.S.C. §1472.

Subdivision (f) of Rule 7004 and subdivisions (g) and (h) of Rule 4 F.R.Civ.P. govern time and proof of service and amendment of process or of proof of service.

Rule 1004 provides for transmission to nonpetitioning partners of a petition filed against the partnership by fewer than all the general partners.

NOTES OF ADVISORY COMMITTEE ON RULES—1987 AMENDMENT

The rule has been broadened to include service of a petition commencing a case ancillary to a foreign proceeding, previously included in Rule 1003(e)(2).

NOTES OF ADVISORY COMMITTEE ON RULES—1991 AMENDMENT

Reference to the Official Form number is deleted in anticipation of future revision and renumbering of the Official Forms.

Rule 4(g) and (h) F.R.Civ.P. made applicable by this rule refers to Rule 4(g) and (h) F.R.Civ.P. in effect on January 1, 1990, notwithstanding any subsequent amendment thereto. See Rule 7004(g).

NOTES OF ADVISORY COMMITTEE ON RULES—1993 AMENDMENT

This rule is amended to delete the reference to the Official Form. The Official Form for the summons was abrogated in 1991. Other amendments are stylistic and make no substantive change.

NOTES OF ADVISORY COMMITTEE ON RULES—1997 AMENDMENT

The amendments to this rule are technical, are promulgated solely to conform to changes in subdivision designations in Rule 4, F.R.Civ.P., and in Rule 7004, and are not intended to effectuate any material change in substance.

In 1996, the letter designation of subdivision (f) of Rule 7004 (Summons; Time Limit for Service) was changed to subdivision (e). In 1993, the provisions of Rule 4, F.R.Civ.P., relating to proof of service contained in Rule 4(g) (Return) and Rule 4(h) (Amendments), were placed in the new subdivision (*l*) of Rule 4 (Proof of Service). The technical amendments to Rule 1010 are designed solely to conform to these new subdivision designations.

The 1996 amendments to Rule 7004 and the 1993 amendments to Rule 4, F.R.Civ.P., have not affected the availability of service by first class mail in accordance with Rule 7004(b) for the service of a summons and petition in an involuntary case commenced under §303 or an ancillary case commenced under §304 of the Code.

*GAP Report on Rule 1010.* These amendments, which are technical and conforming, were not published for comment.

COMMITTEE NOTES ON RULES—2008 AMENDMENT

This rule is amended to implement the 2005 amendments to the Code, which repealed §304 and replaced it with chapter 15 governing ancillary and other cross-border cases. Under chapter 15, a foreign representative commences a case by filing a petition for recognition of a pending foreign nonmain proceeding. The amendment requires service of the summons and petition on the debtor and any entity against whom the representative is seeking provisional relief. Until the court enters a recognition order under §1517, no stay is in effect unless the court enters some form of provisional relief under §1519. Thus, only those entities against whom specific provisional relief is sought need to be served. The court may, however, direct that service be made on additional entities as appropriate.

This rule does not apply to a petition for recognition of a foreign main proceeding.

The rule is also amended by renumbering the prior rule as subdivision (a) and adding a new subdivision (b) requiring any corporate creditor that files or joins an involuntary petition to file a corporate ownership statement.

*Changes Made After Publication.* No changes were made after publication.

REFERENCES IN TEXT

The Federal Rules of Civil Procedure, referred to in subd. (a), are set out in the Appendix to Title 28, Judiciary and Judicial Procedure.

## Rule 1011. Responsive Pleading or Motion in Involuntary and Cross-Border Cases

(a) WHO MAY CONTEST PETITION. The debtor named in an involuntary petition, or a party in interest to a petition for recognition of a foreign proceeding, may contest the petition. In the case of a petition against a partnership under Rule 1004, a nonpetitioning general partner, or a person who is alleged to be a general partner but denies the allegation, may contest the petition.

(b) DEFENSES AND OBJECTIONS; WHEN PRESENTED. Defenses and objections to the petition shall be presented in the manner prescribed by Rule 12 F.R.Civ.P. and shall be filed and served within 21 days after service of the summons, except that if service is made by publication on a party or partner not residing or found within the state in which the court sits, the court shall prescribe the time for filing and serving the response.

(c) EFFECT OF MOTION. Service of a motion under Rule 12(b) F.R.Civ.P. shall extend the time for filing and serving a responsive pleading as permitted by Rule 12(a) F.R.Civ.P.

(d) CLAIMS AGAINST PETITIONERS. A claim against a petitioning creditor may not be asserted in the answer except for the purpose of defeating the petition.

(e) OTHER PLEADINGS. No other pleadings shall be permitted, except that the court may order a reply to an answer and prescribe the time for filing and service.

(f) CORPORATE OWNERSHIP STATEMENT. If the entity responding to the involuntary petition or the petition for recognition of a foreign proceeding is a corporation, the entity shall file with its first appearance, pleading, motion, response, or other request addressed to the court a corporate ownership statement containing the information described in Rule 7007.1.

(As amended Mar. 30, 1987, eff. Aug. 1, 1987; Apr. 26, 2004, eff. Dec. 1, 2004; Apr. 23, 2008, eff. Dec. 1, 2008; Mar. 26, 2009, eff. Dec. 1, 2009.)

NOTES OF ADVISORY COMMITTEE ON RULES—1983

This rule is derived from former Bankruptcy Rule 112. A petition filed by fewer than all the general partners under Rule 1004(b) to have an order for relief entered with respect to the partnership is referred to as a petition against the partnership because of the adversary character of the proceeding it commences. *Cf.* §303(b)(3) of the Code; 2 Collier *Bankruptcy* ¶303.05[5][a] (15th ed. 1981); 2 *id.* ¶¶18.33[2], 18.46 (14th ed. 1966). One who denies an allegation of membership in the firm is nevertheless recognized as a party entitled to contest a petition filed against a partnership under subdivision (b) of Rule 1004 in view of the possible consequences to him of an order for relief against the entity alleged to include him as a member. See §723 of the Code; *Francis v. McNeal*, 228 U.S. 695 (1913); *Manson v. Williams*, 213 U.S. 453 (1909); *Carter v. Whisler*, 275 Fed. 743, 746–747 (8th Cir. 1921). The rule preserves the features of the former Act and Rule 112 and the Code permitting no response by creditors to an involuntary petition or petition against a partnership under Rule 1004(b).

*Subdivision (b):* Rule 12 F.R.Civ.P. has been looked to by the courts as prescribing the mode of making a defense or objection to a petition in bankruptcy. See *Fada of New York, Inc. v. Organization Service Co., Inc.*, 125 F.2d 120. (2d Cir. 1942); *In the Matter of McDougald*, 17 F.R.D. 2, 5 (W.D. Ark. 1955); *In the Matter of Miller*, 6 Fed. Rules Serv. 12f.26, Case No. 1 (N.D. Ohio 1942); *Tatum v. Acadian Production Corp. of La.*, 35 F. Supp. 40, 50 (E.D. La. 1940); 2 Collier, *supra* ¶303.07 (15th ed. 1981); 2 *id.* at 134–40 (14th ed. 1966). As pointed out in the Note accompanying former Bankruptcy Rule 915 an objection that a debtor is neither entitled to the benefits of the Code nor amenable to an involuntary petition goes to jurisdiction of the subject matter and may be made at any time consistent with Rule 12(h)(3) F.R.Civ.P. Nothing in this rule recognizes standing in a creditor or any other person not authorized to contest a petition to raise an objection that a person eligible to file a voluntary petition cannot be the subject of an order for relief on an involuntary petition. See Seligson & King, *Jurisdiction and Venue in Bankruptcy*, 36 Ref.J. 36, 38–40 (1962).

As Collier has pointed out with respect to the Bankruptcy Act, "the mechanics of the provisions in §18a and b relating to time for appearance and pleading are unnecessarily confusing. . . . It would seem, though, to be more straightforward to provide, as does Federal Rule 12(a), that the time to respond runs from the date of service rather than the date of issuance of process." 2 Collier, *supra* at 119. The time normally allowed for the service and filing of an answer or motion under Rule 1011 runs from the date of the issuance of the summons. Compare Rule 7012. Service of the summons and petition will ordinarily be made by mail under Rule 1010 and must be made within 10 days of the issuance of the summons under Rule 7004(e), which governs the time of service. When service is made by publication, the court should fix the time for service and filing of the response in the light of all the circumstances so as to afford a fair opportunity to the debtor to enter a defense or objection without unduly delaying the hearing on the petition. *Cf.* Rule 12(a) F.R.Civ.P.

*Subdivision (c):* Under subdivision (c), the timely service of a motion permitted by Rule 12(b), (e), (f), or (h) F.R.Civ.P. alters the time within which an answer must be filed. If the court denies a motion or postpones its disposition until trial on the merits, the answer must be served within 10 days after notice of the court's action. If the court grants a motion for a more definite statement, the answer may be served any time within 10 days after the service of the more definite statement.

Many of the rules governing adversary proceedings apply to proceedings on a contested petition unless the court otherwise directs as provided in Rule 1018. The specific provisions of this Rule 1011 or 7005, however, govern the filing of an answer or motion responsive to a petition. The rules of Part VII are adaptations of the corresponding Federal Rules of Civil Procedure, and the effect of Rule 1018 is thus to make the provisions of Civil Rules 5, 8, 9, 15, and 56, *inter alia*, generally applicable to the making of defenses and objections to the petition. Rule 1018 follows prior law and practice in this respect. See 2 Collier, *Bankruptcy* ¶¶ 18.39–18.41 (14th ed. 1966).

*Subdivision (d)*. This subdivision adopts the position taken in many cases that an affirmative judgment against a petitioning creditor cannot be sought by a counterclaim filed in an answer to an involuntary petition. See, *e.g.*, *Georgia Jewelers, Inc. v. Bulova Watch Co.*, 302 F.2d 362, 369–70 (5th Cir. 1962); *Associated Electronic Supply Co. of Omaha v. C.B.S. Electronic Sales Corp.*, 288 F.2d 683, 684–85 (8th Cir. 1961). The subdivision follows *Harris v. Capehart-Farnsworth Corp.*, 225 F.2d 268 (8th Cir. 1955), in permitting the debtor to challenge the standing of a petitioner by filing a counterclaim against him. It does not foreclose the court from rejecting a counterclaim that cannot be determined without unduly delaying the decision upon the petition. See *In the Matter of Bichel Optical Laboratories, Inc.*, 299 F. Supp. 545 (D. Minn. 1969).

*Subdivision (e)*. This subdivision makes it clear that no reply needs to be made to an answer, including one asserting a counterclaim, unless the court orders otherwise.

NOTES OF ADVISORY COMMITTEE ON RULES—1987 AMENDMENT

The rule has been broadened to make applicable in ancillary cases the provisions concerning responsive pleadings to involuntary petitions.

COMMITTEE NOTES ON RULES—2004 AMENDMENT

The amendment to Rule 1004 that became effective on December 1, 2002, deleted former subdivision (a) of that rule leaving only the provisions relating to involuntary petitions against partnerships. The rule no longer includes subdivisions. Therefore, this technical amendment changes the reference to Rule 1004(b) to Rule 1004.

COMMITTEE NOTES ON RULES—2008 AMENDMENT

The rule is amended to reflect the 2005 amendments to the Code, which repealed § 304 and added chapter 15. Section 304 covered cases ancillary to foreign proceedings, while chapter 15 governs ancillary and other cross-border cases and introduces the concept of a petition for recognition of a foreign proceeding.

The rule is also amended in tandem with the amendment to Rule 1010 to require the parties responding to an involuntary petition and a petition for recognition of a foreign proceeding to file corporate ownership statements to assist the court in determining whether recusal is necessary.

COMMITTEE NOTES ON RULES—2009 AMENDMENT

The rule is amended to implement changes in connection with the amendment to Rule 9006(a) and the manner by which time is computed under the rules. The deadline in the rule is amended to substitute a deadline that is a multiple of seven days. Throughout the rules, deadlines are amended in the following manner:

- 5-day periods become 7-day periods
- 10-day periods become 14-day periods
- 15-day periods become 14-day periods
- 20-day periods become 21-day periods
- 25-day periods become 28-day periods

*Changes Made After Publication*. No changes were made after publication.

REFERENCES IN TEXT

The Federal Rules of Civil Procedure, referred to in subds. (b) and (c), are set out in the Appendix to Title 28, Judiciary and Judicial Procedure.

**[Rule 1012. Examination of Debtor, Including Discovery, on Issue of Nonpayment of Debts in Involuntary Cases.] (Abrogated Mar. 30, 1987, eff. Aug. 1, 1987)**

NOTES OF ADVISORY COMMITTEE ON RULES—1987

This rule is abrogated. The discovery rules apply whenever an involuntary petition is contested. Rule 1018.

## Rule 1013. Hearing and Disposition of a Petition in an Involuntary Case

(a) CONTESTED PETITION. The court shall determine the issues of a contested petition at the earliest practicable time and forthwith enter an order for relief, dismiss the petition, or enter any other appropriate order.

(b) DEFAULT. If no pleading or other defense to a petition is filed within the time provided by Rule 1011, the court, on the next day, or as soon thereafter as practicable, shall enter an order for the relief requested in the petition.

[(c) ORDER FOR RELIEF] (Abrogated Apr. 22, 1993, eff. Aug. 1, 1993)

(As amended Apr. 30, 1991, eff. Aug. 1, 1991; Apr. 22, 1993, eff. Aug. 1, 1993.)

NOTES OF ADVISORY COMMITTEE ON RULES—1983

This rule is adapted from former Bankruptcy Rule 115(a) and (c) and applies in chapter 7 and 11 cases. The right to trial by jury under § 19a of the Bankruptcy Act has been abrogated and the availability of a trial by jury is within the discretion of the bankruptcy judge pursuant to 28 U.S.C. § 1480(b). Rule 9015 governs the demand for a jury trial.

Subdivision (b) of Rule 1013 is derived from former Bankruptcy Rule 115(c) and § 18(e) of the Bankruptcy Act. If an order for relief is not entered on default, dismissal will ordinarily be appropriate but the court may postpone definitive action. See also Rule 9024 with respect to setting aside an order for relief on default for cause.

Subdivision (e) of former Bankruptcy Rule 115 has not been carried over because its provisions are covered by § 303(i) of the Code.

NOTES OF ADVISORY COMMITTEE ON RULES—1991 AMENDMENT

Reference to the Official Form number is deleted in anticipation of future revision and renumbering of the Official Forms.

NOTES OF ADVISORY COMMITTEE ON RULES—1993 AMENDMENT

*Subdivision (c)* is abrogated because the official form for the order for relief was abrogated in 1991. Other amendments are stylistic and make no substantive change.

## Rule 1014. Dismissal and Change of Venue

(a) DISMISSAL AND TRANSFER OF CASES.

(1) *Cases Filed in Proper District.* If a petition is filed in the proper district, the court, on the timely motion of a party in interest or on its own motion, and after hearing on notice to the petitioners, the United States trustee, and other entities as directed by the court, may transfer the case to any other district if the court determines that the transfer is in the interest of justice or for the convenience of the parties.

(2) *Cases Filed in Improper District.* If a petition is filed in an improper district, the court,

on the timely motion of a party in interest or on its own motion, and after hearing on notice to the petitioners, the United States trustee, and other entities as directed by the court, may dismiss the case or transfer it to any other district if the court determines that transfer is in the interest of justice or for the convenience of the parties.

(b) PROCEDURE WHEN PETITIONS INVOLVING THE SAME DEBTOR OR RELATED DEBTORS ARE FILED IN DIFFERENT COURTS. If petitions commencing cases under the Code are filed in different districts by or against (1) the same debtor, or (2) a partnership and one or more of its general partners, or (3) two or more general partners, or (4) a debtor and an affiliate, on motion filed in the district in which the petition filed first is pending and after hearing on notice to the petitioners, the United States trustee, and other entities as directed by the court, the court may determine, in the interest of justice or for the convenience of the parties, the district or districts in which the case or cases should proceed. Except as otherwise ordered by the court in the district in which the petition filed first is pending, the proceedings on the other petitions shall be stayed by the courts in which they have been filed until the determination is made.

(As amended Mar. 30, 1987, eff. Aug. 1, 1987; Apr. 30, 1991, eff. Aug. 1, 1991; Apr. 30, 2007, eff. Dec. 1, 2007.)

NOTES OF ADVISORY COMMITTEE ON RULES—1983

This rule is derived from former Bankruptcy Rule 116 which contained venue as well as transfer provisions. Public Law 95–598, however, placed the venue provisions in 28 U.S.C. §1472, and no purpose is served by repeating them in this rule. Transfer of cases is provided in 28 U.S.C. §1475 but this rule adds the procedure for obtaining transfer. Pursuant to 28 U.S.C. §1472, proper venue for cases filed under the Code is either the district of domicile, residence, principal place of business, or location of principal assets for 180 days or the longer portion thereof immediately preceding the petition. 28 U.S.C. §1475 permits the court to transfer a case in the interest of justice and for the convenience of the parties. If the venue is improper, the court may retain or transfer the case in the interest of justice and for the convenience of the parties pursuant to 28 U.S.C. §1477.

*Subdivision (a)* of the rule is derived from former Bankruptcy Rule 116(b). It implements 28 U.S.C. §§1475 and 1477 and clarifies the procedure to be followed in requesting and effecting transfer of a case. Subdivision (a) protects the parties against being subjected to a transfer except on a timely motion of a party in interest. If the transfer would result in fragmentation or duplication of administration, increase expense, or delay closing the estate, such a factor would bear on the timeliness of the motion as well as on the propriety of the transfer under the standards prescribed in subdivision (a). Subdivision (a) of the rule requires the interest of justice and the convenience of the parties to be the grounds of any transfer of a case or of the retention of a case filed in an improper district as does 28 U.S.C. §1477. *Cf.* 28 U.S.C. §1404(a) (district court may transfer any civil action "[f]or the convenience of parties and witnesses, in the interest of justice"). It also expressly requires a hearing on notice to the petitioner or petitioners before the transfer of any case may be ordered. Under this rule, a motion by a party in interest is necessary. There is no provision for the court to act on its own initiative.

*Subdivision (b)* is derived from former Bankruptcy Rule 116(c). It authorizes the court in which the first petition is filed under the Code by or against a debtor to entertain a motion seeking a determination whether the case so commenced should continue or be transferred and consolidated or administered jointly with another case commenced by or against the same or related person in another court under a different chapter of the Code. Subdivision (b) is correlated with 28 U.S.C. §1472 which authorizes petitioners to file cases involving a partnership and partners or affiliated debtors.

The reference in subdivision (b) to petitions filed "by" a partner or "by" any other of the persons mentioned is to be understood as referring to voluntary petitions. It is not the purpose of this subdivision to permit more than one case to be filed in the same court because a creditor signing an involuntary petition happens to be a partner, a partnership, or an affiliate of a debtor.

Transfers of adversary proceedings in cases under title 11 are governed by Rule 7087 and 28 U.S.C. §1475.

NOTES OF ADVISORY COMMITTEE ON RULES—1987 AMENDMENT

Both paragraphs 1 and 2 of subdivision (a) are amended to conform to the standard for transfer in 28 U.S.C. §1412. Formerly, 28 U.S.C. §1477 authorized a court either to transfer or retain a case which had been commenced in a district where venue was improper. However, 28 U.S.C. §1412, which supersedes 28 U.S.C. §1477, authorizes only the transfer of a case. The rule is amended to delete the reference to retention of a case commenced in the improper district. Dismissal of a case commenced in the improper district as authorized by 28 U.S.C. §1406 has been added to the rule. If a timely motion to dismiss for improper venue is not filed, the right to object to venue is waived.

The last sentence of the rule has been deleted as unnecessary.

NOTES OF ADVISORY COMMITTEE ON RULES—1991 AMENDMENT

*Subdivision (b)* is amended to provide that a motion for transfer of venue under this subdivision shall be filed in the district in which the first petition is pending. If the case commenced by the first petition has been transferred to another district prior to the filing of a motion to transfer a related case under this subdivision, the motion must be filed in the district to which the first petition had been transferred.

The other amendments to this rule are consistent with the responsibilities of the United States trustee in the supervision and administration of cases pursuant to 28 U.S.C. §586(a)(3). The United States trustee may appear and be heard on issues relating to the transfer of the case or dismissal due to improper venue. See §307 of the Code.

COMMITTEE NOTES ON RULES—2007 AMENDMENT

Courts have generally held that they have the authority to dismiss or transfer cases on their own motion. The amendment recognizes this authority and also provides that dismissal or transfer of the case may take place only after notice and a hearing.

Other amendments are stylistic.

*Changes Made After Publication.* No changes since publication.

### Rule 1015. Consolidation or Joint Administration of Cases Pending in Same Court

(a) CASES INVOLVING SAME DEBTOR. If two or more petitions are pending in the same court by or against the same debtor, the court may order consolidation of the cases.

(b) CASES INVOLVING TWO OR MORE DEBTORS. If a joint petition or two or more petitions are pending in the same court by or against (1) a husband and wife, or (2) a partnership and one or more of its general partners, or (3) two or more general partners, or (4) a debtor and an affiliate, the court may order a joint administration of the estates. Prior to entering an order the court shall give consideration to protecting creditors of different estates against potential conflicts of interest. An order directing joint administration of individual cases of a husband and wife shall, if one spouse has elected the exemptions under §522(b)(2) of the Code and the other has elected the exemptions under §522(b)(3), fix a reasonable time within which either may amend the election so that both shall have elected the same exemptions. The order shall notify the debtors that unless they elect the same exemptions within the time fixed by the court, they will be deemed to have elected the exemptions provided by §522(b)(2).

(c) EXPEDITING AND PROTECTIVE ORDERS. When an order for consolidation or joint administration of a joint case or two or more cases is entered pursuant to this rule, while protecting the rights of the parties under the Code, the court may enter orders as may tend to avoid unnecessary costs and delay.

(As amended Mar. 30, 1987, eff. Aug. 1, 1987; Apr. 23, 2008; eff. Dec. 1, 2008.)

NOTES OF ADVISORY COMMITTEE ON RULES—1983

*Subdivision (a)* of this rule is derived from former Bankruptcy Rule 117(a). It applies to cases when the same debtor is named in both voluntary and involuntary petitions, when husband and wife have filed a joint petition pursuant to §302 of the Code, and when two or more involuntary petitions are filed against the same debtor. It also applies when cases are pending in the same court by virtue of a transfer of one or more petitions from another court. Subdivision (c) allows the court discretion regarding the order of trial of issues raised by two or more involuntary petitions against the same debtor.

*Subdivision (b)* recognizes the propriety of joint administration of estates in certain kinds of cases. The election or appointment of one trustee for two or more jointly administered estates is authorized by Rule 2009. The authority of the court to order joint administration under subdivision (b) extends equally to the situation when the petitions are filed under different sections, *e.g.*, when one petition is voluntary and the other involuntary, and when all of the petitions are filed under the same section of the Code.

Consolidation of cases implies a unitary administration of the estate and will ordinarily be indicated under the circumstances to which subdivision (a) applies. This rule does not deal with the consolidation of cases involving two or more separate debtors. Consolidation of the estates of separate debtors may sometimes be appropriate, as when the affairs of an individual and a corporation owned or controlled by that individual are so intermingled that the court cannot separate their assets and liabilities. Consolidation, as distinguished from joint administration, is neither authorized nor prohibited by this rule since the propriety of consolidation depends on substantive considerations and affects the substantive rights of the creditors of the different estates. For illustrations of the substantive consolidation of separate estates, see *Sampsell v. Imperial Paper & Color Corp.*, 313 U.S. 215 (1941). See also *Chemical Bank N.Y. Trust Co. v. Kheel*, 369 F.2d 845 (2d Cir. 1966); Seligson & Mandell, *Multi-Debtor Petition—Consolidation of Debtors and Due Process of Law*, 73 Com.L.J. 341 (1968); Kennedy, *Insolvency and the Corporate Veil in the United States* in *Proceedings of the 8th International Symposium on Comparative Law* 232, 248–55 (1971).

Joint administration as distinguished from consolidation may include combining the estates by using a single docket for the matters occurring in the administration, including the listing of filed claims, the combining of notices to creditors of the different estates, and the joint handling of other purely administrative matters that may aid in expediting the cases and rendering the process less costly.

*Subdivision (c)* is an adaptation of the provisions of Rule 42(a) F.R.Civ.P. for the purposes of administration of estates under this rule. The rule does not deal with filing fees when an order for the consolidation of cases or joint administration of estates is made.

A joint petition of husband and wife, requiring the payment of a single filing fee, is permitted by §302 of the Code. Consolidation of such a case, however, rests in the discretion of the court; see §302(b) of the Code.

NOTES OF ADVISORY COMMITTEE ON RULES—1987 AMENDMENT

The amendment to subdivision (b) implements the provisions of §522(b) of the Code, as enacted by the 1984 amendments.

COMMITTEE NOTES ON RULES—2008 AMENDMENT

The rule is amended to conform to the change in the numbering of §522(b) of the Code that was made as a part of the 2005 amendments. Former subsections (b)(1) and (b)(2) of §522 were renumbered as subsections (b)(2) and (b)(3), respectively. The rule is amended to make the parallel change.

*Changes Made After Publication.* No changes were made after publication.

## Rule 1016. Death or Incompetency of Debtor

Death or incompetency of the debtor shall not abate a liquidation case under chapter 7 of the Code. In such event the estate shall be administered and the case concluded in the same manner, so far as possible, as though the death or incompetency had not occurred. If a reorganization, family farmer's debt adjustment, or individual's debt adjustment case is pending under chapter 11, chapter 12, or chapter 13, the case may be dismissed; or if further administration is possible and in the best interest of the parties, the case may proceed and be concluded in the same manner, so far as possible, as though the death or incompetency had not occurred.

(As amended Apr. 30, 1991, eff. Aug. 1, 1991.)

NOTES OF ADVISORY COMMITTEE ON RULES—1983

This rule is derived from former Rules 118 and 11-16. In a chapter 11 reorganization case or chapter 13 individual's debt adjustment case, the likelihood is that the case will be dismissed.

NOTES OF ADVISORY COMMITTEE ON RULES—1991 AMENDMENT

This rule is amended to conform to 25 F.R.Civ.P. and to include chapter 12 cases.

## Rule 1017. Dismissal or Conversion of Case; Suspension

(a) VOLUNTARY DISMISSAL; DISMISSAL FOR WANT OF PROSECUTION OR OTHER CAUSE. Except as provided in §§707(a)(3), 707(b), 1208(b), and 1307(b) of the Code, and in Rule 1017(b), (c), and (e), a case shall not be dismissed on motion of the petitioner, for want of prosecution or other cause, or by consent of the parties, before a hearing on notice as provided in Rule 2002. For the purpose of the notice, the debtor shall file a list of creditors with their addresses within the time fixed by the court unless the list was previously filed. If the debtor fails to file the list, the court may order the debtor or another entity to prepare and file it.

(b) DISMISSAL FOR FAILURE TO PAY FILING FEE.

(1) If any installment of the filing fee has not been paid, the court may, after a hearing on notice to the debtor and the trustee, dismiss the case.

(2) If the case is dismissed or closed without full payment of the filing fee, the installments collected shall be distributed in the same manner and proportions as if the filing fee had been paid in full.

(c) DISMISSAL OF VOLUNTARY CHAPTER 7 OR CHAPTER 13 CASE FOR FAILURE TO TIMELY FILE LIST OF CREDITORS, SCHEDULES, AND STATEMENT OF FINANCIAL AFFAIRS. The court may dismiss a voluntary chapter 7 or chapter 13 case under §707(a)(3) or §1307(c)(9) after a hearing on notice served by the United States trustee on the debtor, the trustee, and any other entities as the court directs.

(d) SUSPENSION. The court shall not dismiss a case or suspend proceedings under §305 before a hearing on notice as provided in Rule 2002(a).

(e) DISMISSAL OF AN INDIVIDUAL DEBTOR'S CHAPTER 7 CASE, OR CONVERSION TO A CASE UNDER CHAPTER 11 OR 13, FOR ABUSE. The court may dismiss or, with the debtor's consent, convert an individual debtor's case for abuse under §707(b) only on motion and after a hearing on notice to the debtor, the trustee, the United States trustee, and any other entity as the court directs.

(1) Except as otherwise provided in §704(b)(2), a motion to dismiss a case for abuse under §707(b) or (c) may be filed only within 60 days after the first date set for the meeting of creditors under §341(a), unless, on request filed before the time has expired, the court for cause extends the time for filing the motion to dismiss. The party filing the motion shall set forth in the motion all matters to be considered at the hearing. In addition, a motion to dismiss under §707(b)(1) and (3) shall state with particularity the circumstances alleged to constitute abuse.

(2) If the hearing is set on the court's own motion, notice of the hearing shall be served on the debtor no later than 60 days after the first date set for the meeting of creditors under §341(a). The notice shall set forth all matters to be considered by the court at the hearing.

(f) PROCEDURE FOR DISMISSAL, CONVERSION, OR SUSPENSION.

(1) Rule 9014 governs a proceeding to dismiss or suspend a case, or to convert a case to another chapter, except under §§706(a), 1112(a), 1208(a) or (b), or 1307(a) or (b).

(2) Conversion or dismissal under §§706(a), 1112(a), 1208(b), or 1307(b) shall be on motion filed and served as required by Rule 9013.

(3) A chapter 12 or chapter 13 case shall be converted without court order when the debtor files a notice of conversion under §§1208(a) or 1307(a). The filing date of the notice becomes the date of the conversion order for the purposes of applying §348(c) and Rule 1019. The clerk shall promptly transmit a copy of the notice to the United States trustee.

(As amended Mar. 30, 1987, eff. Aug. 1, 1987; Apr. 30, 1991, eff. Aug. 1, 1991; Apr. 22, 1993, eff. Aug. 1, 1993; Apr. 26, 1999, eff. Dec. 1, 1999; Apr. 17, 2000, eff. Dec. 1, 2000; Apr. 23, 2008, eff. Dec. 1, 2008.)

NOTES OF ADVISORY COMMITTEE ON RULES—1983

*Subdivision (a)* of this rule is derived from former Bankruptcy Rule 120(a). While the rule applies to voluntary and involuntary cases, the "consent of the parties" referred to is that of petitioning creditors and the debtor in an involuntary case. The last sentence recognizes that the court should not be confined to petitioning creditors in its choice of parties on whom to call for assistance in preparing the list of creditors when the debtor fails to do so. This subdivision implements §§303(j), 707, 1112 and 1307 of the Code by specifying the manner of and persons to whom notice shall be given and requiring the court to hold a hearing on the issue of dismissal.

*Subdivision (b)* is derived from former Bankruptcy Rule 120(b). A dismissal under this subdivision can occur only when the petition has been permitted to be filed pursuant to Rule 1006(b). The provision for notice in paragraph (3) is correlated with the provision in Rule 4006 when there is a waiver, denial, or revocation of a discharge. As pointed out in the Note accompanying Rule 4008, the purpose of notifying creditors of a debtor that no discharge has been granted is to correct their assumption to the contrary so that they can take appropriate steps to protect their claims.

*Subdivision (c)* is new and specifies the notice required for a hearing on dismissal or suspension pursuant to §305 of the Code. The suspension to which this subdivision refers is that of the case; it does not concern abstention of the court in hearing an adversary proceeding pursuant to 28 U.S.C. §1478(b).

*Subdivision (d)*. Any proceeding, whether by a debtor or other party, to dismiss or convert a case under §§706, 707, 1112, or 1307 is commenced by a motion pursuant to Rule 9014.

NOTES OF ADVISORY COMMITTEE ON RULES—1987 AMENDMENT

*Subdivision (d)* is amended to provide that dismissal or conversion pursuant to §§706(a), 707(b), 1112(a), and 1307(b) is not automatically a contested matter under Rule 9014. Conversion or dismissal under these sections is initiated by the filing and serving of a motion as required by Rule 9013. No hearing is required on these motions unless the court directs.

Conversion of a chapter 13 case to a chapter 7 case as authorized by §1307(a) is accomplished by the filing of a notice of conversion. The notice of conversion procedure is modeled on the voluntary dismissal provision of Rule 41(a)(1) F.R.Civ.P. Conversion occurs on the filing of the notice. No court order is required.

*Subdivision (e)* is new and provides the procedure to be followed when a court on its own motion has made a preliminary determination that an individual debtor's chapter 7 case may be dismissed pursuant to §707(b) of the Code, which was added by the 1984 amendments. A debtor's failure to attend the hearing is not a ground for dismissal pursuant to §707(b).

NOTES OF ADVISORY COMMITTEE ON RULES AMENDMENT

*Subdivision (a)* is amended to clarify that all entities required to receive notice under Rule 2002, including but not limited to creditors, are entitled to the 20 day notice of the hearing to dismiss the case. The United States trustee receives the notice pursuant to Rule 2002(k).

The word "petition" is changed to "case" in subdivisions (a), (b), and (c) to conform to §§707, 930, 1112, 1208, and 1307.

*Subdivision (d)* is amended to conform to §348(c) of the Code which refers to the "conversion order."

*Subdivisions (a) and (d)* are amended to provide procedures for dismissal or conversion of a chapter 12 case. Procedures for dismissal or conversion under §1208(a) and (b) are the same as the procedures for dismissal or conversion of a chapter 13 case under §1307(a) and (b).

*Subdivision (e)* is amended to conform to the 1986 amendment to §707(b) of the Code which permits the United States trustee to make a motion to dismiss a case for substantial abuse. The time limit for such a motion is added by this subdivision. In general, the facts that are the basis for a motion to dismiss under §707(b) exist at the time the case is commenced and usually can be discovered early in the case by reviewing the debtor's schedules and examining the debtor at the meeting of creditors. Since dismissal for substantial abuse has the effect of denying the debtor a discharge in the chapter 7 case based on matters which may be discovered early, a motion to dismiss under §707(b) is analogous to an objection to discharge pursuant to Rule 4004 and, therefore, should be required to be made within a specified time period. If matters relating to substantial abuse are not discovered within the time period specified in subdivision (e) because of the debtor's false testimony, refusal to obey a court order, fraudulent schedules or other fraud, and the debtor receives a discharge, the debtor's conduct may constitute the basis for revocation of the discharge under §727(d) and (e) of the Code.

NOTES OF ADVISORY COMMITTEE ON RULES—1993 AMENDMENT

*Subdivision (d)* is amended to clarify that the date of the filing of a notice of conversion in a chapter 12 or chapter 13 case is treated as the date of the conversion order for the purpose of applying Rule 1019. Other amendments are stylistic and make no substantive change.

COMMITTEE NOTES ON RULES—1999 AMENDMENT

*Subdivision (b)(3)*, which provides that notice of dismissal for failure to pay the filing fee shall be sent to all creditors within 30 days after the dismissal, is deleted as unnecessary. Rule 2002(f) provides for notice to creditors of the dismissal of a case.

Rule 2002(a) and this rule currently require notice to all creditors of a hearing on dismissal of a voluntary chapter 7 case for the debtor's failure to file a list of creditors, schedules, and statement of financial affairs within the time provided in §707(a)(3) of the Code. A new subdivision (c) is added to provide that the United States trustee, who is the only entity with standing to file a motion to dismiss under §707(a)(3) or §1307(c)(9), is required to serve the motion on only the debtor, the trustee, and any other entities as the court directs. This amendment, and the amendment to Rule 2002, will have the effect of avoiding the expense of sending notices of the motion to all creditors in a chapter 7 case.

New subdivision (f) is the same as current subdivision (d), except that it provides that a motion to suspend all proceedings in a case or to dismiss a case for substantial abuse of chapter 7 under §707(b) is governed by Rule 9014.

Other amendments to this rule are stylistic or for clarification.

*GAP Report on Rule 1017.* No changes since publication, except for stylistic changes in Rule 1017(e) and (f).

COMMITTEE NOTES ON RULES—2000 AMENDMENT

This rule is amended to permit the court to grant a timely request filed by the United States trustee for an extension of time to file a motion to dismiss a chapter 7 case under §707(b), whether the court rules on the request before or after the expiration of the 60-day period.

*Reporter's Note on Text of Rule 1017(e).* The above text of Rule 1017(e) is not based on the text of the rule in effect on this date. The above text embodies amendments that have been promulgated by the Supreme Court in April 1999 and, unless Congress acts with respect to the amendments, will become effective on December 1, 1999.

*GAP Report on Rule 1017(e).* No changes since publication.

COMMITTEE NOTES ON RULES—2008 AMENDMENT

Subdivision (e) is amended to implement the 2005 amendments to §707 of the Code. These statutory amendments permit conversion of a chapter 7 case to a case under chapter 11 or 13, change the basis for dismissal or conversion from "substantial abuse" to "abuse," authorize parties other than the United States trustee to bring motions under §707(b) under certain circumstances, and add §707(c) to create an explicit ground for dismissal based on the request of a victim of a crime of violence or drug trafficking. The conforming amendments to subdivision (e) preserve the time limits already in place for §707(b) motions, except to the extent that §704(b)(2) sets the deadline for the United States trustee to act. In contrast to the grounds for a motion to dismiss under §707(b)(2), which are quite specific, the grounds under §707(b)(1) and (3) are very general. Therefore, to enable the debtor to respond, subdivision (e) requires that motions to dismiss under §707(b)(1) and (3) state with particularity the circumstances alleged to constitute abuse.

*Changes Made After Publication.* No changes were made after publication.

## Rule 1018. Contested Involuntary Petitions; Contested Petitions Commencing Ancillary Cases; Proceedings to Vacate Order for Relief; Applicability of Rules in Part VII Governing Adversary Proceedings

The following rules in Part VII apply to all proceedings relating to a contested involuntary petition, to proceedings relating to a contested petition commencing a case ancillary to a foreign proceeding, and to all proceedings to vacate an order for relief: Rules 7005, 7008–7010, 7015, 7016, 7024–7026, 7028–7037, 7052, 7054, 7056, and 7062, except as otherwise provided in Part I of these rules and unless the court otherwise directs. The court may direct that other rules in Part VII shall also apply. For the purposes of this rule a reference in the Part VII rules to adversary proceedings shall be read as a reference to proceedings relating to a contested involuntary petition, or contested ancillary petition, or proceedings to vacate an order for relief. Reference in the Federal Rules of Civil Procedure to the complaint shall be read as a reference to the petition.

(As amended Mar. 30, 1987, eff. Aug. 1, 1987.)

NOTES OF ADVISORY COMMITTEE ON RULES—1983

The rules in Part VII to which this rule refers are adaptations of the Federal Rules of Civil Procedure for the purpose of governing the procedure in adversary proceedings in cases under the Code. See the Note accompanying Rule 7001 *infra*. Because of the special need for dispatch and expedition in the determination of the issues in an involuntary petition, see *Acme Harvester Co. v. Beekman Lumber Co.*, 222 U.S. 300, 309 (1911), the objective of some of the Federal Rules of Civil Procedure and their adaptations in Part VII to facilitate the settlement of multiple controversies involving many persons in a single lawsuit is not compatible with the exigencies of bankruptcy administration. See *United States F. & G. Co. v. Bray*, 225 U.S. 205, 218 (1912). For that reason Rules 7013, 7014 and 7018–7023 will rarely be appropriate in a proceeding on a contested petition.

Certain terms used in the Federal Rules of Civil Procedure have altered meanings when they are made applicable in cases under the Code by these rules. See Rule 9002 *infra*. This Rule 1018 requires that the terms "adversary proceedings" when used in the rules in Part VII and "complaint" when used in the Federal Rules of Civil Procedure be given altered meanings when they are made applicable to proceedings relating to a contested petition or proceedings to vacate any order for relief. A motion to vacate an order for relief, whether or not made on a petition that was or could have been contested, is governed by the rules in Part VII referred to in this Rule 1018.

NOTES OF ADVISORY COMMITTEE ON RULES—1987 AMENDMENT

Rule 1018 is amended to include within its terms a petition commencing an ancillary case when it is contested. This provision was formerly included in Rule 1003(e)(4).

Although this rule does not contain an explicit authorization for the entry of an order for relief when a debtor refuses to cooperate in discovery relating to a contested involuntary petition, the court has ample power under Rule 37(b) F.R.Civ.P., as incorporated by Rule 7037, to enter an order for relief under appropriate circumstances. Rule 37(b) authorizes the court to enter judgment by default or an order that "facts shall be taken as established."

## Rule 1019. Conversion of a Chapter 11 Reorganization Case, Chapter 12 Family Farmer's Debt Adjustment Case, or Chapter 13 Individual's Debt Adjustment Case to a Chapter 7 Liquidation Case

When a chapter 11, chapter 12, or chapter 13 case has been converted or reconverted to a chapter 7 case:

(1) *Filing of Lists, Inventories, Schedules, Statements.*

(A) Lists, inventories, schedules, and statements of financial affairs theretofore filed shall be deemed to be filed in the chapter 7 case, unless the court directs otherwise. If they have not been previously filed, the debtor shall comply with Rule 1007 as if an order for relief had been entered on an involuntary petition on the date of the entry of the order directing that the case continue under chapter 7.

(B) If a statement of intention is required, it shall be filed within 30 days after entry of the order of conversion or before the first date set for the meeting of creditors, whichever is earlier. The court may grant an extension of time for cause only on written motion filed, or oral request made during a hearing, before the time has expired. Notice of an extension shall be given to the United States trustee and to any committee, trustee, or other party as the court may direct.

(2) *New Filing Periods.* A new time period for filing a motion under §707(b) or (c), a claim, a complaint objecting to discharge, or a complaint to obtain a determination of dischargeability of any debt shall commence under Rules 1017, 3002, 4004, or 4007, but a new time period shall not commence if a chapter 7 case had been converted to a chapter 11, 12, or 13 case and thereafter reconverted to a chapter 7 case and the time for filing a motion under §707(b) or (c), a claim, a complaint objecting to discharge, or a complaint to obtain a determination of the dischargeability of any debt, or any extension thereof, expired in the original chapter 7 case.

(3) *Claims Filed Before Conversion.* All claims actually filed by a creditor before conversion of the case are deemed filed in the chapter 7 case.

(4) *Turnover of Records and Property.* After qualification of, or assumption of duties by the chapter 7 trustee, any debtor in possession or trustee previously acting in the chapter 11, 12, or 13 case shall, forthwith, unless otherwise ordered, turn over to the chapter 7 trustee all records and property of the estate in the possession or control of the debtor in possession or trustee.

(5) *Filing Final Report and Schedule of Postpetition Debts.*

(A) *Conversion of Chapter 11 or Chapter 12 Case.* Unless the court directs otherwise, if a chapter 11 or chapter 12 case is converted to chapter 7, the debtor in possession or, if the debtor is not a debtor in possession, the trustee serving at the time of conversion, shall:

(i) not later than 14 days after conversion of the case, file a schedule of unpaid debts incurred after the filing of the petition and before conversion of the case, including the name and address of each holder of a claim; and

(ii) not later than 30 days after conversion of the case, file and transmit to the United States trustee a final report and account;

(B) *Conversion of Chapter 13 Case.* Unless the court directs otherwise, if a chapter 13 case is converted to chapter 7,

(i) the debtor, not later than 14 days after conversion of the case, shall file a schedule of unpaid debts incurred after the filing of the petition and before conversion of the case, including the name and address of each holder of a claim; and

(ii) the trustee, not later than 30 days after conversion of the case, shall file and transmit to the United States trustee a final report and account;

(C) *Conversion After Confirmation of a Plan.* Unless the court orders otherwise, if a chapter 11, chapter 12, or chapter 13 case is converted to chapter 7 after confirmation of a plan, the debtor shall file:

(i) a schedule of property not listed in the final report and account acquired after the filing of the petition but before conversion, except if the case is converted from chapter 13 to chapter 7 and §348(f)(2) does not apply;

(ii) a schedule of unpaid debts not listed in the final report and account incurred after confirmation but before the conversion; and

(iii) a schedule of executory contracts and unexpired leases entered into or assumed after the filing of the petition but before conversion.

(D) *Transmission to United States Trustee* The clerk shall forthwith transmit to the United States trustee a copy of every schedule filed pursuant to Rule 1019(5).

(6) *Postpetition Claims; Preconversion Administrative Expenses; Notice.* A request for payment of an administrative expense incurred before conversion of the case is timely filed under §503(a) of the Code if it is filed before conversion or a time fixed by the court. If the request is filed by a governmental unit, it is timely if it is filed before conversion or within

the later of a time fixed by the court or 180 days after the date of the conversion. A claim of a kind specified in §348(d) may be filed in accordance with Rules 3001(a)–(d) and 3002. Upon the filing of the schedule of unpaid debts incurred after commencement of the case and before conversion, the clerk, or some other person as the court may direct, shall give notice to those entities listed on the schedule of the time for filing a request for payment of an administrative expense and, unless a notice of insufficient assets to pay a dividend is mailed in accordance with Rule 2002(e), the time for filing a claim of a kind specified in §348(d).

(As amended Mar. 30, 1987, eff. Aug. 1, 1987; Apr. 30, 1991, eff. Aug. 1, 1991; Apr. 23, 1996, eff. Dec. 1, 1996; Apr. 11, 1997, eff. Dec. 1, 1997; Apr. 26, 1999, eff. Dec. 1, 1999; Apr. 23, 2008, eff. Dec. 1, 2008; Mar. 26, 2009, eff. Dec. 1, 2009.)

NOTES OF ADVISORY COMMITTEE ON RULES—1983

This rule is derived from former Bankruptcy Rule 122 and implements §348 of the Code. The rule applies to proceedings in a chapter 7 case following supersession of a case commenced under chapter 11 or 13, whether the latter was initiated by an original petition or was converted from a pending chapter 7 or another chapter case. The rule is not intended to invalidate any action taken in the superseded case before its conversion to chapter 7.

*Paragraph (1):* If requirements applicable in the superseded case respecting the filing of schedules of debts and property, or lists of creditors and inventory, and of statements of financial affairs have been complied with before the order directing conversion to liquidation, these documents will ordinarily provide all the information about the debts, property, financial affairs, and contracts of the debtor needed for the administration of the estate. If the information submitted in the superseded case is inadequate for the purposes of administration, however, the court may direct the preparation of further informational material and the manner and time of its submission pursuant to paragraph (1). If no schedules, lists, inventories, or statements were filed in the superseded case, this paragraph imposes the duty on the debtor to file schedules and a statement of affairs pursuant to Rule 1007 as if an involuntary petition had been filed on the date when the court directed the conversion of the case to a liquidation case.

*Paragraphs (2) and (3).* Paragraph (2) requires notice to be given to all creditors of the order of conversion. The notice is to be included in the notice of the meeting of creditors and Official Form No. 16 may be adapted for use. A meeting of creditors may have been held in the superseded case as required by §341(a) of the Code but that would not dispense with the need to hold one in the ensuing liquidation case. Section 701(a) of the Code permits the court to appoint the trustee acting in the chapter 11 or 13 case as interim trustee in the chapter 7 case. Section 702(a) of the Code allows creditors to elect a trustee but only at the meeting of creditors held under §341. The right to elect a trustee is not lost because the chapter 7 case follows a chapter 11 or 13 case. Thus a meeting of creditors is necessary. The date fixed for the meeting of creditors will control at least the time for filing claims pursuant to Rule 3002(c). That time will remain applicable in the ensuing chapter 7 case except as paragraph (3) provides, if that time had expired in an earlier chapter 7 case which was converted to the chapter 11 or 13 case, it is not revived in the subsequent chapter 7 case. The same is true if the time for filing a complaint objecting to discharge or to determine nondischargeability of a debt had expired. Paragraph (3), however, recognizes that such time may be extended by the court under Rule 4004 or 4007 on motion made within the original prescribed time.

*Paragraph (4)* renders it unnecessary to file anew claims that had been filed in the chapter 11 or 13 case before conversion to chapter 7.

*Paragraph (5)* contemplates that typically, after the court orders conversion of a chapter case to liquidation, a trustee under chapter 7 will forthwith take charge of the property of the estate and proceed expeditiously to liquidate it. The court may appoint the interim trustee in the chapter 7 case pursuant to §701(a) of the Code. If creditors do not elect a trustee under §702, the interim trustee becomes the trustee.

*Paragraph (6)* requires the trustee or debtor in possession acting in the chapter 11 or 13 case to file a final report and schedule of debts incurred in that case. This schedule will provide the information necessary for giving the notice required by paragraph (7) of the rule.

*Paragraph (7)* requires that claims that arose in the chapter 11 or 13 case be filed within 60 days after entry of the order converting the case to one under chapter 7. Claims not scheduled pursuant to paragraph (6) of the rule or arising from the rejection of an executory contract entered into during the chapter case may be filed within a time fixed by the court. Pursuant to §348(c) of the Code, the conversion order is treated as the order for relief to fix the time for the trustee to assume or reject executory contracts under §365(d).

*Paragraph (8)* permits the extension of the time for filing claims when claims are not timely filed but only with respect to any surplus that may remain in the estate. See also §726(a)(2)(C) and (3) of the Code.

NOTES OF ADVISORY COMMITTEE ON RULES—1987 AMENDMENT

*Paragraph (1)* is amended to provide for the filing of a statement of intention in a case converted to chapter 7. Paragraph (1)(B) is added to provide for the filing of the statement of intention when a case is converted to chapter 7. The time for filing the statement of intention and for an extension of that time is governed by §521(2)(A) of the Code. An extension of time for other required filings is governed by Rule 1007(c), which paragraph (1)(A) incorporates by reference. Because of the amendment to Rule 1007(c), the filing of new lists, schedules, and statements is now governed exclusively by Rule 1019(1).

*Paragraph (3)* of the rule is expanded to include the effect of conversion of a chapter 11 or 13 case to a chapter 7 case. On conversion of a case from chapter 11 or 13 to a chapter 7 case, parties have a new period within which to file claims or complaints relating to the granting of the discharge or the dischargeability of a debt. This amendment is consistent with the holding and reasoning of the court in *F & M Marquette Nat'l Bank v. Richards*, 780 F.2d 24 (8th Cir. 1985).

*Paragraph (4)* is amended to deal directly with the status of claims which are properly listed on the schedules filed in a chapter 11 case and deemed filed pursuant to §1111(a) of the Code. Section 1111(a) is only applicable to the chapter 11 case. On conversion of the chapter 11 case to a chapter 7 case, paragraph (4) governs the status of claims filed in the chapter 11 case. The Third Circuit properly construed paragraph (4) as applicable to claims deemed filed in the superseded chapter 11 case. *In re Crouthamel Potato Chip Co.*, 786 F.2d 141 (3d Cir. 1986).

The amendment to paragraph (4) changes that result by providing that only claims that are actually filed in the chapter 11 case are treated as filed in the superseding chapter 7 case. When chapter 11 cases are converted to chapter 7 cases, difficulties in obtaining and verifying the debtors' records are common. It is unfair to the chapter 7 trustee and creditors to require that they be bound by schedules which may not be subject to verification.

*Paragraph (6)* is amended to place the obligation on the chapter 13 debtor to file a schedule of unpaid debts incurred during the superseded chapter 13 case.

NOTES OF ADVISORY COMMITTEE ON RULES—1991 AMENDMENT

This rule is amended to include conversion of a case from chapter 12 to chapter 7 and to implement the United States trustee system.

The amendments to paragraph (1)(A) are stylistic. Reference to the statement of executory contracts is deleted to conform to the amendment to Rule 1007(b)(1) which changes the statement to a schedule of executory contracts and unexpired leases.

*Paragraph (1)(B)* is amended to enable the United States trustee to monitor the progress of the case and to take appropriate action to enforce the debtor's obligation to perform the statement of intention in a timely manner.

*Paragraph (2)* is deleted because notice of conversion of the case is required by Rules 1017(d), 2002(f)(2), and 9022. The United States trustee, who supervises trustees pursuant to 28 U.S.C. §586(a), may give notice of the conversion to the trustee in the superseded case.

*Paragraph (6)*, renumbered as paragraph (5), is amended to reduce to 15 days the time for filing a schedule of postpetition debts and requires inclusion of the name and address of each creditor in connection with the postpetition debt. These changes will enable the clerk to send postpetition creditors a timely notice of the meeting of creditors held pursuant to §341(a) of the Code. The amendments to this paragraph also provide the United States trustee with the final report and account of the superseded case, and with a copy of every schedule filed after conversion of the case. Conversion to chapter 7 terminates the service of the trustee in the superseded case pursuant to §348(e) of the Code. Sections 704(a)(9), 1106(a)(1), 1107(a), 1202(b)(1), 1203 and 1302(b)(1) of the Code require the trustee or debtor in possession to file a final report and account with the court and the United States trustee. The words "with the court" are deleted as unnecessary. See Rules 5005(a) and 9001(3).

*Paragraph (7)*, renumbered as paragraph (6), is amended to conform the time for filing postpetition claims to the time for filing prepetition claims pursuant to paragraph (3) (renumbered as paragraph (2)) of this rule and Rule 3002(c). This paragraph is also amended to eliminate the need for a court order to provide notice of the time for filing claims. It is anticipated that this notice will be given together with the notice of the meeting of creditors. It is amended further to avoid the need to fix a time for filing claims arising under §365(d) if it is a no asset case upon conversion. If assets become available for distribution, the court may fix a time for filing such claims pursuant to Rule 3002(c)(4).

The additions of references to unexpired leases in paragraph (1)(A) and in paragraphs (6) and (7) (renumbered as paragraphs (5) and (6)) are technical amendments to clarify that unexpired leases are included as well as other executory contracts.

NOTES OF ADVISORY COMMITTEE ON RULES—1996 AMENDMENT

*Subdivision (7)* is abrogated to conform to the abrogation of Rule 3002(c)(6).

*GAP Report on Rule 1019.* No changes were made to the text of the rule. The Committee Note was changed to conform to the proposed changes to Rule 3002 (see GAP Report on Rule 3002 below).

NOTES OF ADVISORY COMMITTEE ON RULES—1997 AMENDMENT

The amendments to subdivisions (3) and (5) are technical corrections and stylistic changes. The phrase "superseded case" is deleted because it creates the erroneous impression that conversion of a case results in a new case that is distinct from the original case. Similarly, the phrase "original petition" is deleted because it erroneously implies that there is a second petition with respect to a converted case. See §348 of the Code.

*GAP Report on Rule 1019.* No changes to the published draft.

COMMITTEE NOTES ON RULES—1999 AMENDMENT

*Paragraph (1)(B)* is amended to clarify that a motion for an extension of time to file a statement of intention must be made by written motion filed before the time expires, or by oral request made at a hearing before the time expires.

*Subdivision (6)* is amended to provide that a holder of an administrative expense claim incurred after the commencement of the case, but before conversion to chapter 7, is required to file a request for payment under §503(a) within a time fixed by the court, rather than a proof of claim under §501 and Rules 3001(a)–(d) and 3002. The 180-day period applicable to governmental units is intended to conform to §502(b)(9) of the Code and Rule 3002(c)(1). It is unnecessary for the court to fix a time for filing requests for payment if it appears that there are not sufficient assets to pay preconversion administrative expenses. If a time for filing a request for payment of an administrative expense is fixed by the court, it may be enlarged as provided in Rule 9006(b). If an administrative expense claimant fails to timely file the request, it may be tardily filed under §503(a) if permitted by the court for cause.

The final sentence of Rule 1019(6) is deleted because it is unnecessary in view of the other amendments to this paragraph. If a party has entered into a postpetition contract or lease with the trustee or debtor that constitutes an administrative expense, a timely request for payment must be filed in accordance with this paragraph and §503(b) of the Code. The time for filing a proof of claim in connection with the rejection of any other executory contract or unexpired lease is governed by Rule 3002(c)(4).

The phrase "including the United States, any state, or any subdivision thereof" is deleted as unnecessary. Other amendments to this rule are stylistic.

*GAP Report on Rule 1019.* The proposed amendments to Rule 1019(6) were changed to delete the deadline for filing requests for payment of preconversion administrative expenses that would be applicable in all cases, and to provide instead that the court may fix such a deadline. The committee note was revised to clarify that it is not necessary for the court to fix a deadline where there are insufficient assets to pay preconversion administrative expenses.

COMMITTEE NOTES ON RULES—2008 AMENDMENT

Subdivision (2) is amended to include a new filing period for motions under §707(b) and (c) of the Code when a case is converted to chapter 7. The establishment of a deadline for filing such motions is not intended to express a position as to whether such motions are permitted under the Code.

*Changes Made After Publication.* The Committee Note was amended by adding the second sentence to the Note stating explicitly that the rule was not intended to take a position on whether motions to dismiss a case under §707(b) and (c) are proper in a case that is converted from another chapter.

COMMITTEE NOTES ON RULES—2009 AMENDMENT

The rule is amended to implement changes in connection with the amendment to Rule 9006(a) and the manner by which time is computed under the rules. The deadlines in the rule are amended to substitute a deadline that is a multiple of seven days. Throughout the rules, deadlines are amended in the following manner:

- 5-day periods become 7-day periods
- 10-day periods become 14-day periods
- 15-day periods become 14-day periods
- 20-day periods become 21-day periods
- 25-day periods become 28-day periods

## Rule 1020. Small Business Chapter 11 Reorganization Case

(a) SMALL BUSINESS DEBTOR DESIGNATION voluntary chapter 11 case, the debtor shall state in the petition whether the debtor is a small business debtor. In an involuntary chapter 11 case, the debtor shall file within 14 days after entry of the order for relief a statement as to whether the debtor is a small business debtor. Except as provided in subdivision (c), the status of the case as a small business case shall be in accordance with the debtor's statement under this subdivision, unless and until the court enters an order finding that the debtor's statement is incorrect.

(b) OBJECTING TO DESIGNATION. Except as provided in subdivision (c), the United States trustee or a party in interest may file an objection to the debtor's statement under subdivision (a) no later than 30 days after the conclusion of the meeting of creditors held under §341(a) of the Code, or within 30 days after any amendment to the statement, whichever is later.

(c) APPOINTMENT OF COMMITTEE OF UNSECURED CREDITORS. If a committee of unsecured creditors has been appointed under §1102(a)(1), the case shall proceed as a small business case only if, and from the time when, the court enters an order determining that the committee has not been sufficiently active and representative to provide effective oversight of the debtor and that the debtor satisfies all the other requirements for being a small business. A request for a determination under this subdivision may be filed by the United States trustee or a party in interest only within a reasonable time after the failure of the committee to be sufficiently active and representative. The debtor may file a request for a determination at any time as to whether the committee has been sufficiently active and representative.

(d) PROCEDURE FOR OBJECTION OR DETERMINATION. Any objection or request for a determination under this rule shall be governed by Rule 9014 and served on: the debtor; the debtor's attorney; the United States trustee; the trustee; any committee appointed under §1102 or its authorized agent, or, if no committee of unsecured creditors has been appointed under §1102, the creditors included on the list filed under Rule 1007(d); and any other entity as the court directs.

(Added Apr. 11, 1997, eff. Dec. 1, 1997; amended Apr. 23, 2008, eff. Dec. 1, 2008; Mar. 26, 2009, eff. Dec. 1, 2009.)

NOTES OF ADVISORY COMMITTEE ON RULES—1997

This rule is designed to implement §§1121(e) and 1125(f) that were added to the Code by the Bankruptcy Reform Act of 1994.

*GAP Report on Rule 1020.* The phrase "or by a later date as the court, for cause, may fix" at the end of the published draft was deleted. The general provisions on reducing or extending time periods under Rule 9006 will be applicable.

COMMITTEE NOTES ON RULES—2008 AMENDMENT

Under the Code, as amended in 2005, there are no longer any provisions permitting or requiring a small business debtor to elect to be treated as a small business. Therefore, the election provisions in the rule are eliminated.

The 2005 amendments to the Code include several provisions relating to small business cases under chapter 11. Section 101 includes definitions of "small business debtor" and "small business case." The purpose of the new language in this rule is to provide a procedure for informing the parties, the United States trustee, and the court of whether the debtor is a small business debtor, and to provide procedures for resolving disputes regarding the proper characterization of the debtor. Because it is important to resolve such disputes early in the case, a time limit for objecting to the debtor's self-designation is imposed. Rule 9006(b)(1), which governs enlargement of time, is applicable to the time limits set forth in this rule.

An important factor in determining whether the debtor is a small business debtor is whether the United States trustee has appointed a committee of unsecured creditors under §1102, and whether such a committee is sufficiently active and representative. Subdivision (c), relating to the appointment and activity of a committee of unsecured creditors, is designed to be consistent with the Code's definition of "small business debtor."

*Changes Made After Publication.* No changes were made after publication.

COMMITTEE NOTES ON RULES—2009 AMENDMENT

The rule is amended to implement changes in connection with the amendment to Rule 9006(a) and the manner by which time is computed under the rules. The deadline in the rule is amended to substitute a deadline that is a multiple of seven days. Throughout the rules, deadlines are amended in the following manner:

- 5-day periods become 7-day periods
- 10-day periods become 14-day periods
- 15-day periods become 14-day periods
- 20-day periods become 21-day periods
- 25-day periods become 28-day periods

## Rule 1021. Health Care Business Case

(a) HEALTH CARE BUSINESS DESIGNATION. Unless the court orders otherwise, if a petition in a case under chapter 7, chapter 9, or chapter 11 states that the debtor is a health care business, the case shall proceed as a case in which the debtor is a health care business.

(b) MOTION. The United States trustee or a party in interest may file a motion to determine whether the debtor is a health care business. The motion shall be transmitted to the United States trustee and served on: the debtor; the trustee; any committee elected under §705 or appointed under §1102 of the Code or its authorized agent, or, if the case is a chapter 9 municipality case or a chapter 11 reorganization case and no committee of unsecured creditors has been appointed under §1102, the creditors included on the list filed under Rule 1007(d); and any other entity as the court directs. The motion shall be governed by Rule 9014.

(Added Apr. 23, 2008, eff. Dec. 1, 2008.)

COMMITTEE NOTES ON RULES—2008

Section 101(27A) of the Code, added by the 2005 amendments, defines a health care business. This rule provides procedures for designating the debtor as a health care business. The debtor in a voluntary case, or petitioning creditors in an involuntary case, make that designation by checking the appropriate box on the petition. The rule also provides procedures for resolving disputes regarding the status of the debtor as a health care business.

*Changes Made After Publication.* No changes were made after publication.

## PART II—OFFICERS AND ADMINISTRATION; NOTICES; MEETINGS; EXAMINATIONS; ELECTIONS; ATTORNEYS AND ACCOUNTANTS

### Rule 2001. Appointment of Interim Trustee Before Order for Relief in a Chapter 7 Liquidation Case

(a) APPOINTMENT. At any time following the commencement of an involuntary liquidation case and before an order for relief, the court on written motion of a party in interest may order the appointment of an interim trustee under §303(g) of the Code. The motion shall set forth the necessity for the appointment and may be granted only after hearing on notice to the debtor, the petitioning creditors, the United States trustee, and other parties in interest as the court may designate.

(b) BOND OF MOVANT. An interim trustee may not be appointed under this rule unless the movant furnishes a bond in an amount approved by the court, conditioned to indemnify the debtor for costs, attorney's fee, expenses, and damages allowable under §303(i) of the Code.

(c) ORDER OF APPOINTMENT. The order directing the appointment of an interim trustee shall state the reason the appointment is necessary and shall specify the trustee's duties.

(d) TURNOVER AND REPORT. Following qualification of the trustee selected under §702 of the Code, the interim trustee, unless otherwise ordered, shall (1) forthwith deliver to the trustee all the records and property of the estate in possession or subject to control of the interim trustee and, (2) within 30 days thereafter file a final report and account.

(As amended Mar. 30, 1987, eff. Aug. 1, 1987; Apr. 30, 1991, eff. Aug. 1, 1991.)

NOTES OF ADVISORY COMMITTEE ON RULES—1983

This rule is adapted from former Bankruptcy Rule 201. See also former Chapter X Rule 10-201. In conformity with title 11 of the United States Code, this rule substitutes "interim trustee" for "receiver." Subdivision (a) and (e) of Rule 201 are not included because the provisions contained therein are found in detail in §303(g) of the Code, or they are inconsistent with §701 of the Code. Similarly, the provisions in Rule 201(d) relating to a debtor's counterbond are not included because of their presence in §303(g).

*Subdivision (a)* makes it clear that the court may not on its own motion order the appointment of an interim trustee before an order for relief is entered. Appointment may be ordered only on motion of a party in interest.

*Subdivision (b)* requires those seeking the appointment of an interim trustee to furnish a bond. The bond may be the same one required of petitioning creditors under §303(e) of the Code to indemnify the debtor for damages allowed by the court under §303(i).

*Subdivision (c)* requires that the order specify which duties enumerated in §303(g) shall be performed by the interim trustee. Reference should be made to Rule 2015 for additional duties required of an interim trustee including keeping records and filing periodic reports with the court.

*Subdivision (d)* requires turnover of records and property to the trustee selected under §702 of the Code, after qualification. That trustee may be the interim trustee who becomes the trustee because of the failure of creditors to elect one under §702(d) or the trustee elected by creditors under §702(b), (c).

NOTES OF ADVISORY COMMITTEE ON RULES—1991 AMENDMENT

This rule is amended to conform to §303(g) of the Code which provides that the United States trustee appoints the interim trustee. See Rule X-1003. This rule does not apply to the exercise by the court of the power to act sua sponte pursuant to §105(a) of the Code.

### Rule 2002. Notices to Creditors, Equity Security Holders, Administrators in Foreign Proceedings, Persons Against Whom Provisional Relief is Sought in Ancillary and Other Cross-Border Cases, United States, and United States Trustee

(a) TWENTY-ONE-DAY NOTICES TO PARTIES IN INTEREST. Except as provided in subdivisions (h), (i), (*l*), (p), and (q) of this rule, the clerk, or some other person as the court may direct, shall give the debtor, the trustee, all creditors and indenture trustees at least 21 days' notice by mail of:

(1) the meeting of creditors under §341 or §1104(b) of the Code, which notice, unless the court orders otherwise, shall include the debtor's employer identification number, social security number, and any other federal taxpayer identification number;

(2) a proposed use, sale, or lease of property of the estate other than in the ordinary course of business, unless the court for cause shown shortens the time or directs another method of giving notice;

(3) the hearing on approval of a compromise or settlement of a controversy other than approval of an agreement pursuant to Rule 4001(d), unless the court for cause shown directs that notice not be sent;

(4) in a chapter 7 liquidation, a chapter 11 reorganization case, or a chapter 12 family farmer debt adjustment case, the hearing on the dismissal of the case or the conversion of the case to another chapter, unless the hearing is under §707(a)(3) or §707(b) or is on dismissal of the case for failure to pay the filing fee;

(5) the time fixed to accept or reject a proposed modification of a plan;

(6) a hearing on any entity's request for compensation or reimbursement of expenses if the request exceeds $1,000;

(7) the time fixed for filing proofs of claims pursuant to Rule 3003(c); and

(8) the time fixed for filing objections and the hearing to consider confirmation of a chapter 12 plan.

(b) TWENTY-EIGHT-DAY NOTICES TO P INTEREST. Except as provided in subdivision ( of this rule, the clerk, or some other person as the court may direct, shall give the debtor, the trustee, all creditors and indenture trustees not less than 28 days' notice by mail of the time fixed (1) for filing objections and the hearing to consider approval of a disclosure statement or, under §1125(f), to make a final determination whether the plan provides adequate information so that a separate disclosure statement is not necessary; and (2) for filing objections and the hearing to consider confirmation of a chapter 9, chapter 11, or chapter 13 plan.

(c) CONTENT OF NOTICE.

(1) *Proposed Use, Sale, or Lease of Property* Subject to Rule 6004, the notice of a proposed use, sale, or lease of property required by sub-

division (a)(2) of this rule shall include the time and place of any public sale, the terms and conditions of any private sale and the time fixed for filing objections. The notice of a proposed use, sale, or lease of property, including real estate, is sufficient if it generally describes the property. The notice of a proposed sale or lease of personally identifiable information under § 363(b)(1) of the Code shall state whether the sale is consistent with any policy prohibiting the transfer of the information.

(2) *Notice of Hearing on Compensation.* The notice of a hearing on an application for compensation or reimbursement of expenses required by subdivision (a)(6) of this rule shall identify the applicant and the amounts requested.

(3) *Notice of Hearing on Confirmation When Plan Provides for an Injunction.* If a plan provides for an injunction against conduct not otherwise enjoined under the Code, the notice required under Rule 2002(b)(2) shall:

(A) include in conspicuous language (bold, italic, or underlined text) a statement that the plan proposes an injunction;

(B) describe briefly the nature of the injunction; and

(C) identify the entities that would be subject to the injunction.

(d) NOTICE TO EQUITY SECURITY HOLDERS. In a chapter 11 reorganization case, unless otherwise ordered by the court, the clerk, or some other person as the court may direct, shall in the manner and form directed by the court give notice to all equity security holders of (1) the order for relief; (2) any meeting of equity security holders held pursuant to § 341 of the Code; (3) the hearing on the proposed sale of all or substantially all of the debtor's assets; (4) the hearing on the dismissal or conversion of a case to another chapter; (5) the time fixed for filing objections to and the hearing to consider approval of a disclosure statement; (6) the time fixed for filing objections to and the hearing to consider confirmation of a plan; and (7) the time fixed to accept or reject a proposed modification of a plan.

(e) NOTICE OF NO DIVIDEND. In a chapter 7 liquidation case, if it appears from the schedules that there are no assets from which a dividend can be paid, the notice of the meeting of creditors may include a statement to that effect; that it is unnecessary to file claims; and that if sufficient assets become available for the payment of a dividend, further notice will be given for the filing of claims.

(f) OTHER NOTICES. Except as provided in subdivision (*l*) of this rule, the clerk, or some other person as the court may direct, shall give the debtor, all creditors, and indenture trustees notice by mail of:

(1) the order for relief;

(2) the dismissal or the conversion of the case to another chapter, or the suspension of proceedings under § 305;

(3) the time allowed for filing claims pursuant to Rule 3002;

(4) the time fixed for filing a complaint objecting to the debtor's discharge pursuant to § 727 of the Code as provided in Rule 4004;

(5) the time fixed for filing a complaint to determine the dischargeability of a debt pursuant to § 523 of the Code as provided in Rule 4007;

(6) the waiver, denial, or revocation of a discharge as provided in Rule 4006;

(7) entry of an order confirming a chapter 9, 11, or 12 plan;

(8) a summary of the trustee's final report in a chapter 7 case if the net proceeds realized exceed $1,500;

(9) a notice under Rule 5008 regarding the presumption of abuse;

(10) a statement under § 704(b)(1) as to whether the debtor's case would be presumed to be an abuse under § 707(b); and

(11) the time to request a delay in the entry of the discharge under §§ 1141(d)(5)(C), 1228(f), and 1328(h). Notice of the time fixed for accepting or rejecting a plan pursuant to Rule 3017(c) shall be given in accordance with Rule 3017(d).

(g) ADDRESSING NOTICES.

(1) Notices required to be mailed under Rule 2002 to a creditor, indenture trustee, or equity security holder shall be addressed as such entity or an authorized agent has directed in its last request filed in the particular case. For the purposes of this subdivision—

(A) a proof of claim filed by a creditor or indenture trustee that designates a mailing address constitutes a filed request to mail notices to that address, unless a notice of no dividend has been given under Rule 2002(e) and a later notice of possible dividend under Rule 3002(c)(5) has not been given; and

(B) a proof of interest filed by an equity security holder that designates a mailing address constitutes a filed request to mail notices to that address.

(2) Except as provided in § 342(f) of the Code, if a creditor or indenture trustee has not filed a request designating a mailing address under Rule 2002(g)(1) or Rule 5003(e), the notices shall be mailed to the address shown on the list of creditors or schedule of liabilities, whichever is filed later. If an equity security holder has not filed a request designating a mailing address under Rule 2002(g)(1) or Rule 5003(e), the notices shall be mailed to the address shown on the list of equity security holders.

(3) If a list or schedule filed under Rule 1007 includes the name and address of a legal representative of an infant or incompetent person, and a person other than that representative files a request or proof of claim designating a name and mailing address that differs from the name and address of the representative included in the list or schedule, unless the court orders otherwise, notices under Rule 2002 shall be mailed to the representative included in the list or schedules and to the name and address designated in the request or proof of claim.

(4) Notwithstanding Rule 2002(g)(1)–(3), an entity and a notice provider may agree that when the notice provider is directed by the court to give a notice, the notice provider shall give the notice to the entity in the manner agreed to and at the address or addresses

the entity supplies to the notice provider. That address is conclusively presumed to be a proper address for the notice. The notice provider's failure to use the supplied address does not invalidate any notice that is otherwise effective under applicable law.

(5) A creditor may treat a notice as not having been brought to the creditor's attention under §342(g)(1) only if, prior to issuance of the notice, the creditor has filed a statement that designates the name and address of the person or organizational subdivision of the creditor responsible for receiving notices under the Code, and that describes the procedures established by the creditor to cause such notices to be delivered to the designated person or subdivision.

(h) NOTICES TO CREDITORS WHOSE CLAIMS ARE FILED. In a chapter 7 case, after 90 days following the first date set for the meeting of creditors under §341 of the Code, the court may direct that all notices required by subdivision (a) of this rule be mailed only to the debtor, the trustee, all indenture trustees, creditors that hold claims for which proofs of claim have been filed, and creditors, if any, that are still permitted to file claims by reason of an extension granted pursuant to Rule 3002(c)(1) or (c)(2). In a case where notice of insufficient assets to pay a dividend has been given to creditors pursuant to subdivision (e) of this rule, after 90 days following the mailing of a notice of the time for filing claims pursuant to Rule 3002(c)(5), the court may direct that notices be mailed only to the entities specified in the preceding sentence.

(i) NOTICES TO COMMITTEES. Copies of all notices required to be mailed pursuant to this rule shall be mailed to the committees elected under §705 or appointed under §1102 of the Code or to their authorized agents. Notwithstanding the foregoing subdivisions, the court may order that notices required by subdivision (a)(2), (3) and (6) of this rule be transmitted to the United States trustee and be mailed only to the committees elected under §705 or appointed under §1102 of the Code or to their authorized agents and to the creditors and equity security holders who serve on the trustee or debtor in possession and file a request that all notices be mailed to them. A committee appointed under §1114 shall receive copies of all notices required by subdivisions (a)(1), (a)(5), (b), (f)(2), and (f)(7), and such other notices as the court may direct.

(j) NOTICES TO THE UNITED STATES. Copies of notices required to be mailed to all creditors under this rule shall be mailed (1) in a chapter 11 reorganization case, to the Securities and Exchange Commission at any place the Commission designates, if the Commission has filed either a notice of appearance in the case or a written request to receive notices; (2) in a commodity broker case, to the Commodity Futures Trading Commission at Washington, D.C.; (3) in a chapter 11 case, to the Internal Revenue Service at its address set out in the register maintained under Rule 5003(e) for the district in which the case is pending; (4) if the papers in the case disclose a debt to the United States other than for taxes, to the United States attorney for the district in which the case is pending and to the department, agency, or instrumentality of the United States through which the debtor became indebted; or (5) if the filed papers disclose a stock interest of the United States, to the Secretary of the Treasury at Washington, D.C.

(k) NOTICES TO UNITED STATES TRUSTEE. Unless the case is a chapter 9 municipality case or unless the United States trustee requests otherwise, the clerk, or some other person as the court may direct, shall transmit to the United States trustee notice of the matters described in subdivisions (a)(2), (a)(3), (a)(4), (a)(8), (b), (f)(1), (f)(2), (f)(4), (f)(6), (f)(7), (f)(8), and (q) of this rule and notice of hearings on all applications for compensation or reimbursement of expenses. Notices to the United States trustee shall be transmitted within the time prescribed in subdivision (a) or (b) of this rule. The United States trustee shall also receive notice of any other matter if such notice is requested by the United States trustee or ordered by the court. Nothing in these rules requires the clerk or any other person to transmit to the United States trustee any notice, schedule, report, application or other document in a case under the Securities Investor Protection Act, 15 U.S.C. §78aaa *et. seq.*

(*l*) NOTICE BY PUBLICATION. The court may order notice by publication if it finds that notice by mail is impracticable or that it is desirable to supplement the notice.

(m) ORDERS DESIGNATING MATTER OF NOTICES. The court may from time to time enter orders designating the matters in respect to which, the entity to whom, and the form and manner in which notices shall be sent except as otherwise provided by these rules.

(n) CAPTION. The caption of every notice given under this rule shall comply with Rule 1005. The caption of every notice required to be given by the debtor to a creditor shall include the information required to be in the notice by §342(c) of the Code.

(*o*) NOTICE OF ORDER FOR RELIEF IN CONSUMER CASE. In a voluntary case commenced by an individual debtor whose debts are primarily consumer debts, the clerk or some other person as the court may direct shall give the trustee and all creditors notice by mail of the order for relief within 21 days from the date thereof.

(p) NOTICE TO A CREDITOR WITH A FOREIGN DRESS.

(1) If, at the request of the United States trustee or a party in interest, or on its own initiative, the court finds that a notice mailed within the time prescribed by these rules would not be sufficient to give a creditor with a foreign address to which notices under these rules are mailed reasonable notice under the circumstances, the court may order that the notice be supplemented with notice by other means or that the time prescribed for the notice by mail be enlarged.

(2) Unless the court for cause orders otherwise, a creditor with a foreign address to which notices under this rule are mailed shall be given at least 30 days' notice of the time fixed for filing a proof of claim under Rule 3002(c) or Rule 3003(c).

(3) Unless the court for cause orders otherwise, the mailing address of a creditor with a foreign address shall be determined under Rule 2002(g).

(q) NOTICE OF PETITION FOR RECOGNITION OF FOREIGN PROCEEDING AND OF COURT'S INTENTION TO COMMUNICATE WITH FOREIGN COURTS AND FOREIGN REPRESENTATIVES.

(1) *Notice of Petition for Recognition.* The clerk, or some other person as the court may direct, shall forthwith give the debtor, all persons or bodies authorized to administer foreign proceedings of the debtor, all entities against whom provisional relief is being sought under §1519 of the Code, all parties to litigation pending in the United States in which the debtor is a party at the time of the filing of the petition, and such other entities as the court may direct, at least 21 days' notice by mail of the hearing on the petition for recognition of a foreign proceeding. The notice shall state whether the petition seeks recognition as a foreign main proceeding or foreign nonmain proceeding.

(2) *Notice of Court's Intention to Communicate with Foreign Courts and Foreign Representatives.* The clerk, or some other person as the court may direct, shall give the debtor, all persons or bodies authorized to administer foreign proceedings of the debtor, all entities against whom provisional relief is being sought under §1519 of the Code, all parties to litigation pending in the United States in which the debtor is a party at the time of the filing of the petition, and such other entities as the court may direct, notice by mail of the court's intention to communicate with a foreign court or foreign representative.

(As amended Pub. L. 98–91, §2(a), Aug. 30, 1983, 97 Stat. 607; Pub. L. 98–353, title III, §321, July 10, 1984, 98 Stat. 357; Mar. 30, 1987, eff. Aug. 1, 1987; Apr. 30, 1991, eff. Aug. 1, 1991; Apr. 22, 1993, eff. Aug. 1, 1993; Apr. 23, 1996, eff. Dec. 1, 1996; Apr. 11, 1997, eff. Dec. 1, 1997; Apr. 26, 1999, eff. Dec. 1, 1999; Apr. 17, 2000, eff. Dec. 1, 2000; Apr. 23, 2001, eff. Dec. 1, 2001; Mar. 27, 2003, eff. Dec. 1, 2003; Apr. 26, 2004, eff. Dec. 1, 2004; Apr. 25, 2005, eff. Dec. 1, 2005; Apr. 23, 2008, eff. Dec. 1, 2008; Mar. 26, 2009, eff. Dec. 1, 2009.)

NOTES OF ADVISORY COMMITTEE ON RULES—1983

Some of the notices required by this rule may be given either by the clerk or as the court may otherwise direct. For example, the court may order the trustee or debtor in possession to transmit one or more of the notices required by this rule, such as, notice of a proposed sale of property. See §363(b) of the Code. When publication of notices is required or desirable, reference should be made to Rule 9008.

Notice of the order for relief is required to be given by §342 of the Code and by subdivision (f)(1) of this rule. That notice may be combined with the notice of the meeting of creditors as indicated in Official Form No. 16, the notice and order of the meeting of creditors.

*Subdivision (a)* sets forth the requirement that 20 days notice be given of the significant events in a case under the Bankruptcy Code. The former Act and Rules provided a ten day notice in bankruptcy and Chapter XI cases, and a 20 day notice in a Chapter X case. This rule generally makes uniform the 20 day notice provision except that subdivision (b) contains a 25 day period for certain events in a chapter 9, 11, or 13 case. Generally, Rule 9006 permits reduction of time periods. Since notice by mail is complete on mailing, the requirement of subdivision (a) is satisfied if the notices are deposited in the mail at least 20 days before the event. See Rule 9006(e). The exceptions referred to in the introductory phrase include the modifications in the notice procedure permitted by subdivision (h) as to non-filing creditors, subdivision (i) as to cases where a committee is functioning, and subdivision (k) where compliance with subdivision (a) is impracticable.

The notice of a proposed sale affords creditors an opportunity to object to the sale and raise a dispute for the court's attention. Section 363(b) of the Code permits the trustee or debtor in possession to sell property, other than in the ordinary course of business, only after notice and hearing. If no objection is raised after notice, §102(1) provides that there need not be an actual hearing. Thus, absent objection, there would be no court involvement with respect to a trustee's sale. Once an objection is raised, only the court may pass on it.

Prior to the Code the court could shorten the notice period for a proposed sale of property or dispense with notice. This subdivision (a), permits the 20 day period to be shortened in appropriate circumstances but the rule does not contain a provision allowing the court to dispense with notice. The rule is thus consistent with the Code, §§363(b) and 102(1)(A) of the Code. See 28 U.S.C. §2075. It may be necessary, in certain circumstances, however, to use a method of notice other than mail. Subdivision (a)(2) vests the court with discretion, on cause shown, to order a different method. Reference should also be made to Rule 6004 which allows a different type of notice of proposed sales when the property is of little value.

Notice of the hearing on an application for compensation or reimbursement of expenses totalling $100 or less need not be given. In chapter 13 cases relatively small amounts are sometimes allowed for post-confirmation services and it would not serve a useful purpose to require advance notice.

*Subdivision (b)* is similar to subdivision (a) but lengthens the notice time to 25 days with respect to those events particularly significant in chapter 9, 11 and 13 cases. The additional time may be necessary to formulate objections to a disclosure statement or confirmation of a plan and preparation for the hearing on approval of the disclosure statement or confirmation. The disclosure statement and hearing thereon is only applicable in chapter 9 cases (§901(a) of the Code), and chapter 11 cases (§1125 of the Code).

*Subdivision (c)* specifies certain matters that should be included in the notice of a proposed sale of property and notice of the hearing on an application for allowances. Rule 6004 fixes the time within which parties in interest may file objections to a proposed sale of property.

*Subdivision (d)* relates exclusively to the notices given to equity security holders in chapter 11 cases. Under chapter 11, a plan may impair the interests of the debtor's shareholders or a plan may be a relatively simple restructuring of unsecured debt. In some cases, it is necessary that equity interest holders receive various notices and in other cases there is no purpose to be served. This subdivision indicates that the court is not mandated to order notices but rather that the matter should be treated with some flexibility. The court may decide whether notice is to be given and how it is to be given. Under §341(b) of the Code, a meeting of equity security holders is not required in each case, only when it is ordered by the court. Thus subdivision (d)(2) requires notice only when the court orders a meeting.

In addition to the notices specified in this subdivision, there may be other events or matters arising in a case as to which equity security holders should receive notice. These are situations left to determination by the court.

*Subdivision (e)*, authorizing a notice of the apparent insufficiency of assets for the payment of any dividend, is correlated with Rule 3002(c)(5), which provides for the issuance of an additional notice to creditors if the possibility of a payment later materializes.

*Subdivision (f)* provides for the transmission of other notices to which no time period applies. Clause (1) requires notice of the order for relief; this complements the mandate of §342 of the Code requiring such notice as is appropriate of the order for relief. This notice may be combined with the notice of the meeting of creditors to avoid the necessity of more than one mailing. See Official Form No. 16, notice of meeting of creditors.

*Subdivision (g)* recognizes that an agent authorized to receive notices for a creditor may, without a court order, designate where notices to the creditor he represents should be addressed. Agent includes an officer of a corporation, an attorney at law, or an attorney in fact if the requisite authority has been given him. It should be noted that Official Forms Nos. 17 and 18 do not include an authorization of the holder of a power of attorney to receive notices for the creditor. Neither these forms nor this rule carries any implication that such an authorization may not be given in a power of attorney or that a request for notices to be addressed to both the creditor or his duly authorized agent may not be filed.

*Subdivision (h).* After the time for filing claims has expired in a chapter 7 case, creditors who have not filed their claims in accordance with Rule 3002(c) are not entitled to share in the estate except as they may come within the special provisions of §726 of the Code or Rule 3002(c)(6). The elimination of notice to creditors who have no recognized stake in the estate may permit economies in time and expense. Reduction of the list of creditors to receive notices under this subdivision is discretionary. This subdivision does not apply to the notice of the meeting of creditors.

*Subdivision (i)* contains a list of matters of which notice may be given a creditors' committee or to its authorized agent in lieu of notice to the creditors. Such notice may serve every practical purpose of a notice to all the creditors and save delay and expense. *In re Schulte-United, Inc.*, 59 F.2d 553, 561 (8th Cir. 1932).

*Subdivision (j).* The premise for the requirement that the district director of internal revenue receive copies of notices that all creditors receive in a chapter 11 case is that every debtor is potentially a tax debtor of the United States. Notice to the district director alerts him to the possibility that a tax debtor's estate is about to be liquidated or reorganized and that the debtor may be discharged. When other indebtedness to the United States is indicated, the United States attorney is notified as the person in the best position to protect the interests of the government. In addition, the provision requires notice by mail to the head of any department, agency, or instrumentality of the United States through whose action the debtor became indebted to the United States. This rule is not intended to preclude a local rule from requiring a state or local tax authority to receive some or all of the notices to creditors under these rules.

*Subdivision (k)* specifies two kinds of situations in which notice by publication may be appropriate: (1) when notice by mail is impracticable; and (2) when notice by mail alone is less than adequate. Notice by mail may be impracticable when, for example, the debtor has disappeared or his records have been destroyed and the names and addresses of his creditors are unavailable, or when the number of creditors with nominal claims is very large and the estate to be distributed may be insufficient to defray the costs of issuing the notices. Supplementing notice by mail is also indicated when the debtor's records are incomplete or inaccurate and it is reasonable to believe that publication may reach some of the creditors who would otherwise be missed. Rule 9008 applies when the court directs notice by publication under this rule. Neither clause (2) of subdivision (a) nor subdivision (k) of this rule is concerned with the publication of advertisement to the general public of a sale of property of the estate at public auction under Rule 6004(b). See 3 Collier, *Bankruptcy* 522–23 (14th ed. 1971); 4B *id.* 1165–67 (1967); 2 *id.* ¶363.03 (15th ed. 1981).

*Subdivision (m).* Inclusion in notices to creditors of information as to other names used by the debtor as required by Rule 1005 will assist them in the preparation of their proofs of claim and in deciding whether to file a complaint objecting to the debtor's discharge. Additional names may be listed by the debtor on his statement of affairs when he did not file the petition. The mailing of notices should not be postponed to await a delayed filing of the statement of financial affairs.

NOTES OF ADVISORY COMMITTEE ON RULES—1987 AMENDMENT

*Subdivision (a)* is amended to provide that notice of a hearing on an application for compensation must be given only when the amount requested is in excess of $500.

*Subdivision (d).* A new notice requirement is added as clause (3). When a proposed sale is of all or substantially all of the debtor's assets, it is appropriate that equity security holders be given notice of the proposed sale. The clauses of subdivision (d) are renumbered to accommodate this addition.

*Subdivision (f).* Clause (7) is eliminated. Mailing of a copy of the discharge order is governed by Rule 4004(g).

*Subdivision (g)* is amended to relieve the clerk of the duty to mail notices to the address shown in a proof of claim when a notice of no dividend has been given pursuant to Rule 2002. This amendment avoids the necessity of the clerk searching proofs of claim which are filed in no dividend cases to ascertain whether a different address is shown.

*Subdivision (n)* was enacted by §321 of the 1984 amendments.

NOTES OF ADVISORY COMMITTEE ON RULES—1991 AMENDMENT

*Subdivision (a)(3)* is amended to exclude compromise or settlement agreements concerning adequate protection or which modify or terminate the automatic stay, provide for use of cash collateral, or create a senior or equal lien on collateral to obtain credit. Notice requirements relating to approval of such agreements are governed by Rule 4001(d).

*Subdivision (a)(5)* is amended to include a hearing on dismissal or conversion of a chapter 12 case. This subdivision does not apply when a hearing is not required. It is also amended to avoid the necessity of giving notice to all creditors of a hearing on the dismissal of a consumer debtor's case based on substantial abuse of chapter 7. Such hearings on dismissal under §707(b) of the Code are governed by Rule 1017(e).

*Subdivision (a)(9)* is added to provide for notice of the time fixed for filing objections and the hearing to consider confirmation of a plan in a chapter 12 case. Section 1224 of the Code requires "expedited notice" of the confirmation hearing in a chapter 12 case and requires that the hearing be concluded not later than 45 days after the filing of the plan unless the time is extended for cause. This amendment establishes 20 days as the notice period. The court may shorten this time on its own motion or on motion of a party in interest. The notice includes both the date of the hearing and the date for filing objections, and must be accompanied by a copy of the plan or a summary of the plan in accordance with Rule 3015(d).

*Subdivision (b)* is amended to delete as unnecessary the references to subdivisions (h) and (i).

*Subdivision (d)* does not require notice to equity security holders in a chapter 12 case. The procedural burden of requiring such notice is outweighed by the likelihood that all equity security holders of a family farmer will be informed of the progress of the case without formal notice. Subdivision (d) is amended to recognize that the United States trustee may convene a meeting of equity security holders pursuant to §341(b).

*Subdivision (f)(2)* is amended and subdivision (f)(4) is deleted to require notice of any conversion of the case, whether the conversion is by court order or is effectuated by the debtor filing a notice of conversion pursuant to §§1208(a) or 1307(a). Subdivision (f)(8), renumbered (f)(7), is amended to include entry of an order confirming a chapter 12 plan. Subdivision (f)(9) is amended to increase the amount to $1,500.

*Subdivisions (g) and (j)* are amended to delete the words "with the court" and subdivision (i) is amended to delete the words "with the clerk" because these phrases are unnecessary. See Rules 5005(a) and 9001(3).

*Subdivision (i)* is amended to require that the United States trustee receive notices required by subdivision (a)(2), (3) and (7) of this rule notwithstanding a court order limiting such notice to committees and to creditors and equity security holders who request such notices. Subdivision (i) is amended further to include committees elected pursuant to §705 of the Code and to provide that committees of retired employees appointed in chapter 11 cases receive certain notices.

*Subdivision (k)* is derived from Rule X-1008. The administrative functions of the United States trustee pursuant to 28 U.S.C. §586(a) and standing to be heard on issues under §307 and other sections of the Code require that the United States trustee be informed of developments and issues in every case except chapter 9 cases. The rule omits those notices described in subdivision (a)(1) because a meeting of creditors is convened only by the United States trustee, and those notices described in subdivision (a)(4) (date fixed for filing claims against a surplus), subdivision (a)(6) (time fixed to accept or reject proposed modification of a plan), subdivision (a)(8) (time fixed for filing proofs of claims in chapter 11 cases), subdivision (f)(3) (time fixed for filing claims in chapter 7, 12, and 13 cases), and subdivision (f)(5) (time fixed for filing complaint to determine dischargeability of debt) because these notices do not relate to matters that generally involve the United States trustee. Nonetheless, the omission of these notices does not prevent the United States trustee from receiving such notices upon request. The United States trustee also receives notice of hearings on applications for compensation or reimbursement without regard to the $500 limitation contained in subdivision (a)(7) of this rule. This rule is intended to be flexible in that it permits the United States trustee in a particular judicial district to request notices in certain categories, and to request not to receive notices in other categories, when the practice in that district makes that desirable.

NOTES OF ADVISORY COMMITTEE ON RULES—1993 AMENDMENT

*Subdivision (j)* is amended to avoid the necessity of sending an additional notice to the Washington, D.C. address of the Securities and Exchange Commission if the Commission prefers to have notices sent only to a local office. This change also clarifies that notices required to be mailed pursuant to this rule must be sent to the Securities and Exchange Commission only if it has filed a notice of appearance or has filed a written request. Other amendments are stylistic and make no substantive change.

NOTES OF ADVISORY COMMITTEE ON RULES—1996 AMENDMENT

*Paragraph (a)(4)* is abrogated to conform to the abrogation of Rule 3002(c)(6). The remaining paragraphs of subdivision (a) are renumbered, and references to these paragraphs contained in other subdivisions of this rule are amended accordingly.

*Paragraph (f)(8)* is amended so that a summary of the trustee's final account, which is prepared after distribution of property, does not have to be mailed to the debtor, all creditors, and indenture trustees in a chapter 7 case. Parties are sufficiently protected by receiving a summary of the trustee's final report that informs parties of the proposed distribution of property.

*Subdivision (h)* is amended (1) to provide that an order under this subdivision may not be issued if a notice of no dividend is given pursuant to Rule 2002(e) and the time for filing claims has not expired as provided in Rule 3002(c)(5); (2) to clarify that notices required to be mailed by subdivision (a) to parties other than creditors must be mailed to those entities despite an order issued pursuant to subdivision (h); (3) to provide that if the court, pursuant to Rule 3002(c)(1) or 3002(c)(2), has granted an extension of time to file a proof of claim, the creditor for whom the extension has been granted must continue to receive notices despite an order issued pursuant to subdivision (h); and (4) to delete references to subdivision (a)(4) and Rule 3002(c)(6), which have been abrogated.

Other amendments to this rule are stylistic.

*GAP Report on Rule 2002.* No changes since publication, except for stylistic changes and the correction of a typographical error in the committee note.

NOTES OF ADVISORY COMMITTEE ON RULES—1997 AMENDMENT

*Paragraph (a)(1)* is amended to include notice of a meeting of creditors convened under §1104(b) of the Code for the purpose of electing a trustee in a chapter 11 case. The court for cause shown may order the 20-day period reduced pursuant to Rule 9006(c)(1).

*Subdivision (n)* is amended to conform to the 1994 amendment to §342 of the Code. As provided in §342(c), the failure of a notice given by the debtor to a creditor to contain the information required by §342(c) does not invalidate the legal effect of the notice.

*GAP Report on Rule 2002.* No changes to the published draft.

COMMITTEE NOTES ON RULES—1999 AMENDMENT

*Paragraph (a)(4)* is amended to conform to the amendments to Rule 1017. If the United States trustee files a motion to dismiss a case for the debtor's failure to file the list of creditors, schedules, or the statement of financial affairs within the time specified in §707(a)(3), the amendments to this rule and to Rule 1017 eliminate the requirement that all creditors receive notice of the hearing.

Paragraph (a)(4) is amended further to conform to Rule 1017(b), which requires that notice of the hearing on dismissal of a case for failure to pay the filing fee be served on only the debtor and the trustee.

*Paragraph (f)(2)* is amended to provide for notice of the suspension of proceedings under §305.

*GAP Report on Rule 2002.* No changes since publication.

COMMITTEE NOTES ON RULES—2000 AMENDMENT

*Paragraph (a)(6)* is amended to increase the dollar amount from $500 to $1,000. The amount was last amended in 1987, when it was changed from $100 to $500. The amendment also clarifies that the notice is required only if a particular entity is requesting more than $1,000 as compensation or reimbursement of expenses. If several professionals are requesting compensation or reimbursement, and only one hearing will be held on all applications, notice under paragraph (a)(6) is required only with respect to the entities that have requested more than $1,000. If each applicant requests $1,000 or less, notice under paragraph (a)(6) is not required even though the aggregate amount of all applications to be considered at the hearing is more than $1,000.

If a particular entity had filed prior applications or had received compensation or reimbursement of expenses at an earlier time in the case, the amounts previously requested or awarded are not considered when determining whether the present application exceeds $1,000 for the purpose of applying this rule.

*GAP Report on Rule 2002(a).* No changes since publication.

COMMITTEE NOTES ON RULES—2001 AMENDMENT

*Subdivision (c)(3)* is added to assure that parties given notice of a hearing to consider confirmation of a plan under subdivision (b) are given adequate notice of an injunction provided for in the plan if it would enjoin conduct that is not otherwise enjoined by operation of the Code. The validity and effect of any injunction provided for in a plan are substantive law matters that are beyond the scope of these rules.

The notice requirement of subdivision (c)(3) is not applicable to an injunction contained in a plan if it is substantially the same as an injunction provided under the Code. For example, if a plan contains an injunction against acts to collect a discharged debt from the debtor, Rule 2002(c)(3) would not apply because that conduct would be enjoined under §524(a)(2) upon the debtor's discharge. But if a plan provides that creditors will be enjoined from asserting claims against persons who are not debtors in the case, the notice of the confirmation hearing must include the information required under Rule 2002(c)(3) because that conduct would not be enjoined by operation of the Code. *See* §524(e).

The requirement that the notice identify the entities that would be subject to the injunction requires only reasonable identification under the circumstances. If the entities that would be subject to the injunction cannot be identified by name, the notice may describe them by class or category if reasonable under the circumstances. For example, it may be sufficient for the notice to identify the entities as "all creditors of the debtor" and for the notice to be published in a manner that satisfies due process requirements.

*Subdivision (g)* has been revised to clarify that where a creditor or indenture trustee files both a proof of claim which includes a mailing address and a separate request designating a mailing address, the last paper filed determines the proper address. The amendments also clarify that a request designating a mailing address is effective only with respect to a particular case.

Under Rule 2002(g), a duly filed proof of claim is considered a request designating a mailing address if a notice of no dividend has been given under Rule 2002(e), but has been superseded by a subsequent notice of possible dividend under Rule 3002(c)(5). A duly filed proof of interest is considered a request designating a mailing address of an equity security holder.

Rule 2002(g)(3) is added to assure that notices to an infant or incompetent person under this rule are mailed to the appropriate guardian or other legal representative. Under Rule 1007(m), if the debtor knows that a creditor is an infant or incompetent person, the debtor is required to include in the list and schedule of creditors the name and address of the person upon whom process would be served in an adversary proceeding in accordance with Rule 7004(b)(2). If the infant or incompetent person, or another person, files a request or proof of claim designating a different name and mailing address, the notices would have to be mailed to both names and addresses until the court resolved the issue as to the proper mailing address.

The other amendments to Rule 2002(g) are stylistic.

*Changes Made After Publication and Comments.* In Rule 2002(c)(3), the word "highlighted" was replaced with "underlined" because highlighted documents are difficult to scan electronically for inclusion in the clerks' files. The Committee Note was revised to put in a more prominent position the statement that the validity and effect of any injunction provided for in a plan are substantive matters beyond the scope of the rules.

In Rule 2002(g), no changes were made.

COMMITTEE NOTES ON RULES—2003 AMENDMENT

Subdivision (a)(1) of the rule is amended to direct the clerk or other person giving notice of the §341 or §1104(b) meeting of creditors to include the debtor's full social security number on the notice. Official Form 9, the form of the notice of the meeting of creditors that will become a part of the court's file in the case, will include only the last four digits of the debtor's social security number. This rule, however, directs the clerk to include the full social security number on the notice that is served on the creditors and other identified parties, unless the court orders otherwise in a particular case. This will enable creditors and other parties in interest who are in possession of the debtor's social security number to verify the debtor's identity and proceed accordingly. The filed Official Form 9, however, will not include the debtor's full social security number. This will prevent the full social security number from becoming a part of the court's file in the case, and the number will not be included in the court's electronic records. Creditors who already have the debtor's social security number will be able to verify the existence of a case under the debtor's social security number, but any person searching the electronic case files without the number will not be able to acquire the debtor's social security number.

*Changes Made After Publication and Comments.* The rule amendment was made in response to concerns of both private creditors and taxing authorities that truncating the social security number of a debtor to the last four digits would unduly hamper their ability to identify the debtor and govern their actions accordingly. Therefore, the Advisory Committee amended Rule 2002 to require the clerk to include the debtor's full social security number on the notice informing creditors of the §341 meeting and other significant deadlines in the case. This is essentially a continuation of the practice under the current rules, and the amendment is necessary because of the amendment to Rule 1005 that restricts publication of the social security number on the caption of the petition to the final four digits of the number.

COMMITTEE NOTES ON RULES—2004 AMENDMENT

The rule is amended to reflect that the structure of the Internal Revenue Service no longer includes a District Director. Thus, rather than sending notice to the District Director, the rule now requires that the notices be sent to the location designated by the Service and set out in the register of addresses maintained by the clerk under Rule 5003(e). The other change is stylistic.

COMMITTEE NOTES ON RULES—2005 AMENDMENT

A new paragraph (g)(4) is inserted in the rule. The new paragraph authorizes an entity and a notice provider to agree that the notice provider will give notices to the entity at the address or addresses set out in their agreement. Rule 9001(9) sets out the definition of a notice provider.

The business of many entities is national in scope, and technology currently exists to direct the transmission of notice (both electronically and in paper form) to those entities in an accurate and much more efficient manner than by sending individual notices to the same creditor by separate mailings. The rule authorizes an entity and a notice provider to determine the manner of the service as well as to set the address or addresses to which the notices must be sent. For example, they could agree that all notices sent by the notice provider to the entity must be sent to a single, nationwide electronic or postal address. They could also establish local or regional addresses to which notices would be sent in matters pending in specific districts. Since the entity and notice provider also can agree on the date of the commencement of service under the agreement, there is no need to set a date in the rule after which notices would have to be sent to the address or addresses that the entity establishes. Furthermore, since the entity supplies the address to the notice provider, use of that address is conclusively presumed to be proper. Nonetheless, if that address is not used, the notice still may be effective if the notice is otherwise effective under applicable law. This is the same treatment given under Rule 5003(e) to notices sent to governmental units at addresses other than those set out in that register of addresses.

The remaining subdivisions of Rule 2002(g) continue to govern the addressing of a notice that is not sent pursuant to an agreement described in Rule 2002(g)(4).

*Changes Made After Publication and Comment* changes since publication.

COMMITTEE NOTES ON RULES—2008 AMENDMENT

Subdivision (b) is amended to provide for 25 days' notice of the time for the court to make a final determination whether the plan in a small business case can serve as a disclosure statement. Conditional approval of a disclosure statement in a small business case is governed by Rule 3017.1 and does not require 25 days' notice. The court may consider this matter in a hearing combined with the confirmation hearing in a small business case.

Because of the requirements of Rule 6004(g), subdivision (c)(1) is amended to require that a trustee leasing or selling personally identifiable information under §363(b)(1)(A) or (B) of the Code, as amended in 2005, include in the notice of the lease or sale transaction a statement as to whether the lease or sale is consistent with a policy prohibiting the transfer of the information.

Subdivisions (f)(9) and (10) are new. They reflect the 2005 amendments to §§342(d) and 704(b) of the Code. Section 342(d) requires the clerk to give notice to creditors shortly after the commencement of the case as to whether a presumption of abuse exists. Subdivision (f)(9) adds this notice to the list of notices that the clerk must give. Subdivision (f)(10) implements the amendment to §704(b), which requires the court to provide a copy to all creditors of a statement by the United States trustee or bankruptcy administrator as to whether the debtor's case would be presumed to be an abuse under §707(b) not later than five days after receiving it.

Subdivision (f)(11) is also added to provide notice to creditors of the debtor's filing of a statement in a chapter 11, 12, or 13 case that there is no reasonable cause to believe that §522(q) applies in the case. This allows a creditor who disputes that assertion to request a delay of the entry of the discharge in the case.

Subdivision (g)(2) of the rule is amended because the 2005 amendments to §342(f) of the Code permit creditors in chapter 7 and 13 individual debtor cases to file a notice with any bankruptcy court of the address to which the creditor wishes all notices to be sent. The amendment to Rule 2002(g)(2) therefore only limits application of the subdivision when a creditor files a notice under §342(f).

New subdivision (g)(5) implements §342(g)(1) which was added to the Code in 2005. Section 342(g)(1) allows a creditor to treat a notice as not having been brought to the creditor's attention, and so potentially ineffective, until it is received by a person or organizational subdivision that the creditor has designated to receive notices under the Bankruptcy Code. Under that section, the creditor must have established reasonable procedures for such notices to be delivered to the designated person or subdivision. The rule provides that, in order to challenge a notice under §342(g)(1), a creditor must have filed the name and address of the designated notice recipient, as well as a description of the procedures for directing notices to that recipient, prior to the time that the challenged notice was issued. The filing required by the rule may be made as part of a creditor's filing under §342(f), which allows a creditor to file a notice of the address to be used by all bankruptcy courts or by particular bankruptcy courts to provide notice to the creditor in cases under chapters 7 and 13. Filing the name and address of the designated notice recipient and the procedures for directing notices to that recipient will reduce uncertainty as to the proper party for receiving notice and limit factual disputes as to whether a notice recipient has been designated and as to the nature of procedures adopted to direct notices to the recipient.

Subdivision (k) is amended to add notices given under subdivision (q) to the list of notices which must be served on the United States trustee.

Section 1514(d) of the Code, added by the 2005 amendments, requires that such additional time as is reasonable under the circumstances be given to creditors with foreign addresses with respect to notices and the filing of a proof of claim. Thus, subdivision (p)(1) is added to this rule to give the court flexibility to direct that notice by other means shall supplement notice by mail, or to enlarge the notice period, for creditors with foreign addresses. If cause exists, such as likely delays in the delivery of mailed notices in particular locations, the court may order that notice also be given by email, facsimile, or private courier. Alternatively, the court may enlarge the notice period for a creditor with a foreign address. It is expected that in most situations involving foreign creditors, fairness will not require any additional notice or extension of the notice period. This rule recognizes that the court has discretion to establish procedures to determine, on its own initiative, whether relief under subdivision (p) is appropriate, but that the court is not required to establish such procedures and may decide to act only on request of a party in interest.

Subdivision (p)(2) is added to the rule to grant creditors with a foreign address to which notices are mailed at least 30 days' notice of the time within which to file proofs of claims if notice is mailed to the foreign address, unless the court orders otherwise. If cause exists, such as likely delays in the delivery of notices in particular locations, the court may extend the notice period for creditors with foreign addresses. The court may also shorten the additional notice time if circumstances so warrant. For example, if the court in a chapter 11 case determines that supplementing the notice to a foreign creditor with notice by electronic means, such as email or facsimile, would give the creditor reasonable notice, the court may order that the creditor be given only 20 days' notice in accordance with Rule 2002(a)(7).

Subdivision (p)(3) is added to provide that the court may, for cause, override a creditor's designation of a foreign address under Rule 2002(g). For example, if a party in interest believes that a creditor has wrongfully designated a foreign address to obtain additional time when it has a significant presence in the United States, the party can ask the court to order that notices to that creditor be sent to an address other than the one designated by the foreign creditor.

Subdivision (q) is added to require that notice of the hearing on the petition for recognition of a foreign proceeding be given to the debtor, all administrators in foreign proceedings of the debtor, entities against whom provisional relief is sought, and entities with whom the debtor is engaged in litigation at the time of the commencement of the case. There is no need at this stage of the proceedings to provide notice to all creditors. If the foreign representative should take action to commence a case under another chapter of the Code, the rules governing those proceedings will operate to provide that notice is given to all creditors.

The rule also requires notice of the court's intention to communicate with a foreign court or foreign representative.

*Changes Made After Publication.* Subdivision (g)(2) was amended to provide that the designated address of a governmental unit under Rule 5003(e) establishes an exception to the rule that a creditor's address is to be taken from the debtor's schedules. The fifth and sixth paragraphs of the Committee Note were amended to explain that change.

Subdivision (p)(3) was added to the rule to provide that the court may override a creditor's designation of a foreign mailing address under Rule 2002(g). This will permit a party in interest to seek court relief if a creditor has improperly designated a foreign address.

Subdivision (q)(1) and (2) were amended by adopting language from §101(24) to identify foreign representatives as "all persons or bodies authorized to administer foreign proceedings of the debtor" rather than as "all administrators in foreign proceedings of the debtor." References to Rule 5012 in subdivision (q)(2) and in the Committee Note were deleted.

COMMITTEE NOTES ON RULES—2009 AMENDMENT

The rule is amended to implement changes in connection with the amendment to Rule 9006(a) and the manner by which time is computed under the rules. The deadlines in the rule are amended to substitute a deadline that is a multiple of seven days. Throughout the rules, deadlines are amended in the following manner:

- 5-day periods become 7-day periods
- 10-day periods become 14-day periods
- 15-day periods become 14-day periods
- 20-day periods become 21-day periods
- 25-day periods become 28-day periods

REFERENCES IN TEXT

The Securities Investor Protection Act, referred to in subd. (k), probably means the Securities Investor Protection Act of 1970, Pub. L. 91–598, Dec. 30, 1970, 84 Stat. 1636, as amended, which is classified generally to chapter 2B–1 (§78aaa et seq.) of Title 15, Commerce and Trade. For complete classification of this Act to the Code, see section 78aaa of Title 15 and Tables.

AMENDMENT BY PUBLIC LAW

1984—Subd. (n). Pub. L. 98–353 added subd. (n).

1983—Subd. (f). Pub. L. 98–91 inserted ", or some other person as the Court may direct," after "clerk".

EFFECTIVE DATE OF 1984 AMENDMENT

Amendment by Pub. L. 98–353 effective with respect to cases filed 90 days after July 10, 1984, see section 552(a) of Pub. L. 98–353, set out as a note under section 101 of this title.

EFFECTIVE DATE OF 1983 AMENDMENT

Section 1 of Pub. L. 98–91 provided: "That rule 2002(f) of the Bankruptcy Rules, as proposed by the United States Supreme Court in the order of April 25, 1983, of the Court, shall take effect on August 1, 1983, except as otherwise provided in section 2 [amending subd. (f) of this rule and enacting a provision set out as a note below]."

Section 2(b) of Pub. L. 98–91 provided that: "The amendment made by subsection (a) [amending subd. (f) of this rule] shall take effect on August 1, 1983."

**Rule 2003. Meeting of Creditors or Equity Security Holders**

(a) DATE AND PLACE. Except as otherwise provided in §341(e) of the Code, in a chapter 7 liquidation or a chapter 11 reorganization case, the United States trustee shall call a meeting of creditors to be held no fewer than 21 and no more than 40 days after the order for relief. In a chapter 12 family farmer debt adjustment case, the United States trustee shall call a meeting of creditors to be held no fewer than 21 and no more than 35 days after the order for relief. In a chapter 13 individual's debt adjustment case, the United States trustee shall call a meeting of creditors to be held no fewer than 21 and no more than 50 days after the order for relief. If there is an appeal from or a motion to vacate the order for relief, or if there is a motion to dismiss the case, the United States trustee may set a later date for the meeting. The meeting may be held at a regular place for holding court or at any other place designated by the United States trustee within the district convenient for the parties in interest. If the United States trustee designates a place for the meeting which is not regularly staffed by the United States trustee or an assistant who may preside at the meeting, the meeting may be held not more than 60 days after the order for relief.

(b) ORDER OF MEETING.

(1) *Meeting of Creditors*. The United States trustee shall preside at the meeting of creditors. The business of the meeting shall include the examination of the debtor under oath and, in a chapter 7 liquidation case, may include the election of a creditors' committee and, if the case is not under subchapter V of chapter 7, the election of a trustee. The presiding officer shall have the authority to administer oaths.

(2) *Meeting of Equity Security Holders*. If the United States trustee convenes a meeting of equity security holders pursuant to §341(b) of the Code, the United States trustee shall fix a date for the meeting and shall preside.

(3) *Right To Vote*. In a chapter 7 liquidation case, a creditor is entitled to vote at a meeting if, at or before the meeting, the creditor has filed a proof of claim or a writing setting forth facts evidencing a right to vote pursuant to §702(a) of the Code unless objection is made to the claim or the proof of claim is insufficient on its face. A creditor of a partnership may file a proof of claim or writing evidencing a right to vote for the trustee for the estate of the general partner notwithstanding that a trustee for the estate of the partnership has previously qualified. In the event of an objection to the amount or allowability of a claim for the purpose of voting, unless the court orders otherwise, the United States trustee shall tabulate the votes for each alternative presented by the dispute and, if resolution of such dispute is necessary to determine the result of the election, the tabulations for each alternative shall be reported to the court.

(c) RECORD OF MEETING. Any examination under oath at the meeting of creditors held pursuant to §341(a) of the Code shall be recorded verbatim by the United States trustee using electronic sound recording equipment or other means of recording, and such record shall be preserved by the United States trustee and available for public access until two years after the conclusion of the meeting of creditors. Upon request of any entity, the United States trustee shall certify and provide a copy or transcript of such recording at the entity's expense.

(d) REPORT OF ELECTION AND RESOLUTION OF DISPUTES IN A CHAPTER 7 CASE.

(1) *Report of Undisputed Election*. In a chapter 7 case, if the election of a trustee or a member of a creditors' committee is not disputed, the United States trustee shall promptly file a report of the election, including the name and address of the person or entity elected and a statement that the election is undisputed.

(2) *Disputed Election*. If the election is disputed, the United States trustee shall promptly file a report stating that the election is disputed, informing the court of the nature of the dispute, and listing the name and address of any candidate elected under any alternative presented by the dispute. No later than the date on which the report is filed, the United States trustee shall mail a copy of the report to any party in interest that has made a request to receive a copy of the report. Pending disposition by the court of a disputed election for trustee, the interim trustee shall continue in office. Unless a motion for the resolution of the dispute is filed no later than 14 days after the United States trustee files a report of a disputed election for trustee, the interim trustee shall serve as trustee in the case.

(e) ADJOURNMENT. The meeting may be adjourned from time to time by announcement at the meeting of the adjourned date and time without further written notice.

(f) SPECIAL MEETINGS. The United States trustee may call a special meeting of creditors on request of a party in interest or on the United States trustee's own initiative.

(g) FINAL MEETING. If the United States trustee calls a final meeting of creditors in a case in which the net proceeds realized exceed $1,500, the clerk shall mail a summary of the trustee's final account to the creditors with a notice of the meeting, together with a statement of the amount of the claims allowed. The trustee shall attend the final meeting and shall, if requested, report on the administration of the estate.

(As amended Mar. 30, 1987, eff. Aug. 1, 1987; Apr. 30, 1991, eff. Aug. 1, 1991; Apr. 22, 1993, eff. Aug. 1, 1993; Apr. 26, 1999, eff. Dec. 1, 1999; Mar. 27, 2003, eff. Dec. 1, 2003; Apr. 23, 2008, eff. Dec. 1, 2008; Mar. 26, 2009, eff. Dec. 1, 2009.)

NOTES OF ADVISORY COMMITTEE ON RULES—1983

Section 341(a) of the Code requires a meeting of creditors in a chapter 7, 11 or 13 case, and §341(b) permits the court to order a meeting of equity security holders. A major change from prior law, however, prohibits the judge from attending or presiding over the meeting. Section 341(c).

This rule does not apply either in a case for the reorganization of a railroad or for the adjustment of debts of a municipality. Sections 1161 and 901 render §§341 and 343 inapplicable in these types of cases. Section 341 sets the requirement for a meeting of creditors and §343 provides for the examination of the debtor.

*Subdivision (a).* The meeting is to be held between 20 and 40 days after the date of the order for relief. In a voluntary case, the date of the order for relief is the date of the filing of the petition (§301 of the Code); in an involuntary case, it is the date of an actual order (§303(i) of the Code).

*Subdivision (b)* provides flexibility as to who will preside at the meeting of creditors. The court may designate a person to serve as presiding officer, such as the interim trustee appointed under §701 of the Code. If the court does not designate anyone, the clerk will preside. In either case, creditors may elect a person of their own choosing. In any event, the clerk may remain to record the proceedings and take appearances. Use of the clerk is not contrary to the legislative policy of §341(c). The judge remains insulated from any information coming forth at the meeting and any information obtained by the clerk must not be relayed to the judge.

Although the clerk may preside at the meeting, the clerk is not performing any kind of judicial role, nor should the clerk give any semblance of performing such a role. It would be pretentious for the clerk to ascend the bench, don a robe or be addressed as "your honor". The clerk should not appear to parties or others as any type of judicial officer.

In a chapter 11 case, if a committee of unsecured creditors has been appointed pursuant to §1102(a)(1) of the Code and a chairman has been selected, the chairman will preside or a person, such as the attorney for the committee, may be designated to preside by the chairman.

Since the judge must fix the bond of the trustee but cannot be present at the meeting, the rule allows the creditors to recommend the amount of the bond. They should be able to obtain relevant information concerning the extent of assets of the debtor at the meeting.

Paragraph (1) authorizes the presiding officer to administer oaths. This is important because the debtor's examination must be under oath.

Paragraph (3) of subdivision (b) has application only in a chapter 7 case. That is the only type of case under the Code that permits election of a trustee or committee. In all other cases, no vote is taken at the meeting of creditors. If it is necessary for the court to make a determination with respect to a claim, the meeting may be adjourned until the objection or dispute is resolved.

The second sentence recognizes that partnership creditors may vote for a trustee of a partner's estate along with the separate creditors of the partner. Although §723(c) gives the trustee of a partnership a claim against a partner's estate for the full amount of partnership creditors' claims allowed, the purpose and function of this provision are to simplify distribution and prevent double proof, not to disfranchise partnership creditors in electing a trustee of an estate against which they hold allowable claims.

*Subdivision (c)* requires minutes and a record of the meeting to be maintained by the presiding officer. A verbatim record must be made of the debtor's examination but the rule is flexible as to the means used to record the examination.

*Subdivision (d)* recognizes that the court must be informed immediately about the election or nonelection of a trustee in a chapter 7 case. Pursuant to Rule 2008, the clerk officially informs the trustee of his election or appointment and how he is to qualify. The presiding person has no authority to resolve a disputed election.

For purposes of expediency, the results of the election should be obtained for each alternative presented by the dispute and immediately reported to the court. Thus, when an interested party presents the dispute to the court, its prompt resolution by the court will determine the dispute and a new or adjourned meeting to conduct the election may be avoided. The clerk is not an interested party.

A creditors' committee may be elected only in a chapter 7 case. In chapter 11 cases, a creditors' committee is appointed pursuant to §1102.

While a final meeting is not required, Rule 2002(f)(10) provides for the trustee's final account to be sent to creditors.

NOTES OF ADVISORY COMMITTEE ON RULES—1987 AMENDMENT

*Subdivision (a).* Many courts schedule meetings of creditors at various locations in the district. Because the clerk must schedule meetings at those locations, an additional 20 days for scheduling the meetings is provided under the amended rule.

NOTES OF ADVISORY COMMITTEE ON RULES—1991 AMENDMENT

The amendment to subdivision (a) relating to the calling of the meeting of creditors in a chapter 12 case is consistent with the expedited procedures of chapter 12. Subdivision (a) is also amended to clarify that the United States trustee does not call a meeting of creditors in a chapter 9 case. Pursuant to §901(a) of the Code, §341 is inapplicable in chapter 9 cases. The other amendments to subdivisions (a), (b)(1), and (b)(2) and the additions of subdivisions (f) and (g) are derived from Rule X-1006 and conform to the 1986 amendments to §341 of the Code. The second sentence of subdivision (b)(3) is amended because Rule 2009(e) is abrogated. Although the United States trustee fixes the date for the meeting, the clerk of the bankruptcy court transmits the notice of the meeting unless the court orders otherwise, as prescribed in Rule 2002(a)(1).

Pursuant to §702 and §705 of the Code, creditors may elect a trustee and a committee in a chapter 7 case. Subdivision (b) of this rule provides that the United States trustee shall preside over any election that is held under those sections. The deletion of the last sentence of subdivision (b)(1) does not preclude creditors from recommending to the United States trustee the amount of the trustee's bond when a trustee is elected. Trustees and committees are not elected in chapter 11, 12, and 13 cases.

If an election is disputed, the United States trustee shall not resolve the dispute. For purposes of expediency, the United States trustee shall tabulate the results of the election for each alternative presented by the dispute. However, if the court finds that such tabulation is not feasible under the circumstances, the United States trustee need not tabulate the votes. If such tabulation is feasible and if the disputed vote or votes would affect the result of the election, the tabulations of votes for each alternative presented by the dispute shall be reported to the court. If a motion is made for resolution of the dispute in accordance with subdivision (d) of this rule, the court will determine the issue and another meeting to conduct the election may not be necessary.

*Subdivisions (f) and (g)* are derived from Rule X-1006(d) and (e), except that the amount is increased to $1,500 to conform to the amendment to Rule 2002(f).

NOTES OF ADVISORY COMMITTEE ON RULES—1993 AMENDMENT

*Subdivision (a)* is amended to extend by ten days the time for holding the meeting of creditors in a chapter 13 case. This extension will provide more flexibility for scheduling the meeting of creditors. Other amendments are stylistic and make no substantive change.

COMMITTEE NOTES ON RULES—1999 AMENDMENT

*Subdivision (d)* is amended to require the United States trustee to mail a copy of a report of a disputed election to any party in interest that has requested a copy of it. Also, if the election is for a trustee, the rule as amended will give a party in interest ten days from the filing of the report, rather than from the date of the meeting of creditors, to file a motion to resolve the dispute.

The substitution of "United States trustee" for "presiding officer" is stylistic. Section 341(a) of the Code provides that the United States trustee shall preside at the meeting of creditors. Other amendments are designed to conform to the style of Rule 2007.1(b)(3) regarding the election of a trustee in a chapter 11 case.

*GAP Report on Rule 2003.* No changes since publication.

COMMITTEE NOTES ON RULES—2003 AMENDMENT

The rule is amended to reflect the enactment of subchapter V of chapter 7 of the Code governing multilateral clearing organization liquidations. Section 782 of the Code provides that the designation of a trustee or alternative trustee for the case is made by the Federal Reserve Board. Therefore, the meeting of creditors in those cases cannot include the election of a trustee.

*Changes Made After Publication and Comments.* No changes since publication.

COMMITTEE NOTES ON RULES—2008 AMENDMENT

If the debtor has solicited acceptances to a plan before commencement of the case, §341(e), which was added to the Code by the 2005 amendments, authorizes the court, on request of a party in interest and after notice and a hearing, to order that a meeting of creditors not be convened. The rule is amended to recognize that a meeting of creditors might not be held in those cases.

*Changes Made After Publication.* No changes were made after publication.

COMMITTEE NOTES ON RULES—2009 AMENDMENT

The rule is amended to implement changes in connection with the amendment to Rule 9006(a) and the manner by which time is computed under the rules. The deadlines in the rule are amended to substitute a deadline that is a multiple of seven days. Throughout the rules, deadlines are amended in the following manner:

- 5-day periods become 7-day periods
- 10-day periods become 14-day periods
- 15-day periods become 14-day periods
- 20-day periods become 21-day periods
- 25-day periods become 28-day periods

## Rule 2004. Examination

(a) EXAMINATION ON MOTION. On motion of any party in interest, the court may order the examination of any entity.

(b) SCOPE OF EXAMINATION. The examination of an entity under this rule or of the debtor under §343 of the Code may relate only to the acts, conduct, or property or to the liabilities and financial condition of the debtor, or to any matter which may affect the administration of the debtor's estate, or to the debtor's right to a discharge. In a family farmer's debt adjustment case under chapter 12, an individual's debt adjustment case under chapter 13, or a reorganization case under chapter 11 of the Code, other than for the reorganization of a railroad, the examination may also relate to the operation of any business and the desirability of its continuance, the source of any money or property acquired or to be acquired by the debtor for purposes of consummating a plan and the consideration given or offered therefor, and any other matter relevant to the case or to the formulation of a plan.

(c) COMPELLING ATTENDANCE AND PRODUCTION OF DOCUMENTS. The attendance of an entity for examination and for the production of documents, whether the examination is to be conducted within or without the district in which the case is pending, may be compelled as provided in Rule 9016 for the attendance of a witness at a hearing or trial. As an officer of the court, an attorney may issue and sign a subpoena on behalf of the court for the district in which the examination is to be held if the attorney is admitted to practice in that court or in the court in which the case is pending.

(d) TIME AND PLACE OF EXAMINATION OF DEBTOR. The court may for cause shown and on terms as it may impose order the debtor to be examined under this rule at any time or place it designates, whether within or without the district wherein the case is pending.

(e) MILEAGE. An entity other than a debtor shall not be required to attend as a witness unless lawful mileage and witness fee for one day's attendance shall be first tendered. If the debtor resides more than 100 miles from the place of examination when required to appear for an examination under this rule, the mileage allowed by law to a witness shall be tendered for any distance more than 100 miles from the debtor's residence at the date of the filing of the first petition commencing a case under the Code or the residence at the time the debtor is required to appear for the examination, whichever is the lesser.

(As amended Mar. 30, 1987, eff. Aug. 1, 1987; Apr. 30, 1991, eff. Aug. 1, 1991; Apr. 29, 2002, eff. Dec. 1, 2002.)

NOTES OF ADVISORY COMMITTEE ON RULES

*Subdivision (a)* of this rule is derived from former Bankruptcy Rule 205(a). See generally 2 Collier, *ruptcy* ¶¶343.02, 343.08, 343.13 (15th ed. 1981). It specifies the manner of moving for an examination. The motion may be heard *ex parte* or it may be heard on notice.

*Subdivision (b)* is derived from former Bankruptcy Rules 205(d) and 11-26.

*Subdivision (c)* specifies the mode of compelling attendance of a witness or party for an examination and for the production of evidence under this rule. The subdivision is substantially declaratory of the practice that had developed under §21a of the Act. See 2 Collier, *supra* ¶343.11.

This subdivision will be applicable for the most part to the examination of a person other than the debtor. The debtor is required to appear at the meeting of creditors for examination. The word "person" includes the debtor and this subdivision may be used if necessary to obtain the debtor's attendance for examination.

*Subdivision (d)* is derived from former Bankruptcy Rule 205(f) and is not a limitation on subdivision (c). Any person, including the debtor, served with a subpoena within the range of a subpoena must attend for examination pursuant to subdivision (c). Subdivision (d) applies only to the debtor and a subpoena need not be issued. There are no territorial limits on the service of an order on the debtor. See, *e.g.*, *In re Totem Lodge & Country Club, Inc.*, 134 F. Supp. 158 (S.D.N.Y. 1955).

*Subdivision (e)* is derived from former Bankruptcy Rule 205(g). The lawful mileage and fee for attendance at a United States court as a witness are prescribed by 28 U.S.C. §1821.

*Definition of debtor.* The word "debtor" as used in this rule includes the persons specified in the definition in Rule 9001(5).

*Spousal privilege.* The limitation on the spousal privilege formerly contained in §21a of the Act is not carried over in the Code. For privileges generally, see Rule 501 of the Federal Rules of Evidence made applicable in cases under the Code by Rule 1101 thereof.

NOTES OF ADVISORY COMMITTEE ON RULES—1991 AMENDMENT

This rule is amended to allow the examination in a chapter 12 case to cover the same matters that may be covered in an examination in a chapter 11 or 13 case.

COMMITTEE NOTES ON RULES—2002 AMENDMENT

*Subdivision (c)* is amended to clarify that an examination ordered under Rule 2004(a) may be held outside the district in which the case is pending if the subpoena is issued by the court for the district in which the examination is to be held and is served in the manner provided in Rule 45 F. R. Civ. P., made applicable by Rule 9016.

The subdivision is amended further to clarify that, in addition to the procedures for the issuance of a subpoena set forth in Rule 45 F. R. Civ. P., an attorney may issue and sign a subpoena on behalf of the court for the district in which a Rule 2004 examination is to be held if the attorney is authorized to practice, even if admitted pro hac vice, either in the court in which the case is pending or in the court for the district in which the examination is to be held. This provision supplements the procedures for the issuance of a subpoena set forth in Rule 45(a)(3)(A) and (B) F. R. Civ. P. and is consistent with one of the purposes of the 1991 amendments to Rule 45, to ease the burdens of interdistrict law practice.

*Changes Made After Publication and Comments.* The typographical error was corrected, but no other changes were made.

## Rule 2005. Apprehension and Removal of Debtor to Compel Attendance for Examination

(a) ORDER TO COMPEL ATTENDANCE FOR EXAMINATION. On motion of any party in interest supported by an affidavit alleging (1) that the examination of the debtor is necessary for the proper administration of the estate and that there is reasonable cause to believe that the debtor is about to leave or has left the debtor's residence or principal place of business to avoid examination, or (2) that the debtor has evaded service of a subpoena or of an order to attend for examination, or (3) that the debtor has willfully disobeyed a subpoena or order to attend for examination, duly served, the court may issue to the marshal, or some other officer authorized by law, an order directing the officer to bring the debtor before the court without unnecessary delay. If, after hearing, the court finds the allegations to be true, the court shall thereupon cause the debtor to be examined forthwith. If necessary, the court shall fix conditions for further examination and for the debtor's obedience to all orders made in reference thereto.

(b) REMOVAL. Whenever any order to bring the debtor before the court is issued under this rule and the debtor is found in a district other than that of the court issuing the order, the debtor may be taken into custody under the order and removed in accordance with the following rules:

(1) If the debtor is taken into custody under the order at a place less than 100 miles from the place of issue of the order, the debtor shall be brought forthwith before the court that issued the order.

(2) If the debtor is taken into custody under the order at a place 100 miles or more from the place of issue of the order, the debtor shall be brought without unnecessary delay before the nearest available United States magistrate judge, bankruptcy judge, or district judge. If, after hearing, the magistrate judge, bankruptcy judge, or district judge finds that an order has issued under this rule and that the person in custody is the debtor, or if the person in custody waives a hearing, the magistrate judge, bankruptcy judge, or district judge shall order removal, and the person in custody shall be released on conditions ensuring prompt appearance before the court that issued the order to compel the attendance.

(c) CONDITIONS OF RELEASE. In determining what conditions will reasonably assure attendance or obedience under subdivision (a) of this rule or appearance under subdivision (b) of this rule, the court shall be governed by the provisions and policies of title 18, U.S.C., §3146(a) and (b).

(As amended Mar. 30, 1987, eff. Aug. 1, 1987; Apr. 22, 1993, eff. Aug. 1, 1993.)

NOTES OF ADVISORY COMMITTEE ON RULES—1983

This rule is derived from former Bankruptcy Rule 206. The rule requires the debtor to be examined as soon as possible if allegations of the movant for compulsory examination under this rule are found to be true after a hearing. Subdivision (b) includes in paragraphs (1) and (2) provisions adapted from subdivisions (a) and (b) of Rule 40 of the Federal Rules of Criminal Procedure, which governs the handling of a person arrested in one district on a warrant issued in another. Subdivision (c) incorporates by reference the features of subdivisions (a) and (b) of 18 U.S.C. §3146, which prescribe standards, procedures and factors to be considered in determining conditions of release of accused persons in noncapital cases prior to trial. The word "debtor" as used in this rule includes the persons named in Rule 9001(5).

The affidavit required to be submitted in support of the motion may be subscribed by the unsworn declaration provided for in 28 U.S.C. §1746.

NOTES OF ADVISORY COMMITTEE ON RULES—1993 AMENDMENT

*Subdivision (b)(2)* is amended to conform to §321 of the Judicial Improvements Act of 1990, Pub. L. No. 101–650, which changed the title of "United States magistrate" to "United States magistrate judge." Other amendments are stylistic and make no substantive change.

### Rule 2006. Solicitation and Voting of Proxies in Chapter 7 Liquidation Cases

(a) APPLICABILITY. This rule applies only in a liquidation case pending under chapter 7 of the Code.

(b) DEFINITIONS.

(1) *Proxy*. A proxy is a written power of attorney authorizing any entity to vote the claim or otherwise act as the owner's attorney in fact in connection with the administration of the estate.

(2) *Solicitation of Proxy*. The solicitation of a proxy is any communication, other than one from an attorney to a regular client who owns a claim or from an attorney to the owner of a claim who has requested the attorney to represent the owner, by which a creditor is asked, directly or indirectly, to give a proxy after or in contemplation of the filing of a petition by or against the debtor.

(c) AUTHORIZED SOLICITATION.

(1) A proxy may be solicited only by (A) a creditor owning an allowable unsecured claim against the estate on the date of the filing of the petition; (B) a committee elected pursuant to §705 of the Code; (C) a committee of creditors selected by a majority in number and amount of claims of creditors (i) whose claims are not contingent or unliquidated, (ii) who are not disqualified from voting under §702(a) of the Code and (iii) who were present or represented at a meeting of which all creditors having claims of over $500 or the 100 creditors having the largest claims had at least seven days' notice in writing and of which meeting written minutes were kept and are available reporting the names of the creditors present or represented and voting and the amounts of their claims; or (D) a bona fide trade or credit association, but such association may solicit only creditors who were its members or subscribers in good standing and had allowable unsecured claims on the date of the filing of the petition.

(2) A proxy may be solicited only in writing.

(d) SOLICITATION NOT AUTHORIZED. This rule does not permit solicitation (1) in any interest other than that of general creditors; (2) by or on behalf of any custodian; (3) by the interim trustee or by or on behalf of any entity not qualified to vote under §702(a) of the Code; (4) by or on behalf of an attorney at law; or (5) by or on behalf of a transferee of a claim for collection only.

(e) DATA REQUIRED FROM HOLDERS OF MULTIPLE PROXIES. At any time before the voting commences at any meeting of creditors pursuant to §341(a) of the Code, or at any other time as the court may direct, a holder of two or more proxies shall file and transmit to the United States trustee a verified list of the proxies to be voted and a verified statement of the pertinent facts and circumstances in connection with the execution and delivery of each proxy, including:

(1) a copy of the solicitation;

(2) identification of the solicitor, the forwarder, if the forwarder is neither the solicitor nor the owner of the claim, and the proxyholder, including their connections with the debtor and with each other. If the solicitor, forwarder, or proxyholder is an association, there shall also be included a statement that the creditors whose claims have been solicited and the creditors whose claims are to be voted were members or subscribers in good standing and had allowable unsecured claims on the date of the filing of the petition. If the solicitor, forwarder, or proxyholder is a committee of creditors, the statement shall also set forth the date and place the committee was organized, that the committee was organized in accordance with clause (B) or (C) of paragraph (c)(1) of this rule, the members of the committee, the amounts of their claims, when the claims were acquired, the amounts paid therefor, and the extent to which the claims of the committee members are secured or entitled to priority;

(3) a statement that no consideration has been paid or promised by the proxyholder for the proxy;

(4) a statement as to whether there is any agreement and, if so, the particulars thereof, between the proxyholder and any other entity for the payment of any consideration in connection with voting the proxy, or for the sharing of compensation with any entity, other than a member or regular associate of the proxyholder's law firm, which may be allowed the trustee or any entity for services rendered in the case, or for the employment of any person as attorney, accountant, appraiser, auctioneer, or other employee for the estate;

(5) if the proxy was solicited by an entity other than the proxyholder, or forwarded to the holder by an entity who is neither a solicitor of the proxy nor the owner of the claim, a statement signed and verified by the solicitor or forwarder that no consideration has been paid or promised for the proxy, and whether there is any agreement, and, if so, the particulars thereof, between the solicitor or forwarder and any other entity for the payment of any consideration in connection with voting the proxy, or for sharing compensation with any entity other than a member or regular associate of the solicitor's or forwarder's law firm which may be allowed the trustee or any entity for services rendered in the case, or for the employment of any person as attorney, accountant, appraiser, auctioneer, or other employee for the estate;

(6) if the solicitor, forwarder, or proxyholder is a committee, a statement signed and verified by each member as to the amount and source of any consideration paid or to be paid to such member in connection with the case other than by way of dividend on the member's claim.

(f) ENFORCEMENT OF RESTRICTIONS ON TION. On motion of any party in interest or on its own initiative, the court may determine whether there has been a failure to comply with the provisions of this rule or any other impropriety in connection with the solicitation or voting of a proxy. After notice and a hearing the court may reject any proxy for cause, vacate any order entered in consequence of the voting of any proxy which should have been rejected, or take any other appropriate action.

(As amended Mar. 30, 1987, eff. Aug. 1, 1987; Apr. 30, 1991, eff. Aug. 1, 1991; Mar. 26, 2009, eff. Dec. 1, 2009.)

NOTES OF ADVISORY COMMITTEE ON RULES—1983

This rule is a comprehensive regulation of solicitation and voting of proxies in liquidation cases. It is derived from former Bankruptcy Rule 208. The rule applies only in chapter 7 cases because no voting occurs, other than on a plan, in a chapter 11 case. Former Bankruptcy Rule 208 did not apply to solicitations of acceptances of plans.

Creditor control was a basic feature of the Act and is continued, in part, by the Code. Creditor democracy is perverted and the congressional objective frustrated, however, if control of administration falls into the hands of persons whose principal interest is not in what the estate can be made to yield to the unsecured creditors but in what it can yield to those involved in its administration or in other ulterior objectives.

*Subdivision (b).* The definition of proxy in the first paragraph of subdivision (b) is derived from former Bankruptcy Rule 208.

*Subdivision (c).* The purpose of the rule is to protect creditors against loss of control of administration of their debtors' estates to holders of proxies having interests that differ from those of the creditors. The rule does not prohibit solicitation but restricts it to those who were creditors at the commencement of the case or their freely and fairly selected representatives. The special role occupied by credit and trade associations is recognized in the last clause of subdivision (c)(1). On the assumption that members or subscribers may have affiliated with an association in part for the purpose of obtaining its services as a representative in liquidation proceedings, an established association is authorized to solicit its own members, or its regular customers or clients, who were creditors on the date of the filing of the petition. Although the association may not solicit nonmembers or nonsubscribers for proxies, it may sponsor a meeting of creditors at which a committee entitled to solicit proxies may be selected in accordance with clause (C) of subdivision (c)(1).

Under certain circumstances, the relationship of a creditor, creditors' committee, or association to the estate or the case may be such as to warrant rejection of any proxy solicited by such a person or group. Thus a person who is forbidden by the Code to vote his own claim should be equally disabled to solicit proxies from creditors. Solicitation by or on behalf of the debtor has been uniformly condemned, *e.g.*, *In re White*, 15 F.2d 371 (9th Cir. 1926), as has solicitation on behalf of a preferred creditor, *Matter of Law*, 13 Am.B.R. 650 (S.D. Ill. 1905). The prohibition on solicitation by a receiver or his attorney made explicit by General Order 39 has been collaterally supported by rulings rejecting proxies solicited by a receiver in equity, *In re Western States Bldg.-Loan Ass'n*, 54 F.2d 415 (S.D. Cal. 1931), and by an assignee for the benefit of creditors, *Lines v. Falstaff Brewing Co.*, 233 F.2d 927 (9th Cir. 1956).

*Subdivision (d)* prohibits solicitation by any person or group having a relationship described in the preceding paragraph. It also makes no exception for attorneys or transferees of claims for collection. The rule does not undertake to regulate communications between an attorney and his regular client or between an attorney and a creditor who has asked the attorney to represent him in a proceeding under the Code, but any other communication by an attorney or any other person or group requesting a proxy from the owner of a claim constitutes a regulated solicitation. Solicitation by an attorney of a proxy from a creditor who was not a client prior to the solicitation is objectionable not only as unethical conduct as recognized by such cases as *In the Matter of Darland Company*, 184 F. Supp. 760 (S.D. Iowa 1960) but also and more importantly because the practice carries a substantial risk that administration will fall into the hands of those whose interest is in obtaining fees from the estate rather than securing dividends for creditors. The same risk attaches to solicitation by the holder of a claim for collection only.

*Subdivision (e).* The regulation of solicitation and voting of proxies is achieved by the rule principally through the imposition of requirements of disclosure on the holders of two or more proxies. The disclosures must be made to the clerk before the meeting at which the proxies are to be voted to afford the clerk or a party in interest an opportunity to examine the circumstances accompanying the acquisition of the proxies in advance of any exercise of the proxies. In the light of the examination the clerk or a party in interest should bring to the attention of the judge any question that arises and the judge may permit the proxies that comply with the rule to be voted and reject those that do not unless the holders can effect or establish compliance in such manner as the court shall prescribe. The holders of single proxies are excused from the disclosure requirements because of the insubstantiality of the risk that such proxies have been solicited, or will be voted, in an interest other than that of general creditors.

Every holder of two or more proxies must include in the submission a verified statement that no consideration has been paid or promised for the proxy, either by the proxyholder or the solicitor or any forwarder of the proxy. Any payment or promise of consideration for a proxy would be conclusive evidence of a purpose to acquire control of the administration of an estate for an ulterior purpose. The holder of multiple proxies must also include in the submission a verified statement as to whether there is any agreement by the holder, the solicitor, or any forwarder of the proxy for the employment of any person in the administration of an estate or for the sharing of any compensation allowed in connection with the administration of the estate. The provisions requiring these statements implement the policy of the Code expressed in §504 as well as the policy of this rule to deter the acquisition of proxies for the purpose of obtaining a share in the outlays for administration. Finally the facts as to any consideration moving or promised to any member of a committee which functions as a solicitor, forwarder, or proxyholder must be disclosed by the proxyholder. Such information would be of significance to the court in evaluating the purpose of the committee in obtaining, transmitting, or voting proxies.

*Subdivision (f)* has counterparts in the local rules referred to in the Advisory Committee's Note to former Bankruptcy Rule 208. Courts have been accorded a wide range of discretion in the handling of disputes involving proxies. Thus the referee was allowed to reject proxies and to proceed forthwith to hold a scheduled election at the same meeting. *E.g.*, *In re Portage Wholesale Co.*, 183 F.2d 959 (7th Cir. 1950); *In re McGill*, 106 Fed. 57 (6th Cir. 1901); *In re Deena Woolen Mills, Inc.*, 114 F. Supp. 260, 273 (D. Me. 1953); *In re Finlay*, 3 Am.B.R. 738 (S.D.N.Y. 1900). The bankruptcy judge may postpone an election to permit a determination of issues presented by a dispute as to proxies and to afford those creditors whose proxies are rejected an opportunity to give new proxies or to attend an adjourned meeting to vote their own claims. *Cf. In the Matter of Lenrick Sales, Inc* F.2d 439, 442–43 (3d Cir.), cert. denied, 389 U.S. 822 (1967); *In the Matter of Construction Supply Corp.* 221 F. Supp. 124, 128 (E.D. Va. 1963). This rule is not intended to restrict the scope of the court's discretion in the handling of disputes as to proxies.

NOTES OF ADVISORY COMMITTEE ON RULES—1991 AMENDMENT

This rule is amended to give the United States trustee information in connection with proxies so that the United States trustee may perform responsibilities as presiding officer at the §341 meeting of creditors. See Rule 2003.

The words "with the clerk" are deleted as unnecessary. See Rules 5005(a) and 9001(3).

COMMITTEE NOTES ON RULES—2009 AMENDMENT

The rule is amended to implement changes in connection with the amendment to Rule 9006(a) and the manner by which time is computed under the rules. The deadline in the rule is amended to substitute a deadline that is a multiple of seven days. Throughout the rules, deadlines are amended in the following manner:

- 5-day periods become 7-day periods
- 10-day periods become 14-day periods
- 15-day periods become 14-day periods
- 20-day periods become 21-day periods
- 25-day periods become 28-day periods

## Rule 2007. Review of Appointment of Creditors' Committee Organized Before Commencement of the Case

(a) MOTION TO REVIEW APPOINTMENT. If a committee appointed by the United States trustee pursuant to §1102(a) of the Code consists of the members of a committee organized by creditors before the commencement of a chapter 9 or chapter 11 case, on motion of a party in interest and after a hearing on notice to the United States trustee and other entities as the court may direct, the court may determine whether the appointment of the committee satisfies the requirements of §1102(b)(1) of the Code.

(b) SELECTION OF MEMBERS OF COMMITTEE. The court may find that a committee organized by unsecured creditors before the commencement of a chapter 9 or chapter 11 case was fairly chosen if:

(1) it was selected by a majority in number and amount of claims of unsecured creditors who may vote under §702(a) of the Code and were present in person or represented at a meeting of which all creditors having unsecured claims of over $1,000 or the 100 unsecured creditors having the largest claims had at least seven days' notice in writing, and of which meeting written minutes reporting the names of the creditors present or represented and voting and the amounts of their claims were kept and are available for inspection;

(2) all proxies voted at the meeting for the elected committee were solicited pursuant to Rule 2006 and the lists and statements required by subdivision (e) thereof have been transmitted to the United States trustee; and

(3) the organization of the committee was in all other respects fair and proper.

(c) FAILURE TO COMPLY WITH REQUIREMENTS FOR APPOINTMENT. After a hearing on notice pursuant to subdivision (a) of this rule, the court shall direct the United States trustee to vacate the appointment of the committee and may order other appropriate action if the court finds that such appointment failed to satisfy the requirements of §1102(b)(1) of the Code.

(As amended Mar. 30, 1987, eff. Aug. 1, 1987; Apr. 30, 1991, eff. Aug. 1, 1991; Mar. 26, 2009, eff. Dec. 1, 2009.)

NOTES OF ADVISORY COMMITTEE ON RULES—1983

Section 1102(b)(1) of the Code permits the court to appoint as the unsecured creditors' committee, the committee that was selected by creditors before the order for relief. This provision recognizes the propriety of continuing a "prepetition" committee in an official capacity. Such a committee, however, must be found to have been fairly chosen and representative of the different kinds of claims to be represented.

*Subdivision (a)* does not necessarily require a hearing but does require a party in interest to bring to the court's attention the fact that a prepetition committee had been organized and should be appointed. An application would suffice for this purpose. Party in interest would include the committee, any member of the committee, or any of its agents acting for the committee. Whether or not notice of the application should be given to any other party is left to the discretion of the court.

*Subdivision (b)* implements §1102(b)(1). The Code provision allows the court to appoint, as the official §1102(a) committee, a "prepetition" committee if its members were fairly chosen and the committee is representative of the different kinds of claims. This subdivision of the rule indicates some of the factors the court may consider in determining whether the requirements of §1102(b)(1) have been satisfied. In effect, the subdivision provides various factors which are similar to those set forth in Rule 2006 with respect to the solicitation and voting of proxies in a chapter 7 liquidation case.

NOTES OF ADVISORY COMMITTEE ON RULES—1987 AMENDMENT

The rule is amended to conform to the 1984 amendments to §1102(b)(1) of the Code.

NOTES OF ADVISORY COMMITTEE ON RULES—1991 AMENDMENT

This rule is amended to conform to the 1986 amendments to §1102(a). The United States trustee appoints committees pursuant to §1102 in chapter 11 cases. Section 1102 is applicable in chapter 9 cases pursuant to §901(a).

Although §1102(b)(1) of the Code permits the United States trustee to appoint a prepetition committee as the statutory committee if its members were fairly chosen and it is representative of the different kinds of claims to be represented, the amendment to this rule provides a procedure for judicial review of the appointment. The factors that may be considered by the court in determining whether the committee was fairly chosen are not new. A finding that a prepetition committee has not been fairly chosen does not prohibit the appointment of some or all of its members to the creditors' committee. Although this rule deals only with judicial review of the appointment of prepetition committees, it does not preclude judicial review under Rule 2020 regarding the appointment of other committees.

COMMITTEE NOTES ON RULES—2009 AMENDMENT

The rule is amended to implement changes in connection with the amendment to Rule 9006(a) and the manner by which time is computed under the rules. The deadline in the rule is amended to substitute a deadline that is a multiple of seven days. Throughout the rules, deadlines are amended in the following manner:

- 5-day periods become 7-day periods
- 10-day periods become 14-day periods
- 15-day periods become 14-day periods
- 20-day periods become 21-day periods
- 25-day periods become 28-day periods

## Rule 2007.1. Appointment of Trustee or Examiner in a Chapter 11 Reorganization Case

(a) ORDER TO APPOINT TRUSTEE OR E

In a chapter 11 reorganization case, a motion for an order to appoint a trustee or an examiner under §1104(a) or §1104(c) of the Code shall be made in accordance with Rule 9014.

(b) ELECTION OF TRUSTEE.

(1) *Request for an Election.* A request to convene a meeting of creditors for the purpose of electing a trustee in a chapter 11 reorganization case shall be filed and transmitted to the United States trustee in accordance with Rule 5005 within the time prescribed by §1104(b) of

the Code. Pending court approval of the person elected, any person appointed by the United States trustee under §1104(d) and approved in accordance with subdivision (c) of this rule shall serve as trustee.

(2) *Manner of Election and Notice.* An election of a trustee under §1104(b) of the Code shall be conducted in the manner provided in Rules 2003(b)(3) and 2006. Notice of the meeting of creditors convened under §1104(b) shall be given as provided in Rule 2002. The United States trustee shall preside at the meeting. A proxy for the purpose of voting in the election may be solicited only by a committee of creditors appointed under §1102 of the Code or by any other party entitled to solicit a proxy pursuant to Rule 2006.

(3) *Report of Election and Resolution of Disputes.*

(A) *Report of Undisputed Election.* If no dispute arises out of the election, the United States trustee shall promptly file a report certifying the election, including the name and address of the person elected and a statement that the election is undisputed. The report shall be accompanied by a verified statement of the person elected setting forth that person's connections with the debtor, creditors, any other party in interest, their respective attorneys and accountants, the United States trustee, or any person employed in the office of the United States trustee.

(B) *Dispute Arising Out of an Election.* If a dispute arises out of an election, the United States trustee shall promptly file a report stating that the election is disputed, informing the court of the nature of the dispute, and listing the name and address of any candidate elected under any alternative presented by the dispute. The report shall be accompanied by a verified statement by each candidate elected under each alternative presented by the dispute, setting forth the person's connections with the debtor, creditors, any other party in interest, their respective attorneys and accountants, the United States trustee, or any person employed in the office of the United States trustee. Not later than the date on which the report of the disputed election is filed, the United States trustee shall mail a copy of the report and each verified statement to any party in interest that has made a request to convene a meeting under §1104(b) or to receive a copy of the report, and to any committee appointed under §1102 of the Code.

(c) APPROVAL OF APPOINTMENT. An order approving the appointment of a trustee or an examiner under §1104(d) of the Code shall be made on application of the United States trustee. The application shall state the name of the person appointed and, to the best of the applicant's knowledge, all the person's connections with the debtor, creditors, any other parties in interest, their respective attorneys and accountants, the United States trustee, or persons employed in the office of the United States trustee. The application shall state the names of the parties in interest with whom the United States trustee consulted regarding the appointment. The application shall be accompanied by a verified statement of the person appointed setting forth the person's connections with the debtor, creditors, any other party in interest, their respective attorneys and accountants, the United States trustee, or any person employed in the office of the United States trustee.

(Added Apr. 30, 1991, eff. Aug. 1, 1991; amended Apr. 11, 1997, eff. Dec. 1, 1997; Apr. 23, 2008, eff. Dec. 1, 2008.)

NOTES OF ADVISORY COMMITTEE ON RULES—1991

This rule is added to implement the 1986 amendments to §1104 of the Code regarding the appointment of a trustee or examiner in a chapter 11 case. A motion for an order to appoint a trustee or examiner is a contested matter. Although the court decides whether the appointment is warranted under the particular facts of the case, it is the United States trustee who makes the appointment pursuant to §1104(c) of the Code. The appointment is subject to approval of the court, however, which may be obtained by application of the United States trustee. Section 1104(c) of the Code requires that the appointment be made after consultation with parties in interest and that the person appointed be disinterested.

The requirement that connections with the United States trustee or persons employed in the United States trustee's office be revealed is not intended to enlarge the definition of "disinterested person" in §101(13) of the Code, to supersede executive regulations or other laws relating to appointments by United States trustees, or to otherwise restrict the United States trustee's discretion in making appointments. This information is required, however, in the interest of full disclosure and confidence in the appointment process and to give the court all information that may be relevant to the exercise of judicial discretion in approving the appointment of a trustee or examiner in a chapter 11 case.

NOTES OF ADVISORY COMMITTEE ON RULES—1997 AMENDMENT

This rule is amended to implement the 1994 amendments to §1104 of the Code regarding the election of a trustee in a chapter 11 case.

Eligibility for voting in an election for a chapter 11 trustee is determined in accordance with Rule 2003(b)(3). Creditors whose claims are deemed filed under §1111(a) are treated for voting purposes as creditors who have filed proofs of claim.

Proxies for the purpose of voting in the election may be solicited only by a creditors' committee appointed under §1102 or by any other party entitled to solicit proxies pursuant to Rule 2006. Therefore, a trustee or examiner who has served in the case, or a committee of equity security holders appointed under §1102, may not solicit proxies.

The procedures for reporting disputes to the court derive from similar provisions in Rule 2003(d) applicable to chapter 7 cases. An election may be disputed by a party in interest or by the United States trustee. For example, if the United States trustee believes that the person elected is ineligible to serve as trustee because the person is not "disinterested," the United States trustee should file a report disputing the election.

The word "only" is deleted from subdivision (b), redesignated as subdivision (c), to avoid any negative inference with respect to the availability of procedures for obtaining review of the United States trustee's acts or failure to act pursuant to Rule 2020.

*GAP Report on Rule 2017.1.* The published draft of proposed new subdivision (b)(3) of Rule 2017.1 [2007.1], and the Committee Note, was substantially revised to implement Mr. Patchan's recommendations (described above), to clarify how a disputed election will be reported, and to make stylistic improvements.

COMMITTEE NOTES ON RULES—2008 AMENDMENT

Under §1104(b)(2) of the Code, as amended in 2005, if an eligible, disinterested person is elected to serve as trustee in a chapter 11 case, the United States trustee is directed to file a report certifying the election. The person elected does not have to be appointed to the position. Rather, the filing of the report certifying the election itself constitutes the appointment. The section further provides that in the event of a dispute in the election of a trustee, the court must resolve the matter. The rule is amended to be consistent with §1104(b)(2).

When the United States trustee files a report certifying the election of a trustee, the person elected must provide a verified statement, similar to the statement required of professional persons under Rule 2014, disclosing connections with parties in interest and certain other persons connected with the case. Although court approval of the person elected is not required, the disclosure of the person's connections will enable parties in interest to determine whether the person is disinterested.

*Changes Made After Publication.* No changes were made after publication.

## Rule 2007.2. Appointment of Patient Care Ombudsman in a Health Care Business Case

(a) ORDER TO APPOINT PATIENT CARE OMBUDSMAN. In a chapter 7, chapter 9, or chapter 11 case in which the debtor is a health care business, the court shall order the appointment of a patient care ombudsman under §333 of the Code, unless the court, on motion of the United States trustee or a party in interest filed no later than 21 days after the commencement of the case or within another time fixed by the court, finds that the appointment of a patient care ombudsman is not necessary under the specific circumstances of the case for the protection of patients.

(b) MOTION FOR ORDER TO APPOINT OMBUDSMAN. If the court has found that the appointment of an ombudsman is not necessary, or has terminated the appointment, the court, on motion of the United States trustee or a party in interest, may order the appointment at a later time if it finds that the appointment has become necessary to protect patients.

(c) NOTICE OF APPOINTMENT. If a patient care ombudsman is appointed under §333, the United States trustee shall promptly file a notice of the appointment, including the name and address of the person appointed. Unless the person appointed is a State Long-Term Care Ombudsman, the notice shall be accompanied by a verified statement of the person appointed setting forth the person's connections with the debtor, creditors, patients, any other party in interest, their respective attorneys and accountants, the United States trustee, and any person employed in the office of the United States trustee.

(d) TERMINATION OF APPOINTMENT. On motion of the United States trustee or a party in interest, the court may terminate the appointment of a patient care ombudsman if the court finds that the appointment is not necessary to protect patients.

(e) MOTION. A motion under this rule shall be governed by Rule 9014. The motion shall be transmitted to the United States trustee and served on: the debtor; the trustee; any committee elected under §705 or appointed under §1102 of the Code or its authorized agent, or, if the case is a chapter 9 municipality case or a chapter 11 reorganization case and no committee of unsecured creditors has been appointed under §1102, on the creditors included on the list filed under Rule 1007(d); and such other entities as the court may direct.

(Added Apr. 23, 2008, eff. Dec. 1, 2008; amended Mar. 26, 2009, eff. Dec. 1, 2009.)

COMMITTEE NOTES ON RULES—2008

Section 333 of the Code, added by the 2005 amendments, requires the court to order the appointment of a health care ombudsman within the first 30 days of a health care business case, unless the court finds that the appointment is not necessary for the protection of patients. The rule recognizes this requirement and provides a procedure by which a party may obtain a court order finding that the appointment of a patient care ombudsman is unnecessary. In the absence of a timely motion under subdivision (a) of this rule, the court will enter an order directing the United States trustee to appoint the ombudsman.

Subdivision (b) recognizes that, despite a previous order finding that a patient care ombudsman is not necessary, circumstances of the case may change or newly discovered evidence may demonstrate the necessity of an ombudsman to protect the interests of patients. In that event, a party may move the court for an order directing the appointment of an ombudsman.

When the appointment of a patient care ombudsman is ordered, the United States trustee is required to appoint a disinterested person to serve in that capacity. Court approval of the appointment is not required, but subdivision (c) requires the person appointed, if not a State Long-Term Care Ombudsman, to file a verified statement similar to the statement filed by professional persons under Rule 2014 so that parties in interest will have information relevant to disinterestedness. If a party believes that the person appointed is not disinterested, it may file a motion asking the court to find that the person is not eligible to serve.

Subdivision (d) permits parties in interest to move for the termination of the appointment of a patient care ombudsman. If the movant can show that there no longer is any need for the ombudsman, the court may order the termination of the appointment.

*Changes Made After Publication.* No changes were made after publication.

COMMITTEE NOTES ON RULES—2009 AMENDMENT

The rule is amended to implement changes in connection with the amendment to Rule 9006(a) and the manner by which time is computed under the rules. The deadline in the rule is amended to substitute a deadline that is a multiple of seven days. Throughout the rules, deadlines are amended in the following manner:

- 5-day periods become 7-day periods
- 10-day periods become 14-day periods
- 15-day periods become 14-day periods
- 20-day periods become 21-day periods
- 25-day periods become 28-day periods

## Rule 2008. Notice to Trustee of Selection

The United States trustee shall immediately notify the person selected as trustee how to qualify and, if applicable, the amount of the trustee's bond. A trustee that has filed a blanket bond pursuant to Rule 2010 and has been selected as trustee in a chapter 7, chapter 12, or chapter 13 case that does not notify the court and the United States trustee in writing of rejection of the office within seven days after receipt of notice of selection shall be deemed to have accepted the office. Any other person selected as trustee shall notify the court and the United States trustee in writing of acceptance of the office within seven days after receipt of notice of selection or shall be deemed to have rejected the office.

(As amended Mar. 30, 1987, eff. Aug. 1, 1987; Apr. 30, 1991, eff. Aug. 1, 1991; Mar. 26, 2009, eff. Dec. 1, 2009.)

NOTES OF ADVISORY COMMITTEE ON RULES—1983

This rule is adapted from former Bankruptcy Rule 209(c). The remainder of that rule is inapplicable because its provisions are covered by §§701–703, 321 of the Code.

If the person selected as trustee accepts the office, he must qualify within five days after his selection, as required by §322(a) of the Code.

In districts having a standing trustee for chapter 13 cases, a blanket acceptance of the appointment would be sufficient for compliance by the standing trustee with this rule.

NOTES OF ADVISORY COMMITTEE ON RULES—1987 AMENDMENT

The rule is amended to eliminate the need for a standing chapter 13 trustee or member of the panel of chapter 7 trustees to accept or reject an appointment.

NOTES OF ADVISORY COMMITTEE ON RULES—1991 AMENDMENT

The amendments to this rule relating to the United States trustee are derived from Rule X-1004(a) and conform to the 1986 amendments to the Code and 28 U.S.C. §586 which provide that the United States trustee appoints and supervises trustees, and in a chapter 7 case presides over any election of a trustee. This rule applies when a trustee is either appointed or elected. This rule is also amended to provide for chapter 12 cases.

COMMITTEE NOTES ON RULES—2009 AMENDMENT

The rule is amended to implement changes in connection with the amendment to Rule 9006(a) and the manner by which time is computed under the rules. The deadline in the rule is amended to substitute a deadline that is a multiple of seven days. Throughout the rules, deadlines are amended in the following manner:

- 5-day periods become 7-day periods
- 10-day periods become 14-day periods
- 15-day periods become 14-day periods
- 20-day periods become 21-day periods
- 25-day periods become 28-day periods

## Rule 2009. Trustees for Estates When Joint Administration Ordered

(a) ELECTION OF SINGLE TRUSTEE FOR ESTATES BEING JOINTLY ADMINISTERED. If the court orders a joint administration of two or more estates under Rule 1015(b), creditors may elect a single trustee for the estates being jointly administered, unless the case is under subchapter V of chapter 7 of the Code.

(b) RIGHT OF CREDITORS TO ELECT SEPARATE TRUSTEE. Notwithstanding entry of an order for joint administration under Rule 1015(b), the creditors of any debtor may elect a separate trustee for the estate of the debtor as provided in §702 of the Code, unless the case is under subchapter V of chapter 7.

(c) APPOINTMENT OF TRUSTEES FOR ESTATES BEING JOINTLY ADMINISTERED.

(1) *Chapter 7 Liquidation Cases.* Except in a case governed by subchapter V of chapter 7, the United States trustee may appoint one or more interim trustees for estates being jointly administered in chapter 7 cases.

(2) *Chapter 11 Reorganization Cases.* If the appointment of a trustee is ordered, the United States trustee may appoint one or more trustees for estates being jointly administered in chapter 11 cases.

(3) *Chapter 12 Family Farmer's Debt Adjustment Cases.* The United States trustee may appoint one or more trustees for estates being jointly administered in chapter 12 cases.

(4) *Chapter 13 Individual's Debt Adjustment Cases.* The United States trustee may appoint one or more trustees for estates being jointly administered in chapter 13 cases.

(d) POTENTIAL CONFLICTS OF INTEREST. On a showing that creditors or equity security holders of the different estates will be prejudiced by conflicts of interest of a common trustee who has been elected or appointed, the court shall order the selection of separate trustees for estates being jointly administered.

(e) SEPARATE ACCOUNTS. The trustee or trustees of estates being jointly administered shall keep separate accounts of the property and distribution of each estate.

(As amended Mar. 30, 1987, eff. Aug. 1, 1987; Apr. 30, 1991, eff. Aug. 1, 1991; Mar. 27, 2003, eff. Dec. 1, 2003.)

NOTES OF ADVISORY COMMITTEE ON RULES—1983

This rule is applicable in chapter 7 cases and, in part, in chapter 11 and 13 cases. The provisions in subdivisions (a) and (b) concerning creditor election of a trustee apply only in a chapter 7 case because it is only pursuant to §702 of the Code that creditors may elect a trustee. Subdivision (c) of the rule applies in chapter 11 and 13 as well as chapter 7 cases; pursuant to §1104 of the Code, the court may order the appointment of a trustee on application of a party in interest and, pursuant to §1163 of the Code, the court must appoint a trustee in a railroad reorganization case. Subdivision (c) should not be taken as an indication that more than one trustee may be appointed for a single debtor. Section 1104(c) permits only one trustee for each estate. In a chapter 13 case, if there is no standing trustee, the court is to appoint a person to serve as trustee pursuant to §1302 of the Code. There is no provision for a trustee in a chapter 9 case, except for a very limited purpose; see §926 of the Code.

This rule recognizes that economical and expeditious administration of two or more estates may be facilitated not only by the selection of a single trustee for a partnership and its partners, but by such selection whenever estates are being jointly administered pursuant to Rule 1015. See *In the Matter of International Oil Co.*, 427 F.2d 186, 187 (2d Cir. 1970). The rule is derived from former §5c of the Act and former Bankruptcy Rule 210. The premise of §5c of the Act was that notwithstanding the potentiality of conflict between the interests of the creditors of the partners and those of the creditors of the partnership, the conflict is not sufficiently serious or frequent in most cases to warrant the selection of separate trustees for the firm and the several partners. Even before the proviso was added to §5c of the Act in 1938 to permit the creditors of a general partner to elect their separate trustee for his estate, it was held that the court had discretion to permit such an election or to make a separate appointment when a conflict of interest was recognized. *Wood*, 248 Fed. 246, 249–50 (6th Cir.), cert. denied, 247 U.S. 512 (1918); 4 Collier, *Bankruptcy* ¶723.04 (15th ed. 1980). The rule retains in subdivision (e) the features of the practice respecting the selection of a trustee that was developed under §5 of the Act. Subdivisions (a) and (c) permit the court to authorize election of a single trustee or to make a single appointment when joint administration of estates of other kinds of debtors is ordered, but subdivision (d) requires the court to make a preliminary evaluation of the risks of conflict of interest. If after the election or appointment of a common trustee a conflict of interest materializes, the court must take appropriate action to deal with it.

*Subdivision (f)* is derived from §5e of the Act and former Bankruptcy Rule 210(f) and requires that the common trustee keep a separate account for each estate in all cases that are jointly administered.

NOTES OF ADVISORY COMMITTEE ON RULES—1991 AMENDMENT

One or more trustees may be appointed for estates being jointly administered in chapter 12 cases.

The amendments to this rule are derived from Rule X-1005 and are necessary because the United States trustee, rather than the court, has responsibility for appointing trustees pursuant to §§701, 1104, 1202, and 1302 of the Code.

If separate trustees are ordered for chapter 7 estates pursuant to subdivision (d), separate and successor trustees should be chosen as prescribed in §703 of the Code. If the occasion for another election arises, the United States trustee should call a meeting of creditors for this purpose. An order to select separate trustees does not disqualify an appointed or elected trustee from serving for one of the estates.

*Subdivision (e)* is abrogated because the exercise of discretion by the United States trustee, who is in the Executive Branch, is not subject to advance restriction by rule of court. United States v. Cox, 342 F.2d 167 (5th Cir. 1965), *cert. denied*, 365 U.S. 863 (1965); United States v. Frumento, 409 F.Supp. 136, 141 (E.D.Pa.), *aff'd*, 563 F.2d 1083 (3d Cir. 1977), *cert. denied*, 434 U.S. 1072 (1977); see, Smith v. United States, 375 F.2d 243 (5th Cir. 1967); House Report No. 95-595, 95th Cong., 1st Sess. 110 (1977). However, a trustee appointed by the United States trustee may be removed by the court for cause. See §324 of the Code. Subdivision (d) of this rule, as amended, is consistent with §324. Subdivision (f) is redesignated as subdivision (e).

COMMITTEE NOTES ON RULES—2003 AMENDMENT

The rule is amended to reflect the enactment of subchapter V of chapter 7 of the Code governing multilateral clearing organization liquidations. Section 782 of the Code provides that the designation of a trustee or alternative trustee for the case is made by the Federal Reserve Board. Therefore, neither the United States trustee nor the creditors can appoint or elect a trustee in these cases.

Other amendments are stylistic.

*Changes Made After Publication and Comments.* No changes since publication.

## Rule 2010. Qualification by Trustee; Proceeding on Bond

(a) BLANKET BOND. The United States trustee may authorize a blanket bond in favor of the United States conditioned on the faithful performance of official duties by the trustee or trustees to cover (1) a person who qualifies as trustee in a number of cases, and (2) a number of trustees each of whom qualifies in a different case.

(b) PROCEEDING ON BOND. A proceeding on the trustee's bond may be brought by any party in interest in the name of the United States for the use of the entity injured by the breach of the condition.

(As amended Mar. 30, 1987, eff. Aug. 1, 1987; Apr. 30, 1991, eff. Aug. 1, 1991.)

NOTES OF ADVISORY COMMITTEE ON RULES—1983

*Subdivisions (a) and (b).* Subdivision (a) gives authority for approval by the court of a single bond to cover (1) a person who qualifies as trustee in a number of cases, and (2) a number of trustees each of whom qualifies in a different case. The cases need not be related in any way. Substantial economies can be effected if a single bond covering a number of different cases can be issued and approved at one time. When a blanket bond is filed, the trustee qualifies under subdivision (b) of the rule by filing an acceptance of the office.

*Subdivision (c)* prescribes the evidentiary effect of a certified copy of an order approving the trustee's bond given by a trustee under this rule or, when a blanket bond has been authorized, of a certified copy of acceptance. This rule supplements the Federal Rules of Evidence, which apply in bankruptcy cases. See Rule 1101 of the Federal Rules of Evidence. The order of approval should conform to Official Form No. 25. See, however, §549(c) of the Code which provides only for the filing of the petition in the real estate records to serve as constructive notice of the pendency of the case. See also Rule 2011 which prescribes the evidentiary effect of a certificate that the debtor is a debtor in possession.

*Subdivision (d)* is derived from former Bankruptcy Rule 212(f). Reference should be made to §322(a) and (d) of the Code which requires the bond to be filed with the bankruptcy court and places a two year limitation for the commencement of a proceeding on the bond. A bond filed under this rule should conform to Official Form No. 25. A proceeding on the bond of a trustee is governed by the rules in Part VII. See the Note accompanying Rule 7001. See also Rule 9025.

NOTES OF ADVISORY COMMITTEE ON RULES—1987 AMENDMENT

*Subdivision (b)* is deleted because of the amendment to Rule 2008.

NOTES OF ADVISORY COMMITTEE ON RULES—1991 AMENDMENT

This rule is amended to conform to the 1986 amendment of §322 of the Code. The United States trustee determines the amount and sufficiency of the trustee's bond. The amendment to subdivision (a) is derived from Rule X-1004(b).

*Subdivision (b)* is abrogated because an order approving a bond is no longer necessary in view of the 1986 amendments to §322 of the Code. Subdivision (c) is redesignated as subdivision (b).

## Rule 2011. Evidence of Debtor in Possession or Qualification of Trustee

(a) Whenever evidence is required that a debtor is a debtor in possession or that a trustee has qualified, the clerk may so certify and the certificate shall constitute conclusive evidence of that fact.

(b) If a person elected or appointed as trustee does not qualify within the time prescribed by §322(a) of the Code, the clerk shall so notify the court and the United States trustee.

(As amended Apr. 30, 1991, eff. Aug. 1, 1991.)

NOTES OF ADVISORY COMMITTEE ON RULES

This rule prescribes the evidentiary effect of a certificate issued by the clerk that the debtor is a debtor in possession. See Official Form No. 26. Only chapter 11 of the Code provides for a debtor in possession. See §1107(a) of the Code. If, however, a trustee is appointed in the chapter 11 case, there will not be a debtor in possession. See §§1101(1), 1105 of the Code.

NOTES OF ADVISORY COMMITTEE ON RULES AMENDMENT

This rule is amended to provide a procedure for proving that a trustee has qualified in accordance with §322 of the Code. *Subdivision (b)* is added so that the court and the United States trustee will be informed if the person selected as trustee pursuant to §§701, 702, 1104,

1202, 1302, or 1163 fails to qualify within the time prescribed in §322(a).

## Rule 2012. Substitution of Trustee or Successor Trustee; Accounting

(a) TRUSTEE. If a trustee is appointed in a chapter 11 case or the debtor is removed as debtor in possession in a chapter 12 case, the trustee is substituted automatically for the debtor in possession as a party in any pending action, proceeding, or matter.

(b) SUCCESSOR TRUSTEE. When a trustee dies, resigns, is removed, or otherwise ceases to hold office during the pendency of a case under the Code (1) the successor is automatically substituted as a party in any pending action, proceeding, or matter; and (2) the successor trustee shall prepare, file, and transmit to the United States trustee an accounting of the prior administration of the estate.

(As amended Mar. 30, 1987, eff. Aug. 1, 1987; Apr. 30, 1991, eff. Aug. 1, 1991.)

NOTES OF ADVISORY COMMITTEE ON RULES—1983

Paragraph (1) of this rule implements §325 of the Code. It provides that a pending action or proceeding continues without abatement and that the trustee's successor is automatically substituted as a party whether it be another trustee or the debtor returned to possession, as such party.

Paragraph (2) places it within the responsibility of a successor trustee to file an accounting of the prior administration of the estate. If an accounting is impossible to obtain from the prior trustee because of death or lack of cooperation, prior reports submitted in the earlier administration may be updated.

NOTES OF ADVISORY COMMITTEE ON RULES—1987 AMENDMENT

*Subdivision (a)* is new. The subdivision provides for the substitution of a trustee appointed in a chapter 11 case for the debtor in possession in any pending litigation.

The original provisions of the rule are now in subdivision (b).

NOTES OF ADVISORY COMMITTEE ON RULES—1991 AMENDMENT

*Subdivision (a)* is amended to include any chapter 12 case in which the debtor is removed as debtor in possession pursuant to §1204(a) of the Code.

*Subdivision (b)* is amended to require that the accounting of the prior administration which must be filed with the court is also transmitted to the United States trustee who is responsible for supervising the administration of cases and trustees. See 28 U.S.C. §586(a)(3). Because a court order is not required for the appointment of a successor trustee, requiring the court to fix a time for filing the accounting is inefficient and unnecessary. The United States trustee has supervisory powers over trustees and may require the successor trustee to file the accounting within a certain time period. If the successor trustee fails to file the accounting within a reasonable time, the United States trustee or a party in interest may take appropriate steps including a request for an appropriate court order. See 28 U.S.C. §586(a)(3)(G). The words "with the court" are deleted in subdivision (b)(2) as unnecessary. See Rules 5005(a) and 9001(3).

## Rule 2013. Public Record of Compensation Awarded to Trustees, Examiners, and Professionals

(a) RECORD TO BE KEPT. The clerk shall maintain a public record listing fees awarded by the court (1) to trustees and attorneys, accountants, appraisers, auctioneers and other professionals employed by trustees, and (2) to examiners. The record shall include the name and docket number of the case, the name of the individual or firm receiving the fee and the amount of the fee awarded. The record shall be maintained chronologically and shall be kept current and open to examination by the public without charge. "Trustees," as used in this rule, does not include debtors in possession.

(b) SUMMARY OF RECORD. At the close of each annual period, the clerk shall prepare a summary of the public record by individual or firm name, to reflect total fees awarded during the preceding year. The summary shall be open to examination by the public without charge. The clerk shall transmit a copy of the summary to the United States trustee.

(As amended Mar. 30, 1987, eff. Aug. 1, 1987; Apr. 30, 1991, eff. Aug. 1, 1991.)

NOTES OF ADVISORY COMMITTEE ON RULES—1983

This rule is adapted from former Rule 213. The first sentence of that rule is omitted because of the provisions in 28 U.S.C. §§586 and 604(f) creating panels of private trustees.

The rule is not applicable to standing trustees serving in chapter 13 cases. See §1302 of the Code.

A basic purpose of the rule is to prevent what Congress has defined as "cronyism." Appointment or employment, whether in a chapter 7 or 11 case, should not center among a small select group of individuals unless the circumstances are such that it would be warranted. The public record of appointments to be kept by the clerk will provide a means for monitoring the appointment process.

*Subdivision (b)* provides a convenient source for public review of fees paid from debtors' estates in the bankruptcy courts. Thus, public recognition of appointments, fairly distributed and based on professional qualifications and expertise, will be promoted and notions of improper favor dispelled. This rule is in keeping with the findings of the Congressional subcommittees as set forth in the House Report of the Committee on the Judiciary, No. 95–595, 95th Cong., 1st Sess. 89–99 (1977). These findings included the observations that there were frequent appointments of the same person, contacts developed between the bankruptcy bar and the courts, and an unusually close relationship between the bar and the judges developed over the years. A major purpose of the new statute is to dilute these practices and instill greater public confidence in the system. Rule 2013 implements that laudatory purpose.

NOTES OF ADVISORY COMMITTEE ON RULES—1987 AMENDMENT

In subdivisions (b) and (c) the word awarded is substituted for the word paid. While clerks do not know if fees are paid, they can determine what fees are awarded by the court.

NOTES OF ADVISORY COMMITTEE ON RULES—1991 AMENDMENT

*Subdivision (a)* is deleted. The matter contained in this subdivision is more properly left for regulation by the United States trustee. When appointing trustees and examiners and when monitoring applications for employment of auctioneers, appraisers and other professionals, the United States trustee should be sensitive to disproportionate or excessive fees received by any person.

*Subdivision (b)*, redesignated as subdivision (a), is amended to reflect the fact that the United States trustee appoints examiners subject to court approval.

*Subdivision (c)*, redesignated as subdivision (b), is amended to furnish the United States trustee with a copy of the annual summary which may assist that office in the performance of its responsibilities under 28 U.S.C. §586 and the Code.

The rule is not applicable to standing trustees serving in chapter 12 cases. See §1202 of the Code.

## Rule 2014. Employment of Professional Persons

(a) APPLICATION FOR AND ORDER OF EMPLOYMENT. An order approving the employment of attorneys, accountants, appraisers, auctioneers, agents, or other professionals pursuant to §327, §1103, or §1114 of the Code shall be made only on application of the trustee or committee. The application shall be filed and, unless the case is a chapter 9 municipality case, a copy of the application shall be transmitted by the applicant to the United States trustee. The application shall state the specific facts showing the necessity for the employment, the name of the person to be employed, the reasons for the selection, the professional services to be rendered, any proposed arrangement for compensation, and, to the best of the applicant's knowledge, all of the person's connections with the debtor, creditors, any other party in interest, their respective attorneys and accountants, the United States trustee, or any person employed in the office of the United States trustee. The application shall be accompanied by a verified statement of the person to be employed setting forth the person's connections with the debtor, creditors, any other party in interest, their respective attorneys and accountants, the United States trustee, or any person employed in the office of the United States trustee.

(b) SERVICES RENDERED BY MEMBER OR ASSOCIATE OF FIRM OF ATTORNEYS OR ACCOUNTANTS. If, under the Code and this rule, a law partnership or corporation is employed as an attorney, or an accounting partnership or corporation is employed as an accountant, or if a named attorney or accountant is employed, any partner, member, or regular associate of the partnership, corporation, or individual may act as attorney or accountant so employed, without further order of the court.

(As amended Mar. 30, 1987, eff. Aug. 1, 1987; Apr. 30, 1991, eff. Aug. 1, 1991.)

NOTES OF ADVISORY COMMITTEE ON RULES—1983

*Subdivision (a)* is adapted from the second sentence of former Bankruptcy Rule 215(a). The remainder of that rule is covered by §327 of the Code.

*Subdivision (b)* is derived from former Bankruptcy Rule 215(f). The compensation provisions are set forth in §504 of the Code.

NOTES OF ADVISORY COMMITTEE ON RULES—1991 AMENDMENT

This rule is amended to include retention of professionals by committees of retired employees pursuant to §1114 of the Code.

The United States trustee monitors applications filed under §327 of the Code and may file with the court comments with respect to the approval of such applications. See 28 U.S.C. §586(a)(3)(H). The United States trustee also monitors creditors' committees in accordance with 28 U.S.C. §586(a)(3)(E). The addition of the second sentence of subdivision (a) is designed to enable the United States trustee to perform these duties.

*Subdivision (a)* is also amended to require disclosure of the professional's connections with the United States trustee or persons employed in the United States trustee's office. This requirement is not intended to prohibit the employment of such persons in all cases or to enlarge the definition of "disinterested person" in §101(13) of the Code. However, the court may consider a connection with the United States trustee's office as a factor when exercising its discretion. Also, this information should be revealed in the interest of full disclosure and confidence in the bankruptcy system, especially since the United States trustee monitors and may be heard on applications for compensation and reimbursement of professionals employed under this rule.

The United States trustee appoints committees pursuant to §1102 of the Code which is applicable in chapter 9 cases under §901. In the interest of full disclosure and confidence in the bankruptcy system, a connection between the United States trustee and a professional employed by the committee should be revealed in every case, including a chapter 9 case. However, since the United States trustee does not have any role in the employment of professionals in chapter 9 cases, it is not necessary in such cases to transmit to the United States trustee a copy of the application under subdivision (a) of this rule. See 28 U.S.C. §586(a)(3)(H).

## Rule 2015. Duty to Keep Records, Make Reports, and Give Notice of Case or Change of Status

(a) TRUSTEE OR DEBTOR IN POSSESSION. A trustee or debtor in possession shall:

(1) in a chapter 7 liquidation case and, if the court directs, in a chapter 11 reorganization case file and transmit to the United States trustee a complete inventory of the property of the debtor within 30 days after qualifying as a trustee or debtor in possession, unless such an inventory has already been filed;

(2) keep a record of receipts and the disposition of money and property received;

(3) file the reports and summaries required by §704(8) of the Code which shall include a statement, if payments are made to employees, of the amounts of deductions for all taxes required to be withheld or paid for and in behalf of employees and the place where these amounts are deposited;

(4) as soon as possible after the commencement of the case, give notice of the case to every entity known to be holding money or property subject to withdrawal or order of the debtor, including every bank, savings or building and loan association, public utility company, and landlord with whom the debtor has a deposit, and to every insurance company which has issued a policy having a cash surrender value payable to the debtor, except that notice need not be given to any entity who has knowledge or has previously been notified of the case;

(5) in a chapter 11 reorganization case, on or before the last day of the month after each calendar quarter during which there is a duty to pay fees under 28 U.S.C. §1930(a)(6), file and transmit to the United States trustee a statement of any disbursements made during that quarter and of any fees payable under 28 U.S.C. §1930(a)(6) for that quarter; and

(6) in a chapter 11 small business case, unless the court, for cause, sets another reporting interval, file and transmit to the United States trustee for each calendar month after the order for relief, on the appropriate Official Form, the report required by §308. If the order for relief is within the first 15 days of a cal-

endar month, a report shall be filed for the portion of the month that follows the order for relief. If the order for relief is after the 15th day of a calendar month, the period for the remainder of the month shall be included in the report for the next calendar month. Each report shall be filed no later than 21 days after the last day of the calendar month following the month covered by the report. The obligation to file reports under this subparagraph terminates on the effective date of the plan, or conversion or dismissal of the case.

(b) CHAPTER 12 TRUSTEE AND DEBTOR IN POSSESSION. In a chapter 12 family farmer's debt adjustment case, the debtor in possession shall perform the duties prescribed in clauses (2)–(4) of subdivision (a) of this rule and, if the court directs, shall file and transmit to the United States trustee a complete inventory of the property of the debtor within the time fixed by the court. If the debtor is removed as debtor in possession, the trustee shall perform the duties of the debtor in possession prescribed in this paragraph.

(c) CHAPTER 13 TRUSTEE AND DEBTOR.

(1) *Business Cases.* In a chapter 13 individual's debt adjustment case, when the debtor is engaged in business, the debtor shall perform the duties prescribed by clauses (2)–(4) of subdivision (a) of this rule and, if the court directs, shall file and transmit to the United States trustee a complete inventory of the property of the debtor within the time fixed by the court.

(2) *Nonbusiness Cases.* In a chapter 13 individual's debt adjustment case, when the debtor is not engaged in business, the trustee shall perform the duties prescribed by clause (2) of subdivision (a) of this rule.

(d) FOREIGN REPRESENTATIVE. In a case in which the court has granted recognition of a foreign proceeding under chapter 15, the foreign representative shall file any notice required under §1518 of the Code within 14 days after the date when the representative becomes aware of the subsequent information.

(e) TRANSMISSION OF REPORTS. In a chapter 11 case the court may direct that copies or summaries of annual reports and copies or summaries of other reports shall be mailed to the creditors, equity security holders, and indenture trustees. The court may also direct the publication of summaries of any such reports. A copy of every report or summary mailed or published pursuant to this subdivision shall be transmitted to the United States trustee.

(As amended Mar. 30, 1987, eff. Aug. 1, 1987; Apr. 30, 1991, eff. Aug. 1, 1991; Apr. 23, 1996, eff. Dec. 1, 1996; Apr. 29, 2002, eff. Dec. 1, 2002; Apr. 23, 2008, eff. Dec. 1, 2008; Mar. 26, 2009, eff. Dec. 1, 2009.)

NOTES OF ADVISORY COMMITTEE ON RULES—1983

This rule combines the provisions found in former Rules 218, 10–208, 11–30 and 13–208 of the Rules of Bankruptcy Procedure. It specifies various duties which are in addition to those required by §§704, 1106, 1302 and 1304 of the Code.

In *subdivision (a)* the times permitted to be fixed by the court in clause (3) for the filing of reports and summaries may be fixed by local rule or order.

*Subdivision (b).* This subdivision prescribes duties on either the debtor or trustee in chapter 13 cases, depending on whether or not the debtor is engaged in business (§1304 of the Code). The duty of giving notice prescribed by subdivision (a)(4) is not included in a nonbusiness case because of its impracticability.

*Subdivision (c)* is derived from former Chapter X Rule 10–208(c) which, in turn, was derived from §190 of the Act. The equity security holders to whom the reports should be sent are those of record at the time of transmittal of such reports.

NOTES OF ADVISORY COMMITTEE ON RULES—1987 AMENDMENT

*Subdivision (a)* is amended to add as a duty of the trustee or debtor in possession the filing of a notice of or a copy of the petition. The filing of such notice or a copy of the petition is essential to the protection of the estate from unauthorized post-petition conveyances of real property. Section 549(c) of the Code protects the title of a good faith purchaser for fair equivalent value unless the notice or copy of the petition is filed.

NOTES OF ADVISORY COMMITTEE ON RULES—1991 AMENDMENT

This rule is amended to provide the United States trustee with information needed to perform supervisory responsibilities in accordance with 28 U.S.C. §586(a)(3) and to exercise the right to raise, appear and be heard on issues pursuant to §307 of the Code.

*Subdivision (a)(3)* is amended to conform to the 1986 amendments to §704(8) of the Code and the United States trustee system. It may not be necessary for the court to fix a time to file reports if the United States trustee requests that they be filed within a specified time and there is no dispute regarding such time.

*Subdivision (a)(5)* is deleted because the filing of a notice of or copy of the petition to protect real property against unauthorized postpetition transfers in a particular case is within the discretion of the trustee.

The new subdivision (a)(5) was added to enable the United States trustee, parties in interest, and the court to determine the appropriate quarterly fee required by 28 U.S.C. §1930(a)(6). The requirements of subdivision (a)(5) should be satisfied whenever possible by including this information in other reports filed by the trustee or debtor in possession. Nonpayment of the fee may result in dismissal or conversion of the case pursuant to §1112(b) of the Code.

Rule X–1007(b), which provides that the trustee or debtor in possession shall cooperate with the United States trustee by furnishing information that the United States trustee reasonably requires, is deleted as unnecessary. The deletion of Rule X–1007(b) should not be construed as a limitation of the powers of the United States trustee or of the duty of the trustee or debtor in possession to cooperate with the United States trustee in the performance of the statutory responsibilities of that office.

*Subdivision (a)(6)* is abrogated as unnecessary. See §1106(a)(7) of the Code.

*Subdivision (a)(7)* is abrogated. The closing of a chapter 11 case is governed by Rule 3022.

New *subdivision (b)*, which prescribes the duties of the debtor in possession and trustee in a chapter 12 case, does not prohibit additional reporting requirements pursuant to local rule or court order.

NOTES OF ADVISORY COMMITTEE ON RULES—1996 AMENDMENT

*Subdivision (a)(1)* provides that the trustee in a chapter 7 case and, if the court directs, the trustee or debtor in possession in a chapter 11 case, is required to file and transmit to the United States trustee a complete inventory of the debtor's property within 30 days after qualifying as trustee or debtor in possession, unless such an inventory has already been filed. Subdivisions (b) and (c) are amended to clarify that a debtor in possession and trustee in a chapter 12 case, and a debtor in a chapter 13 case where the debtor is engaged in business, are not required to file and transmit to the United States trustee a complete inventory of the property of the debtor unless the court so directs. If the court so directs, the court also fixes the time limit for filing and transmitting the inventory.

*GAP Report on Rule 2015.* No changes since publication, except for a stylistic change in the first sentence of the committee note.

COMMITTEE NOTES ON RULES—2002 AMENDMENT

*Subdivision (a)(5)* is amended to provide that the duty to file quarterly disbursement reports continues only so long as there is an obligation to make quarterly payments to the United States trustee under 28 U.S.C. §1930(a)(6).

Other amendments are stylistic.

*Changes Made After Publication and Comments.* No changes were made.

COMMITTEE NOTES ON RULES—2008 AMENDMENT

Subparagraph (a)(6) implements §308 of the Code, added by the 2005 amendments. That section requires small business chapter 11 debtors to file periodic financial and operating reports, and the rule sets the time for filing those reports and requires the use of an Official Form for the report. The obligation to file reports under this rule does not relieve the trustee or debtor of any other obligations to provide information or documents to the United States trustee.

The rule also is amended to fix the time for the filing of notices under §1518, added to the Code in 2005. Former subdivision (d) is renumbered as subdivision (e).

Other changes are stylistic.

*Changes Made After Publication.* No changes were made after publication.

COMMITTEE NOTES ON RULES—2009 AMENDMENT

The rule is amended to implement changes in connection with the amendment to Rule 9006(a) and the manner by which time is computed under the rules. The deadlines in the rule are amended to substitute a deadline that is a multiple of seven days. Throughout the rules, deadlines are amended in the following manner:

- 5-day periods become 7-day periods
- 10-day periods become 14-day periods
- 15-day periods become 14-day periods
- 20-day periods become 21-day periods
- 25-day periods become 28-day periods

## Rule 2015.1. Patient Care Ombudsman

(a) REPORTS. A patient care ombudsman, at least 14 days before making a report under §333(b)(2) of the Code, shall give notice that the report will be made to the court, unless the court orders otherwise. The notice shall be transmitted to the United States trustee, posted conspicuously at the health care facility that is the subject of the report, and served on: the debtor; the trustee; all patients; and any committee elected under §705 or appointed under §1102 of the Code or its authorized agent, or, if the case is a chapter 9 municipality case or a chapter 11 reorganization case and no committee of unsecured creditors has been appointed under §1102, on the creditors included on the list filed under Rule 1007(d); and such other entities as the court may direct. The notice shall state the date and time when the report will be made, the manner in which the report will be made, and, if the report is in writing, the name, address, telephone number, email address, and website, if any, of the person from whom a copy of the report may be obtained at the debtor's expense.

(b) AUTHORIZATION TO REVIEW CONFIDENTIAL PATIENT RECORDS. A motion by a patient care ombudsman under §333(c) to review confidential patient records shall be governed by Rule 9014, served on the patient and any family member or other contact person whose name and address have been given to the trustee or the debtor for the purpose of providing information regarding the patient's health care, and transmitted to the United States trustee subject to applicable nonbankruptcy law relating to patient privacy. Unless the court orders otherwise, a hearing on the motion may not be commenced earlier than 14 days after service of the motion.

(Added Apr. 23, 2008, eff. Dec. 1, 2008; amended Mar. 26, 2009, eff. Dec. 1, 2009.)

COMMITTEE NOTES ON RULES—2008

This rule is new and implements §333 of the Code, added by the 2005 amendments. Subdivision (a) is designed to give parties in interest, including patients or their representatives, sufficient notice so that they will be able to review written reports or attend hearings at which reports are made. The rule permits a notice to relate to a single report or to periodic reports to be given during the case. For example, the ombudsman may give notice that reports will be made at specified intervals or dates during the case.

Subdivision (a) of the rule also requires that the notice be posted conspicuously at the health care facility in a place where it will be seen by patients and their families or others visiting the patients. This may require posting in common areas and patient rooms within the facility. Because health care facilities and the patients they serve can vary greatly, the locations of the posted notice should be tailored to the specific facility that is the subject of the report.

Subdivision (b) requires the ombudsman to notify the patient and the United States trustee that the ombudsman is seeking access to confidential patient records so that they will be able to appear and be heard on the matter. This procedure should assist the court in reaching its decision both as to access to the records and appropriate restrictions on that access to ensure continued confidentiality. Notices given under this rule are subject to the provisions of applicable federal and state law that relate to the protection of patients' privacy, such as the Health Insurance Portability and Accountability Act of 1996, Pub. L. No. 104–191 (HIPAA).

*Changes Made After Publication.* Two stylistic changes were made to the rule. The reference to the court's authority to order otherwise was moved from the beginning to the end of the first sentence of subdivision (a). On line 19, the word "patient" was substituted for "health" to be consistent with the Code.

COMMITTEE NOTES ON RULES—2009 AMENDMENT

The rule is amended to implement changes in connection with the amendment to Rule 9006(a) and the manner by which time is computed under the rules. The deadlines in the rule are amended to substitute a deadline that is a multiple of seven days. Throughout the rules, deadlines are amended in the following manner:

- 5-day periods become 7-day periods
- 10-day periods become 14-day periods
- 15-day periods become 14-day periods
- 20-day periods become 21-day periods
- 25-day periods become 28-day periods

## Rule 2015.2. Transfer of Patient in Health Care Business Case

Unless the court orders otherwise, if the debtor is a health care business, the trustee may not transfer a patient to another health care business under §704(a)(12) of the Code unless the trustee gives at least 14 days' notice of the transfer to the patient care ombudsman, if any, the patient, and any family member or other contact person whose name and address has been given to the trustee or the debtor for the purpose of providing information regarding the patient's health care. The notice is subject to applicable nonbankruptcy law relating to patient privacy.

(Added Apr. 23, 2008, eff. Dec. 1, 2008; amended Mar. 26, 2009, eff. Dec. 1, 2009.)

COMMITTEE NOTES ON RULES—2008

This rule is new. Section 704(a)(12), added to the Code by the 2005 amendments, authorizes the trustee to relocate patients when a health care business debtor's facility is in the process of being closed. The Code permits the trustee to take this action without the need for any court order, but the notice required by this rule will enable a patient care ombudsman appointed under §333, or a patient who contends that the trustee's actions violate §704(a)(12), to have those issues resolved before the patient is transferred.

This rule also permits the court to enter an order dispensing with or altering the notice requirement in proper circumstances. For example, a facility could be closed immediately, or very quickly, such that 10 days' notice would not be possible in some instances. In that event, the court may shorten the time required for notice.

Notices given under this rule are subject to the provisions of applicable federal and state law that relate to the protection of patients' privacy, such as the Health Insurance Portability and Accountability Act of 1996, Pub. L. No. 104–191 (HIPAA).

*Changes Made After Publication.* No changes were made after publication.

COMMITTEE NOTES ON RULES—2009 AMENDMENT

The rule is amended to implement changes in connection with the amendment to Rule 9006(a) and the manner by which time is computed under the rules. The deadline in the rule is amended to substitute a deadline that is a multiple of seven days. Throughout the rules, deadlines are amended in the following manner:

- 5-day periods become 7-day periods
- 10-day periods become 14-day periods
- 15-day periods become 14-day periods
- 20-day periods become 21-day periods
- 25-day periods become 28-day periods

**Rule 2015.3. Reports of Financial Information on Entities in Which a Chapter 11 Estate Holds a Controlling or Substantial Interest**

(a) REPORTING REQUIREMENT. In a chapter 11 case, the trustee or debtor in possession shall file periodic financial reports of the value, operations, and profitability of each entity that is not a publicly traded corporation or a debtor in a case under title 11, and in which the estate holds a substantial or controlling interest. The reports shall be prepared as prescribed by the appropriate Official Form, and shall be based upon the most recent information reasonably available to the trustee or debtor in possession.

(b) TIME FOR FILING; SERVICE. The first report required by this rule shall be filed no later than seven days before the first date set for the meeting of creditors under §341 of the Code. Subsequent reports shall be filed no less frequently than every six months thereafter, until the effective date of a plan or the case is dismissed or converted. Copies of the report shall be served on the United States trustee, any committee appointed under §1102 of the Code, and any other party in interest that has filed a request therefor.

(c) PRESUMPTION OF SUBSTANTIAL OR CONTROLLING INTEREST; JUDICIAL DETERMINATION. For purposes of this rule, an entity of which the estate controls or owns at least a 20 percent interest, shall be presumed to be an entity in which the estate has a substantial or controlling interest. An entity in which the estate controls or owns less than a 20 percent interest shall be presumed not to be an entity in which the estate has a substantial or controlling interest. Upon motion, the entity, any holder of an interest therein, the United States trustee, or any other party in interest may seek to rebut either presumption, and the court shall, after notice and a hearing, determine whether the estate's interest in the entity is substantial or controlling.

(d) MODIFICATION OF REPORTING REQUIREMENT. The court may, after notice and a hearing, vary the reporting requirement established by subdivision (a) of this rule for cause, including that the trustee or debtor in possession is not able, after a good faith effort, to comply with those reporting requirements, or that the information required by subdivision (a) is publicly available.

(e) NOTICE AND PROTECTIVE ORDERS. No later than 14 days before filing the first report required by this rule, the trustee or debtor in possession shall send notice to the entity in which the estate has a substantial or controlling interest, and to all holders—known to the trustee or debtor in possession—of an interest in that entity, that the trustee or debtor in possession expects to file and serve financial information relating to the entity in accordance with this rule. The entity in which the estate has a substantial or controlling interest, or a person holding an interest in that entity, may request protection of the information under §107 of the Code.

(f) EFFECT OF REQUEST. Unless the court orders otherwise, the pendency of a request under subdivisions (c), (d), or (e) of this rule shall not alter or stay the requirements of subdivision (a).

(Added Apr. 23, 2008, eff. Dec. 1, 2008; amended Mar. 26, 2009, eff. Dec. 1, 2009.)

COMMITTEE NOTES ON RULES—2008

This rule implements §419 of the Bankruptcy Abuse Prevention and Consumer Protection Act of 2005 ("BAPCPA"). Reports are to be made on the appropriate Official Form. While §419 of BAPCPA places the obligation to report upon the "debtor," this rule extends the obligation to include cases in which a trustee has been appointed. The court can order that the reports not be filed in appropriate circumstances, such as when the information that would be included in these reports is already available to interested parties.

*Changes After Publication.* In subdivision (e), the 20 day period was changed to 14 days. This better reconciles the timing of the notice and the scheduling of the §341 meeting of creditors, and it is also consistent with the upcoming time computation amendments.

COMMITTEE NOTES ON RULES—2009 AMENDMENT

The rule is amended to implement changes in connection with the amendment to Rule 9006(a) and the manner by which time is computed under the rules. The deadline in the rule is amended to substitute a deadline that is a multiple of seven days. Throughout the rules, deadlines are amended in the following manner:

- 5-day periods become 7-day periods
- 10-day periods become 14-day periods

- 15-day periods become 14-day periods
- 20-day periods become 21-day periods
- 25-day periods become 28-day periods

### Rule 2016. Compensation for Services Rendered and Reimbursement of Expenses

(a) APPLICATION FOR COMPENSATION OR REIMBURSEMENT. An entity seeking interim or final compensation for services, or reimbursement of necessary expenses, from the estate shall file an application setting forth a detailed statement of (1) the services rendered, time expended and expenses incurred, and (2) the amounts requested. An application for compensation shall include a statement as to what payments have theretofore been made or promised to the applicant for services rendered or to be rendered in any capacity whatsoever in connection with the case, the source of the compensation so paid or promised, whether any compensation previously received has been shared and whether an agreement or understanding exists between the applicant and any other entity for the sharing of compensation received or to be received for services rendered in or in connection with the case, and the particulars of any sharing of compensation or agreement or understanding therefor, except that details of any agreement by the applicant for the sharing of compensation as a member or regular associate of a firm of lawyers or accountants shall not be required. The requirements of this subdivision shall apply to an application for compensation for services rendered by an attorney or accountant even though the application is filed by a creditor or other entity. Unless the case is a chapter 9 municipality case, the applicant shall transmit to the United States trustee a copy of the application.

(b) DISCLOSURE OF COMPENSATION PAID OR PROMISED TO ATTORNEY FOR DEBTOR. Every attorney for a debtor, whether or not the attorney applies for compensation, shall file and transmit to the United States trustee within 14 days after the order for relief, or at another time as the court may direct, the statement required by §329 of the Code including whether the attorney has shared or agreed to share the compensation with any other entity. The statement shall include the particulars of any such sharing or agreement to share by the attorney, but the details of any agreement for the sharing of the compensation with a member or regular associate of the attorney's law firm shall not be required. A supplemental statement shall be filed and transmitted to the United States trustee within 14 days after any payment or agreement not previously disclosed.

(c) DISCLOSURE OF COMPENSATION PAID OR PROMISED TO BANKRUPTCY PETITION PREPARER. Before a petition is filed, every bankruptcy petition preparer for a debtor shall deliver to the debtor, the declaration under penalty of perjury required by §110(h)(2). The declaration shall disclose any fee, and the source of any fee, received from or on behalf of the debtor within 12 months of the filing of the case and all unpaid fees charged to the debtor. The declaration shall also describe the services performed and documents prepared or caused to be prepared by the bankruptcy petition preparer. The declaration shall be filed with the petition. The petition preparer shall file a supplemental statement within 14 days after any payment or agreement not previously disclosed.

(As amended Mar. 30, 1987, eff. Aug. 1, 1987; Apr. 30, 1991, eff. Aug. 1, 1991; Mar. 27, 2003, eff. Dec. 1, 2003; Mar. 26, 2009, eff. Dec. 1, 2009.)

#### NOTES OF ADVISORY COMMITTEE ON RULES—1983

This rule is derived from former Rule 219. Many of the former rule's requirements are, however, set forth in the Code. Section 329 requires disclosure by an attorney of transactions with the debtor, §330 sets forth the bases for allowing compensation, and §504 prohibits sharing of compensation. This rule implements those various provisions.

*Subdivision (a)* includes within its provisions a committee, member thereof, agent, attorney or accountant for the committee when compensation or reimbursement of expenses is sought from the estate.

Regular associate of a law firm is defined in Rule 9001(9) to include any attorney regularly employed by, associated with, or counsel to that law firm. Firm is defined in Rule 9001(6) to include a partnership or professional corporation.

#### NOTES OF ADVISORY COMMITTEE ON RULES—1987 AMENDMENT

*Subdivision (a)* is amended to change "person" to "entity". There are occasions in which a governmental unit may be entitled to file an application under this rule. The requirement that the application contain a "detailed statement of services rendered, time expended and expenses incurred" gives to the court authority to ensure that the application is both comprehensive and detailed. No amendments are made to delineate further the requirements of the application because the amount of detail to be furnished is a function of the nature of the services rendered and the complexity of the case.

*Subdivision (b)* is amended to require that the attorney for the debtor file the §329 statement before the meeting of creditors. This will assist the parties in conducting the examination of the debtor. In addition, the amended rule requires the attorney to supplement the §329 statement if an undisclosed payment is made to the attorney or a new or amended agreement is entered into by the debtor and the attorney.

#### NOTES OF ADVISORY COMMITTEE ON RULES AMENDMENT

*Subdivision (a)* is amended to enable the United States trustee to perform the duty to monitor applications for compensation and reimbursement filed under §330 of the Code. See 28 U.S.C. §586(a)(3)(A).

*Subdivision (b)* is amended to give the United States trustee the information needed to determine whether to request appropriate relief based on excessive fees under §329(b) of the Code. See Rule 2017.

The words "with the court" are deleted in subdivisions (a) and (b) as unnecessary. See Rules 5005(a) and 9001(3).

#### COMMITTEE NOTES ON RULES—2003 AMENDMENT

This rule is amended by adding subdivision (c) to implement §110(h)(1) of the Code.

*Changes Made After Publication and Comments* changes since publication.

#### COMMITTEE NOTES ON RULES—2009 AMENDMENT

The rule is amended to implement changes in connection with the amendment to Rule 9006(a) and the manner by which time is computed under the rules. The deadline in the rule is amended to substitute a deadline that is a multiple of seven days. Throughout the rules, deadlines are amended in the following manner:

- 5-day periods become 7-day periods
- 10-day periods become 14-day periods

- 15-day periods become 14-day periods
- 20-day periods become 21-day periods
- 25-day periods become 28-day periods

Subdivision (c) is amended to reflect the 2005 amendment to §110(h)(1) of the Bankruptcy Code which now requires that the declaration be filed with the petition. The statute previously required that the petition preparer file the declaration within 10 days after the filing of the petition. The amendment to the rule also corrects the cross reference to §110(h)(1), which was redesignated as subparagraph (h)(2) of §110 by the 2005 amendment to the Code.

Other changes are stylistic.

## Rule 2017. Examination of Debtor's Transactions with Debtor's Attorney

(a) PAYMENT OR TRANSFER TO ATTORNEY BEFORE ORDER FOR RELIEF. On motion by any party in interest or on the court's own initiative, the court after notice and a hearing may determine whether any payment of money or any transfer of property by the debtor, made directly or indirectly and in contemplation of the filing of a petition under the Code by or against the debtor or before entry of the order for relief in an involuntary case, to an attorney for services rendered or to be rendered is excessive.

(b) PAYMENT OR TRANSFER TO ATTORNEY AFTER ORDER FOR RELIEF. On motion by the debtor, the United States trustee, or on the court's own initiative, the court after notice and a hearing may determine whether any payment of money or any transfer of property, or any agreement therefor, by the debtor to an attorney after entry of an order for relief in a case under the Code is excessive, whether the payment or transfer is made or is to be made directly or indirectly, if the payment, transfer, or agreement therefor is for services in any way related to the case.

(As amended Mar. 30, 1987, eff. Aug. 1, 1987; Apr. 30, 1991, eff. Aug. 1, 1991.)

NOTES OF ADVISORY COMMITTEE ON RULES—1983

This rule is derived from §60d of the Act and former Bankruptcy Rule 220 and implements §329 of the Code. Information required to be disclosed by the attorney for a debtor by §329 of the Code and by the debtor in his Statement of Financial Affairs (Item 15 of Form No. 7, Item 20 of Form No. 8) will assist the court in determining whether to proceed under this rule. Section 60d was enacted in recognition of "the temptation of a failing debtor to deal too liberally with his property in employing counsel to protect him in view of financial reverses and probable failure." *In re Wood & Henderson*, 210 U.S. 246, 253 (1908). This rule, like §60d of the Act and §329 of the Code, is premised on the need for and appropriateness of judicial scrutiny of arrangements between a debtor and his attorney to protect the creditors of the estate and the debtor against overreaching by an officer of the court who is in a peculiarly advantageous position to impose on both the creditors and his client. 2 Collier, *Bankruptcy* ¶329.02 (15th ed. 1980); MacLachlan, *Bankruptcy* 318 (1956). Rule 9014 applies to any contested matter arising under this rule.

This rule is not to be construed to permit post-petition payments or transfers which may be avoided under other provisions of the Code.

NOTES OF ADVISORY COMMITTEE ON RULES—1991 AMENDMENT

This rule is amended to include within subdivision (a) a payment or transfer of property by the debtor to an attorney after the filing of an involuntary petition but before the order for relief. Any party in interest should be able to make a motion for a determination of whether such payment or transfer is excessive because the funds or property transferred may be property of the estate.

The United States trustee supervises and monitors the administration of bankruptcy cases other than chapter 9 cases and pursuant to §307 of the Code may raise, appear and be heard on issues relating to fees paid to the debtor's attorney. It is consistent with that role to expect the United States trustee to review statements filed under Rule 2016(b) and to file motions relating to excessive fees pursuant to §329 of the Code.

## Rule 2018. Intervention; Right to Be Heard

(a) PERMISSIVE INTERVENTION. In a case under the Code, after hearing on such notice as the court directs and for cause shown, the court may permit any interested entity to intervene generally or with respect to any specified matter.

(b) INTERVENTION BY ATTORNEY GENERAL OF A STATE. In a chapter 7, 11, 12, or 13 case, the Attorney General of a State may appear and be heard on behalf of consumer creditors if the court determines the appearance is in the public interest, but the Attorney General may not appeal from any judgment, order, or decree in the case.

(c) CHAPTER 9 MUNICIPALITY CASE. The Secretary of the Treasury of the United States may, or if requested by the court shall, intervene in a chapter 9 case. Representatives of the state in which the debtor is located may intervene in a chapter 9 case with respect to matters specified by the court.

(d) LABOR UNIONS. In a chapter 9, 11, or 12 case, a labor union or employees' association, representative of employees of the debtor, shall have the right to be heard on the economic soundness of a plan affecting the interests of the employees. A labor union or employees' association which exercises its right to be heard under this subdivision shall not be entitled to appeal any judgment, order, or decree relating to the plan, unless otherwise permitted by law.

(e) SERVICE ON ENTITIES COVERED BY T RULE. The court may enter orders governing the service of notice and papers on entities permitted to intervene or be heard pursuant to this rule.

(As amended Mar. 30, 1987, eff. Aug. 1, 1987; Apr. 30, 1991, eff. Aug. 1, 1991.)

NOTES OF ADVISORY COMMITTEE ON RULES—1983

This rule is derived from former Rules 8-210, 9-15 and 10-210 and it implements §§1109 and 1164 of the Code.

Pursuant to §1109 of the Code, parties in interest have a right to be heard and the Securities and Exchange Commission may raise and be heard on any issue but it may not take an appeal. That section is applicable in chapter 9 cases (§901 of the Code) and in chapter 11 cases, including cases under subchapter IV thereof for the reorganization of a railroad.

In a railroad reorganization case under subchapter IV of chapter 11, §1164 also gives the right to be heard to the Interstate Commerce Commission, the Department of Transportation and any state or local regulatory commission with jurisdiction over the debtor, but these entities may not appeal.

This rule does not apply in adversary proceedings. For intervention in adversary proceedings, see Rule 7024. The rules do not provide any right of compensation to or reimbursement of expenses for intervenors or others covered by this rule. Section 503(b)(3)(D) and (4) is not applicable to the entities covered by this rule.

*Subdivision (a)* is derived from former Chapter VIII Rule 8–210 and former Chapter X Rule 10–210. It permits intervention of an entity (see §101(14), (21) of the Code) not otherwise entitled to do so under the Code or this rule. Such a party seeking to intervene must show cause therefor.

*Subdivision (b)* specifically grants the appropriate state's Attorney General the right to appear and be heard on behalf of consumer creditors when it is in the public interest. See House Rep. No. 95–595, 95th Cong., 1st Sess. (1977) 189. While "consumer creditor" is not defined in the Code or elsewhere, it would include the type of individual entitled to priority under §507(a)(5) of the Code, that is, an individual who has deposited money for the purchase, lease or rental of property or the purchase of services for the personal, family, or household use of the individual. It would also include individuals who purchased or leased property for such purposes in connection with which there may exist claims for breach of warranty.

This subdivision does not grant the Attorney General the status of party in interest. In other contexts, the Attorney General will, of course, be a party in interest as for example, in representing a state in connection with a tax claim.

*Subdivision (c)* recognizes the possible interests of the Secretary of the Treasury or of the state of the debtor's locale when a municipality is the debtor. It is derived from former Chapter IX Rule 9–15 and §85(d) of the Act.

*Subdivision (d)* is derived from former Chapter X Rule 10–210 which, in turn, was derived from §206 of the Act. Section 206 has no counterpart in the Code.

*Subdivision (e)* is derived from former Chapter VIII Rule 8–210(d). It gives the court flexibility in directing the type of future notices to be given intervenors.

NOTES OF ADVISORY COMMITTEE ON RULES—1987 AMENDMENT

*Subdivision (d)* is amended to make it clear that the prohibition against appeals by labor unions is limited only to their participation in connection with the hearings on the plan as provided in subdivision (d). If a labor union would otherwise have the right to file an appeal or to be a party to an appeal, this rule does not preclude the labor union from exercising that right.

NOTES OF ADVISORY COMMITTEE ON RULES—1991 AMENDMENT

*Subdivisions (b) and (d)* are amended to include chapter 12.

## Rule 2019. Representation of Creditors and Equity Security Holders in Chapter 9 Municipality and Chapter 11 Reorganization Cases

(a) DATA REQUIRED. In a chapter 9 municipality or chapter 11 reorganization case, except with respect to a committee appointed pursuant to §1102 or 1114 of the Code, every entity or committee representing more than one creditor or equity security holder and, unless otherwise directed by the court, every indenture trustee, shall file a verified statement setting forth (1) the name and address of the creditor or equity security holder; (2) the nature and amount of the claim or interest and the time of acquisition thereof unless it is alleged to have been acquired more than one year prior to the filing of the petition; (3) a recital of the pertinent facts and circumstances in connection with the employment of the entity or indenture trustee, and, in the case of a committee, the name or names of the entity or entities at whose instance, directly or indirectly, the employment was arranged or the committee was organized or agreed to act; and (4) with reference to the time of the employment of the entity, the organization or formation of the committee, or the appearance in the case of any indenture trustee, the amounts of claims or interests owned by the entity, the members of the committee or the indenture trustee, the times when acquired, the amounts paid therefor, and any sales or other disposition thereof. The statement shall include a copy of the instrument, if any, whereby the entity, committee, or indenture trustee is empowered to act on behalf of creditors or equity security holders. A supplemental statement shall be filed promptly, setting forth any material changes in the facts contained in the statement filed pursuant to this subdivision.

(b) FAILURE TO COMPLY; EFFECT. On motion of any party in interest or on its own initiative, the court may (1) determine whether there has been a failure to comply with the provisions of subdivision (a) of this rule or with any other applicable law regulating the activities and personnel of any entity, committee, or indenture trustee or any other impropriety in connection with any solicitation and, if it so determines, the court may refuse to permit that entity, committee, or indenture trustee to be heard further or to intervene in the case; (2) examine any representation provision of a deposit agreement, proxy, trust mortgage, trust indenture, or deed of trust, or committee or other authorization, and any claim or interest acquired by any entity or committee in contemplation or in the course of a case under the Code and grant appropriate relief; and (3) hold invalid any authority, acceptance, rejection, or objection given, procured, or received by an entity or committee who has not complied with this rule or with §1125(b) of the Code.

(As amended Mar. 30, 1987, eff. Aug. 1, 1987; Apr. 30, 1991, eff. Aug. 1, 1991.)

NOTES OF ADVISORY COMMITTEE ON RULES—1983

This rule is a comprehensive regulation of representation in chapter 9 municipality and in chapter 11 reorganization cases. It is derived from §§209–213 of the Act and former Chapter X Rule 10–211.

*Subdivision (b)* is derived from §§212, 213 of the Act. As used in clause (2), "other authorization" would include a power or warrant of attorney which are specifically mentioned in §212 of the Act. This rule deals with representation provisions in mortgages, trust deeds, etc. to protect the beneficiaries from unfair practices and the like. It does not deal with the validation or invalidation of security interests generally. If immediate compliance is not possible, the court may permit a representative to be heard on a specific matter, but there is no implicit waiver of compliance on a permanent basis.

NOTES OF ADVISORY COMMITTEE ON RULES AMENDMENT

*Subdivision (a)* is amended to exclude from the requirements of this rule committees of retired employees appointed pursuant to §1114 of the Code. The words "with the clerk" are deleted as unnecessary. See Rules 5005(a) and 9001(3).

## Rule 2020. Review of Acts by United States Trustee

A proceeding to contest any act or failure to act by the United States trustee is governed by Rule 9014.

(Added Apr. 30, 1991, eff. Aug. 1, 1991.)

NOTES OF ADVISORY COMMITTEE ON RULES—1991

The United States trustee performs administrative functions, such as the convening of the meeting of creditors and the appointment of trustees and committees. Most of the acts of the United States trustee are not controversial and will go unchallenged. However, the United States trustee is not a judicial officer and does not resolve disputes regarding the propriety of its own actions. This rule, which is new, provides a procedure for judicial review of the United States trustee's acts or failure to act in connection with the administration of the case. For example, if the United States trustee schedules a §341 meeting to be held 90 days after the petition is filed, and a party in interest wishes to challenge the propriety of that act in view of §341(a) of the Code and Rule 2003 which requires that the meeting be held not more than 40 days after the order for relief, this rule permits the party to do so by motion.

This rule provides for review of acts already committed by the United States trustee, but does not provide for advisory opinions in advance of the act. This rule is not intended to limit the discretion of the United States trustee, provided that the United States trustee's act is authorized by, and in compliance with, the Code, title 28, these rules, and other applicable law.

## PART III—CLAIMS AND DISTRIBUTION TO CREDITORS AND EQUITY INTEREST HOLDERS; PLANS

### Rule 3001. Proof of Claim

(a) FORM AND CONTENT. A proof of claim is a written statement setting forth a creditor's claim. A proof of claim shall conform substantially to the appropriate Official Form.

(b) WHO MAY EXECUTE. A proof of claim shall be executed by the creditor or the creditor's authorized agent except as provided in Rules 3004 and 3005.

(c) CLAIM BASED ON A WRITING. When a claim, or an interest in property of the debtor securing the claim, is based on a writing, the original or a duplicate shall be filed with the proof of claim. If the writing has been lost or destroyed, a statement of the circumstances of the loss or destruction shall be filed with the claim.

(d) EVIDENCE OF PERFECTION OF SECURITY INTEREST. If a security interest in property of the debtor is claimed, the proof of claim shall be accompanied by evidence that the security interest has been perfected.

(e) TRANSFERRED CLAIM.

(1) *Transfer of Claim Other Than for Security Before Proof Filed.* If a claim has been transferred other than for security before proof of the claim has been filed, the proof of claim may be filed only by the transferee or an indenture trustee.

(2) *Transfer of Claim Other than for Security after Proof Filed.* If a claim other than one based on a publicly traded note, bond, or debenture has been transferred other than for security after the proof of claim has been filed, evidence of the transfer shall be filed by the transferee. The clerk shall immediately notify the alleged transferor by mail of the filing of the evidence of transfer and that objection thereto, if any, must be filed within 21 days of the mailing of the notice or within any additional time allowed by the court. If the alleged transferor files a timely objection and the court finds, after notice and a hearing, that the claim has been transferred other than for security, it shall enter an order substituting the transferee for the transferor. If a timely objection is not filed by the alleged transferor, the transferee shall be substituted for the transferor.

(3) *Transfer of Claim for Security Before Proof Filed.* If a claim other than one based on a publicly traded note, bond, or debenture has been transferred for security before proof of the claim has been filed, the transferor or transferee or both may file a proof of claim for the full amount. The proof shall be supported by a statement setting forth the terms of the transfer. If either the transferor or the transferee files a proof of claim, the clerk shall immediately notify the other by mail of the right to join in the filed claim. If both transferor and transferee file proofs of the same claim, the proofs shall be consolidated. If the transferor or transferee does not file an agreement regarding its relative rights respecting voting of the claim, payment of dividends thereon, or participation in the administration of the estate, on motion by a party in interest and after notice and a hearing, the court shall enter such orders respecting these matters as may be appropriate.

(4) *Transfer of Claim for Security after Proof Filed.* If a claim other than one based on a publicly traded note, bond, or debenture has been transferred for security after the proof of claim has been filed, evidence of the terms of the transfer shall be filed by the transferee. The clerk shall immediately notify the alleged transferor by mail of the filing of the evidence of transfer and that objection thereto, if any, must be filed within 21 days of the mailing of the notice or within any additional time allowed by the court. If a timely objection is filed by the alleged transferor, the court, after notice and a hearing, shall determine whether the claim has been transferred for security. If the transferor or transferee does not file an agreement regarding its relative rights respecting voting of the claim, payment of dividends thereon, or participation in the administration of the estate, on motion by a party in interest and after notice and a hearing, the court shall enter such orders respecting these matters as may be appropriate.

(5) *Service of Objection or Motion; Notice of Hearing.* A copy of an objection filed pursuant to paragraph (2) or (4) or a motion filed pursuant to paragraph (3) or (4) of this subdivision together with a notice of a hearing shall be mailed or otherwise delivered to the transferor or transferee, whichever is appropriate, at least 30 days prior to the hearing.

(f) EVIDENTIARY EFFECT. A proof of claim executed and filed in accordance with these rules shall constitute prima facie evidence of the validity and amount of the claim.

(g)[1] To the extent not inconsistent with the United States Warehouse Act or applicable State law, a warehouse receipt, scale ticket, or similar document of the type routinely issued as evidence of title by a grain storage facility, as defined in section 557 of title 11, shall constitute

[1] So in original. Subsec. (g) enacted without a catchline.

prima facie evidence of the validity and amount of a claim of ownership of a quantity of grain.

(As amended Pub. L. 98–353, title III, §354, July 10, 1984, 98 Stat. 361; Apr. 30, 1991, eff. Aug. 1, 1991; Mar. 26, 2009, eff. Dec. 1, 2009.)

NOTES OF ADVISORY COMMITTEE ON RULES—1983

This rule is adapted from former Bankruptcy Rules 301 and 302. The Federal Rules of Evidence, made applicable to cases under the Code by Rule 1101, do not prescribe the evidentiary effect to be accorded particular documents. Subdivision (f) of this rule supplements the Federal Rules of Evidence as they apply to cases under the Code.

*Subdivision (c).* This subdivision is similar to former Bankruptcy Rule 302(c) and continues the requirement for the filing of any written security agreement and provides that the filing of a duplicate of a writing underlying a claim authenticates the claim with the same effect as the filing of the original writing. *Cf.* Rules 1001(4) and 1003 of F.R. of Evid. Subdivision (d) together with the requirement in the first sentence of subdivision (c) for the filing of any written security agreement, is designed to facilitate the determination whether the claim is secured and properly perfected so as to be valid against the trustee.

*Subdivision (d).* "Satisfactory evidence" of perfection, which is to accompany the proof of claim, would include a duplicate of an instrument filed or recorded, a duplicate of a certificate of title when a security interest is perfected by notation on such a certificate, a statement that pledged property has been in possession of the secured party since a specified date, or a statement of the reasons why no action was necessary for perfection. The secured creditor may not be required to file a proof of claim under this rule if he is not seeking allowance of a claim for a deficiency. But see §506(d) of the Code.

*Subdivision (e).* The rule recognizes the differences between an unconditional transfer of a claim and a transfer for the purpose of security and prescribes a procedure for dealing with the rights of the transferor and transferee when the transfer is for security. The rule clarifies the procedure to be followed when a transfer precedes or follows the filing of the petition. The interests of sound administration are served by requiring the post-petition transferee to file with the proof of claim a statement of the transferor acknowledging the transfer and the consideration for the transfer. Such a disclosure will assist the court in dealing with evils that may arise out of post-bankruptcy traffic in claims against an estate. *Monroe v. Scofield*, 135 F.2d 725 (10th Cir. 1943); *In re Philadelphia & Western Ry.*, 64 F. Supp. 738 (E.D. Pa. 1946); *cf. In re Latham Lithographic Corp.*, 107 F.2d 749 (2d Cir. 1939). Both paragraphs (1) and (3) of this subdivision, which deal with a transfer before the filing of a proof of claim, recognize that the transferee may be unable to obtain the required statement from the transferor, but in that event a sound reason for such inability must accompany the proof of claim filed by the transferee.

Paragraphs (3) and (4) clarify the status of a claim transferred for the purpose of security. An assignee for security has been recognized as a rightful claimant in bankruptcy. *Feder v. John Engelhorn & Sons*, 202 F.2d 411 (2d Cir. 1953). An assignor's right to file a claim notwithstanding the assignment was sustained in *In re R & L Engineering Co.*, 182 F. Supp. 317 (S.D. Cal. 1960). Facilitation of the filing of proofs by both claimants as holders of interests in a single claim is consonant with equitable treatment of the parties and sound administration. See *In re Latham Lithographic Corp.*, 107 F.2d 749 (2d Cir. 1939).

Paragraphs (2) and (4) of subdivision (e) deal with the transfer of a claim after proof has been filed. Evidence of the terms of the transfer required to be disclosed to the court will facilitate the court's determination of the appropriate order to be entered because of the transfer.

Paragraph (5) describes the procedure to be followed when an objection is made by the transferor to the transferee's filed evidence of transfer.

NOTES OF ADVISORY COMMITTEE ON RULES—1987

*Subdivision (g)* was added by §354 of the 1984 amendments.

NOTES OF ADVISORY COMMITTEE ON RULES—1991 AMENDMENT

*Subdivision (a)* is amended in anticipation of future revision and renumbering of the Official Forms.

*Subdivision (e)* is amended to limit the court's role to the adjudication of disputes regarding transfers of claims. If a claim has been transferred prior to the filing of a proof of claim, there is no need to state the consideration for the transfer or to submit other evidence of the transfer. If a claim has been transferred other than for security after a proof of claim has been filed, the transferee is substituted for the transferor in the absence of a timely objection by the alleged transferor. In that event, the clerk should note the transfer without the need for court approval. If a timely objection is filed, the court's role is to determine whether a transfer has been made that is enforceable under nonbankruptcy law. This rule is not intended either to encourage or discourage postpetition transfers of claims or to affect any remedies otherwise available under nonbankruptcy law to a transferor or transferee such as for misrepresentation in connection with the transfer of a claim. "After notice and a hearing" as used in subdivision (e) shall be construed in accordance with paragraph (5).

The words "with the clerk" in subdivision (e)(2) and (e)(4) are deleted as unnecessary. See Rules 5005(a) and 9001(3).

COMMITTEE NOTES ON RULES—2009 AMENDMENT

The rule is amended to implement changes in connection with the amendment to Rule 9006(a) and the manner by which time is computed under the rules. The deadlines in the rule are amended to substitute a deadline that is a multiple of seven days. Throughout the rules, deadlines are amended in the following manner:

- 5-day periods become 7-day periods
- 10-day periods become 14-day periods
- 15-day periods become 14-day periods
- 20-day periods become 21-day periods
- 25-day periods become 28-day periods

REFERENCES IN TEXT

The United States Warehouse Act, referred to in subd. (g), is Part C of act Aug. 11, 1916, ch. 313, 39 Stat. 486, as amended, which is classified generally to chapter 10 (§241 et seq.) of Title 7, Agriculture. For complete classification of this Act to the Code, see Short Title note set out under section 241 of Title 7 and Tables.

AMENDMENT BY PUBLIC LAW

1984—Subd. (g). Pub. L. 98–353 added subd. (g).

EFFECTIVE DATE OF 1984 AMENDMENT

Amendment by Pub. L. 98–353 effective with respect to cases filed 90 days after July 10, 1984, see section 552(a) of Pub. L. 98–353, set out as a note under section 101 of this title.

## Rule 3002. Filing Proof of Claim or Interest

(a) NECESSITY FOR FILING. An unsecured creditor or an equity security holder must file a proof of claim or interest for the claim or interest to be allowed, except as provided in Rules 1019(3), 3003, 3004, and 3005.

(b) PLACE OF FILING. A proof of claim or interest shall be filed in accordance with Rule 5005.

(c) TIME FOR FILING. In a chapter 7 liquidation, chapter 12 family farmer's debt adjustment, or chapter 13 individual's debt adjustment case, a proof of claim is timely filed if it is filed not later than 90 days after the first date set for the meeting of creditors called under §341(a) of the Code, except as follows:

(1) A proof of claim filed by a governmental unit, other than for a claim resulting from a tax return filed under §1308, is timely filed if it is filed not later than 180 days after the date of the order for relief. A proof of claim filed by a governmental unit for a claim resulting from a tax return filed under §1308 is timely filed if it is filed no later than 180 days after the date of the order for relief or 60 days after the date of the filing of the tax return. The court may, for cause, enlarge the time for a governmental unit to file a proof of claim only upon motion of the governmental unit made before expiration of the period for filing a timely proof of claim.

(2) In the interest of justice and if it will not unduly delay the administration of the case, the court may extend the time for filing a proof of claim by an infant or incompetent person or the representative of either.

(3) An unsecured claim which arises in favor of an entity or becomes allowable as a result of a judgment may be filed within 30 days after the judgment becomes final if the judgment is for the recovery of money or property from that entity or denies or avoids the entity's interest in property. If the judgment imposes a liability which is not satisfied, or a duty which is not performed within such period or such further time as the court may permit, the claim shall not be allowed.

(4) A claim arising from the rejection of an executory contract or unexpired lease of the debtor may be filed within such time as the court may direct.

(5) If notice of insufficient assets to pay a dividend was given to creditors under Rule 2002(e), and subsequently the trustee notifies the court that payment of a dividend appears possible, the clerk shall give at least 90 days' notice by mail to creditors of that fact and of the date by which proofs of claim must be filed.

(6) If notice of the time to file a proof of claim has been mailed to a creditor at a foreign address, on motion filed by the creditor before or after the expiration of the time, the court may extend the time by not more than 60 days if the court finds that the notice was insufficient under the circumstances to give the creditor a reasonable time to file a proof of claim.

(As amended Mar. 30, 1987, eff. Aug. 1, 1987; Apr. 30, 1991, eff. Aug. 1, 1991; Apr. 23, 1996, eff. Dec. 1, 1996; Apr. 23, 2008, eff. Dec. 1, 2008.)

NOTES OF ADVISORY COMMITTEE ON RULES—1983

*Subdivision (a)* of this rule is substantially a restatement of the general requirement that claims be proved and filed. The exceptions refer to Rule 3003 providing for the filing of claims in chapter 9 and 11 cases, and to Rules 3004 and 3005 authorizing claims to be filed by the debtor or trustee and the filing of a claim by a contingent creditor of the debtor.

A secured claim need not be filed or allowed under §502 or §506(d) unless a party in interest has requested a determination and allowance or disallowance under §502.

*Subdivision (c)* is adapted from former Bankruptcy Rule 302(e) but changes the time limits on the filing of claims in chapter 7 and 13 cases from six months to 90 days after the first date set for the meeting of creditors. The special rule for early filing by a secured creditor in a chapter 13 case, in former Rule 13-302(e)(1) is not continued.

Although the claim of a secured creditor may have arisen before the petition, a judgment avoiding the security interest may not have been entered until after the time for filing claims has expired. Under Rule 3002(c)(3) the creditor who did not file a secured claim may nevertheless file an unsecured claim within the time prescribed. A judgment does not become final for the purpose of starting the 30 day period provided for by paragraph (3) until the time for appeal has expired or, if an appeal is taken, until the appeal has been disposed of. *In re Tapp*, 61 F. Supp. 594 (W.D. Ky. 1945).

Paragraph (1) is derived from former Bankruptcy Rule 302(e). The governmental unit may move for an extension of the 90 day period. Pursuant to §501(c) of the Code, if the government does not file its claim within the proper time period, the debtor or trustee may file on its behalf. An extension is not needed by the debtor or trustee because the right to file does not arise until the government's time has expired.

Paragraph (4) is derived from former chapter rules. (See, *e.g.*, Rule 11-33(a)(2)(B). In light of the reduced time it is necessary that a party with a claim arising from the rejection of an executory contract have sufficient time to file that claim. This clause allows the court to fix an appropriate time.

Paragraph (5) of subdivision (c) is correlated with the provision in Rule 2002(e) authorizing notification to creditors of estates from which no dividends are anticipated. The clause permits creditors who have refrained from filing claims after receiving notification to be given an opportunity to file when subsequent developments indicate the possibility of a dividend. The notice required by this clause must be given in the manner provided in Rule 2002. The information relating to the discovery of assets will usually be obtained by the clerk from the trustee's interim reports or special notification by the trustee.

Provision is made in Rule 2002(a) and (h) for notifying all creditors of the fixing of a time for filing claims against a surplus under paragraph (6). This paragraph does not deal with the distribution of the surplus. Reference must also be made to §726(a)(2)(C) and (3) which permits distribution on late filed claims.

Paragraph (6) is only operative in a chapter 7 case. In chapter 13 cases, the plan itself provides the distribution to creditors which is not necessarily dependent on the size of the estate.

NOTES OF ADVISORY COMMITTEE ON RULES—1987 AMENDMENT

*Subdivision (a)* is amended by adding a reference to Rule 1019(4). Rule 1019(4) provides that claims actually filed by a creditor in a chapter 11 or 13 case shall be treated as filed in a superseding chapter 7 case. Claims deemed filed in a chapter 11 case pursuant to §1111(a) of the Code are not considered as filed in a superseding chapter 7 case. The creditor must file a claim in the superseding chapter 7 case.

NOTES OF ADVISORY COMMITTEE ON RULES—1991 AMENDMENT

*Subdivision (a)* is amended to conform to the renumbering of subdivisions of Rule 1019. Subdivision (c) is amended to include chapter 12 cases. Subdivision (c)(4) is amended to clarify that it includes a claim arising from the rejection of an unexpired lease.

NOTES OF ADVISORY COMMITTEE ON RULES—1996 AMENDMENT

The amendments are designed to conform to §§502(b)(9) and 726(a) of the Code as amended by the Bankruptcy Reform Act of 1994.

The Reform Act amended §726(a)(1) and added §502(b)(9) to the Code to govern the effects of a tardily filed claim. Under §502(b)(9), a tardily filed claim must be disallowed if an objection to the proof of claim is filed, except to the extent that a holder of a tardily filed claim is entitled to distribution under §726(a)(1), (2), or (3).

The phrase "in accordance with this rule" is deleted from Rule 3002(a) to clarify that the effect of filing a proof of claim after the expiration of the time prescribed in Rule 3002(c) is governed by §502(b)(9) of the Code, rather than by this rule.

Section 502(b)(9) of the Code provides that a claim of a governmental unit shall be timely filed if it is filed "before 180 days after the date of the order for relief" or such later time as the Bankruptcy Rules provide. To avoid any confusion as to whether a governmental unit's proof of claim is timely filed under §502(b)(9) if it is filed on the 180th day after the order for relief, paragraph (1) of subdivision (c) provides that a governmental unit's claim is timely if it is filed not later than 180 days after the order for relief.

References to "the United States, a state, or subdivision thereof" in paragraph (1) of subdivision (c) are changed to "governmental unit" to avoid different treatment among foreign and domestic governments.

*GAP Report on Rule 3002.* After publication of the proposed amendments, the Bankruptcy Reform Act of 1994 amended sections 726 and 502(b) of the Code to clarify the rights of creditors who tardily file a proof of claim. In view of the Reform Act, proposed new subdivision (d) of Rule 3002 has been deleted from the proposed amendments because it is no longer necessary. In addition, subdivisions (a) and (c) have been changed after publication to clarify that the effect of tardily filing a proof of claim is governed by §502(b)(9) of the Code, rather than by this rule.

The amendments to §502(b) also provide that a governmental unit's proof of claim is timely filed if it is filed before 180 days after the order for relief. Proposed amendments to Rule 3002(c)(1) were added to the published amendments to conform to this statutory change and to avoid any confusion as to whether a claim by a governmental unit is timely if it is filed on the 180th day.

The committee note has been re-written to explain the rule changes designed to conform to the Reform Act.

COMMITTEE NOTES ON RULES—2008 AMENDMENT

Subdivision (c)(1) is amended to reflect the addition of §1308 to the Bankruptcy Code in 2005. This provision requires that chapter 13 debtors file tax returns during the pendency of the case, and imposes bankruptcy-related consequences if debtors fail to do so. Subdivision (c)(1) provides additional time for governmental units to file a proof of claim for tax obligations with respect to tax returns filed during the pendency of a chapter 13 case. The amendment also allows the governmental unit to move for additional time to file a proof of claim prior to expiration of the applicable filing period.

Subdivision (c)(5) of the rule is amended to set a new period for providing notice to creditors that they may file a proof of claim in a case in which they were previously informed that there was no need to file a claim. Under Rule 2002(e), if it appears that there will be no distribution to creditors, the creditors are notified of this fact and are informed that if assets are later discovered and a distribution is likely that a new notice will be given to the creditors. This second notice is prescribed by Rule 3002(c)(5). The rule is amended to direct the clerk to give at least 90 days' notice of the time within which creditors may file a proof of claim. Setting the deadline in this manner allows the notices being sent to creditors to be more accurate regarding the deadline than was possible under the prior rule. The rule previously began the 90 day notice period from the time of the mailing of the notice, a date that could vary and generally would not even be known to the creditor. Under the amended rule, the notice will identify a specific bar date for filing proofs of claim thereby being more helpful to the creditors.

Subdivision (c)(6) is added to give the court discretion to extend the time for filing a proof of claim for a creditor who received notice of the time to file the claim at a foreign address, if the court finds that the notice was not sufficient, under the particular circumstances, to give the foreign creditor a reasonable time to file a proof of claim. This amendment is designed to comply with §1514(d), added to the Code by the 2005 amendments, and requires that the rules and orders of the court provide such additional time as is reasonable under the circumstances for foreign creditors to file claims in cases under all chapters of the Code.

Other changes are stylistic.

*Changes Made After Publication.* Subdivision (c)(1) was amended to allow governmental units to move for an enlargement of the time to file a proof of claim. The Committee Note was amended to describe this addition to the rule.

## Rule 3003. Filing Proof of Claim or Equity Security Interest in Chapter 9 Municipality or Chapter 11 Reorganization Cases

(a) APPLICABILITY OF RULE. This rule applies in chapter 9 and 11 cases.

(b) SCHEDULE OF LIABILITIES AND LIST OF EQUITY SECURITY HOLDERS.

(1) *Schedule of Liabilities.* The schedule of liabilities filed pursuant to §521(1) of the Code shall constitute prima facie evidence of the validity and amount of the claims of creditors, unless they are scheduled as disputed, contingent, or unliquidated. It shall not be necessary for a creditor or equity security holder to file a proof of claim or interest except as provided in subdivision (c)(2) of this rule.

(2) *List of Equity Security Holders.* The list of equity security holders filed pursuant to Rule 1007(a)(3) shall constitute prima facie evidence of the validity and amount of the equity security interests and it shall not be necessary for the holders of such interests to file a proof of interest.

(c) FILING PROOF OF CLAIM.

(1) *Who May File.* Any creditor or indenture trustee may file a proof of claim within the time prescribed by subdivision (c)(3) of this rule.

(2) *Who Must File.* Any creditor or equity security holder whose claim or interest is not scheduled or scheduled as disputed, contingent, or unliquidated shall file a proof of claim or interest within the time prescribed by subdivision (c)(3) of this rule; any creditor who fails to do so shall not be treated as a creditor with respect to such claim for the purposes of voting and distribution.

(3) *Time for Filing.* The court shall fix and for cause shown may extend the time within which proofs of claim or interest may be filed. Notwithstanding the expiration of such time, a proof of claim may be filed to the extent and under the conditions stated in Rule 3002(c)(2), (c)(3), (c)(4), and (c)(6).

(4) *Effect of Filing Claim or Interest.* A proof of claim or interest executed and filed in accordance with this subdivision shall supersede any scheduling of that claim or interest pursuant to §521(a)(1) of the Code.

(5) *Filing by Indenture Trustee.* An indenture trustee may file a claim on behalf of all known

or unknown holders of securities issued pursuant to the trust instrument under which it is trustee.

(d) PROOF OF RIGHT TO RECORD STATUS. For the purposes of Rules 3017, 3018 and 3021 and for receiving notices, an entity who is not the record holder of a security may file a statement setting forth facts which entitle that entity to be treated as the record holder. An objection to the statement may be filed by any party in interest.

(As amended Mar. 30, 1987, eff. Aug. 1, 1987; Apr. 30, 1991, eff. Aug. 1, 1991; Apr. 23, 2008, eff. Dec. 1, 2008.)

NOTES OF ADVISORY COMMITTEE ON RULES—1983

*Subdivision (a).* This rule applies only in chapter 9 and chapter 11 cases. It is adapted from former Chapter X Rule 10–401 and provides an exception to the requirement for filing proofs of claim and interest as expressed in §§925 and 1111(a) of the Code.

*Subdivision (b).* This general statement implements §§925 and 1111(a) of the Code.

*Subdivision (c).* This subdivision permits, in paragraph (1), the filing of a proof of claim but does not make it mandatory. Paragraph (2) requires, as does the Code, filing when a claim is scheduled as disputed, contingent, or unliquidated as to amount. It is the creditor's responsibility to determine if the claim is accurately listed. Notice of the provision of this rule is provided for in Official Form No. 16, the order for the meeting of creditors. In an appropriate case the court may order creditors whose claims are scheduled as disputed, contingent, or unliquidated be notified of that fact but the procedure is left to the discretion of the court.

*Subdivision (d)* is derived from former Chapter X Rule 10–401(f).

Except with respect to the need and time for filing claims, the other aspects concerning claims covered by Rules 3001 and 3002 are applicable in chapter 9 and 11 cases.

Holders of equity security interests need not file proofs of interest. Voting and distribution participation is dependent on ownership as disclosed by the appropriate records of a transfer agent or the corporate or other business records at the time prescribed in Rules 3017 and 3021.

NOTES OF ADVISORY COMMITTEE ON RULES—1991 AMENDMENT

Paragraph (3) of subdivision (c) is amended to permit the late filing of claims by infants or incompetent persons under the same circumstances that permit late filings in cases under chapter 7, 12, or 13. The amendment also provides sufficient time in which to file a claim that arises from a postpetition judgment against the claimant for the recovery of money or property or the avoidance of a lien. It also provides for purposes of clarification that upon rejection of an executory contract or unexpired lease, the court shall set a time for filing a claim arising therefrom despite prior expiration of the time set for filing proofs of claim.

The caption of paragraph (4) of subdivision (c) is amended to indicate that it applies to a proof of claim.

COMMITTEE NOTES ON RULES—2008 AMENDMENT

Subdivision (c)(3) is amended to implement §1514(d) of the Code, which was added by the 2005 amendments. It makes the new Rule 3002(c)(6) applicable in chapter 9 and chapter 11 cases. This change was necessary so that creditors with foreign addresses be provided such additional time as is reasonable under the circumstances to file proofs of claims.

*Changes Made After Publication.* No changes were made after publication.

## Rule 3004. Filing of Claims by Debtor or Trustee

If a creditor does not timely file a proof of claim under Rule 3002(c) or 3003(c), the debtor or trustee may file a proof of the claim within 30 days after the expiration of the time for filing claims prescribed by Rule 3002(c) or 3003(c), whichever is applicable. The clerk shall forthwith give notice of the filing to the creditor, the debtor and the trustee.

(As amended Mar. 30, 1987, eff. Aug. 1, 1987; Apr. 25, 2005, eff. Dec. 1, 2005.)

NOTES OF ADVISORY COMMITTEE ON RULES—1983

This rule is adapted from former Bankruptcy Rule 303 but conforms with the changes made by §501(c) of the Code. Rule 303 permitted only the filing of tax and wage claims by the debtor. Section 501(c) of the Code, however, permits the filing by the debtor or trustee on behalf of any creditor.

It is the policy of the Code that debtors' estates should be administered for the benefit of creditors without regard to the dischargeability of their claims. After their estates have been closed, however, discharged debtors may find themselves saddled with liabilities, particularly for taxes, which remain unpaid because of the failure of creditors holding nondischargeable claims to file proofs of claim and receive distributions thereon. The result is that the debtor is deprived of an important benefit of the Code without any fault or omission on the debtor's part and without any objective of the Code being served thereby.

Section 501(c) of the Code authorizes a debtor or trustee to file a proof of claim for any holder of a claim. Although all claims may not be nondischargeable, it may be difficult to determine, in particular, whether tax claims survive discharge. See Plumb, *Federal Tax Liens and Priorities in Bankruptcy*, 43 Ref. J. 37, 43–44 (1969); 1 Collier, *Bankruptcy* ¶17.14 (14th ed. 1967); 3 *id.* ¶523.06 (15th ed. 1979). To eliminate the necessity of the resolution of this troublesome issue, the option accorded the debtor by the Code does not depend on the nondischargeability of the claim. No serious administrative problems and no unfairness to creditors seemed to develop from adoption of Rule 303, the forerunner to §501(c). The authority to file is conditioned on the creditor's failure to file the proof of claim on or before the first date set for the meeting of creditors, which is the date a claim must ordinarily be filed in order to be voted in a chapter 7 case. Notice to the creditor is provided to enable him to file a proof of claim pursuant to Rule 3002, which proof, when filed, would supersede the proof filed by the debtor or trustee. Notice to the trustee would serve to alert the trustee to the special character of the proof and the possible need for supplementary evidence of the validity and amount of the claim. If the trustee does not qualify until after a proof of claim is filed by the debtor pursuant to this rule, he should be notified as soon as practicable thereafter.

To the extent the claim is allowed and dividends paid thereon, it will be reduced or perhaps paid in full. If the claim is also filed pursuant to Rule 3005, only one distribution thereon may be made. As expressly required by Rule 3005 and by the purpose of this rule such distribution must diminish the claim.

NOTES OF ADVISORY COMMITTEE ON RULES—1987 AMENDMENT

Under the rule as amended, the debtor or trustee in a chapter 7 or 13 case has 120 days from the first date set for the meeting of creditors to file a claim for the creditor. During the first 90 days of that period the creditor in a chapter 7 or 13 case may file a claim as provided by Rule 3002(c). If the creditor fails to file a claim, the debtor or trustee shall have an additional 30 days thereafter to file the claim. A proof of claim filed by a creditor supersedes a claim filed by the debtor or trustee only if it is timely filed within the 90 days allowed under Rule 3002(c).

COMMITTEE NOTES ON RULES—2005 AMENDMENT

The rule is amended to conform to §501(c) of the Code. Under that provision, the debtor or trustee may file proof of a claim if the creditor fails to do so in a timely fashion. The rule previously authorized the debtor and the trustee to file a claim as early as the day after the first date set for the meeting of creditors under §341(a). Under the amended rule, the debtor and trustee must wait until the creditor's opportunity to file a claim has expired. Providing the debtor and the trustee with the opportunity to file a claim ensures that the claim will participate in any distribution in the case. This is particularly important for claims that are nondischargeable.

Since the debtor and trustee cannot file a proof of claim until after the creditor's time to file has expired, the rule no longer permits the creditor to file a proof of claim that will supersede the claim filed by the debtor or trustee. The rule leaves to the courts the issue of whether to permit subsequent amendment of such proof of claim.

Other changes are stylistic.

*Changes Made After Publication and Comment.* No changes were made after publication. The Advisory Committee concluded that Mr. Van Allsburg's suggestion goes beyond the scope of the published proposal. Consequently, the Committee declined to adopt the suggestion but may consider it in greater detail at a future meeting.

## Rule 3005. Filing of Claim, Acceptance, or Rejection by Guarantor, Surety, Indorser, or Other Codebtor

(a) FILING OF CLAIM. If a creditor does not timely file a proof of claim under Rule 3002(c) or 3003(c), any entity that is or may be liable with the debtor to that creditor, or who has secured that creditor, may file a proof of the claim within 30 days after the expiration of the time for filing claims prescribed by Rule 3002(c) or Rule 3003(c) whichever is applicable. No distribution shall be made on the claim except on satisfactory proof that the original debt will be diminished by the amount of distribution.

(b) FILING OF ACCEPTANCE OR REJECTION; SUBSTITUTION OF CREDITOR. An entity which has filed a claim pursuant to the first sentence of subdivision (a) of this rule may file an acceptance or rejection of a plan in the name of the creditor, if known, or if unknown, in the entity's own name but if the creditor files a proof of claim within the time permitted by Rule 3003(c) or files a notice prior to confirmation of a plan of the creditor's intention to act in the creditor's own behalf, the creditor shall be substituted for the obligor with respect to that claim.

(As amended Mar. 30, 1987, eff. Aug. 1, 1987; Apr. 30, 1991, eff. Aug. 1, 1991; Apr. 25, 2005, eff. Dec. 1, 2005.)

NOTES OF ADVISORY COMMITTEE ON RULES—1983

This rule is adapted from former Rules 304 and 10–402. Together with §501(b) of the Code, the rule makes clear that anyone who may be liable on a debt of the debtor, including a surety, guarantor, indorser, or other codebtor, is authorized to file in the name of the creditor of the debtor.

*Subdivision (a).* Rule 3002(c) provides the time period for filing proofs of claim in chapter 7 and 13 cases; Rule 3003(c) provides the time, when necessary, for filing claims in a chapter 9 or 11 case.

*Subdivision (b).* This subdivision applies in chapter 9 and 11 cases as distinguished from chapter 7 cases. It permits voting for or against a plan by an obligor who files a claim in place of the creditor.

NOTES OF ADVISORY COMMITTEE ON RULES—1991 AMENDMENT

The words "with the court" in subdivision (b) are deleted as unnecessary. See Rules 5005(a) and 9001(3).

COMMITTEE NOTES ON RULES—2005 AMENDMENT

The rule is amended to delete the last sentence of subdivision (a). The sentence is unnecessary because if a creditor has filed a timely claim under Rule 3002 or 3003(c), the codebtor cannot file a proof of such claim. The codebtor, consistent with §501(b) of the Code, may file a proof of such claim only after the creditor's time to file has expired. Therefore, the rule no longer permits the creditor to file a superseding claim. The rule leaves to the courts the issue of whether to permit subsequent amendment of the proof of claim.

The amendment conforms the rule to §501(b) by deleting language providing that the codebtor files proof of the claim in the name of the creditor.

Other amendments are stylistic.

*Changes Made After Publication and Comment:*

(a) The reference on line 2 of Rule 3005 to "Rule 3002 or 3003(c)" was changed to read "Rule 3002(c) or 3003(c)" to make it parallel to the language in Rule 3004.

(b) The phrase "file a proof of the claim" from line 7 of the proposed rule was moved up to line 4 of the proposed amendment immediately after the word "may". This makes the structure of Rules 3004 and 3005 more consistent.

## Rule 3006. Withdrawal of Claim; Effect on Acceptance or Rejection of Plan

A creditor may withdraw a claim as of right by filing a notice of withdrawal, except as provided in this rule. If after a creditor has filed a proof of claim an objection is filed thereto or a complaint is filed against that creditor in an adversary proceeding, or the creditor has accepted or rejected the plan or otherwise has participated significantly in the case, the creditor may not withdraw the claim except on order of the court after a hearing on notice to the trustee or debtor in possession, and any creditors' committee elected pursuant to §705(a) or appointed pursuant to §1102 of the Code. The order of the court shall contain such terms and conditions as the court deems proper. Unless the court orders otherwise, an authorized withdrawal of a claim shall constitute withdrawal of any related acceptance or rejection of a plan.

(As amended Apr. 30, 1991, eff. Aug. 1, 1991.)

NOTES OF ADVISORY COMMITTEE ON RULES

This rule is derived from former Rules 305 and 10–404.

Since 1938 it has generally been held that Rule 41 F.R.Civ.P. governs the withdrawal of a proof of claim. *In re Empire Coal Sales Corp.*, 45 F. Supp. 974, 976 (S.D.N.Y.), aff'd sub nom. *Kleid v. Ruthbell Coal Co* F.2d 372, 373 (2d Cir. 1942); *Kelso v. MacLaren* 867, 870 (8th Cir. 1941); *In re Hills*, 35 F. Supp. 532, 533 (W.D. Wash. 1940). Accordingly, the cited cases held that after an objection has been filed a proof of claim may be withdrawn only subject to approval by the court. This constitutes a restriction of the right of withdrawal as recognized by some though by no means all of the cases antedating the promulgation of the Federal Rules of Civil Procedure. See 3 Collier *ruptcy*, ¶57.12 (14th ed. 1961); Note, 20 Bost. U. L. Rev. 121 (1940).

The filing of a claim does not commence an adversary proceeding but the filing of an objection to the claim initiates a contest that must be disposed of by the court. This rule recognizes the applicability of the considerations underlying Rule 41(a) F.R.Civ.P. to the withdrawal of a claim after it has been put in issue by an objection. Rule 41(a)(2) F.R.Civ.P. requires leave of court to obtain dismissal over the objection of a defendant who has pleaded a counterclaim prior to the service of the plaintiff's motion to dismiss. Although the applicability of this provision to the withdrawal of a claim was assumed in *Conway v. Union Bank of Switzerland*, 204 F.2d 603, 608 (2d Cir. 1953), *Kleid v. Ruthbell Coal Co., supra*, *Kelso v. MacLaren, supra*, and *In re Hills, supra*, this rule vests discretion in the court to grant, deny, or condition the request of a creditor to withdraw, without regard to whether the trustee has filed a merely defensive objection or a complaint seeking an affirmative recovery of money or property from the creditor.

A number of pre-1938 cases sustained denial of a creditor's request to withdraw proof of claim on the ground of estoppel or election of remedies. 2 Remington, *Bankruptcy* 186 (Henderson ed. 1956); *cf.* 3 Collier, *supra* ¶57.12, at 201 (1964). Voting a claim for a trustee was an important factor in the denial of a request to withdraw in *Standard Varnish Works v. Haydock*, 143 Fed. 318, 319–20 (6th Cir. 1906), and *In re Cann*, 47 F.2d 661, 662 (W.D. Pa. 1931). And it has frequently been recognized that a creditor should not be allowed to withdraw a claim after accepting a dividend. *In re Friedmann*, 1 Am. B. R. 510, 512 (Ref., S.D.N.Y. 1899); 3 Collier 205 (1964); *cf. In re O'Gara Coal Co.*, 12 F.2d 426, 429 (7th Cir.), cert. denied, 271 U.S. 683 (1926). It was held in *Industrial Credit Co. v. Hazen*, 222 F.2d 225 (8th Cir. 1955), however, that although a claimant had participated in the first meeting of creditors and in the examination of witnesses, the creditor was entitled under Rule 41(a)(1) F.R.Civ.P. to withdraw the claim as of right by filing a notice of withdrawal before the trustee filed an objection under §57g of the Act. While this rule incorporates the post-1938 case law referred to in the first paragraph of this note, it rejects the inference drawn in the *Hazen* case that Rule 41(a) F.R.Civ.P. supersedes the pre-1938 case law that vests discretion in the court to deny or restrict withdrawal of a claim by a creditor on the ground of estoppel or election of remedies. While purely formal or technical participation in a case by a creditor who has filed a claim should not deprive the creditor of the right to withdraw the claim, a creditor who has accepted a dividend or who has voted in the election of a trustee or otherwise participated actively in proceedings in a case should be permitted to withdraw only with the approval of the court on terms it deems appropriate after notice to the trustee. 3 Collier 205–06 (1964).

NOTES OF ADVISORY COMMITTEE ON RULES—1991 AMENDMENT

This amendment is stylistic. Notice of the hearing need not be given to committees of equity security holders appointed pursuant to §1102 or committees of retired employees appointed pursuant to §1114 of the Code.

## Rule 3007. Objections to Claims

(a) OBJECTIONS TO CLAIMS. An objection to the allowance of a claim shall be in writing and filed. A copy of the objection with notice of the hearing thereon shall be mailed or otherwise delivered to the claimant, the debtor or debtor in possession, and the trustee at least 30 days prior to the hearing.

(b) DEMAND FOR RELIEF REQUIRING AN ADVERSARY PROCEEDING. A party in interest shall not include a demand for relief of a kind specified in Rule 7001 in an objection to the allowance of a claim, but may include the objection in an adversary proceeding.

(c) LIMITATION ON JOINDER OF CLAIMS OBJECTIONS. Unless otherwise ordered by the court or permitted by subdivision (d), objections to more than one claim shall not be joined in a single objection.

(d) OMNIBUS OBJECTION. Subject to subdivision (e), objections to more than one claim may be joined in an omnibus objection if all the claims were filed by the same entity, or the objections are based solely on the grounds that the claims should be disallowed, in whole or in part, because:

(1) they duplicate other claims;

(2) they have been filed in the wrong case;

(3) they have been amended by subsequently filed proofs of claim;

(4) they were not timely filed;

(5) they have been satisfied or released during the case in accordance with the Code, applicable rules, or a court order;

(6) they were presented in a form that does not comply with applicable rules, and the objection states that the objector is unable to determine the validity of the claim because of the noncompliance;

(7) they are interests, rather than claims; or

(8) they assert priority in an amount that exceeds the maximum amount under §507 of the Code.

(e) REQUIREMENTS FOR OMNIBUS OBJECTION. An omnibus objection shall:

(1) state in a conspicuous place that claimants receiving the objection should locate their names and claims in the objection;

(2) list claimants alphabetically, provide a cross-reference to claim numbers, and, if appropriate, list claimants by category of claims;

(3) state the grounds of the objection to each claim and provide a cross-reference to the pages in the omnibus objection pertinent to the stated grounds;

(4) state in the title the identity of the objector and the grounds for the objections;

(5) be numbered consecutively with other omnibus objections filed by the same objector; and

(6) contain objections to no more than 100 claims.

(f) FINALITY OF OBJECTION. The finality of any order regarding a claim objection included in an omnibus objection shall be determined as though the claim had been subject to an individual objection.

(As amended Apr. 30, 1991, eff. Aug. 1, 1991; Apr. 30, 2007, eff. Dec. 1, 2007.)

NOTES OF ADVISORY COMMITTEE ON RULES—1983

This rule is derived from §47a(8) of the Act and former Bankruptcy Rule 306. It prescribes the manner in which an objection to a claim shall be made and notice of the hearing thereon given to the claimant. The requirement of a writing does not apply to an objection to the allowance of a claim for the purpose of voting for a trustee or creditors' committee in a chapter 7 case. See Rule 2003.

The contested matter initiated by an objection to a claim is governed by rule 9014, unless a counterclaim by the trustee is joined with the objection to the claim. The filing of a counterclaim ordinarily commences an adversary proceeding subject to the rules in Part VII.

While the debtor's other creditors may make objections to the allowance of a claim, the demands of orderly and expeditious administration have led to a recognition that the right to object is generally exercised by the trustee. Pursuant to §502(a) of the Code, however, any party in interest may object to a claim. But under §704 the trustee, if any purpose would be served thereby, has the duty to examine proofs of claim and object to improper claims.

By virtue of the automatic allowance of a claim not objected to, a dividend may be paid on a claim which may thereafter be disallowed on objection made pursuant to this rule. The amount of the dividend paid before the disallowance in such event would be recoverable by the trustee in an adversary proceeding.

NOTES OF ADVISORY COMMITTEE ON RULES—1991 AMENDMENT

The words "with the court" are deleted as unnecessary. See Rules 5005(a) and 9001(3).

COMMITTEE NOTES ON RULES—2007 AMENDMENT

The rule is amended in a number of ways. First, the amendment prohibits a party in interest from including in a claim objection a request for relief that requires an adversary proceeding. A party in interest may, however, include an objection to the allowance of a claim in an adversary proceeding. Unlike a contested matter, an adversary proceeding requires the service of a summons and complaint, which puts the defendant on notice of the potential for an affirmative recovery. Permitting the plaintiff in the adversary proceeding to include an objection to a claim would not unfairly surprise the defendant as might be the case if the action were brought as a contested matter that included an action to obtain relief of a kind specified in Rule 7001.

The rule as amended does not require that a party include an objection to the allowance of a claim in an adversary proceeding. If a claim objection is filed separately from a related adversary proceeding, the court may consolidate the objection with the adversary proceeding under Rule 7042.

The rule also is amended to authorize the filing of a pleading that joins objections to more than one claim. Such filings present a significant opportunity for the efficient administration of large cases, but the rule includes restrictions on the use of these omnibus objections to ensure the protection of the due process rights of the claimants.

Unless the court orders otherwise, objections to more than one claim may be joined in a single pleading only if all of the claims were filed by the same entity, or if the objections are based solely on the grounds set out in subdivision (d) of the rule. Objections of the type listed in subdivision (d) often can be resolved without material factual or legal disputes. Objections to multiple claims permitted under the rule must comply with the procedural requirements set forth in subdivision (e). Among those requirements is the requirement in subdivision (e)(5) that these omnibus objections be consecutively numbered. Since these objections may not join more than 100 objections in any one omnibus objection, there may be a need for several omnibus objections to be filed in a particular case. Consecutive numbering of each omnibus objection and the identification of the objector in the title of the objection is essential to keep track of the objections on the court's docket. For example, the objections could be titled Debtor in Possession's First Omnibus Objection to Claims, Debtor in Possession's Second Omnibus Objection to Claims, Creditors' Committee's First Omnibus Objection to Claims, and so on. Titling the objections in this manner should avoid confusion and aid in tracking the objections on the docket.

Subdivision (f) provides that an order resolving an objection to any particular claim is treated, for purposes of finality, as if the claim had been the subject of an individual objection. A party seeking to appeal any such order is neither required, nor permitted, to await the court's resolution of all other joined objections. The rule permits the joinder of objections for convenience, and that convenience should not impede timely review of a court's decision with respect to each claim. Whether the court's action as to a particular objection is final, and the consequences of that finality, are not addressed by this amendment. Moreover, use of an omnibus objection generally does not preclude the objecting party from raising a subsequent objection to the claim on other grounds. See Restatement (Second) of Judgments §26(1)(d) (1982) (generally applicable rule barring multiple actions based on same transaction or series of transactions is overridden when a statutory scheme permits splitting of claims).

*Changes Made After Publication.* There were several changes made to the rule after its publication. The Advisory Committee declined to follow Mr. Sabino's suggestion, concluding that the rule as proposed includes sufficient flexibility, and that expanding the flexibility might lead to excessive deviation from the appropriate format for omnibus claims objections. The Advisory Committee also declined to follow Mr. Horsley's suggestion because the deadline for filing a proof of claim varies based on the nature of the creditor (governmental units have different deadlines from other creditors) as well as on the chapter under which the case is pending. The Advisory Committee rejected Judge Grant's suggestion that a party proposing an omnibus claims objection be required to demonstrate some special cause to allow the joinder of the objections. The Advisory Committee concluded that the rule includes sufficient protections for claimants such that omnibus objections should be allowed without the need for a special showing by the claims objector that joinder is proper.

The Advisory Committee did accept several of Judge Grant's suggestions, and the rule was amended by deleting the grounds for objection to claims based on the filing of a superceding proof of claim under proposed subdivision (d)(3) and the transfer of claims under proposed subdivision (d)(4). Subdivision (d)(3) now permits objections to claims that have been amended by a subsequently filed proof of claim and the paragraphs within subdivision (d) have been renumbered to reflect the deletion. The Committee Note also no longer includes any reliance on §502(j) for the statement indicating that a subsequent claim objection can be filed to a claim that was previously included in an omnibus claim objection.

## Rule 3008. Reconsideration of Claims

A party in interest may move for reconsideration of an order allowing or disallowing a claim against the estate. The court after a hearing on notice shall enter an appropriate order.

NOTES OF ADVISORY COMMITTEE ON RULES

Section 502(j) of the Code deals only with the reconsideration of allowed claims as did former §57k of the Act and General Order 21(b). It had sometimes been held that a referee had no jurisdiction to reconsider a disallowed claim, or the amount or priority of an allowed claim, at the instance of the claimant. See, *In re Gouse*, 7 F. Supp. 106 (M.D. Pa. 1934); *In re Tomlinson & Dye, Inc.*, 3 F. Supp. 800 (N.D. Okla. 1933). This view disregarded §2a(2) of the Act and the "ancient and elementary power" of a referee as a court to reconsider orders. *In re Pottasch Brow. Co., Inc.*, 79 F.2d 613, 616 (2d Cir. 1935); *Castaner v. Mora*, 234 F.2d 710 (1st Cir. 1956). This rule recognizes, as did former Bankruptcy Rule 307, the power of the court to reconsider an order of disallowance on appropriate motion.

Reconsideration of a claim that has been previously allowed or disallowed after objection is discretionary with the court. The right to seek reconsideration of an allowed claim, like the right to object to its allowance, is generally exercised by the trustee if one has qualified and is performing the duties of that office with reasonable diligence and fidelity. A request for reconsideration of a disallowance would, on the other hand, ordinarily come from the claimant.

A proof of claim executed and filed in accordance with the rules in this Part III is prima facie evidence of the validity and the amount of the claim notwithstanding a motion for reconsideration of an order of allowance. Failure to respond does not constitute an admission, though it may be deemed a consent to a reconsideration. *In re Goble Boat Co.*, 190 Fed. 92 (N.D.N.Y. 1911). The court may decline to reconsider an order of allowance or disallowance without notice to any adverse party and without affording any hearing to the movant. If a motion to reconsider is granted, notice and hearing must be afforded to parties in interest before the previous action in the claim taken in respect to the claim may be vacated or modified. After reconsideration, the court may allow or disallow the claim, increase or decrease the amount of a prior allowance, accord the claim a priority different from that originally assigned it, or enter any other appropriate order.

The rule expands §502(j) which provides for reconsideration of an allowance only before the case is closed. Authorities have disagreed as to whether reconsideration may be had after a case has been reopened. Compare 3 Collier *Bankruptcy* ¶57.23[4] (14th ed. 1964), see generally 3 *id.* ¶502.10 (15th ed. 1979), with 2 Remington, *Bankruptcy* 498 (Henderson ed. 1956). If a case is reopened as provided in §350(b) of the Code, reconsideration of the allowance or disallowance of a claim may be sought and granted in accordance with this rule.

## Rule 3009. Declaration and Payment of Dividends in a Chapter 7 Liquidation Case

In a chapter 7 case, dividends to creditors shall be paid as promptly as practicable. Dividend checks shall be made payable to and mailed to each creditor whose claim has been allowed, unless a power of attorney authorizing another entity to receive dividends has been executed and filed in accordance with Rule 9010. In that event, dividend checks shall be made payable to the creditor and to the other entity and shall be mailed to the other entity.

(As amended Mar. 30, 1987, eff. Aug. 1, 1987; Apr. 22, 1993, eff. Aug. 1, 1993.)

### NOTES OF ADVISORY COMMITTEE ON RULES—1983

This rule is derived from former Rules 308 and 11-35(a). The preparation of records showing dividends declared and to whom payable is subject to prescription by the Director of the Administrative Office pursuant to Rule 5003(e). The rule governs distributions to creditors having priority as well as to general unsecured creditors. Notwithstanding the detailed statutory provisions regulating the declaration of dividends, a necessarily wide discretion over this matter has been recognized to reside in the court. See 3A Collier, *Bankruptcy* ¶65.03 (14th ed. 1975): 1 *Proceedings of Seminar for Newly Appointed Referees in Bankruptcy* 173 (1964). Although the rule leaves to the discretion of the court the amount and the times of dividend payments, it recognizes the creditors' right to as prompt payment as practicable.

The second and third sentences of the rule make explicit the method of payment of dividends and afford protection of the interests of the creditor and the holder of a power of attorney authorized to receive payment.

The rule does not permit variance at local option. This represents a marked change from former Bankruptcy Rule 308.

### NOTES OF ADVISORY COMMITTEE ON RULES—1993 AMENDMENT

This rule is amended to delete the requirement that the court approve the amounts and times of distributions in chapter 7 cases. This change recognizes the role of the United States trustee in supervising trustees. Other amendments are stylistic and make no substantive change.

## Rule 3010. Small Dividends and Payments in Chapter 7 Liquidation, Chapter 12 Family Farmer's Debt Adjustment, and Chapter 13 Individual's Debt Adjustment Cases

(a) CHAPTER 7 CASES. In a chapter 7 case no dividend in an amount less than $5 shall be distributed by the trustee to any creditor unless authorized by local rule or order of the court. Any dividend not distributed to a creditor shall be treated in the same manner as unclaimed funds as provided in §347 of the Code.

(b) CHAPTER 12 AND CHAPTER 13 CASES. In a chapter 12 or chapter 13 case no payment in an amount less than $15 shall be distributed by the trustee to any creditor unless authorized by local rule or order of the court. Funds not distributed because of this subdivision shall accumulate and shall be paid whenever the accumulation aggregates $15. Any funds remaining shall be distributed with the final payment.

(As amended Mar. 30, 1987, eff. Aug. 1, 1987; Apr. 30, 1991, eff. Aug. 1, 1991.)

### NOTES OF ADVISORY COMMITTEE ON RULES—1983

This rule permits a court to eliminate the disproportionate expense and inconvenience incurred by the issuance of a dividend check of less than $5 (or $15 in a chapter 13 case). Creditors are more irritated than pleased to receive such small dividends, but the money is held subject to their specific request as are unclaimed dividends under §347(a) of the Code. When the trustee deposits undistributed dividends pursuant to a direction in accordance with this rule the trustee should file with the clerk a list of the names and addresses, so far as known, of the persons entitled to the money so deposited and the respective amounts payable to them pursuant to Rule 3011. In a chapter 13 case, the small dividend will accumulate and will be payable at the latest, with the final dividend. Local rule or order may change the practice permitted in this rule and, in that connection, the order may be incorporated in the order confirming a chapter 13 plan.

### NOTES OF ADVISORY COMMITTEE ON RULES—1991 AMENDMENT

*Subdivision (b)* is amended to include chapter 12 cases.

## Rule 3011. Unclaimed Funds in Chapter 7 Liquidation, Chapter 12 Family Farmer's Debt Adjustment, and Chapter 13 Individual's Debt Adjustment Cases

The trustee shall file a list of all known names and addresses of the entities and the amounts which they are entitled to be paid from remaining property of the estate that is paid into court pursuant to §347(a) of the Code.

(As amended Mar. 30, 1987, eff. Aug. 1, 1987; Apr. 30, 1991, eff. Aug. 1, 1991.)

### NOTES OF ADVISORY COMMITTEE ON RULES—1983

This rule is derived from former Bankruptcy Rule 310. The operative provisions of that rule, however, are contained in §347(a) of the Code, requiring the trustee to stop payment of checks remaining unpaid 90 days after distribution. The rule adds the requirement of filing a list of the names and addresses of the persons entitled to these dividends. This rule applies in a chapter 7 or 13 case but not in a chapter 9 or 11 case. The latter cases are governed by §347(b) of the Code which provides for unclaimed distributions to be returned to the debtor or other entity acquiring the assets of the debtor.

NOTES OF ADVISORY COMMITTEE ON RULES—1991 AMENDMENT

The title of this rule is amended to include chapter 12 cases. The words "with the clerk" are deleted as unnecessary. See Rules 5005(a) and 9001(3).

## Rule 3012. Valuation of Security

The court may determine the value of a claim secured by a lien on property in which the estate has an interest on motion of any party in interest and after a hearing on notice to the holder of the secured claim and any other entity as the court may direct.

(As amended Mar. 30, 1987, eff. Aug. 1, 1987.)

NOTES OF ADVISORY COMMITTEE ON RULES—1983

Pursuant to § 506(a) of the Code, secured claims are to be valued and allowed as secured to the extent of the value of the collateral and unsecured, to the extent it is enforceable, for the excess over such value. The valuation of secured claims may become important in different contexts *e.g.*, to determine the issue of adequate protection under § 361, impairment under § 1124, or treatment of the claim in a plan pursuant to § 1129(b) of the Code. This rule permits the issue to be raised on motion by a party in interest. The secured creditor is entitled to notice of the hearing on the motion and the court may direct that others in the case also receive such notice.

An adversary proceeding is commenced when the validity, priority, or extent of a lien is at issue as prescribed by Rule 7001. That proceeding is relevant to the basis of the lien itself while valuation under Rule 3012 would be for the purposes indicated above.

## Rule 3013. Classification of Claims and Interests

For the purposes of the plan and its acceptance, the court may, on motion after hearing on notice as the court may direct, determine classes of creditors and equity security holders pursuant to §§ 1122, 1222(b)(1), and 1322(b)(1) of the Code.

(As amended Apr. 30, 1991, eff. Aug. 1, 1991.)

NOTES OF ADVISORY COMMITTEE ON RULES—1983

Sections 1122 and 1322(b)(1) set the standards for classifying claims and interests but provide that such classification is accomplished in the plan. This rule does not change the standards; rather it recognizes that it may be desirable or necessary to establish proper classification before a plan can be formulated. It provides for a court hearing on such notice as the court may direct.

NOTES OF ADVISORY COMMITTEE ON RULES—1991 AMENDMENT

This rule is amended to include chapter 12 cases.

## Rule 3014. Election Under § 1111(b) by Secured Creditor in Chapter 9 Municipality or Chapter 11 Reorganization Case

An election of application of § 1111(b)(2) of the Code by a class of secured creditors in a chapter 9 or 11 case may be made at any time prior to the conclusion of the hearing on the disclosure statement or within such later time as the court may fix. If the disclosure statement is conditionally approved pursuant to Rule 3017.1, and a final hearing on the disclosure statement is not held, the election of application of § 1111(b)(2) may be made not later than the date fixed pursuant to Rule 3017.1(a)(2) or another date the court may fix. The election shall be in writing and signed unless made at the hearing on the disclosure statement. The election, if made by the majorities required by § 1111(b)(1)(A)(i), shall be binding on all members of the class with respect to the plan.

(As amended Apr. 11, 1997, eff. Dec. 1, 1997.)

NOTES OF ADVISORY COMMITTEE ON RULES—1983

Pursuant to § 1111(b)(1) of the Code, a nonrecourse secured loan is converted, automatically, into a recourse loan thereby entitling the creditor to an unsecured deficiency claim if the value of the collateral is less than the debt. The class, however, may retain the loan as a nonrecourse loan by electing application of § 1111(b)(2) by the majorities stated in § 1111(b)(1)(A)(i). That section does not specify any time periods for making the election.

Rule 3014 provides that if no agreement is negotiated, the election of § 1111(b)(2) of the Code may be made at any time prior to conclusion of the hearing on the disclosure statement. Once the hearing has been concluded, it would be too late for a secured creditor class to demand different treatment unless the court has fixed a later time. This would be the case if, for example, a public class of secured creditors should have an approved disclosure statement prior to electing under § 1111(b).

Generally it is important that the proponent of a plan ascertain the position of the secured creditor class before a plan is proposed. The secured creditor class must know the prospects of its treatment under the plan before it can intelligently determine its rights under § 1111(b). The rule recognizes that there may be negotiations between the proponent of the plan and the secured creditor leading to a representation of desired treatment under § 1111(b). If that treatment is approved by the requisite majorities of the class and culminates in a written, signed statement filed with the court, that statement becomes binding and the class may not thereafter demand different treatment under § 1111(b) with respect to that plan. The proponent of the plan is thus enabled to seek approval of the disclosure statement and transmit the plan for voting in anticipation of confirmation. Only if that plan is not confirmed may the class of secured creditors thereafter change its prior election.

While this rule and the Code refer to a class of secured creditors it should be noted that ordinarily each secured creditor is in a separate and distinct class. In that event, the secured creditor has the sole power to determine application of § 1111(b) with respect to that claim.

NOTES OF ADVISORY COMMITTEE ON RULES AMENDMENT

This amendment provides a deadline for electing application of § 1111(b)(2) in a small business case in which a conditionally approved disclosure statement is finally approved without a hearing.

*GAP Report on Rule 3014.* No changes to the published draft.

## Rule 3015. Filing, Objection to Confirmation, and Modification of a Plan in a Chapter 12 Family Farmer's Debt Adjustment or a Chapter 13 Individual's Debt Adjustment Case

(a) CHAPTER 12 PLAN. The debtor may file a chapter 12 plan with the petition. If a plan is not filed with the petition, it shall be filed within the time prescribed by § 1221 of the Code.

(b) CHAPTER 13 PLAN. The debtor may file a chapter 13 plan with the petition. If a plan is not filed with the petition, it shall be filed within 14 days thereafter, and such time may not be further extended except for cause shown and on notice as the court may direct. If a case is converted to chapter 13, a plan shall be filed within 14 days thereafter, and such time may not be further extended except for cause shown and on notice as the court may direct.

(c) DATING. Every proposed plan and any modification thereof shall be dated.

(d) NOTICE AND COPIES. The plan or a summary of the plan shall be included with each notice of the hearing on confirmation mailed pursuant to Rule 2002. If required by the court, the debtor shall furnish a sufficient number of copies to enable the clerk to include a copy of the plan with the notice of the hearing.

(e) TRANSMISSION TO UNITED STATES TRUSTEE. The clerk shall forthwith transmit to the United States trustee a copy of the plan and any modification thereof filed pursuant to subdivision (a) or (b) of this rule.

(f) OBJECTION TO CONFIRMATION; DETERMINATION OF GOOD FAITH IN THE ABSENCE OF AN OBJECTION. An objection to confirmation of a plan shall be filed and served on the debtor, the trustee, and any other entity designated by the court, and shall be transmitted to the United States trustee, before confirmation of the plan. An objection to confirmation is governed by Rule 9014. If no objection is timely filed, the court may determine that the plan has been proposed in good faith and not by any means forbidden by law without receiving evidence on such issues.

(g) MODIFICATION OF PLAN AFTER CONFIRMATION. A request to modify a plan pursuant to §1229 or §1329 of the Code shall identify the proponent and shall be filed together with the proposed modification. The clerk, or some other person as the court may direct, shall give the debtor, the trustee, and all creditors not less than 21 days' notice by mail of the time fixed for filing objections and, if an objection is filed, the hearing to consider the proposed modification, unless the court orders otherwise with respect to creditors who are not affected by the proposed modification. A copy of the notice shall be transmitted to the United States trustee. A copy of the proposed modification, or a summary thereof, shall be included with the notice. If required by the court, the proponent shall furnish a sufficient number of copies of the proposed modification, or a summary thereof, to enable the clerk to include a copy with each notice. Any objection to the proposed modification shall be filed and served on the debtor, the trustee, and any other entity designated by the court, and shall be transmitted to the United States trustee. An objection to a proposed modification is governed by Rule 9014.

(As amended Apr. 30, 1991, eff. Aug. 1, 1991; Apr. 22, 1993, eff. Aug. 1, 1993; Mar. 26, 2009, eff. Dec. 1, 2009.)

NOTES OF ADVISORY COMMITTEE ON RULES—1983

Section 1321 provides only that the "debtor shall file a plan." No time periods are specified, nor is any other detail provided. The rule requires a chapter 13 plan to be filed either with the petition or within 15 days thereafter. The court may, for cause, extend the time. The rule permits a summary of the plan to be transmitted with the notice of the hearing on confirmation. The court may, however, require the plan itself to be transmitted and the debtor to supply enough copies for this purpose. In the former rules under Chapter XIII the plan would accompany the notice of the first meeting of creditors. It is more important for the plan or a summary of its terms to be sent with the notice of the confirmation hearing. At that hearing objections to the plan will be heard by the court.

NOTES OF ADVISORY COMMITTEE ON RULES—1991 AMENDMENT

This rule is amended to include chapter 12 plans. Section 1221 of the Code requires the debtor to file a chapter 12 plan not later than 90 days after the order for relief, except that the court may extend the period if an extension is "substantially justified."

*Subdivision (e)* enables the United States trustee to monitor chapter 12 and chapter 13 plans pursuant to 28 U.S.C. §586(a)(3)(C).

NOTES OF ADVISORY COMMITTEE ON RULES—1993 AMENDMENT

*Subdivision (b)* is amended to provide a time limit for filing a plan after a case has been converted to chapter 13. The substitution of "may" for "shall" is stylistic and makes no substantive change.

*Subdivision (d)* is amended to clarify that the plan or a summary of the plan must be included with each notice of the confirmation hearing in a chapter 12 case pursuant to Rule 2002(a).

*Subdivision (f)* is added to expand the scope of the rule to govern objections to confirmation in chapter 12 and chapter 13 cases. The subdivision also is amended to include a provision that permits the court, in the absence of an objection, to determine that the plan has been proposed in good faith and not by any means forbidden by law without the need to receive evidence on these issues. These matters are now governed by Rule 3020.

*Subdivision (g)* is added to provide a procedure for post-confirmation modification of chapter 12 and chapter 13 plans. These procedures are designed to be similar to the procedures for confirmation of plans. However, if no objection is filed with respect to a proposed modification of a plan after confirmation, the court is not required to hold a hearing. See §1229(b)(2) and §1329(b)(2) which provide that the plan as modified becomes the plan unless, after notice and a hearing, such modification is disapproved. See §102(1). The notice of the time fixed for filing objections to the proposed modification should set a date for a hearing to be held in the event that an objection is filed.

Amendments to the title of this rule are stylistic and make no substantive change.

COMMITTEE NOTES ON RULES—2009 AMENDMENT

The rule is amended to implement changes in connection with the amendment to Rule 9006(a) and the manner by which time is computed under the rules. The deadlines in the rule are amended to substitute a deadline that is a multiple of seven days. Throughout the rules, deadlines are amended in the following manner:

- 5-day periods become 7-day periods
- 10-day periods become 14-day periods
- 15-day periods become 14-day periods
- 20-day periods become 21-day periods
- 25-day periods become 28-day periods

## Rule 3016. Filing of Plan and Disclosure Statement in a Chapter 9 Municipality or Chapter 11 Reorganization Case

(a) IDENTIFICATION OF PLAN. Every proposed plan and any modification thereof shall be dated and, in a chapter 11 case, identified with the name of the entity or entities submitting or filing it.

(b) DISCLOSURE STATEMENT. In a chapter 9 or 11 case, a disclosure statement under §1125 of the Code or evidence showing compliance with §1126(b) shall be filed with the plan or within a time fixed by the court, unless the plan is intended to provide adequate information under §1125(f)(1). If the plan is intended to provide adequate information under §1125(f)(1), it shall be so designated and Rule 3017.1 shall apply as if the plan is a disclosure statement.

(c) INJUNCTION UNDER A PLAN. If a plan provides for an injunction against conduct not otherwise enjoined under the Code, the plan and disclosure statement shall describe in specific and conspicuous language (bold, italic, or underlined text) all acts to be enjoined and identify the entities that would be subject to the injunction.

(d) STANDARD FORM SMALL BUSINESS DISCLOSURE STATEMENT AND PLAN. In a small business case, the court may approve a disclosure statement and may confirm a plan that conform substantially to the appropriate Official Forms or other standard forms approved by the court.

(As amended Mar. 30, 1987, eff. Aug. 1, 1987; Apr. 30, 1991, eff. Aug. 1, 1991; Apr. 23, 1996, eff. Dec. 1, 1996; Apr. 23, 2001, eff. Dec. 1, 2001; Apr. 23, 2008, eff. Dec. 1, 2008.)

NOTES OF ADVISORY COMMITTEE ON RULES—1983

This rule implements the Code provisions concerning the filing of plans in chapters 9 and 11.

*Chapter 9 Cases.* Section 941 provides that the debtor may file a plan with the petition or thereafter but within a time fixed by the court. A rule, therefore, is unnecessary to specify the time for filing chapter 9 plans.

*Chapter 11 Nonrailroad Cases.* Section 1121 contains detailed provisions with respect to who may file a chapter 11 plan and, in part, the time period. Section 1121(a) permits a debtor to file a plan with the petition or at any time during the case. Section 1121(b) and (c) grants exclusive periods of 120 days and 180 days for the debtor to file and obtain acceptance of a plan. Failure to take advantage of these periods or the appointment of a trustee would permit other parties in interest to file a plan. These statutory provisions are not repeated in the rules.

*Chapter 11 Railroad Cases.* Pursuant to subchapter IV of chapter 11, §1121 of the Code is applicable in railroad cases; see §§1161, 103(g). A trustee, however, is to be appointed in every case; thus, pursuant to §1121(c), any party in interest may file a plan. See discussion of subdivision (a) of this rule, *infra.*

*Subdivision (a).* Section 1121(c), while permitting parties in interest a limited right to file plans, does not provide any time limitation. This subdivision sets as the deadline, the conclusion of the hearing on the disclosure statement. The court may, however, grant additional time. It is derived from former Chapter X Rule 10–301(c)(2) which used, as the cut-off time, the conclusion of the hearing on approval of a plan. As indicated, *supra,* §1121(a) permits a debtor to file a plan at any time during the chapter 11 case. Under §1121(c), parties other than a debtor may file a plan only after a trustee is appointed or the debtor's exclusive time expires.

*Subdivision (b)* requires plans to be properly identified.

*Subdivision (c).* This provision is new. In chapter 9 and 11 cases (including railroad reorganization cases) postpetition solicitation of votes on a plan requires transmittal of a disclosure statement, the contents of which have been approved by the court. See §1125 of the Code. A prepetition solicitation must either have been in conformity with applicable nonbankruptcy law or, if none, the disclosure must have been of adequate information as set forth in §1125 of the Code. See §1126(b). Subdivision (c) of this rule provides the time for filing the disclosure statement or evidence of compliance with §1126(b) which ordinarily will be with the plan but the court may allow a later time or the court may, pursuant to the last sentence, fix a time certain. Rule 3017 deals with the hearing on the disclosure statement. The disclosure statement, pursuant to §1125 is to contain adequate information. "Adequate information" is defined in §1125(a) as information that would permit a reasonable creditor or equity security holder to make an informed judgment on the plan.

NOTES OF ADVISORY COMMITTEE ON RULES—1991 AMENDMENT

*Subdivision (a)* is amended to enlarge the time for filing competing plans. A party in interest may not file a plan without leave of court only if an order approving a disclosure statement relating to another plan has been entered and a decision on confirmation of the plan has not been entered. This subdivision does not fix a deadline beyond which a debtor may not file a plan.

NOTES OF ADVISORY COMMITTEE ON RULES—1996 AMENDMENT

Section 1121(c) gives a party in interest the right to file a chapter 11 plan after expiration of the period when only the debtor may file a plan. Under §1121(d), the exclusive period in which only the debtor may file a plan may be extended, but only if a party in interest so requests and the court, after notice and a hearing, finds cause for an extension. Subdivision (a) is abrogated because it could have the effect of extending the debtor's exclusive period for filing a plan without satisfying the requirements of §1121(d). The abrogation of subdivision (a) does not affect the court's discretion with respect to the scheduling of hearings on the approval of disclosure statements when more than one plan has been filed.

The amendment to subdivision (c), redesignated as subdivision (b), is stylistic.

*GAP Report on Rule 3016.* No changes since publication, except for a stylistic change.

COMMITTEE NOTES ON RULES—2001 AMENDMENT

*Subdivision (c)* is added to assure that entities whose conduct would be enjoined under a plan, rather than by operation of the Code, are given adequate notice of the proposed injunction. The validity and effect of any injunction are substantive law matters that are beyond the scope of these rules.

Specific and conspicuous language is not necessary if the injunction contained in the plan is substantially the same as an injunction provided under the Code. For example, if a plan contains an injunction against acts to collect a discharged debt from the debtor, Rule 3016(c) would not apply because that conduct would be enjoined nonetheless under §524(a)(2). But if a plan provides that creditors will be permanently enjoined from asserting claims against persons who are not debtors in the case, the plan and disclosure statement must highlight the injunctive language and comply with the requirements of Rule 3016(c). *See* §524(e).

The requirement in this rule that the plan and disclosure statement identify the entities that would be subject to the injunction requires reasonable identification under the circumstances. If the entities that would be subject to the injunction cannot be identified by name, the plan and disclosure statement may describe them by class or category. For example, it may be sufficient to identify the subjects of the injunction as "all creditors of the debtor."

*Changes Made After Publication and Comments* word "highlighted" in the parenthesis was replaced with "underlined" because highlighted documents are difficult to scan electronically for inclusion in the clerks' files. The Committee Note was revised to put in a more prominent position the statement that the validity and effect of any injunction provided for in a plan are substantive matters beyond the scope of the rules. Other stylistic changes were made to the Committee Note.

COMMITTEE NOTES ON RULES—2008 AMENDMENT

Subdivision (b) is amended to recognize that, in 2005, §1125(f)(1) was added to the Code to provide that the plan proponent in a small business case need not file a disclosure statement if the plan itself includes adequate information and the court finds that a separate disclosure statement is unnecessary. If the plan is intended to provide adequate information in a small business case, it may be conditionally approved as a disclosure statement under Rule 3017.1 and is subject to all other rules applicable to disclosure statements in small business cases.

Subdivision (d) is added to the rule to implement §433 of the Bankruptcy Abuse Prevention and Consumer Protection Act of 2005 which requires the promulgation of Official Forms for plans and disclosure statements in small business cases. Section 1125(f)(2) of the Code provides that the court may approve a disclosure statement submitted on the appropriate Official Form or on a standard form approved by the court. The rule takes no position on whether a court may require a local standard form disclosure statement or plan of reorganization in lieu of the Official Forms.

Other amendments are stylistic.

*Changes Made After Publication.* No changes were made after publication.

## Rule 3017. Court Consideration of Disclosure Statement in a Chapter 9 Municipality or Chapter 11 Reorganization Case

(a) HEARING ON DISCLOSURE STATEMENT AND OBJECTIONS. Except as provided in Rule 3017.1, after a disclosure statement is filed in accordance with Rule 3016(b), the court shall hold a hearing on at least 28 days' notice to the debtor, creditors, equity security holders and other parties in interest as provided in Rule 2002 to consider the disclosure statement and any objections or modifications thereto. The plan and the disclosure statement shall be mailed with the notice of the hearing only to the debtor, any trustee or committee appointed under the Code, the Securities and Exchange Commission and any party in interest who requests in writing a copy of the statement or plan. Objections to the disclosure statement shall be filed and served on the debtor, the trustee, any committee appointed under the Code, and any other entity designated by the court, at any time before the disclosure statement is approved or by an earlier date as the court may fix. In a chapter 11 reorganization case, every notice, plan, disclosure statement, and objection required to be served or mailed pursuant to this subdivision shall be transmitted to the United States trustee within the time provided in this subdivision.

(b) DETERMINATION ON DISCLOSURE STATEMENT. Following the hearing the court shall determine whether the disclosure statement should be approved.

(c) DATES FIXED FOR VOTING ON PLAN AND CONFIRMATION. On or before approval of the disclosure statement, the court shall fix a time within which the holders of claims and interests may accept or reject the plan and may fix a date for the hearing on confirmation.

(d) TRANSMISSION AND NOTICE TO UNITED STATES TRUSTEE, CREDITORS, AND EQUITY SECURITY HOLDERS. Upon approval of a disclosure statement,—[1] except to the extent that the court orders otherwise with respect to one or more unimpaired classes of creditors or equity security holders—the debtor in possession, trustee, proponent of the plan, or clerk as the court orders shall mail to all creditors and equity security holders, and in a chapter 11 reorganization case shall transmit to the United States trustee,

(1) the plan or a court-approved summary of the plan;

(2) the disclosure statement approved by the court;

(3) notice of the time within which acceptances and rejections of the plan may be filed; and

(4) any other information as the court may direct, including any court opinion approving the disclosure statement or a court-approved summary of the opinion.

In addition, notice of the time fixed for filing objections and the hearing on confirmation shall be mailed to all creditors and equity security holders in accordance with Rule 2002(b), and a form of ballot conforming to the appropriate Official Form shall be mailed to creditors and equity security holders entitled to vote on the plan. If the court opinion is not transmitted or only a summary of the plan is transmitted, the court opinion or the plan shall be provided on request of a party in interest at the plan proponent's expense. If the court orders that the disclosure statement and the plan or a summary of the plan shall not be mailed to any unimpaired class, notice that the class is designated in the plan as unimpaired and notice of the name and address of the person from whom the plan or summary of the plan and disclosure statement may be obtained upon request and at the plan proponent's expense, shall be mailed to members of the unimpaired class together with the notice of the time fixed for filing objections to and the hearing on confirmation. For the purposes of this subdivision, creditors and equity security holders shall include holders of stock, bonds, debentures, notes, and other securities of record on the date the order approving the disclosure statement is entered or another date fixed by the court, for cause, after notice and a hearing.

(e) TRANSMISSION TO BENEFICIAL HOLDERS OF SECURITIES. At the hearing held pursuant to subdivision (a) of this rule, the court shall consider the procedures for transmitting the documents and information required by subdivision (d) of this rule to beneficial holders of stock, bonds, debentures, notes, and other securities, determine the adequacy of the procedures, and enter any orders the court deems appropriate.

(f) NOTICE AND TRANSMISSION OF DOCUMENTS TO ENTITIES SUBJECT TO AN INJUNCTION UNDER A PLAN. If a plan provides for an injunction against conduct not otherwise enjoined under the Code and an entity that would be subject to the injunction is not a creditor or equity security holder, at the hearing held under Rule 3017(a), the court shall consider procedures for providing the entity with:

(1) at least 28 days' notice of the time fixed for filing objections and the hearing on confirmation of the plan containing the information described in Rule 2002(c)(3); and

(2) to the extent feasible, a copy of the plan and disclosure statement.

[1] So in original. The comma probably should not appear.

(As amended Mar. 30, 1987, eff. Aug. 1, 1987; Apr. 30, 1991, eff. Aug. 1, 1991; Apr. 11, 1997, eff. Dec. 1, 1997; Apr. 23, 2001, eff. Dec. 1, 2001; Mar. 26, 2009, eff. Dec. 1, 2009.)

NOTES OF ADVISORY COMMITTEE ON RULES—1983

This rule is adapted from former Rule 10–303 which dealt with the approval of a Chapter X plan by the court. There is no requirement for plan approval in a chapter 9 or 11 case under the Code but there is the requirement that a disclosure statement containing adequate financial information be approved by the court after notice and a hearing before votes on a plan are solicited. Section 1125(b) of the Code is made applicable in chapter 9 cases by §901(a). It is also applicable in railroad reorganization cases under subchapter IV of chapter 11; see §1161 of the Code.

*Subdivision (a)* of this rule provides for the hearing on the disclosure statement. Thus, a hearing would be required in all cases; whether it may be ex parte would depend on the circumstances of the case, but a mere absence of objections would not eliminate the need for a hearing; see §102(1) of the Code.

No provision similar to former Rule 10–303(f) is included. That subdivision together with former Rule 10–304 prohibited solicitation of votes until after entry of an order approving the plan. Section 1125(b) of the Code explicitly provides that votes on a plan may not be solicited until a disclosure statement approved by the court is transmitted. Pursuant to the change in rulemaking power, a comparable provision in this rule is unnecessary. 28 U.S.C. §2075.

Copies of the disclosure statement and plan need not be mailed with the notice of the hearing or otherwise transmitted prior to the hearing except with respect to the parties explicitly set forth in the subdivision.

It should be noted that, by construction, the singular includes the plural. Therefore, the phrase "plan or plans" or "disclosure statement or statements" has not been used although the possibility of multiple plans and statements is recognized.

*Subdivision (d)* permits the court to require a party other than the clerk of the bankruptcy court to bear the responsibility for transmitting the notices and documents specified in the rule when votes on the plan are solicited. Ordinarily the person responsible for such mailing will be the proponent of the plan. In rare cases the clerk may be directed to mail these documents, particularly when the trustee would have the responsibility but there is insufficient money in the estate to enable the trustee to perform this task.

NOTES OF ADVISORY COMMITTEE ON RULES—1987 AMENDMENT

*Subdivision (d).* Section 1125(c) of the Code requires that the entire approved disclosure statement be provided in connection with voting on a plan. The court is authorized by §1125(c) to approve different disclosure statements for different classes. Although the rule does not permit the mailing of a summary of the disclosure statement in place of the approved disclosure statement, the court may approve a summary of the disclosure statement to be mailed with the complete disclosure statement to those voting on the plan.

NOTES OF ADVISORY COMMITTEE ON RULES—1991 AMENDMENT

This rule is amended to enable the United States trustee to monitor and comment with regard to chapter 11 disclosure statements and plans. The United States trustee does not perform these functions in a chapter 9 municipal debt adjustment case. See 28 U.S.C. §586(a)(3)(B).

*Subdivision (d)* is amended to give the court the discretion to direct that one or more unimpaired classes shall not receive disclosure statements, plans, or summaries of plans. Members of unimpaired classes are not entitled to vote on the plan. Although disclosure statements enable members of unimpaired classes to make informed judgments as to whether to object to confirmation because of lack of feasibility or other grounds, in an unusual case the court may direct that disclosure statements shall not be sent to such classes if to do so would not be feasible considering the size of the unimpaired classes and the expense of printing and mailing. In any event, all creditors are entitled to notice of the time fixed for filing objections and notice of the hearing to consider confirmation of the plan pursuant to Rule 2002(b) and the requirement of such notice may not be excused with respect to unimpaired classes. The amendment to subdivision (d) also ensures that the members of unimpaired classes who do not receive such documents will have sufficient information so that they may request these documents in advance of the hearing on confirmation. The amendment to subdivision (d) is not intended to give the court the discretion to dispense with the mailing of the plan and disclosure statement to governmental units holding claims entitled to priority under §507(a)(7) because they may not be classified. See §1123(a)(1).

The words "with the court" in subdivision (a) are deleted as unnecessary. See Rules 5005(a) and 9001(3). Reference to the Official Form number in subdivision (d) is deleted in anticipation of future revision and renumbering of the Official Forms.

*Subdivision (e)* is designed to ensure that appropriate measures are taken for the plan, disclosure statement, ballot and other materials which are required to be transmitted to creditors and equity security holders under this rule to reach the beneficial holders of securities held in nominee name. Such measures may include orders directing the trustee or debtor in possession to reimburse the nominees out of the funds of the estate for the expenses incurred by them in distributing materials to beneficial holders. In most cases, the plan proponent will not know the identities of the beneficial holders and therefore it will be necessary to rely on the nominal holders of the securities to distribute the plan materials to the beneficial owners.

NOTES OF ADVISORY COMMITTEE ON RULES—1997 AMENDMENT

*Subdivision (a)* is amended to provide that it does not apply to the extent provided in new Rule 3017.1, which applies in small business cases.

*Subdivision (d)* is amended to provide flexibility in fixing the record date for the purpose of determining the holders of securities who are entitled to receive documents pursuant to this subdivision. For example, if there may be a delay between the oral announcement of the judge's order approving the disclosure statement and entry of the order on the court docket, the court may fix the date on which the judge orally approves the disclosure statement as the record date so that the parties may expedite preparation of the lists necessary to facilitate the distribution of the plan, disclosure statement, ballots, and other related documents.

The court may set a record date pursuant to subdivision (d) only after notice and a hearing as provided in §102(1) of the Code. Notice of a request for an order fixing the record date may be included in the notice of the hearing to consider approval of the disclosure statement mailed pursuant to Rule 2002(b).

If the court fixes a record date pursuant to subdivision (d) with respect to the holders of securities, and the holders are impaired by the plan, the judge also should order that the same record date applies for the purpose of determining eligibility for voting pursuant to Rule 3018(a).

Other amendments to this rule are stylistic.

*GAP Report on Rule 3017.* No changes to the published draft.

COMMITTEE NOTES ON RULES—2001 AMENDMENT

*Subdivision (f)* is added to assure that entities whose conduct would be enjoined under a plan, rather than by operation of the Code, and who will not receive the documents listed in subdivision (d) because they are neither creditors nor equity security holders, are provided with adequate notice of the proposed injunction. It does not address any substantive law issues relating to the validity or effect of any injunction provided under a plan, or any due process or other constitutional issues relating to notice. These issues are beyond the scope of these rules and are left for judicial determination.

This rule recognizes the need for adequate notice to subjects of an injunction, but that reasonable flexibility under the circumstances may be required. If a known and identifiable entity would be subject to the injunction, and the notice, plan, and disclosure statement could be mailed to that entity, the court should require that they be mailed at the same time that the plan, disclosure statement and related documents are mailed to creditors under Rule 3017(d). If mailing notices and other documents is not feasible because the entities subject to the injunction are described in the plan and disclosure statement by class or category and they cannot be identified individually by name and address, the court may require that notice under Rule 3017(f)(1) be published.

*Changes Made After Publication and Comments.* No changes were made in the text of the proposed amendments since publication. The Committee Note was revised to put in a more prominent position the statement that the rule does not address related substantive law issues which are beyond the scope of the rules.

COMMITTEE NOTES ON RULES—2009 AMENDMENT

The rule is amended to implement changes in connection with the amendment to Rule 9006(a) and the manner by which time is computed under the rules. The deadlines in the rule are amended to substitute a deadline that is a multiple of seven days. Throughout the rules, deadlines are amended in the following manner:

- 5-day periods become 7-day periods
- 10-day periods become 14-day periods
- 15-day periods become 14-day periods
- 20-day periods become 21-day periods
- 25-day periods become 28-day periods

## Rule 3017.1. Court Consideration of Disclosure Statement in a Small Business Case

(a) CONDITIONAL APPROVAL OF DISCLOSURE STATEMENT. In a small business case, the court may, on application of the plan proponent or on its own initiative, conditionally approve a disclosure statement filed in accordance with Rule 3016. On or before conditional approval of the disclosure statement, the court shall:

(1) fix a time within which the holders of claims and interests may accept or reject the plan;

(2) fix a time for filing objections to the disclosure statement;

(3) fix a date for the hearing on final approval of the disclosure statement to be held if a timely objection is filed; and

(4) fix a date for the hearing on confirmation.

(b) APPLICATION OF RULE 3017. Rule 3017(a), (b), (c), and (e) do not apply to a conditionally approved disclosure statement. Rule 3017(d) applies to a conditionally approved disclosure statement, except that conditional approval is considered approval of the disclosure statement for the purpose of applying Rule 3017(d).

(c) FINAL APPROVAL.

(1) *Notice.* Notice of the time fixed for filing objections and the hearing to consider final approval of the disclosure statement shall be given in accordance with Rule 2002 and may be combined with notice of the hearing on confirmation of the plan.

(2) *Objections.* Objections to the disclosure statement shall be filed, transmitted to the United States trustee, and served on the debtor, the trustee, any committee appointed under the Code and any other entity designated by the court at any time before final approval of the disclosure statement or by an earlier date as the court may fix.

(3) *Hearing.* If a timely objection to the disclosure statement is filed, the court shall hold a hearing to consider final approval before or combined with the hearing on confirmation of the plan.

(Added Apr. 11, 1997, eff. Dec. 1, 1997; amended Apr. 23, 2008, eff. Dec. 1, 2008.)

NOTES OF ADVISORY COMMITTEE ON RULES—1997

This rule is added to implement §1125(f) that was added to the Code by the Bankruptcy Reform Act of 1994.

The procedures for electing to be considered a small business are set forth in Rule 1020. If the debtor is a small business and has elected to be considered a small business, §1125(f) permits the court to conditionally approve a disclosure statement subject to final approval after notice and a hearing. If a disclosure statement is conditionally approved, and no timely objection to the disclosure statement is filed, it is not necessary for the court to hold a hearing on final approval.

*GAP Report on Rule 3017.1.* No change to the published draft.

COMMITTEE NOTES ON RULES—2008 AMENDMENT

Section 101 of the Code, as amended in 2005, defines a "small business case" and "small business debtor," and eliminates any need to elect that status. Therefore, the reference in the rule to an election is deleted.

As provided in the amendment to Rule 3016(b), a plan intended to provide adequate information in a small business case under §1125(f)(1) may be conditionally approved and is otherwise treated as a disclosure statement under this rule.

*Changes Made After Publication.* No changes were made after publication.

## Rule 3018. Acceptance or Rejection of Plan in a Chapter 9 Municipality or a Chapter 11 Reorganization Case

(a) ENTITIES ENTITLED TO ACCEPT OR REJECT PLAN; TIME FOR ACCEPTANCE OR REJECTION plan may be accepted or rejected in accordance with §1126 of the Code within the time fixed by the court pursuant to Rule 3017. Subject to subdivision (b) of this rule, an equity security holder or creditor whose claim is based on a security of record shall not be entitled to accept or reject a plan unless the equity security holder or creditor is the holder of record of the security on the date the order approving the disclosure statement is entered or on another date fixed by the court, for cause, after notice and a hearing. For cause shown, the court after notice and hearing may permit a creditor or equity security holder to change or withdraw an acceptance or rejection. Notwithstanding objection to a claim or interest, the court after notice and hearing may temporarily allow the claim or interest in an amount which the court deems proper for the purpose of accepting or rejecting a plan.

(b) ACCEPTANCES OR REJECTIONS OBTAINED FORE PETITION. An equity security holder or creditor whose claim is based on a security of record who accepted or rejected the plan before the commencement of the case shall not be deemed to have accepted or rejected the plan pursuant to §1126(b) of the Code unless the equity security holder or creditor was the holder of record of the security on the date specified in the solicitation of such acceptance or rejection for the purposes of such solicitation. A holder of a claim or interest who has accepted or rejected a plan before the commencement of the case under the Code shall not be deemed to have accepted or rejected the plan if the court finds after notice and hearing that the plan was not transmitted to substantially all creditors and equity security holders of the same class, that an unreasonably short time was prescribed for such creditors and equity security holders to accept or reject the plan, or that the solicitation was not in compliance with §1126(b) of the Code.

(c) FORM OF ACCEPTANCE OR REJECTION. An acceptance or rejection shall be in writing, identify the plan or plans accepted or rejected, be signed by the creditor or equity security holder or an authorized agent, and conform to the appropriate Official Form. If more than one plan is transmitted pursuant to Rule 3017, an acceptance or rejection may be filed by each creditor or equity security holder for any number of plans transmitted and if acceptances are filed for more than one plan, the creditor or equity security holder may indicate a preference or preferences among the plans so accepted.

(d) ACCEPTANCE OR REJECTION BY PARTIALLY SECURED CREDITOR. A creditor whose claim has been allowed in part as a secured claim and in part as an unsecured claim shall be entitled to accept or reject a plan in both capacities.

(As amended Mar. 30, 1987, eff. Aug. 1, 1987; Apr. 30, 1991, eff. Aug. 1, 1991; Apr. 22, 1993, eff. Aug. 1, 1993; Apr. 11, 1997, eff. Dec. 1, 1997.)

NOTES OF ADVISORY COMMITTEE ON RULES—1983

This rule applies in chapter 9, 11 and 13 cases under the Code. The references in the rule to equity security holders will not, however, be relevant in chapter 9 or 13 cases. The rule will be of little utility in a chapter 13 case because only secured creditors may be requested to vote on a plan; unsecured creditors are not entitled to vote; see §1325(a)(4), (5) of the Code.

*Subdivision (a)* is derived from former Rule 10–305(a). It substitutes, in a reorganization case, entry of the order approving the disclosure statement for the order approving a plan in conformity with the differences between Chapter X and chapter 11. In keeping with the underlying theory it continues to recognize that the lapse of time between the filing of the petition and entry of such order will normally be significant and, during that interim, bonds and equity interests can change ownership.

*Subdivision (b)* recognizes the former Chapter XI practice permitting a plan and acceptances to be filed with the petition, as does §1126(b) of the Code. However, because a plan under chapter 11 may affect shareholder interests, there should be reference to a record date of ownership. In this instance the appropriate record date is that used in the prepetition solicitation materials because it is those acceptances or rejections which are being submitted to the court.

While §1126(c), (d), and (e) prohibits use of an acceptance or rejection not procured in good faith, the added provision in subdivision (b) of the rule is somewhat more detailed. It would prohibit use of prepetition acceptances or rejections when some but not all impaired creditors or equity security holders are solicited or when they are not given a reasonable opportunity to submit their acceptances or rejections. This provision together with §1126(e) gives the court the power to nullify abusive solicitation procedures.

*Subdivision (c).* It is possible that multiple plans may be before the court for confirmation. Pursuant to §1129(c) of the Code, the court may confirm only one plan but is required to consider the preferences expressed by those accepting the plans in determining which one to confirm.

Subdivisions (d) and (e) of former Rule 10–305 are not continued since comparable provisions are contained in the statute; see §1126(c), (d), (e).

It should be noted that while the singular "plan" is used throughout, by construction the plural is included; see §102(7).

NOTES OF ADVISORY COMMITTEE ON RULES—1991 AMENDMENT

*Subdivisions (a) and (b)* are amended to delete provisions that duplicate §1126 of the Code. An entity who is not a record holder of a security, but who claims that it is entitled to be treated as a record holder, may file a statement pursuant to Rule 3003(d).

*Subdivision (a)* is amended further to allow the court to permit a creditor or equity security holder to change or withdraw an acceptance or rejection for cause shown whether or not the time fixed for voting has expired.

*Subdivision (b)* is also amended to give effect to a prepetition acceptance or rejection if solicitation requirements were satisfied with respect to substantially all members of the same class, instead of requiring proper solicitation with respect to substantially all members of all classes.

*Subdivision (c)* is amended to delete the Official Form number in anticipation of future revision and renumbering of the Official Forms.

NOTES OF ADVISORY COMMITTEE ON RULES—1993 AMENDMENT

The title of this rule is amended to indicate that it applies only in a chapter 9 or a chapter 11 case. The amendment of the word "Plans" to "Plan" is stylistic.

NOTES OF ADVISORY COMMITTEE ON RULES—1997 AMENDMENT

*Subdivision (a)* is amended to provide flexibility in fixing the record date for the purpose of determining the holders of securities who are entitled to vote on the plan. For example, if there may be a delay between the oral announcement of the judge's decision approving the disclosure statement and entry of the order on the court docket, the court may fix the date on which the judge orally approves the disclosure statement as the record date for voting purposes so that the parties may expedite preparation of the lists necessary to facilitate the distribution of the plan, disclosure statement, ballots, and other related documents in connection with the solicitation of votes.

The court may set a record date pursuant to subdivision (a) only after notice and a hearing as provided in §102(1) of the Code. Notice of a request for an order fixing the record date may be included in the notice of the hearing to consider approval of the disclosure statement mailed pursuant to Rule 2002(b).

If the court fixes the record date for voting purposes, the judge also should order that the same record date shall apply for the purpose of distributing the documents required to be distributed pursuant to Rule 3017(d).

*GAP Report on Rule 3018.* No changes to the published draft.

## Rule 3019. Modification of Accepted Plan in a Chapter 9 Municipality or a Chapter 11 Reorganization Case

(a) MODIFICATION OF PLAN BEFORE C TION. In a chapter 9 or chapter 11 case, after a plan has been accepted and before its confirmation, the proponent may file a modification of the plan. If the court finds after hearing on notice to the trustee, any committee appointed under the Code, and any other entity designated by the court that the proposed modification does not adversely change the treatment of the claim of any creditor or the interest of any equity security holder who has not accepted in writing the modification, it shall be deemed accepted by all creditors and equity security holders who have previously accepted the plan.

(b) MODIFICATION OF PLAN AFTER CONFIRMATION IN INDIVIDUAL DEBTOR CASE. If the debtor is an individual, a request to modify the plan under §1127(e) of the Code is governed by Rule 9014. The request shall identify the proponent and shall be filed together with the proposed modification. The clerk, or some other person as the court may direct, shall give the debtor, the trustee, and all creditors not less than 21 days' notice by mail of the time fixed to file objections and, if an objection is filed, the hearing to consider the proposed modification, unless the court orders otherwise with respect to creditors who are not affected by the proposed modification. A copy of the notice shall be transmitted to the United States trustee, together with a copy of the proposed modification. Any objection to the proposed modification shall be filed and served on the debtor, the proponent of the modification, the trustee, and any other entity designated by the court, and shall be transmitted to the United States trustee.

(As amended Mar. 30, 1987, eff. Aug. 1, 1987; Apr. 22, 1993, eff. Aug. 1, 1993; Apr. 23, 2008, eff. Dec. 1, 2008; Mar. 26, 2009, eff. Dec. 1, 2009.)

NOTES OF ADVISORY COMMITTEE ON RULES—1983

This rule implements §§942, 1127 and 1323 of the Code. For example, §1127 provides for modification before and after confirmation but does not deal with the minor modifications that do not adversely change any rights. The rule makes clear that a modification may be made, after acceptance of the plan without submission to creditors and equity security holders if their interests are not affected. To come within this rule, the modification should be one that does not change the rights of a creditor or equity security holder as fixed in the plan before modification.

NOTES OF ADVISORY COMMITTEE ON RULES—1993 AMENDMENT

This rule is amended to limit its application to chapter 9 and chapter 11 cases. Modification of plans after confirmation in chapter 12 and chapter 13 cases is governed by Rule 3015. The addition of the comma in the second sentence is stylistic and makes no substantive change.

COMMITTEE NOTES ON RULES—2008 AMENDMENT

The 2005 amendments to §1127 of the Code provide for modification of a confirmed plan in an individual debtor chapter 11 case. Therefore, the rule is amended to establish the procedure for filing and objecting to a proposed modification of a confirmed plan.

*Changes Made After Publication.* The last sentence of the published rule provided that an objection to modification of a plan is governed by Rule 9014. The sentence is deleted and the reference to Rule 9014 is moved to the first sentence of subdivision (b) of the rule. The Committee Note was revised to make the reference to the 2005 amendments to the Bankruptcy Code consistent with their identification in other Committee Notes.

COMMITTEE NOTES ON RULES—2009 AMENDMENT

The rule is amended to implement changes in connection with the amendment to Rule 9006(a) and the manner by which time is computed under the rules. The deadline in the rule is amended to substitute a deadline that is a multiple of seven days. Throughout the rules, deadlines are amended in the following manner:

- 5-day periods become 7-day periods
- 10-day periods become 14-day periods
- 15-day periods become 14-day periods
- 20-day periods become 21-day periods
- 25-day periods become 28-day periods

## Rule 3020. Deposit; Confirmation of Plan in a Chapter 9 Municipality or Chapter 11 Reorganization Case

(a) DEPOSIT. In a chapter 11 case, prior to entry of the order confirming the plan, the court may order the deposit with the trustee or debtor in possession of the consideration required by the plan to be distributed on confirmation. Any money deposited shall be kept in a special account established for the exclusive purpose of making the distribution.

(b) OBJECTION TO AND HEARING ON CONFIRMATION IN A CHAPTER 9 OR CHAPTER 11 CASE.

(1) *Objection.* An objection to confirmation of the plan shall be filed and served on the debtor, the trustee, the proponent of the plan, any committee appointed under the Code, and any other entity designated by the court, within a time fixed by the court. Unless the case is a chapter 9 municipality case, a copy of every objection to confirmation shall be transmitted by the objecting party to the United States trustee within the time fixed for filing objections. An objection to confirmation is governed by Rule 9014.

(2) *Hearing.* The court shall rule on confirmation of the plan after notice and hearing as provided in Rule 2002. If no objection is timely filed, the court may determine that the plan has been proposed in good faith and not by any means forbidden by law without receiving evidence on such issues.

(c) ORDER OF CONFIRMATION.

(1) The order of confirmation shall conform to the appropriate Official Form. If the plan provides for an injunction against conduct not otherwise enjoined under the Code, the order of confirmation shall (1) describe in reasonable detail all acts enjoined; (2) be specific in its terms regarding the injunction; and (3) identify the entities subject to the injunction.

(2) Notice of entry of the order of confirmation shall be mailed promptly to the debtor, the trustee, creditors, equity security holders, other parties in interest, and, if known, to any identified entity subject to an injunction provided for in the plan against conduct not otherwise enjoined under the Code.

(3) Except in a chapter 9 municipality case, notice of entry of the order of confirmation shall be transmitted to the United States trustee as provided in Rule 2002(k).

(d) RETAINED POWER. Notwithstanding the entry of the order of confirmation, the court may issue any other order necessary to administer the estate.

(e) STAY OF CONFIRMATION ORDER. An order confirming a plan is stayed until the expiration of 14 days after the entry of the order, unless the court orders otherwise.

(As amended Mar. 30, 1987, eff. Aug. 1, 1987; Apr. 30, 1991, eff. Aug. 1, 1991; Apr. 22, 1993, eff. Aug. 1, 1993; Apr. 26, 1999, eff. Dec. 1, 1999; Apr. 23, 2001, eff. Dec. 1, 2001; Mar. 26, 2009, eff. Dec. 1, 2009.)

NOTES OF ADVISORY COMMITTEE ON RULES—1983

This rule is adapted from former Rules 10–307, 11–38, and 13–213. It applies to cases filed under chapters 9, 11 and 13. Certain subdivisions of the earlier rules have not been included, such as, a subdivision revesting title in the debtor because §541 of the Code does not transfer title out of the debtor as did §70a of the Bankruptcy Act; see also §§1141(b), 1327(b). Subdivision (b) of former Rule 13–213 is not included because its provisions are contained in the statute; see §§1322, 1325(b), 105.

*Subdivision (a)* gives discretion to the court to require in chapter 11 cases the deposit of any consideration to be distributed on confirmation. If money is to be distributed, it is to be deposited in a special account to assure that it will not be used for any other purpose. The Code is silent in chapter 11 with respect to the need to make a deposit or the person with whom any deposit is to be made. Consequently, there is no statutory authority for any person to act in a capacity similar to the disbursing agent under former Chapter XI practice. This rule provides that only the debtor in possession or trustee should be appointed as the recipient of the deposit. Any consideration other than money, *e.g.*, notes or stock may be given directly to the debtor in possession or trustee and need not be left in any kind of special account. In chapter 9 cases, §944(b) provides for deposit with a disbursing agent appointed by the court of any consideration to be distributed under the plan.

*Subdivision (d)* clarifies the authority of the court to conclude matters pending before it prior to confirmation and to continue to administer the estate as necessary, *e.g.*, resolving objections to claims.

NOTES OF ADVISORY COMMITTEE ON RULES—1991 AMENDMENT

The United States trustee monitors chapter 11, chapter 12, and chapter 13 plans and has standing to be heard regarding confirmation of a plan. See 28 U.S.C. §586(a)(3). The amendments to subdivisions (b)(1) and (c) of this rule facilitate that role of the United States trustee. Subdivision (b)(1) is also amended to require service on the proponent of the plan of objections to confirmation. The words "with the court" in subdivision (b)(1) are deleted as unnecessary. See Rules 5005(a) and 9001(3).

In a chapter 12 case, the court is required to conduct and conclude the hearing on confirmation of the plan within the time prescribed in §1224 of the Code.

*Subdivision (c)* is also amended to require that the confirmation order be mailed to the trustee. Reference to the Official Form number is deleted in anticipation of future revision and renumbering of the Official Forms.

NOTES OF ADVISORY COMMITTEE ON RULES—1993 AMENDMENT

This rule is amended to limit its application to chapter 9 and chapter 11 cases. The procedures relating to confirmation of plans in chapter 12 and chapter 13 cases are provided in Rule 3015. Other amendments are stylistic and make no substantive change.

COMMITTEE NOTES ON RULES—1999 AMENDMENT

*Subdivision (e)* is added to provide sufficient time for a party to request a stay pending appeal of an order confirming a plan under chapter 9 or chapter 11 of the Code before the plan is implemented and an appeal becomes moot. Unless the court orders otherwise, any transfer of assets, issuance of securities, and cash distributions provided for in the plan may not be made before the expiration of the 10-day period. The stay of the confirmation order under subdivision (e) does not affect the time for filing a notice of appeal from the confirmation order in accordance with Rule 8002.

The court may, in its discretion, order that Rule 3020(e) is not applicable so that the plan may be implemented and distributions may be made immediately. Alternatively, the court may order that the stay under Rule 3020(e) is for a fixed period less than 10 days.

*GAP Report on Rule 3020.* No changes since publication.

COMMITTEE NOTES ON RULES—2001 AMENDMENT

*Subdivision (c)* is amended to provide notice to an entity subject to an injunction provided for in a plan against conduct not otherwise enjoined by operation of the Code. This requirement is not applicable to an injunction contained in a plan if it is substantially the same as an injunction provided under the Code. The validity and effect of any injunction provided for in a plan are substantive law matters that are beyond the scope of these rules.

The requirement that the order of confirmation identify the entities subject to the injunction requires only reasonable identification under the circumstances. If the entities that would be subject to the injunction cannot be identified by name, the order may describe them by class or category if reasonable under the circumstances. For example, it may be sufficient to identify the entities as "all creditors of the debtor."

*Changes Made After Publication and Comments.* No changes were made in the text of the proposed amendments. The Committee Note was revised to put in a more prominent position the statement that the validity and effect of injunctions provided for in plans is beyond the scope of the rules.

COMMITTEE NOTES ON RULES—2009 AMENDMENT

The rule is amended to implement changes in connection with the amendment to Rule 9006(a) and the manner by which time is computed under the rules. The deadline in the rule is amended to substitute a deadline that is a multiple of seven days. Throughout the rules, deadlines are amended in the following manner:

- 5-day periods become 7-day periods
- 10-day periods become 14-day periods
- 15-day periods become 14-day periods
- 20-day periods become 21-day periods
- 25-day periods become 28-day periods

## Rule 3021. Distribution Under Plan

Except as provided in Rule 3020(e), after a plan is confirmed, distribution shall be made to creditors whose claims have been allowed, to interest holders whose interests have not been disallowed, and to indenture trustees who have filed claims under Rule 3003(c)(5) that have been allowed. For purposes of this rule, creditors include holders of bonds, debentures, notes, and other debt securities, and interest holders include the holders of stock and other equity securities, of record at the time of commencement of distribution, unless a different time is fixed by the plan or the order confirming the plan.

(As amended Apr. 11, 1997, eff. Dec. 1, 1997; Apr. 26, 1999, eff. Dec. 1, 1999.)

NOTES OF ADVISORY COMMITTEE ON RULES

This rule is derived from former Chapter X Rule 10–405(a). Subdivision (b) of that rule is covered by §1143 of the Code.

NOTES OF ADVISORY COMMITTEE ON RULES AMENDMENT

This rule is amended to provide flexibility in fixing the record date for the purpose of making distributions to holders of securities of record. In a large case, it may be impractical for the debtor to determine the holders of record with respect to publicly held securities and also to make distributions to those holders at the same time. Under this amendment, the plan or the order confirming the plan may fix a record date for distributions that is earlier than the date on which distributions commence.

This rule also is amended to treat holders of bonds, debentures, notes, and other debt securities the same as any other creditors by providing that they shall receive a distribution only if their claims have been allowed. Finally, the amendments clarify that distributions are to be made to all interest holders—not only those that are within the definition of "equity security holders" under § 101 of the Code—whose interests have not been disallowed.

*GAP Report on Rule 3021.* No changes to the published draft.

COMMITTEE NOTES ON RULES—1999 AMENDMENT

This amendment is to conform to the amendments to Rule 3020 regarding the ten-day stay of an order confirming a plan in a chapter 9 or chapter 11 case. The other amendments are stylistic.

*GAP Report on Rule 3021.* No changes since publication.

## Rule 3022. Final Decree in Chapter 11 Reorganization Case

After an estate is fully administered in a chapter 11 reorganization case, the court, on its own motion or on motion of a party in interest, shall enter a final decree closing the case.

(As amended Mar. 30, 1987, eff. Aug. 1, 1987; Apr. 30, 1991, eff. Aug. 1, 1991.)

NOTES OF ADVISORY COMMITTEE ON RULES—1983

Section 350 of the Code requires the court to close the case after the estate is fully administered and the trustee has been discharged. Section 1143 places a five year limitation on the surrender of securities when required for participation under a plan but this provision should not delay entry of the final decree.

NOTES OF ADVISORY COMMITTEE ON RULES—1991 AMENDMENT

Entry of a final decree closing a chapter 11 case should not be delayed solely because the payments required by the plan have not been completed. Factors that the court should consider in determining whether the estate has been fully administered include (1) whether the order confirming the plan has become final, (2) whether deposits required by the plan have been distributed, (3) whether the property proposed by the plan to be transferred has been transferred, (4) whether the debtor or the successor of the debtor under the plan has assumed the business or the management of the property dealt with by the plan, (5) whether payments under the plan have commenced, and (6) whether all motions, contested matters, and adversary proceedings have been finally resolved.

The court should not keep the case open only because of the possibility that the court's jurisdiction may be invoked in the future. A final decree closing the case after the estate is fully administered does not deprive the court of jurisdiction to enforce or interpret its own orders and does not prevent the court from reopening the case for cause pursuant to § 350(b) of the Code. For example, on motion of a party in interest, the court may reopen the case to revoke an order of confirmation procured by fraud under § 1144 of the Code. If the plan or confirmation order provides that the case shall remain open until a certain date or event because of the likelihood that the court's jurisdiction may be required for specific purposes prior thereto, the case should remain open until that date or event.

# PART IV—THE DEBTOR: DUTIES AND BENEFITS

## Rule 4001. Relief from Automatic Stay; Prohibiting or Conditioning the Use, Sale, or Lease of Property; Use of Cash Collateral; Obtaining Credit; Agreements

(a) RELIEF FROM STAY; PROHIBITING OR CONDITIONING THE USE, SALE, OR LEASE OF PROPERTY.

(1) *Motion.* A motion for relief from an automatic stay provided by the Code or a motion to prohibit or condition the use, sale, or lease of property pursuant to § 363(e) shall be made in accordance with Rule 9014 and shall be served on any committee elected pursuant to § 705 or appointed pursuant to § 1102 of the Code or its authorized agent, or, if the case is a chapter 9 municipality case or a chapter 11 reorganization case and no committee of unsecured creditors has been appointed pursuant to § 1102, on the creditors included on the list filed pursuant to Rule 1007(d), and on such other entities as the court may direct.

(2) *Ex Parte Relief.* Relief from a stay under § 362(a) or a request to prohibit or condition the use, sale, or lease of property pursuant to § 363(e) may be granted without prior notice only if (A) it clearly appears from specific facts shown by affidavit or by a verified motion that immediate and irreparable injury, loss, or damage will result to the movant before the adverse party or the attorney for the adverse party can be heard in opposition, and (B) the movant's attorney certifies to the court in writing the efforts, if any, which have been made to give notice and the reasons why notice should not be required. The party obtaining relief under this subdivision and § 362(f) or § 363(e) shall immediately give oral notice thereof to the trustee or debtor in possession and to the debtor and forthwith mail or otherwise transmit to such adverse party or parties a copy of the order granting relief. On two days notice to the party who obtained relief from the stay without notice or on shorter notice to that party as the court may prescribe, the adverse party may appear and move reinstatement of the stay or reconsideration of the order prohibiting or conditioning the use, sale, or lease of property. In that event, the court shall proceed expeditiously to hear and determine the motion.

(3) *Stay of Order.* An order granting a motion for relief from an automatic stay made in accordance with Rule 4001(a)(1) is stayed until the expiration of 14 days after the entry of the order, unless the court orders otherwise.

(b) USE OF CASH COLLATERAL.

(1) *Motion; Service.*

(A) *Motion.* A motion for authority to use cash collateral shall be made in accordance with Rule 9014 and shall be accompanied by a proposed form of order.

(B) *Contents.* The motion shall consist of or (if the motion is more than five pages in length) begin with a concise statement of the relief requested, not to exceed five pages, that lists or summarizes, and sets out the location within the relevant documents of, all material provisions, including:

(i) the name of each entity with an interest in the cash collateral;

(ii) the purposes for the use of the cash collateral;

(iii) the material terms, including duration, of the use of the cash collateral; and

(iv) any liens, cash payments, or other adequate protection that will be provided to each entity with an interest in the cash collateral or, if no additional adequate protection is proposed, an explanation of why each entity's interest is adequately protected.

(C) *Service.* The motion shall be served on: (1) any entity with an interest in the cash collateral; (2) any committee elected under §705 or appointed under §1102 of the Code, or its authorized agent, or, if the case is a chapter 9 municipality case or a chapter 11 reorganization case and no committee of unsecured creditors has been appointed under §1102, the creditors included on the list filed under Rule 1007(d); and (3) any other entity that the court directs.

(2) *Hearing.* The court may commence a final hearing on a motion for authorization to use cash collateral no earlier than 14 days after service of the motion. If the motion so requests, the court may conduct a preliminary hearing before such 14-day period expires, but the court may authorize the use of only that amount of cash collateral as is necessary to avoid immediate and irreparable harm to the estate pending a final hearing.

(3) *Notice.* Notice of hearing pursuant to this subdivision shall be given to the parties on whom service of the motion is required by paragraph (1) of this subdivision and to such other entities as the court may direct.

(c) OBTAINING CREDIT.

(1) *Motion; Service.*

(A) *Motion.* A motion for authority to obtain credit shall be made in accordance with Rule 9014 and shall be accompanied by a copy of the credit agreement and a proposed form of order.

(B) *Contents.* The motion shall consist of or (if the motion is more than five pages in length) begin with a concise statement of the relief requested, not to exceed five pages, that lists or summarizes, and sets out the location within the relevant documents of, all material provisions of the proposed credit agreement and form of order, including interest rate, maturity, events of default, liens, borrowing limits, and borrowing conditions. If the proposed credit agreement or form of order includes any of the provisions listed below, the concise statement shall also: briefly list or summarize each one; identify its specific location in the proposed agreement and form of order; and identify any such provision that is proposed to remain in effect if interim approval is granted, but final relief is denied, as provided under Rule 4001(c)(2). In addition, the motion shall describe the nature and extent of each provision listed below:

(i) a grant of priority or a lien on property of the estate under §364(c) or (d);

(ii) the providing of adequate protection or priority for a claim that arose before the commencement of the case, including the granting of a lien on property of the estate to secure the claim, or the use of property of the estate or credit obtained under §364 to make cash payments on account of the claim;

(iii) a determination of the validity, enforceability, priority, or amount of a claim that arose before the commencement of the case, or of any lien securing the claim;

(iv) a waiver or modification of Code provisions or applicable rules relating to the automatic stay;

(v) a waiver or modification of any entity's authority or right to file a plan, seek an extension of time in which the debtor has the exclusive right to file a plan, request the use of cash collateral under §363(c), or request authority to obtain credit under §364;

(vi) the establishment of deadlines for filing a plan of reorganization, for approval of a disclosure statement, for a hearing on confirmation, or for entry of a confirmation order;

(vii) a waiver or modification of the applicability of nonbankruptcy law relating to the perfection of a lien on property of the estate, or on the foreclosure or other enforcement of the lien;

(viii) a release, waiver, or limitation on any claim or other cause of action belonging to the estate or the trustee, including any modification of the statute of limitations or other deadline to commence an action;

(ix) the indemnification of any entity;

(x) a release, waiver, or limitation of any right under §506(c); or

(xi) the granting of a lien on any claim or cause of action arising under §§544,[1] 545, 547, 548, 549, 553(b), 723(a), or 724(a).

(C) *Service.* The motion shall be served on: (1) any committee elected under §705 or appointed under §1102 of the Code, or its authorized agent, or, if the case is a chapter 9 municipality case or a chapter 11 reorganization case and no committee of unsecured creditors has been appointed under §1102, on the creditors included on the list filed under Rule 1007(d); and (2) on any other entity that the court directs.

(2) *Hearing.* The court may commence a final hearing on a motion for authority to obtain credit no earlier than 14 days after service of the motion. If the motion so requests, the court may conduct a hearing before such 14-day period expires, but the court may authorize the obtaining of credit only to the extent necessary to avoid immediate and irreparable harm to the estate pending a final hearing.

(3) *Notice.* Notice of hearing pursuant to this subdivision shall be given to the parties on whom service of the motion is required by paragraph (1) of this subdivision and to such other entities as the court may direct.

[1] So in original. Probably should be only one section symbol.

(d) AGREEMENT RELATING TO RELIEF FROM THE AUTOMATIC STAY, PROHIBITING OR CONDITIONING THE USE, SALE, OR LEASE OF PROPERTY, PROVIDING ADEQUATE PROTECTION, USE OF CASH COLLATERAL, AND OBTAINING CREDIT.

(1) *Motion; Service.*

(A) *Motion.* A motion for approval of any of the following shall be accompanied by a copy of the agreement and a proposed form of order:

(i) an agreement to provide adequate protection;

(ii) an agreement to prohibit or condition the use, sale, or lease of property;

(iii) an agreement to modify or terminate the stay provided for in §362;

(iv) an agreement to use cash collateral; or

(v) an agreement between the debtor and an entity that has a lien or interest in property of the estate pursuant to which the entity consents to the creation of a lien senior or equal to the entity's lien or interest in such property.

(B) *Contents.* The motion shall consist of or (if the motion is more than five pages in length) begin with a concise statement of the relief requested, not to exceed five pages, that lists or summarizes, and sets out the location within the relevant documents of, all material provisions of the agreement. In addition, the concise statement shall briefly list or summarize, and identify the specific location of, each provision in the proposed form of order, agreement, or other document of the type listed in subdivision (c)(1)(B). The motion shall also describe the nature and extent of each such provision.

(C) *Service.* The motion shall be served on: (1) any committee elected under §705 or appointed under §1102 of the Code, or its authorized agent, or, if the case is a chapter 9 municipality case or a chapter 11 reorganization case and no committee of unsecured creditors has been appointed under §1102, on the creditors included on the list filed under Rule 1007(d); and (2) on any other entity the court directs.

(2) *Objection.* Notice of the motion and the time within which objections may be filed and served on the debtor in possession or trustee shall be mailed to the parties on whom service is required by paragraph (1) of this subdivision and to such other entities as the court may direct. Unless the court fixes a different time, objections may be filed within 15 days of the mailing of notice.

(3) *Disposition; Hearing.* If no objection is filed, the court may enter an order approving or disapproving the agreement without conducting a hearing. If an objection is filed or if the court determines a hearing is appropriate, the court shall hold a hearing on no less than five days' notice to the objector, the movant, the parties on whom service is required by paragraph (1) of this subdivision and such other entities as the court may direct.

(4) *Agreement in Settlement of Motion.* The court may direct that the procedures prescribed in paragraphs (1), (2), and (3) of this subdivision shall not apply and the agreement may be approved without further notice if the court determines that a motion made pursuant to subdivisions (a), (b), or (c) of this rule was sufficient to afford reasonable notice of the material provisions of the agreement and opportunity for a hearing.

(As amended Mar. 30, 1987, eff. Aug. 1, 1987; Apr. 30, 1991, eff. Aug. 1, 1991; Apr. 26, 1999, eff. Dec. 1, 1999; Apr. 30, 2007; eff. Dec. 1, 2007; Mar. 26, 2009, eff. Dec. 1, 2009.)

NOTES OF ADVISORY COMMITTEE ON RULES—1983

This rule implements §362 of the Code which set forth provisions regarding the automatic stay that arises on the filing of a petition. That section and this rule are applicable in chapters 7, 9, 11 and 13 cases. It also implements §363(c)(2) concerning use of cash collateral.

*Subdivision (a)* transforms with respect to the automatic stay what was an adversary proceeding under the former rules to motion practice. The Code provides automatic stays in several sections, *e.g.*, §§362(a), 1301(a), and in §362(d) provides some grounds for relief from the stay. This rule specifies that the pleading seeking relief is by means of a motion. Thus the time period in Rule 7012 to answer a complaint would not be applicable and shorter periods may be fixed. Section 362(e) requires the preliminary hearing to be concluded within 30 days of it inception, rendering ordinary complaint and answer practice inappropriate.

This subdivision also makes clear that a motion under Rule 9014 is the proper procedure for a debtor to seek court permission to use cash collateral. See §363(c)(2). Pursuant to Rule 5005, the motion should be filed in the court in which the case in pending. The court or local rule may specify the persons to be served with the motion for relief from the stay; see Rule 9013.

*Subdivision (b)* of the rule fills a procedural void left by §362. Pursuant to §362(e), the automatic stay is terminated 30 days after a motion for relief is made unless the court continues the stay as a result of a final hearing or, pending final hearing, after a preliminary hearing. If a preliminary hearing is held, §362(e) requires the final hearing to be commenced within 30 days after the preliminary hearing. Although the expressed legislative intent is to require expeditious resolution of a secured party's motion for relief, §362 is silent as to the time within which the final hearing must be concluded. Subdivision (b) imposes a 30 day deadline on the court to resolve the dispute.

At the final hearing, the stay is to be terminated, modified, annulled, or conditioned for cause, which includes, *inter alia*, lack of adequate protection; §362(d). The burden of proving adequate protection is on the party opposing relief from the stay; §362(g)(2). Adequate protection is exemplified in §361.

*Subdivision (c)* implements §362(f) which permits ex parte relief from the stay when there will be irreparable damage. This subdivision sets forth the procedure to be followed when relief is sought under §362(f). It is derived from former Bankruptcy Rule 601(d).

NOTES OF ADVISORY COMMITTEE ON RULES—1987 AMENDMENT

The scope of this rule is expanded and the former subdivisions (a), (b) and (c) are now combined in subdivision (a). The new subdivision (a)(2) is amended to conform to the 1984 amendments to §362(e) of the Code.

*Subdivision (b)* deals explicitly with the procedures which follow after a motion to use cash collateral is made and served. Filing shall be pursuant to Rule 5005. Service of the motion may be made by any method authorized by Rule 7004 and, if service is by mail, service is complete on mailing. Rule 9006(e). Under subdivision (b)(2), the court may commence a final hearing on the motion within 15 days of service. Rule 9006(f) does not extend this 15 day period when service of the motion is by mail because the party served is not required to act within the 15 day period. In addition to service of the motion, notice of the hearing must be given. Rule 9007 authorizes the court to direct the form and manner of giving notice that is appropriate to the circumstances.

Section 363(c)(3) authorizes the court to conduct a preliminary hearing and to authorize the use of cash collateral "if there is a reasonable likelihood that the trustee will prevail at a final hearing." Subdivision (b)(2) of the rule permits a preliminary hearing to be held earlier than 15 days after service. Any order authorizing the use of cash collateral shall be limited to the amount necessary to protect the estate until a final hearing is held.

The objective of subdivision (b) is to accommodate both the immediate need of the debtor and the interest of the secured creditor in the cash collateral. The time for holding the final hearing may be enlarged beyond the 15 days prescribed when required by the circumstances.

The motion for authority to use cash collateral shall include (1) the amount of cash collateral sought to be used; (2) the name and address of each entity having an interest in the cash collateral; (3) the name and address of the entity in control or having possession of the cash collateral; (4) the facts demonstrating the need to use the cash collateral; and (5) the nature of the protection to be provided those having an interest in the cash collateral. If a preliminary hearing is requested, the motion shall also include the amount of cash collateral sought to be used pending final hearing and the protection to be provided.

Notice of the preliminary and final hearings may be combined. This rule does not limit the authority of the court under §363(c)(2)(B) and §102(1).

*Subdivision (c)* is new. The service, hearing, and notice requirements are similar to those imposed by subdivision (b). The motion to obtain credit shall include the amount and type of the credit to be extended, the name and address of the lender, the terms of the agreement, the need to obtain the credit, and the efforts made to obtain credit from other sources. If the motion is to obtain credit pursuant to §364(c) or (d), the motion shall describe the collateral, if any, and the protection for any existing interest in the collateral which may be affected by the proposed agreement.

*Subdivision (d)* is new. In the event the 15 day period for filing objections to the approval of an agreement of the parties described in this subdivision is too long, the parties either may move for a reduction of the period under Rule 9006(c)(1) or proceed under subdivision (b) or (c), if applicable. Rule 9006(c)(1) requires that cause be shown for the reduction of the period in which to object. In applying this criterion the court may consider the option of proceeding under subdivision (b) or (c) and grant a preliminary hearing and relief pending final hearing.

NOTES OF ADVISORY COMMITTEE ON RULES—1991 AMENDMENT

*Subdivision (a)* is expanded to include a request to prohibit or condition the use, sale, or lease of property as is necessary to provide adequate protection of a property interest pursuant to §363(e) of the Code.

Notice of the motion for relief from the automatic stay or to prohibit or condition the use, sale, or lease of property must be served on the entities entitled to receive notice of a motion to approve an agreement pursuant to subdivision (d). If the movant and the adverse party agree to settle the motion and the terms of the agreement do not materially differ from the terms set forth in the movant's motion papers, the court may approve the agreement without further notice pursuant to subdivision (d)(4).

*Subdivision (a)(2)* is deleted as unnecessary because of §362(e) of the Code.

*Subdivisions (b)(1), (c)(1), and (d)(1)* are amended to require service on committees that are elected in chapter 7 cases. Service on committees of retired employees appointed under §1114 of the Code is not required. These subdivisions are amended further to clarify that, in the absence of a creditors' committee, service on the creditors included on the list filed pursuant to Rule 1007(d) is required only in chapter 9 and chapter 11 cases. The other amendments to subdivision (d)(1) are for consistency of style and are not substantive.

*Subdivision (d)(4)* is added to avoid the necessity of further notice and delay for the approval of an agreement in settlement of a motion for relief from an automatic stay, to prohibit or condition the use, sale, or lease of property, for use of cash collateral, or for authority to obtain credit if the entities entitled to notice have already received sufficient notice of the scope of the proposed agreement in the motion papers and have had an opportunity to be heard. For example, if a trustee makes a motion to use cash collateral and proposes in the original motion papers to provide adequate protection of the interest of the secured party by granting a lien on certain equipment, and the secured creditor subsequently agrees to terms that are within the scope of those proposed in the motion, the court may enter an order approving the agreement without further notice if the entities that received the original motion papers have had a reasonable opportunity to object to the granting of the motion to use cash collateral.

If the motion papers served under subdivision (a), (b), or (c) do not afford notice sufficient to inform the recipients of the material provisions of the proposed agreement and opportunity for a hearing, approval of the settlement agreement may not be obtained unless the procedural requirements of subdivision (d)(1), (d)(2), and (d)(3) are satisfied. If the 15 day period for filing objections to the approval of the settlement agreement is too long under the particular circumstances of the case, the court may shorten the time for cause under Rule 9006(c)(1).

COMMITTEE NOTES ON RULES—1999 AMENDMENT

*Paragraph (a)(3)* is added to provide sufficient time for a party to request a stay pending appeal of an order granting relief from an automatic stay before the order is enforced or implemented. The stay under paragraph (a)(3) is not applicable to orders granted ex parte in accordance with Rule 4001(a)(2).

The stay of the order does not affect the time for filing a notice of appeal in accordance with Rule 8002. While the enforcement and implementation of an order granting relief from the automatic stay is temporarily stayed under paragraph (a)(3), the automatic stay continues to protect the debtor, and the moving party may not foreclose on collateral or take any other steps that would violate the automatic stay.

The court may, in its discretion, order that Rule 4001(a)(3) is not applicable so that the prevailing party may immediately enforce and implement the order granting relief from the automatic stay. Alternatively, the court may order that the stay under Rule 4001(a)(3) is for a fixed period less than 10 days.

*GAP Report on Rule 4001.* No changes since publication.

COMMITTEE NOTES ON RULES—2007 AMENDMENT

The rule is amended to require that parties seeking authority to use cash collateral, to obtain credit, and to obtain approval of agreements to provide adequate protection, modify or terminate the stay, or to grant a senior or equal lien on property, submit with those requests a proposed order granting the relief, and that they provide more extensive notice to interested parties of a number of specified terms. The motion must either not exceed five pages in length, or, if it is longer, begin with a concise statement of five pages or less, that summarizes or lists the material provisions and which will assist the court and interested parties in understanding the nature of the relief requested. The concise statement must also set out the location within the documents of the summarized or listed provisions. The parties to agreements and lending offers frequently have concise summaries of their transactions that contain a list of the material provisions of the agreements, even if the agreements themselves are very lengthy. A similar summary should allow the court and interested parties to understand the relief requested.

In addition to the concise statement, the rule requires that motions under subdivisions (c) and (d) state whether the movant is seeking approval of any of the provisions listed in subdivision (c)(1)(B), and where those provisions are located in the documents. The rule is intended to enhance the ability of the court and interested parties to find and evaluate those provisions.

The rule also provides that any motion for authority to obtain credit must identify any provision listed in subdivision (c)(1)(B)(i)–(xi) that is proposed to remain effective if the court grants the motion on an interim basis under Rule 4001(c)(2), but later denies final relief.

Other amendments are stylistic.

*Changes Made After Publication.*

1. The introductory language in subdivisions (b)(1)(B), (c)(1)(B), and (d)(1)(B) was revised to clarify that the motions filed under the rule can be either no more than five pages long or begin with a concise statement of that length. This permits the continued use of forms that have been effective in smaller cases. Subdivision (c)(1)(B) also is amended to require that the motion identify any provisionally approved term that would remain in effect even if the court denies the permanent relief requested.

2. A new subparagraph (c)(1)(B)(vi) was inserted into the rule and the remaining subparagraphs were renumbered accordingly. The new subparagraph requires that the motion identify any provisions setting deadlines for filing and confirming reorganization plans and disclosure statements.

3. Subdivisions (c)(1)(C) and (d)(1)(C) of the proposed rule were deleted as unnecessary. The court has whatever authority Rule 9024 provides, and making an explicit reference to that rule in these subdivisions brings unnecessary attention to Rule 9024 and could create a different standard of review under that rule than would apply in other instances. The Advisory Committee did not intend either consequence, so the subdivisions were deleted.

4. Subdivision (d)(1)(A) was restyled to form a vertical list of the motions subject to that provision.

COMMITTEE NOTES ON RULES—2009 AMENDMENT

The rule is amended to implement changes in connection with the amendment to Rule 9006(a) and the manner by which time is computed under the rules. The deadlines in the rule are amended to substitute a deadline that is a multiple of seven days. Throughout the rules, deadlines are amended in the following manner:

- 5-day periods become 7-day periods
- 10-day periods become 14-day periods
- 15-day periods become 14-day periods
- 20-day periods become 21-day periods
- 25-day periods become 28-day periods

## Rule 4002. Duties of Debtor

(a) IN GENERAL. In addition to performing other duties prescribed by the Code and rules, the debtor shall:

(1) attend and submit to an examination at the times ordered by the court;

(2) attend the hearing on a complaint objecting to discharge and testify, if called as a witness;

(3) inform the trustee immediately in writing as to the location of real property in which the debtor has an interest and the name and address of every person holding money or property subject to the debtor's withdrawal or order if a schedule of property has not yet been filed pursuant to Rule 1007;

(4) cooperate with the trustee in the preparation of an inventory, the examination of proofs of claim, and the administration of the estate; and

(5) file a statement of any change of the debtor's address.

(b) INDIVIDUAL DEBTOR'S DUTY TO PROVIDE DOCUMENTATION.

(1) *Personal Identification.* Every individual debtor shall bring to the meeting of creditors under § 341:

(A) a picture identification issued by a governmental unit, or other personal identifying information that establishes the debtor's identity; and

(B) evidence of social-security number(s), or a written statement that such documentation does not exist.

(2) *Financial Information.* Every individual debtor shall bring to the meeting of creditors under § 341, and make available to the trustee, the following documents or copies of them, or provide a written statement that the documentation does not exist or is not in the debtor's possession:

(A) evidence of current income such as the most recent payment advice;

(B) unless the trustee or the United States trustee instructs otherwise, statements for each of the debtor's depository and investment accounts, including checking, savings, and money market accounts, mutual funds and brokerage accounts for the time period that includes the date of the filing of the petition; and

(C) documentation of monthly expenses claimed by the debtor if required by § 707(b)(2)(A) or (B).

(3) *Tax Return.* At least 7 days before the first date set for the meeting of creditors under § 341, the debtor shall provide to the trustee a copy of the debtor's federal income tax return for the most recent tax year ending immediately before the commencement of the case and for which a return was filed, including any attachments, or a transcript of the tax return, or provide a written statement that the documentation does not exist.

(4) *Tax Returns Provided to Creditors.* If a creditor, at least 14 days before the first date set for the meeting of creditors under § 341, requests a copy of the debtor's tax return that is to be provided to the trustee under subdivision (b)(3), the debtor, at least 7 days before the first date set for the meeting of creditors under § 341, shall provide to the requesting creditor a copy of the return, including any attachments, or a transcript of the tax return, or provide a written statement that the documentation does not exist.

(5) *Confidentiality of Tax Information.* The debtor's obligation to provide tax returns under Rule 4002(b)(3) and (b)(4) is subject to procedures for safeguarding the confidentiality of tax information established by the Director of the Administrative Office of the United States Courts.

(As amended Mar. 30, 1987, eff. Aug. 1, 1987; Apr. 23, 2008, eff. Dec. 1 2008; Mar. 26, 2009, eff. Dec. 1, 2009.)

NOTES OF ADVISORY COMMITTEE ON RULES—1983

This rule should be read together with §§343 and 521 of the Code and Rule 1007, all of which impose duties on the debtor. Clause (3) of this rule implements the provisions of Rule 2015(a).

NOTES OF ADVISORY COMMITTEE ON RULES—1987 AMENDMENT

New clause (5) of the rule imposes on the debtor the duty to advise the clerk of any change of the debtor's address.

COMMITTEE NOTES ON RULES—2008 AMENDMENT

This rule is amended to implement §521(a)(1)(B)(iv) and (e)(2), added to the Code by the 2005 amendments. These Code amendments expressly require the debtor to file with the court, or provide to the trustee, specific documents. The amendments to the rule implement these obligations and establish a time frame for creditors to make requests for a copy of the debtor's Federal income tax return. The rule also requires the debtor to provide documentation in support of claimed expenses under §707(b)(2)(A) and (B).

Subdivision (b) of the rule is also amended to require the debtor to cooperate with the trustee by providing materials and documents necessary to assist the trustee in the performance of the trustee's duties. Nothing in the rule, however, is intended to limit or restrict the debtor's duties under §521, or to limit the access of the Attorney General to any information provided by the debtor in the case. Subdivision (b)(2) does not require that the debtor create documents or obtain documents from third parties; rather, the debtor's obligation is to bring to the meeting of creditors under §341 the documents which the debtor possesses. Under subdivision (b)(2)(B), the trustee or the United States trustee can instruct debtors that they need not provide the documents described in that subdivision. Under subdivisions (b)(3) and (b)(4), the debtor must obtain and provide copies of tax returns or tax transcripts to the appropriate person, unless no such documents exist. Any written statement that the debtor provides indicating either that documents do not exist or are not in the debtor's possession must be verified or contain an unsworn declaration as required under Rule 1008.

Because the amendment implements the debtor's duty to cooperate with the trustee, the materials provided to the trustee would not be made available to any other party in interest at the §341 meeting of creditors other than the Attorney General. Some of the documents may contain otherwise private information that should not be disseminated. For example, pay stubs and financial account statements might include the social-security numbers of the debtor and the debtor's spouse and dependents, as well as the names of the debtor's children. The debtor should redact all but the last four digits of all social-security numbers and the names of any minors when they appear in these documents. This type of information would not usually be needed by creditors and others who may be attending the meeting. If a creditor perceives a need to review specific documents or other evidence, the creditor may proceed under Rule 2004.

Tax information produced under this rule is subject to procedures for safeguarding confidentiality established by the Director of the Administrative Office of the United States Courts.

*Changes Made After Publication.* The second paragraph of the Committee Note was amended to clarify that the debtor's duty to provide copies of tax returns or tax transcripts are governed by a different standard than the debtor's duty to provide other financial information.

COMMITTEE NOTES ON RULES—2009 AMENDMENT

The rule is amended to implement changes in connection with the amendment to Rule 9006(a) and the manner by which time is computed under the rules. The deadline in the rule is amended to substitute a deadline that is a multiple of seven days. Throughout the rules, deadlines are amended in the following manner:

- 5-day periods become 7-day periods
- 10-day periods become 14-day periods
- 15-day periods become 14-day periods
- 20-day periods become 21-day periods
- 25-day periods become 28-day periods

## Rule 4003. Exemptions

(a) CLAIM OF EXEMPTIONS. A debtor shall list the property claimed as exempt under §522 of the Code on the schedule of assets required to be filed by Rule 1007. If the debtor fails to claim exemptions or file the schedule within the time specified in Rule 1007, a dependent of the debtor may file the list within 30 days thereafter.

(b) OBJECTING TO A CLAIM OF EXEMPTIONS.

(1) Except as provided in paragraphs (2) and (3), a party in interest may file an objection to the list of property claimed as exempt within 30 days after the meeting of creditors held under §341(a) is concluded or within 30 days after any amendment to the list or supplemental schedules is filed, whichever is later. The court may, for cause, extend the time for filing objections if, before the time to object expires, a party in interest files a request for an extension.

(2) The trustee may file an objection to a claim of exemption at any time prior to one year after the closing of the case if the debtor fraudulently asserted the claim of exemption. The trustee shall deliver or mail the objection to the debtor and the debtor's attorney, and to any person filing the list of exempt property and that person's attorney.

(3) An objection to a claim of exemption based on §522(q) shall be filed before the closing of the case. If an exemption is first claimed after a case is reopened, an objection shall be filed before the reopened case is closed.

(4) A copy of any objection shall be delivered or mailed to the trustee, the debtor and the debtor's attorney, and the person filing the list and that person's attorney.

(c) BURDEN OF PROOF. In any hearing under this rule, the objecting party has the burden of proving that the exemptions are not properly claimed. After hearing on notice, the court shall determine the issues presented by the objections.

(d) AVOIDANCE BY DEBTOR OF TRANSFERS OF EXEMPT PROPERTY. A proceeding by the debtor to avoid a lien or other transfer of property exempt under §522(f) of the Code shall be by motion in accordance with Rule 9014. Notwithstanding the provisions of subdivision (b), a creditor may object to a motion filed under §522(f) by challenging the validity of the exemption asserted to be impaired by the lien.

(As amended Mar. 30, 1987, eff. Aug. 1, 1987; Apr. 30, 1991, eff. Aug. 1, 1991; Apr. 17, 2000, eff. Dec. 1, 2000; Apr. 23, 2008, eff. Dec. 1, 2008.)

NOTES OF ADVISORY COMMITTEE ON RULES

This rule is derived from §522(1) of the Code and, in part, former Bankruptcy Rule 403. The Code changes the thrust of that rule by making it the burden of the debtor to list his exemptions and the burden of parties in interest to raise objections in the absence of which "the property claimed as exempt on such list is exempt;" § 522(1).

*Subdivision (a).* While § 522(1) refers to a list of property claimed as exempt, the rule incorporates such a list as part of Official Form No. 6, the schedule of the debtor's assets, rather than requiring a separate list and filing. Rule 1007, to which subdivision (a) refers, requires that schedule to be filed within 15 days after the order for relief, unless the court extends the time.

Section 522(1) also provides that a dependent of the debtor may file the list if the debtor fails to do so. Subdivision (a) of the rule allows such filing from the expiration of the debtor's time until 30 days thereafter. Dependent is defined in § 522(a)(1).

*Subdivision (d)* provides that a proceeding by the debtor, permitted by § 522(f) of the Code, is a contested matter rather than the more formal adversary proceeding. Proceedings within the scope of this subdivision are distinguished from proceedings brought by the trustee to avoid transfers. The latter are classified as adversary proceedings by Rule 7001.

NOTES OF ADVISORY COMMITTEE ON RULES—1991 AMENDMENT

*Subdivision (b)* is amended to facilitate the filing of objections to exemptions claimed on a supplemental schedule filed under Rule 1007(h).

COMMITTEE NOTES ON RULES—2000 AMENDMENT

This rule is amended to permit the court to grant a timely request for an extension of time to file objections to the list of claimed exemptions, whether the court rules on the request before or after the expiration of the 30-day period. The purpose of this amendment is to avoid the harshness of the present rule which has been construed to deprive a bankruptcy court of jurisdiction to grant a timely request for an extension if it has failed to rule on the request within the 30-day period. See *In re Laurain*, 113 F.3d 595 (6th Cir. 1997), *Matter of Stoulig*, 45 F.3d 957 (5th Cir. 1995), *In re Brayshaw*, 912 F.2d 1255 (10th Cir. 1990). The amendments clarify that the extension may be granted only for cause. The amendments also conform the rule to § 522(*l*) of the Code by recognizing that any party in interest may file an objection or request for an extension of time under this rule. Other amendments are stylistic.

*GAP Report on Rule 4003(b).* The words "trustee or creditor" were replaced by "party in interest" to conform to § 522(*l*) of the Bankruptcy Code which permits any party in interest to object to claimed exemptions. Style revisions also were made to the published draft.

COMMITTEE NOTES ON RULES—2008 AMENDMENT

Subdivision (b) is rewritten to include four paragraphs.

Subdivision (b)(2) is added to the rule to permit the trustee to object to an exemption at any time up to one year after the closing of the case if the debtor fraudulently claimed the exemption. Extending the deadline for trustees to object to an exemption when the exemption claim has been fraudulently made will permit the court to review and, in proper circumstances, deny improperly claimed exemptions, thereby protecting the legitimate interests of creditors and the bankruptcy estate. However, similar to the deadline set in § 727(e) of the Code for revoking a discharge which was fraudulently obtained, an objection to an exemption that was fraudulently claimed must be filed within one year after the closing of the case. Subdivision (b)(2) extends the objection deadline only for trustees.

Subdivision (b)(3) is added to the rule to reflect the addition of subsection (q) to § 522 of the Code by the 2005 Act. Section 522(q) imposes a $136,875 limit on a state homestead exemption if the debtor has been convicted of a felony or owes a debt arising from certain causes of action. Other revised provisions of the Code, such as § 727(a)(12) and § 1328(h), suggest that the court may consider issues relating to § 522(q) late in the case, and the 30-day period for objections would not be appropriate for this provision.

Subdivision (d) is amended to clarify that a creditor with a lien on property that the debtor is attempting to avoid on the grounds that the lien impairs an exemption may raise in defense to the lien avoidance action any objection to the debtor's claimed exemption. The right to object is limited to an objection to the exemption of the property subject to the lien and for purposes of the lien avoidance action only. The creditor may not object to other exemption claims made by the debtor. Those objections, if any, are governed by Rule 4003(b).

Other changes are stylistic.

*Changes Made After Publication.* The deadline for filing objections to exemptions under subdivision (b)(1) was returned to 30 days after the conclusion of the § 341 meeting of creditors rather than the 60 day period proposed in the published rule. The second paragraph of the Committee Note which discussed this change was therefore deleted. Subdivisions (b)(2) and (b)(3) were amended to add the debtor and the debtor's attorney to the list of persons to whom objections to exemptions must be delivered.

## Rule 4004. Grant or Denial of Discharge

(a) TIME FOR FILING COMPLAINT OBJECTING TO DISCHARGE; NOTICE OF TIME FIXED. In a chapter 7 liquidation case a complaint objecting to the debtor's discharge under § 727(a) of the Code shall be filed no later than 60 days after the first date set for the meeting of creditors under § 341(a). In a chapter 11 reorganization case, the complaint shall be filed no later than the first date set for the hearing on confirmation. At least 28 days' notice of the time so fixed shall be given to the United States trustee and all creditors as provided in Rule 2002(f) and (k) and to the trustee and the trustee's attorney.

(b) EXTENSION OF TIME. On motion of any party in interest, after hearing on notice, the court may for cause extend the time to file a complaint objecting to discharge. The motion shall be filed before the time has expired.

(c) GRANT OF DISCHARGE.

(1) In a chapter 7 case, on expiration of the time fixed for filing a complaint objecting to discharge and the time fixed for filing a motion to dismiss the case under Rule 1017(e), the court shall forthwith grant the discharge unless:

(A) the debtor is not an individual;

(B) a complaint objecting to the discharge has been filed;

(C) the debtor has filed a waiver under § 727(a)(10);

(D) a motion to dismiss the case under § 707 is pending;

(E) a motion to extend the time for filing a complaint objecting to the discharge is pending;

(F) a motion to extend the time for filing a motion to dismiss the case under Rule 1017(e)(1) is pending;

(G) the debtor has not paid in full the filing fee prescribed by 28 U.S.C. § 1930(a) and any other fee prescribed by the Judicial Conference of the United States under 28 U.S.C. § 1930(b) that is payable to the clerk upon the commencement of a case under the Code, unless the court has waived the fees under 28 U.S.C. § 1930(f);

(H) the debtor has not filed with the court a statement of completion of a course concerning personal financial management as required by Rule 1007(b)(7);

(I) a motion to delay or postpone discharge under §727(a)(12) is pending;

(J) a motion to enlarge the time to file a reaffirmation agreement under Rule 4008(a) is pending;

(K) a presumption has arisen under §524(m) that a reaffirmation agreement is an undue hardship; or

(L) a motion is pending to delay discharge, because the debtor has not filed with the court all tax documents required to be filed under §521(f).

(2) Notwithstanding Rule 4004(c)(1), on motion of the debtor, the court may defer the entry of an order granting a discharge for 30 days and, on motion within that period, the court may defer entry of the order to a date certain.

(3) If the debtor is required to file a statement under Rule 1007(b)(8), the court shall not grant a discharge earlier than 30 days after the statement is filed.

(d) APPLICABILITY OF RULES IN PART VII. A proceeding commenced by a complaint objecting to discharge is governed by Part VII of these rules.

(e) ORDER OF DISCHARGE. An order of discharge shall conform to the appropriate Official Form.

(f) REGISTRATION IN OTHER DISTRICTS. An order of discharge that has become final may be registered in any other district by filing a certified copy of the order in the office of the clerk of that district. When so registered the order of discharge shall have the same effect as an order of the court of the district where registered.

(g) NOTICE OF DISCHARGE. The clerk shall promptly mail a copy of the final order of discharge to those specified in subdivision (a) of this rule.

(As amended Mar. 30, 1987, eff. Aug. 1, 1987; Apr. 30, 1991, eff. Aug. 1, 1991; Apr. 23, 1996, eff. Dec. 1, 1996; Apr. 26, 1999, eff. Dec. 1, 1999; Apr. 17, 2000, eff. Dec. 1, 2000; Apr. 29, 2002, eff. Dec. 1, 2002; Apr. 23, 2008, eff. Dec. 1, 2008; Mar. 26, 2009, eff. Dec. 1, 2009.)

NOTES OF ADVISORY COMMITTEE ON RULES—1983

This rule is adapted from former Bankruptcy Rule 404.

*Subdivisions (a) and (b)* of this rule prescribe the procedure for determining whether a discharge will be granted pursuant to §727 of the Code. The time fixed by subdivision (a) may be enlarged as provided in subdivision (b).

The notice referred to in subdivision (a) is required to be given by mail and addressed to creditors as provided in Rule 2002.

An extension granted on a motion pursuant to subdivision (b) of the rule would ordinarily benefit only the movant, but its scope and effect would depend on the terms of the extension.

*Subdivision (c).* If a complaint objecting to discharge is filed, the court's grant or denial of the discharge will be entered at the conclusion of the proceeding as a judgment in accordance with Rule 9021. The inclusion of the clause in subdivision (c) qualifying the duty of the court to grant a discharge when a waiver has been filed is in accord with the construction of the Code. 4 Collier, *Bankruptcy* ¶727.12 (15th ed. 1979).

The last sentence of subdivision (c) takes cognizance of §524(c) of the Code which authorizes a debtor to enter into enforceable reaffirmation agreements only prior to entry of the order of discharge. Immediate entry of that order after expiration of the time fixed for filing complaints objecting to discharge may render it more difficult for a debtor to settle pending litigation to determine the dischargeability of a debt and execute a reaffirmation agreement as part of a settlement.

*Subdivision (d).* An objection to discharge is required to be made by a complaint, which initiates an adversary proceeding as provided in Rule 7003. Pursuant to Rule 5005, the complaint should be filed in the court in which the case is pending.

*Subdivision (e).* Official Form No. 27 to which subdivision (e) refers, includes notice of the effects of a discharge specified in §524(a) of the Code.

*Subdivision (f).* Registration may facilitate the enforcement of the order of discharge in a district other than that in which it was entered. See 2 Moore's *Federal Practice* ¶1.04[2] (2d ed. 1967). Because of the nationwide service of process authorized by Rule 7004, however, registration of the order of discharge is not necessary under these rules to enable a discharged debtor to obtain relief against a creditor proceeding anywhere in the United States in disregard of the injunctive provisions of the order of discharge.

*Subdivision (g).* Notice of discharge should be mailed promptly after the order becomes final so that creditors may be informed of entry of the order and of its injunctive provisions. Rule 2002 specifies the manner of the notice and persons to whom the notice is to be given.

NOTES OF ADVISORY COMMITTEE ON RULES—1991 AMENDMENT

This rule is amended to conform to §727(c) which gives the United States trustee the right to object to discharge. This amendment is derived from Rule X-1008(a)(1) and is consistent with Rule 2002. The amendment to subdivision (c) is to prevent a timely motion to dismiss a chapter 7 case for substantial abuse from becoming moot merely because a discharge order has been entered. Reference to the Official Form number in subdivision (e) is deleted in anticipation of future revision and renumbering of the Official Forms.

NOTES OF ADVISORY COMMITTEE ON RULES—1996 AMENDMENT

*Subsection (c)* is amended to delay entry of the order of discharge if a motion pursuant to Rule 4004(b) to extend the time for filing a complaint objecting to discharge is pending. Also, this subdivision is amended to delay entry of the discharge order if the debtor has not paid in full the filing fee and the administrative fee required to be paid upon the commencement of the case. If the debtor is authorized to pay the fees in installments in accordance with Rule 1006, the discharge order will not be entered until the final installment has been paid.

The other amendments to this rule are stylistic.

*GAP Report on Rule 4004.* No changes have been made since publication, except for stylistic changes.

COMMITTEE NOTES ON RULES—1999 AMENDMENT

*Subdivision (a)* is amended to clarify that, in a chapter 7 case, the deadline for filing a complaint objecting to discharge under §727(a) is 60 days after the first date set for the meeting of creditors, whether or not the meeting is held on that date. The time for filing the complaint is not affected by any delay in the commencement or conclusion of the meeting of creditors. This amendment does not affect the right of any party in interest to file a motion for an extension of time to file a complaint objecting to discharge in accordance with Rule 4004(b).

The substitution of the word "filed" for "made" in subdivision (b) is intended to avoid confusion regarding the time when a motion is "made" for the purpose of applying these rules. *See, e.g., In re Coggin*, 30 F.3d 1443 (11th Cir. 1994). As amended, this rule requires that a motion for an extension of time for filing a complaint objecting to discharge be *filed* before the time has expired.

Other amendments to this rule are stylistic.

*GAP Report on Rule 4004.* No changes since publication.

COMMITTEE NOTES ON RULES—2000 AMENDMENT

*Subdivision (c)* is amended so that a discharge will not be granted while a motion requesting an extension of time to file a motion to dismiss the case under § 707(b) is pending. Other amendments are stylistic.

*GAP Report on Rule 4004(c).* No changes since publication except for style revisions.

COMMITTEE NOTES ON RULES—2002 AMENDMENT

*Subdivision (c)(1)(D)* is amended to provide that the filing of a motion to dismiss under § 707 of the Bankruptcy Code postpones the entry of the discharge. Under the present version of the rule, only motions to dismiss brought under § 707(b) cause the postponement of the discharge. This amendment would change the result in cases such as *In re Tanenbaum*, 210 B.R. 182 (Bankr. D. Colo. 1997).

*Changes Made After Publication and Comments.* No changes were made.

COMMITTEE NOTES ON RULES—2008 AMENDMENT

Subdivision (c)(1)(G) is amended to reflect the fee waiver provision in 28 U.S.C. § 1930, added by the 2005 amendments.

Subdivision (c)(1)(H) is new. It reflects the 2005 addition to the Code of §§ 727(a)(11) and 1328(g), which require that individual debtors complete a course in personal financial management as a condition to the entry of a discharge. Including this requirement in the rule helps prevent the inadvertent entry of a discharge when the debtor has not complied with this requirement. If a debtor fails to file the required statement regarding a personal financial management course, the clerk will close the bankruptcy case without the entry of a discharge.

Subdivision (c)(1)(I) is new. It reflects the 2005 addition to the Code of § 727(a)(12). This provision is linked to § 522(q). Section 522(q) limits the availability of the homestead exemption for individuals who have been convicted of a felony or who owe a debt arising from certain causes of action within a particular time frame. The existence of reasonable cause to believe that § 522(q) may be applicable to the debtor constitutes grounds for withholding the discharge.

Subdivision (c)(1)(J) is new. It accommodates the deadline for filing a reaffirmation agreement established by Rule 4008(a).

Subdivision (c)(1)(K) is new. It reflects the 2005 revisions to § 524 of the Code that alter the requirements for approval of reaffirmation agreements. Section 524(m) sets forth circumstances under which a reaffirmation agreement is presumed to be an undue hardship. This triggers an obligation to review the presumption and may require notice and a hearing. Subdivision (c)(1)(J) has been added to prevent the discharge from being entered until the court approves or disapproves the reaffirmation agreement in accordance with § 524(m).

Subdivision (c)(1)(L) is new. It implements § 1228(a) of Public Law Number 109–8, an uncodified provision of the Bankruptcy Abuse Prevention and Consumer Protection Act of 2005, which prohibits entry of a discharge unless required tax documents have been provided to the court.

Subdivision (c)(3) is new. It postpones the entry of the discharge of an individual debtor in a case under chapter 11, 12, or 13 if there is a question as to the applicability of § 522(q) of the Code. The postponement provides an opportunity for a creditor to file a motion to limit the debtor's exemption under that provision.

Other changes are stylistic.

*Changes Made After Publication.* No changes were made after publication.

COMMITTEE NOTES ON RULES—2009 AMENDMENT

The rule is amended to implement changes in connection with the amendment to Rule 9006(a) and the manner by which time is computed under the rules. The deadline in the rule is amended to substitute a deadline that is a multiple of seven days. Throughout the rules, deadlines are amended in the following manner:

- 5-day periods become 7-day periods
- 10-day periods become 14-day periods
- 15-day periods become 14-day periods
- 20-day periods become 21-day periods
- 25-day periods become 28-day periods

## Rule 4005. Burden of Proof in Objecting to Discharge

At the trial on a complaint objecting to a discharge, the plaintiff has the burden of proving the objection.

(As amended Mar. 30, 1987, eff. Aug. 1, 1987.)

NOTES OF ADVISORY COMMITTEE ON RULES—1983

This rule does not address the burden of going forward with the evidence. Subject to the allocation by the rule of the initial burden of producing evidence and the ultimate burden of persuasion, the rule leaves to the courts the formulation of rules governing the shift of the burden of going forward with the evidence in the light of considerations such as the difficulty of proving the nonexistence of a fact and of establishing a fact as to which the evidence is likely to be more accessible to the debtor than to the objector. *See, e.g., In re Haggerty*, 165 F.2d 977, 979–80 (2d Cir. 1948); *Federal Provision Co. v. Ershowsky*, 94 F.2d 574, 575 (2d Cir. 1938); *In re Riceputo*, 41 F. Supp. 926, 927–28 (E.D.N.Y. 1941).

## Rule 4006. Notice of No Discharge

If an order is entered: denying a discharge; revoking a discharge; approving a waiver of discharge; or, in the case of an individual debtor, closing the case without the entry of a discharge, the clerk shall promptly notify all parties in interest in the manner provided by Rule 2002.

(As amended Mar. 30, 1987, eff. Aug. 1, 1987; Apr. 23, 2008, eff. Dec. 1, 2008.)

NOTES OF ADVISORY COMMITTEE ON RULES—1983

The suspension by § 108(c) of the Code of the statute of limitations affecting any debt of a debtor terminates within 30 days after the debtor is denied a discharge or otherwise loses his right to a discharge. If, however, a debtor's failure to receive a discharge does not come to the attention of his creditors until after the statutes of limitations have run, the debtor obtains substantially the same benefits from his bankruptcy as a debtor who is discharged.

This rule requires the clerk to notify creditors if a debtor fails to obtain a discharge because a waiver of discharge was filed under § 727(a)(10) or as a result of an order denying or revoking the discharge under § 727(a) or (d).

COMMITTEE NOTES ON RULES—2008 AMENDMENT

This amendment was necessary because the 2005 amendments to the Code require that individual debtors in a chapter 7 or 13 case complete a course in personal financial management as a condition to the entry of a discharge. If the debtor fails to complete the course, the case may be closed and no discharge will be entered. Reopening the case is governed by § 350 and Rule 5010. The rule is amended to provide notice to parties in interest, including the debtor, that no discharge was entered.

*Changes Made After Publication.* No changes were made after publication.

## Rule 4007. Determination of Dischargeability of a Debt

(a) PERSONS ENTITLED TO FILE COMPLAINT. A debtor or any creditor may file a complaint to obtain a determination of the dischargeability of any debt.

(b) TIME FOR COMMENCING PROCEEDING OTHER THAN UNDER §523(c) OF THE CODE. A complaint other than under §523(c) may be filed at any time. A case may be reopened without payment of an additional filing fee for the purpose of filing a complaint to obtain a determination under this rule.

(c) TIME FOR FILING COMPLAINT UNDER §523(c) IN A CHAPTER 7 LIQUIDATION, CHAPTER 11 REORGANIZATION, CHAPTER 12 FAMILY FARMER'S DEBT ADJUSTMENT CASE, OR CHAPTER 13 INDIVIDUAL'S DEBT ADJUSTMENT CASE; NOTICE OF TIME FIXED. Except as otherwise provided in subdivision (d), a complaint to determine the dischargeability of a debt under §523(c) shall be filed no later than 60 days after the first date set for the meeting of creditors under §341(a). The court shall give all creditors no less than 30 days' notice of the time so fixed in the manner provided in Rule 2002. On motion of a party in interest, after hearing on notice, the court may for cause extend the time fixed under this subdivision. The motion shall be filed before the time has expired.

(d) TIME FOR FILING COMPLAINT UNDER §523(a)(6) IN A CHAPTER 13 INDIVIDUAL'S DEBT ADJUSTMENT CASE; NOTICE OF TIME FIXED. On motion by a debtor for a discharge under §1328(b), the court shall enter an order fixing the time to file a complaint to determine the dischargeability of any debt under §523(a)(6) and shall give no less than 30 days' notice of the time fixed to all creditors in the manner provided in Rule 2002. On motion of any party in interest, after hearing on notice, the court may for cause extend the time fixed under this subdivision. The motion shall be filed before the time has expired.

(e) APPLICABILITY OF RULES IN PART VII. A proceeding commenced by a complaint filed under this rule is governed by Part VII of these rules.

(As amended Mar. 30, 1987, eff. Aug. 1, 1987; Apr. 30, 1991, eff. Aug. 1, 1991; Apr. 26, 1999, eff. Dec. 1, 1999; Apr. 23, 2008, eff. Dec. 1, 2008.)

NOTES OF ADVISORY COMMITTEE ON RULES—1983

This rule prescribes the procedure to be followed when a party requests the court to determine dischargeability of a debt pursuant to §523 of the Code.

Although a complaint that comes within §523(c) must ordinarily be filed before determining whether the debtor will be discharged, the court need not determine the issues presented by the complaint filed under this rule until the question of discharge has been determined under Rule 4004. A complaint filed under this rule initiates an adversary proceeding as provided in Rule 7003.

*Subdivision (b)* does not contain a time limit for filing a complaint to determine the dischargeability of a type of debt listed as nondischargeable under §523(a)(1), (3), (5), (7), (8), or (9). Jurisdiction over this issue on these debts is held concurrently by the bankruptcy court and any appropriate nonbankruptcy forum.

*Subdivision (c)* differs from subdivision (b) by imposing a deadline for filing complaints to determine the issue of dischargeability of debts set out in §523(a)(2), (4) or (6) of the Code. The bankruptcy court has exclusive jurisdiction to determine dischargeability of these debts. If a complaint is not timely filed, the debt is discharged. See §523(c).

*Subdivision (e).* The complaint required by this subdivision should be filed in the court in which the case is pending pursuant to Rule 5005.

NOTES OF ADVISORY COMMITTEE ON RULES—1991 AMENDMENT

*Subdivision (a)* is amended to delete the words "with the court" as unnecessary. See Rules 5005(a) and 9001(3).

*Subdivision (c)* is amended to apply in chapter 12 cases the same time period that applies in chapter 7 and 11 cases for filing a complaint under §523(c) of the Code to determine dischargeability of certain debts. Under §1228(a) of the Code, a chapter 12 discharge does not discharge the debts specified in §523(a) of the Code.

COMMITTEE NOTES ON RULES—1999 AMENDMENT

*Subdivision (c)* is amended to clarify that the deadline for filing a complaint to determine the dischargeability of a debt under §523(c) of the Code is 60 days after the first date set for the meeting of creditors, whether or not the meeting is held on that date. The time for filing the complaint is not affected by any delay in the commencement or conclusion of the meeting of creditors. This amendment does not affect the right of any party in interest to file a motion for an extension of time to file a complaint to determine the dischargeability of a debt in accordance with this rule.

The substitution of the word "filed" for "made" in the final sentences of subdivisions (c) and (d) is intended to avoid confusion regarding the time when a motion is "made" for the purpose of applying these rules. *See, e.g., In re Coggin*, 30 F.3d 1443 (11th Cir. 1994). As amended, these subdivisions require that a motion for an extension of time be *filed* before the time has expired.

The other amendments to this rule are stylistic.

*GAP Report on Rule 4007.* No changes since publication, except for stylistic changes in the heading of Rule 4007(d).

COMMITTEE NOTES ON RULES—2008 AMENDMENT

Subdivision (c) is amended because of the 2005 amendments to §1328(a) of the Code. This revision expands the exceptions to discharge upon completion of a chapter 13 plan. Subdivision (c) extends to chapter 13 the same time limits applicable to other chapters of the Code with respect to the two exceptions to discharge that have been added to §1328(a) and that are within §523(c).

The amendment to subdivision (d) reflects the 2005 amendments to §1328(a) that expands the exceptions to discharge upon completion of a chapter 13 plan, including two out of three of the provisions that fall within §523(c). However, the 2005 revisions to §1328(a) do not include a reference to §523(a)(6), which is the third provision to which §523(c) refers. Thus, subdivision (d) is now limited to that provision.

*Changes Made After Publication.* No changes were made after publication.

## Rule 4008. Filing of Reaffirmation Agreement; Statement in Support of Reaffirmation Agreement

(a) FILING OF REAFFIRMATION AGREEMENT reaffirmation agreement shall be filed no later than 60 days after the first date set for the meeting of creditors under §341(a) of the Code. The reaffirmation agreement shall be accompanied by a cover sheet, prepared as prescribed by the appropriate Official Form. The court may, at any time and in its discretion, enlarge the time to file a reaffirmation agreement.

(b) STATEMENT IN SUPPORT OF REAFFIRMATION AGREEMENT. The debtor's statement required under §524(k)(6)(A) of the Code shall be accompanied by a statement of the total income and expenses stated on schedules I and J. If there is a difference between the total income and expenses stated on those schedules and the statement required under §524(k)(6)(A), the statement required by this subdivision shall include an explanation of the difference.

(As amended Apr. 30, 1991, eff. Aug. 1, 1991; Apr. 23, 2008, eff. Dec. 1, 2008; Mar. 26, 2009, eff. Dec. 1, 2009.)

NOTES OF ADVISORY COMMITTEE ON RULES—1983

Section 524(d) of the Code requires the court to hold a hearing to inform an individual debtor concerning the granting or denial of discharge and the law applicable to reaffirmation agreements.

The notice of the §524(d) hearing may be combined with the notice of the meeting of creditors or entered as a separate order.

The expression "not more than" contained in the first sentence of the rule is for the explicit purpose of requiring the hearing to occur within that time period and cannot be extended.

NOTES OF ADVISORY COMMITTEE ON RULES—1991 AMENDMENT

This rule is changed to conform to §524(d) of the Code as amended in 1986. A hearing under §524(d) is not mandatory unless the debtor desires to enter into a reaffirmation agreement.

COMMITTEE NOTES ON RULES—2008 AMENDMENT

This rule is amended to establish a deadline for filing reaffirmation agreements. The Code sets out a number of prerequisites to the enforceability of reaffirmation agreements. Among those requirements, §524(k)(6)(A) provides that each reaffirmation agreement must be accompanied by a statement indicating the debtor's ability to make the payments called for by the agreement. In the event that this statement reflects an insufficient income to allow payment of the reaffirmed debt, §524(m) provides that a presumption of undue hardship arises, allowing the court to disapprove the reaffirmation agreement, but only after a hearing conducted prior to the entry of discharge. Rule 4004(c)(1)(K) accommodates this provision by delaying the entry of discharge where a presumption of undue hardship arises. However, in order for that rule to be effective, the reaffirmation agreement itself must be filed before the entry of discharge. Under Rule 4004(c)(1) discharge is to be entered promptly after the expiration of the time for filing a complaint objecting to discharge, which, under Rule 4004(a), is 60 days after the first date set for the meeting of creditors under §341(a). Accordingly, that date is set as the deadline for filing a reaffirmation agreement.

Any party may file the agreement with the court. Thus, whichever party has a greater incentive to enforce the agreement usually will file it. In the event that the parties are unable to file a reaffirmation agreement in a timely fashion, the rule grants the court broad discretion to permit a late filing. A corresponding change to Rule 4004(c)(1)(J) accommodates such an extension by providing for a delay in the entry of discharge during the pendency of a motion to extend the time for filing a reaffirmation agreement.

Rule 4008 is also amended by deleting provisions regarding the timing of any reaffirmation and discharge hearing. As noted above, §524(m) itself requires that hearings on undue hardship be conducted prior to the entry of discharge. In other respects, including hearings to approve reaffirmation agreements of unrepresented debtors under §524(c)(6), the rule leaves discretion to the court to set the hearing at a time appropriate for the particular circumstances presented in the case and consistent with the scheduling needs of the parties.

*Changes Made After Publication.* The only change was stylistic. The phrase "of the Code" was added to subdivision (b).

COMMITTEE NOTES ON RULES—2009 AMENDMENT

Subdivision (a) of the rule is amended to require that the entity filing the reaffirmation agreement with the court also include Official Form 27, the Reaffirmation Agreement Cover Sheet. The form includes information necessary for the court to determine whether the proposed reaffirmation agreement is presumed to be an undue hardship for the debtor under §524(m) of the Code.

*Changes Made After Publication.* No changes since publication.

## PART V—COURTS AND CLERKS

### Rule 5001. Courts and Clerks' Offices

(a) COURTS ALWAYS OPEN. The courts shall be deemed always open for the purpose of filing any pleading or other proper paper, issuing and returning process, and filing, making, or entering motions, orders and rules.

(b) TRIALS AND HEARINGS; ORDERS IN CHAMBERS. All trials and hearings shall be conducted in open court and so far as convenient in a regular court room. Except as otherwise provided in 28 U.S.C. §152(c), all other acts or proceedings may be done or conducted by a judge in chambers and at any place either within or without the district; but no hearing, other than one ex parte, shall be conducted outside the district without the consent of all parties affected thereby.

(c) CLERK'S OFFICE. The clerk's office with the clerk or a deputy in attendance shall be open during business hours on all days except Saturdays, Sundays and the legal holidays listed in Rule 9006(a).

(As amended Mar. 30, 1987, eff. Aug. 1, 1987; Apr. 30, 1991, eff. Aug. 1, 1991; Apr. 23, 2008, eff. Dec. 1, 2008.)

NOTES OF ADVISORY COMMITTEE ON RULES—1983

This rule is adapted from subdivisions (a), (b) and (c) of Rule 77 F.R.Civ.P.

NOTES OF ADVISORY COMMITTEE ON RULES—1987 AMENDMENT

Rule 9001, as amended, defines court to mean the bankruptcy judge or district judge before whom a case or proceeding is pending. Clerk means the bankruptcy clerk, if one has been appointed for the district; if a bankruptcy clerk has not been appointed, clerk means clerk of the district court.

NOTES OF ADVISORY COMMITTEE ON RULES—1991 AMENDMENT

*Subdivision (c)* is amended to refer to Rule 9006(a) for a list of legal holidays. Reference to F.R.Civ.P. is not necessary for this purpose.

COMMITTEE NOTES ON RULES—2008 AMENDMENT

The rule is amended to permit bankruptcy judges to hold hearings outside of the district in which the case is pending to the extent that the circumstances lead to the authorization of the court to take such action under the 2005 amendment to 28 U.S.C. §152(c). Under that provision, bankruptcy judges may hold court outside of their districts in emergency situations and when the business of the court otherwise so requires. This amendment to the rule is intended to implement the legislation.

*Changes Made After Publication.* No changes were made after publication.

## Rule 5002. Restrictions on Approval of Appointments

(a) APPROVAL OF APPOINTMENT OF RELATIVES PROHIBITED. The appointment of an individual as a trustee or examiner pursuant to §1104 of the Code shall not be approved by the court if the individual is a relative of the bankruptcy judge approving the appointment or the United States trustee in the region in which the case is pending. The employment of an individual as an attorney, accountant, appraiser, auctioneer, or other professional person pursuant to §§327, 1103, or 1114 shall not be approved by the court if the individual is a relative of the bankruptcy judge approving the employment. The employment of an individual as attorney, accountant, appraiser, auctioneer, or other professional person pursuant to §§327, 1103, or 1114 may be approved by the court if the individual is a relative of the United States trustee in the region in which the case is pending, unless the court finds that the relationship with the United States trustee renders the employment improper under the circumstances of the case. Whenever under this subdivision an individual may not be approved for appointment or employment, the individual's firm, partnership, corporation, or any other form of business association or relationship, and all members, associates and professional employees thereof also may not be approved for appointment or employment.

(b) JUDICIAL DETERMINATION THAT APPROVAL OF APPOINTMENT OR EMPLOYMENT IS IMPROPER. A bankruptcy judge may not approve the appointment of a person as a trustee or examiner pursuant to §1104 of the Code or approve the employment of a person as an attorney, accountant, appraiser, auctioneer, or other professional person pursuant to §§327, 1103, or 1114 of the Code if that person is or has been so connected with such judge or the United States trustee as to render the appointment or employment improper.

(As amended Apr. 29, 1985, eff. Aug. 1, 1985; Apr. 30, 1991, eff. Aug. 1, 1991.)

NOTES OF ADVISORY COMMITTEE ON RULES—1983

This rule is adapted from former Bankruptcy Rule 505(a). The scope of the prohibition on appointment or employment is expanded to include an examiner appointed under §1104 of the Code and attorneys and other professional persons whose employment must be approved by the court under §327 or §1103.

The rule supplements two statutory provisions. Under 18 U.S.C. §1910, it is a criminal offense for a judge to appoint a relative as a trustee and, under 28 U.S.C. §458, a person may not be "appointed to or employed in any office or duty in any court" if he is a relative of any judge of that court. The rule prohibits the appointment or employment of a relative of a bankruptcy judge in a case pending before that bankruptcy judge or before other bankruptcy judges sitting within the district.

A relative is defined in §101(34) of the Code to be an "individual related by affinity or consanguinity within the third degree as determined by the common law, or individual in a step or adoptive relationship within such third degree." Persons within the third degree under the common law system are as follows: first degree—parents, brothers and sisters, and children; second degree—grandparents, uncles and aunts, first cousins, nephews and nieces, and grandchildren; third degree—great grandparents, great uncles and aunts, first cousins once removed, second cousins, grand nephews and nieces, great grandchildren. Rule 9001 incorporates the definitions of §101 of the Code.

In order for the policy of this rule to be meaningfully implemented, it is necessary to extend the prohibition against appointment or employment to the firm or other business association of the ineligible person and to those affiliated with the firm or business association. "Firm" is defined in Rule 9001 to include a professional partnership or corporation of attorneys or accountants. All other types of business and professional associations and relationships are covered by this rule.

NOTES OF ADVISORY COMMITTEE ON RULES—1985 AMENDMENT

The amended rule is divided into two subdivisions. Subdivision (a) applies to relatives of bankruptcy judges and subdivision (b) applies to persons who are or have been connected with bankruptcy judges. Subdivision (a) permits no judicial discretion; subdivision (b) allows judicial discretion. In both subdivisions of the amended rule "bankruptcy judge" has been substituted for "judge". The amended rule makes clear that it only applies to relatives of, or persons connected with, the bankruptcy judge. See *In re Hilltop Sand and Gravel, Inc.*, 35 B.R. 412 (N.D. Ohio 1983).

*Subdivision (a).* The original rule prohibited all bankruptcy judges in a district from appointing or approving the employment of (i) a relative of any bankruptcy judge serving in the district, (ii) the firm or business association of any ineligible relative and (iii) any member or professional employee of the firm or business association of an ineligible relative. In addition, the definition of relative, the third degree relationship under the common law, is quite broad. The restriction on the employment opportunities of relatives of bankruptcy judges was magnified by the fact that many law and accounting firms have practices and offices spanning the nation.

Relatives are not eligible for appointment or employment when the bankruptcy judge to whom they are related makes the appointment or approves the employment. Canon 3(b)(4) of the Code of Judicial Conduct, which provides that the judge "shall exercise his power of appointment only on the basis of merit, avoiding nepotism and favoritism," should guide a bankruptcy judge when a relative of a judge of the same bankruptcy court is considered for appointment or employment.

*Subdivision (b),* derived from clause (2) of the original rule, makes a person ineligible for appointment or employment if the person is so connected with a bankruptcy judge making the appointment or approving the employment as to render the appointment or approval of employment improper. The caption and text of the subdivision emphasize that application of the connection test is committed to the sound discretion of the bankruptcy judge who is to make the appointment or approve the employment. All relevant circumstances are to be taken into account by the court. The most important of those circumstances include: the nature and duration of the connection with the bankruptcy judge; whether the connection still exists, and, if not, when it was terminated; and the type of appointment or employment. These and other considerations must be carefully evaluated by the bankruptcy judge.

The policy underlying subdivision (b) is essentially the same as the policy embodied in the Code of Judicial Conduct. Canon 2 of the Code of Judicial Conduct instructs a judge to avoid impropriety and the appearance of impropriety, and Canon 3(b)(4) provides that the judge "should exercise his power of appointment only on the basis of merit, avoiding nepotism and favoritism." Subdivision (b) alerts the potential appointee or employee and party seeking approval of employment to consider the possible relevance or impact of subdivision (b) and indicates to them that appropriate disclosure must be made to the bankruptcy court before accepting appointment or employment. The information required may be made a part of the application for approval of employment. See Rule 2014(a).

Subdivision (b) departs from the former rule in an important respect: a firm or business association is not prohibited from appointment or employment merely because an individual member or employee of the firm or business association is ineligible under subdivision (b).

The emphasis given to the bankruptcy court's judicial discretion in applying subdivision (b) and the absence of a *per se* extension of ineligibility to the firm or business association or any ineligible individual complement the amendments to subdivision (a). The change is intended to moderate the prior limitation on the employment opportunities of attorneys, accountants and other professional persons who are or who have been connected in some way with the bankruptcy judge. For example, in all but the most unusual situations service as a law clerk to a bankruptcy judge is not the type of connection which alone precludes appointment or employment. Even if a bankruptcy judge determines that it is improper to appoint or approve the employment of a former law clerk in the period immediately after completion of the former law clerk's service with the judge, the firm which employs the former law clerk will, absent other circumstances, be eligible for employment. In each instance all the facts must be considered by the bankruptcy judge.

Subdivision (b) applies to persons connected with a bankruptcy judge. "Person" is defined in §101 of the Bankruptcy Code to include an "individual, partnership and corporation". A partnership or corporation may be appointed or employed to serve in a bankruptcy case. If a bankruptcy judge is connected in some way with a partnership or corporation, it is necessary for the court to determine whether the appointment or employment of that partnership or corporation is proper.

The amended rule does not regulate professional relationships which do not require approval of a bankruptcy judge. Disqualification of the bankruptcy judge pursuant to 28 U.S.C. §455 may, however, be appropriate. Under Rule 5004(a), a bankruptcy judge may find that disqualification from only some aspect of the case, rather than the entire case, is necessary. A situation may also arise in which the disqualifying circumstance only comes to light after services have been performed. Rule 5004(b) provides that if compensation from the estate is sought for these services, the bankruptcy judge is disqualified from awarding compensation.

NOTES OF ADVISORY COMMITTEE ON RULES—1991 AMENDMENT

The 1986 amendments to the Code provide that the United States trustee shall appoint trustees in chapter 7, chapter 12, and chapter 13 cases without the necessity of court approval. This rule is not intended to apply to the appointment of trustees in those cases because it would be inappropriate for a court rule to restrict in advance the exercise of discretion by the executive branch. See Committee Note to Rule 2009.

In chapter 11 cases, a trustee or examiner is appointed by the United States trustee after consultation with parties in interest and subject to court approval. Subdivision (a), as amended, prohibits the approval of the appointment of an individual as a trustee or examiner if the person is a relative of the United States trustee making the appointment or the bankruptcy judge approving the appointment.

The United States trustee neither appoints nor approves the employment of professional persons employed pursuant to §§327, 1103, or 1114 of the Code. Therefore, subdivision (a) is not a prohibition against judicial approval of employment of a professional person who is a relative of the United States trustee. However, the United States trustee monitors applications for compensation and reimbursement of expenses and may raise, appear and be heard on issues in the case. Employment of relatives of the United States trustee may be approved unless the court finds, after considering the relationship and the particular circumstances of the case, that the relationship would cause the employment to be improper. As used in this rule, "improper" includes the appearance of impropriety.

United States trustee is defined to include a designee or assistant United States trustee. See Rule 9001. Therefore, subdivision (a) is applicable if the person appointed as trustee or examiner or the professional to be employed is a relative of a designee of the United States trustee or any assistant United States trustee in the region in which the case is pending.

This rule is not exclusive of other laws or rules regulating ethical conduct. See, e.g., 28 CFR §45.735-5.

## Rule 5003. Records Kept By the Clerk

(a) BANKRUPTCY DOCKETS. The clerk shall keep a docket in each case under the Code and shall enter thereon each judgment, order, and activity in that case as prescribed by the Director of the Administrative Office of the United States Courts. The entry of a judgment or order in a docket shall show the date the entry is made.

(b) CLAIMS REGISTER. The clerk shall keep in a claims register a list of claims filed in a case when it appears that there will be a distribution to unsecured creditors.

(c) JUDGMENTS AND ORDERS. The clerk shall keep, in the form and manner as the Director of the Administrative Office of the United States Courts may prescribe, a correct copy of every final judgment or order affecting title to or lien on real property or for the recovery of money or property, and any other order which the court may direct to be kept. On request of the prevailing party, a correct copy of every judgment or order affecting title to or lien upon real or personal property or for the recovery of money or property shall be kept and indexed with the civil judgments of the district court.

(d) INDEX OF CASES; CERTIFICATE OF SEARCH. The clerk shall keep indices of all cases and adversary proceedings as prescribed by the Director of the Administrative Office of the United States Courts. On request, the clerk shall make a search of any index and papers in the clerk's custody and certify whether a case or proceeding has been filed in or transferred to the court or if a discharge has been entered in its records.

(e) REGISTER OF MAILING ADDRESSES OF F ERAL AND STATE GOVERNMENTAL UNITS AND C TAIN TAXING AUTHORITIES. The United States or the state or territory in which the court is located may file a statement designating its mailing address. The United States, state, territory, or local governmental unit responsible for collecting taxes within the district in which the case is pending may also file a statement designating an address for service of requests under §505(b) of the Code, and the designation shall describe where further information concerning additional requirements for filing such requests may be found. The clerk shall keep, in the form and manner as the Director of the Administrative Office of the United States Courts may prescribe, a register that includes the mailing addresses designated under the first sentence of this subdivision, and a separate register of the addresses designated for the service of requests under §505(b) of the Code. The clerk is not required to include in any single register more than one mailing address for each department, agency, or instrumentality of the United States or the state or territory. If more than one address for a department, agency, or instrumentality is included in the register, the clerk shall also include information that would enable a user of the register to determine the circumstances when each address is applicable, and mailing notice to only one applicable address is sufficient to provide effective notice. The clerk shall update the register annually, effective January 2 of each year. The mailing address in the register is conclusively presumed to be a proper address for the governmental unit, but the failure to use that mailing address does not invalidate any notice that is otherwise effective under applicable law.

(f) OTHER BOOKS AND RECORDS OF THE CLERK. The clerk shall keep any other books and records required by the Director of the Administrative Office of the United States Courts.

(As amended Mar. 30, 1987, eff. Aug. 1, 1987; Apr. 17, 2000, eff. Dec. 1, 2000; Apr. 23, 2008, eff. Dec. 1, 2008.)

NOTES OF ADVISORY COMMITTEE ON RULES—1983

This rule consolidates former Bankruptcy Rules 504 and 507. The record-keeping duties of the referee under former Bankruptcy Rule 504 are transferred to the clerk. Subdivisions (a), (c), (d) and (e) are similar to subdivisions (a)–(d) of Rule 79 F.R.Civ.P.

*Subdivision (b)* requires that filed claims be listed on a claims register only when there may be a distribution to unsecured creditors. Compilation of the list for no asset or nominal asset cases would serve no purpose.

Rule 2013 requires the clerk to maintain a public record of fees paid from the estate and an annual summary thereof.

Former Bankruptcy Rules 507(d) and 508, which made materials in the clerk's office and files available to the public, are not necessary because § 107 of the Code guarantees public access to files and dockets of cases under the Code.

NOTES OF ADVISORY COMMITTEE ON RULES—1987 AMENDMENT

*Subdivision (a)* has been made more specific.

*Subdivision (c)* is amended to require that on the request of the prevailing party the clerk of the district court shall keep and index bankruptcy judgments and orders affecting title to or lien upon real or personal property or for the recovery of money or property with the civil judgments of the district court. This requirement is derived from former Rule 9021(b). The Director of the Administrative Office will provide guidance to the bankruptcy and district court clerks regarding appropriate paperwork and retention procedures.

COMMITTEE NOTES ON RULES—2000 AMENDMENT

*Subdivision (e)* is added to provide a source where debtors, their attorneys, and other parties may go to determine whether the United States or the state or territory in which the court is located has filed a statement designating a mailing address for notice purposes. By using the address in the register—which must be available to the public—the sender is assured that the mailing address is proper. But the use of an address that differs from the address included in the register does not invalidate the notice if it is otherwise effective under applicable law.

The register may include a separate mailing address for each department, agency, or instrumentality of the United States or the state or territory. This rule does not require that addresses of municipalities or other local governmental units be included in the register, but the clerk may include them.

Although it is important for the register to be kept current, debtors, their attorneys, and other parties should be able to rely on mailing addresses listed in the register without the need to continuously inquire as to new or amended addresses. Therefore, the clerk must update the register, but only once each year.

To avoid unnecessary cost and burden on the clerk and to keep the register a reasonable length, the clerk is not required to include more than one mailing address for a particular agency, department, or instrumentality of the United States or the state or territory. But if more than one address is included, the clerk is required to include information so that a person using the register could determine when each address should be used. In any event, the inclusion of more than one address for a particular department, agency, or instrumentality does not impose on a person sending a notice the duty to send it to more than one address.

*GAP Report on Rule 5003.* No changes since publication.

COMMITTEE NOTES ON RULES—2008 AMENDMENT

The rule is amended to implement § 505(b)(1) of the Code added by the 2005 amendments, which allows a taxing authority to designate an address to use for the service of requests under that subsection. Under the amendment, the clerk is directed to maintain a separate register for mailing addresses of governmental units solely for the service of requests under § 505(b). This register is in addition to the register of addresses of governmental units already maintained by the clerk. The clerk is required to keep only one address for a governmental unit in each register.

*Changes Made After Publication.* Subdivision (e) was amended to clarify that the clerk must maintain a separate mailing address register that contains the addresses to which notices pertaining to actions under § 505 of the Code are to be sent.

## Rule 5004. Disqualification

(a) DISQUALIFICATION OF JUDGE. A bankruptcy judge shall be governed by 28 U.S.C. § 455, and disqualified from presiding over the proceeding or contested matter in which the disqualifying circumstances[1] arises or, if appropriate, shall be disqualified from presiding over the case.

(b) DISQUALIFICATION OF JUDGE FROM ALLOWING COMPENSATION. A bankruptcy judge shall be disqualified from allowing compensation to a person who is a relative of the bankruptcy judge or with whom the judge is so connected as to render it improper for the judge to authorize such compensation.

(As amended Apr. 29, 1985, eff. Aug. 1, 1985; Mar. 30, 1987, eff. Aug. 1, 1987.)

NOTES OF ADVISORY COMMITTEE ON RULES

*Subdivision (a).* Disqualification of a bankruptcy judge is governed by 28 U.S.C. § 455. That section provides that the judge "shall disqualify himself in any proceeding in which his impartiality might reasonably be questioned" or under certain other circumstances. In a case under the Code it is possible that the disqualifying circumstance will be isolated to an adversary proceeding or contested matter. The rule makes it clear that when the disqualifying circumstance is limited in that way the judge need only disqualify himself from presiding over that adversary proceeding or contested matter.

It is possible, however, that even if the disqualifying circumstance arises in connection with an adversary proceeding, the effect will be so pervasive that disqualification from presiding over the case is appropriate. This distinction is consistent with the definition of "proceeding" in 28 U.S.C. § 455(d)(1).

[1] So in original. Probably should be "circumstance".

*Subdivision (b)* precludes a bankruptcy judge from allowing compensation from the estate to a relative or other person closely associated with the judge. The subdivision applies where the judge has not appointed or approved the employment of the person requesting compensation. Perhaps the most frequent application of the subdivision will be in the allowance of administrative expenses under §503(b)(3)–(5) of the Code. For example, if an attorney or accountant is retained by an indenture trustee who thereafter makes a substantial contribution in a chapter 11 case, the attorney or accountant may seek compensation under §503(b)(4). If the attorney or accountant is a relative of or associated with the bankruptcy judge, the judge may not allow compensation to the attorney or accountant. Section 101(34) defines relative and Rule 9001 incorporates the definitions of the Code. See the Advisory Committee's Note to Rule 5002.

NOTES OF ADVISORY COMMITTEE ON RULES—1985 AMENDMENT

Subdivision (a) was affected by the Bankruptcy Amendments and Federal Judgeship Act of 1984, P.L. 98–353, 98 Stat. 333. The 1978 Bankruptcy Reform Act, P.L. 95–598, included bankruptcy judges in the definition of United States judges in 28 U.S.C. §451 and they were therefore subject to the provisions of 28 U.S.C. §455. This was to become effective on April 1, 1984, P.L. 95–598, §404(b). Section 113 of P.L. 98–353, however, appears to have rendered the amendment to 28 U.S.C. §451 ineffective. Subdivision (a) of the rule retains the substance and intent of the earlier draft by making bankruptcy judges subject to 28 U.S.C. §455.

The word "associated" in subdivision (b) has been changed to "connected" in order to conform with Rule 5002(b).

NOTES OF ADVISORY COMMITTEE ON RULES—1987 AMENDMENT

The rule is amended to be gender neutral. The bankruptcy judge before whom the matter is pending determines whether disqualification is required.

## Rule 5005. Filing and Transmittal of Papers

(a) FILING.

(1) *Place of Filing.* The lists, schedules, statements, proofs of claim or interest, complaints, motions, applications, objections and other papers required to be filed by these rules, except as provided in 28 U.S.C. §1409, shall be filed with the clerk in the district where the case under the Code is pending. The judge of that court may permit the papers to be filed with the judge, in which event the filing date shall be noted thereon, and they shall be forthwith transmitted to the clerk. The clerk shall not refuse to accept for filing any petition or other paper presented for the purpose of filing solely because it is not presented in proper form as required by these rules or any local rules or practices.

(2) *Filing by Electronic Means.* A court may by local rule permit or require documents to be filed, signed, or verified by electronic means that are consistent with technical standards, if any, that the Judicial Conference of the United States establishes. A local rule may require filing by electronic means only if reasonable exceptions are allowed. A document filed by electronic means in compliance with a local rule constitutes a written paper for the purpose of applying these rules, the Federal Rules of Civil Procedure made applicable by these rules, and §107 of the Code.

(b) TRANSMITTAL TO THE UNITED STATES TRUSTEE.

(1) The complaints, motions, applications, objections and other papers required to be transmitted to the United States trustee by these rules shall be mailed or delivered to an office of the United States trustee, or to another place designated by the United States trustee, in the district where the case under the Code is pending.

(2) The entity, other than the clerk, transmitting a paper to the United States trustee shall promptly file as proof of such transmittal a verified statement identifying the paper and stating the date on which it was transmitted to the United States trustee.

(3) Nothing in these rules shall require the clerk to transmit any paper to the United States trustee if the United States trustee requests in writing that the paper not be transmitted.

(c) ERROR IN FILING OR TRANSMITTAL. A paper intended to be filed with the clerk but erroneously delivered to the United States trustee, the trustee, the attorney for the trustee, a bankruptcy judge, a district judge, the clerk of the bankruptcy appellate panel, or the clerk of the district court shall, after the date of its receipt has been noted thereon, be transmitted forthwith to the clerk of the bankruptcy court. A paper intended to be transmitted to the United States trustee but erroneously delivered to the clerk, the trustee, the attorney for the trustee, a bankruptcy judge, a district judge, the clerk of the bankruptcy appellate panel, or the clerk of the district court shall, after the date of its receipt has been noted thereon, be transmitted forthwith to the United States trustee. In the interest of justice, the court may order that a paper erroneously delivered shall be deemed filed with the clerk or transmitted to the United States trustee as of the date of its original delivery.

(As amended Mar. 30, 1987, eff. Aug. 1, 1987; Apr. 30, 1991, eff. Aug. 1, 1991; Apr. 22, 1993, eff. Aug. 1, 1993; Apr. 23, 1996, eff. Dec. 1, 1996; Apr. 12, 2006, eff. Dec. 1, 2006.)

NOTES OF ADVISORY COMMITTEE ON RULES—1983

*Subdivision (a)* is an adaptation of Rule 5(e) F.R.Civ.P. Sections 301–304 of the Code and Rules 1002 and 1003 require that cases under the Code be commenced by filing a petition "with the bankruptcy court." Other sections of the Code and other rules refer to or contemplate filing but there is no specific reference to filing with the bankruptcy court. For example, §501 of the Code requires filing of proofs of claim and Rule 3016(c) requires the filing of a disclosure statement. This subdivision applies to all situations in which filing is required. Except when filing in another district is authorized by 28 U.S.C. §1473, all papers, including complaints commencing adversary proceedings, must be filed in the court where the case under the Code is pending.

*Subdivision (b)* is the same as former Bankruptcy Rule 509(c).

NOTES OF ADVISORY COMMITTEE ON RULES—1987 AMENDMENT

*Subdivision (a)* is amended to conform with the 1984 amendments.

NOTES OF ADVISORY COMMITTEE ON RULES—1991 AMENDMENT

*Subdivision (b)(1)* is flexible in that it permits the United States trustee to designate a place or places for receiving papers within the district in which the case is pending. Transmittal of papers to the United States trustee may be accomplished by mail or delivery, including delivery by courier, and the technical requirements for service of process are not applicable. Although papers relating to a proceeding commenced in another district pursuant to 28 U.S.C. §1409 must be filed with the clerk in that district, the papers required to be transmitted to the United States trustee must be mailed or delivered to the United States trustee in the district in which the case under the Code is pending. The United States trustee in the district in which the case is pending monitors the progress of the case and should be informed of all developments in the case wherever the developments take place.

*Subdivision (b)(2)* requires that proof of transmittal to the United States trustee be filed with the clerk. If papers are served on the United States trustee by mail or otherwise, the filing of proof of service would satisfy the requirements of this subdivision. This requirement enables the court to assure that papers are actually transmitted to the United States trustee in compliance with the rules. When the rules require that a paper be transmitted to the United States trustee and proof of transmittal has not been filed with the clerk, the court should not schedule a hearing or should take other appropriate action to assure that the paper is transmitted to the United States trustee. The filing of the verified statement with the clerk also enables other parties in interest to determine whether a paper has been transmitted to the United States trustee.

*Subdivision (b)(3)* is designed to relieve the clerk of any obligation under these rules to transmit any paper to the United States trustee if the United States trustee does not wish to receive it.

*Subdivision (c)* is amended to include the erroneous delivery of papers intended to be transmitted to the United States trustee.

NOTES OF ADVISORY COMMITTEE ON RULES—1993 AMENDMENT

*Subdivision (a)* is amended to conform to the 1991 amendment to Rule 5(e) F.R.Civ.P. It is not a suitable role for the office of the clerk to refuse to accept for filing papers not conforming to requirements of form imposed by these rules or by local rules or practices. The enforcement of these rules and local rules is a role for a judge. This amendment does not require the clerk to accept for filing papers sent to the clerk's office by facsimile transmission.

NOTES OF ADVISORY COMMITTEE ON RULES—1996 AMENDMENT

The rule is amended to permit, but not require, courts to adopt local rules that allow filing, signing, or verifying of documents by electronic means. However, such local rules must be consistent with technical standards, if any, promulgated by the Judicial Conference of the United States.

An important benefit to be derived by permitting filing by electronic means is that the extensive volume of paper received and maintained as records in the clerk's office will be reduced substantially. With the receipt of electronic data transmissions by computer, the clerk may maintain records electronically without the need to reproduce them in tangible paper form.

Judicial Conference standards governing the technological aspects of electronic filing will result in uniformity among judicial districts to accommodate an increasingly national bar. By delegating to the Judicial Conference the establishment and future amendment of national standards for electronic filing, the Supreme Court and Congress will be relieved of the burden of reviewing and promulgating detailed rules dealing with complex technological standards. Another reason for leaving to the Judicial Conference the formulation of technological standards for electronic filing is that advances in computer technology occur often, and changes in the technological standards may have to be implemented more frequently than would be feasible by rule amendment under the Rules Enabling Act process.

It is anticipated that standards established by the Judicial Conference will govern technical specifications for electronic data transmission, such as requirements relating to the formatting of data, speed of transmission, means to transmit copies of supporting documentation, and security of communication procedures. In addition, before procedures for electronic filing are implemented, standards must be established to assure the proper maintenance and integrity of the record and to provide appropriate access and retrieval mechanisms. These matters will be governed by local rules until system-wide standards are adopted by the Judicial Conference.

Rule 9009 requires that the Official Forms shall be observed and used "with alterations as may be appropriate." Compliance with local rules and any Judicial Conference standards with respect to the formatting or presentation of electronically transmitted data, to the extent that they do not conform to the Official Forms, would be an appropriate alteration within the meaning of Rule 9009.

These rules require that certain documents be in writing. For example, Rule 3001 states that a proof of claim is a "written statement." Similarly, Rule 3007 provides that an objection to a claim "shall be in writing." Pursuant to the new subdivision (a)(2), any requirement under these rules that a paper be written may be satisfied by filing the document by electronic means, notwithstanding the fact that the clerk neither receives nor prints a paper reproduction of the electronic data.

Section 107(a) of the Code provides that a "paper" filed in a case is a public record open to examination by an entity at reasonable times without charge, except as provided in §107(b). The amendment to subdivision (a)(2) provides that an electronically filed document is to be treated as such a public record.

Although under subdivision (a)(2) electronically filed documents may be treated as written papers or as signed or verified writings, it is important to emphasize that such treatment is only for the purpose of applying these rules. In addition, local rules and Judicial Conference standards regarding verification must satisfy the requirements of 28 U.S.C. §1746.

*GAP Report on Rule 5005.* No changes since publication.

COMMITTEE NOTES ON RULES—2006 AMENDMENT

*Subdivision (a).* Amended Rule 5005(a)(2) acknowledges that many courts have required electronic filing by means of a standing order, procedures manual, or local rule. These local practices reflect the advantages that courts and most litigants realize from electronic filings. Courts requiring electronic filing must make reasonable exceptions for persons for whom electronic filing of documents constitutes an unreasonable denial of access to the courts. Experience with the rule will facilitate convergence on uniform exceptions in an amended Rule 5005(a)(2).

*Subdivision (c).* The rule is amended to include the clerk of the bankruptcy appellate panel among the list of persons required to transmit to the proper person erroneously filed or transmitted papers. The amendment is necessary because the bankruptcy appellate panels were not in existence at the time of the original promulgation of the rule. The amendment also inserts the district judge on the list of persons required to transmit papers intended for the United States trustee but erroneously sent to another person. The district judge is included in the list of persons who must transmit papers to the clerk of the bankruptcy court in the first part of the rule, and there is no reason to exclude the district judge from the list of persons who must transmit erroneously filed papers to the United States trustee.

*Changes Made After Publication.* The published version of the Rule did not include the sentence set out on lines 7–10 above [sic]. The Advisory Committee concluded, based on the written comments received and additonal Advisory Committee consideration, that the text of the rule should include a statement regarding the need for courts to protect access to the courts for those whose status might not allow for electronic participation in cases. The published version had relegated this notion to the Committee Note, but further deliberations led to the conclusion that this matter is too important to leave to the Committee Note and instead should be included in the text of the rule.

REFERENCES IN TEXT

The Federal Rules of Civil Procedure, referred to in subd. (a)(2), are set out in the Appendix to Title 28, Judiciary and Judicial Procedure.

## Rule 5006. Certification of Copies of Papers

The clerk shall issue a certified copy of the record of any proceeding in a case under the Code or of any paper filed with the clerk on payment of any prescribed fee.

(As amended Apr. 30, 1991, eff. Aug. 1, 1991.)

NOTES OF ADVISORY COMMITTEE ON RULES—1983

Fees for certification and copying are fixed by the Judicial Conference under 28 U.S.C. §1930(b).

Rule 1101 F. R. Evid. makes the Federal Rules of Evidence applicable to cases under the Code. Rule 1005 F. R. Evid. allows the contents of an official record or of a paper filed with the court to be proved by a duly certified copy. A copy certified and issued in accordance with Rule 5006 is accorded authenticity by Rule 902(4) F. R. Evid.

## Rule 5007. Record of Proceedings and Transcripts

(a) FILING OF RECORD OR TRANSCRIPT. The reporter or operator of a recording device shall certify the original notes of testimony, tape recording, or other original record of the proceeding and promptly file them with the clerk. The person preparing any transcript shall promptly file a certified copy.

(b) TRANSCRIPT FEES. The fees for copies of transcripts shall be charged at rates prescribed by the Judicial Conference of the United States. No fee may be charged for the certified copy filed with the clerk.

(c) ADMISSIBILITY OF RECORD IN EVIDENCE. A certified sound recording or a transcript of a proceeding shall be admissible as prima facie evidence to establish the record.

(As amended Mar. 30, 1987, eff. Aug. 1, 1987; Apr. 30, 1991, eff. Aug. 1, 1991.)

NOTES OF ADVISORY COMMITTEE ON RULES—1983

This rule supplements 28 U.S.C. §773. A record of proceedings before the bankruptcy judge is to be made whenever practicable. By whatever means the record is made, subdivision (a) requires that the preparer of the record certify and file the original notes, tape recording, or other form of sound recording of the proceedings. Similarly, if a transcript is requested, the preparer is to file a certified copy with the clerk.

*Subdivision (b)* is derived from 28 U.S.C. §753(f).

*Subdivision (c)* is derived from former Bankruptcy Rule 511(c). This subdivision extends to a sound recording the same evidentiary status as a transcript under 28 U.S.C. §773(b).

NOTES OF ADVISORY COMMITTEE ON RULES—1991 AMENDMENT

The words "with the clerk" in the final sentence of subdivision (a) are deleted as unnecessary. See Rules 5005(a) and 9001(3).

## Rule 5008. Notice Regarding Presumption of Abuse in Chapter 7 Cases of Individual Debtors

If a presumption of abuse has arisen under §707(b) in a chapter 7 case of an individual with primarily consumer debts, the clerk shall within 10 days after the date of the filing of the petition notify creditors of the presumption of abuse in accordance with Rule 2002. If the debtor has not filed a statement indicating whether a presumption of abuse has arisen, the clerk shall within 10 days after the date of the filing of the petition notify creditors that the debtor has not filed the statement and that further notice will be given if a later filed statement indicates that a presumption of abuse has arisen. If a debtor later files a statement indicating that a presumption of abuse has arisen, the clerk shall notify creditors of the presumption of abuse as promptly as practicable.

(Added Apr. 23, 2008, eff. Dec. 1, 2008.)

NOTES OF ADVISORY COMMITTEE ON RULES—1991

This rule [Rule 5008. Funds of the Estate; abrogated Apr. 30, 1991, eff. Aug. 1, 1991] is abrogated in view of the amendments to §345(b) of the Code and the role of the United States trustee in approving bonds and supervising trustees.

COMMITTEE NOTES ON RULES—2008

This rule is new. The 2005 amendments to §342 of the Code require that clerks give written notice to all creditors not later than 10 days after the date of the filing of the petition that a presumption of abuse has arisen under §707(b). A statement filed by the debtor will be the source of the clerk's information about the presumption of abuse. This rule enables the clerk to meet its obligation to send the notice within the statutory time period set forth in §342. In the event that the court receives the debtor's statement after the clerk has sent the first notice, and the debtor's statement indicates a presumption of abuse, the rule requires that the clerk send a second notice.

*Changes Made After Publication.* No changes were made after publication.

## Rule 5009. Closing Chapter 7 Liquidation, Chapter 12 Family Farmer's Debt Adjustment, and Chapter 13 Individual's Debt Adjustment Cases

If in a chapter 7, chapter 12, or chapter 13 case the trustee has filed a final report and final account and has certified that the estate has been fully administered, and if within 30 days no objection has been filed by the United States trustee or a party in interest, there shall be a presumption that the estate has been fully administered.

(As amended Apr. 30, 1991, eff. Aug. 1, 1991.)

NOTES OF ADVISORY COMMITTEE ON RULES—1983

This rule is the same as §350(a) of the Code. An estate may be closed even though the period allowed by Rule 3002(c) for filing claims has not expired. The closing of a case may be expedited when a notice of no dividends is given under Rule 2002(e). Dismissal of a case for want of prosecution or failure to pay filing fees is governed by Rule 1017.

NOTES OF ADVISORY COMMITTEE ON RULES—1991 AMENDMENT

The final report and account of the trustee is required to be filed with the court and the United States trustee under §§704(9), 1202(b)(1), and 1302(b)(1) of the Code. This amendment facilitates the United States trustee's performance of statutory duties to supervise trustees and administer cases under chapters 7, 12, and 13 pursuant to 28 U.S.C. §586. In the absence of a timely objection by the United States trustee or a party in interest, the court may discharge the trustee and close the case pursuant to §350(a) without the need to review the final report and account or to determine the merits of the trustee's certification that the estate has been fully administered.

Rule 3022 governs the closing of chapter 11 cases.

### Rule 5010. Reopening Cases

A case may be reopened on motion of the debtor or other party in interest pursuant to §350(b) of the Code. In a chapter 7, 12, or 13 case a trustee shall not be appointed by the United States trustee unless the court determines that a trustee is necessary to protect the interests of creditors and the debtor or to insure efficient administration of the case.

(As amended Mar. 30, 1987, eff. Aug. 1, 1987; Apr. 30, 1991, eff. Aug. 1, 1991.)

NOTES OF ADVISORY COMMITTEE ON RULES—1983

Section 350(b) of the Code provides: "A case may be reopened in the court in which such case was closed to administer assets, to accord relief to the debtor, or for other cause."

Rule 9024, which incorporates Rule 60 F.R.Civ.P., exempts motions to reopen cases under the Code from the one year limitation of Rule 60(b).

Although a case has been closed the court may sometimes act without reopening the case. Under Rule 9024, clerical errors in judgments, orders, or other parts of the record or errors therein caused by oversight or omission may be corrected. A judgment determined to be non-dischargeable pursuant to Rule 4007 may be enforced after a case is closed by a writ of execution obtained pursuant to Rule 7069.

NOTES OF ADVISORY COMMITTEE ON RULES—1987 AMENDMENT

In order to avoid unnecessary cost and delay, the rule is amended to permit reopening of a case without the appointment of a trustee when the services of a trustee are not needed.

NOTES OF ADVISORY COMMITTEE ON RULES—1991 AMENDMENT

This rule is amended to conform to the 1986 amendments to the Code that give the United States trustee the duty to appoint trustees in chapter 7, 12 and 13 cases. See §§701, 702(d), 1202(a), and 1302(a) of the Code. In most reopened cases, a trustee is not needed because there are no assets to be administered. Therefore, in the interest of judicial economy, this rule is amended so that a motion will not be necessary unless the United States trustee or a party in interest seeks the appointment of a trustee in the reopened case.

### Rule 5011. Withdrawal and Abstention from Hearing a Proceeding

(a) WITHDRAWAL. A motion for withdrawal of a case or proceeding shall be heard by a district judge.

(b) ABSTENTION FROM HEARING A PROCEEDING. A motion for abstention pursuant to 28 U.S.C. §1334(c) shall be governed by Rule 9014 and shall be served on the parties to the proceeding.

(c) EFFECT OF FILING OF MOTION FOR WITHDRAWAL OR ABSTENTION. The filing of a motion for withdrawal of a case or proceeding or for abstention pursuant to 28 U.S.C. §1334(c) shall not stay the administration of the case or any proceeding therein before the bankruptcy judge except that the bankruptcy judge may stay, on such terms and conditions as are proper, proceedings pending disposition of the motion. A motion for a stay ordinarily shall be presented first to the bankruptcy judge. A motion for a stay or relief from a stay filed in the district court shall state why it has not been presented to or obtained from the bankruptcy judge. Relief granted by the district judge shall be on such terms and conditions as the judge deems proper.

(Added Mar. 30, 1987, eff. Aug. 1, 1987; amended Apr. 30, 1991, eff. Aug. 1, 1991.)

NOTES OF ADVISORY COMMITTEE ON RULES—1987

Motions for withdrawal pursuant to 28 U.S.C. §157(d) or abstention pursuant to 28 U.S.C. §1334(c), like all other motions, are to be filed with the clerk as required by Rule 5005(a). If a bankruptcy clerk has been appointed for the district, all motions are filed with the bankruptcy clerk. The method for forwarding withdrawal motions to the district court will be established by administrative procedures.

*Subdivision (a).* Section 157(d) permits the district court to order withdrawal on its own motion or the motion of a party. Subdivision (a) of this rule makes it clear that the bankruptcy judge will not conduct hearings on a withdrawal motion. The withdrawal decision is committed exclusively to the district court.

*Subdivision (b).* A decision to abstain under 28 U.S.C. §1334(c) is not appealable. The district court is vested originally with jurisdiction and the decision to relinquish that jurisdiction must ultimately be a matter for the district court. The bankruptcy judge ordinarily will be in the best position to evaluate the grounds asserted for abstention. This subdivision (b) provides that the initial hearing on the motion is before the bankruptcy judge. The procedure for review of the report and recommendation are governed by Rule 9033.

This rule does not apply to motions under §305 of the Code for abstention from hearing a case. Judicial decisions will determine the scope of the bankruptcy judge's authority under §305.

*Subdivision (c).* Unless the court so orders, proceedings are not stayed when motions are filed for withdrawal or for abstention from hearing a proceeding. Because of the district court's authority over cases and proceedings, the subdivision authorizes the district court to order a stay or modify a stay ordered by the bankruptcy judge.

NOTES OF ADVISORY COMMITTEE ON RULES AMENDMENT

*Subdivision (b)* is amended to delete the restriction that limits the role of the bankruptcy court to the filing of a report and recommendation for disposition of a motion for abstention under 28 U.S.C. §1334(c)(2). This amendment is consistent with §309(b) of the Judicial Improvements Act of 1990 which amended §1334(c)(2) so that it allows an appeal to the district court of a bankruptcy court's order determining an abstention motion. This subdivision is also amended to clarify that the motion is a contested matter governed by Rule 9014 and that it must be served on all parties to the proceeding which is the subject of the motion.

## PART VI—COLLECTION AND LIQUIDATION OF THE ESTATE

### Rule 6001. Burden of Proof As to Validity of Postpetition Transfer

Any entity asserting the validity of a transfer under §549 of the Code shall have the burden of proof.

NOTES OF ADVISORY COMMITTEE ON RULES—1983

This rule is derived from former Bankruptcy Rule 603. The Act contained, in §70d, a provision placing the burden of proof on the same person as did Rule 603. The Code does not contain any directive with respect to the burden of proof. This omission, in all probability, resulted from the intention to leave matters affecting evidence to these rules. See H. Rep. No. 95–595, 95th Cong. 1st Sess. (1977) 293.

## Rule 6002. Accounting by Prior Custodian of Property of the Estate

(a) ACCOUNTING REQUIRED. Any custodian required by the Code to deliver property in the custodian's possession or control to the trustee shall promptly file and transmit to the United States trustee a report and account with respect to the property of the estate and the administration thereof.

(b) EXAMINATION OF ADMINISTRATION. On the filing and transmittal of the report and account required by subdivision (a) of this rule and after an examination has been made into the superseded administration, after notice and a hearing, the court shall determine the propriety of the administration, including the reasonableness of all disbursements.

(As amended Mar. 30, 1987, eff. Aug. 1, 1987; Apr. 30, 1991, eff. Aug. 1, 1991; Apr. 22, 1993, eff. Aug. 1, 1993.)

NOTES OF ADVISORY COMMITTEE ON RULES—1983

"Custodian" is defined in §101(10) of the Code. The definition includes a trustee or receiver appointed in proceedings not under the Code, as well as an assignee for the benefit of creditors.

This rule prescribes the procedure to be followed by a custodian who under §543 of the Code is required to deliver property to the trustee and to account for its disposition. The examination under subdivision (b) may be initiated (1) on the motion of the custodian required to account under subdivision (a) for an approval of his account and discharge thereon, (2) on the motion of, or the filing of an objection to the custodian's account by, the trustee or any other party in interest, or (3) on the court's own initiative. Rule 9014 applies to any contested matter arising under this rule.

Section 543(d) is similar to an abstention provision. It grants the bankruptcy court discretion to permit the custodian to remain in possession and control of the property. In that event, the custodian is excused from complying with §543(a)–(c) and thus would not be required to turn over the property to the trustee. When there is no duty to turn over to the trustee, Rule 6002 would not be applicable.

NOTES OF ADVISORY COMMITTEE ON RULES—1991 AMENDMENT

This rule is amended to enable the United States trustee to review, object to, or to otherwise be heard regarding the custodian's report and accounting. See §§307 and 543 of the Code.

NOTES OF ADVISORY COMMITTEE ON RULES—1993 AMENDMENT

*Subdivision (b)* is amended to conform to the language of §102(1) of the Code.

## Rule 6003. Interim and Final Relief Immediately Following the Commencement of the Case—Applications for Employment; Motions for Use, Sale, or Lease of Property; and Motions for Assumption or Assignment of Executory Contracts

Except to the extent that relief is necessary to avoid immediate and irreparable harm, the court shall not, within 21 days after the filing of the petition, grant relief regarding the following:

(a) an application under Rule 2014;

(b) a motion to use, sell, lease, or otherwise incur an obligation regarding property of the estate, including a motion to pay all or part of a claim that arose before the filing of the petition, but not a motion under Rule 4001; and

(c) a motion to assume or assign an executory contract or unexpired lease in accordance with §365.

(Added Apr. 30, 2007; eff. Dec. 1, 2007; amended Mar. 26, 2009, eff. Dec. 1, 2009.)

NOTES OF ADVISORY COMMITTEE ON RULES—1991

This rule [Former Rule 6003—Disbursement of Money of the Estate (Abrogated Apr. 30, 1991, eff. Aug. 1, 1991)] is abrogated in view of the role of the United States trustee in supervising trustees. Use of estate funds by a trustee or debtor in possession is governed by §363 of the Code.

COMMITTEE NOTES ON RULES—2007

There can be a flurry of activity during the first days of a bankruptcy case. This activity frequently takes place prior to the formation of a creditors' committee, and it also can include substantial amounts of materials for the court and parties in interest to review and evaluate. This rule is intended to alleviate some of the time pressures present at the start of a case so that full and close consideration can be given to matters that may have a fundamental impact on the case.

The rule provides that the court cannot grant relief on applications for the employment of professional persons, motions for the use, sale, or lease of property of the estate other than such a motion under Rule 4001, and motions to assume or assign executory contracts and unexpired leases for the first 20 days of the case, unless granting relief is necessary to avoid immediate and irreparable harm. This standard is taken from Rule 4001(b)(2) and (c)(2), and decisions under those provisions should provide guidance for the application of this provision.

This rule does not govern motions and applications made more than 20 days after the filing of the petition.

*Changes After Publication.* Subdivision (c) was amended by deleting the reference to the rejection of executory contracts or unexpired leases. The rule, as revised, now limits only the assumption or assignment of executory contracts or unexpired leases in that subdivision.

COMMITTEE NOTES ON RULES—2009 AMENDMENT

The rule is amended to implement changes in connection with the amendment to Rule 9006(a) and the manner by which time is computed under the rules. The deadline in the rule is amended to substitute a deadline that is a multiple of seven days. Throughout the rules, deadlines are amended in the following manner:

- 5-day periods become 7-day periods
- 10-day periods become 14-day periods
- 15-day periods become 14-day periods
- 20-day periods become 21-day periods
- 25-day periods become 28-day periods

## Rule 6004. Use, Sale, or Lease of Property

(a) NOTICE OF PROPOSED USE, SALE, OR LEASE OF PROPERTY. Notice of a proposed use, sale, or lease of property, other than cash collateral, not in the ordinary course of business shall be given pursuant to Rule 2002(a)(2), (c)(1), (i), and (k) and, if applicable, in accordance with §363(b)(2) of the Code.

(b) OBJECTION TO PROPOSAL. Except as provided in subdivisions (c) and (d) of this rule, an objection to a proposed use, sale, or lease of property shall be filed and served not less than seven days before the date set for the proposed action or within the time fixed by the court. An objection to the proposed use, sale, or lease of property is governed by Rule 9014.

(c) SALE FREE AND CLEAR OF LIENS AND OTHER INTERESTS. A motion for authority to sell property free and clear of liens or other interests shall be made in accordance with Rule 9014 and shall be served on the parties who have liens or other interests in the property to be sold. The notice required by subdivision (a) of this rule shall include the date of the hearing on the motion and the time within which objections may be filed and served on the debtor in possession or trustee.

(d) SALE OF PROPERTY UNDER $2,500. Notwithstanding subdivision (a) of this rule, when all of the nonexempt property of the estate has an aggregate gross value less than $2,500, it shall be sufficient to give a general notice of intent to sell such property other than in the ordinary course of business to all creditors, indenture trustees, committees appointed or elected pursuant to the Code, the United States trustee and other persons as the court may direct. An objection to any such sale may be filed and served by a party in interest within 14 days of the mailing of the notice, or within the time fixed by the court. An objection is governed by Rule 9014.

(e) HEARING. If a timely objection is made pursuant to subdivision (b) or (d) of this rule, the date of the hearing thereon may be set in the notice given pursuant to subdivision (a) of this rule.

(f) CONDUCT OF SALE NOT IN THE ORDINARY COURSE OF BUSINESS.

(1) *Public or Private Sale.* All sales not in the ordinary course of business may be by private sale or by public auction. Unless it is impracticable, an itemized statement of the property sold, the name of each purchaser, and the price received for each item or lot or for the property as a whole if sold in bulk shall be filed on completion of a sale. If the property is sold by an auctioneer, the auctioneer shall file the statement, transmit a copy thereof to the United States trustee, and furnish a copy to the trustee, debtor in possession, or chapter 13 debtor. If the property is not sold by an auctioneer, the trustee, debtor in possession, or chapter 13 debtor shall file the statement and transmit a copy thereof to the United States trustee.

(2) *Execution of Instruments.* After a sale in accordance with this rule the debtor, the trustee, or debtor in possession, as the case may be, shall execute any instrument necessary or ordered by the court to effectuate the transfer to the purchaser.

(g) SALE OF PERSONALLY IDENTIFIABLE INFORMATION.

(1) *Motion.* A motion for authority to sell or lease personally identifiable information under §363(b)(1)(B) shall include a request for an order directing the United States trustee to appoint a consumer privacy ombudsman under §332. Rule 9014 governs the motion which shall be served on: any committee elected under §705 or appointed under §1102 of the Code, or if the case is a chapter 11 reorganization case and no committee of unsecured creditors has been appointed under §1102, on the creditors included on the list of creditors filed under Rule 1007(d); and on such other entities as the court may direct. The motion shall be transmitted to the United States trustee.

(2) *Appointment.* If a consumer privacy ombudsman is appointed under §332, no later than seven days before the hearing on the motion under §363(b)(1)(B), the United States trustee shall file a notice of the appointment, including the name and address of the person appointed. The United States trustee's notice shall be accompanied by a verified statement of the person appointed setting forth the person's connections with the debtor, creditors, any other party in interest, their respective attorneys and accountants, the United States trustee, or any person employed in the office of the United States trustee.

(h) STAY OF ORDER AUTHORIZING USE, SALE, OR LEASE OF PROPERTY. An order authorizing the use, sale, or lease of property other than cash collateral is stayed until the expiration of 14 days after entry of the order, unless the court orders otherwise.

(As amended Mar. 30, 1987, eff. Aug. 1, 1987; Apr. 30, 1991, eff. Aug. 1, 1991; Apr. 26, 1999, eff. Dec. 1, 1999; Apr. 23, 2008, eff. Dec. 1, 2008; Mar. 26, 2009, eff. Dec. 1, 2009.)

NOTES OF ADVISORY COMMITTEE ON RULES—1983

*Subdivisions (a) and (b).* Pursuant to §363(b) of the Code, a trustee or debtor in possession may use, sell, or lease property other than in the ordinary course of business only after notice and hearing. Rule 2002(a), (c) and (i) specifies the time when notice of sale is to be given, the contents of the notice and the persons to whom notice is to be given of sales of property. Subdivision (a) makes those provisions applicable as well to notices for proposed use and lease of property.

The Code does not provide the time within which parties may file objections to a proposed sale. Subdivision (b) of the rule requires the objection to be in writing and filed not less than five days before the proposed action is to take place. The objection should also be served within that time on the person who is proposing to take the action which would be either the trustee or debtor in possession. This time period is subject to change by the court. In some instances there is a need to conduct a sale in a short period of time and the court is given discretion to tailor the requirements to the circumstances.

*Subdivision (c).* In some situations a notice of sale for different pieces of property to all persons specified in Rule 2002(a) may be uneconomic and inefficient. This is particularly true in some chapter 7 liquidation cases when there is property of relatively little value which must be sold by the trustee. Subdivision (c) allows a general notice of intent to sell when the aggregate value of the estate's property is less than $2,500. The gross value is the value of the property without regard to the amount of any debt secured by a lien on the property. It is not necessary to give a detailed notice specifying the time and place of a particular sale. Thus, the requirements of Rule 2002(c) need not be met. If this method of providing notice of sales is used, the subdivision specifies that parties in interest may serve and file objections to the proposed sale of any property within the class and the time for service and filing is fixed at not later than 15 days after mailing the notice. The court may fix a different time. Subdivision (c) would have little utility in chapter 11 cases. Pursuant to Rule 2002(i), the court can limit notices of sale to the creditors' committee appointed under §1102 of the Code and the same burdens present in a small chapter 7 case would not exist.

*Subdivision (d).* If a timely objection is filed, a hearing is required with respect to the use, sale, or lease of property. Subdivision (d) renders the filing of an objection tantamount to requesting a hearing so as to require a hearing pursuant to §§363(b) and 102(1)(B)(i).

*Subdivision (e)* is derived in part from former Bankruptcy Rule 606(b) but does not carry forward the requirement of that rule that court approval be obtained for sales of property. Pursuant to §363(b) court approval is not required unless timely objection is made to the proposed sale. The itemized statement or information required by the subdivision is not necessary when it would be impracticable to prepare it or set forth the information. For example, a liquidation sale of retail goods although not in the ordinary course of business may be on a daily ongoing basis and only summaries may be available.

The duty imposed by paragraph (2) does not affect the power of the bankruptcy court to order third persons to execute instruments transferring property purchased at a sale under this subdivision. See, *e.g., In re Rosenberg*, 138 F.2d 409 (7th Cir. 1943).

NOTES OF ADVISORY COMMITTEE ON RULES—1987 AMENDMENT

*Subdivision (a)* is amended to conform to the 1984 amendments to §363(b)(2) of the Code.

*Subdivision (b)* is amended to provide that an objection to a proposed use, sale, or lease of property creates a contested matter governed by Rule 9014. A similar amendment is made to subdivision (d), which was formerly subdivision (c).

*Subdivision (c)* is new. Section 363(f) provides that sales free and clear of liens or other interests are only permitted if one of the five statutory requirements is satisfied. Rule 9013 requires that a motion state with particularity the grounds relied upon by the movant. A motion for approval of a sale free and clear of liens or other interests is subject to Rule 9014, service must be made on the parties holding liens or other interests in the property, and notice of the hearing on the motion and the time for filing objections must be included in the notice given under subdivision (a).

NOTES OF ADVISORY COMMITTEE ON RULES—1991 AMENDMENT

This rule is amended to provide notice to the United States trustee of a proposed use, sale or lease of property not in the ordinary course of business. See Rule 2002(k). Subdivision (f)(1) is amended to enable the United States trustee to monitor the progress of the case in accordance with 28 U.S.C. §586(a)(3)(G).

The words "with the clerk" in subdivision (f)(1) are deleted as unnecessary. See Rules 5005(a) and 9001(3).

COMMITTEE NOTES ON RULES—1999 AMENDMENT

*Subdivision (g)* is added to provide sufficient time for a party to request a stay pending appeal of an order authorizing the use, sale, or lease of property under §363(b) of the Code before the order is implemented. It does not affect the time for filing a notice of appeal in accordance with Rule 8002.

Rule 6004(g) does not apply to orders regarding the use of cash collateral and does not affect the trustee's right to use, sell, or lease property without a court order to the extent permitted under §363 of the Code.

The court may, in its discretion, order that Rule 6004(g) is not applicable so that the property may be used, sold, or leased immediately in accordance with the order entered by the court. Alternatively, the court may order that the stay under Rule 6004(g) is for a fixed period less than 10 days.

*GAP Report on Rule 6004.* No changes since publication.

COMMITTEE NOTES ON RULES—2008 AMENDMENT

The rule is amended by inserting a new subdivision (g) to implement §§332 and 363(b)(1)(B) of the Code, added by the 2005 amendments. This rule governs the proposed transfer of personally identifiable information in a manner inconsistent with any policy covering the transfer of the information. Rule 2002(c)(1) requires the seller to state in the notice of the sale or lease whether the transfer is consistent with and policy governing the transfer of the information.

Under §332 of the Code, the consumer privacy ombudsman must be appointed at least five days prior to the hearing on a sale or lease of personally identifiable information. In an appropriate case, the consumer privacy ombudsman may seek a continuance of the hearing on the proposed sale to perform the tasks required of the ombudsman by §332 of the Code.

Former subdivision (g) is redesignated as subdivision (h).

*Changes Made After Publication.* The Committee Note was amended to highlight the connection between this rule and Rule 2002 with regard to the obligation to provide notice of proposed transactions. It was also amended to recognize the ability of the consumer privacy ombudsman to seek a continuance of a hearing on the proposed sale of personally identifiable information.

COMMITTEE NOTES ON RULES—2009 AMENDMENT

The rule is amended to implement changes in connection with the amendment to Rule 9006(a) and the manner by which time is computed under the rules. The deadlines in the rule are amended to substitute a deadline that is a multiple of seven days. Throughout the rules, deadlines are amended in the following manner:

- 5-day periods become 7-day periods
- 10-day periods become 14-day periods
- 15-day periods become 14-day periods
- 20-day periods become 21-day periods
- 25-day periods become 28-day periods

## Rule 6005. Appraisers and Auctioneers

The order of the court approving the employment of an appraiser or auctioneer shall fix the amount or rate of compensation. No officer or employee of the Judicial Branch of the United States or the United States Department of Justice shall be eligible to act as appraiser or auctioneer. No residence or licensing requirement shall disqualify an appraiser or auctioneer from employment.

(As amended Apr. 30, 1991, eff. Aug. 1, 1991.)

NOTES OF ADVISORY COMMITTEE ON RULES—1983

This rule is derived from former Bankruptcy Rule 606(c) and implements §327 of the Code. Pursuant to §327, the trustee or debtor in possession may employ one or more appraisers or auctioneers, subject to court approval. This rule requires the court order approving such employment to fix the amount or rate of compensation. The second sentence of the former rule is retained to continue to safeguard against imputations of favoritism which detract from public confidence in bankruptcy administration. The final sentence is to guard against imposition of parochial requirements not warranted by any consideration having to do with sound bankruptcy administration.

Reference should also be made to Rule 2013(a) regarding the limitation on employment of appraisers and auctioneers, and Rule 2014(a) regarding the application for appointment of an appraiser or auctioneer.

## Rule 6006. Assumption, Rejection or Assignment of an Executory Contract or Unexpired Lease

(a) PROCEEDING TO ASSUME, REJECT, OR SIGN. A proceeding to assume, reject, or assign an executory contract or unexpired lease, other than as part of a plan, is governed by Rule 9014.

(b) PROCEEDING TO REQUIRE TRUSTEE TO A A proceeding by a party to an executory contract or unexpired lease in a chapter 9 municipality case, chapter 11 reorganization case, chapter 12 family farmer's debt adjustment case, or chapter 13 individual's debt adjustment case, to require the trustee, debtor in possession, or debtor to determine whether to assume or reject the contract or lease is governed by Rule 9014.

(c) NOTICE. Notice of a motion made pursuant to subdivision (a) or (b) of this rule shall be given to the other party to the contract or lease, to other parties in interest as the court may direct, and, except in a chapter 9 municipality case, to the United States trustee.

(d) STAY OF ORDER AUTHORIZING ASSIGNMENT. An order authorizing the trustee to assign an executory contract or unexpired lease under §365(f) is stayed until the expiration of 14 days after the entry of the order, unless the court orders otherwise.

(e) LIMITATIONS. The trustee shall not seek authority to assume or assign multiple executory contracts or unexpired leases in one motion unless: (1) all executory contracts or unexpired leases to be assumed or assigned are between the same parties or are to be assigned to the same assignee; (2) the trustee seeks to assume, but not assign to more than one assignee, unexpired leases of real property; or (3) the court otherwise authorizes the motion to be filed. Subject to subdivision (f), the trustee may join requests for authority to reject multiple executory contracts or unexpired leases in one motion.

(f) OMNIBUS MOTIONS. A motion to reject or, if permitted under subdivision (e), a motion to assume or assign multiple executory contracts or unexpired leases that are not between the same parties shall:

(1) state in a conspicuous place that parties receiving the omnibus motion should locate their names and their contracts or leases listed in the motion;

(2) list parties alphabetically and identify the corresponding contract or lease;

(3) specify the terms, including the curing of defaults, for each requested assumption or assignment;

(4) specify the terms, including the identity of each assignee and the adequate assurance of future performance by each assignee, for each requested assignment;

(5) be numbered consecutively with other omnibus motions to assume, assign, or reject executory contracts or unexpired leases; and

(6) be limited to no more than 100 executory contracts or unexpired leases.

(g) FINALITY OF DETERMINATION. The finality of any order respecting an executory contract or unexpired lease included in an omnibus motion shall be determined as though such contract or lease had been the subject of a separate motion.

(As amended Mar. 30, 1987, eff. Aug. 1, 1987; Apr. 30, 1991, eff. Aug. 1, 1991; Apr. 22, 1993, eff. Aug. 1, 1993; Apr. 26, 1999, eff. Dec. 1, 1999; Apr. 30 2007; eff. Dec. 1, 2007; Mar. 26, 2009, eff. Dec. 1, 2009.)

NOTES OF ADVISORY COMMITTEE ON RULES—1983

Section 365(a) of the Code requires court approval for the assumption or rejection of an executory contract by the trustee or debtor in possession. The trustee or debtor in possession may also assign an executory contract, §365(f)(1), but must first assume the contract, §365(f)(2). Rule 6006 provides a procedure for obtaining court approval. It does not apply to the automatic rejection of contracts which are not assumed in chapter 7 liquidation cases within 60 days after the order for relief, or to the assumption or rejection of contracts in a plan pursuant to §1123(b)(2) or §1322(b)(7).

*Subdivision (a)* by referring to Rule 9014 requires a motion to be brought for the assumption, rejection, or assignment of an executory contract. Normally, the motion will be brought by the trustee, debtor in possession or debtor in a chapter 9 or chapter 13 case. The authorization to assume a contract and to assign it may be sought in a single motion and determined by a single order.

*Subdivision (b)* makes applicable the same motion procedure when the other party to the contract seeks to require the chapter officer to take some action. Section 365(d)(2) recognizes that this procedure is available to these contractual parties. This provision of the Code and subdivision of the rule apply only in chapter 9, 11 and 13 cases. A motion is not necessary in chapter 7 cases because in those cases a contract is deemed rejected if the trustee does not timely assume it.

*Subdivision (c)* provides for the court to set a hearing on a motion made under subdivision (a) or (b). The other party to the contract should be given appropriate notice of the hearing and the court may order that other parties in interest, such as a creditors' committee, also be given notice.

NOTES OF ADVISORY COMMITTEE ON RULES—1987 AMENDMENT

*Subdivisions (a) and (b)* are amended to conform to the 1984 amendment to §365 of the Code, which governs assumption or rejection of time share interests.

Section 1113, governing collective bargaining agreements, was added to the Code in 1984. It sets out requirements that must be met before a collective bargaining agreement may be rejected. The application to reject a collective bargaining agreement referred to in §1113 shall be made by motion. The motion to reject creates a contested matter under Rule 9014, and service is made pursuant to Rule 7004 on the representative of the employees. The time periods set forth in §1113(d) govern the scheduling of the hearing and disposition of a motion to reject the agreement.

NOTES OF ADVISORY COMMITTEE ON RULES—1991 AMENDMENT

References to time share interests are deleted as unnecessary. Time share interests are within the scope of this rule to the extent that they are governed by §365 of the Code.

*Subdivision (b)* is amended to include chapter 12 cases.

*Subdivision (c)* is amended to enable the United States trustee to appear and be heard on the issues relating to the assumption or rejection of executory contracts and unexpired leases. See §§307, 365, and 1113 of the Code.

NOTES OF ADVISORY COMMITTEE ON RULES AMENDMENT

This rule is amended to delete the requirement for an actual hearing when no request for a hearing is made. See Rule 9014.

COMMITTEE NOTES ON RULES—1999 AMENDMENT

*Subdivision (d)* is added to provide sufficient time for a party to request a stay pending appeal of an order authorizing the assignment of an executory contract or unexpired lease under §365(f) of the Code before the assignment is consummated. The stay under subdivision (d) does not affect the time for filing a notice of appeal in accordance with Rule 8002.

The court may, in its discretion, order that Rule 6006(d) is not applicable so that the executory contract or unexpired lease may be assigned immediately in accordance with the order entered by the court. Alternatively, the court may order that the stay under Rule 6006(d) is for a fixed period less than 10 days.

*GAP Report on Rule 6006.* No changes since publication.

COMMITTEE NOTES ON RULES—2007 AMENDMENT

The rule is amended to authorize the use of omnibus motions to reject multiple executory contracts and unexpired leases. In some cases there may be numerous executory contracts and unexpired leases, and this rule permits the combining of up to one hundred of these contracts and leases in a single motion to initiate the contested matter.

The rule also is amended to authorize the use of a single motion to assume or assign executory contracts and unexpired leases (i) when such contracts and leases are with a single nondebtor party, (ii) when such contracts and leases are being assigned to the same assignee, (iii) when the trustee proposes to assume, but not assign to more than one assignee, real property leases, or (iv) the court authorizes the filing of a joint motion to assume or to assume and assign executory contracts and unexpired leases under other circumstances that are not specifically recognized in the rule.

An omnibus motion to assume, assign, or reject multiple executory contracts and unexpired leases must comply with the procedural requirements set forth in subdivision (f) of the rule, unless the court orders otherwise. These requirements are intended to ensure that the nondebtor parties to the contracts and leases receive effective notice of the motion. Among those requirements is the requirement in subdivision (f)(5) that these motions be consecutively numbered (*e.g.*, Debtor in Possession's First Omnibus Motion for Authority to Assume Executory Contracts and Unexpired Leases, Debtor in Possession's Second Omnibus Motion for Authority to Assume Executory Contracts and Unexpired Leases, etc.). There may be a need for several of these motions in a particular case. Numbering the motions consecutively is essential to keep track of these motions on the court's docket and should avoid confusion that might otherwise result from similar or identically-titled motions.

Subdivision (g) of the rule provides that the finality of any order respecting an executory contract or unexpired lease included in an omnibus motion shall be determined as though such contract or lease had been the subject of a separate motion. A party seeking to appeal any such order is neither required, nor permitted, to await the court's resolution of all other contracts or leases included in the omnibus motion to obtain appellate review of the order. The rule permits the listing of multiple contracts or leases for convenience, and that convenience should not impede timely review of the court's decision with respect to each contract or lease.

*Changes After Publication.* Subdivision (e) of the proposed rule was amended as suggested by the NBC to insert a third category of requests that the trustee may make under an omnibus motion. The list of categories was numbered, and the new category is set out in (e)(2).

COMMITTEE NOTES ON RULES—2009 AMENDMENT

The rule is amended to implement changes in connection with the amendment to Rule 9006(a) and the manner by which time is computed under the rules. The deadline in the rule is amended to substitute a deadline that is a multiple of seven days. Throughout the rules, deadlines are amended in the following manner:

- 5-day periods become 7-day periods
- 10-day periods become 14-day periods
- 15-day periods become 14-day periods
- 20-day periods become 21-day periods
- 25-day periods become 28-day periods

## Rule 6007. Abandonment or Disposition of Property

(a) NOTICE OF PROPOSED ABANDONMENT OR DISPOSITION; OBJECTIONS; HEARING. Unless otherwise directed by the court, the trustee or debtor in possession shall give notice of a proposed abandonment or disposition of property to the United States trustee, all creditors, indenture trustees, and committees elected pursuant to §705 or appointed pursuant to §1102 of the Code. A party in interest may file and serve an objection within 14 days of the mailing of the notice, or within the time fixed by the court. If a timely objection is made, the court shall set a hearing on notice to the United States trustee and to other entities as the court may direct.

(b) MOTION BY PARTY IN INTEREST. A party in interest may file and serve a motion requiring the trustee or debtor in possession to abandon property of the estate.

[(c) HEARING] (Abrogated Apr. 22, 1993, eff. Aug. 1, 1993)

(As amended Mar. 30, 1987, eff. Aug. 1, 1987; Apr. 30, 1991, eff. Aug. 1, 1991; Apr. 22, 1993, eff. Aug. 1, 1993; Mar. 26, 2009, eff. Dec. 1, 2009.)

NOTES OF ADVISORY COMMITTEE ON RULES—1983

Sections 554 and 725 of the Code permit and require abandonment and disposition of property of the estate. Pursuant to §554, the trustee may abandon property but only after notice and hearing. This section is applicable in chapter 7, 11 and 13 cases. Section 725 requires the trustee to dispose of property in which someone other than the estate has an interest, prior to final distribution. It applies only in chapter 7 cases. Notice and hearing are also required conditions. Section 102(1) provides that "notice and hearing" is construed to mean appropriate notice and an opportunity for a hearing. Neither §554 nor §725 specify to whom the notices are to be sent. This rule does not apply to §554(c). Pursuant to that subsection, property is deemed abandoned if it is not administered. A hearing is not required by the statute.

*Subdivision (a)* requires the notices to be sent to all creditors, indenture trustees, and committees elected under §705 or appointed under §1102 of the Code. This may appear burdensome, expensive and inefficient but the subdivision is in keeping with the Code's requirement for notice and the Code's intent to remove the bankruptcy judge from undisputed matters. The burden, expense and inefficiency can be alleviated in large measure by incorporating the notice into or together with the notice of the meeting of creditors so that separate notices would not be required.

*Subdivision (b)* implements §554(b) which specifies that a party in interest may request an order that the trustee abandon property. The rule specifies that the request be by motion and, pursuant to the Code, lists the parties who should receive notice.

*Subdivision (c)* requires a hearing when an objection under subdivision (a) is filed or a motion under subdivision (b) is made. Filing of an objection is sufficient to require a hearing; a separate or joined request for a hearing is unnecessary since the objection itself is tantamount to such a request.

NOTES OF ADVISORY COMMITTEE ON RULES—1991 AMENDMENT

This rule is amended to conform to the 1986 amendments to 28 U.S.C. §586(a) and to the Code. The United States trustee monitors the progress of the case and has standing to raise, appear and be heard on the issues relating to the abandonment or other disposition of property. See §§307 and 554 of the Code. Committees of retired employees appointed under §1114 are not entitled to notice under subdivision (a) of this rule.

NOTES OF ADVISORY COMMITTEE ON RULES—1993 AMENDMENT

This rule is amended to clarify that when a motion is made pursuant to subdivision (b), a hearing is not required if a hearing is not requested or if there is no opposition to the motion. See Rule 9014. Other amendments are stylistic and make no substantive change.

COMMITTEE NOTES ON RULES—2009 AMENDMENT

The rule is amended to implement changes in connection with the amendment to Rule 9006(a) and the manner by which time is computed under the rules. The deadline in the rule is amended to substitute a deadline that is a multiple of seven days. Throughout the rules, deadlines are amended in the following manner:

- 5-day periods become 7-day periods
- 10-day periods become 14-day periods
- 15-day periods become 14-day periods
- 20-day periods become 21-day periods
- 25-day periods become 28-day periods

### Rule 6008. Redemption of Property from Lien or Sale

On motion by the debtor, trustee, or debtor in possession and after hearing on notice as the court may direct, the court may authorize the redemption of property from a lien or from a sale to enforce a lien in accordance with applicable law.

NOTES OF ADVISORY COMMITTEE ON RULES—1983

This rule is derived from former Bankruptcy Rule 609. No provision in the Code addresses the trustee's right of redemption. Ordinarily the secured creditor should be given notice of the trustee's motion so that any objection may be raised to the proposed redemption.

The rule applies also to a debtor exercising a right of redemption pursuant to §722. A proceeding under that section is governed by Rule 9014.

### Rule 6009. Prosecution and Defense of Proceedings by Trustee or Debtor in Possession

With or without court approval, the trustee or debtor in possession may prosecute or may enter an appearance and defend any pending action or proceeding by or against the debtor, or commence and prosecute any action or proceeding in behalf of the estate before any tribunal.

NOTES OF ADVISORY COMMITTEE ON RULES—1983

This rule is derived from former Bankruptcy Rule 610.

### Rule 6010. Proceeding to Avoid Indemnifying Lien or Transfer to Surety

If a lien voidable under §547 of the Code has been dissolved by the furnishing of a bond or other obligation and the surety thereon has been indemnified by the transfer of, or the creation of a lien upon, nonexempt property of the debtor, the surety shall be joined as a defendant in any proceeding to avoid the indemnifying transfer or lien. Such proceeding is governed by the rules in Part VII.

(As amended Apr. 30, 1991, eff. Aug. 1, 1991.)

NOTES OF ADVISORY COMMITTEE ON RULES—1983

This rule is derived from former Bankruptcy Rule 612.

NOTES OF ADVISORY COMMITTEE ON RULES—1991 AMENDMENT

This rule is amended to conform to §550(a) of the Code which provides that the trustee may recover the property transferred in a voidable transfer. The value of the property may be recovered in lieu of the property itself only if the court so orders.

### Rule 6011. Disposal of Patient Records in Health Care Business Case

(a) NOTICE BY PUBLICATION UNDER §351(1)(A). A notice regarding the claiming or disposing of patient records under §351(1)(A) shall not identify any patient by name or other identifying information, but shall:

(1) identify with particularity the health care facility whose patient records the trustee proposes to destroy;

(2) state the name, address, telephone number, email address, and website, if any, of a person from whom information about the patient records may be obtained;

(3) state how to claim the patient records; and

(4) state the date by which patient records must be claimed, and that if they are not so claimed the records will be destroyed.

(b) NOTICE BY MAIL UNDER §351(1)(B). Subject to applicable nonbankruptcy law relating to patient privacy, a notice regarding the claiming or disposing of patient records under §351(1)(B) shall, in addition to including the information in subdivision (a), direct that a patient's family member or other representative who receives the notice inform the patient of the notice. Any notice under this subdivision shall be mailed to the patient and any family member or other contact person whose name and address have been given to the trustee or the debtor for the purpose of providing information regarding the patient's health care, to the Attorney General of the State where the health care facility is located, and to any insurance company known to have provided health care insurance to the patient.

(c) PROOF OF COMPLIANCE WITH NOTICE REQUIREMENT. Unless the court orders the trustee to file proof of compliance with §351(1)(B) under seal, the trustee shall not file, but shall maintain, the proof of compliance for a reasonable time.

(d) REPORT OF DESTRUCTION OF RECORDS. The trustee shall file, no later than 30 days after the destruction of patient records under §351(3), a report certifying that the unclaimed records have been destroyed and explaining the method used to effect the destruction. The report shall not identify any patient by name or other identifying information.

(Added Apr. 23, 2008, eff. Dec. 1, 2008.)

COMMITTEE NOTES ON RULES—2008

This rule is new. It implements §351(1), which was added to the Code by the 2005 amendments. That provision requires the trustee to notify patients that their patient records will be destroyed if they remain unclaimed for one year after the publication of a notice in an appropriate newspaper. The Code provision also requires that individualized notice be sent to each patient and to the patient's family member or other contact person.

The variety of health care businesses and the range of current and former patients present the need for flexibility in the creation and publication of the notices that will be given. Nevertheless, there are some matters that must be included in any notice being given to patients, their family members, and contact persons to ensure that sufficient information is provided to these persons regarding the trustee's intent to dispose of patient records. Subdivision (a) of this rule lists the minimum requirements for notices given under §351(1)(A), and subdivision (b) governs the form of notices under §351(1)(B). Notices given under this rule are subject to provisions under applicable federal and state law that relate to the protection of patients' privacy, such as the Health Insurance Portability and Accountability Act of 1996, Pub. L. No. 104–191 (HIPAA).

Subdivision (c) directs the trustee to maintain proof of compliance with §351(1)(B), but because the proof of compliance may contain patient names that should or must remain confidential, it prohibits filing the proof of compliance unless the court orders the trustee to file it under seal.

Subdivision (d) requires the trustee to file a report with the court regarding the destruction of patient records. This certification is intended to ensure that the trustee properly completed the destruction process. However, because the report will be filed with the court and ordinarily will be available to the public under §107, the names, addresses, and other identifying information of patients are not to be included in the report to protect patient privacy.

*Changes Made After Publication.* Subdivision (b)(2) was amended to add the Attorney General of the State where a health care facility is located to the list of entities entitled to notice of the disposal of patient records.

## PART VII—ADVERSARY PROCEEDINGS

### Rule 7001. Scope of Rules of Part VII

An adversary proceeding is governed by the rules of this Part VII. The following are adversary proceedings:

(1) a proceeding to recover money or property, other than a proceeding to compel the debtor to deliver property to the trustee, or a proceeding under §554(b) or §725 of the Code, Rule 2017, or Rule 6002;

(2) a proceeding to determine the validity, priority, or extent of a lien or other interest in property, other than a proceeding under Rule 4003(d);

(3) a proceeding to obtain approval under §363(h) for the sale of both the interest of the estate and of a co-owner in property;

(4) a proceeding to object to or revoke a discharge;

(5) a proceeding to revoke an order of confirmation of a chapter 11, chapter 12, or chapter 13 plan;

(6) a proceeding to determine the dischargeability of a debt;

(7) a proceeding to obtain an injunction or other equitable relief, except when a chapter 9, chapter 11, chapter 12, or chapter 13 plan provides for the relief;

(8) a proceeding to subordinate any allowed claim or interest, except when a chapter 9, chapter 11, chapter 12, or chapter 13 plan provides for subordination;

(9) a proceeding to obtain a declaratory judgment relating to any of the foregoing; or

(10) a proceeding to determine a claim or cause of action removed under 28 U.S.C. §1452.

(As amended Mar. 30, 1987, eff. Aug. 1, 1987; Apr. 30, 1991, eff. Aug. 1, 1991; Apr. 26, 1999, eff. Dec. 1, 1999.)

NOTES OF ADVISORY COMMITTEE ON RULES—1983

The rules in Part VII govern the procedural aspects of litigation involving the matters referred to in this Rule 7001. Under Rule 9014 some of the Part VII rules also apply to contested matters.

These Part VII rules are based on the premise that to the extent possible practice before the bankruptcy courts and the district courts should be the same. These rules either incorporate or are adaptations of most of the Federal Rules of Civil Procedure. Although the Part VII rules of the former Bankruptcy Rules also relied heavily on the F.R.Civ.P., the former Part VII rules departed from the civil practice in two significant ways: a trial or pretrial conference had to be scheduled as soon as the adversary proceeding was filed and pleadings had to be filed within periods shorter than those established by the F.R.Civ.P. These departures from the civil practice have been eliminated.

The content and numbering of these Part VII rules correlates to the content and numbering of the F.R.Civ.P. Most, but not all, of the F.R.Civ.P. have a comparable Part VII rule. When there is no Part VII rule with a number corresponding to a particular F.R.Civ.P., Parts V and IX of these rules must be consulted to determine if one of the rules in those parts deals with the subject. The list below indicates the F.R.Civ.P., or subdivision thereof, covered by a rule in either Part V or Part IX.

| F.R.Civ.P. | Rule in Part V or IX |
|---|---|
| 6 | 9006 |
| 7(b) | 9013 |
| 10(a) | 9004(b) |
| 11 | 9011 |
| 38,39 | 9015(a)–(e) |
| 47–51 | 9015(f) |
| 43,44,44.1 | 9017 |
| 45 | 9016 |
| 58 | 9021 |
| 59 | 9023 |
| 60 | 9024 |
| 61 | 9005 |
| 63 | 9028 |
| 77(a),(b),(c) | 5001 |
| 77(d) | 9022(d) |
| 79(a)–(d) | 5003 |
| 81(c) | 9027 |
| 83 | 9029 |
| 92 | 9030 |

Proceedings to which the rules in Part VII apply directly include those brought to avoid transfers by the debtor under §§544, 545, 547, 548 and 549 of the Code; subject to important exceptions, proceedings to recover money or property; proceedings on bonds under Rules 5008(d) and 9025; proceedings under Rule 4004 to determine whether a discharge in a chapter 7 or 11 case should be denied because of an objection grounded on §727 and proceedings in a chapter 7 or 13 case to revoke a discharge as provided in §§727(d) or 1328(e); and proceedings initiated pursuant to §523(c) of the Code to determine the dischargeability of a particular debt. Those proceedings were classified as adversary proceedings under former Bankruptcy Rule 701.

Also included as adversary proceedings are proceedings to revoke an order of confirmation of a plan in a chapter 11 or 13 case as provided in §§1144 and 1330, to subordinate under §510(c), other than as part of a plan, an allowed claim or interest, and to sell under §363(h) both the interest of the estate and a co-owner in property.

Declaratory judgments with respect to the subject matter of the various adversary proceedings are also adversary proceedings.

Any claim or cause of action removed to a bankruptcy court pursuant to 28 U.S.C. §1478 is also an adversary proceeding.

Unlike former Bankruptcy Rule 701, requests for relief from an automatic stay do not commence an adversary proceeding. Section 362(e) of the Code and Rule 4001 establish an expedited schedule for judicial disposition of requests for relief from the automatic stay. The formalities of the adversary proceeding process and the time for serving pleadings are not well suited to the expedited schedule. The motion practice prescribed in Rule 4001 is best suited to such requests because the court has the flexibility to fix hearing dates and other deadlines appropriate to the particular situation.

Clause (1) contains important exceptions. A person with an interest in property in the possession of the trustee or debtor in possession may seek to recover or reclaim that property under §554(b) or §725 of the Code. Since many attempts to recover or reclaim property under these two sections do not generate disputes, application of the formalities of the Part VII Rules is not appropriate. Also excluded from adversary proceedings is litigation arising from an examination under Rule 2017 of a debtor's payments of money or transfers of property to an attorney representing the debtor in a case under the Code or an examination of a superseded administration under Rule 6002.

Exemptions and objections thereto are governed by Rule 4003. Filing of proofs of claim and the allowances thereof are governed by Rules 3001–3005, and objections to claims are governed by Rule 3007. When an objection to a claim is joined with a demand for relief of the kind specified in this Rule 7001, the matter becomes an adversary proceeding. See Rule 3007.

NOTES OF ADVISORY COMMITTEE ON RULES—1987 AMENDMENT

Another exception is added to clause (1). A trustee may proceed by motion to recover property from the debtor.

NOTES OF ADVISORY COMMITTEE ON RULES—1991 AMENDMENT

Clauses (5) and (8) are amended to include chapter 12 plans.

COMMITTEE NOTES ON RULES—1999 AMENDMENT

This rule is amended to recognize that an adversary proceeding is not necessary to obtain injunctive or other equitable relief that is provided for in a plan under circumstances in which substantive law permits the relief. Other amendments are stylistic.

*GAP Report on Rule 7001.* No changes since publication, except for stylistic changes.

## Rule 7002. References to Federal Rules of Civil Procedure

Whenever a Federal Rule of Civil Procedure applicable to adversary proceedings makes reference to another Federal Rule of Civil Procedure, the reference shall be read as a reference to the Federal Rule of Civil Procedure as modified in this Part VII.

NOTES OF ADVISORY COMMITTEE ON RULES—1983

Rules 5, 12, 13, 14, 25, 27, 30, 41 and 52 F.R.Civ.P. are made applicable to adversary proceedings by Part VII. Each of those rules contains a cross reference to another Federal Rule; however, the Part VII rule which incorporates the cross-referenced Federal Rule modifies the Federal Rule in some way. Under this Rule 7002 the cross reference is to the Federal Rule as modified by Part VII. For example, Rule 5 F.R.Civ.P., which is made applicable to adversary proceedings by Rule 7005, contains a reference to Rule 4 F.R.Civ.P. Under this Rule 7002, the cross reference is to Rule 4 F.R.Civ.P. as modified by Rule 7004.

Rules 7, 10, 12, 13, 14, 19, 22, 23.2, 24–37, 41, 45, 49, 50, 52, 55, 59, 60, 62 F.R.Civ.P. are made applicable to adversary proceedings by Part VII or generally to cases under the Code by Part IX. Each of those Federal Rules contains a cross reference to another Federal Rule which is not modified by the Part VII or Part IX rule which makes the cross-referenced Federal Rule applicable. Since the cross-referenced rule is not modified by a Part VII rule this Rule 7002 does not apply.

REFERENCES IN TEXT

The Federal Rules of Civil Procedure, referred to in text, are set out in the Appendix to Title 28, Judiciary and Judicial Procedure.

## Rule 7003. Commencement of Adversary Proceeding

Rule 3 F.R.Civ.P. applies in adversary proceedings.

NOTES OF ADVISORY COMMITTEE ON RULES—1983

Rule 5005(a) requires that a complaint commencing an adversary proceeding be filed with the court in which the case under the Code is pending unless 28 U.S.C. §1473 authorizes the filing of the complaint in another district.

REFERENCES IN TEXT

The Federal Rules of Civil Procedure, referred to in text, are set out in the Appendix to Title 28, Judiciary and Judicial Procedure.

## Rule 7004. Process; Service of Summons, Complaint

(a) SUMMONS; SERVICE; PROOF OF SERVICE.

(1) Except as provided in Rule 7004(a)(2), Rule 4(a), (b), (c)(1), (d)(1), (e)–(j), (*l*), and (m) F.R.Civ.P. applies in adversary proceedings. Personal service under Rule 4(e)–(j) F.R.Civ.P. may be made by any person at least 18 years of age who is not a party, and the summons may be delivered by the clerk to any such person.

(2) The clerk may sign, seal, and issue a summons electronically by putting an "s/" before the clerk's name and including the court's seal on the summons.

(b) SERVICE BY FIRST CLASS MAIL. Except as provided in subdivision (h), in addition to the methods of service authorized by Rule 4(e)–(j) F.R.Civ.P., service may be made within the United States by first class mail postage prepaid as follows:

(1) Upon an individual other than an infant or incompetent, by mailing a copy of the summons and complaint to the individual's dwelling house or usual place of abode or to the place where the individual regularly conducts a business or profession.

(2) Upon an infant or an incompetent person, by mailing a copy of the summons and complaint to the person upon whom process is prescribed to be served by the law of the state in which service is made when an action is brought against such a defendant in the courts of general jurisdiction of that state. The summons and complaint in that case shall be addressed to the person required to be served at that person's dwelling house or usual place of abode or at the place where the person regularly conducts a business or profession.

(3) Upon a domestic or foreign corporation or upon a partnership or other unincorporated association, by mailing a copy of the summons and complaint to the attention of an officer, a managing or general agent, or to any other agent authorized by appointment or by law to receive service of process and, if the agent is one authorized by statute to receive service and the statute so requires, by also mailing a copy to the defendant.

(4) Upon the United States, by mailing a copy of the summons and complaint addressed to the civil process clerk at the office of the United States attorney for the district in which the action is brought and by mailing a

copy of the summons and complaint to the Attorney General of the United States at Washington, District of Columbia, and in any action attacking the validity of an order of an officer or an agency of the United States not made a party, by also mailing a copy of the summons and complaint to that officer or agency. The court shall allow a reasonable time for service pursuant to this subdivision for the purpose of curing the failure to mail a copy of the summons and complaint to multiple officers, agencies, or corporations of the United States if the plaintiff has mailed a copy of the summons and complaint either to the civil process clerk at the office of the United States attorney or to the Attorney General of the United States.

(5) Upon any officer or agency of the United States, by mailing a copy of the summons and complaint to the United States as prescribed in paragraph (4) of this subdivision and also to the officer or agency. If the agency is a corporation, the mailing shall be as prescribed in paragraph (3) of this subdivision of this rule. The court shall allow a reasonable time for service pursuant to this subdivision for the purpose of curing the failure to mail a copy of the summons and complaint to multiple officers, agencies, or corporations of the United States if the plaintiff has mailed a copy of the summons and complaint either to the civil process clerk at the office of the United States attorney or to the Attorney General of the United States. If the United States trustee is the trustee in the case and service is made upon the United States trustee solely as trustee, service may be made as prescribed in paragraph (10) of this subdivision of this rule.

(6) Upon a state or municipal corporation or other governmental organization thereof subject to suit, by mailing a copy of the summons and complaint to the person or office upon whom process is prescribed to be served by the law of the state in which service is made when an action is brought against such a defendant in the courts of general jurisdiction of that state, or in the absence of the designation of any such person or office by state law, then to the chief executive officer thereof.

(7) Upon a defendant of any class referred to in paragraph (1) or (3) of this subdivision of this rule, it is also sufficient if a copy of the summons and complaint is mailed to the entity upon whom service is prescribed to be served by any statute of the United States or by the law of the state in which service is made when an action is brought against such a defendant in the court of general jurisdiction of that state.

(8) Upon any defendant, it is also sufficient if a copy of the summons and complaint is mailed to an agent of such defendant authorized by appointment or by law to receive service of process, at the agent's dwelling house or usual place of abode or at the place where the agent regularly carries on a business or profession and, if the authorization so requires, by mailing also a copy of the summons and complaint to the defendant as provided in this subdivision.

(9) Upon the debtor, after a petition has been filed by or served upon the debtor and until the case is dismissed or closed, by mailing a copy of the summons and complaint to the debtor at the address shown in the petition or to such other address as the debtor may designate in a filed writing.

(10) Upon the United States trustee, when the United States trustee is the trustee in the case and service is made upon the United States trustee solely as trustee, by mailing a copy of the summons and complaint to an office of the United States trustee or another place designated by the United States trustee in the district where the case under the Code is pending.

(c) SERVICE BY PUBLICATION. If a party to an adversary proceeding to determine or protect rights in property in the custody of the court cannot be served as provided in Rule 4(e)–(j) F.R.Civ.P. or subdivision (b) of this rule, the court may order the summons and complaint to be served by mailing copies thereof by first class mail, postage prepaid, to the party's last known address, and by at least one publication in such manner and form as the court may direct.

(d) NATIONWIDE SERVICE OF PROCESS. The summons and complaint and all other process except a subpoena may be served anywhere in the United States.

(e) SUMMONS: TIME LIMIT FOR SERVICE WITHIN THE UNITED STATES. Service made under Rule 4(e), (g), (h)(1), (i), or (j)(2) F.R.Civ.P. shall be by delivery of the summons and complaint within 14 days after the summons is issued. If service is by any authorized form of mail, the summons and complaint shall be deposited in the mail within 14 days after the summons is issued. If a summons is not timely delivered or mailed, another summons shall be issued and served. This subdivision does not apply to service in a foreign country.

(f) PERSONAL JURISDICTION. If the exercise of jurisdiction is consistent with the Constitution and laws of the United States, serving a summons or filing a waiver of service in accordance with this rule or the subdivisions of Rule 4 F.R.Civ.P. made applicable by these rules is effective to establish personal jurisdiction over the person of any defendant with respect to a case under the Code or a civil proceeding arising under the Code, or arising in or related to a case under the Code.

(g) SERVICE ON DEBTOR'S ATTORNEY. If the debtor is represented by an attorney, whenever service is made upon the debtor under this Rule, service shall also be made upon the debtor's attorney by any means authorized under Rule 5(b) F.R.Civ.P.

(h) SERVICE OF PROCESS ON AN INSURED DEPOSI TORY INSTITUTION. Service on an insured depository institution (as defined in section 3 of the Federal Deposit Insurance Act) in a contested matter or adversary proceeding shall be made by certified mail addressed to an officer of the institution unless—

(1) the institution has appeared by its attorney, in which case the attorney shall be served by first class mail;

(2) the court orders otherwise after service upon the institution by certified mail of notice of an application to permit service on the institution by first class mail sent to an offi-

cer of the institution designated by the institution; or

(3) the institution has waived in writing its entitlement to service by certified mail by designating an officer to receive service.

(As amended Mar. 30, 1987, eff. Aug. 1, 1987; Apr. 30, 1991, eff. Aug. 1, 1991; Pub. L. 103–394, title I, §114, Oct. 22, 1994, 108 Stat. 4118; Apr. 23, 1996, eff. Dec. 1, 1996; Apr. 26, 1999, eff. Dec. 1, 1999; Apr. 25, 2005, eff. Dec. 1, 2005; Apr. 12, 2006, eff. Dec. 1, 2006; Mar. 26, 2009, eff. Dec. 1, 2009.)

NOTES OF ADVISORY COMMITTEE ON RULES—1983

*Subdivision (a)* of the rule, by incorporation of Rule 4(a), (b), (d), (e) and (g)–(i) F.R.Civ.P., governs the mechanics of issuance of a summons and its form, the manner of service on parties and their representatives, and service in foreign countries.

*Subdivision (b)*, which is the same as former Rule 704(c), authorizes service of process by first class mail postage prepaid. This rule retains the modes of service contained in former Bankruptcy Rule 704. The former practice, in effect since 1976, has proven satisfactory.

*Subdivision (c)* is derived from former Bankruptcy Rule 704(d)(2).

*Subdivision (d)*. Nationwide service of process is authorized by subdivision (d).

*Subdivision (e)* authorizes service by delivery on individuals and corporations in foreign countries if the party to be served is the debtor or any person required to perform the duties of the debtor and certain other persons, the adversary proceeding involves property in the custody of the bankruptcy court, or if federal or state law authorizes such service in a foreign country.

*Subdivision (f)*. The requirement of former Bankruptcy Rule 704 that the summons be served within 10 days is carried over into these rules by subdivision (f).

NOTES OF ADVISORY COMMITTEE ON RULES—1987 AMENDMENT

*Subdivision (a)* is amended to make Rule 4(j) F.R.Civ.P. applicable to service of the summons. If service is not completed within 120 days of the filing of the complaint, the complaint may be dismissed.

Technical amendments are made to subdivisions (a), (b), (e), and (f) to conform to recent amendments to Rule 4 F.R.Civ.P.

NOTES OF ADVISORY COMMITTEE ON RULES—1991 AMENDMENT

The United States trustee may serve as trustee in a case pursuant to 28 U.S.C. §586(a)(2) and §§701(a)(2), 1202(a), and 1302(a) of the Code. This rule is amended to avoid the necessity of mailing copies of a summons and complaint or other pleadings to the Attorney General and to the United States attorney when service on the United States trustee is required only because the United States trustee is acting as a case trustee. For example, a proceeding commenced by a creditor to dismiss a case for unreasonable delay under §707(a) is governed by Rule 9014 which requires service on the trustee pursuant to the requirements of Rule 7004 for the service of a summons and complaint. The Attorney General and the United States attorney would have no interest in receiving a copy of the motion to dismiss. Mailing to the office of the United States trustee when acting as the case trustee is sufficient in such cases.

The words "with the court" in subdivision (b)(9) are deleted as unnecessary. See Rules 5005(a) and 9001(3).

The new paragraph (10) of subdivision (b) does not affect requirements for service of process on the United States trustee when sued or otherwise a party to a litigation unrelated to its capacity as a trustee. If a proceeding is commenced against the United States trustee which is unrelated to the United States trustee's role as trustee, the requirements of paragraph (5) of subdivision (b) of this rule would apply.

*Subdivision (g)* is added in anticipation of substantial amendment to, and restructuring of subdivisions of, Rule 4 F.R.Civ.P. Any amendment to Rule 4 will not affect service in bankruptcy cases and proceedings until further amendment to the Bankruptcy Rules. On January 1, 1990, Rule 4 F.R.Civ.P. read as follows:

RULE 4 F.R.CIV.P.

PROCESS

(a) SUMMONS: ISSUANCE. Upon the filing of the complaint the clerk shall forthwith issue a summons and deliver the summons to the plaintiff or the plaintiff's attorney, who shall be responsible for prompt service of the summons and a copy of the complaint. Upon request of the plaintiff separate or additional summons shall issue against any defendants.

(b) SAME: FORM. The summons shall be signed by the clerk, be under the seal of the court, contain the name of the court and the names of the parties, be directed to the defendant, state the name and address of the plaintiff's attorney, if any, otherwise the plaintiff's address, and the time within which these rules require the defendant to appear and defend, and shall notify the defendant that in case of the defendant's failure to do so judgment by default will be rendered against the defendant for the relief demanded in the complaint. When, under Rule 4(e), service is made pursuant to a statute or rule of court of a state, the summons, or notice, or order in lieu of summons shall correspond as nearly as may be to that required by the statute or rule.

(c) SERVICE.

(1) [Not applicable.]

(2)(A) [Not applicable.]

(B) [Not applicable.]

(C) A summons and complaint may be served upon a defendant of any class referred to in paragraph (1) or (3) of subdivision (d) of this rule—

(i) pursuant to the law of the State in which the district court is held for the service of summons or other like process upon such defendant in an action brought in the courts of general jurisdiction of that State, or

(ii) [Not applicable.]

(D) [Not applicable.]

(E) [Not applicable.]

(3) [Not applicable.]

(d) SUMMONS AND COMPLAINT: PERSON TO BE SERVED. The summons and complaint shall be served together. The plaintiff shall furnish the person making service with such copies as are necessary. Service shall be made as follows:

(1) Upon an individual other than an infant or an incompetent person, by delivering a copy of the summons and of the complaint to the individual personally or by leaving copies thereof at the individual's dwelling house or usual place of abode with some person of suitable age and discretion then residing therein or by delivering a copy of the summons and of the complaint to an agent authorized by appointment or by law to receive service of process.

(2) Upon an infant or an incompetent person, by serving the summons and complaint in the manner prescribed by the law of the state in which the service is made for the service of summons or other like process upon any such defendant in an action brought in the courts of general jurisdiction of that state.

(3) Upon a domestic or foreign corporation or upon a partnership or other unincorporated association which is subject to suit under a common name, by delivering a copy of the summons and of the complaint to an officer, a managing or general agent, or to any other agent authorized by appointment or by law to receive service of process and, if the agent is one authorized by statute to receive service and the statute so requires, by also mailing a copy to the defendant.

(4) Upon the United States, by delivering a copy of the summons and of the complaint to the United States attorney for the district in which the action is

brought or to an assistant United States attorney or clerical employee designated by the United States attorney in a writing filed with the clerk of the court and by sending a copy of the summons and of the complaint by registered or certified mail to the Attorney General of the United States at Washington, District of Columbia, and in any action attacking the validity of an order of an officer or agency of the United States not made a party, by also sending a copy of the summons and of the complaint by registered or certified mail to such officer or agency.

(5) Upon an officer or agency of the United States, by serving the United States and by sending a copy of the summons and of the complaint by registered or certified mail to such officer or agency. If the agency is a corporation the copy shall be delivered as provided in paragraph (3) of this subdivision of this rule.

(6) Upon a state or municipal corporation or other governmental organization thereof subject to suit, by delivering a copy of the summons and of the complaint to the chief executive officer thereof or by serving the summons and complaint in the manner prescribed by the law of that state for the service of summons or other like process upon any such defendant.

(e) SUMMONS: SERVICE UPON PARTY NOT INHABITANT OF OR FOUND WITHIN STATE. Whenever a statute of the United States or an order of court thereunder provides for service of a summons, or of a notice, or of an order in lieu of summons upon a party not an inhabitant of or found within the state in which the district court is held, service may be made under the circumstances and in the manner prescribed by the statute or order, or, if there is no provision therein prescribing the manner of service, in a manner stated in this rule. Whenever a statute or rule of court of the state in which the district court is held provides (1) for service of a summons, or of a notice, or of an order in lieu of summons upon a party not an inhabitant of or found within the state, or (2) for service upon or notice to such a party to appear and respond or defend in an action by reason of the attachment or garnishment or similar seizure of the party's property located within the state, service may in either case be made under the circumstances and in the manner prescribed in the statute or rule.

(f) [Not applicable.]

(g) RETURN. The person serving the process shall make proof of service thereof to the court promptly and in any event within the time during which the person served must respond to the process. If service is made by a person other than a United States marshal or deputy United States marshal, such person shall make affidavit thereof. If service is made under subdivision (c)(2)(C)(ii) of this rule, return shall be made by the sender's filing with the court the acknowledgment received pursuant to such subdivision. Failure to make proof of service does not affect the validity of the service.

(h) AMENDMENT. At any time in its discretion and upon such terms as it deems just, the court may allow any process or proof of service thereof to be amended, unless it clearly appears that material prejudice would result to the substantial rights of the party against whom the process issued.

(i) ALTERNATIVE PROVISIONS FOR SERVICE IN A FOREIGN COUNTRY.

(1) *Manner.* When the federal or state law referred to in subdivision (e) of this rule authorizes service upon a party not an inhabitant of or found within the state in which the district court is held, and service is to be effected upon the party in a foreign country, it is also sufficient if service of the summons and complaint is made: (A) in the manner prescribed by the law of the foreign country for service in that country in an action in any of its courts of general jurisdiction; or (B) as directed by the foreign authority in response to a letter rogatory, when service in either case is reasonably calculated to give actual notice; or (C) upon an individual, by delivery to the individual personally, and upon a corporation or partnership or association, by delivery to an officer, a managing or general agent; or (D) by any form of mail, requiring a signed receipt, to be addressed and dispatched by the clerk of the court to the party to be served; or (E) as directed by order of the court. Service under (C) or (E) above may be made by any person who is not a party and is not less than 18 years of age or who is designated by order of the district court or by the foreign court. On request, the clerk shall deliver the summons to the plaintiff for transmission to the person or the foreign court or officer who will make the service.

(2) *Return.* Proof of service may be made as prescribed by subdivision (g) of this rule, or by the law of the foreign country, or by order of the court. When service is made pursuant to subparagraph (1)(D) of this subdivision, proof of service shall include a receipt signed by the addressee or other evidence of delivery to the addressee satisfactory to the court.

(j) SUMMONS: TIME LIMIT FOR SERVICE. If a service of the summons and complaint is not made upon a defendant within 120 days after the filing of the complaint and the party on whose behalf such service was required cannot show good cause why such service was not made within that period, the action shall be dismissed as to that defendant without prejudice upon the court's own initiative with notice to such party or upon motion. This subdivision shall not apply to service in a foreign country pursuant to subdivision (i) of this rule.

NOTES OF ADVISORY COMMITTEE ON RULES—1996 AMENDMENT

The purpose of these amendments is to conform the rule to the 1993 revisions of Rule 4 F.R.Civ.P. and to make stylistic improvements. Rule 7004, as amended, continues to provide for service by first class mail as an alternative to the methods of personal service provided in Rule 4 F.R.Civ.P., except as provided in the new subdivision (h).

Rule 4(d)(2) F.R.Civ.P. provides a procedure by which the plaintiff may request by first class mail that the defendant waive service of the summons. This procedure is not applicable in adversary proceedings because it is not necessary in view of the availability of service by mail pursuant to Rule 7004(b). However, if a written waiver of service of a summons is made in an adversary proceeding, Rule 4(d)(1) F.R.Civ.P. applies so that the defendant does not thereby waive any objection to the venue or the jurisdiction of the court over the person of the defendant.

*Subdivisions (b)(4) and (b)(5)* are amended to conform to the 1993 amendments to Rule 4(i)(3) F.R.Civ.P., which protect the plaintiff from the hazard of losing a substantive right because of failure to comply with the requirements of multiple service when the United States or an officer, agency, or corporation of the United States is a defendant. These subdivisions also are amended to require that the summons and complaint be addressed to the civil process clerk at the office of the United States attorney.

*Subdivision (e),* which has governed service in a foreign country, is abrogated and Rule 4(f) and (h)(2) F.R.Civ.P., as substantially revised in 1993, are made applicable in adversary proceedings.

The new subdivision (f) is consistent with the 1993 amendments to F.R.Civ.P. 4(k)(2). It clarifies that service or filing a waiver of service in accordance with this rule or the applicable subdivisions of F.R.Civ.P. 4 is sufficient to establish personal jurisdiction over the defendant. See the committee note to the 1993 amendments to Rule 4 F.R.Civ.P.

*Subdivision (g)* is abrogated. This subdivision was promulgated in 1991 so that anticipated revisions to Rule 4 F.R.Civ.P. would not affect service of process in adversary proceedings until further amendment to Rule 7004.

*Subdivision (h)* and the first phrase of subdivision (b) were added by §114 of the Bankruptcy Reform Act of 1994, Pub. L. No. 103–394, 108 Stat. 4106.

*GAP Report on Rule 7004.* After publication of the proposed amendments, Rule 7004(b) was amended and Rule

7004(h) was added by the Bankruptcy Reform Act of 1994 to provide for service by certified mail on an insured depository institution. The above draft includes those statutory amendments (without underlining new language or striking former language). No other changes have been made since publication, except for stylistic changes.

COMMITTEE NOTES ON RULES—1999 AMENDMENT

*Subdivision (e)* is amended so that the ten-day time limit for service of a summons does not apply if the summons is served in a foreign country.

*GAP Report on Rule 7004.* No changes since publication.

COMMITTEE NOTES ON RULES—2005 AMENDMENT

This amendment specifically authorizes the clerk to issue a summons electronically. In some bankruptcy cases the trustee or debtor in possession may commence hundreds of adversary proceedings simultaneously, and permitting the electronic signing and sealing of the summonses for those proceedings increases the efficiency of the clerk's office without any negative impact on any party. The rule only authorizes electronic issuance of the summons. It does not address the service requirements for the summons. Those requirements are set out elsewhere in Rule 7004, and nothing in Rule 7004(a)(2) should be construed as authorizing electronic service of a summons.

*Changes Made After Publication and Comment.* No changes were made after publication.

COMMITTEE NOTES ON RULES—2006 AMENDMENT

Under current Rule 7004, an entity may serve a summons and complaint upon the debtor by personal service or by mail. If the entity chooses to serve the debtor by mail, it must also serve a copy of the summons and complaint on the debtor's attorney by mail. If the entity effects personal service on the debtor, there is no requirement that the debtor's attorney also be served.

*Subdivision (b)(9).* The rule is amended to delete the reference in subdivision (b)(9) to the debtor's address as set forth in the statement of financial affairs. In 1991, the Official Form of the statement of financial affairs was revised and no longer includes a question regarding the debtor's current residence. Since that time, Official Form 1, the petition, has required the debtor to list both the debtor's residence and mailing address. Therefore, the subdivision is amended to delete the statement of financial affairs as a document that might contain an address at which the debtor can be served.

*Subdivision (g).* The rule is amended to require service on the debtor's attorney whenever the debtor is served with a summons and complaint. The amendment makes this change by deleting that portion of Rule 7004(b)(9) that requires service on the debtor's attorney when the debtor is served by mail, and relocates the obligation to serve the debtor's attorney into new subdivision (g). Service on the debtor's attorney is not limited to mail service, but may be accomplished by any means permitted under Rule 5(b) F.R.Civ.P.

*Changes Made After Publication.* The Committee Note was amended to add the final [second] paragraph of the Note. The new paragraph describes the reason for the deletion of the reference in the rule to the statement of affairs as a source for the debtor's address. This was a secondary reason for amending the rule, and even in the absence of public comment on the proposed amendment, the Advisory Committee believes that the additional explanation in the Committee Note is appropriate.

COMMITTEE NOTES ON RULES—2009 AMENDMENT

The rule is amended to implement changes in connection with the amendment to Rule 9006(a) and the manner by which time is computed under the rules. The deadlines in the rule are amended to substitute a deadline that is a multiple of seven days. Throughout the rules, deadlines are amended in the following manner:

- 5-day periods become 7-day periods
- 10-day periods become 14-day periods
- 15-day periods become 14-day periods
- 20-day periods become 21-day periods
- 25-day periods become 28-day periods

REFERENCES IN TEXT

The Federal Rules of Civil Procedure, referred to in text, are set out in the Appendix to Title 28, Judiciary and Judicial Procedure.

Section 3 of the Federal Deposit Insurance Act, referred to in subd. (h), is classified to section 1813 of Title 12, Banks and Banking.

AMENDMENT BY PUBLIC LAW

1994—Subd. (b). Pub. L. 103–394, §114(1), substituted "Except as provided in subdivision (h), in addition" for "In addition".

Subd. (h). Pub. L. 103–394, §114(2), added subd. (h).

EFFECTIVE DATE OF 1994 AMENDMENT

Amendment by Pub. L. 103–394 effective Oct. 22, 1994, and not applicable with respect to cases commenced under this title before Oct. 22, 1994, see section 702 of Pub. L. 103–394, set out as a note under section 101 of this title.

## Rule 7005. Service and Filing of Pleadings and Other Papers

Rule 5 F.R.Civ.P. applies in adversary proceedings.

NOTES OF ADVISORY COMMITTEE ON RULES—1983

Rule 5 F.R.Civ.P. refers to Rule 4 F.R.Civ.P. Pursuant to Rule 7002 this reference is to Rule 4 F.R.Civ.P. as incorporated and modified by Rule 7004.

REFERENCES IN TEXT

The Federal Rules of Civil Procedure, referred to in text, are set out in the Appendix to Title 28, Judiciary and Judicial Procedure.

## Rule 7007. Pleadings Allowed

Rule 7 F.R.Civ.P. applies in adversary proceedings.

REFERENCES IN TEXT

The Federal Rules of Civil Procedure, referred to in text, are set out in the Appendix to Title 28, Judiciary and Judicial Procedure.

## Rule 7007.1. Corporate Ownership Statement

(a) REQUIRED DISCLOSURE. Any corporation that is a party to an adversary proceeding, other than the debtor or a governmental unit, shall file two copies of a statement that identifies any corporation, other than a governmental unit, that directly or indirectly owns 10% or more of any class of the corporation's equity interests, or states that there are no entities to report under this subdivision.

(b) TIME FOR FILING. A party shall file the statement required under Rule 7007.1(a) with its first appearance, pleading, motion, response, or other request addressed to the court. A party shall file a supplemental statement promptly upon any change in circumstances that this rule requires the party to identify or disclose.

(Added Mar. 27, 2003, eff. Dec. 1, 2003; amended Apr. 30, 2007; eff. Dec. 1, 2007.)

COMMITTEE NOTES ON RULES—2003

This rule is derived from Rule 26.1 of the Federal Rules of Appellate Procedure. The information that parties shall supply will support properly informed disqualification decisions in situations that call for automatic disqualification under Canon 3C(1)(c) of the Code of Conduct for United States Judges. This rule does not cover all of the circumstances that may call for disqualification under the subjective financial interest standard of Canon 3C, and does not deal at all with other circumstances that may call for disqualification. Nevertheless, the required disclosures are calculated to reach the majority of circumstances that are likely to call for disqualification under Canon 3C(1)(c).

The rule directs nongovernmental corporate parties to list those corporations that hold significant ownership interests in them. This includes listing membership interests in limited liability companies and similar entities that fall under the definition of a corporation in Bankruptcy Code §101.

Under subdivision (b), parties must file the statement with the first document that they file in any adversary proceeding. The rule also requires parties and other persons to file supplemental statements promptly whenever changed circumstances require disclosure of new or additional information.

The rule does not prohibit the adoption of local rules requiring disclosures beyond those called for in Rule 7007.1.

*Changes Made After Publication and Comments.* No changes since publication.

COMMITTEE NOTES ON RULES—2007 AMENDMENT

The rule is amended to clarify that a party must file a corporate ownership statement with its initial paper filed with the court in an adversary proceeding. The party's initial filing may be a document that is not a "pleading" as defined in Rule 7 F. R. Civ. P., which is made applicable in adversary proceedings by Rule 7007. The amendment also brings Rule 7007.1 more closely in line with Rule 7.1 F. R. Civ. P.

*Changes After Publication.* No changes were made after publication.

## Rule 7008. General Rules of Pleading

(a) APPLICABILITY OF RULE 8 F.R.CIV.P. Rule 8 F.R.Civ.P. applies in adversary proceedings. The allegation of jurisdiction required by Rule 8(a) shall also contain a reference to the name, number, and chapter of the case under the Code to which the adversary proceeding relates and to the district and division where the case under the Code is pending. In an adversary proceeding before a bankruptcy judge, the complaint, counterclaim, cross-claim, or third-party complaint shall contain a statement that the proceeding is core or non-core and, if non-core, that the pleader does or does not consent to entry of final orders or judgment by the bankruptcy judge.

(b) ATTORNEY'S FEES. A request for an award of attorney's fees shall be pleaded as a claim in a complaint, cross-claim, third-party complaint, answer, or reply as may be appropriate.

(As amended Mar. 30, 1987, eff. Aug. 1, 1987.)

NOTES OF ADVISORY COMMITTEE ON RULES—1987 AMENDMENT

Proceedings before a bankruptcy judge are either core or non-core. 28 U.S.C. §157. A bankruptcy judge may enter a final order or judgment in a core proceeding. In a non-core proceeding, absent consent of the parties, the bankruptcy judge may not enter a final order or judgment but may only submit proposed findings of fact and conclusions of law to the district judge who will enter the final order or judgment. 28 U.S.C. §157(c)(1). The amendment to subdivision (a) of this rule requires an allegation as to whether a proceeding is core or non-core. A party who alleges that the proceeding is non-core shall state whether the party does or does not consent to the entry of a final order or judgment by the bankruptcy judge. Failure to include the statement of consent does not constitute consent. Only express consent in the pleadings or otherwise is effective to authorize entry of a final order or judgment by the bankruptcy judge in a non-core proceeding. Amendments to Rule 7012 require that the defendant admit or deny the allegation as to whether the proceeding is core or non-core.

REFERENCES IN TEXT

The Federal Rules of Civil Procedure, referred to in subd. (a), are set out in the Appendix to Title 28, Judiciary and Judicial Procedure.

## Rule 7009. Pleading Special Matters

Rule 9 F.R.Civ.P. applies in adversary proceedings.

REFERENCES IN TEXT

The Federal Rules of Civil Procedure, referred to in text, are set out in the Appendix to Title 28, Judiciary and Judicial Procedure.

## Rule 7010. Form of Pleadings

Rule 10 F.R.Civ.P. applies in adversary proceedings, except that the caption of each pleading in such a proceeding shall conform substantially to the appropriate Official Form.

(As amended Apr. 30, 1991, eff. Aug. 1, 1991.)

NOTES OF ADVISORY COMMITTEE ON RULES—1991 AMENDMENT

Reference to the Official Form number is deleted in anticipation of future revision and renumbering of the Official Forms.

REFERENCES IN TEXT

The Federal Rules of Civil Procedure, referred to in text, are set out in the Appendix to Title 28, Judiciary and Judicial Procedure.

## Rule 7012. Defenses and Objections—When and How Presented—By Pleading or Motion—Motion for Judgment on the Pleadings

(a) WHEN PRESENTED. If a complaint is duly served, the defendant shall serve an answer within 30 days after the issuance of the summons, except when a different time is prescribed by the court. The court shall prescribe the time for service of the answer when service of a complaint is made by publication or upon a party in a foreign country. A party served with a pleading stating a cross-claim shall serve an answer thereto within 21 days after service. The plaintiff shall serve a reply to a counterclaim in the answer within 21 days after service of the answer or, if a reply is ordered by the court, within 21 days after service of the order, unless the order otherwise directs. The United States or an officer or agency thereof shall serve an answer to a complaint within 35 days after the issuance of the summons, and shall serve an answer to a cross-claim, or a reply to a counterclaim, within 35 days after service upon the United States attorney of the pleading in which the claim is asserted. The service of a motion permitted under this rule alters these periods of time as follows, unless a different time is fixed by order of the court: (1) if the court denies the motion or postpones its disposition until the trial on the merits, the responsive pleading shall be served within 14 days after notice of the court's action; (2) if the court grants a motion for a more definite statement, the responsive pleading shall be served within 14 days after the service of a more definite statement.

(b) APPLICABILITY OF RULE 12(b)–(i) F.R.CIV.P. Rule 12(b)–(i) F.R.Civ.P. applies in adversary proceedings. A responsive pleading shall admit or deny an allegation that the proceeding is core or non-core. If the response is that the proceeding is non-core, it shall include a statement that the party does or does not consent to entry of final orders or judgment by the bankruptcy judge. In non-core proceedings final orders and judgments shall not be entered on the bankruptcy judge's order except with the express consent of the parties.

(As amended Mar. 30, 1987, eff. Aug. 1, 1987; Apr. 23, 2008, eff. Dec. 1, 2008; Mar. 26, 2009, eff. Dec. 1, 2009.)

NOTES OF ADVISORY COMMITTEE ON RULES—1983

*Subdivision (a)* continues the practice of former Bankruptcy Rule 712(a) by requiring that the answer to a complaint be filed within 30 days after the issuance of the summons. Under Rule 7004(f), the summons must be served within 10 days of issuance. The other pleading periods in adversary proceedings are the same as those in civil actions before the district courts, except that the United States is allowed 35 rather than 60 days to respond.

Rule 12(b)(7) and (h)(2) F.R.Civ.P. refers to Rule 19 F.R.Civ.P. Pursuant to Rule 7002 these references are to Rule 19 F.R.Civ.P. as incorporated and modified by Rule 7019.

NOTES OF ADVISORY COMMITTEE ON RULES—1987 AMENDMENT

The amendment to subdivision (b) requires a response to the allegation that the proceeding is core or non-core. A final order of judgment may not be entered in a non-core proceeding heard by a bankruptcy judge unless all parties expressly consent. 28 U.S.C. §157(c).

COMMITTEE NOTES ON RULES—2008 AMENDMENT

The rule is amended to conform to the changes made to the Federal Rules of Civil Procedure through the restyling of those rules effective on December 1, 2007.

COMMITTEE NOTES ON RULES—2009 AMENDMENT

The rule is amended to implement changes in connection with the amendment to Rule 9006(a) and the manner by which time is computed under the rules. The deadlines in the rule are amended to substitute a deadline that is a multiple of seven days. Throughout the rules, deadlines are amended in the following manner:

- 5-day periods become 7-day periods
- 10-day periods become 14-day periods
- 15-day periods become 14-day periods
- 20-day periods become 21-day periods
- 25-day periods become 28-day periods

REFERENCES IN TEXT

The Federal Rules of Civil Procedure, referred to in subd. (b), are set out in the Appendix to Title 28, Judiciary and Judicial Procedure.

### Rule 7013. Counterclaim and Cross-Claim

Rule 13 F.R.Civ.P. applies in adversary proceedings, except that a party sued by a trustee or debtor in possession need not state as a counterclaim any claim that the party has against the debtor, the debtor's property, or the estate, unless the claim arose after the entry of an order for relief. A trustee or debtor in possession who fails to plead a counterclaim through oversight, inadvertence, or excusable neglect, or when justice so requires, may by leave of court amend the pleading, or commence a new adversary proceeding or separate action.

(As amended Mar. 30, 1987, eff. Aug. 1, 1987.)

NOTES OF ADVISORY COMMITTEE ON RULES—1983

Rule 13(h) F.R.Civ.P. refers to Rule 19 F.R.Civ.P. Pursuant to Rule 7002 this reference is to Rule 19 F.R.Civ.P. as incorporated and modified by Rule 7019.

REFERENCES IN TEXT

The Federal Rules of Civil Procedure, referred to in text, are set out in the Appendix to Title 28, Judiciary and Judicial Procedure.

### Rule 7014. Third-Party Practice

Rule 14 F.R.Civ.P. applies in adversary proceedings.

NOTES OF ADVISORY COMMITTEE ON RULES—1983

This rule does not purport to deal with questions of jurisdiction. The scope of the jurisdictional grant under 28 U.S.C. §1471 and whether the doctrines of pendent or ancillary jurisdiction are applicable to adversary proceedings will be determined by the courts.

Rule 14 F.R.Civ.P. refers to Rules 12 and 13 F.R.Civ.P. Pursuant to Rule 7002 those references are to Rules 12 and 13 as incorporated and modified by Rules 7012 and 7013.

REFERENCES IN TEXT

The Federal Rules of Civil Procedure, referred to in text, are set out in the Appendix to Title 28, Judiciary and Judicial Procedure.

### Rule 7015. Amended and Supplemental Pleadings

Rule 15 F.R.Civ.P. applies in adversary proceedings.

REFERENCES IN TEXT

The Federal Rules of Civil Procedure, referred to in text, are set out in the Appendix to Title 28, Judiciary and Judicial Procedure.

### Rule 7016. Pre-Trial Procedure; Formulating Issues

Rule 16 F.R.Civ.P. applies in adversary proceedings.

REFERENCES IN TEXT

The Federal Rules of Civil Procedure, referred to in text, are set out in the Appendix to Title 28, Judiciary and Judicial Procedure.

### Rule 7017. Parties Plaintiff and Defendant; Capacity

Rule 17 F.R.Civ.P. applies in adversary proceedings, except as provided in Rule 2010(b).

(As amended Apr. 30, 1991, eff. Aug. 1, 1991.)

NOTES OF ADVISORY COMMITTEE ON RULES

Rules 2010(d) and 5008(d), which implement §§322 and 345 of the Code, authorize a party in interest to prosecute a claim on the bond of a trustee or depository in the name of the United States.

NOTES OF ADVISORY COMMITTEE ON RULES AMENDMENT

Reference to Rule 5008(d) is deleted because of the abrogation of Rule 5008.

REFERENCES IN TEXT

The Federal Rules of Civil Procedure, referred to in text, are set out in the Appendix to Title 28, Judiciary and Judicial Procedure.

## Rule 7018. Joinder of Claims and Remedies

Rule 18 F.R.Civ.P. applies in adversary proceedings.

REFERENCES IN TEXT

The Federal Rules of Civil Procedure, referred to in text, are set out in the Appendix to Title 28, Judiciary and Judicial Procedure.

## Rule 7019. Joinder of Persons Needed for Just Determination

Rule 19 F.R.Civ.P. applies in adversary proceedings, except that (1) if an entity joined as a party raises the defense that the court lacks jurisdiction over the subject matter and the defense is sustained, the court shall dismiss such entity from the adversary proceedings and (2) if an entity joined as a party properly and timely raises the defense of improper venue, the court shall determine, as provided in 28 U.S.C. §1412, whether that part of the proceeding involving the joined party shall be transferred to another district, or whether the entire adversary proceeding shall be transferred to another district.

(As amended Mar. 30, 1987, eff. Aug. 1, 1987.)

NOTES OF ADVISORY COMMITTEE ON RULES—1983

This rule addresses a situation different from that encountered by the district court when its jurisdiction is based on diversity of citizenship under 28 U.S.C. §1332. Joining of a party whose citizenship is the same as that of an adversary destroys the district court's jurisdiction over the entire civil action but under 28 U.S.C. §1471 the attempted joinder of such a person would not affect the bankruptcy court's jurisdiction over the original adversary proceeding.

NOTES OF ADVISORY COMMITTEE ON RULES—1987 AMENDMENT

The rule is amended to delete the reference to retention of the adversary proceeding if venue is improper. See 28 U.S.C. §1412.

REFERENCES IN TEXT

The Federal Rules of Civil Procedure, referred to in text, are set out in the Appendix to Title 28, Judiciary and Judicial Procedure.

## Rule 7020. Permissive Joinder of Parties

Rule 20 F.R.Civ.P. applies in adversary proceedings.

REFERENCES IN TEXT

The Federal Rules of Civil Procedure, referred to in text, are set out in the Appendix to Title 28, Judiciary and Judicial Procedure.

## Rule 7021. Misjoinder and Non-Joinder of Parties

Rule 21 F.R.Civ.P. applies in adversary proceedings.

REFERENCES IN TEXT

The Federal Rules of Civil Procedure, referred to in text, are set out in the Appendix to Title 28, Judiciary and Judicial Procedure.

## Rule 7022. Interpleader

Rule 22(a) F.R.Civ.P. applies in adversary proceedings. This rule supplements—and does not limit—the joinder of parties allowed by Rule 7020.

(As amended Apr. 23, 2008, eff. Dec. 1, 2008.)

COMMITTEE NOTES ON RULES—2008 AMENDMENT

The rule is amended to conform to the changes made to the Federal Rules of Civil Procedure through the restyling of those rules effective on December 1, 2007.

REFERENCES IN TEXT

The Federal Rules of Civil Procedure, referred to in text, are set out in the Appendix to Title 28, Judiciary and Judicial Procedure.

## Rule 7023. Class Proceedings

Rule 23 F.R.Civ.P. applies in adversary proceedings.

REFERENCES IN TEXT

The Federal Rules of Civil Procedure, referred to in text, are set out in the Appendix to Title 28, Judiciary and Judicial Procedure.

## Rule 7023.1. Derivative Actions

Rule 23.1 F.R.Civ.P. applies in adversary proceedings.

(As amended Apr. 23, 2008, eff. Dec. 1, 2008.)

COMMITTEE NOTES ON RULES—2008 AMENDMENT

The rule is amended to conform to the changes made to the Federal Rules of Civil Procedure through the restyling of those rules effective on December 1, 2007.

REFERENCES IN TEXT

The Federal Rules of Civil Procedure, referred to in text, are set out in the Appendix to Title 28, Judiciary and Judicial Procedure.

## Rule 7023.2. Adversary Proceedings Relating to Unincorporated Associations

Rule 23.2 F.R.Civ.P. applies in adversary proceedings.

REFERENCES IN TEXT

The Federal Rules of Civil Procedure, referred to in text, are set out in the Appendix to Title 28, Judiciary and Judicial Procedure.

## Rule 7024. Intervention

Rule 24 F.R.Civ.P. applies in adversary proceedings.

NOTES OF ADVISORY COMMITTEE ON RULES—1983

A person may seek to intervene in the case under the Code or in an adversary proceeding relating to the case under the Code. Intervention in a case under the Code is governed by Rule 2018 and intervention in an adversary proceeding is governed by this rule. Intervention in a case and intervention in an adversary proceeding must be sought separately.

REFERENCES IN TEXT

The Federal Rules of Civil Procedure, referred to in text, are set out in the Appendix to Title 28, Judiciary and Judicial Procedure.

## Rule 7025. Substitution of Parties

Subject to the provisions of Rule 2012, Rule 25 F.R.Civ.P. applies in adversary proceedings.

NOTES OF ADVISORY COMMITTEE ON RULES—1983

Rule 25 F.R.Civ.P. refers to Rule 4 F.R.Civ.P. Pursuant to Rule 7002 that reference is to Rule 4 as incorporated and modified by Rule 7004.

REFERENCES IN TEXT

The Federal Rules of Civil Procedure, referred to in text, are set out in the Appendix to Title 28, Judiciary and Judicial Procedure.

### Rule 7026. General Provisions Governing Discovery

Rule 26 F.R.Civ.P. applies in adversary proceedings.

REFERENCES IN TEXT

The Federal Rules of Civil Procedure, referred to in text, are set out in the Appendix to Title 28, Judiciary and Judicial Procedure.

### Rule 7027. Depositions Before Adversary Proceedings or Pending Appeal

Rule 27 F.R.Civ.P. applies to adversary proceedings.

NOTES OF ADVISORY COMMITTEE ON RULES—1983

Rule 27(a)(2) F.R.Civ.P. refers to Rule 4 F.R.Civ.P. Pursuant to Rule 7002 the reference is to Rule 4 F.R.Civ.P. as incorporated and modified by Rule 7004.

REFERENCES IN TEXT

The Federal Rules of Civil Procedure, referred to in text, are set out in the Appendix to Title 28, Judiciary and Judicial Procedure.

### Rule 7028. Persons Before Whom Depositions May Be Taken

Rule 28 F.R.Civ.P. applies in adversary proceedings.

REFERENCES IN TEXT

The Federal Rules of Civil Procedure, referred to in text, are set out in the Appendix to Title 28, Judiciary and Judicial Procedure.

### Rule 7029. Stipulations Regarding Discovery Procedure

Rule 29 F.R.Civ.P. applies in adversary proceedings.

REFERENCES IN TEXT

The Federal Rules of Civil Procedure, referred to in text, are set out in the Appendix to Title 28, Judiciary and Judicial Procedure.

### Rule 7030. Depositions Upon Oral Examination

Rule 30 F.R.Civ.P. applies in adversary proceedings.

NOTES OF ADVISORY COMMITTEE ON RULES—1983

Rule 30 F.R.Civ.P. refers to Rule 4 F.R.Civ.P. Pursuant to Rule 7002 that reference is a reference to Rule 4 F.R.Civ.P. as incorporated and modified by Rule 7004.

REFERENCES IN TEXT

The Federal Rules of Civil Procedure, referred to in text, are set out in the Appendix to Title 28, Judiciary and Judicial Procedure.

### Rule 7031. Deposition Upon Written Questions

Rule 31 F.R.Civ.P. applies in adversary proceedings.

REFERENCES IN TEXT

The Federal Rules of Civil Procedure, referred to in text, are set out in the Appendix to Title 28, Judiciary and Judicial Procedure.

### Rule 7032. Use of Depositions in Adversary Proceedings

Rule 32 F.R.Civ.P. applies in adversary proceedings.

REFERENCES IN TEXT

The Federal Rules of Civil Procedure, referred to in text, are set out in the Appendix to Title 28, Judiciary and Judicial Procedure.

### Rule 7033. Interrogatories to Parties

Rule 33 F.R.Civ.P. applies in adversary proceedings.

REFERENCES IN TEXT

The Federal Rules of Civil Procedure, referred to in text, are set out in the Appendix to Title 28, Judiciary and Judicial Procedure.

### Rule 7034. Production of Documents and Things and Entry Upon Land for Inspection and Other Purposes

Rule 34 F.R.Civ.P. applies in adversary proceedings.

REFERENCES IN TEXT

The Federal Rules of Civil Procedure, referred to in text, are set out in the Appendix to Title 28, Judiciary and Judicial Procedure.

### Rule 7035. Physical and Mental Examination of Persons

Rule 35 F.R.Civ.P. applies in adversary proceedings.

REFERENCES IN TEXT

The Federal Rules of Civil Procedure, referred to in text, are set out in the Appendix to Title 28, Judiciary and Judicial Procedure.

### Rule 7036. Requests for Admission

Rule 36 F.R.Civ.P. applies in adversary proceedings.

REFERENCES IN TEXT

The Federal Rules of Civil Procedure, referred to in text, are set out in the Appendix to Title 28, Judiciary and Judicial Procedure.

### Rule 7037. Failure to Make Discovery: Sanctions

Rule 37 F.R.Civ.P. applies in adversary proceedings.

REFERENCES IN TEXT

The Federal Rules of Civil Procedure, referred to in text, are set out in the Appendix to Title 28, Judiciary and Judicial Procedure.

### Rule 7040. Assignment of Cases for Trial

Rule 40 F.R.Civ.P. applies in adversary proceedings.

REFERENCES IN TEXT

The Federal Rules of Civil Procedure, referred to in text, are set out in the Appendix to Title 28, Judiciary and Judicial Procedure.

### Rule 7041. Dismissal of Adversary Proceedings

Rule 41 F.R.Civ.P. applies in adversary proceedings, except that a complaint objecting to the debtor's discharge shall not be dismissed at the plaintiff's instance without notice to the trustee, the United States trustee, and such other persons as the court may direct, and only on order of the court containing terms and conditions which the court deems proper.

(As amended Apr. 30, 1991, eff. Aug. 1, 1991.)

NOTES OF ADVISORY COMMITTEE ON RULES—1983

Dismissal of a complaint objecting to a discharge raises special concerns because the plaintiff may have been induced to dismiss by an advantage given or promised by the debtor or someone acting in his interest. Some courts by local rule or order have required the debtor and his attorney or the plaintiff to file an affidavit that nothing has been promised to the plaintiff in consideration of the withdrawal of the objection. By specifically authorizing the court to impose conditions in the order of dismissal this rule permits the continuation of this salutary practice.

Rule 41 F.R.Civ.P. refers to Rule 19 F.R.Civ.P. Pursuant to Rule 7002 that reference is to Rule 19 F.R.Civ.P. as incorporated and modified by Rule 7019.

NOTES OF ADVISORY COMMITTEE ON RULES—1991 AMENDMENT

The United States trustee has standing to object to the debtor's discharge pursuant to §727(c) and may have refrained from commencing an adversary proceeding objecting to discharge within the time limits provided in Rule 4004 only because another party commenced such a proceeding. The United States trustee may oppose dismissal of the original proceeding.

The rule is also amended to clarify that the court may direct that other persons receive notice of a plaintiff's motion to dismiss a complaint objecting to discharge.

REFERENCES IN TEXT

The Federal Rules of Civil Procedure, referred to in text, are set out in the Appendix to Title 28, Judiciary and Judicial Procedure.

### Rule 7042. Consolidation of Adversary Proceedings; Separate Trials

Rule 42 F.R.Civ.P. applies in adversary proceedings.

REFERENCES IN TEXT

The Federal Rules of Civil Procedure, referred to in text, are set out in the Appendix to Title 28, Judiciary and Judicial Procedure.

### Rule 7052. Findings by the Court

Rule 52 F.R.Civ.P. applies in adversary proceedings, except that any motion under subdivision (b) of that rule for amended or additional findings shall be filed no later than 14 days after entry of judgment. In these proceedings, the reference in Rule 52 F.R.Civ.P. to the entry of judgment under Rule 58 F.R.Civ.P. shall be read as a reference to the entry of a judgment or order under Rule 5003(a).

(As amended Mar. 26, 2009, eff. Dec. 1, 2009.)

NOTES OF ADVISORY COMMITTEE ON RULES—1983

Rule 52(a) F.R.Civ.P. refers to Rule 12 F.R.Civ.P. Pursuant to Rule 7002 this reference is to Rule 12 F.R.Civ.P. as incorporated and modified by Rule 7012.

COMMITTEE NOTES ON RULES—2009 AMENDMENT

The rule is amended by limiting the time for filing post judgment motions for amended or additional findings. In 2009, Rule 52 F. R. Civ. P. was amended to extend the deadline for filing those post judgment motions to no later than 28 days after entry of the judgment. That deadline corresponds to the 30-day deadline for filing a notice of appeal in a civil case under Rule 4(a)(1)(A) F. R. App. P. In a bankruptcy case, the deadline for filing a notice of appeal is 14 days. Therefore, the 28-day deadline for filing a motion for amended or additional findings would effectively override the notice of appeal deadline under Rule 8002(a) but for this amendment.

The rule is amended to clarify that the reference in Rule 52 F. R. Civ. P. to Rule 58 F. R. Civ. P. and its provisions is construed as a reference to the entry of a judgment or order under Rule 5003(a).

*Changes Made After Publication.* No changes since publication.

REFERENCES IN TEXT

The Federal Rules of Civil Procedure, referred to in text, are set out in the Appendix to Title 28, Judiciary and Judicial Procedure.

### Rule 7054. Judgments; Costs

(a) JUDGMENTS. Rule 54(a)–(c) F.R.Civ.P. applies in adversary proceedings.

(b) COSTS. The court may allow costs to the prevailing party except when a statute of the United States or these rules otherwise provides. Costs against the United States, its officers and agencies shall be imposed only to the extent permitted by law. Costs may be taxed by the clerk on one day's notice; on motion served within five days thereafter, the action of the clerk may be reviewed by the court.

REFERENCES IN TEXT

The Federal Rules of Civil Procedure, referred to in subd. (a), are set out in the Appendix to Title 28, Judiciary and Judicial Procedure.

### Rule 7055. Default

Rule 55 F.R.Civ.P. applies in adversary proceedings.

REFERENCES IN TEXT

The Federal Rules of Civil Procedure, referred to in text, are set out in the Appendix to Title 28, Judiciary and Judicial Procedure.

### Rule 7056. Summary Judgment

Rule 56 F.R.Civ.P. applies in adversary proceedings.

REFERENCES IN TEXT

The Federal Rules of Civil Procedure, referred to in text, are set out in the Appendix to Title 28, Judiciary and Judicial Procedure.

### Rule 7058. Entering Judgment in Adversary Proceeding

Rule 58 F.R.Civ.P. applies in adversary proceedings. In these proceedings, the reference in Rule 58 F.R.Civ.P. to the civil docket shall be read as a reference to the docket maintained by the clerk under Rule 5003(a).

(Added Mar. 26, 2009, eff. Dec. 1, 2009.)

COMMITTEE NOTES ON RULES—2009

This rule makes Rule 58 F.R.Civ.P. applicable in adversary proceedings and is added in connection with the amendments to Rule 9021.

*Changes Made After Publication.* No changes since publication.

REFERENCES IN TEXT

The Federal Rules of Civil Procedure, referred to in text, are set out in the Appendix to Title 28, Judiciary and Judicial Procedure.

## Rule 7062. Stay of Proceedings to Enforce a Judgment

Rule 62 F.R.Civ.P. applies in adversary proceedings.

(As amended Apr. 30, 1991, eff. Aug. 1, 1991; Apr. 26, 1999, eff. Dec. 1, 1999.)

NOTES OF ADVISORY COMMITTEE ON RULES—1983

The additional exceptions set forth in this rule make applicable to those matters the consequences contained in Rule 62(c) and (d) with respect to orders in actions for injunctions.

NOTES OF ADVISORY COMMITTEE ON RULES—1991 AMENDMENT

This rule is amended to include as additional exceptions to Rule 62(a) an order granting relief from the automatic stay of actions against codebtors provided by §1201 of the Code, the sale or lease of property of the estate under §363, and the assumption or assignment of an executory contract under §365.

COMMITTEE NOTES ON RULES—1999 AMENDMENT

The additional exceptions to Rule 62(a) consist of orders that are issued in contested matters. These exceptions are deleted from this rule because of the amendment to Rule 9014 that renders this rule inapplicable in contested matters unless the court orders otherwise. *See also* the amendments to Rules 3020, 3021, 4001, 6004, and 6006 that delay the implementation of certain types of orders for a period of ten days unless the court otherwise directs.

*GAP Report on Rule 7062.* No changes since publication.

REFERENCES IN TEXT

The Federal Rules of Civil Procedure, referred to in text, are set out in the Appendix to Title 28, Judiciary and Judicial Procedure.

## Rule 7064. Seizure of Person or Property

Rule 62 F.R.Civ.P. applies in adversary proceedings.

REFERENCES IN TEXT

The Federal Rules of Civil Procedure, referred to in text, are set out in the Appendix to Title 28, Judiciary and Judicial Procedure.

## Rule 7065. Injunctions

Rule 65 F.R.Civ.P. applies in adversary proceedings, except that a temporary restraining order or preliminary injunction may be issued on application of a debtor, trustee, or debtor in possession without compliance with Rule 65(c).

REFERENCES IN TEXT

The Federal Rules of Civil Procedure, referred to in text, are set out in the Appendix to Title 28, Judiciary and Judicial Procedure.

## Rule 7067. Deposit in Court

Rule 67 F.R.Civ.P. applies in adversary proceedings.

REFERENCES IN TEXT

The Federal Rules of Civil Procedure, referred to in text, are set out in the Appendix to Title 28, Judiciary and Judicial Procedure.

## Rule 7068. Offer of Judgment

Rule 68 F.R.Civ.P. applies in adversary proceedings.

REFERENCES IN TEXT

The Federal Rules of Civil Procedure, referred to in text, are set out in the Appendix to Title 28, Judiciary and Judicial Procedure.

## Rule 7069. Execution

Rule 69 F.R.Civ.P. applies in adversary proceedings.

REFERENCES IN TEXT

The Federal Rules of Civil Procedure, referred to in text, are set out in the Appendix to Title 28, Judiciary and Judicial Procedure.

## Rule 7070. Judgment for Specific Acts; Vesting Title

Rule 70 F.R.Civ.P. applies in adversary proceedings and the court may enter a judgment divesting the title of any party and vesting title in others whenever the real or personal property involved is within the jurisdiction of the court.

(As amended Mar. 30, 1987, eff. Aug. 1, 1987.)

NOTES OF ADVISORY COMMITTEE ON RULES—1987 AMENDMENT

The reference to court is used in the amendment because the district court may preside over an adversary proceeding.

REFERENCES IN TEXT

The Federal Rules of Civil Procedure, referred to in text, are set out in the Appendix to Title 28, Judiciary and Judicial Procedure.

## Rule 7071. Process in Behalf of and Against Persons Not Parties

Rule 71 F.R.Civ.P. applies in adversary proceedings.

REFERENCES IN TEXT

The Federal Rules of Civil Procedure, referred to in text, are set out in the Appendix to Title 28, Judiciary and Judicial Procedure.

## Rule 7087. Transfer of Adversary Proceeding

On motion and after a hearing, the court may transfer an adversary proceeding or any part thereof to another district pursuant to 28 U.S.C. §1412, except as provided in Rule 7019(2).

(As amended Mar. 30, 1987, eff. Aug. 1, 1987.)

NOTES OF ADVISORY COMMITTEE ON RULES AMENDMENT

The reference to the venue section of title 28 is amended to conform to the 1984 amendments to title 28.

# PART VIII—APPEALS TO DISTRICT COURT OR BANKRUPTCY APPELLATE PANEL

## Rule 8001. Manner of Taking Appeal; Voluntary Dismissal; Certification to Court of Appeals

(a) APPEAL AS OF RIGHT; HOW TAKEN
peal from a judgment, order, or decree of a bankruptcy judge to a district court or bankruptcy appellate panel as permitted by 28 U.S.C. §158(a)(1) or (a)(2) shall be taken by filing a no-

tice of appeal with the clerk within the time allowed by Rule 8002. An appellant's failure to take any step other than timely filing a notice of appeal does not affect the validity of the appeal, but is ground only for such action as the district court or bankruptcy appellate panel deems appropriate, which may include dismissal of the appeal. The notice of appeal shall (1) conform substantially to the appropriate Official Form, (2) contain the names of all parties to the judgment, order, or decree appealed from and the names, addresses, and telephone numbers of their respective attorneys, and (3) be accompanied by the prescribed fee. Each appellant shall file a sufficient number of copies of the notice of appeal to enable the clerk to comply promptly with Rule 8004.

(b) APPEAL BY LEAVE; HOW TAKEN. An appeal from an interlocutory judgment, order, or decree of a bankruptcy judge as permitted by 28 U.S.C. §158(a)(3) shall be taken by filing a notice of appeal, as prescribed in subdivision (a) of this rule, accompanied by a motion for leave to appeal prepared in accordance with Rule 8003 and with proof of service in accordance with Rule 8008.

(c) VOLUNTARY DISMISSAL.

(1) *Before Docketing.* If an appeal has not been docketed, the appeal may be dismissed by the bankruptcy judge on the filing of a stipulation for dismissal signed by all the parties, or on motion and notice by the appellant.

(2) *After Docketing.* If an appeal has been docketed and the parties to the appeal sign and file with the clerk of the district court or the clerk of the bankruptcy appellate panel an agreement that the appeal be dismissed and pay any court costs or fees that may be due, the clerk of the district court or the clerk of the bankruptcy appellate panel shall enter an order dismissing the appeal. An appeal may also be dismissed on motion of the appellant on terms and conditions fixed by the district court or bankruptcy appellate panel.

[(d) EFFECT OF TAKING A DIRECT APPEAL TO THE COURT OF APPEALS] (Abrogated Mar. 30, 1987, eff. Aug. 1, 1987)

(e) ELECTION TO HAVE APPEAL HEARD BY DISTRICT COURT INSTEAD OF BANKRUPTCY APPELLATE PANEL; WITHDRAWAL OF ELECTION.

(1) *Separate Writing for Election.* An election to have an appeal heard by the district court under 28 U.S.C. §158(c)(1) may be made only by a statement of election contained in a separate writing filed within the time prescribed by 28 U.S.C. §158(c)(1).

(2) *Withdrawal of Election.* A request to withdraw the election may be filed only by written stipulation of all the parties to the appeal or their attorneys of record. Upon such a stipulation, the district court may either transfer the appeal to the bankruptcy appellate panel or retain the appeal in the district court.

(f) CERTIFICATION FOR DIRECT APPEAL TO COURT OF APPEALS.

(1) *Timely Appeal Required.* A certification of a judgment, order, or decree of a bankruptcy court to a court of appeals under 28 U.S.C. §158(d)(2) shall not be effective until a timely appeal has been taken in the manner required by subdivisions (a) or (b) of this rule and the notice of appeal has become effective under Rule 8002.

(2) *Court Where Certification Made and Filed.* A certification that a circumstance specified in 28 U.S.C. §158(d)(2)(A)(i)–(iii) exists shall be filed in the court in which a matter is pending for purposes of 28 U.S.C. §158(d)(2) and this rule. A matter is pending in a bankruptcy court until the docketing, in accordance with Rule 8007(b), of an appeal taken under 28 U.S.C. §158(a)(1) or (2), or the grant of leave to appeal under 28 U.S.C. §158(a)(3). A matter is pending in a district court or bankruptcy appellate panel after the docketing, in accordance with Rule 8007(b), of an appeal taken under 28 U.S.C. §158(a)(1) or (2), or the grant of leave to appeal under 28 U.S.C. §158(a)(3).

(A) *Certification by Court on Request or Court's Own Initiative.*

(i) Before Docketing or Grant of Leave to Appeal. Only a bankruptcy court may make a certification on request or on its own initiative while the matter is pending in the bankruptcy court.

(ii) After Docketing or Grant of Leave to Appeal. Only the district court or bankruptcy appellate panel involved may make a certification on request of the parties or on its own initiative while the matter is pending in the district court or bankruptcy appellate panel.

(B) *Certification by All Appellants and Appellees Acting Jointly.* A certification by all the appellants and appellees, if any, acting jointly may be made by filing the appropriate Official Form with the clerk of the court in which the matter is pending. The certification may be accompanied by a short statement of the basis for the certification, which may include the information listed in subdivision (f)(3)(C) of this rule.

(3) *Request for Certification; Filing; Service; Contents.*

(A) A request for certification shall be filed, within the time specified by 28 U.S.C. §158(d)(2), with the clerk of the court in which the matter is pending.

(B) Notice of the filing of a request for certification shall be served in the manner required for service of a notice of appeal under Rule 8004.

(C) A request for certification shall include the following:

(i) the facts necessary to understand the question presented;

(ii)the question itself;

(iii) the relief sought;

(iv) the reasons why the appeal should be allowed and is authorized by statute or rule, including why a circumstance specified in 28 U.S.C. §158(d)(2)(A)(i)–(iii) exists; and

(v) an attached copy of the judgment, order, or decree complained of and any related opinion or memorandum.

(D) A party may file a response to a request for certification or a cross request within 14 days after the notice of the request is served, or another time fixed by the court.

(E) Rule 9014 does not govern a request, cross request, or any response. The matter shall be submitted without oral argument unless the court otherwise directs.

(F) A certification of an appeal under 28 U.S.C. §158(d)(2) shall be made in a separate document served on the parties.

(4) *Certification on Court's Own Initiative.*

(A) A certification of an appeal on the court's own initiative under 28 U.S.C. §158(d)(2) shall be made in a separate document served on the parties in the manner required for service of a notice of appeal under Rule 8004. The certification shall be accompanied by an opinion or memorandum that contains the information required by subdivision (f)(3)(C)(i)–(iv) of this rule.

(B) A party may file a supplementary short statement of the basis for certification within 14 days after the certification.

(5) *Duties of Parties After Certification.* A petition for permission to appeal in accordance with F.R.App.P. 5 shall be filed no later than 30 days after a certification has become effective as provided in subdivision (f)(1).

(As amended Mar. 30, 1987, eff. Aug. 1, 1987; Apr. 30, 1991, eff. Aug. 1, 1991; Apr. 11, 1997, eff. Dec. 1, 1997; Apr. 23, 2008, eff. Dec. 1, 2008; Mar. 26, 2009, eff. Dec. 1, 2009.)

NOTES OF ADVISORY COMMITTEE ON RULES—1983

These rules in Part VIII apply only to appeals to the district courts or bankruptcy appellate panels. Subsequent appeals to the courts of appeals, or direct appeals by agreement of the parties under 28 U.S.C. §1293(b), are governed by the Federal Rules of Appellate Procedure.

*Subdivisions (a) and (b)* require that a notice of appeal be filed whenever a litigant seeks to secure appellate review by the district court or bankruptcy appellate panel. An appeal from an interlocutory order which will be heard only if leave is granted under 28 U.S.C. §§1334(b) or 1482(b) is taken by filing a notice of appeal accompanied by a motion for leave to appeal which complies with the requirements set forth in Rule 8003. Rule 8003 also governs other aspects of interlocutory appeals.

*Subdivision (c)* is an adaptation of Rule 42 F.R.App.P.

*Subdivision (d)* deals with the situation in which an appellant perfects an appeal to the district court or a bankruptcy appellate panel and also a direct appeal pursuant to 28 U.S.C. §1293(b) to the court of appeals. This subdivision provides that once the appeal to the court of appeals is taken, a notice of appeal to the district court or bankruptcy appellate panel shall be dismissed and, if the first appeal is to the district court or bankruptcy appellate panel, the first appeal shall be dismissed. Paragraph (3) gives an appellant or cross appellant an opportunity to file an appeal to the district court or bankruptcy appellate panel if the court of appeals dismisses the direct appeal because the judgment, order, or decree appealed from is not final. Since the court of appeals has determined the judgment, order, or decree is not final, the new appeal is an appeal for which leave is necessary.

NOTES OF ADVISORY COMMITTEE ON RULES—1987 AMENDMENT

*Subdivisions (a) and (b)* are amended to conform to the 1984 amendments.

*Subdivision (d)* is abrogated because there is no direct appeal to the court of appeals under 28 U.S.C. §158, as enacted by the 1984 amendments.

*Subdivision (e)* is new. Section 158(b)(1) of title 28 authorizes the circuit councils to establish bankruptcy appellate panels. Appeals may not be heard by these panels unless the district court authorizes the referral and all parties to the appeal consent. This rule requires that the parties consent to such an appeal; however, the method of consenting to an appeal may be the subject of a rule promulgated by a circuit council under Rule 8018.

NOTES OF ADVISORY COMMITTEE ON RULES—1991 AMENDMENT

Reference to the Official Form number is deleted in anticipation of future revision and renumbering of the Official Forms.

NOTES OF ADVISORY COMMITTEE ON RULES—1997 AMENDMENT

This rule is amended to conform to the Bankruptcy Reform Act of 1994 which amended 28 U.S.C. §158. As amended, a party may—without obtaining leave of the court—appeal from an interlocutory order or decree of the bankruptcy court issued under §1121(d) of the Code increasing or reducing the time periods referred to in §1121.

*Subdivision (e)* is amended to provide the procedure for electing under 28 U.S.C. §158(c)(1) to have an appeal heard by the district court instead of the bankruptcy appellate panel service. This subdivision is applicable only if a bankruptcy appellate panel service is authorized under 28 U.S.C. §158(b) to hear the appeal.

*GAP Report on Rule 8001.* The heading of subdivision (e) is amended to clarify that it applies to the election to have an appeal heard by the district court instead of the BAP. The final paragraph of the Committee Note is revised to clarify that subdivision (e) is applicable only if a BAP is authorized to hear the appeal.

COMMITTEE NOTES ON RULES—2008 AMENDMENT

Subdivision (e) is amended by redesignating the subdivision as (e)(1) and adding new subdivision (e)(2). Subdivision (e)(2) explicitly recognizes the district court's authority to transfer an appeal to the bankruptcy appellate panel on two conditions: first, all of the parties to the appeal must have agreed to request the withdrawal of the election to have the district court hear the appeal; and, second, the district court must decide whether to grant the request for withdrawal. The district court has discretion either to keep the case or transfer it to the bankruptcy appellate panel, which will prevent strategic behavior by parties and avoid the wasting of judicial resources.

Subdivision (f) is added to the rule to implement the 2005 amendments to 28 U.S.C. §158(d). That section authorizes appeals directly to the court of appeals, with that court's consent, upon certification that a ground for the appeal exists under §158(d)(2)(A)(i)–(iii). Certification can be made by the court on its own initiative under subdivision (f)(4), or in response to a request of a party or a majority of the appellants and appellees (if any) under subdivision (f)(3). Certification also can be made by all of the appellants and appellees under subdivision (f)(2)(B). Under subdivision (f)(1), certification is effective only when a timely appeal is commenced under subdivision (a) or (b), and a notice of appeal has been timely filed under Rule 8002. These actions will provide sufficient notice of the appeal to the circuit clerk, so the rule dispenses with the uncodified temporary procedural requirements set out in §1233(b)(4) of the Bankruptcy Abuse Prevention and Consumer Protection Act of 2005, Pub. L. No. 109–8.

The rule adopts a bright-line test for identifying the court in which a matter is pending. Under subdivision (f)(2), the bright-line chosen is the "docketing" under Rule 8007(b) of an appeal of an interlocutory order or decree under 28 U.S.C. §158(a)(2) or a final judgment, order or decree under 28 U.S.C. §158(a)(1), or the granting of leave to appeal any other interlocutory judgment, order or decree under 28 U.S.C. §158(a)(3), whichever is earlier.

To ensure that parties are aware of a certification, the rule requires either that it be made on the Official

Form (if being made by all of the parties to the appeal) or on a separate document (whether the certification is made on the court's own initiative or in response to a request by a party). This is particularly important because the rule adopts the bankruptcy practice established by Rule 8001(a) and (b) of requiring a notice of appeal in every instance, including interlocutory orders, of appeals from bankruptcy court orders, judgments, and decrees. Because this requirement is satisfied by filing the notice of appeal that takes the appeal to the district court or bankruptcy appellate panel in the first instance, the rule does not require a separate notice of appeal if a certification occurs after a district court or bankruptcy appellate panel decision.

A certification under subdivision (f)(1) does not place the appeal in the circuit court. Rather, the court of appeals must first authorize the direct appeal. Subdivision (f)(5) therefore provides that any party intending to pursue the appeal in the court of appeals must seek that permission under Rule 5 of the Federal Rules of Appellate Procedure. Subdivision (f)(5) requires that the petition for permission to appeal be filed within 30 days after an effective certification.

*Changes Made After Publication.* The second paragraph of the Committee Note was amended to identify more specifically the different ways in which the certification of a direct appeal to the court of appeals.

COMMITTEE NOTES ON RULES—2009 AMENDMENT

The rule is amended to implement changes in connection with the amendment to Rule 9006(a) and the manner by which time is computed under the rules. The deadlines in the rule are amended to substitute a deadline that is a multiple of seven days. Throughout the rules, deadlines are amended in the following manner:

- 5-day periods become 7-day periods
- 10-day periods become 14-day periods
- 15-day periods become 14-day periods
- 20-day periods become 21-day periods
- 25-day periods become 28-day periods

REFERENCES IN TEXT

The Federal Rules of Appellate Procedure, referred to in subd. (f)(5), are set out in the Appendix to Title 28, Judiciary and Judicial Procedure.

## Rule 8002. Time for Filing Notice of Appeal

(a) FOURTEEN-DAY PERIOD. The notice of appeal shall be filed with the clerk within 14 days of the date of the entry of the judgment, order, or decree appealed from. If a timely notice of appeal is filed by a party, any other party may file a notice of appeal within 14 days of the date on which the first notice of appeal was filed, or within the time otherwise prescribed by this rule, whichever period last expires. A notice of appeal filed after the announcement of a decision or order but before entry of the judgment, order, or decree shall be treated as filed after such entry and on the day thereof. If a notice of appeal is mistakenly filed with the district court or the bankruptcy appellate panel, the clerk of the district court or the clerk of the bankruptcy appellate panel shall note thereon the date on which it was received and transmit it to the clerk and it shall be deemed filed with the clerk on the date so noted.

(b) EFFECT OF MOTION ON TIME FOR APPEAL. If any party makes a timely motion of a type specified immediately below, the time for appeal for all parties runs from the entry of the order disposing of the last such motion outstanding. This provision applies to a timely motion:

(1) to amend or make additional findings of fact under Rule 7052, whether or not granting the motion would alter the judgment;

(2) to alter or amend the judgment under Rule 9023;

(3) for a new trial under Rule 9023; or

(4) for relief under Rule 9024 if the motion is filed no later than 14 days after the entry of judgment. A notice of appeal filed after announcement or entry of the judgment, order, or decree but before disposition of any of the above motions is ineffective to appeal from the judgment, order, or decree, or part thereof, specified in the notice of appeal, until the entry of the order disposing of the last such motion outstanding. Appellate review of an order disposing of any of the above motions requires the party, in compliance with Rule 8001, to amend a previously filed notice of appeal. A party intending to challenge an alteration or amendment of the judgment, order, or decree shall file a notice, or an amended notice, of appeal within the time prescribed by this Rule 8002 measured from the entry of the order disposing of the last such motion outstanding. No additional fees will be required for filing an amended notice.

(c) EXTENSION OF TIME FOR APPEAL.

(1) The bankruptcy judge may extend the time for filing the notice of appeal by any party, unless the judgment, order, or decree appealed from:

(A) grants relief from an automatic stay under § 362, § 922, § 1201, or § 1301;

(B) authorizes the sale or lease of property or the use of cash collateral under § 363;

(C) authorizes the obtaining of credit under § 364;

(D) authorizes the assumption or assignment of an executory contract or unexpired lease under § 365;

(E) approves a disclosure statement under § 1125; or

(F) confirms a plan under § 943, § 1129, § 1225, or § 1325 of the Code.

(2) A request to extend the time for filing a notice of appeal must be made by written motion filed before the time for filing a notice of appeal has expired, except that such a motion filed not later than 21 days after the expiration of the time for filing a notice of appeal may be granted upon a showing of excusable neglect. An extension of time for filing a notice of appeal may not exceed 21 days from the expiration of the time for filing a notice of appeal otherwise prescribed by this rule or 14 days from the date of entry of the order granting the motion, whichever is later.

(As amended Mar. 30, 1987, eff. Aug. 1, 1987; Apr. 30, 1991, eff. Aug. 1, 1991; Apr. 29, 1994, eff. Aug. 1, 1994; Apr. 11, 1997, eff. Dec. 1, 1997; Mar. 26, 2009, eff. Dec. 1, 2009.)

NOTES OF ADVISORY COMMITTEE ON RULES—1983

This rule is an adaptation of Rule 4(a) F.R.App.P. The time to appeal from a judgment, order, or decree of a bankruptcy judge is 10 days, rather than the 30 days provided for in the civil practice. The shortened time is specified in order to obtain prompt appellate review, often important to the administration of a case under the Code. If a timely notice of appeal is filed, other parties have an additional 10 days within which to file a notice of appeal. A notice of appeal filed within the additional 10 day period by an appellee is a cross appeal.

but there is a separate appeal if a non-appellee files a notice of appeal within that 10 day period. The district courts and bankruptcy appellate panels have inherent authority to consolidate appeals.

*Subdivision (b)* is essentially the same as Rule 4(a)(4) of the F.R.App.P.

*Subdivision (c)* is similar to former Bankruptcy Rule 802(c). To expedite the disposition of appeals the maximum extension of time is 20 days instead of the 30 days provided by Rule 4(a)(5) of the F.R.App.P. Subject to the exceptions set forth in subdivision (c), the court may extend the time for taking an appeal when a motion for extension is filed after the expiration of the original 10 day period but no later than 20 days after the expiration of the original 10 day period. Orders of the bankruptcy court relating to the sale of property, extension of credit, confirmation of a plan, dismissal or conversion of the case, and approval of the disclosure statement are of such significance to the administration of the case, the parties in interest, and third parties that this subdivision requires that either an appeal or a motion for extension be filed within the original 10 day period.

If a timely notice of appeal is not filed, no appeal may be taken later. Former Bankruptcy Rule 803, which provided that a referee's judgment became final when the appeal period expired, has been omitted as unnecessary.

NOTES OF ADVISORY COMMITTEE ON RULES—1991 AMENDMENT

*Subdivision (a)* is amended to conform to F.R.App.P. 4(a)(2) which is designed to avoid the loss of the right to appeal when a notice of appeal is filed prematurely.

*Subdivision (b)(1)* is deleted because Rule 9015 was abrogated in 1987.

NOTES OF ADVISORY COMMITTEE ON RULES—1994 AMENDMENT

These amendments are intended to conform to the 1993 amendments to F.R.App.P. 4(a)(4) and 6(b)(2)(i).

This rule as amended provides that a notice of appeal filed before the disposition of a specified postjudgment motion will become effective upon disposition of the motion. A notice filed before the filing of one of the specified motions or after the filing of a motion but before disposition of the motion is, in effect, suspended until the motion is disposed of, whereupon, the previously filed notice effectively places jurisdiction in the district court or bankruptcy appellate panel.

Because a notice of appeal will ripen into an effective appeal upon disposition of a postjudgment motion, in some instances there will be an appeal from a judgment that has been altered substantially because the motion was granted in whole or in part. The appeal may be dismissed for want of prosecution when the appellant fails to meet the briefing schedule. But, the appellee may also move to strike the appeal. When responding to such a motion, the appellant would have an opportunity to state that, even though some relief sought in a postjudgment motion was granted, the appellant still plans to pursue the appeal. Because the appellant's response would provide the appellee with sufficient notice of the appellant's intentions, the rule does not require an additional notice of appeal in that situation.

The amendment provides that a notice of appeal filed before the disposition of a postjudgment tolling motion is sufficient to bring the judgment, order, or decree specified in the original notice of appeal to the district court or bankruptcy appellate panel. If the judgment is altered upon disposition of a postjudgment motion, however, and if a party who has previously filed a notice of appeal wishes to appeal from the disposition of the motion, the party must amend the notice to so indicate. When a party files an amended notice, no additional fees are required because the notice is an amendment of the original and not a new notice of appeal.

*Subdivision (b)* is also amended to include, among motions that extend the time for filing a notice of appeal, a motion under Rule 9024 that is filed within 10 days after entry of judgment. The addition of this motion conforms to a similar amendment to F.R.App.P. 4(a)(4) made in 1993, except that a Rule 9024 motion does not toll the time to appeal unless it is filed within the 10-day period. The reason for providing that the motion extends the time to appeal only if it is *filed* within the 10-day period is to enable the court and the parties in interest to determine solely from the court records whether the time to appeal has been extended by a motion for relief under Rule 9024.

NOTES OF ADVISORY COMMITTEE ON RULES—1997 AMENDMENT

*Subdivision (c)* is amended to provide that a request for an extension of time to file a notice of appeal must be *filed* within the applicable time period. This amendment will avoid uncertainty as to whether the mailing of a motion or an oral request in court is sufficient to request an extension of time, and will enable the court and the parties in interest to determine solely from the court records whether a timely request for an extension has been made.

The amendments also give the court discretion to permit a party to file a notice of appeal more than 20 days after expiration of the time to appeal otherwise prescribed, but only if the motion was timely filed and the notice of appeal is filed within a period not exceeding 10 days after entry of the order extending the time. This amendment is designed to protect parties that file timely motions to extend the time to appeal from the harshness of the present rule as demonstrated in *In re Mouradick*, 13 F.3d 326 (9th Cir. 1994), where the court held that a notice of appeal filed within the 3-day period expressly prescribed by an order granting a timely motion for an extension of time did not confer jurisdiction on the appellate court because the notice of appeal was not filed within the 20-day period specified in subdivision (c).

The subdivision is amended further to prohibit any extension of time to file a notice of appeal—even if the motion for an extension is filed before the expiration of the original time to appeal—if the order appealed from grants relief from the automatic stay, authorizes the sale or lease of property, use of cash collateral, obtaining of credit, or assumption or assignment of an executory contract or unexpired lease under § 365, or approves a disclosure statement or confirms a plan. These types of orders are often relied upon immediately after they are entered and should not be reviewable on appeal after the expiration of the original appeal period under Rule 8002(a) and (b).

*GAP Report on Rule 8002.* No changes to the published draft.

COMMITTEE NOTES ON RULES—2009 AMENDMENT

The rule is amended to implement changes in connection with the amendment to Rule 9006(a) and the manner by which time is computed under the rules. The deadlines in the rule are amended to substitute a deadline that is a multiple of seven days. Throughout the rules, deadlines are amended in the following manner:

- 5-day periods become 7-day periods
- 10-day periods become 14-day periods
- 15-day periods become 14-day periods
- 20-day periods become 21-day periods
- 25-day periods become 28-day periods

## Rule 8003. Leave to Appeal

(a) CONTENT OF MOTION; ANSWER. A motion for leave to appeal under 28 U.S.C. § 158(a) shall contain: (1) a statement of the facts necessary to an understanding of the questions to be presented by the appeal; (2) a statement of those questions and of the relief sought; (3) a statement of the reasons why an appeal should be granted; and (4) a copy of the judgment, order, or decree complained of and of any opinion or memorandum relating thereto. Within 14 days after service of the motion, an adverse party may file with the clerk an answer in opposition.

(b) TRANSMITTAL; DETERMINATION OF MOTION. The clerk shall transmit the notice of appeal, the motion for leave to appeal and any answer thereto to the clerk of the district court or the clerk of the bankruptcy appellate panel as soon as all parties have filed answers or the time for filing an answer has expired. The motion and answer shall be submitted without oral argument unless otherwise ordered.

(c) APPEAL IMPROPERLY TAKEN REGARDED AS A MOTION FOR LEAVE TO APPEAL. If a required motion for leave to appeal is not filed, but a notice of appeal is timely filed, the district court or bankruptcy appellate panel may grant leave to appeal or direct that a motion for leave to appeal be filed. The district court or the bankruptcy appellate panel may also deny leave to appeal but in so doing shall consider the notice of appeal as a motion for leave to appeal. Unless an order directing that a motion for leave to appeal be filed provides otherwise, the motion shall be filed within 14 days of entry of the order.

(d) REQUIREMENT OF LEAVE TO APPEAL. If leave to appeal is required by 28 U.S.C. §158(a) and has not earlier been granted, the authorization of a direct appeal by a court of appeals under 28 U.S.C. §158(d)(2) shall be deemed to satisfy the requirement for leave to appeal.

(As amended Mar. 30, 1987, eff. Aug. 1, 1987; Apr. 23, 2008, eff. Dec. 1, 2008; Mar. 26, 2009, eff. Dec. 1, 2009.)

NOTES OF ADVISORY COMMITTEE ON RULES—1983

*Subdivisions (a) and (b)* of this rule are derived from Rules 5 and 6 F.R.App.P. The motion for leave to appeal is addressed to the district court or the bankruptcy appellate panel, although filed with the clerk of the bankruptcy court.

*Subdivision (c)* provides that if a party mistakenly believes the order appealed from is final and files only a notice of appeal, the appeal is not automatically dismissed. The district court or bankruptcy appellate panel has the options to direct that a motion be filed, to decide exclusively on the papers already filed to grant leave to appeal, or to deny leave to appeal. Cf. 28 U.S.C. §2103.

COMMITTEE NOTES ON RULES—2008 AMENDMENT

The rule is amended to add subdivision (d) to solve the jurisdictional problem that could otherwise ensue when a district court or bankruptcy appellate panel has not granted leave to appeal under 28 U.S.C. §158(a)(3). If the court of appeals accepts the appeal, the requirement of leave to appeal is deemed satisfied. However, if the court of appeals does not authorize a direct appeal, the question of whether to grant leave to appeal remains a matter to be resolved by the district court or the bankruptcy appellate panel.

*Changes Made After Publication.* No changes were made after publication.

COMMITTEE NOTES ON RULES—2009 AMENDMENT

The rule is amended to implement changes in connection with the amendment to Rule 9006(a) and the manner by which time is computed under the rules. The deadlines in the rule are amended to substitute a deadline that is a multiple of seven days. Throughout the rules, deadlines are amended in the following manner:

- 5-day periods become 7-day periods
- 10-day periods become 14-day periods
- 15-day periods become 14-day periods
- 20-day periods become 21-day periods
- 25-day periods become 28-day periods

## Rule 8004. Service of the Notice of Appeal

The clerk shall serve notice of the filing of a notice of appeal by mailing a copy thereof to counsel of record of each party other than the appellant or, if a party is not represented by counsel, to the party's last known address. Failure to serve notice shall not affect the validity of the appeal. The clerk shall note on each copy served the date of the filing of the notice of appeal and shall note in the docket the names of the parties to whom copies are mailed and the date of the mailing. The clerk shall forthwith transmit to the United States trustee a copy of the notice of appeal, but failure to transmit such notice shall not affect the validity of the appeal.

(As amended Mar. 30, 1987, eff. Aug. 1, 1987; Apr. 30, 1991, eff. Aug. 1, 1991.)

NOTES OF ADVISORY COMMITTEE ON RULES—1983

This rule is an adaptation of Rule 3(d) F.R.App.P.

NOTES OF ADVISORY COMMITTEE ON RULES—1991 AMENDMENT

This rule is amended to keep the United States trustee informed of the progress of the case.

## Rule 8005. Stay Pending Appeal

A motion for a stay of the judgment, order, or decree of a bankruptcy judge, for approval of a supersedeas bond, or for other relief pending appeal must ordinarily be presented to the bankruptcy judge in the first instance. Notwithstanding Rule 7062 but subject to the power of the district court and the bankruptcy appellate panel reserved hereinafter, the bankruptcy judge may suspend or order the continuation of other proceedings in the case under the Code or make any other appropriate order during the pendency of an appeal on such terms as will protect the rights of all parties in interest. A motion for such relief, or for modification or termination of relief granted by a bankruptcy judge, may be made to the district court or the bankruptcy appellate panel, but the motion shall show why the relief, modification, or termination was not obtained from the bankruptcy judge. The district court or the bankruptcy appellate panel may condition the relief it grants under this rule on the filing of a bond or other appropriate security with the bankruptcy court. When an appeal is taken by a trustee, a bond or other appropriate security may be required, but when an appeal is taken by the United States or an officer or agency thereof or by direction of any department of the Government of the United States a bond or other security shall not be required.

(As amended Mar. 30, 1987, eff. Aug. 1, 1987.)

NOTES OF ADVISORY COMMITTEE ON RULES—1983

The first, third, and fourth sentences of this rule are adaptations of Rule 8(a) and (b) F.R.App.P. The second sentence of the rule is derived from §39(c) of the Bankruptcy Act and confers on the bankruptcy judge discretion respecting the stay or continuation of other proceedings in the case while an appeal is pending.

The last sentence of the rule, which specifically subjects a trustee to the same kind of security requirements as other litigants, is derived from former Bankruptcy Rule 805. The exemption of the United States from the bond or security requirements is the same as the exemption contained in Rule 62(e) F.R.Civ.P.

Sections 363(m) and 364(e) of the Code provide that unless an order approving a sale of property, or authorizing the obtaining of credit or the incurring of debt is stayed pending appeal, the sale of property to a good faith purchaser or a good faith extension of credit, with or without any priority or lien, shall not be affected by the reversal or modification of such order on appeal, whether or not the purchaser or creditor knows of the pendency of the appeal.

### Rule 8006. Record and Issues on Appeal

Within 14 days after filing the notice of appeal as provided by Rule 8001(a), entry of an order granting leave to appeal, or entry of an order disposing of the last timely motion outstanding of a type specified in Rule 8002(b), whichever is later, the appellant shall file with the clerk and serve on the appellee a designation of the items to be included in the record on appeal and a statement of the issues to be presented. Within 14 days after the service of the appellant's statement the appellee may file and serve on the appellant a designation of additional items to be included in the record on appeal and, if the appellee has filed a cross appeal, the appellee as cross appellant shall file and serve a statement of the issues to be presented on the cross appeal and a designation of additional items to be included in the record. A cross appellee may, within 14 days of service of the cross appellant's statement, file and serve on the cross appellant a designation of additional items to be included in the record. The record on appeal shall include the items so designated by the parties, the notice of appeal, the judgment, order, or decree appealed from, and any opinion, findings of fact, and conclusions of law of the court. Any party filing a designation of the items to be included in the record shall provide to the clerk a copy of the items designated or, if the party fails to provide the copy, the clerk shall prepare the copy at the party's expense. If the record designated by any party includes a transcript of any proceeding or a part thereof, the party shall, immediately after filing the designation, deliver to the reporter and file with the clerk a written request for the transcript and make satisfactory arrangements for payment of its cost. All parties shall take any other action necessary to enable the clerk to assemble and transmit the record.

(As amended Mar. 30, 1987, eff. Aug. 1, 1987; Apr. 30, 1991, eff. Aug. 1, 1991; Apr. 29, 1994, eff. Aug. 1, 1994; Mar. 26, 2009, eff. Dec. 1, 2009.)

NOTES OF ADVISORY COMMITTEE ON RULES—1983

This rule is an adaptation of Rule 10(b) F.R.App.P. The last sentence of the rule is derived from Rule 11(a) F.R.App.P.

NOTES OF ADVISORY COMMITTEE ON RULES—1991 AMENDMENT

The seven-day time periods are changed to 10 days to conform to Rule 75(b)(2) F.R.Civ.P. and Rule 10(b)(3) F.R.App.P. The amendment requiring a party to provide a copy of the items designated for the record is to facilitate the amendments to Rule 8007 providing for retention by the bankruptcy clerk of the original record.

NOTES OF ADVISORY COMMITTEE ON RULES—1994 AMENDMENT

The amendment to the first sentence of this rule is made together with the amendment to Rule 8002(b), which provides, in essence, that certain specified postjudgment motions suspend a filed notice of appeal until the disposition of the last of such motions. The purpose of this amendment is to suspend the 10-day period for filing and serving a designation of the record and statement of the issues if a timely postjudgment motion is made and a notice of appeal is suspended under Rule 8002(b). The 10-day period set forth in the first sentence of this rule begins to run when the order disposing of the last of such postjudgment motions outstanding is entered. The other amendments to this rule are stylistic.

COMMITTEE NOTES ON RULES—2009 AMENDMENT

The rule is amended to implement changes in connection with the amendment to Rule 9006(a) and the manner by which time is computed under the rules. The deadlines in the rule are amended to substitute a deadline that is a multiple of seven days. Throughout the rules, deadlines are amended in the following manner:

- 5-day periods become 7-day periods
- 10-day periods become 14-day periods
- 15-day periods become 14-day periods
- 20-day periods become 21-day periods
- 25-day periods become 28-day periods

### Rule 8007. Completion and Transmission of the Record; Docketing of the Appeal

(a) DUTY OF REPORTER TO PREPARE AND FILE TRANSCRIPT. On receipt of a request for a transcript, the reporter shall acknowledge on the request the date it was received and the date on which the reporter expects to have the transcript completed and shall transmit the request, so endorsed, to the clerk or the clerk of the bankruptcy appellate panel. On completion of the transcript the reporter shall file it with the clerk and, if appropriate, notify the clerk of the bankruptcy appellate panel. If the transcript cannot be completed within 30 days of receipt of the request the reporter shall seek an extension of time from the clerk or the clerk of the bankruptcy appellate panel and the action of the clerk shall be entered in the docket and the parties notified. If the reporter does not file the transcript within the time allowed, the clerk or the clerk of the bankruptcy appellate panel shall notify the bankruptcy judge.

(b) DUTY OF CLERK TO TRANSMIT RECORD; DOCKETING OF APPEAL. When the record is complete for purposes of appeal, the clerk shall transmit a copy thereof forthwith to the clerk of the district court or the clerk of the bankruptcy appellate panel. On receipt of the transmission the clerk of the district court or the clerk of the bankruptcy appellate panel shall enter the appeal in the docket and give notice promptly to all parties to the judgment, order, or decree appealed from of the date on which the appeal was docketed. If the bankruptcy appellate panel directs that additional copies of the record be furnished, the clerk of the bankruptcy appellate panel shall notify the appellant and, if the appellant fails to provide the copies, the clerk shall prepare the copies at the expense of the appellant.

(c) RECORD FOR PRELIMINARY HEARING to the time the record is transmitted a party moves in the district court or before the bankruptcy appellate panel for dismissal, for a stay pending appeal, for additional security on the bond on appeal or on a supersedeas bond, or for any intermediate order, the clerk at the request of any party to the appeal shall transmit to the clerk of the district court or the clerk of the bankruptcy appellate panel a copy of the parts of the record as any party to the appeal shall designate.

(As amended Mar. 30, 1987, eff. Aug. 1, 1987; Apr. 30, 1991, eff. Aug. 1, 1991.)

NOTES OF ADVISORY COMMITTEE ON RULES—1983

*Subdivision (a)* is an adaptation of Rule 11(b) F.R.App.P.

*Subdivision (b)* is similar to former Bankruptcy Rule 807. The duty of the clerk of the bankruptcy court to transmit the record as soon as the record is complete is derived from the second paragraph of Rule 11(b) F.R.App.P. The last sentence of the subdivision applies to appeals to bankruptcy appellate panels. Additional copies of the record may be needed when the appendix to the brief required under Rule 8009(b) is not adequate in the judgment of the bankruptcy appellate panel for disposition of the appeal. If additional copies are required, the appellant will arrange for the production of the copies; if the appellant fails to do so, the clerk of the bankruptcy appellate panel shall prepare the copies at the expense of the appellant.

*Subdivision (c)* is derived from subdivisions (c), (e) and (f) of Rule 11 F.R.App.P. and subdivision (d) is essentially the same as Rule 11(b) F.R.App.P.

NOTES OF ADVISORY COMMITTEE ON RULES—1991 AMENDMENT

This rule is amended to require that the bankruptcy clerk retain the original record and transmit a copy of the record to the clerk of the district court or bankruptcy appellate panel. Transmission of the original documents may cause disruption in the continuing administration of the case in the bankruptcy court.

## Rule 8008. Filing and Service

(a) FILING. Papers required or permitted to be filed with the clerk of the district court or the clerk of the bankruptcy appellate panel may be filed by mail addressed to the clerk, but filing is not timely unless the papers are received by the clerk within the time fixed for filing, except that briefs are deemed filed on the day of mailing. An original and one copy of all papers shall be filed when an appeal is to the district court; an original and three copies shall be filed when an appeal is to a bankruptcy appellate panel. The district court or bankruptcy appellate panel may require that additional copies be furnished. Rule 5005(a)(2) applies to papers filed with the clerk of the district court or the clerk of the bankruptcy appellate panel if filing by electronic means is authorized by local rule promulgated pursuant to Rule 8018.

(b) SERVICE OF ALL PAPERS REQUIRED. Copies of all papers filed by any party and not required by these rules to be served by the clerk of the district court or the clerk of the bankruptcy appellate panel shall, at or before the time of filing, be served by the party or a person acting for the party on all other parties to the appeal. Service on a party represented by counsel shall be made on counsel.

(c) MANNER OF SERVICE. Service may be personal or by mail. Personal service includes delivery of the copy to a clerk or other responsible person at the office of counsel. Service by mail is complete on mailing.

(d) PROOF OF SERVICE. Papers presented for filing shall contain an acknowledgment of service by the person served or proof of service in the form of a statement of the date and manner of service and of the names of the persons served, certified by the person who made service. The clerk of the district court or the clerk of the bankruptcy appellate panel may permit papers to be filed without acknowledgment or proof of service but shall require the acknowledgment or proof of service to be filed promptly thereafter.

(As amended Mar. 30, 1987, eff. Aug. 1, 1987; Apr. 23, 1996, eff. Dec. 1, 1996.)

NOTES OF ADVISORY COMMITTEE ON RULES—1983

This rule is an adaptation of Rule 25 F.R.App.P. Motions, briefs, appendices when required, statements, and any other filed paper must be accompanied by the specified number of copies. Rules 8001 and 8004 govern the number of copies of the notice of appeal which must be filed.

NOTES OF ADVISORY COMMITTEE ON RULES—1996 AMENDMENT

This rule is amended to permit, but not require, district courts and, where bankruptcy appellate panels have been authorized, circuit councils to adopt local rules that allow filing of documents by electronic means, subject to the limitations contained in Rule 5005(a)(2). See the committee note to the amendments to Rule 5005. Other amendments to this rule are stylistic.

*GAP Report on Rule 8008.* No changes since publication, except for stylistic changes.

## Rule 8009. Briefs and Appendix; Filing and Service

(a) BRIEFS. Unless the district court or the bankruptcy appellate panel by local rule or by order excuses the filing of briefs or specifies different time limits:

(1) The appellant shall serve and file a brief within 14 days after entry of the appeal on the docket pursuant to Rule 8007.

(2) The appellee shall serve and file a brief within 14 days after service of the brief of appellant. If the appellee has filed a cross appeal, the brief of the appellee shall contain the issues and argument pertinent to the cross appeal, denominated as such, and the response to the brief of the appellant.

(3) The appellant may serve and file a reply brief within 14 days after service of the brief of the appellee, and if the appellee has cross-appealed, the appellee may file and serve a reply brief to the response of the appellant to the issues presented in the cross appeal within 14 days after service of the reply brief of the appellant. No further briefs may be filed except with leave of the district court or the bankruptcy appellate panel.

(b) APPENDIX TO BRIEF. If the appeal is to a bankruptcy appellate panel, the appellant shall serve and file with the appellant's brief excerpts of the record as an appendix, which shall include the following:

(1) The complaint and answer or other equivalent pleadings;

(2) Any pretrial order;

(3) The judgment, order, or decree from which the appeal is taken;

(4) Any other orders relevant to the appeal;

(5) The opinion, findings of fact, or conclusions of law filed or delivered orally by the court and citations of the opinion if published;

(6) Any motion and response on which the court rendered decision;

(7) The notice of appeal;

(8) The relevant entries in the bankruptcy docket; and

(9) The transcript or portion thereof, if so required by a rule of the bankruptcy appellate panel.

An appellee may also serve and file an appendix which contains material required to be included by the appellant but omitted by appellant.

(As amended Mar. 30, 1987, eff. Aug. 1, 1987; Mar. 26, 2009, eff. Dec. 1, 2009.)

NOTES OF ADVISORY COMMITTEE ON RULES—1983

*Subdivision (a)* of this rule is adapted from Rules 28(a) and 31(a) F.R.App.P. The introductory clause of the rule recognizes the desirability of allowing local and individual variation in the filing of briefs. The numbered paragraphs prescribe shorter periods than the corresponding periods allowed by Rule 31(a) F.R.App.P.

*Subdivision (b)*, which is similar to an interim rule for bankruptcy appellate panels promulgated by the Ninth Circuit, applies only when an appeal is to an appellate panel. The appellant must prepare an appendix to the brief which contains the documents relevant to the appeal. With the appendix available to each member of the appellate panel, it is unlikely that multiple copies of the record will be necessary. The last sentence of the subdivision enables the appellee to correct an omission of the appellant.

Rule 30 F.R.App.P., which governs the preparation of the appendix in appeals taken to the courts of appeals, specifies fewer documents which must be included in the appendix but permits the parties to include any other material.

NOTES OF ADVISORY COMMITTEE ON RULES—1987 AMENDMENT

The amendment to Rule 8007(c) permits a rule of the bankruptcy appellate panel to provide that the record is to be retained rather than transmitted. The new paragraph (9) of subdivision (b) of this rule complements Rule 8007(c) by authorizing a rule of the panel to require inclusion of the transcript or a portion thereof in the appendix.

COMMITTEE NOTES ON RULES—2009 AMENDMENT

The rule is amended to implement changes in connection with the amendment to Rule 9006(a) and the manner by which time is computed under the rules. The deadlines in the rule are amended to substitute a deadline that is a multiple of seven days. Throughout the rules, deadlines are amended in the following manner:

- 5-day periods become 7-day periods
- 10-day periods become 14-day periods
- 15-day periods become 14-day periods
- 20-day periods become 21-day periods
- 25-day periods become 28-day periods

## Rule 8010. Form of Briefs; Length

(a) FORM OF BRIEFS. Unless the district court or the bankruptcy appellate panel by local rule otherwise provides, the form of brief shall be as follows:

(1) *Brief of the Appellant*. The brief of the appellant shall contain under appropriate headings and in the order here indicated:

(A) A table of contents, with page references, and a table of cases alphabetically arranged, statutes and other authorities cited, with references to the pages of the brief where they are cited.

(B) A statement of the basis of appellate jurisdiction.

(C) A statement of the issues presented and the applicable standard of appellate review.

(D) A statement of the case. The statement shall first indicate briefly the nature of the case, the course of the proceedings, and the disposition in the court below. There shall follow a statement of the facts relevant to the issues presented for review, with appropriate references to the record.

(E) An argument. The argument may be preceded by a summary. The argument shall contain the contentions of the appellant with respect to the issues presented, and the reasons therefor, with citations to the authorities, statutes and parts of the record relied on.

(F) A short conclusion stating the precise relief sought.

(2) *Brief of the Appellee*. The brief of the appellee shall conform to the requirements of paragraph (1)(A)–(E) of this subdivision, except that a statement of the basis of appellate jurisdiction, of the issues, or of the case need not be made unless the appellee is dissatisfied with the statement of the appellant.

(b) REPRODUCTION OF STATUTES, RULES, REGULATIONS, OR SIMILAR MATERIAL. If determination of the issues presented requires reference to the Code or other statutes, rules, regulations, or similar material, relevant parts thereof shall be reproduced in the brief or in an addendum or they may be supplied to the court in pamphlet form.

(c) LENGTH OF BRIEFS. Unless the district court or the bankruptcy appellate panel by local rule or order otherwise provides, principal briefs shall not exceed 50 pages, and reply briefs shall not exceed 25 pages, exclusive of pages containing the table of contents, tables of citations and any addendum containing statutes, rules, regulations, or similar material.

NOTES OF ADVISORY COMMITTEE ON RULES

This rule is derived from subdivisions (a), (b), (c), and (f) of Rule 28 F.R.App.P.

When an appeal is to a bankruptcy appellate panel and an appendix is filed pursuant to Rule 8009(b) and reference is made in a brief to parts of the record included in the appendix, the reference should be to the appropriate pages of the appendix at which those parts appear.

## Rule 8011. Motions

(a) CONTENT OF MOTIONS; RESPONSE; R request for an order or other relief shall be made by filing with the clerk of the district court or the clerk of the bankruptcy appellate panel a motion for such order or relief with proof of service on all other parties to the appeal. The motion shall contain or be accompanied by any matter required by a specific provision of these rules governing such a motion, shall state with particularity the grounds on which it is based, and shall set forth the order or relief sought. If a motion is supported by briefs, affidavits or other papers, they shall be served and filed with the motion. Any party may file a response in opposition to a motion other than one for a procedural order within seven days after service of the motion, but the district court or the bankruptcy appellate panel may shorten or extend the time for responding to any motion.

(b) DETERMINATION OF MOTIONS FOR PROCEDURAL ORDERS. Notwithstanding subdivision (a) of this rule, motions for procedural orders, including any motion under Rule 9006, may be acted on at any time, without awaiting a response thereto and without hearing. Any party adversely affected by such action may move for reconsideration, vacation, or modification of the action.

(c) DETERMINATION OF ALL MOTIONS. All motions will be decided without oral argument unless the court orders otherwise. A motion for a stay, or for other emergency relief may be denied if not presented promptly.

(d) EMERGENCY MOTIONS. Whenever a movant requests expedited action on a motion on the ground that, to avoid irreparable harm, relief is needed in less time than would normally be required for the district court or bankruptcy appellate panel to receive and consider a response, the word "Emergency" shall precede the title of the motion. The motion shall be accompanied by an affidavit setting forth the nature of the emergency. The motion shall state whether all grounds advanced in support thereof were submitted to the bankruptcy judge and, if any grounds relied on were not submitted, why the motion should not be remanded to the bankruptcy judge for reconsideration. The motion shall include the office addresses and telephone numbers of moving and opposing counsel and shall be served pursuant to Rule 8008. Prior to filing the motion, the movant shall make every practicable effort to notify opposing counsel in time for counsel to respond to the motion. The affidavit accompanying the motion shall also state when and how opposing counsel was notified or if opposing counsel was not notified why it was not practicable to do so.

(e) POWER OF A SINGLE JUDGE TO ENTERTAIN MOTIONS. A single judge of a bankruptcy appellate panel may grant or deny any request for relief which under these rules may properly be sought by motion, except that a single judge may not dismiss or otherwise decide an appeal or a motion for leave to appeal. The action of a single judge may be reviewed by the panel.

NOTES OF ADVISORY COMMITTEE ON RULES—1983

Subdivisions (a), (b) and (e) of this rule conform substantially to subdivisions (a), (b) and (c) of Rule 27 F.R.App.P. Subdivisions (c) and (d) are taken from Rule 13(c) and (d) of the Rules of the First Circuit governing appeals to bankruptcy appellate panels.

## Rule 8012. Oral Argument

Oral argument shall be allowed in all cases unless the district judge or the judges of the bankruptcy appellate panel unanimously determine after examination of the briefs and record, or appendix to the brief, that oral argument is not needed. Any party shall have an opportunity to file a statement setting forth the reason why oral argument should be allowed.

Oral argument will not be allowed if (1) the appeal is frivolous; (2) the dispositive issue or set of issues has been recently authoritatively decided; or (3) the facts and legal arguments are adequately presented in the briefs and record and the decisional process would not be significantly aided by oral argument.

NOTES OF ADVISORY COMMITTEE ON RULES—1983

This rule is derived from Rule 34(a) F.R.App.P. The other details of oral argument which are covered by the remaining subdivisions of Rule 34 F.R.App.P are not in these rules and are left to local rule or order of the court.

## Rule 8013. Disposition of Appeal; Weight Accorded Bankruptcy Judge's Findings of Fact

On an appeal the district court or bankruptcy appellate panel may affirm, modify, or reverse a bankruptcy judge's judgment, order, or decree or remand with instructions for further proceedings. Findings of fact, whether based on oral or documentary evidence, shall not be set aside unless clearly erroneous, and due regard shall be given to the opportunity of the bankruptcy court to judge the credibility of the witnesses.

(As amended Mar. 30, 1987, eff. Aug. 1, 1987.)

NOTES OF ADVISORY COMMITTEE ON RULES—1983

This rule accords to the findings of a bankruptcy judge the same weight given the findings of a district judge under Rule 52 F.R.Civ.P. See also Rules 7052(a) and 9014.

NOTES OF ADVISORY COMMITTEE ON RULES—1987 AMENDMENT

The amendment to this rule conforms the appellate review standard to Rule 52 F.R.Civ.P., as amended in August 1985.

## Rule 8014. Costs

Except as otherwise provided by law, agreed to by the parties, or ordered by the district court or the bankruptcy appellate panel, costs shall be taxed against the losing party on an appeal. If a judgment is affirmed or reversed in part, or is vacated, costs shall be allowed only as ordered by the court. Costs incurred in the production of copies of briefs, the appendices, and the record and in the preparation and transmission of the record, the cost of the reporter's transcript, if necessary for the determination of the appeal, the premiums paid for cost of supersedeas bonds or other bonds to preserve rights pending appeal and the fee for filing the notice of appeal shall be taxed by the clerk as costs of the appeal in favor of the party entitled to costs under this rule.

(As amended Mar. 30, 1987, eff. Aug. 1, 1987.)

NOTES OF ADVISORY COMMITTEE ON RULES—1983

This rule is an adaptation of Rule 39(a), (c) and (e) of the F.R.App.P. Under this rule all costs are taxed by the clerk of the bankruptcy court.

## Rule 8015. Motion for Rehearing

Unless the district court or the bankruptcy appellate panel by local rule or by court order otherwise provides, a motion for rehearing may be filed within 14 days after entry of the judgment of the district court or the bankruptcy appellate panel. If a timely motion for rehearing is filed, the time for appeal to the court of appeals for all parties shall run from the entry of the order denying rehearing or the entry of subsequent judgment.

(As amended Mar. 30, 1987, eff. Aug. 1, 1987; Mar. 26, 2009, eff. Dec. 1, 2009.)

NOTES OF ADVISORY COMMITTEE ON RULES—1983

This is an adaptation of the first sentence of Rule 40(a) F.R.App.P. The filing of a motion for rehearing does not toll the time for taking an appeal to the court of appeals from the district court or the bankruptcy appellate panel. Appeals from a district court or a bankruptcy appellate panel are to the appropriate court of appeals. Under Rule 4(a)(4) F.R.App.P. the filing of post-trial motions in the district court has the effect of vitiating any prior notice of appeal and, on the district court's disposition of those post-trial motions, a new appeal period starts. Rule 4 F.R.App.P. does not, however, contain any provision which stays or otherwise alters the time for taking an appeal to the court of appeals when a motion for rehearing is filed under Rule 8015 with the district court or bankruptcy appellate panel.

NOTES OF ADVISORY COMMITTEE ON RULES—1987 AMENDMENT

The amendment, which is derived from Rule 8002(b), Rule 4(a)(4) F.R.App.P., and Rule 11.1 Sup.Ct.R., clarifies the effect of the filing of a timely motion for rehearing. If a timely motion is filed, the appeal period to the court of appeals begins to run on the entry of an order denying the motion or the entry of a subsequent judgment.

COMMITTEE NOTES ON RULES—2009 AMENDMENT

The rule is amended to implement changes in connection with the amendment to Rule 9006(a) and the manner by which time is computed under the rules. The deadline in the rule is amended to substitute a deadline that is a multiple of seven days. Throughout the rules, deadlines are amended in the following manner:

- 5-day periods become 7-day periods
- 10-day periods become 14-day periods
- 15-day periods become 14-day periods
- 20-day periods become 21-day periods
- 25-day periods become 28-day periods

## Rule 8016. Duties of Clerk of District Court and Bankruptcy Appellate Panel

(a) ENTRY OF JUDGMENT. The clerk of the district court or the clerk of the bankruptcy appellate panel shall prepare, sign and enter the judgment following receipt of the opinion of the court or the appellate panel or, if there is no opinion, following the instruction of the court or the appellate panel. The notation of a judgment in the docket constitutes entry of judgment.

(b) NOTICE OF ORDERS OR JUDGMENTS; RETURN OF RECORD. Immediately on the entry of a judgment or order the clerk of the district court or the clerk of the bankruptcy appellate panel shall transmit a notice of the entry to each party to the appeal, to the United States trustee, and to the clerk, together with a copy of any opinion respecting the judgment or order, and shall make a note of the transmission in the docket. Original papers transmitted as the record on appeal shall be returned to the clerk on disposition of the appeal.

(As amended Mar. 30, 1987, eff. Aug. 1, 1987; Apr. 30, 1991, eff. Aug. 1, 1991.)

NOTES OF ADVISORY COMMITTEE ON RULES—1983

Subdivision (a) of this rule is adapted from Rule 36 F.R.App.P. Subdivision (b) is similar to subdivisions (c) and (d) of Rule 45 F.R.App.P.

NOTES OF ADVISORY COMMITTEE ON RULES—1991 AMENDMENT

*Subdivision (b)* is amended to enable the United States trustee to monitor the progress of the case. The requirements of this subdivision apply to an order of the district court or bankruptcy appellate panel staying its judgment pending appeal to the court of appeals pursuant to Rule 8017(b).

## Rule 8017. Stay of Judgment of District Court or Bankruptcy Appellate Panel

(a) AUTOMATIC STAY OF JUDGMENT ON APPEAL. Judgments of the district court or the bankruptcy appellate panel are stayed until the expiration of 14 days after entry, unless otherwise ordered by the district court or the bankruptcy appellate panel.

(b) STAY PENDING APPEAL TO THE COURT OF APPEALS. On motion and notice to the parties to the appeal, the district court or the bankruptcy appellate panel may stay its judgment pending an appeal to the court of appeals. The stay shall not extend beyond 30 days after the entry of the judgment of the district court or the bankruptcy appellate panel unless the period is extended for cause shown. If before the expiration of a stay entered pursuant to this subdivision there is an appeal to the court of appeals by the party who obtained the stay, the stay shall continue until final disposition by the court of appeals. A bond or other security may be required as a condition to the grant or continuation of a stay of the judgment. A bond or other security may be required if a trustee obtains a stay but a bond or security shall not be required if a stay is obtained by the United States or an officer or agency thereof or at the direction of any department of the Government of the United States.

(c) POWER OF COURT OF APPEALS NOT LIMITED. This rule does not limit the power of a court of appeals or any judge thereof to stay proceedings during the pendency of an appeal or to suspend, modify, restore, or grant an injunction during the pendency of an appeal or to make any order appropriate to preserve the status quo or the effectiveness of the judgment subsequently to be entered.

(As amended Mar. 26, 2009, eff. Dec. 1, 2009.)

NOTES OF ADVISORY COMMITTEE ON RULES

This rule is derived from Rule 62 F.R.Civ.P. and Rule 41 F.R.App.P.

*Subdivision (a)* accords to the parties to an appeal 10 days within which to decide whether to pursue an appeal to the court of appeals. In ordinary civil litigation there is a similar opportunity. Rule 62(a) F.R.Civ.P. automatically stays enforcement of a district court's judgment in a civil action and Rule 41(a) F.R.App.P. provides that the mandate of the court of appeals shall not issue for 21 days, unless the court otherwise directs. The district court or bankruptcy appellate panel may reduce the 10 day period of this subdivision.

*Subdivision (b)* vests in the district courts and the bankruptcy appellate panels the same authority the courts of appeals have under Rule 41(b) F.R.App.P. to stay their judgments pending appeal. Perfection of an appeal to the court of appeals while a stay entered by the district court or bankruptcy appellate panel is in effect results in the automatic continuation of that stay during the course of the appeal in the court of appeals.

*Subdivision (c)* is the same as Rule 62(g) F.R.Civ.P.

COMMITTEE NOTES ON RULES—2009 AMENDMENT

The rule is amended to implement changes in connection with the amendment to Rule 9006(a) and the manner by which time is computed under the rules. The deadline in the rule is amended to substitute a deadline that is a multiple of seven days. Throughout the rules, deadlines are amended in the following manner:

- 5-day periods become 7-day periods
- 10-day periods become 14-day periods
- 15-day periods become 14-day periods
- 20-day periods become 21-day periods
- 25-day periods become 28-day periods

### Rule 8018. Rules by Circuit Councils and District Courts; Procedure When There is No Controlling Law

(a) LOCAL RULES BY CIRCUIT COUNCILS AND DISTRICT COURTS.

(1) Circuit councils which have authorized bankruptcy appellate panels pursuant to 28 U.S.C. §158(b) and the district courts may, acting by a majority of the judges of the council or district court, make and amend rules governing practice and procedure for appeals from orders or judgments of bankruptcy judges to the respective bankruptcy appellate panel or district court consistent with—but not duplicative of—Acts of Congress and the rules of this Part VIII. Local rules shall conform to any uniform numbering system prescribed by the Judicial Conference of the United States. Rule 83 F.R.Civ.P. governs the procedure for making and amending rules to govern appeals.

(2) A local rule imposing a requirement of form shall not be enforced in a manner that causes a party to lose rights because of a nonwillful failure to comply with the requirement.

(b) PROCEDURE WHEN THERE IS NO CONTROLLING LAW. A bankruptcy appellate panel or district judge may regulate practice in any manner consistent with federal law, these rules, Official Forms, and local rules of the circuit council or district court. No sanction or other disadvantage may be imposed for noncompliance with any requirement not in federal law, federal rules, Official Forms, or the local rules of the circuit council or district court unless the alleged violator has been furnished in the particular case with actual notice of the requirement.

(As amended Mar. 30, 1987, eff. Aug. 1, 1987; Apr. 27, 1995, eff. Dec. 1, 1995.)

NOTES OF ADVISORY COMMITTEE ON RULES—1983

This rule is similar to Rule 47 F.R.App.P. and Rule 83 F.R.Civ.P. Local rules governing procedure before the bankruptcy courts may be promulgated under Rule 9028.

NOTES OF ADVISORY COMMITTEE ON RULES—1987 AMENDMENT

Rule 83 F.R.Civ.P. was amended in August 1985 to require greater participation by the public in the rule making process. The amendment to Rule 8018 incorporates Rule 83 F.R.Civ.P. Under 28 U.S.C. §158(b)(2), appeals may be taken to a bankruptcy appellate panel only if the district court so authorizes. If a district court does not authorize appeals to the bankruptcy appellate panel, appeals will be to the district court. This rule is amended to authorize district courts to promulgate rules for appeals.

NOTES OF ADVISORY COMMITTEE ON RULES—1995 AMENDMENT

The amendments to this rule conform to the amendments to Rule 9029. See Committee Note to the amendments to Rule 9029.

REFERENCES IN TEXT

The Federal Rules of Civil Procedure, referred to in subd. (a)(1), are set out in the Appendix to Title 28, Judiciary and Judicial Procedure.

### Rule 8019. Suspension of Rules in Part VIII

In the interest of expediting decision or for other cause, the district court or the bankruptcy appellate panel may suspend the requirements or provisions of the rules in Part VIII, except Rules 8001, 8002 and 8013, and may order proceedings in accordance with the direction.

(As amended Mar. 30, 1987, eff. Aug. 1, 1987.)

NOTES OF ADVISORY COMMITTEE ON RULES—1983

This rule is derived from Rule 2 F.R.App.P.

### Rule 8020. Damages and Costs for Frivolous Appeal

If a district court or bankruptcy appellate panel determines that an appeal from an order, judgment, or decree of a bankruptcy judge is frivolous, it may, after a separately filed motion or notice from the district court or bankruptcy appellate panel and reasonable opportunity to respond, award just damages and single or double costs to the appellee.

(Added Apr. 11, 1997, eff. Dec. 1, 1997.)

NOTES OF ADVISORY COMMITTEE ON RULES—1997

This rule is added to clarify that a district court hearing an appeal, or a bankruptcy appellate panel, has the authority to award damages and costs to an appellee if it finds that the appeal is frivolous. By conforming to the language of Rule 38 F.R.App.P., this rule recognizes that the authority to award damages and costs in connection with frivolous appeals is the same for district courts sitting as appellate courts, bankruptcy appellate panels, and courts of appeals.

*GAP Report on Rule 8020.* No changes to the published draft.

## PART IX—GENERAL PROVISIONS

### Rule 9001. General Definitions

The definitions of words and phrases in §101, §902 and §1101 and the rules of construction in §102 of the Code govern their use in these rules. In addition, the following words and phrases used in these rules have the meanings indicated:

(1) "Bankruptcy clerk" means a clerk appointed pursuant to 28 U.S.C. §156(b).

(2) "Bankruptcy Code" or "Code" means title 11 of the United States Code.

(3) "Clerk" means bankruptcy clerk, if one has been appointed, otherwise clerk of the district court.

(4) "Court" or "judge" means the judicial officer before whom a case or proceeding is pending.

(5) "Debtor." When any act is required by these rules to be performed by a debtor or

when it is necessary to compel attendance of a debtor for examination and the debtor is not a natural person: (A) if the debtor is a corporation, "debtor" includes, if designated by the court, any or all of its officers, members of its board of directors or trustees or of a similar controlling body, a controlling stockholder or member, or any other person in control; (B) if the debtor is a partnership, "debtor" includes any or all of its general partners or, if designated by the court, any other person in control.

(6) "Firm" includes a partnership or professional corporation of attorneys or accountants.

(7) "Judgment" means any appealable order.

(8) "Mail" means first class, postage prepaid.

(9) "Notice provider" means any entity approved by the Administrative Office of the United States Courts to give notice to creditors under Rule 2002(g)(4).

(10) "Regular associate" means any attorney regularly employed by, associated with, or counsel to an individual or firm.

(11) "Trustee" includes a debtor in possession in a chapter 11 case.

(12) "United States trustee" includes an assistant United States trustee and any designee of the United States trustee.

(As amended Mar. 30, 1987, eff. Aug. 1, 1987; Apr. 30, 1991, eff. Aug. 1, 1991; Apr. 25, 2005, eff. Dec. 1, 2005.)

NOTES OF ADVISORY COMMITTEE ON RULES—1987 AMENDMENT

The terms "bankruptcy clerk" and "clerk" have been defined to reflect that unless otherwise stated, for the purpose of these rules, the terms are meant to identify the court officer for the bankruptcy records. If a bankruptcy clerk is appointed, all filings are made with the bankruptcy clerk. If one has not been appointed, all filings are with the clerk of the district court. Rule 5005.

The rule is also amended to include a definition of "court or judge". Since a case or proceeding may be before a bankruptcy judge or a judge of the district court, "court or judge" is defined to mean the judicial officer before whom the case or proceeding is pending.

NOTES OF ADVISORY COMMITTEE ON RULES—1991 AMENDMENT

Section 582 of title 28 provides that the Attorney General may appoint one or more assistant United States trustees in any region when the public interest so requires. This rule is amended to clarify that an assistant United States trustee, as well as any designee of the United States trustee, is included within the meaning of "United States trustee" in the rules.

COMMITTEE NOTES ON RULES—2005 AMENDMENT

The rule is amended to add the definition of a notice provider and to renumber the final three definitions in the rule. A notice provider is an entity approved by the Administrative Office of the United States Courts to enter into agreements with entities to give notice to those entities in the form and manner agreed to by those parties. The new definition supports the amendment to Rule 2002(g)(4) that authorizes a notice provider to give notices under Rule 2002.

Many entities conduct business on a national scale and receive vast numbers of notices in bankruptcy cases throughout the country. Those entities can agree with a notice provider to receive their notices in a form and at an address or addresses that the creditor and notice provider agree upon. There are processes currently in use that provide substantial assurance that notices are not misdirected. Any notice provider would have to demonstrate to the Administrative Office of the United States Courts that it could provide the service in a manner that ensures the proper delivery of notice to creditors. Once the Administrative Office of the United States Courts approves the notice provider to enter into agreements with creditors, the notice provider and other entities can establish the relationship that will govern the delivery of notices in cases as provided in Rule 2002(g)(4).

*Changes Made After Publication and Comment.* No changes since publication.

REFERENCES IN TEXT

The Bankruptcy Act of 1898 as amended, referred to in pars. (1) and (2), is act July 1, 1898, ch. 541, 30 Stat. 544, as amended, which was classified generally to former Title 11, Bankruptcy. Sections 1(10) and 2a of this Act were classified to sections 1(10) and 11(a), respectively, of former Title 11. The Act was repealed effective Oct. 1, 1979, by Pub. L. 95–598, §§401(a), 402(a), Nov. 6, 1978, 92 Stat. 2682, section 101 of which enacted revised Title 11.

## Rule 9002. Meanings of Words in the Federal Rules of Civil Procedure When Applicable to Cases Under the Code

The following words and phrases used in the Federal Rules of Civil Procedure made applicable to cases under the Code by these rules have the meanings indicated unless they are inconsistent with the context:

(1) "Action" or "civil action" means an adversary proceeding or, when appropriate, a contested petition, or proceedings to vacate an order for relief or to determine any other contested matter.

(2) "Appeal" means an appeal as provided by 28 U.S.C. §158.

(3) "Clerk" or "clerk of the district court" means the court officer responsible for the bankruptcy records in the district.

(4) "District Court," "trial court," "court," "district judge," or "judge" means bankruptcy judge if the case or proceeding is pending before a bankruptcy judge.

(5) "Judgment" includes any order appealable to an appellate court.

(As amended Mar. 30, 1987, eff. Aug. 1, 1987; Apr. 22, 1993, eff. Aug. 1, 1993.)

REFERENCES IN TEXT

The Federal Rules of Civil Procedure, referred to in text, are set out in the Appendix to Title 28, Judiciary and Judicial Procedure.

NOTES OF ADVISORY COMMITTEE ON RULES AMENDMENT

This rule is revised to include the words "district judge" in anticipation of amendments to the Federal Rules of Civil Procedure.

## Rule 9003. Prohibition of Ex Parte Contacts

(a) GENERAL PROHIBITION. Except as otherwise permitted by applicable law, any examiner, any party in interest, and any attorney, accountant, or employee of a party in interest shall refrain from ex parte meetings and communications with the court concerning matters affecting a particular case or proceeding.

(b) UNITED STATES TRUSTEE. Except as otherwise permitted by applicable law, the United States trustee and assistants to and employees or agents of the United States trustee shall refrain from ex parte meetings and communications with the court concerning matters affecting a particular case or proceeding. This rule does not preclude communications with the court to discuss general problems of administration and improvement of bankruptcy administration, including the operation of the United States trustee system.

(As amended Mar. 30, 1987, eff. Aug. 1, 1987; Apr. 30, 1991, eff. Aug. 1, 1991.)

NOTES OF ADVISORY COMMITTEE ON RULES—1983

This rule regulates the actions of parties in interest and their attorneys or others employed by parties in interest. This regulation of the conduct of parties in interest and their representative is designed to insure that the bankruptcy system operates fairly and that no appearance of unfairness is created. See H. Rep. No. 95–595, 95th Cong., 1st Sess. 95 et seq. (1977).

This rule is not a substitute for or limitation of any applicable canon of professional responsibility or judicial conduct. See, *e.g.*, Canon 7, EC7–35, Disciplinary Rule 7–110(B) of the Code of Professional Responsibility: "Generally, in adversary proceedings a lawyer should not communicate with a judge relative to a matter pending before, or which is to be brought before, a tribunal over which he presides in circumstances which might have the effect or give the appearance of granting undue advantage to one party;" and Canon 3A(4) of the Code of Judicial Conduct: "A judge should . . . neither initiate nor consider ex parte or other communications concerning a pending or impending proceeding."

NOTES OF ADVISORY COMMITTEE ON RULES—1987 AMENDMENT

This rule is amended to apply to both the bankruptcy judges and the district judges of the district.

NOTES OF ADVISORY COMMITTEE ON RULES—1991 AMENDMENT

*Subdivision (a)* is amended to extend to examiners the prohibition on ex parte meetings and communications with the court.

*Subdivision (b)* is derived from Rule X–1010.

## Rule 9004. General Requirements of Form

(a) LEGIBILITY; ABBREVIATIONS. All petitions, pleadings, schedules and other papers shall be clearly legible. Abbreviations in common use in the English language may be used.

(b) CAPTION. Each paper filed shall contain a caption setting forth the name of the court, the title of the case, the bankruptcy docket number, and a brief designation of the character of the paper.

NOTES OF ADVISORY COMMITTEE ON RULES—1983

*Subdivision (b).* Additional requirements applicable to the caption for a petition are found in Rule 1005, to the caption for notices to creditors in Rule 2002(m), and to the caption for a pleading or other paper filed in an adversary proceeding in Rule 7010. Failure to comply with this or any other rule imposing a merely formal requirement does not ordinarily result in the loss of rights. See Rule 9005.

## Rule 9005. Harmless Error

Rule 61 F.R.Civ.P. applies in cases under the Code. When appropriate, the court may order the correction of any error or defect or the cure of any omission which does not affect substantial rights.

REFERENCES IN TEXT

The Federal Rules of Civil Procedure, referred to in text, are set out in the Appendix to Title 28, Judiciary and Judicial Procedure.

## Rule 9005.1. Constitutional Challenge to a Statute—Notice, Certification, and Intervention

Rule 5.1 F.R.Civ.P. applies in cases under the Code.

(Added Apr. 30, 2007, eff. Dec. 1, 2007.)

COMMITTEE NOTES ON RULES—2007

The rule is added to adopt the new rule added to the Federal Rules of Civil Procedure. The new Civil Rule replaces Rule 24(c) F. R. Civ. P., so the cross reference to Civil Rule 24 contained in Rule 7024 is no longer sufficient to bring the provisions of new Civil Rule 5.1 into adversary proceedings. This rule also makes Civil Rule 5.1 applicable to all contested matters and other proceedings within the bankruptcy case.

*Changes After Publication.* No changes were made after publication.

REFERENCES IN TEXT

The Federal Rules of Civil Procedure, referred to in text, are set out in the Appendix to Title 28, Judiciary and Judicial Procedure.

## Rule 9006. Computing and Extending Time

(a) COMPUTING TIME. The following rules apply in computing any time period specified in these rules, in the Federal Rules of Civil Procedure, in any local rule or court order, or in any statute that does not specify a method of computing time.

(1) *Period Stated in Days or a Longer Unit.* When the period is stated in days or a longer unit of time:

(A) exclude the day of the event that triggers the period;

(B) count every day, including intermediate Saturdays, Sundays, and legal holidays; and

(C) include the last day of the period, but if the last day is a Saturday, Sunday, or legal holiday, the period continues to run until the end of the next day that is not a Saturday, Sunday, or legal holiday.

(2) *Period Stated in Hours.* When the period is stated in hours:

(A) begin counting immediately on the occurrence of the event that triggers the period;

(B) count every hour, including hours during intermediate Saturdays, Sundays, and legal holidays; and

(C) if the period would end on a Saturday, Sunday, or legal holiday, then continue the period until the same time on the next day that is not a Saturday, Sunday, or legal holiday.

(3) *Inaccessibility of Clerk's Office.* Unless the court orders otherwise, if the clerk's office is inaccessible:

(A) on the last day for filing under Rule 9006(a)(1), then the time for filing is extended to the first accessible day that is not a Saturday, Sunday, or legal holiday; or

(B) during the last hour for filing under Rule 9006(a)(2), then the time for filing is extended to the same time on the first accessible day that is not a Saturday, Sunday, or legal holiday.

(4) *"Last Day" Defined.* Unless a different time is set by a statute, local rule, or order in the case, the last day ends:

(A) for electronic filing, at midnight in the court's time zone; and

(B) for filing by other means, when the clerk's office is scheduled to close.

(5) *"Next Day" Defined.* The "next day" is determined by continuing to count forward when the period is measured after an event and backward when measured before an event.

(6) *"Legal Holiday" Defined.* "Legal holiday" means:

(A) the day set aside by statute for observing New Year's Day, Martin Luther King Jr.'s Birthday, Washington's Birthday, Memorial Day, Independence Day, Labor Day, Columbus Day, Veterans' Day, Thanksgiving Day, or Christmas Day;

(B) any day declared a holiday by the President or Congress; and

(C) for periods that are measured after an event, any other day declared a holiday by the state where the district court is located. (In this rule, "state" includes the District of Columbia and any United States commonwealth or territory.)

(b) ENLARGEMENT.

(1) *In General.* Except as provided in paragraphs (2) and (3) of this subdivision, when an act is required or allowed to be done at or within a specified period by these rules or by a notice given thereunder or by order of court, the court for cause shown may at any time in its discretion (1) with or without motion or notice order the period enlarged if the request therefor is made before the expiration of the period originally prescribed or as extended by a previous order or (2) on motion made after the expiration of the specified period permit the act to be done where the failure to act was the result of excusable neglect.

(2) *Enlargement Not Permitted.* The court may not enlarge the time for taking action under Rules 1007(d), 2003(a) and (d), 7052, 9023, and 9024.

(3) *Enlargement Governed By Other Rules.* The court may enlarge the time for taking action under Rules 1006(b)(2), 1017(e), 3002(c), 4003(b), 4004(a), 4007(c), 4008(a), 8002, and 9033, only to the extent and under the conditions stated in those rules. In addition, the court may enlarge the time to file the statement required under Rule 1007(b)(7), and to file schedules and statements in a small business case under §1116(3) of the Code, only to the extent and under the conditions stated in Rule 1007(c).

(c) REDUCTION.

(1) *In General.* Except as provided in paragraph (2) of this subdivision, when an act is required or allowed to be done at or within a specified time by these rules or by a notice given thereunder or by order of court, the court for cause shown may in its discretion with or without motion or notice order the period reduced.

(2) *Reduction Not Permitted.* The court may not reduce the time for taking action under Rules 2002(a)(7), 2003(a), 3002(c), 3014, 3015, 4001(b)(2), (c)(2), 4003(a), 4004(a), 4007(c), 4008(a), 8002, and 9033(b). In addition, the court may not reduce the time under Rule 1007(c) to file the statement required by Rule 1007(b)(7).

(d) FOR MOTIONS—AFFIDAVITS. A written motion, other than one which may be heard ex parte, and notice of any hearing shall be served not later than seven days before the time specified for such hearing, unless a different period is fixed by these rules or by order of the court. Such an order may for cause shown be made on ex parte application. When a motion is supported by affidavit, the affidavit shall be served with the motion; and, except as otherwise provided in Rule 9023, opposing affidavits may be served not later than one day before the hearing, unless the court permits them to be served at some other time.

(e) TIME OF SERVICE. Service of process and service of any paper other than process or of notice by mail is complete on mailing.

(f) ADDITIONAL TIME AFTER SERVICE BY MAIL OR UNDER RULE 5(b)(2)(D), (E), OR (F) F.R.CIV.P. When there is a right or requirement to act or undertake some proceedings within a prescribed period after service and that service is by mail or under Rule 5(b)(2)(D), (E), or (F) F.R.Civ.P., three days are added after the prescribed period would otherwise expire under Rule 9006(a).

(g) GRAIN STORAGE FACILITY CASES. This rule shall not limit the court's authority under §557 of the Code to enter orders governing procedures in cases in which the debtor is an owner or operator of a grain storage facility.

(As amended Mar. 30, 1987, eff. Aug. 1, 1987; Apr. 25, 1989, eff. Aug. 1, 1989; Apr. 30, 1991, eff. Aug. 1, 1991; Apr. 23, 1996, eff. Dec. 1, 1996; Apr. 26, 1999, eff. Dec. 1, 1999; Apr. 23, 2001, eff. Dec. 1, 2001; Apr. 25, 2005, eff. Dec. 1, 2005; Apr. 23, 2008, eff. Dec. 1, 2008; Mar. 26, 2009, eff. Dec. 1, 2009.)

NOTES OF ADVISORY COMMITTEE ON RULES

*Subdivision (a).* This rule is an adaptation of Rule 6 F.R.Civ.P. It governs the time for acts to be done and proceedings to be had in cases under the Code and any litigation arising therein.

*Subdivision (b)* is patterned after Rule 6(b) F.R.Civ.P. and Rule 26(b) F.R.App.P.

Paragraph (1) of this subdivision confers on the court discretion generally to authorize extensions of time for doing acts required or allowed by these rules or orders of court. The exceptions to this general authority to extend the time are contained in paragraphs (2) and (3).

In the interest of prompt administration of bankruptcy cases certain time periods may not be extended. Paragraph (2) lists the rules which establish time periods which may not be extended: Rule 1007(d), time for filing a list of 20 largest creditors; Rule 1017(b)(3), 30 day period for sending notice of dismissal for failure to pay the filing fee; Rule 1019(2), 20 day period for notice of conversion to a chapter 7 case; Rule 2003(a), meeting of creditors not more than 40 days after order for relief; Rule 2003(d), 10 days for filing a motion for resolution of an election dispute; Rule 3014, time for the §1111(b)(2) election; Rule 4001(b), expiration of stay 30 days following the commencement of final hearing; Rule 7052(b), 10 day period to move to amend findings of fact; Rule 9015(f), 20 day period to move for judgment notwithstanding the verdict; Rule 9023, 10 day period to move for a new trial; and Rule 9024, time to move for relief from judgment.

Many rules which establish a time for doing an act also contain a specific authorization and standard for granting an extension of time and, in some cases, limit the length of an extension. In some instances it would be inconsistent with the objective of the rule and sound administration of the case to permit extension under Rule 9006(b)(1), but with respect to the other rules it is appropriate that the power to extend time be supplemented by Rule 9006(b)(1). Unless a rule which contains a specific authorization to extend time is listed in paragraph (3) of this subdivision, an extension of the time may be granted under paragraph (1) of this subdivision. If a rule is included in paragraph (3) an extension may not be granted under paragraph (1). The following rules are listed in paragraph (3): Rule 1006(b)(2), time for paying the filing fee in installments; Rule 3002(c), 90 day period for filing a claim in a chapter 7 or 13 case; Rule 4003(b), 30 days for filing objections to a claim of exemptions; Rule 4004(a), 60 day period to object to a discharge; Rule 4007(b), 60 day period to file a dischargeability complaint; and Rule 8002, 10 days for filing a notice of appeal.

*Subdivision (c).* Paragraph (1) of this subdivision authorizes the reduction of the time periods established by these rules or an order of the court. Excluded from this general authority are the time periods established by the rules referred to in paragraph (2) of the subdivision: Rule 2002 (a) and (b), 20 day and 25 day notices of certain hearings and actions in the case; Rule 2003(a), meeting of creditors to be not less than 20 days after the order for relief; Rule 3002(c), 90 days for filing a claim in a chapter 7 or 13 case; Rule 3014, time for §1111(b)(2) election; Rule 3015, 10 day period after filing of petition to file a chapter 13 plan; Rule 4003(a), 15 days for a dependent to claim exemptions; Rule 4004(a), 60 day period to object to a discharge; Rule 4007(c), 60 day period to file a dischargeability complaint; and Rule 8002, 10 days for filing a notice of appeal. Reduction of the time periods fixed in the rules referred to in this subdivision would be inconsistent with the purposes of those rules and would cause harmful uncertainty.

*Subdivision (d)* is derived from Rule 6(d) F.R.Civ.P. The reference is to Rule 9023 instead of to Rule 59(c) F.R.Civ.P. because Rule 9023 incorporates Rule 59 F.R.Civ.P. but excepts therefrom motions to reconsider orders allowing and disallowing claims.

*Subdivision (f)* is new and is the same as Rule 6(e) F.R.Civ.P.

NOTES OF ADVISORY COMMITTEE ON RULES—1987 AMENDMENT

*Subdivision (a)* is amended to conform to the 1984 amendments to Rule 6 F.R.Civ.P.

*Subdivision (b).* The reference to Rule 4001(b) in paragraph (3) is deleted because of the amendments made to Rule 4001. Rule 9033, which is new, contains specific provisions governing the extension of time to file objections to proposed findings of fact and conclusions of law. Rule 9033 is added to the rules referred to in paragraph (3).

*Subdivision (c).* Rule 4001(b)(2) and (c)(2) provide that a final hearing on a motion to use cash collateral or a motion for authority to obtain credit may be held no earlier than 15 days after the filing of the motion. These two rules are added to paragraph (2) to make it clear that the 15 day period may not be reduced. Rule 9033 is also added to paragraph (2).

*Subdivision (g)* is new. Under §557 of the Code, as enacted by the 1984 amendments, the court is directed to expedite grain storage facility cases. This subdivision makes it clear this rule does not limit the court's authority under §557.

The original Advisory Committee Note to this rule included the 25 day notice period of Rule 2002(b) as a time period which may not be reduced under Rule 9006(c)(2). This was an error.

NOTES OF ADVISORY COMMITTEE ON RULES—1989 AMENDMENT

Prior to 1987, subdivision (a) provided that intermediate weekends and legal holidays would not be counted in the computation of a time period if the prescribed or allowed time was less than 7 days. This rule was amended in 1987 to conform to Fed. R. Civ. P. 6(a) which provides for the exclusion of intermediate weekends and legal holidays if the time prescribed or allowed is less than 11 days. An undesirable result of the 1987 amendment was that 10-day time periods prescribed in the interest of prompt administration of bankruptcy cases were extended to at least 14 calendar days.

As a result of the present amendment, 10-day time periods prescribed or allowed will no longer be extended to at least 14 calendar days because of intermediate weekends and legal holidays.

NOTES OF ADVISORY COMMITTEE ON RULES—1991 AMENDMENT

As a result of the 1989 amendment to this rule, the method of computing time under subdivision (a) is not the same as the method of computing time under Rule 6(a) F.R.Civ.P. Subdivision (a) is amended to provide that it governs the computation of time periods prescribed by the Federal Rules of Civil Procedure when the Bankruptcy Rules make a civil rule applicable to a bankruptcy case or proceeding.

*Subdivision (b)(2)* is amended because of the deletion of Rule 1019(2). Reference to Rule 9015(f) is deleted because of the abrogation of Rule 9015 in 1987.

*Subdivision (b)(3)* is amended to limit the enlargement of time regarding dismissal of a chapter 7 case for substantial abuse in accordance with Rule 1017(e).

NOTES OF ADVISORY COMMITTEE ON RULES—1996 AMENDMENT

Subdivision (c)(2) is amended to conform to the abrogation of Rule 2002(a)(4) and the renumbering of Rule 2002(a)(8) to Rule 2002(a)(7).

*GAP Report on Rule 9006.* No changes since publication, except for a stylistic change.

COMMITTEE NOTES ON RULES—1999 AMENDMENT

Rule 9006(b)(2) is amended to conform to the abrogation of Rule 1017(b)(3).

*GAP Report on Rule 9006.* The proposed amendment to Rule 9006(b)(2) has been added as a technical change to conform to the abrogation of Rule 1017(b)(3). The proposed amendment to Rule 9006(c)(2), providing that the time under Rule 1019(6) to file a request for payment of an administrative expense after a case is converted to chapter 7 could not be reduced by the court, was deleted. The proposed amendments to Rule 1019(6) have been changed so that the court will fix the time for filing the request for payment. Since the court will fix the time limit, the court should have the power to reduce it. *See* GAP Report to Rule 1019(6).

COMMITTEE NOTES ON RULES—2001 AMENDMENT

Rule 5(b) F. R. Civ. P., which is made applicable in adversary proceedings by Rule 7005, is being restyled and amended to authorize service by electronic means—or any other means not otherwise authorized under Rule 5(b)—if consent is obtained from the person served. The amendment to Rule 9006(f) is intended to extend the three-day "mail rule" to service under Rule 5(b)(2)(D), including service by electronic means. The three-day rule also will apply to service under Rule 5(b)(2)(C) F. R. Civ. P. when the person served has no known address and the paper is served by leaving a copy with the clerk of the court.

*Changes Made After Publication and Comments* No changes were made.

COMMITTEE NOTES ON RULES—2005 AMENDMENT

Rule 9006(f) is amended, consistent with a corresponding amendment to Rule 6(e) of the F.R. Civ. P., to clarify the method of counting the number of days to respond after service either by mail or under Civil Rule 5(b)(2)(C) or (D). Three days are added after the prescribed period expires. If, before the application of Rule 9006(f), the prescribed period is less than 8 days, intervening Saturdays, Sundays, and legal holidays are excluded from the calculation under Rule 9006(a). Some illustrations may be helpful.

Under existing Rule 9006(a), assuming that there are no legal holidays and that a response is due in seven days, if a paper is filed on a Monday, the seven day response period commences on Tuesday and concludes on Wednesday of the next week. Adding three days to the end of the period would extend it to Saturday, but because the response period ends on a weekend, the response day would be the following Monday, two weeks after the filing of the initial paper. If the paper is filed on a Tuesday, the seven-day response period would end on the following Thursday, and the response time would also be the following Monday. If the paper is mailed on a Wednesday, the initial seven-day period would expire nine days later on a Friday, but the response would again be due on the following Monday because of Rule 9006(f). If the paper is mailed on a Thursday, however, the seven day period ends on Monday, eleven days after the mailing of the service because of the exclusion of the two intervening Saturdays and Sundays. The response is due three days later on the following Thursday. If the paper is mailed on a Friday, the seven day period would conclude on a Tuesday, and the response is due three days later on a Friday.

No other change in the system of counting time is intended.

Other changes are stylistic.

*Changes Made After Publication and Comment.* The phrase "would otherwise expire under Rule 9006(a)" was added to the end of the rule to clarify further that the three day extension is to be added to the end of the period that is established under the counting provisions of Rule 9006(a). This also maintains a parallel construction with Civil Rule 6(e) in which the same addition to the rule was made after the public comment period.

COMMITTEE NOTES ON RULES—2008 AMENDMENT

Subdivision (b)(3) is amended to implement §1116(3) of the Code, as amended by the 2005 amendments, which places specific limits on the extension of time for filing schedules and statements of financial affairs in a small business case.

Subdivisions (b)(3) and (c)(2) are amended to provide that enlargement or reduction of the time to file the statement of completion of a personal financial management course required by Rule 1007(b)(7) are governed by Rule 1007(c). Likewise, the amendments to subdivisions (b)(3) and (c)(2) recognize that the enlargement of time to file a reaffirmation agreement is governed by Rule 4008(a), and that reduction of the time provided under that rule is not permitted.

Other amendments are stylistic.

*Changes Made After Publication.* Subdivision (b)(3) was amended to provide that Rule 9006 does not govern the enlargement of time to file a reaffirmation agreement, the statement required under Rule 1007(b)(7), or the time to file schedules and statements of financial affairs in small business cases. The title of subdivision (b)(3) was also amended to more accurately describe the operation of the provision. Subdivision (c)(2) was amended to recognize that the court may not reduce the time under Rule 1007(c) to file the statement required by Rule 1007(b)(7).

COMMITTEE NOTES ON RULES—2009 AMENDMENT

*Subdivision (a).* Subdivision (a) has been amended to simplify and clarify the provisions that describe how deadlines are computed. Subdivision (a) governs the computation of any time period found in a Federal Rule of Bankruptcy Procedure, a Federal Rule of Civil Procedure, a statute, a local rule, or a court order. In accordance with Bankruptcy Rule 9029(a), a local rule may not direct that a deadline be computed in a manner inconsistent with subdivision (a).

The time-computation provisions of subdivision (a) apply only when a time period must be computed. They do not apply when a fixed time to act is set. The amendments thus carry forward the approach taken in *Violette v. P.A. Days, Inc.*, 427 F.3d 1015, 1016 (6th Cir. 2005) (holding that Civil Rule 6(a) "does not apply to situations where the court has established a specific calendar day as a deadline"), and reject the contrary holding of *In re American Healthcare Management, Inc.*, 900 F.2d 827, 832 (5th Cir. 1990) (holding that Bankruptcy Rule 9006(a) governs treatment of date-certain deadline set by court order). If, for example, the date for filing is "no later than November 1, 2007," subdivision (a) does not govern. But if a filing is required to be made "within 10 days" or "within 72 hours," subdivision (a) describes how that deadline is computed.

Subdivision (a) does not apply when computing a time period set by a statute if the statute specifies a method of computing time. *See, e.g.*, 11 U.S.C. §527(a)(2) (debt relief agencies must provide a written notice to an assisted person "not later than 3 business days" after providing bankruptcy assistance services).

*Subdivision (a)(1).* New subdivision (a)(1) addresses the computation of time periods that are stated in days. It also applies to time periods that are stated in weeks, months, or years. *See, e.g.*, Federal Rule of Civil Procedure 60(c)(1) made applicable to bankruptcy cases under Rule 9024. Subdivision (a)(1)(B)'s directive to "count every day" is relevant only if the period is stated in days (not weeks, months, or years).

Under former Rule 9006(a), a period of eight days or more was computed differently than a period of less than eight days. Intermediate Saturdays, Sundays, and legal holidays were included in computing the longer periods, but excluded in computing the shorter periods. Former Rule 9006(a) thus made computing deadlines unnecessarily complicated and led to counterintuitive results.

Under new subdivision (a)(1), all deadlines stated in days (no matter the length) are computed in the same way. The day of the event that triggers the deadline is not counted. All other days—including intermediate Saturdays, Sundays, and legal holidays—are counted, with only one exception: If the period ends on a Saturday, Sunday, or legal holiday, then the deadline falls on the next day that is not a Saturday, Sunday, or legal holiday. An illustration is provided below in the discussion of subdivision (a)(5). Subdivision (a)(3) addresses filing deadlines that expire on a day when the clerk's office is inaccessible.

Where subdivision (a) formerly referred to the "act, event, or default" that triggers the deadline, new subdivision (a) refers simply to the "event" that triggers the deadline; this change in terminology is adopted for brevity and simplicity, and is not intended to change meaning.

Periods previously expressed as less than eight days will be shortened as a practical matter by the decision to count intermediate Saturdays, Sundays, and legal holidays in computing all periods. Many of those periods have been lengthened to compensate for the change. *See, e.g.*, Rules 2008 (trustee's duty to notify court of acceptance of the appointment within five days is extended to seven days); 6004(b) (time for filing and service of objection to proposed use, sale or lease of property extended from five days prior to the hearing to seven days prior to the hearing); and 9006(d) (time for giving notice of a hearing extended from five days prior to the hearing to seven days).

Most of the 10-day periods were adjusted to meet the change in computation method by setting 14 days as the new period. *See, e.g.*, Rules 1007(h) (10-day period to file supplemental schedule for property debtor becomes entitled to acquire after the commencement of the case is extended to 14 days); 3020(e) (10-day stay of order confirming a chapter 11 plan extended to 14 days); 8002(a) (10-day period in which to file notice of appeal extended to 14 days). A 14-day period also has the advantage that the final day falls on the same day of the week as the event that triggered the period—the14th day after a Monday, for example, is a Monday. This advantage of using week-long periods led to adopting seven-day periods to replace some of the periods set at less than 10 days, 21-day periods to replace 20-day periods, and 28-day periods to replace 25-day periods.Thirty-day and longer periods, however, were generally retained without change.

*Subdivision (a)(2).* New subdivision (a)(2) addresses the computation of time periods that are stated in hours. No such deadline currently appears in the Federal Rules of Bankruptcy Procedure. But some statutes contain deadlines stated in hours, as do some court orders issued in expedited proceedings.

Under subdivision (a)(2), a deadline stated in hours starts to run immediately on the occurrence of the event that triggers the deadline. The deadline generally ends when the time expires. If, however, the time period expires at a specific time (say, 2:17 p.m.) on a Saturday, Sunday, or legal holiday, then the deadline is extended to the same time (2:17 p.m.) on the next day that is not a Saturday, Sunday, or legal holiday. Periods stated in hours are not to be "rounded up" to the next whole hour. Subdivision (a)(3) addresses situations when the clerk's office is inaccessible during the last hour before a filing deadline expires.

Subdivision (a)(2)(B) directs that every hour be counted. Thus, for example, a 72-hour period that commences at 10:23 a.m. on Friday, November 2, 2007, will run until 9:23 a.m. on Monday, November 5; the discrepancy in start and end times in this example results from the intervening shift from daylight saving time to standard time.

*Subdivision (a)(3).* When determining the last day of a filing period stated in days or a longer unit of time, a day on which the clerk's office is not accessible because of the weather or another reason is treated like a Saturday, Sunday, or legal holiday. When determining the end of a filing period stated in hours, if the clerk's office is inaccessible during the last hour of the filing period computed under subdivision (a)(2) then the period is extended to the same time on the next day that is not a weekend, holiday, or day when the clerk's office is inaccessible.

Subdivision (a)(3)'s extensions apply "[u]nless the court orders otherwise." In some circumstances, the court might not wish a period of inaccessibility to trigger a full 24-hour extension; in those instances, the court can specify a briefer extension.

The text of the rule no longer refers to "weather or other conditions" as the reason for the inaccessibility of the clerk's office. The reference to "weather" was deleted from the text to underscore that inaccessibility can occur for reasons unrelated to weather, such as an outage of the electronic filing system. Weather can still be a reason for inaccessibility of the clerk's office. The rule does not attempt to define inaccessibility. Rather, the concept will continue to develop through caselaw. *See, e.g.*, William G. Phelps, *When Is Office of Clerk of Court Inaccessible Due to Weather or Other Conditions for Purpose of Computing Time Period for Filing Papers under Rule 6(a) of Federal Rules of Civil Procedure*, 135 A.L.R. Fed. 259 (1996) (collecting cases). In addition, many local provisions address inaccessibility for purposes of electronic filing. *See, e.g.*, D. Kan. Rule 5.4.11 ("A Filing User whose filing is made untimely as the result of a technical failure may seek appropriate relief from the court.").

*Subdivision (a)(4).* New subdivision (a)(4) defines the end of the last day of a period for purposes of subdivision (a)(1). Subdivision (a)(4) does not apply in computing periods stated in hours under subdivision (a)(2), and does not apply if a different time is set by a statute, local rule, or order in the case. A local rule may provide, for example, that papers filed in a drop box after the normal hours of the clerk's office are filed as of the day that is date-stamped on the papers by a device in the drop box.

28 U.S.C. §452 provides that "[a]ll courts of the United States shall be deemed always open for the purpose of filing proper papers, issuing and returning process, and making motions and orders." A corresponding provision exists in Rule 5001(a). Some courts have held that these provisions permit an after-hours filing by handing the papers to an appropriate official. *See, e.g., Casalduc v. Diaz*, 117 F.2d 915, 917 (1st Cir. 1941). Subdivision (a)(4) does not address the effect of the statute on the question of after-hours filing; instead, the rule is designed to deal with filings in the ordinary course without regard to Section 452.

*Subdivision (a)(5).* New subdivision (a)(5) defines the "next" day for purposes of subdivisions (a)(1)(C) and (a)(2)(C). The Federal Rules of Bankruptcy Procedure contain both forward-looking time periods and backward-looking time periods. A forward-looking time period requires something to be done within a period of time *after* an event. *See, e.g.*, Rules 1007(c) (["]the schedules, statements, and other documents shall be filed by the debtor within 14 days of the entry of the order for relief"); 1019(5)(B)(ii) ("the trustee, not later than 30 days after conversion of the case, shall file and transmit to the United States trustee a final report and account"); and 7012(a) ("If a complaint is duly served, the defendant shall serve an answer within 30 days after the issuance of the summons, except when a different time is prescribed by the court.").

A backward-looking time period requires something to be done within a period of time *before* an event. *See, e.g.*, Rules 6004(b) ("an objection to a proposed use, sale, or lease of property shall be filed and served not less than seven days before the date set for the proposed action"); 9006(d) ("A written motion, other than one which may be heard ex parte, and notice of any hearing shall be served not later than seven days before the time specified for such hearing"). In determining what is the "next" day for purposes of subdivisions (a)(1)(C) and (a)(2)(C), one should continue counting in the same direction—that is, forward when computing a forward-looking period and backward when computing a backward-looking period. If, for example, a filing is due within 10 days *after* an event, and the tenth day falls on Saturday, September 1, 2007, then the filing is due on Tuesday, September 4, 2007 (Monday, September 3, is Labor Day). But if a filing is due 10 days *before* an event, and the tenth day falls on Saturday, September 1, then the filing is due on Friday, August 31.

*Subdivision (a)(6).* New subdivision (a)(6) defines "legal holiday" for purposes of the Federal Rules of Bankruptcy Procedure, including the time-computation provisions of subdivision (a). Subdivision (a)(6) continues to include within the definition of "legal holiday" days that are declared a holiday by the President or Congress.

For forward-counted periods—*i.e.*, periods that are measured after an event—subdivision (a)(6)(C) includes certain state holidays within the definition of legal holidays, and defines the term "state"—for purposes of subdivision (a)(6)—to include the District of Columbia and any commonwealth or territory of the United States. Thus, for purposes of subdivision (a)(6)'s definition of "legal holiday," "state" includes the District of Columbia, Guam, American Samoa, the U.S. Virgin Islands, the Commonwealth of Puerto Rico, and the Commonwealth of the Northern Mariana Islands.

However, state legal holidays are not recognized in computing backward-counted periods. For both forward- and backward-counted periods, the rule thus protects those who may be unsure of the effect of state holidays. For forward-counted deadlines, treating state holidays the same as federal holidays extends the deadline. Thus, someone who thought that the federal courts might be closed on a state holiday would be safeguarded against an inadvertent late filing. In contrast, for backward-counted deadlines, not giving state holidays the treatment of federal holidays allows filing on the state holiday itself rather than the day before. Take, for example, Monday, April 21, 2008 (Patriot's Day, a legal holiday in the relevant state). If a filing is due 14 days after an event, and the fourteenth day is April 21, then the filing is due on Tuesday, April 22 because Monday, April 21 counts as a legal holiday. But if a filing is due 14 days before an event, and the fourteenth day is April 21, the filing is due on Monday, April 21; the fact that April 21 is a state holiday does not make April 21 a legal holiday for purposes of computing this backward-counted deadline. But note that if the clerk's office is inaccessible on Monday, April 21, then subdivision (a)(3) extends the April 21 filing deadline forward to the next accessible day that is not a Saturday, Sunday or legal holiday—no earlier than Tuesday, April 22.

*Changes Made After Publication.* The reference to Rule 6(a)(1) in subdivision (a)(3)(A) at line 50 of the rule as it was published was corrected by referring instead to Rule 9006(a)(1).

The Standing Committee changed Rule 9006(a)(6) to exclude state holidays from the definition of "legal holiday" for purposes of computing backward-counted periods; conforming changes were made to the Committee Note to subdivision (a)(6). In addition, the term "possession" was deleted from the definition of "state" in subdivision (a)(6), and a conforming change was made to the Committee Note.

[*Subdivision (d).*] The rule is amended to implement changes in connection with the amendment to Rule 9006(a) and the manner by which time is computed under the rules. The deadline in the rule is amended to substitute a deadline that is a multiple of seven days. Throughout the rules, deadlines are amended in the following manner:

- 5-day periods become 7-day periods
- 10-day periods become 14-day periods
- 15-day periods become 14-day periods
- 20-day periods become 21-day periods
- 25-day periods become 28-day periods

Subdivision (f) is amended to conform to the changes made to Rule 5(b)(2) of the Federal Rules of Civil Procedure as a part of the Civil Rules Restyling Project. As a part of that project, subparagraphs (b)(2)(C) and (D) of that rule were rewritten as subparagraphs (b)(2)(D), (E), and (F). The cross reference to those rules contained in subdivision (f) of this rule is corrected by this amendment.

REFERENCES IN TEXT

The Federal Rules of Civil Procedure, referred to in subds. (a) and (f), are set out in the Appendix to Title 28, Judiciary and Judicial Procedure.

### Rule 9007. General Authority to Regulate Notices

When notice is to be given under these rules, the court shall designate, if not otherwise specified herein, the time within which, the entities to whom, and the form and manner in which the notice shall be given. When feasible, the court may order any notices under these rules to be combined.

(As amended Mar. 30, 1987, eff. Aug. 1, 1987.)

### Rule 9008. Service or Notice by Publication

Whenever these rules require or authorize service or notice by publication, the court shall, to the extent not otherwise specified in these rules, determine the form and manner thereof, including the newspaper or other medium to be used and the number of publications.

### Rule 9009. Forms

Except as otherwise provided in Rule 3016(d), the Official Forms prescribed by the Judicial Conference of the United States shall be observed and used with alterations as may be appropriate. Forms may be combined and their contents rearranged to permit economies in their use. The Director of the Administrative Office of the United States Courts may issue additional forms for use under the Code. The forms shall be construed to be consistent with these rules and the Code.

(As amended Apr. 30, 1991, eff. Aug. 1, 1991; Apr. 23, 2008, eff. Dec. 1, 2008.)

NOTES OF ADVISORY COMMITTEE ON RULES—1983

The rule continues the obligatory character of the Official Forms in the interest of facilitating the processing of the paperwork of bankruptcy administration, but provides that Official Forms will be prescribed by the Judicial Conference of the United States. The Supreme Court and the Congress will thus be relieved of the burden of considering the large number of complex forms used in bankruptcy practice. The use of the Official Forms has generally been held subject to a "rule of substantial compliance" and some of these rules, for example Rule 1002, specifically state that the filed document need only "conform substantially" to the Official Form. See also Rule 9005. The second sentence recognizes the propriety of combining and rearranging Official Forms to take advantage of technological developments and resulting economies.

The Director of the Administrative Office is authorized to issue additional forms for the guidance of the bar.

NOTES OF ADVISORY COMMITTEE ON RULES—1991 AMENDMENT

Rule 9029 [9009] is amended to clarify that local court rules may not prohibit or limit the use of the Official Forms.

COMMITTEE NOTES ON RULES—2008 AMENDMENT

The rule is amended to provide that a plan proponent in a small business chapter 11 case need not use an Official Form of a plan of reorganization and disclosure statement. The use of those forms is optional, and under Rule 3016(d) the proponent may submit a plan and disclosure statement in those cases that does not conform to the Official Forms.

*Changes Made After Publication.* No changes were made after publication.

### Rule 9010. Representation and Appearances; Powers of Attorney

(a) AUTHORITY TO ACT PERSONALLY OR BY TORNEY. A debtor, creditor, equity security holder, indenture trustee, committee or other party may (1) appear in a case under the Code and act either in the entity's own behalf or by an attorney authorized to practice in the court, and (2) perform any act not constituting the practice of law, by an authorized agent, attorney in fact, or proxy.

(b) NOTICE OF APPEARANCE. An attorney appearing for a party in a case under the Code shall file a notice of appearance with the attorney's name, office address and telephone number, unless the attorney's appearance is otherwise noted in the record.

(c) POWER OF ATTORNEY. The authority of any agent, attorney in fact, or proxy to represent a creditor for any purpose other than the execution and filing of a proof of claim or the acceptance or rejection of a plan shall be evidenced by a power of attorney conforming substantially to the appropriate Official Form. The execution of any such power of attorney shall be acknowledged before one of the officers enumerated in 28 U.S.C. §459, §953, Rule 9012, or a person authorized to administer oaths under the laws of the state where the oath is administered.

(As amended Mar. 30, 1987, eff. Aug. 1, 1987; Apr. 30, 1991, eff. Aug. 1, 1991.)

NOTES OF ADVISORY COMMITTEE ON RULES—1983

This rule is substantially the same as former Bankruptcy Rule 910 and does not purport to change prior holdings prohibiting a corporation from appearing *pro se*. See *In re Las Colinas Development Corp.*, 585 F.2d 7 (1st Cir. 1978).

NOTES OF ADVISORY COMMITTEE ON RULES—1987 AMENDMENT

*Subdivision (c)* is amended to include a reference to Rule 9012 which is amended to authorize a bankruptcy judge or clerk to administer oaths.

NOTES OF ADVISORY COMMITTEE ON RULES—1991 AMENDMENT

References to Official Form numbers in subdivision (c) are deleted in anticipation of future revision and renumbering of the Official Forms.

## Rule 9011. Signing of Papers; Representations to the Court; Sanctions; Verification and Copies of Papers

(a) SIGNATURE. Every petition, pleading, written motion, and other paper, except a list, schedule, or statement, or amendments thereto, shall be signed by at least one attorney of record in the attorney's individual name. A party who is not represented by an attorney shall sign all papers. Each paper shall state the signer's address and telephone number, if any. An unsigned paper shall be stricken unless omission of the signature is corrected promptly after being called to the attention of the attorney or party.

(b) REPRESENTATIONS TO THE COURT. By presenting to the court (whether by signing, filing, submitting, or later advocating) a petition, pleading, written motion, or other paper, an attorney or unrepresented party is certifying that to the best of the person's knowledge, information, and belief, formed after an inquiry reasonable under the circumstances,—[1]

(1) it is not being presented for any improper purpose, such as to harass or to cause unnecessary delay or needless increase in the cost of litigation;

(2) the claims, defenses, and other legal contentions therein are warranted by existing law or by a nonfrivolous argument for the extension, modification, or reversal of existing law or the establishment of new law;

(3) the allegations and other factual contentions have evidentiary support or, if specifically so identified, are likely to have evidentiary support after a reasonable opportunity for further investigation or discovery; and

(4) the denials of factual contentions are warranted on the evidence or, if specifically so identified, are reasonably based on a lack of information or belief.

(c) SANCTIONS. If, after notice and a reasonable opportunity to respond, the court determines that subdivision (b) has been violated, the court may, subject to the conditions stated below, impose an appropriate sanction upon the attorneys, law firms, or parties that have violated subdivision (b) or are responsible for the violation.

(1) *How Initiated.*

(A) *By Motion.* A motion for sanctions under this rule shall be made separately from other motions or requests and shall describe the specific conduct alleged to violate subdivision (b). It shall be served as provided in Rule 7004. The motion for sanctions may not be filed with or presented to the court unless, within 21 days after service of the motion (or such other period as the court may prescribe), the challenged paper, claim, defense, contention, allegation, or denial is not withdrawn or appropriately corrected, except that this limitation shall not apply if the conduct alleged is the filing of a petition in violation of subdivision (b). If warranted, the court may award to the party prevailing on the motion the reasonable expenses and attorney's fees incurred in presenting or opposing the motion. Absent exceptional circumstances, a law firm shall be held jointly responsible for violations committed by its partners, associates, and employees.

(B) *On Court's Initiative.* On its own initiative, the court may enter an order describing the specific conduct that appears to violate subdivision (b) and directing an attorney, law firm, or party to show cause why it has not violated subdivision (b) with respect thereto.

(2) *Nature of Sanction; Limitations.* A sanction imposed for violation of this rule shall be limited to what is sufficient to deter repetition of such conduct or comparable conduct by others similarly situated. Subject to the limitations in subparagraphs (A) and (B), the sanction may consist of, or include, directives of a nonmonetary nature, an order to pay a penalty into court, or, if imposed on motion and warranted for effective deterrence, an order directing payment to the movant of some or all of the reasonable attorneys' fees and other expenses incurred as a direct result of the violation.

(A) Monetary sanctions may not be awarded against a represented party for a violation of subdivision (b)(2).

(B) Monetary sanctions may not be awarded on the court's initiative unless the court issues its order to show cause before a voluntary dismissal or settlement of the claims made by or against the party which is, or whose attorneys are, to be sanctioned.

(3) *Order.* When imposing sanctions, the court shall describe the conduct determined to constitute a violation of this rule and explain the basis for the sanction imposed.

(d) INAPPLICABILITY TO DISCOVERY. Subdivisions (a) through (c) of this rule do not apply to disclosures and discovery requests, responses, objections, and motions that are subject to the provisions of Rules 7026 through 7037.

(e) VERIFICATION. Except as otherwise specifically provided by these rules, papers filed in a case under the Code need not be verified. Whenever verification is required by these rules, an unsworn declaration as provided in 28 U.S.C. §1746 satisfies the requirement of verification.

[1] So in original. The comma probably should not appear.

(f) COPIES OF SIGNED OR VERIFIED PAPERS. When these rules require copies of a signed or verified paper, it shall suffice if the original is signed or verified and the copies are conformed to the original.

(As amended Mar. 30, 1987, eff. Aug. 1, 1987; Apr. 30, 1991, eff. Aug. 1, 1991; Apr. 11, 1997, eff. Dec. 1, 1997.)

NOTES OF ADVISORY COMMITTEE ON RULES—1983

*Subdivision (a).* Excepted from the papers which an attorney for a debtor must sign are lists, schedules, statements of financial affairs, statements of executory contracts, Chapter 13 Statements and amendments thereto. Rule 1008 requires that these documents be verified by the debtor. Although the petition must also be verified, counsel for the debtor must sign the petition. See Official Form No. 1. An unrepresented party must sign all papers.

The last sentence of this subdivision authorizes a broad range of sanctions.

The word "document" is used in this subdivision to refer to all papers which the attorney or party is required to sign.

*Subdivision (b)* extends to all papers filed in cases under the Code the policy of minimizing reliance on the formalities of verification which is reflected in the third sentence of Rule 11 F.R.Civ.P. The second sentence of subdivision (b) permits the substitution of an unsworn declaration for the verification. See 28 U.S.C. §1746. Rules requiring verification or an affidavit are as follows: Rule 1008, petitions, schedules, statements of financial affairs, Chapter 13 Statements and amendments; Rule 2006(e), list of multiple proxies and statement of facts and circumstances regarding their acquisition; Rule 4001(c), motion for ex parte relief from stay; Rule 7065, incorporating Rule 65(b) F.R.Civ.P. governing issuance of temporary restraining order; Rule 8011(d), affidavit in support of emergency motion on appeal.

NOTES OF ADVISORY COMMITTEE ON RULES—1987 AMENDMENT

The statement of intention of the debtor under §521(2) of the Code is added to the documents which counsel is not required to sign.

NOTES OF ADVISORY COMMITTEE ON RULES—1991 AMENDMENT

*Subdivision (a)* is amended to conform to Rule 11 F.R.Civ.P. where appropriate, but also to clarify that it applies to the unnecessary delay or needless increase in the cost of the administration of the case. Deletion of the references to specific statements that are excluded from the scope of this subdivision is stylistic. As used in subdivision (a) of this rule, "statement" is limited to the statement of financial affairs and the statement of intention required to be filed under Rule 1007. Deletion of the reference to the Chapter 13 Statement is consistent with the amendment to Rule 1007(b).

NOTES OF ADVISORY COMMITTEE ON RULES—1997 AMENDMENT

This rule is amended to conform to the 1993 changes to F.R.Civ.P. 11. For an explanation of these amendments, see the advisory committee note to the 1993 amendments to F.R.Civ.P. 11.

The "safe harbor" provision contained in subdivision (c)(1)(A), which prohibits the filing of a motion for sanctions unless the challenged paper is not withdrawn or corrected within a prescribed time after service of the motion, does not apply if the challenged paper is a petition. The filing of a petition has immediate serious consequences, including the imposition of the automatic stay under §362 of the Code, which may not be avoided by the subsequent withdrawal of the petition. In addition, a petition for relief under chapter 7 or chapter 11 may not be withdrawn unless the court orders dismissal of the case for cause after notice and a hearing.

*GAP Report on Rule 9011.* The proposed amendments to subdivision (a) were revised to clarify that a party not represented by an attorney must sign lists, schedules, and statements, as well as other papers that are filed.

## Rule 9012. Oaths and Affirmations

(a) PERSONS AUTHORIZED TO ADMINISTER OATHS. The following persons may administer oaths and affirmations and take acknowledgments: a bankruptcy judge, clerk, deputy clerk, United States trustee, officer authorized to administer oaths in proceedings before the courts of the United States or under the laws of the state where the oath is to be taken, or a diplomatic or consular officer of the United States in any foreign country.

(b) AFFIRMATION IN LIEU OF OATH. When in a case under the Code an oath is required to be taken a solemn affirmation may be accepted in lieu thereof.

(As amended Mar. 30, 1987, eff. Aug. 1, 1987; Apr. 30, 1991, eff. Aug. 1, 1991.)

NOTES OF ADVISORY COMMITTEE ON RULES—1983

This rule is derived from Rule 43(d) F.R.Civ.P.

The provisions of former Bankruptcy Rule 912(a) relating to who may administer oaths have been deleted as unnecessary. Bankruptcy judges and the clerks and deputy clerks of bankruptcy courts are authorized by statute to administer oaths and affirmations and to take acknowledgments. 28 U.S.C. §§459, 953. A person designated to preside at the meeting of creditors has authority under Rule 2003(b)(1) to administer the oath. Administration of the oath at a deposition is governed by Rule 7028.

NOTES OF ADVISORY COMMITTEE ON RULES—1987 AMENDMENT

*Subdivision (a)* has been added to the rule to authorize bankruptcy judges and clerks to administer oaths.

NOTES OF ADVISORY COMMITTEE ON RULES—1991 AMENDMENT

This rule is amended to conform to the 1986 amendment to §343 which provides that the United States trustee may administer the oath to the debtor at the §341 meeting. This rule also allows the United States trustee to administer oaths and affirmations and to take acknowledgments in other situations. This amendment also affects Rule 9010(c) relating to the acknowledgment of a power of attorney. The words "United States trustee" include a designee of the United States trustee pursuant to Rule 9001 and §102(9) of the Code.

## Rule 9013. Motions: Form and Service

A request for an order, except when an application is authorized by these rules, shall be by written motion, unless made during a hearing. The motion shall state with particularity the grounds therefor, and shall set forth the relief or order sought. Every written motion other than one which may be considered ex parte shall be served by the moving party on the trustee or debtor in possession and on those entities specified by these rules or, if service is not required or the entities to be served are not specified by these rules, the moving party shall serve the entities the court directs.

(As amended Mar. 30, 1987, eff. Aug. 1, 1987.)

NOTES OF ADVISORY COMMITTEE ON RULES—1983

This rule is derived from Rule 5(a) and Rule 7(b)(1) F.R.Civ.P. Except when an application is specifically authorized by these rules, for example an application under Rule 2014 for approval of the employment of a professional, all requests for court action must be made by motion.

## Rule 9014. Contested Matters

(a) MOTION. In a contested matter not otherwise governed by these rules, relief shall be requested by motion, and reasonable notice and opportunity for hearing shall be afforded the party against whom relief is sought. No response is required under this rule unless the court directs otherwise.

(b) SERVICE. The motion shall be served in the manner provided for service of a summons and complaint by Rule 7004. Any paper served after the motion shall be served in the manner provided by Rule 5(b) F. R. Civ. P.

(c) APPLICATION OF PART VII RULES. Except as otherwise provided in this rule, and unless the court directs otherwise, the following rules shall apply: 7009, 7017, 7021, 7025, 7026, 7028-7037, 7041, 7042, 7052, 7054-7056, 7064, 7069, and 7071. The following subdivisions of Fed. R. Civ. P. 26, as incorporated by Rule 7026, shall not apply in a contested matter unless the court directs otherwise: 26(a)(1) (mandatory disclosure), 26(a)(2) (disclosures regarding expert testimony) and 26(a)(3) (additional pre-trial disclosure), and 26(f) (mandatory meeting before scheduling conference/discovery plan). An entity that desires to perpetuate testimony may proceed in the same manner as provided in Rule 7027 for the taking of a deposition before an adversary proceeding. The court may at any stage in a particular matter direct that one or more of the other rules in Part VII shall apply. The court shall give the parties notice of any order issued under this paragraph to afford them a reasonable opportunity to comply with the procedures prescribed by the order.

(d) TESTIMONY OF WITNESSES. Testimony of witnesses with respect to disputed material factual issues shall be taken in the same manner as testimony in an adversary proceeding.

(e) ATTENDANCE OF WITNESSES. The court shall provide procedures that enable parties to ascertain at a reasonable time before any scheduled hearing whether the hearing will be an evidentiary hearing at which witnesses may testify.

(As amended Mar. 30, 1987, eff. Aug. 1, 1987; Apr. 26, 1999, eff. Dec. 1, 1999; Apr. 29, 2002, eff. Dec. 1, 2002; Apr. 26, 2004, eff. Dec. 1, 2004.)

NOTES OF ADVISORY COMMITTEE ON RULES—1983

Rules 1017(d), 3020(b)(1), 4001(a), 4003(d), and 6006(a), which govern respectively dismissal or conversion of a case, objections to confirmation of a plan, relief from the automatic stay and the use of cash collateral, avoidance of a lien under §552(f) of the Code, and the assumption or rejection of executory contracts or unexpired leases, specifically provide that litigation under those rules shall be as provided in Rule 9014. This rule also governs litigation in other contested matters.

Whenever there is an actual dispute, other than an adversary proceeding, before the bankruptcy court, the litigation to resolve that dispute is a contested matter. For example, the filing of an objection to a proof of claim, to a claim of exemption, or to a disclosure statement creates a dispute which is a contested matter. Even when an objection is not formally required, there may be a dispute. If a party in interest opposes the amount of compensation sought by a professional, there is a dispute which is a contested matter.

When the rules of Part VII are applicable to a contested matter, reference in the Part VII rules to adversary proceedings is to be read as a reference to a contested matter. See Rule 9002(1).

COMMITTEE NOTES ON RULES—1999 AMENDMENT

This rule is amended to delete Rule 7062 from the list of Part VII rules that automatically apply in a contested matter.

Rule 7062 provides that Rule 62 F.R.Civ.P., which governs stays of proceedings to enforce a judgment, is applicable in adversary proceedings. The provisions of Rule 62, including the ten-day automatic stay of the enforcement of a judgment provided by Rule 62(a) and the stay as a matter of right by posting a supersedeas bond provided in Rule 62(d), are not appropriate for most orders granting or denying motions governed by Rule 9014.

Although Rule 7062 will not apply automatically in contested matters, the amended rule permits the court, in its discretion, to order that Rule 7062 apply in a particular matter, and Rule 8005 gives the court discretion to issue a stay or any other appropriate order during the pendency of an appeal on such terms as will protect the rights of all parties in interest. In addition, amendments to Rules 3020, 4001, 6004, and 6006 automatically stay certain types of orders for a period of ten days, unless the court orders otherwise.

*GAP Report on Rule 9014.* No changes since publication.

COMMITTEE NOTES ON RULES—2002 AMENDMENT

The list of Part VII rules that are applicable in a contested matter is extended to include Rule 7009 on pleading special matters, and Rule 7017 on real parties in interest, infants and incompetent persons, and capacity. The discovery rules made applicable in adversary proceedings apply in contested matters unless the court directs otherwise.

*Subdivision (b)* is amended to permit parties to serve papers, other than the original motion, in the manner provided in Rule 5(b) F.R. Civ.P. When the court requires a response to the motion, this amendment will permit service of the response in the same manner as an answer is served in an adversary proceeding.

*Subdivision (d)* is added to clarify that if the motion cannot be decided without resolving a disputed material issue of fact, an evidentiary hearing must be held at which testimony of witnesses is taken in the same manner as testimony is taken in an adversary proceeding or at a trial in a district court civil case. Rule 43(a), rather than Rule 43(e), F.R. Civ.P. would govern the evidentiary hearing on the factual dispute. Under Rule 9017, the Federal Rules of Evidence also apply in a contested matter. Nothing in the rule prohibits a court from resolving any matter that is submitted on affidavits by agreement of the parties.

*Subdivision (e).* Local procedures for hearings and other court appearances in a contested matter vary from district to district. In some bankruptcy courts, an evidentiary hearing at which witnesses may testify usually is held at the first court appearance in the contested matter. In other courts, it is customary for the court to delay the evidentiary hearing on disputed factual issues until some time after the initial hearing date. In order to avoid unnecessary expense and inconvenience, it is important for attorneys to know whether they should bring witnesses to a court appearance. The purpose of the final sentence of this rule is to require that the court provide a mechanism that will enable attorneys to know at a reasonable time before a scheduled hearing whether it will be necessary for witnesses to appear in court on that particular date.

Other amendments to this rule are stylistic.

*Changes Made After Publication and Comments:*

The Advisory Committee made two changes to subdivision (d) after considering the comments received addressing the proposed rule. First, the word "material" is inserted to make explicit that which was implied in the published version of the proposed rule. Second, the reference to F.R.Civ.P. 43(a) was removed. The purpose of proposed subdivision (d) was to recognize that testimony should be taken in the same manner in both contested matters and adversary proceedings. The revision to the published rule states this more directly.

The Committee Note was amended to reflect the changes made in the text of the rule.

COMMITTEE NOTES ON RULES—2004 AMENDMENT

The rule is amended to provide that the mandatory disclosure requirements of Fed. R. Civ. P. 26, as incorporated by Rule 7026, do not apply in contested matters. The typically short time between the commencement and resolution of most contested matters makes the mandatory disclosure provisions of Rule 26 ineffective. Nevertheless, the court may by local rule or by order in a particular case provide that these provisions of the rule apply in a contested matter.

*Changes Made After Publication.* No changes since publication.

REFERENCES IN TEXT

The Federal Rules of Civil Procedure, referred to in subds. (b) and (c), are set out in the Appendix to Title 28, Judiciary and Judicial Procedure.

## Rule 9015. Jury Trials

(a) APPLICABILITY OF CERTAIN FEDERAL RULES OF CIVIL PROCEDURE. Rules 38, 39, 47–49, and 51, F.R.Civ.P., and Rule 81(c) F.R.Civ.P. insofar as it applies to jury trials, apply in cases and proceedings, except that a demand made under Rule 38(b) F.R.Civ.P. shall be filed in accordance with Rule 5005.

(b) CONSENT TO HAVE TRIAL CONDUCTED BY BANKRUPTCY JUDGE. If the right to a jury trial applies, a timely demand has been filed pursuant to Rule 38(b) F.R.Civ.P., and the bankruptcy judge has been specially designated to conduct the jury trial, the parties may consent to have a jury trial conducted by a bankruptcy judge under 28 U.S.C. §157(e) by jointly or separately filing a statement of consent within any applicable time limits specified by local rule.

(c) APPLICABILITY OF RULE 50 F.R.CIV.P. Rule 50 F.R.Civ.P. applies in cases and proceedings, except that any renewed motion for judgment or request for a new trial shall be filed no later than 14 days after the entry of judgment.

(Added Apr. 11, 1997, eff. Dec. 1, 1997; amended Mar. 26, 2009, eff. Dec. 1, 2009.)

NOTES OF ADVISORY COMMITTEE ON RULES—1997

This rule provides procedures relating to jury trials. This rule is not intended to expand or create any right to trial by jury where such right does not otherwise exist.

*GAP Report on Rule 9015.* No changes to the published draft.

COMMITTEE NOTES ON RULES—2009 AMENDMENT

The rule is amended by deleting Rule 50 F.R.Civ.P. from the list in subdivision (a) of rules made applicable in cases and proceedings. However, subdivision (c) is added to make Rule 50 applicable in cases and proceedings, but it limits the time for filing certain post judgment motions to 14 days after the entry of judgment. The amendment is necessary because Rule 50 F.R.Civ.P. was amended in 2009 to extend the deadline for the filing of these post judgment motions to 28 days. That deadline corresponds to the 30-day deadline for filing a notice of appeal in a civil case under Rule 4(a)(1)(A) F.R.App.P. In a bankruptcy case, the deadline for filing a notice of appeal is 14 days. Therefore, the 28-day deadline for filing these post judgment motions would effectively override the notice of appeal deadline under Rule 8002(a) but for this amendment.

Other amendments are stylistic.

REFERENCES IN TEXT

The Federal Rules of Civil Procedure, referred to in text, are set out in the Appendix to Title 28, Judiciary and Judicial Procedure.

## Rule 9016. Subpoena

Rule 45 F.R.Civ.P. applies in cases under the Code.

(As amended Mar. 30, 1987, eff. Aug. 1, 1987.)

NOTES OF ADVISORY COMMITTEE ON RULES—1983

Although Rule 7004(d) authorizes nationwide service of process, Rule 45 F.R.Civ.P. limits the subpoena power to the judicial district and places outside the district which are within 100 miles of the place of trial or hearing.

REFERENCES IN TEXT

The Federal Rules of Civil Procedure, referred to in text, are set out in the Appendix to Title 28, Judiciary and Judicial Procedure.

## Rule 9017. Evidence

The Federal Rules of Evidence and Rules 43, 44 and 44.1 F.R.Civ.P. apply in cases under the Code.

NOTES OF ADVISORY COMMITTEE ON RULES—1983

Sections 251 and 252 of Public Law 95–598, amended Rule 1101 of the Federal Rules of Evidence to provide that the Federal Rules of Evidence apply in bankruptcy courts and to any case or proceeding under the Code. Rules 43, 44 and 44.1 of the F.R.Civ.P., which supplement the Federal Rules of Evidence, are by this rule made applicable to cases under the Code.

Examples of bankruptcy rules containing matters of an evidentiary nature are: Rule 2011, evidence of debtor retained in possession; Rule 3001(f), proof of claim constitutes prima facie evidence of the amount and validity of a claim; and Rule 5007(c), sound recording of court proceedings constitutes the record of the proceedings.

REFERENCES IN TEXT

The Federal Rules of Evidence and the Federal Rules of Civil Procedure, referred to in text, are set out in the Appendix to Title 28, Judiciary and Judicial Procedure.

## Rule 9018. Secret, Confidential, Scandalous, or Defamatory Matter

On motion or on its own initiative, with or without notice, the court may make any order which justice requires (1) to protect the estate or any entity in respect of a trade secret or other confidential research, development, or commercial information, (2) to protect any entity against scandalous or defamatory matter contained in any paper filed in a case under the Code, or (3) to protect governmental matters that are made confidential by statute or regulation. If an order is entered under this rule without notice, any entity affected thereby may move to vacate or modify the order, and after a hearing on notice the court shall determine the motion.

(As amended Mar. 30, 1987, eff. Aug. 1, 1987.)

NOTES OF ADVISORY COMMITTEE ON RULES—1983

This rule provides the procedure for invoking the court's power under § 107 of the Code.

## Rule 9019. Compromise and Arbitration

(a) COMPROMISE. On motion by the trustee and after notice and a hearing, the court may approve a compromise or settlement. Notice shall be given to creditors, the United States trustee, the debtor, and indenture trustees as provided in Rule 2002 and to any other entity as the court may direct.

(b) AUTHORITY TO COMPROMISE OR SETTLE CONTROVERSIES WITHIN CLASSES. After a hearing on such notice as the court may direct, the court may fix a class or classes of controversies and authorize the trustee to compromise or settle controversies within such class or classes without further hearing or notice.

(c) ARBITRATION. On stipulation of the parties to any controversy affecting the estate the court may authorize the matter to be submitted to final and binding arbitration.

(As amended Mar. 30, 1987, eff. Aug. 1, 1987; Apr. 30, 1991, eff. Aug. 1, 1991; Apr. 22, 1993, eff. Aug. 1, 1993.)

NOTES OF ADVISORY COMMITTEE ON RULES—1983

Subdivisions (a) and (c) of this rule are essentially the same as the provisions of former Bankruptcy Rule 919 and subdivision (b) is the same as former Rule 8–514(b), which was applicable to railroad reorganizations. Subdivision (b) permits the court to deal efficiently with a case in which there may be a large number of settlements.

NOTES OF ADVISORY COMMITTEE ON RULES—1991 AMENDMENT

This rule is amended to enable the United States trustee to object or otherwise be heard in connection with a proposed compromise or settlement and otherwise to monitor the progress of the case.

NOTES OF ADVISORY COMMITTEE ON RULES—1993 AMENDMENT

*Subdivision (a)* is amended to conform to the language of § 102(1) of the Code. Other amendments are stylistic and make no substantive change.

## Rule 9020. Contempt Proceedings

Rule 9014 governs a motion for an order of contempt made by the United States trustee or a party in interest.

(As amended Mar. 30, 1987, eff. Aug. 1, 1987; Apr. 30, 1991, eff. Aug. 1, 1991; Apr. 23, 2001, eff. Dec. 1, 2001.)

NOTES OF ADVISORY COMMITTEE ON RULES—1983

Section 1481 of Title 28 provides that a bankruptcy court "may not . . . punish a criminal contempt not committed in the presence of the judge of the court or warranting a punishment of imprisonment." Rule 9020 does not enlarge the power of bankruptcy courts.

*Subdivision (a)* is adapted from former Bankruptcy Rule 920 and Rule 42 F.R.Crim.P. Paragraph (1) of the subdivision permits summary imposition of punishment for contempt if the conduct is in the presence of the court and is of such nature that the conduct "obstruct[s] the administration of justice." See 18 U.S.C. § 401(a). Cases interpreting Rule 42(a) F.R.Crim.P. have held that when criminal contempt is in question summary disposition should be the exception: summary disposition should be reserved for situations where it is necessary to protect the judicial institution. 3 Wright, *Federal Practice & Procedure—Criminal* § 707 (1969). Those cases are equally pertinent to the application of this rule and, therefore, contemptuous conduct in the presence of the judge may often be punished only after the notice and hearing requirements of subdivision (b) are satisfied.

If the bankruptcy court concludes it is without power to punish or to impose the proper punishment for conduct which constitutes contempt, subdivision (a)(3) authorizes the bankruptcy court to certify the matter to the district court.

*Subdivision (b)* makes clear that when a person has a constitutional or statutory right to a jury trial in a criminal contempt matter this rule in no way affects that right. See *Frank v. United States*, 395 U.S. 147 (1969).

The Federal Rules of Civil Procedure do not specifically provide the procedure for the imposition of civil contempt sanctions. The decisional law governing the procedure for imposition of civil sanctions by the district courts will be equally applicable to the bankruptcy courts.

NOTES OF ADVISORY COMMITTEE ON RULES—1987 AMENDMENT

The United States Bankruptcy Courts, as constituted under the Bankruptcy Reform Act of 1978, were courts of law, equity, and admiralty with an inherent contempt power, but former 28 U.S.C. § 1481 restricted the criminal contempt power of bankruptcy judges. Under the 1984 amendments, bankruptcy judges are judicial officers of the district court, 28 U.S.C. §§ 151, 152(a)(1). There are no decisions by the courts of appeals concerning the authority of bankruptcy judges to punish for either civil or criminal contempt under the 1984 amendments. This rule, as amended, recognizes that bankruptcy judges may not have the power to punish for contempt.

Sound judicial administration requires that the initial determination of whether contempt has been committed should be made by the bankruptcy judge. If timely objections are not filed to the bankruptcy judge's order, the order has the same force and effect as an order of the district court. If objections are filed within 10 days of service of the order, the district court conducts a de novo review pursuant to Rule 9033 and any order of contempt is entered by the district court on completion of the court's review of the bankruptcy judge's order.

NOTES OF ADVISORY COMMITTEE ON RULES—1991 AMENDMENT

The words "with the clerk" in subdivision (c) are deleted as unnecessary. See Rules 5005(a) and 9001(3).

COMMITTEE NOTES ON RULES—2001 AMENDMENT

The amendments to this rule cover a motion for an order of contempt filed by the United States trustee or a party in interest. This rule, as amended, does not address a contempt proceeding initiated by the court sua sponte.

Whether the court is acting on motion under this rule or is acting sua sponte, these amendments are not intended to extend, limit, or otherwise affect either the contempt power of a bankruptcy judge or the role of the district judge regarding contempt orders. Issues relating to the contempt power of bankruptcy judges are substantive and are left to statutory and judicial development, rather than procedural rules.

This rule, as amended in 1987, delayed for ten days from service the effectiveness of a bankruptcy judge's order of contempt and rendered the order subject to de novo review by the district court. These limitations on contempt orders were added to the rule in response to the Bankruptcy Amendments and Federal Judgeship Act of 1984, Pub. L. No. 98-353, 98 Stat. 333, which provides that bankruptcy judges are judicial officers of the district court, but does not specifically mention contempt power. *See* 28 U.S.C. §151. As explained in the committee note to the 1987 amendments to this rule, no decisions of the courts of appeals existed concerning the authority of a bankruptcy judge to punish for either civil or criminal contempt under the 1984 Act and, therefore, the rule as amended in 1987 "recognizes that bankruptcy judges may not have the power to punish for contempt." Committee Note to 1987 Amendments to Rule 9020.

Since 1987, several courts of appeals have held that bankruptcy judges have the power to issue civil contempt orders. *See, e.g., Matter of Terrebonne Fuel and Lube, Inc.*, 108 F.3d 609 (5th Cir. 1997); *In re Rainbow Magazine, Inc.*, 77 F.3d 278 (9th Cir. 1996). Several courts have distinguished between a bankruptcy judge's civil contempt power and criminal contempt power. *See, e.g., Matter of Terrebonne Fuel and Lube, Inc.*, 108 F.3d at 613, n. 3 ("[a]lthough we find that bankruptcy judge's [sic] can find a party in civil contempt, we must point out that bankruptcy courts lack the power to hold persons in criminal contempt."). For other decisions regarding criminal contempt power, *see, e.g., In re Ragar*, 3 F.3d 1174 (8th Cir. 1993); *Matter of Hipp, Inc.*, 895 F.2d 1503 (5th Cir. 1990). To the extent that Rule 9020, as amended in 1987, delayed the effectiveness of civil contempt orders and required de novo review by the district court, the rule may have been unnecessarily restrictive in view of judicial decisions recognizing that bankruptcy judges have the power to hold parties in civil contempt.

Subdivision (d), which provides that the rule shall not be construed to impair the right to trial by jury, is deleted as unnecessary and is not intended to deprive any party of the right to a jury trial when it otherwise exists.

*Changes Made After Publication and Comments.* No changes were made in the text of the proposed amendments. Stylistic changes were made to the Committee Note.

## Rule 9021. Entry of Judgment

A judgment or order is effective when entered under Rule 5003.

(As amended Mar. 30, 1987, eff. Aug. 1, 1987; Mar. 26, 2009, eff. Dec. 1, 2009.)

NOTES OF ADVISORY COMMITTEE ON RULES—1983

*Subdivision (a).* This rule is derived from Rule 58 F.R.Civ.P. The requirement that a judgment entered in an adversary proceeding or contested matter be set forth on a separate document is to eliminate uncertainty as to whether an opinion or memorandum of the court is a judgment. There is no sound reason to require that every order in a case under the Code be evidenced by a separate document.

*Subdivision (b)* establishes a procedure for entering a judgment of a bankruptcy court for the recovery of money or property in an index of judgments kept by the clerk of the district court. It clarifies the availability of the same remedies for the enforcement of a bankruptcy court judgment as those provided for the enforcement of a district court judgment. See 28 U.S.C. §§1961–63. When indexed in accordance with subdivision (b) of this rule a judgment of the bankruptcy court may be found by anyone searching for liens of record in the judgment records of the district court. Certification of a copy of the judgment to the clerk of the district court provides a basis for registration of the judgment pursuant to 28 U.S.C. §1963 in any other district. When so registered, the judgment may be enforced by issuance of execution and orders for supplementary proceedings that may be served anywhere within the state where the registering court sits. See 7 Moore, *Federal Practice* 2409–11 (2d ed. 1971). The procedures available in the district court are not exclusive, however, and the holder of a judgment entered by the bankruptcy court may use the remedies under Rules 7069 and 7070 even if the judgment is indexed by the clerk of the district court.

*Subdivision (c)* makes it clear that when a district court hears a matter reserved to it by 28 U.S.C. §§1471, 1481, its judgments are entered in the district court's civil docket and in the docket of the bankruptcy court. When the district court acts as an appellate court, Rule 8016(a) governs the entry of judgments on appeal.

NOTES OF ADVISORY COMMITTEE ON RULES—1987 AMENDMENT

Former subdivision (a) was derived from Rule 58 F.R.Civ.P. As amended, Rule 9021 adopts Rule 58. The reference in Rule 58 to Rule 79(a) F.R.Civ.P. is to be read as a reference to Rule 5003.

COMMITTEE NOTES ON RULES—2009 AMENDMENT

The rule is amended in connection with the amendment that adds Rule 7058. The entry of judgment in adversary proceedings is governed by Rule 7058, and the entry of a judgment or order in all other proceedings is governed by this rule.

*Changes Made After Publication.* No changes since publication.

REFERENCES IN TEXT

The Federal Rules of Civil Procedure, referred to in text, are set out in the Appendix to Title 28, Judiciary and Judicial Procedure.

## Rule 9022. Notice of Judgment or Order

(a) JUDGMENT OR ORDER OF BANKRUPTCY JUDGE. Immediately on the entry of a judgment or order the clerk shall serve a notice of entry in the manner provided in Rule 5(b) F.R.Civ.P. on the contesting parties and on other entities as the court directs. Unless the case is a chapter 9 municipality case, the clerk shall forthwith transmit to the United States trustee a copy of the judgment or order. Service of the notice shall be noted in the docket. Lack of notice of the entry does not affect the time to appeal or relieve or authorize the court to relieve a party for failure to appeal within the time allowed, except as permitted in Rule 8002.

(b) JUDGMENT OR ORDER OF DISTRICT JUDGE. Notice of a judgment or order entered by a district judge is governed by Rule 77(d) F.R.Civ.P. Unless the case is a chapter 9 municipality case, the clerk shall forthwith transmit to the United States trustee a copy of a judgment or order entered by a district judge.

(As amended Mar. 30, 1987, eff. Aug. 1, 1987; Apr. 30, 1991, eff. Aug. 1, 1991; Apr. 23, 2001, eff. Dec. 1, 2001.)

NOTES OF ADVISORY COMMITTEE ON RULES

*Subdivision (a)* of this rule is an adaptation of Rule 77(d) F.R.Civ.P.

*Subdivision (b)* complements Rule 9021(b). When a district court acts as an appellate court, Rule 8016(b) requires the clerk to give notice of the judgment on appeal.

NOTES OF ADVISORY COMMITTEE ON RULES AMENDMENT

This rule is amended to enable the United States trustee to be informed of all developments in the case so that administrative and supervisory functions provided in 28 U.S.C. §586(a) may be performed.

COMMITTEE NOTES ON RULES—2001 AMENDMENT

Rule 5(b) F.R.Civ.P., which is made applicable in adversary proceedings by Rule 7005, is being restyled and amended to authorize service by electronic means—or any other means not otherwise authorized under Rule 5(b)—if consent is obtained from the person served. The amendment to Rule 9022(a) authorizes the clerk to serve notice of entry of a judgment or order by electronic means if the person served consents, or to use any other means of service authorized under Rule 5(b), including service by mail. This amendment conforms to the amendments made to Rule 77(d) F.R.Civ.P.

*Changes Made After Publication and Comments.* No changes were made.

REFERENCES IN TEXT

The Federal Rules of Civil Procedure, referred to in subd. (b), are set out in the Appendix to Title 28, Judiciary and Judicial Procedure.

## Rule 9023. New Trials; Amendment of Judgments

Except as provided in this rule and Rule 3008, Rule 59 F.R.Civ.P. applies in cases under the Code. A motion for a new trial or to alter or amend a judgment shall be filed, and a court may on its own order a new trial, no later than 14 days after entry of judgment.

(As amended Mar. 26, 2009, eff. Dec. 1, 2009.)

NOTES OF ADVISORY COMMITTEE ON RULES—1983

Rule 59 F.R.Civ.P. regulates motions for a new trial and amendment of judgment. Those motions must be served within 10 days of the entry of judgment. No similar time limit is contained in Rule 3008 which governs reconsideration of claims.

COMMITTEE NOTES ON RULES—2009 AMENDMENT

The rule is amended to limit to 14 days the time for a party to file a post judgment motion for a new trial and for the court to order sua sponte a new trial. In 2009, Rule 59 F. R. Civ. P. was amended to extend the deadline for these actions to 28 days after the entry of judgment. That deadline corresponds to the 30-day deadline for filing a notice of appeal in a civil case under Rule 4(a)(1)(A) F.R.App.P. In a bankruptcy case, however, the deadline for filing a notice of appeal is 14 days. Therefore, the 28-day deadline for filing a motion for a new trial or a motion to alter or amend a judgment would effectively override the notice of appeal deadline under Rule 8002(a) but for this amendment.

REFERENCES IN TEXT

The Federal Rules of Civil Procedure, referred to in text, are set out in the Appendix to Title 28, Judiciary and Judicial Procedure.

## Rule 9024. Relief from Judgment or Order

Rule 60 F.R.Civ.P. applies in cases under the Code except that (1) a motion to reopen a case under the Code or for the reconsideration of an order allowing or disallowing a claim against the estate entered without a contest is not subject to the one year limitation prescribed in Rule 60(c), (2) a complaint to revoke a discharge in a chapter 7 liquidation case may be filed only within the time allowed by §727(e) of the Code, and (3) a complaint to revoke an order confirming a plan may be filed only within the time allowed by §1144, §1230, or §1330.

(As amended Apr. 30, 1991, eff. Aug. 1, 1991; Apr. 23, 2008, eff. Dec. 1, 2008.)

NOTES OF ADVISORY COMMITTEE ON RULES—1983

Motions to reopen cases are governed by Rule 5010. Reconsideration of orders allowing and disallowing claims is governed by Rule 3008. For the purpose of this rule all orders of the bankruptcy court are subject to Rule 60 F.R.Civ.P.

Pursuant to §727(e) of the Code a complaint to revoke a discharge must be filed within one year of the entry of the discharge or, when certain grounds of revocation are asserted, the later of one year after the entry of the discharge or the date the case is closed. Under §1144 and §1330 of the Code a party must file a complaint to revoke an order confirming a chapter 11 or 13 plan within 180 days of its entry. Clauses (2) and (3) of this rule make it clear that the time periods established by §§727(e), 1144 and 1330 of the Code may not be circumvented by the invocation of F.R.Civ.P. 60(b).

NOTES OF ADVISORY COMMITTEE ON RULES—1991 AMENDMENT

Clause (3) is amended to include a reference to §1230 of the Code which contains time limitations relating to revocation of confirmation of a chapter 12 plan. The time periods prescribed by §1230 may not be circumvented by the invocation of F.R.Civ.P. 60(b).

COMMITTEE NOTES ON RULES—2008 AMENDMENT

The rule is amended to conform to the changes made to the Federal Rules of Civil Procedure through the restyling of those rules effective on December 1, 2007.

REFERENCES IN TEXT

The Federal Rules of Civil Procedure, referred to in text, are set out in the Appendix to Title 28, Judiciary and Judicial Procedure.

## Rule 9025. Security: Proceedings Against Sureties

Whenever the Code or these rules require or permit the giving of security by a party, and security is given in the form of a bond or stipulation or other undertaking with one or more sureties, each surety submits to the jurisdiction of the court, and liability may be determined in an adversary proceeding governed by the rules in Part VII.

NOTES OF ADVISORY COMMITTEE ON RULES—1983

This rule is an adaptation of Rule 65.1 F.R.Civ.P. and applies to any surety on a bond given pursuant to §303(e) of the Code, Rules 2001, 2010, 5008, 7062, 7065, 8005, or any other rule authorizing the giving of such security.

## Rule 9026. Exceptions Unnecessary

Rule 46 F.R.Civ.P. applies in cases under the Code.

REFERENCES IN TEXT

The Federal Rules of Civil Procedure, referred to in text, are set out in the Appendix to Title 28, Judiciary and Judicial Procedure.

## Rule 9027. Removal

(a) NOTICE OF REMOVAL.

(1) *Where Filed; Form and Content.* A notice of removal shall be filed with the clerk for the district and division within which is located the state or federal court where the civil action is pending. The notice shall be signed pursuant to Rule 9011 and contain a short and plain statement of the facts which entitle the party filing the notice to remove, contain a statement that upon removal of the claim or cause of action the proceeding is core or non-core and, if non-core, that the party filing the notice does or does not consent to entry of final orders or judgment by the bankruptcy judge, and be accompanied by a copy of all process and pleadings.

(2) *Time for Filing; Civil Action Initiated Before Commencement of the Case Under the Code.* If the claim or cause of action in a civil action is pending when a case under the Code is commenced, a notice of removal may be filed only within the longest of (A) 90 days after the order for relief in the case under the Code, (B) 30 days after entry of an order terminating a stay, if the claim or cause of action in a civil action has been stayed under §362 of the Code, or (C) 30 days after a trustee qualifies in a chapter 11 reorganization case but not later than 180 days after the order for relief.

(3) *Time for filing; civil action initiated after commencement of the case under the Code.* If a claim or cause of action is asserted in another court after the commencement of a case under the Code, a notice of removal may be filed with the clerk only within the shorter of (A) 30 days after receipt, through service or otherwise, of a copy of the initial pleading setting forth the claim or cause of action sought to be removed, or (B) 30 days after receipt of the summons if the initial pleading has been filed with the court but not served with the summons.

(b) NOTICE. Promptly after filing the notice of removal, the party filing the notice shall serve a copy of it on all parties to the removed claim or cause of action.

(c) FILING IN NON-BANKRUPTCY COURT. Promptly after filing the notice of removal, the party filing the notice shall file a copy of it with the clerk of the court from which the claim or cause of action is removed. Removal of the claim or cause of action is effected on such filing of a copy of the notice of removal. The parties shall proceed no further in that court unless and until the claim or cause of action is remanded.

(d) REMAND. A motion for remand of the removed claim or cause of action shall be governed by Rule 9014 and served on the parties to the removed claim or cause of action.

(e) PROCEDURE AFTER REMOVAL.

(1) After removal of a claim or cause of action to a district court the district court or, if the case under the Code has been referred to a bankruptcy judge of the district, the bankruptcy judge, may issue all necessary orders and process to bring before it all proper parties whether served by process issued by the court from which the claim or cause of action was removed or otherwise.

(2) The district court or, if the case under the Code has been referred to a bankruptcy judge of the district, the bankruptcy judge, may require the party filing the notice of removal to file with the clerk copies of all records and proceedings relating to the claim or cause of action in the court from which the claim or cause of action was removed.

(3) Any party who has filed a pleading in connection with the removed claim or cause of action, other than the party filing the notice of removal, shall file a statement admitting or denying any allegation in the notice of removal that upon removal of the claim or cause of action the proceeding is core or non-core. If the statement alleges that the proceeding is non-core, it shall state that the party does or does not consent to entry of final orders or judgment by the bankruptcy judge. A statement required by this paragraph shall be signed pursuant to Rule 9011 and shall be filed not later than 14 days after the filing of the notice of removal. Any party who files a statement pursuant to this paragraph shall mail a copy to every other party to the removed claim or cause of action.

(f) PROCESS AFTER REMOVAL. If one or more of the defendants has not been served with process, the service has not been perfected prior to removal, or the process served proves to be defective, such process or service may be completed or new process issued pursuant to Part VII of these rules. This subdivision shall not deprive any defendant on whom process is served after removal of the defendant's right to move to remand the case.

(g) APPLICABILITY OF PART VII. The rules of Part VII apply to a claim or cause of action removed to a district court from a federal or state court and govern procedure after removal. Repleading is not necessary unless the court so orders. In a removed action in which the defendant has not answered, the defendant shall answer or present the other defenses or objections available under the rules of Part VII within 21 days following the receipt through service or otherwise of a copy of the initial pleading setting forth the claim for relief on which the action or proceeding is based, or within 21 days following the service of summons on such initial pleading, or within seven days following the filing of the notice of removal, whichever period is longest.

(h) RECORD SUPPLIED. When a party is entitled to copies of the records and proceedings in any civil action or proceeding in a federal or a state court, to be used in the removed civil action or proceeding, and the clerk of the federal or state court, on demand accompanied by payment or tender of the lawful fees, fails to deliver certified copies, the court may, on affidavit reciting the facts, direct such record to be supplied by affidavit or otherwise. Thereupon the proceedings, trial and judgment may be had in the court, and all process awarded, as if certified copies had been filed.

(i) ATTACHMENT OR SEQUESTRATION

TIES. When a claim or cause of action is removed to a district court, any attachment or sequestration of property in the court from which the claim or cause of action was removed shall hold the property to answer the final judgment or decree in the same manner as the property would have been held to answer final judgment or decree had it been rendered by the court from which the claim or cause of action was removed. All bonds, undertakings, or security given by either party to the claim or cause of action prior to its removal shall remain valid and effectual notwithstanding such removal. All injunctions issued, orders entered and other proceedings had prior to removal shall remain in full force and effect until dissolved or modified by the court.

(As amended Mar. 30, 1987, eff. Aug. 1, 1987; Apr. 30, 1991, eff. Aug. 1, 1991; Apr. 29, 2002, eff. Dec. 1, 2002; Mar. 26, 2009, eff. Dec. 1, 2009.)

NOTES OF ADVISORY COMMITTEE ON RULES

Under 28 U.S.C. §1478(a) "any claim or cause of action in a civil action, other than a proceeding before the

United States Tax Court or a civil action by a Government unit to enforce [a] . . . regulatory or police power" may be removed "if the bankruptcy courts have jurisdiction over such claim or cause of action." This rule specifies how removal is accomplished, the procedure thereafter, and the procedure to request remand of the removed claim or cause of action. If the claim or cause of action which is removed to the bankruptcy court is subject to the automatic stay of §362 of the Code, the litigation may not proceed in the bankruptcy court until relief from the stay is granted.

The subdivisions of this rule conform substantially to 28 U.S.C. §§1446–1450 and Rule 81(a) F.R.Civ.P. pertaining to removal to the district courts.

*Subdivision (a)(1)* is derived from 28 U.S.C. §1446(a).

*Subdivisions (a)(2) and (a)(3)* are derived from paragraphs one and two of 28 U.S.C. §1446(b). Timely exercise of the right to remove is as important in bankruptcy cases as in removals from a state court to a district court.

*Subdivision (a)(2)* governs the situation in which there is litigation pending and a party to the litigation becomes a debtor under the Code. Frequently, removal would be of little utility in such cases because the pending litigation will be stayed by §362(a) on commencement of the case under the Code. As long as the stay remains in effect there is no reason to impose a time limit for removal to the bankruptcy court and, therefore, clause (B) of subdivision (a)(2) provides that a removal application may be filed within 30 days of entry of an order terminating the stay. Parties to stayed litigation will not be required to act immediately on commencement of a case under the Code to protect their right to remove. If the pending litigation is not stayed by §362(a) of the Code, the removal application must ordinarily be filed within 90 days of the order for relief. Clause (C) contains an alternative period for a chapter 11 case. If a trustee is appointed, the removal application may be filed within 30 days of the trustee's qualification, provided that the removal application is filed not more than 180 days after the order for relief.

The removal application must be filed within the longest of the three possible periods. For example, in a chapter 11 case if the 90 day period expires but a trustee is appointed shortly thereafter, the removal application may be filed within 30 days of the trustee's qualification but not later than 180 days after the order for relief. Nevertheless, if the claim or cause of action in the civil action is stayed under §362, the application may be filed after the 180 day period expires, provided the application is filed within 30 days of an order terminating the stay.

*Subdivision (a)(3)* applies to the situation in which the case under the Code is pending when the removable claim or cause of action is asserted in a civil action initiated in other than the bankruptcy court. The time for filing the application for removal begins to run on receipt of the first pleading containing the removable claim or cause of action. Only litigation not stayed by the Code or by court order may properly be initiated after the case under the Code is commenced. See *e.g.*, §362(a).

*Subdivision (b).* With one exception, this subdivision is the same as 28 U.S.C. §1446(d). The exemption from the bond requirement is enlarged to include a trustee or debtor in possession. Complete exemption from the bond requirement for removal is appropriate because of the limited resources which may be available at the beginning of a case and the small probability that an action will be improperly removed.

Recovery on the bond is permitted only when the removal was improper. If the removal is proper but the bankruptcy court orders the action remanded on equitable grounds, 28 U.S.C. §1478(b), there is no recovery on the bond.

*Subdivisions (c) and (d)* are patterned on 28 U.S.C. §1446(e).

*Subdivision (e).* There is no provision in the Federal Rules of Civil Procedure for seeking remand. The first sentence of this subdivision requires that a request for remand be by motion and that the moving party serve all other parties; however, no hearing is required. In recognition of the intrusion of the removal practice on the state and federal courts from which claims or causes of action are removed, the subdivision directs the bankruptcy court to decide remand motions as soon as practicable. The last sentence of this subdivision is derived from 28 U.S.C. §1446(c)

*Subdivisions (f) and (g)*, with appropriate changes to conform them to the bankruptcy context, are the same as 28 U.S.C. §1447(a) and (b) and 28 U.S.C. §1448, respectively.

*Subdivisions (h) and (i)* are taken from Rule 81(c) F.R.Civ.P.

*Subdivisions (j) and (k)* are derived from 28 U.S.C. §1449 and §1450, respectively.

Remand orders of bankruptcy judges are not appealable. 28 U.S.C. §1478(b).

This rule does not deal with the question whether a single plaintiff or defendant may remove a claim or cause of action if there are two or more plaintiffs or defendants. See 28 U.S.C. §1478.

NOTES OF ADVISORY COMMITTEE ON RULES—1987 AMENDMENT

Section 1452 of title 28, with certain exceptions, provides for removal of claims or causes of action in civil actions pending in state or federal courts when the claim or cause of action is within the jurisdiction conferred by 28 U.S.C. §1334. An order granting or denying a motion for remand is not appealable. 28 U.S.C. §1452(b). Under subdivision (e), as amended, the district court must enter the order on the remand motion; however, the bankruptcy judge conducts the initial hearing on the motion and files a report and recommendation. The parties may file objections. Review of the report and recommendation is pursuant to Rule 9033.

*Subdivision (f)* has been amended to provide that if there has been a referral pursuant to 28 U.S.C. §157(a) the bankruptcy judge will preside over the removed civil action.

*Subdivision (i)* has been abrogated consistent with the abrogation of Rule 9015.

NOTES OF ADVISORY COMMITTEE ON RULES—1991 AMENDMENT

The abrogation of subdivision (b) is consistent with the repeal of 28 U.S.C. §1446(d). The changes substituting the notice of removal for the application for removal conform to the 1988 amendments to 28 U.S.C. §1446.

Rules 7008(a) and 7012(b) were amended in 1987 to require parties to allege in pleadings whether a proceeding is core or non-core and, if non-core, whether the parties consent to the entry of final orders or judgment by the bankruptcy judge. Subdivision (a)(1) is amended and subdivision (f)(3) is added to require parties to a removed claim or cause of action to make the same allegations. The party filing the notice of removal must include the allegation in the notice and the other parties who have filed pleadings must respond to the allegation in a separate statement filed within 10 days after removal. However, if a party to the removed claim or cause of action has not filed a pleading prior to removal, there is no need to file a separate statement under subdivision (f)(3) because the allegation must be included in the responsive pleading filed pursuant to Rule 7012(b).

Subdivision (e), redesignated as subdivision (d), is amended to delete the restriction that limits the role of the bankruptcy court to the filing of a report and recommendation for disposition of a motion for remand under 28 U.S.C. §1452(b). This amendment is consistent with §309(c) of the Judicial Improvements Act of 1990, which amended §1452(b) so that it allows an appeal to the district court of a bankruptcy court's order determining a motion for remand. This subdivision is also amended to clarify that the motion is a contested matter governed by Rule 9014. The words "filed with the clerk" are deleted as unnecessary. See Rules 5005(a) and 9001(3).

COMMITTEE NOTES ON RULES—2002 AMENDMENT

*Subdivision (a)(3)* is amended to clarify that if a claim or cause of action is initiated after the commencement of a bankruptcy case, the time limits for filing a notice of removal of the claim or cause of action apply whether the case is still pending or has been suspended, dismissed, or closed.

*Changes Made After Publication and Comments.* No changes were made.

COMMITTEE NOTES ON RULES—2009 AMENDMENT

The rule is amended to implement changes in connection with the amendment to Rule 9006(a) and the manner by which time is computed under the rules. The deadlines in the rule are amended to substitute a deadline that is a multiple of seven days. Throughout the rules, deadlines are amended in the following manner:

- 5-day periods become 7-day periods
- 10-day periods become 14-day periods
- 15-day periods become 14-day periods
- 20-day periods become 21-day periods
- 25-day periods become 28-day periods

## Rule 9028. Disability of a Judge

Rule 63 F.R.Civ.P. applies in cases under the Code.

(As amended Mar. 30, 1987, eff. Aug. 1, 1987.)

NOTES OF ADVISORY COMMITTEE ON RULES—1983

This rule is an adaptation of Rule 63 F.R.Civ.P.

NOTES OF ADVISORY COMMITTEE ON RULES—1987 AMENDMENT

Rule 9028 has been changed to adopt the procedures contained in Rule 63 of the Federal Rules of Civil Procedure for substituting a judge in the event of disability.

REFERENCES IN TEXT

The Federal Rules of Civil Procedure, referred to in text, are set out in the Appendix to Title 28, Judiciary and Judicial Procedure.

## Rule 9029. Local Bankruptcy Rules; Procedure When There is No Controlling Law

(a) LOCAL BANKRUPTCY RULES.

(1) Each district court acting by a majority of its district judges may make and amend rules governing practice and procedure in all cases and proceedings within the district court's bankruptcy jurisdiction which are consistent with—but not duplicative of—Acts of Congress and these rules and which do not prohibit or limit the use of the Official Forms. Rule 83 F.R.Civ.P. governs the procedure for making local rules. A district court may authorize the bankruptcy judges of the district, subject to any limitation or condition it may prescribe and the requirements of 83 F.R.Civ.P., to make and amend rules of practice and procedure which are consistent with—but not duplicative of—Acts of Congress and these rules and which do not prohibit or limit the use of the Official Forms. Local rules shall conform to any uniform numbering system prescribed by the Judicial Conference of the United States.

(2) A local rule imposing a requirement of form shall not be enforced in a manner that causes a party to lose rights because of a nonwillful failure to comply with the requirement.

(b) PROCEDURE WHEN THERE IS NO CONTROLLING LAW. A judge may regulate practice in any manner consistent with federal law, these rules, Official Forms, and local rules of the district. No sanction or other disadvantage may be imposed for noncompliance with any requirement not in federal law, federal rules, Official Forms, or the local rules of the district unless the alleged violator has been furnished in the particular case with actual notice of the requirement.

(As amended Mar. 30, 1987, eff. Aug. 1, 1987; Apr. 30, 1991, eff. Aug. 1, 1991; Apr. 27, 1995, eff. Dec. 1, 1995.)

NOTES OF ADVISORY COMMITTEE ON RULES—1983

This rule is an adaptation of Rule 83 F.R.Civ.P. and Rule 57(a) F.R.Crim.P. Under this rule bankruptcy courts may make local rules which govern practice before those courts. Circuit councils and district courts are authorized by Rule 8018 to make local rules governing appellate practice.

NOTES OF ADVISORY COMMITTEE ON RULES—1987 AMENDMENT

Rule 9029 is amended to authorize the district court to promulgate local rules governing bankruptcy practice. This rule, as amended, permits the district court to authorize the bankruptcy judges to promulgate or recommend local rules for adoption by the district court.

Effective August 1, 1985, Rule 83 F.R.Civ.P., governing adoption of local rules, was amended to achieve greater participation by the bar, scholars, and the public in the rule making process; to authorize the judicial council to abrogate local rules; and to make certain that single-judge standing orders are not inconsistent with these rules or local rules. Rule 9029 has been amended to incorporate Rule 83. The term "court" in the last sentence of the rule includes the judges of the district court and the bankruptcy judges of the district. Rule 9001(4).

NOTES OF ADVISORY COMMITTEE ON RULES—1991 AMENDMENT

This rule is amended to make it clear that the Official Forms must be accepted in every bankruptcy court.

NOTES OF ADVISORY COMMITTEE ON RULES AMENDMENT

*Subdivision (a).* This rule is amended to reflect the requirement that local rules be consistent not only with applicable national rules but also with Acts of Congress. The amendment also states that local rules should not repeat applicable national rules and Acts of Congress.

The amendment also requires that the numbering of local rules conform with any uniform numbering system that may be prescribed by the Judicial Conference. Lack of uniform numbering might create unnecessary traps for counsel and litigants. A uniform numbering system would make it easier for an increasingly national bar and for litigants to locate a local rule that applies to a particular procedural issue.

Paragraph (2) of subdivision (a) is new. Its aim is to protect against loss of rights in the enforcement of local rules relating to matters of form. For example, a party should not be deprived of a right to a jury trial because its attorney, unaware of—or forgetting—a local rule directing that jury demands be noted in the caption of the case, includes a jury demand only in the body of the pleading. The proscription of paragraph (2) is narrowly drawn—covering only violations that are not willful and only those involving local rules directed to matters of form. It does not limit the court's power to impose substantive penalties upon a party if it or its attorney stubbornly or repeatedly violates a local rule, even one involving merely a matter of form. Nor does it affect the court's power to enforce local rules that involve more than mere matters of form—for example, a local rule requiring that a party demand a jury trial within a specified time period to avoid waiver of the right to a trial by jury.

*Subdivision (b).* This rule provides flexibility to the court in regulating practice when there is no controlling law. Specifically, it permits the court to regulate practice in any manner consistent with federal law, with rules adopted under 28 U.S.C. §2075, with Official Forms, and with the district's local rules.

This rule recognizes that courts rely on multiple directives to control practice. Some courts regulate practice through the published Federal Rules and the local rules of the court. Some courts also have used internal operating procedures, standing orders, and other internal directives. Although such directives continue to be authorized, they can lead to problems. Counsel or litigants may be unaware of various directives. In addition, the sheer volume of directives may impose an unreasonable barrier. For example, it may be difficult to obtain copies of the directives. Finally, counsel or litigants may be unfairly sanctioned for failing to comply with a directive. For these reasons, the amendment to this rule disapproves imposing any sanction or other disadvantage on a person for noncompliance with such an internal directive, unless the alleged violator has been furnished in a particular case with actual notice of the requirement.

There should be no adverse consequence to a party or attorney for violating special requirements relating to practice before a particular judge unless the party or attorney has actual notice of those requirements. Furnishing litigants with a copy outlining the judge's practices—or attaching instructions to a notice setting a case for conference or trial—would suffice to give actual notice, as would an order in a case specifically adopting by reference a judge's standing order and indicating how copies can be obtained.

REFERENCES IN TEXT

The Federal Rules of Civil Procedure, referred to in subd. (a)(1), are set out in the Appendix to Title 28, Judiciary and Judicial Procedure.

## Rule 9030. Jurisdiction and Venue Unaffected

These rules shall not be construed to extend or limit the jurisdiction of the courts or the venue of any matters therein.

(As amended Mar. 30, 1987, eff. Aug. 1, 1987.)

NOTES OF ADVISORY COMMITTEE ON RULES—1983

The rule is an adaptation of Rule 82 F.R.Civ.P.

## Rule 9031. Masters Not Authorized

Rule 53 F.R.Civ.P. does not apply in cases under the Code.

NOTES OF ADVISORY COMMITTEE ON RULES—1983

This rule precludes the appointment of masters in cases and proceedings under the Code.

REFERENCES IN TEXT

The Federal Rules of Civil Procedure, referred to in text, are set out in the Appendix to Title 28, Judiciary and Judicial Procedure.

## Rule 9032. Effect of Amendment of Federal Rules of Civil Procedure

The Federal Rules of Civil Procedure which are incorporated by reference and made applicable by these rules shall be the Federal Rules of Civil Procedure in effect on the effective date of these rules and as thereafter amended, unless otherwise provided by such amendment or by these rules.

(As amended Apr. 30, 1991, eff. Aug. 1, 1991.)

NOTES OF ADVISORY COMMITTEE ON RULES—1991 AMENDMENT

This rule is amended to provide flexibility so that the Bankruptcy Rules may provide that subsequent amendments to a Federal Rule of Civil Procedure made applicable by these rules are not effective with regard to Bankruptcy Code cases or proceedings. For example, in view of the anticipated amendments to, and restructuring of, Rule 4 F.R.Civ.P., Rule 7004(g) will prevent such changes from affecting Bankruptcy Code cases until the Advisory Committee on Bankruptcy Rules has an opportunity to consider such amendments and to make appropriate recommendations for incorporating such amendments into the Bankruptcy Rules.

REFERENCES IN TEXT

The Federal Rules of Civil Procedure, referred to in text, are set out in the Appendix to Title 28, Judiciary and Judicial Procedure.

The effective date of these rules, referred to in text, is Aug. 1, 1983. See Effective Date note set out prec. Rule 1001 of this Appendix.

## Rule 9033. Review of Proposed Findings of Fact and Conclusions of Law in Non-Core Proceedings

(a) SERVICE. In non-core proceedings heard pursuant to 28 U.S.C. §157(c)(1), the bankruptcy judge shall file proposed findings of fact and conclusions of law. The clerk shall serve forthwith copies on all parties by mail and note the date of mailing on the docket.

(b) OBJECTIONS: TIME FOR FILING. Within 14 days after being served with a copy of the proposed findings of fact and conclusions of law a party may serve and file with the clerk written objections which identify the specific proposed findings or conclusions objected to and state the grounds for such objection. A party may respond to another party's objections within 14 days after being served with a copy thereof. A party objecting to the bankruptcy judge's proposed findings or conclusions shall arrange promptly for the transcription of the record, or such portions of it as all parties may agree upon or the bankruptcy judge deems sufficient, unless the district judge otherwise directs.

(c) EXTENSION OF TIME. The bankruptcy judge may for cause extend the time for filing objections by any party for a period not to exceed 21 days from the expiration of the time otherwise prescribed by this rule. A request to extend the time for filing objections must be made before the time for filing objections has expired, except that a request made no more than 21 days after the expiration of the time for filing objections may be granted upon a showing of excusable neglect.

(d) STANDARD OF REVIEW. The district judge shall make a de novo review upon the record or, after additional evidence, of any portion of the bankruptcy judge's findings of fact or conclusions of law to which specific written objection has been made in accordance with this rule. The district judge may accept, reject, or modify the proposed findings of fact or conclusions of law, receive further evidence, or recommit the matter to the bankruptcy judge with instructions.

(Added Mar. 30, 1987, eff. Aug. 1, 1987; amended Mar. 26, 2009, eff. Dec. 1, 2009.)

NOTES OF ADVISORY COMMITTEE ON RULES—1987

Section 157(c)(1) of title 28 requires a bankruptcy judge to submit proposed findings of fact and conclusions of law to the district court when the bankruptcy judge has heard a non-core proceeding. This rule, which is modeled on Rule 72 F.R.Civ.P., provides the procedure for objecting to, and for review by, the district court of specific findings and conclusions.

*Subdivision (a)* requires the clerk to serve a copy of the proposed findings and conclusions on the parties. The bankruptcy clerk, or the district court clerk if there is no bankruptcy clerk in the district, shall serve a copy of the proposed findings and conclusions on all parties.

*Subdivision (b)* is derived from Rule 72(b) F.R.Civ.P. which governs objections to a recommended disposition by a magistrate.

*Subdivision (c)* is similar to Rule 8002(c) of the Bankruptcy Rules and provides for granting of extensions of time to file objections to proposed findings and conclusions.

*Subdivision (d)* adopts the de novo review provisions of Rule 72(b) F.R.Civ.P.

COMMITTEE NOTES ON RULES—2009 AMENDMENT

The rule is amended to implement changes in connection with the amendment to Rule 9006(a) and the manner by which time is computed under the rules. The deadlines in the rule are amended to substitute a deadline that is a multiple of seven days. Throughout the rules, deadlines are amended in the following manner:

- 5-day periods become 7-day periods
- 10-day periods become 14-day periods
- 15-day periods become 14-day periods
- 20-day periods become 21-day periods
- 25-day periods become 28-day periods

## Rule 9034. Transmittal of Pleadings, Motion Papers, Objections, and Other Papers to the United States Trustee

Unless the United States trustee requests otherwise or the case is a chapter 9 municipality case, any entity that files a pleading, motion, objection, or similar paper relating to any of the following matters shall transmit a copy thereof to the United States trustee within the time required by these rules for service of the paper:

(a) a proposed use, sale, or lease of property of the estate other than in the ordinary course of business;

(b) the approval of a compromise or settlement of a controversy;

(c) the dismissal or conversion of a case to another chapter;

(d) the employment of professional persons;

(e) an application for compensation or reimbursement of expenses;

(f) a motion for, or approval of an agreement relating to, the use of cash collateral or authority to obtain credit;

(g) the appointment of a trustee or examiner in a chapter 11 reorganization case;

(h) the approval of a disclosure statement;

(i) the confirmation of a plan;

(j) an objection to, or waiver or revocation of, the debtor's discharge;

(k) any other matter in which the United States trustee requests copies of filed papers or the court orders copies transmitted to the United States trustee.

(Added Apr. 30, 1991, eff. Aug. 1, 1991.)

NOTES OF ADVISORY COMMITTEE ON RULES—1991

Section 307 of the Code gives the United States trustee the right to appear and be heard on issues in cases and proceedings under the Code. This rule is intended to keep the United States trustee informed of certain developments and disputes in which the United States trustee may wish to be heard. This rule, which derives from Rule X-1008, also enables the United States trustee to monitor the progress of the case in accordance with 28 U.S.C. §586(a). The requirement to transmit copies of certain pleadings, motion papers and other documents is intended to be flexible in that the United States trustee in a particular judicial district may request copies of papers in certain categories, and may request not to receive copies of documents in other categories, when the practice in that district makes that desirable. When the rules require that a paper be served on particular parties, the time period in which service is required is also applicable to transmittal to the United States trustee.

Although other rules require that certain notices be transmitted to the United States trustee, this rule goes further in that it requires the transmittal to the United States trustee of other papers filed in connection with these matters. This rule is not an exhaustive list of the matters of which the United States trustee may be entitled to receive notice.

## Rule 9035. Applicability of Rules in Judicial Districts in Alabama and North Carolina

In any case under the Code that is filed in or transferred to a district in the State of Alabama or the State of North Carolina and in which a United States trustee is not authorized to act, these rules apply to the extent that they are not inconsistent with any federal statute effective in the case.

(Added Apr. 30, 1991, eff. Aug. 1, 1991; amended Apr. 11, 1997, eff. Dec. 1, 1997.)

NOTES OF ADVISORY COMMITTEE ON RULES—1991

Section 302(d)(3) of the Bankruptcy Judges, United States Trustees, and Family Farmer Bankruptcy Act of 1986 provides that amendments to the Code relating to United States trustees and quarterly fees required under 28 U.S.C. §1930(a)(6) do not become effective in any judicial district in the States of Alabama and North Carolina until the district elects to be included in the United States trustee system, or October 1, 1992, whichever occurs first, unless Congress extends the deadline. If the United States trustee system becomes effective in these districts, the transition provisions in the 1986 Act will govern the application of the United States trustee amendments to cases that are pending at that time. See §302(d)(3)(F). The statute, and not the bankruptcy court, determines whether a United States trustee is authorized to act in a particular case.

Section 302(d)(3)(I) of the 1986 Act authorizes the Judicial Conference of the United States to promulgate regulations governing the appointment of bankruptcy administrators to supervise the administration of estates and trustees in cases in the districts in Alabama and North Carolina until the provisions of the Act relating to the United States trustee take effect in these districts. Pursuant to this authority, in September 1987, the Judicial Conference promulgated regulations governing the selection and appointment of bankruptcy administrators and regulations governing the establishment, duties, and functions of bankruptcy administrators. Guidelines relating to the bankruptcy administrator program have been prescribed by the Director of the Administrative Office of the United States Courts.

Many of these rules were amended to implement the United States trustee system in accordance with the 1986 Act. Since the provisions of the 1986 Act relating to the United States trustee system are not effective in cases in Alabama and North Carolina in which a bankruptcy administrator is serving, rules referring to United States trustees are at least partially inconsistent with the provisions of the Bankruptcy Code and title 28 of the United States Code effective in such cases.

In determining the applicability of these rules in cases in Alabama and North Carolina in which a United States trustee is not authorized to act, the following guidelines should be followed:

(1) The following rules do not apply because they are inconsistent with the provisions of the Code or title 28 in these cases: 1002(b), 1007(1), 1009(c), 2002(k), 2007.1(b), 2015(a)(6), 2020, 3015(b), 5005(b), 7004(b)(10), 9003(b), and 9034.

(2) The following rules are partially inconsistent with the provisions of the Code effective in these cases and, therefore, are applicable with the following modifications:

(a) *Rule 2001(a) and (c)*—The court, rather than the United States trustee, appoints the interim trustee.

(b) *Rule 2003*—The duties of the United States trustee relating to the meeting of creditors or equity security holders are performed by the officer determined in accordance with regulations of the Judicial Conference, guidelines of the Director of the Administrative Office, local rules or court orders.

(c) *Rule 2007*—The court, rather than the United States trustee, appoints committees in chapter 9 and chapter 11 cases.

(d) *Rule 2008*—The bankruptcy administrator, rather than the United States trustee, informs the trustee of how to qualify.

(e) *Rule 2009(c) and (d)*—The court, rather than the United States trustee, appoints interim trustees in chapter 7 cases and trustees in chapter 11, 12 and 13 cases.

(f) *Rule 2010*—The court, rather than the United States trustee, determines the amount and sufficiency of the trustee's bond.

(g) *Rule 5010*—The court, rather than the United States trustee, appoints the trustee when a case is reopened.

(3) All other rules are applicable because they are consistent with the provisions of the Code and title 28 effective in these cases, except that any reference to the United States trustee is not applicable and should be disregarded.

Many of the amendments to the rules are designed to give the United States trustee, a member of the Executive Branch, notice of certain developments and copies of petitions, schedules, pleadings, and other papers. In contrast, the bankruptcy administrator is an officer in the Judicial Branch and matters relating to notice of developments and access to documents filed in the clerk's office are governed by regulations of the Judicial Conference of the United States, guidelines of the Administrative Office of the United States Courts, local rules, and court orders. Also, requirements for disclosure of connections with the bankruptcy administrator in applications for employment of professional persons, restrictions on appointments of relatives of bankruptcy administrators, effects of erroneously filing papers with the bankruptcy administrator, and other matters not covered by these rules may be governed by regulations of the Judicial Conference, guidelines of the Director of the Administrative Office, local rules, and court orders.

This rule will cease to have effect if a United States trustee is authorized in every case in the districts in Alabama and North Carolina.

NOTES OF ADVISORY COMMITTEE ON RULES—1997 AMENDMENT

Certain statutes that are not codified in title 11 or title 28 of the United States Code, such as § 105 of the Bankruptcy Reform Act of 1994, Pub. L. 103–394, 108 Stat. 4106, relate to bankruptcy administrators in the judicial districts of North Carolina and Alabama. This amendment makes it clear that the Bankruptcy Rules do not apply to the extent that they are inconsistent with these federal statutes.

*GAP Report on Rule 9035.* No changes to the published draft.

## Rule 9036. Notice by Electronic Transmission

Whenever the clerk or some other person as directed by the court is required to send notice by mail and the entity entitled to receive the notice requests in writing that, instead of notice by mail, all or part of the information required to be contained in the notice be sent by a specified type of electronic transmission, the court may direct the clerk or other person to send the information by such electronic transmission. Notice by electronic means is complete on transmission.

(Added Apr. 22, 1993, eff. Aug. 1, 1993; amended Apr. 25, 2005, eff. Dec. 1, 2005.)

NOTES OF ADVISORY COMMITTEE ON RULES—1993

This rule is added to provide flexibility for banks, credit card companies, taxing authorities, and other entities that ordinarily receive notices by mail in a large volume of bankruptcy cases, to arrange to receive by electronic transmission all or part of the information required to be contained in such notices.

The use of electronic technology instead of mail to send information to creditors and interested parties will be more convenient and less costly for the sender and the receiver. For example, a bank that receives by mail, at different locations, notices of meetings of creditors pursuant to Rule 2002(a) in thousands of cases each year may prefer to receive only the vital information ordinarily contained in such notices by electronic transmission to one computer terminal.

The specific means of transmission must be compatible with technology available to the sender and the receiver. Therefore, electronic transmission of notices is permitted only upon request of the entity entitled to receive the notice, specifying the type of electronic transmission, and only if approved by the court.

Electronic transmission pursuant to this rule completes the notice requirements. The creditor or interested party is not thereafter entitled to receive the relevant notice by mail.

COMMITTEE NOTES ON RULES—2005 AMENDMENT

The rule is amended to delete the requirement that the sender of an electronic notice must obtain electronic confirmation that the notice was received. The amendment provides that notice is complete upon transmission. When the rule was first promulgated, confirmation of receipt of electronic notices was commonplace. In the current electronic environment, very few internet service providers offer the confirmation of receipt service. Consequently, compliance with the rule may be impossible, and the rule could discourage the use of electronic noticing.

Confidence in the delivery of email text messages now rivals or exceeds confidence in the delivery of printed materials. Therefore, there is no need for confirmation of receipt of electronic messages just as there is no such requirement for paper notices.

*Changes Made After Publication and Comment* No changes since publication.

## Rule 9037. Privacy Protection For Filings Made with the Court

(a) REDACTED FILINGS. Unless the court orders otherwise, in an electronic or paper filing made with the court that contains an individual's social-security number, taxpayer-identification number, or birth date, the name of an individual, other than the debtor, known to be and identified as a minor, or a financial-account number, a party or nonparty making the filing may include only:

(1) the last four digits of the social-security number and taxpayer-identification number;

(2) the year of the individual's birth;

(3) the minor's initials; and

(4) the last four digits of the financial-account number.

(b) EXEMPTIONS FROM THE REDACTION REQUIREMENT. The redaction requirement does not apply to the following:

(1) a financial-account number that identifies the property allegedly subject to forfeiture in a forfeiture proceeding;

(2) the record of an administrative or agency proceeding unless filed with a proof of claim;

(3) the official record of a state-court proceeding;

(4) the record of a court or tribunal, if that record was not subject to the redaction requirement when originally filed;

(5) a filing covered by subdivision (c) of this rule; and

(6) a filing that is subject to §110 of the Code.

(c) FILINGS MADE UNDER SEAL. The court may order that a filing be made under seal without redaction. The court may later unseal the filing or order the entity that made the filing to file a redacted version for the public record.

(d) PROTECTIVE ORDERS. For cause, the court may by order in a case under the Code:

(1) require redaction of additional information; or

(2) limit or prohibit a nonparty's remote electronic access to a document filed with the court.

(e) OPTION FOR ADDITIONAL UNREDACTED FILING UNDER SEAL. An entity making a redacted filing may also file an unredacted copy under seal. The court must retain the unredacted copy as part of the record.

(f) OPTION FOR FILING A REFERENCE LIST. A filing that contains redacted information may be filed together with a reference list that identifies each item of redacted information and specifies an appropriate identifier that uniquely corresponds to each item listed. The list must be filed under seal and may be amended as of right. Any reference in the case to a listed identifier will be construed to refer to the corresponding item of information.

(g) WAIVER OF PROTECTION OF IDENTIFIERS. An entity waives the protection of subdivision (a) as to the entity's own information by filing it without redaction and not under seal.

(Added Apr. 30, 2007, eff. Dec. 1, 2007.)

COMMITTEE NOTES ON RULES—2007

The rule is adopted in compliance with section 205(c)(3) of the E-Government Act of 2002, Public Law No. 107-347. Section 205(c)(3) requires the Supreme Court to prescribe rules "to protect privacy and security concerns relating to electronic filing of documents and the public availability . . . of documents filed electronically." The rule goes further than the E-Government Act in regulating paper filings even when they are not converted to electronic form, but the number of filings that remain in paper form is certain to diminish over time. Most districts scan paper filings into the electronic case file, where they become available to the public in the same way as documents initially filed in electronic form. It is electronic availability, not the form of the initial filing, that raises the privacy and security concerns addressed in the E-Government Act.

The rule is derived from and implements the policy adopted by the Judicial Conference in September 2001 to address the privacy concerns resulting from public access to electronic case files. *See* http://www.privacy.uscourts.gov/Policy.htm. The Judicial Conference policy is that documents in case files generally should be made available electronically to the same extent they are available at the courthouse, provided that certain "personal data identifiers" are not included in the public file.

While providing for the public filing of some information, such as the last four digits of an account number, the rule does not intend to establish a presumption that this information never could or should be protected. For example, it may well be necessary in individual cases to prevent remote access by nonparties to any part of an account number or social-security number. It may also be necessary to protect information not covered by the redaction requirement—such as driver's license numbers and alien registration numbers—in a particular case. In such cases, protection may be sought under subdivision (c) or (d). Moreover, the rule does not affect the protection available under other rules, such as Rules 16 and 26(c) of the Federal Rules of Civil Procedure, or under other sources of protective authority.

Any personal information not otherwise protected by sealing or redaction will be made available over the internet. Counsel should therefore notify clients of this fact so that an informed decision may be made on what information is to be included in a document filed with the court.

An individual debtor's full social-security number or taxpayer-identification number is included on the notice of the §341 meeting of creditors sent to creditors. Of course, that is not filed with the court, see Rule 1007(f) (the debtor "submits" this information), and the copy of the notice that is filed with the court does not include the full social-security number or taxpayer-identification number. Thus, since the full social-security number or taxpayer-identification number is not filed with the court, it is not available to a person searching that record.

The clerk is not required to review documents filed with the court for compliance with this rule. As subdivision (a) recognizes, the responsibility to redact filings rests with counsel, parties, and others who make filings with the court.

Subdivision (d) recognizes the court's inherent authority to issue a protective order to prevent remote access to private or sensitive information and to require redaction of material in addition to that which would be redacted under subdivision (a) of the rule. These orders may be issued whenever necessary either by the court on its own motion, or on motion of a party in interest.

Subdivision (e) allows an entity that makes a redacted filing to file an unredacted document under seal. This provision is derived from section 205(c)(3)(iv) of the E-Government Act. Subdivision (f) allows the option to file a reference list of redacted information. This provision is derived from section 205(c)(3)(v) of the E-Government Act, as amended in 2004.

In accordance with the E-Government Act, subdivision (f) of the rule refers to "redacted" information. The term "redacted" is intended to govern a filing that is prepared with abbreviated identifiers in the first instance, as well as a filing in which a personal identifier is edited after its preparation.

Subdivision (g) allows an entity to waive the protections of the rule as to that entity's own information by filing it in unredacted form. An entity may elect to waive the protection if, for example, it is determined that the costs of redaction outweigh the benefits to privacy. As to financial account numbers, the instructions to Schedules E and F of Official Form 6 note that the debtor may elect to include the complete account number on those schedules rather than limit the number to the final four digits. Including the complete number would operate as a waiver by the debtor under subdivision (g) as to the full information that the debtor set out on those schedules. The waiver operates only to the extent of the information that the entity filed without redaction. If an entity files an unredacted identifier by mistake, it may seek relief from the court.

Trial exhibits are subject to the redaction requirements of Rule 9037 to the extent they are filed with the court. Trial exhibits that are not initially filed with the court must be redacted in accordance with this rule if and when they are filed as part of an appeal or for other reasons.

*Changes After Publication.* Rule 9037 is intended to parallel as closely as possible Civil Rule 5.2 and Criminal Rule 49.1. The Advisory Committees have worked together to maintain as much consistency as possible in the three versions of the rule. The rule has been revised to implement the several style revisions suggested by the Style Subcommittee of the Standing Committee. Subdivision (b) was reorganized and renumbered. Subdivisions (b)(1) and (b)(3) were added in response to suggestions by the Department of Justice. Subdivision (b)(4), formerly subdivision (b)(2), was amended in response to the suggestion of the Committee on Court Administration and Case Management so that the subdivision now refers to court records that become a part of the record in the pending matter. The term "entity" has been substituted for "person" in subdivision (c) and for "party" in subdivisions (e) and (f) to conform the rule to the definitions provided in the Bankruptcy Code.

## [PART X—UNITED STATES TRUSTEES]
(Abrogated Apr. 30, 1991, eff. Aug. 1, 1991)

## OFFICIAL FORMS

[NOTE: *These official forms should be observed and used with such alterations as may be appropriate to suit the circumstances. See Rule 9009.]*

### INTRODUCTION AND GENERAL INSTRUCTIONS

Rule 9009 of the Federal Rules of Bankruptcy Procedure states that the Official Forms prescribed by the Judicial Conference of the United States "shall be observed and used." The Official Forms, accordingly, are obligatory in character.

Rule 9009 expressly permits the user of the Official Forms to make such "alterations as may be appropriate," and the use of the Official Forms has been held to be subject to a "rule of substantial compliance." Some rules, for example Fed.R.Bankr.P. 3001(a), specifically state that the filed document need only "conform substantially" to the Official Form. A document for which an Official Form is prescribed generally will meet the standard of substantial compliance if the document contains the complete substance, that is, all of the information required by the Official Form.

Rule 9009 also expressly permits the contents of Official Forms to be rearranged, and the format of the Official Forms traditionally has been quite flexible. The forms of the voluntary petition, the schedules, and the statement of financial affairs are printed and sold by private publishers. Design features such as type face, type size, layout, and side and top margins were not prescribed by the Judicial Conference, but rather left to the professional judgment of each publisher.

A great deal of variation, accordingly, has developed. Some publishers also add forms that are not official but which have been drafted by the publisher. A form for a chapter 13 plan, for example, frequently is included with commercially printed packages of forms for filing cases under chapter 13, although there is no Official Form for this purpose. The variety of formats has accelerated since the introduction of computer software for generating the petitions, schedules, and statements of affairs. It is the policy of the Judicial Conference that such diversity is desirable and should be encouraged.

The sheer volume of bankruptcy cases, however, has compelled the Judicial Conference, for the first time, to prescribe the format of certain Official Forms. In particular, the format of Form 1, the Voluntary Petition, now is prescribed. This format is designed to assist the clerk of the bankruptcy court to enter the case in the court's computer database and ensures that all required information is available to both the clerk and the United States trustee at the inception of the case. The rule of substantial compliance continues to apply, however. Accordingly, publishers may vary the size and style of the type and may alter the size and shape of the boxes on the form, within the bounds of that rule.

The Official Forms of the petitions, schedules, and statement of financial affairs, (Forms 1, 5, 6, and 7), are to be printed on one side of the paper only. Each page is to be prepunched with two holes at the top, and sufficient top margin allowed so that neither caption nor text is destroyed or obscured. Compliance with these standards will facilitate both the securing of the papers in the case file and review of the file by the public.

Although Rule 9009 permits alteration, for most of the Official Forms, alteration will be appropriate only in rare circumstances. The special forms for chapter 11 cases, on the other hand, seldom will be used without alterations. Forms 12 through 15, while legally sufficient in any chapter 11 case, are intended by the Judicial Conference, and most often will be used, as a framework for drafting a document specially tailored to the particular case. These alterations generally will take the form of additions to the prescribed elements.

Rule 9009 provides for a balance of prescribed substance, to which full adherence is expected in all but the most unusual cases, and flexible formatting, under which requirements are kept to the minimum necessary for proper operation of the courts and the bankruptcy system. While Rule 9009 recognizes the overall need for flexibility, Rule 9029 makes it clear that the Official Forms must be accepted in every bankruptcy court.

Under Rule 9029, courts may not reject documents presented for filing in novel or unfamiliar formats if those documents contain the substance prescribed by the Official Form and meet the requirements for one-sided printing, pre-punched holes, and adequate top margins. Nor are courts authorized to impose local forms which vary in substance from the Official Forms or reject papers presented for filing on Official Forms on the basis that the proffered documents differ from a locally preferred version.

### SPECIAL INSTRUCTIONS FOR COMPUTER-GENERATED FORMS

In Form 1, the Voluntary Petition, if a box contains multiple choices, a computer-generated petition that shows only the choice made is acceptable for filing. All sections of the petition must be shown and completed, however, unless instructions on the Official Form of the petition state that the box is applicable only to cases filed under a chapter other than the one selected by the debtor. If the debtor has no information to provide for a particular box, for example if the debtor has no prior bankruptcies to report, a computer-generated petition should so indicate by stating "None."

Form 6, the Schedules, on which the debtor reports all of the debtor's assets and liabilities, has been prescribed in a columnar format. Columns help to organize the information which the debtor is required to report and should be used when the printed schedules are completed on a typewriter. In a computerized law office, however, the organizational structure of the schedules can be built into the computer program, and a rigid columnar format may be a hindrance rather than a help.

Schedules generated by computer which provide all of the information requested by the prescribed form are fully acceptable, regardless of the format of the printed page. The information must be appropriately labeled, however. In Schedule B, for example, all of the categories of personal property must be printed on the filed document together with the debtor's response to each. The space occupied by each category may be expanded, however, so that attachments are not needed. Instructions provided on the printed forms can simply be built into the computer program; they need not be reprinted on the filed document.

Form 7, the Statement of Financial Affairs, contains a series of questions which direct the debtor to answer by furnishing information. If the answer to a question is "None," or the question is not applicable, an affirmative statement to that effect is required. To assure that the trustee and the creditors can review the debtor's statement properly, the complete text of each question must be printed on the filed document.

Form 9, the Notice of Filing under the Bankruptcy Code, Meeting of Creditors, and Fixing of Dates, will be prepared by the clerk of the bankruptcy court in most cases. The form is designed for use with automated printing and mailing equipment. Two free lines, which do not appear on the printed blank form, have been programmed into the form. Courts may use this space to add local information, such as directions for obtaining copies of the debtor's schedules.

[Introduction and General Instructions provided by the Advisory Committee on Bankruptcy Rules of the Judicial Conference, June 28, 1990, H. Doc. 102–80, pp. 507, 534, 102d Congress, 1st Session.]

B 1 (Official Form 1) (1/08)

**United States Bankruptcy Court**

**Voluntary Petition**

| | |
|---|---|
| Name of Debtor (if individual, enter Last, First, Middle): | Name of Joint Debtor (Spouse) (Last, First, Middle): |
| All Other Names used by the Debtor in the last 8 years (include married, maiden, and trade names): | All Other Names used by the Joint Debtor in the last 8 years (include married, maiden, and trade names): |
| Last four digits of Soc. Sec. or Indvidual-Taxpayer I.D. (ITIN) No./Complete EIN (if more than one, state all): | Last four digits of Soc. Sec. or Individual-Taxpayer I.D. (ITIN) No./Complete EIN (if more than one, state all): |
| Street Address of Debtor (No. and Street, City, and State): ZIP CODE | Street Address of Joint Debtor (No. and Street, City, and State): ZIP CODE |
| County of Residence or of the Principal Place of Business: | County of Residence or of the Principal Place of Business: |
| Mailing Address of Debtor (if different from street address): ZIP CODE | Mailing Address of Joint Debtor (if different from street address): ZIP CODE |

Location of Principal Assets of Business Debtor (if different from street address above): ZIP CODE

**Type of Debtor**
(Form of Organization)
(Check **one** box.)

☐ Individual (includes Joint Debtors)
*See Exhibit D on page 2 of this form.*
☐ Corporation (includes LLC and LLP)
☐ Partnership
☐ Other (If debtor is not one of the above entities, check this box and state type of entity below.)

**Nature of Business**
(Check **one** box.)

☐ Health Care Business
☐ Single Asset Real Estate as defined in 11 U.S.C. § 101(51B)
☐ Railroad
☐ Stockbroker
☐ Commodity Broker
☐ Clearing Bank
☐ Other

**Tax-Exempt Entity**
(Check box, if applicable.)

☐ Debtor is a tax-exempt organization under Title 26 of the United States Code (the Internal Revenue Code).

**Chapter of Bankruptcy Code Under Which the Petition is Filed** (Check **one** box.)

☐ Chapter 7
☐ Chapter 9
☐ Chapter 11
☐ Chapter 12
☐ Chapter 13
☐ Chapter 15 Petition for Recognition of a Foreign Main Proceeding
☐ Chapter 15 Petition for Recognition of a Foreign Nonmain Proceeding

**Nature of Debts**
(Check one box.)

☐ Debts are primarily consumer debts, defined in 11 U.S.C. § 101(8) as "incurred by an individual primarily for a personal, family, or house-hold purpose."
☐ Debts are primarily business debts.

**Filing Fee** (Check one box.)

☐ Full Filing Fee attached.

☐ Filing Fee to be paid in installments (applicable to individuals only). Must attach signed application for the court's consideration certifying that the debtor is unable to pay fee except in installments. Rule 1006(b). See Official Form 3A.

☐ Filing Fee waiver requested (applicable to chapter 7 individuals only). Must attach signed application for the court's consideration. See Official Form 3B.

**Chapter 11 Debtors**

**Check one box:**
☐ Debtor is a small business debtor as defined in 11 U.S.C. § 101(51D).

☐ Debtor is not a small business debtor as defined in 11 U.S.C. § 101(51D).

**Check if:**
☐ Debtor's aggregate noncontingent liquidated debts (excluding debts owed to insiders or affiliates) are less than $2,190,000.

**Check all applicable boxes:**
☐ A plan is being filed with this petition.
☐ Acceptances of the plan were solicited prepetition from one or more classes of creditors, in accordance with 11 U.S.C. § 1126(b).

**Statistical/Administrative Information**

**THIS SPACE IS FOR COURT USE ONLY**

☐ Debtor estimates that funds will be available for distribution to unsecured creditors.
☐ Debtor estimates that, after any exempt property is excluded and administrative expenses paid, there will be no funds available for distribution to unsecured creditors.

Estimated Number of Creditors

| ☐ | ☐ | ☐ | ☐ | ☐ | ☐ | ☐ | ☐ | ☐ | ☐ |
|---|---|---|---|---|---|---|---|---|---|
| 1-49 | 50-99 | 100-199 | 200-999 | 1,000-5,000 | 5,001-10,000 | 10,001-25,000 | 25,001-50,000 | 50,001-100,000 | Over 100,000 |

Estimated Assets

| ☐ | ☐ | ☐ | ☐ | ☐ | ☐ | ☐ | ☐ | ☐ | ☐ |
|---|---|---|---|---|---|---|---|---|---|
| $0 to $50,000 | $50,001 to $100,000 | $100,001 to $500,000 | $500,001 to $1 million | $1,000,001 to $10 million | $10,000,001 to $50 million | $50,000,001 to $100 million | $100,000,001 to $500 million | $500,000,001 to $1 billion | More than $1 billion |

Estimated Liabilities

| ☐ | ☐ | ☐ | ☐ | ☐ | ☐ | ☐ | ☐ | ☐ | ☐ |
|---|---|---|---|---|---|---|---|---|---|
| $0 to $50,000 | $50,001 to $100,000 | $100,001 to $500,000 | $500,001 to $1 million | $1,000,001 to $10 million | $10,000,001 to $50 million | $50,000,001 to $100 million | $100,000,001 to $500 million | $500,000,001 to $1 billion | More than $1 billion |

B 1 (Official Form 1) (1/08) Page 2

| **Voluntary Petition**<br>*(This page must be completed and filed in every case.)* | Name of Debtor(s): | |
|---|---|---|
| **All Prior Bankruptcy Cases Filed Within Last 8 Years** (If more than two, attach additional sheet.) | | |
| Location Where Filed: | Case Number: | Date Filed: |
| Location Where Filed: | Case Number: | Date Filed: |
| **Pending Bankruptcy Case Filed by any Spouse, Partner, or Affiliate of this Debtor** (If more than one, attach additional sheet.) | | |
| Name of Debtor: | Case Number: | Date Filed: |
| District: | Relationship: | Judge: |

**Exhibit A**

(To be completed if debtor is required to file periodic reports (e.g., forms 10K and 10Q) with the Securities and Exchange Commission pursuant to Section 13 or 15(d) of the Securities Exchange Act of 1934 and is requesting relief under chapter 11.)

☐ Exhibit A is attached and made a part of this petition.

**Exhibit B**

(To be completed if debtor is an individual whose debts are primarily consumer debts.)

I, the attorney for the petitioner named in the foregoing petition, declare that I have informed the petitioner that [he or she] may proceed under chapter 7, 11, 12, or 13 of title 11, United States Code, and have explained the relief available under each such chapter. I further certify that I have delivered to the debtor the notice required by 11 U.S.C. § 342(b).

X ______________________________

Signature of Attorney for Debtor(s) (Date)

**Exhibit C**

Does the debtor own or have possession of any property that poses or is alleged to pose a threat of imminent and identifiable harm to public health or safety?

☐ Yes, and Exhibit C is attached and made a part of this petition.

☐ No.

**Exhibit D**

(To be completed by every individual debtor. If a joint petition is filed, each spouse must complete and attach a separate Exhibit D.)

☐ Exhibit D completed and signed by the debtor is attached and made a part of this petition.

If this is a joint petition:

☐ Exhibit D also completed and signed by the joint debtor is attached and made a part of this petition.

**Information Regarding the Debtor - Venue**

(Check any applicable box.)

☐ Debtor has been domiciled or has had a residence, principal place of business, or principal assets in this District for 180 days immediately preceding the date of this petition or for a longer part of such 180 days than in any other District.

☐ There is a bankruptcy case concerning debtor's affiliate, general partner, or partnership pending in this District.

☐ Debtor is a debtor in a foreign proceeding and has its principal place of business or principal assets in the United States in this District, or has no principal place of business or assets in the United States but is a defendant in an action or proceeding [in a federal or state court] in this District, or the interests of the parties will be served in regard to the relief sought in this District.

**Certification by a Debtor Who Resides as a Tenant of Residential Property**

(Check all applicable boxes.)

☐ Landlord has a judgment against the debtor for possession of debtor's residence. (If box checked, complete the following.)

______________________________

(Name of landlord that obtained judgment)

______________________________

(Address of landlord)

☐ Debtor claims that under applicable nonbankruptcy law, there are circumstances under which the debtor would be permitted to cure the entire monetary default that gave rise to the judgment for possession, after the judgment for possession was entered, and

☐ Debtor has included with this petition the deposit with the court of any rent that would become due during the 30-day period after the filing of the petition.

☐ Debtor certifies that he/she has served the Landlord with this certification. (11 U.S.C. § 362(l)).

B 1 (Official Form) 1 (1/08) **Page 3**

| **Voluntary Petition**<br>*(This page must be completed and filed in every case.)* | Name of Debtor(s): |
|---|---|

**Signatures**

**Signature(s) of Debtor(s) (Individual/Joint)**

I declare under penalty of perjury that the information provided in this petition is true and correct.

[If petitioner is an individual whose debts are primarily consumer debts and has chosen to file under chapter 7] I am aware that I may proceed under chapter 7, 11, 12 or 13 of title 11, United States Code, understand the relief available under each such chapter, and choose to proceed under chapter 7.

[If no attorney represents me and no bankruptcy petition preparer signs the petition] I have obtained and read the notice required by 11 U.S.C. § 342(b).

I request relief in accordance with the chapter of title 11, United States Code, specified in this petition.

X ______________________________

Signature of Debtor

X ______________________________

Signature of Joint Debtor

______________________________

Telephone Number (if not represented by attorney)

______________________________

Date

**Signature of a Foreign Representative**

I declare under penalty of perjury that the information provided in this petition is true and correct, that I am the foreign representative of a debtor in a foreign proceeding, and that I am authorized to file this petition.

(Check only **one** box.)

☐ I request relief in accordance with chapter 15 of title 11, United States Code. Certified copies of the documents required by 11 U.S.C. § 1515 are attached.

☐ Pursuant to 11 U.S.C. § 1511, I request relief in accordance with the chapter of title 11 specified in this petition. A certified copy of the order granting recognition of the foreign main proceeding is attached.

X ______________________________

(Signature of Foreign Representative)

______________________________

(Printed Name of Foreign Representative)

______________________________

Date

**Signature of Attorney***

X ______________________________

Signature of Attorney for Debtor(s)

______________________________

Printed Name of Attorney for Debtor(s)

______________________________

Firm Name

______________________________

Address

______________________________

______________________________

______________________________

Telephone Number

______________________________

Date

*In a case in which § 707(b)(4)(D) applies, this signature also constitutes a certification that the attorney has no knowledge after an inquiry that the information in the schedules is incorrect.

**Signature of Debtor (Corporation/Partnership)**

I declare under penalty of perjury that the information provided in this petition is true and correct, and that I have been authorized to file this petition on behalf of the debtor.

The debtor requests the relief in accordance with the chapter of title 11, United States Code, specified in this petition.

X ______________________________

Signature of Authorized Individual

______________________________

Printed Name of Authorized Individual

______________________________

Title of Authorized Individual

______________________________

Date

**Signature of Non-Attorney Bankruptcy Petition Preparer**

I declare under penalty of perjury that: (1) I am a bankruptcy petition preparer as defined in 11 U.S.C. § 110; (2) I prepared this document for compensation and have provided the debtor with a copy of this document and the notices and information required under 11 U.S.C. §§ 110(b), 110(h), and 342(b); and, (3) if rules or guidelines have been promulgated pursuant to 11 U.S.C. § 110(h) setting a maximum fee for services chargeable by bankruptcy petition preparers, I have given the debtor notice of the maximum amount before preparing any document for filing for a debtor or accepting any fee from the debtor, as required in that section. Official Form 19 is attached.

______________________________

Printed Name and title, if any, of Bankruptcy Petition Preparer

______________________________

Social-Security number (If the bankruptcy petition preparer is not an individual, state the Social-Security number of the officer, principal, responsible person or partner of the bankruptcy petition preparer.) (Required by 11 U.S.C. § 110.)

______________________________

Address

______________________________

X ______________________________

______________________________

Date

Signature of bankruptcy petition preparer or officer, principal, responsible person, or partner whose Social-Security number is provided above.

Names and Social-Security numbers of all other individuals who prepared or assisted in preparing this document unless the bankruptcy petition preparer is not an individual.

If more than one person prepared this document, attach additional sheets conforming to the appropriate official form for each person.

*A bankruptcy petition preparer's failure to comply with the provisions of title 11 and the Federal Rules of Bankruptcy Procedure may result in fines or imprisonment or both. 11 U.S.C. § 110; 18 U.S.C. § 156.*

B 1A (Official Form 1, Exhibit A) (9/97)

*[If debtor is required to file periodic reports (e.g., forms 10K and 10Q) with the Securities and Exchange Commission pursuant to Section 13 or 15(d) of the Securities Exchange Act of 1934 and is requesting relief under chapter 11 of the Bankruptcy Code, this Exhibit "A" shall be completed and attached to the petition.]*

# UNITED STATES BANKRUPTCY COURT

In re ______________________, ) Case No. __________

Debtor )

)

) Chapter 11

## EXHIBIT "A" TO VOLUNTARY PETITION

1. If any of the debtor's securities are registered under Section 12 of the Securities Exchange Act of 1934, the SEC file number is ______________.

2. The following financial data is the latest available information and refers to the debtor's condition on ______________.

a. Total assets $ __________

b. Total debts (including debts listed in 2.c., below) $ __________

c. Debt securities held by more than 500 holders:

| | | | | Approximate number of holders: |
|---|---|---|---|---|
| secured ☐ | unsecured ☐ | subordinated ☐ | $ __________ | __________ |
| secured ☐ | unsecured ☐ | subordinated ☐ | $ __________ | __________ |
| secured ☐ | unsecured ☐ | subordinated ☐ | $ __________ | __________ |
| secured ☐ | unsecured ☐ | subordinated ☐ | $ __________ | __________ |
| secured ☐ | unsecured ☐ | subordinated ☐ | $ __________ | __________ |

d. Number of shares of preferred stock __________ __________

e. Number of shares common stock __________ __________

Comments, if any:

3. Brief description of debtor's business:

4. List the names of any person who directly or indirectly owns, controls, or holds, with power to vote, 5% or more of the voting securities of debtor: ______________________________

B 1C (Official Form 1, Exhibit C) (9/01)

*[If, to the best of the debtor's knowledge, the debtor owns or has possession of property that poses or is alleged to pose a threat of imminent and identifiable harm to the public health or safety, attach this Exhibit "C" to the petition.]*

# UNITED STATES BANKRUPTCY COURT

| | | |
|---|---|---|
| In re ______________________________, | ) | Case No. ____________ |
| Debtor | ) | |
| | ) | |
| | ) | Chapter ____________ |

## EXHIBIT "C" TO VOLUNTARY PETITION

1. Identify and briefly describe all real or personal property owned by or in possession of the debtor that, to the best of the debtor's knowledge, poses or is alleged to pose a threat of imminent and identifiable harm to the public health or safety (attach additional sheets if necessary):

2. With respect to each parcel of real property or item of personal property identified in question 1, describe the nature and location of the dangerous condition, whether environmental or otherwise, that poses or is alleged to pose a threat of imminent and identifiable harm to the public health or safety (attach additional sheets if necessary):

B 1D (Official Form 1, Exhibit D) (12/09)

# UNITED STATES BANKRUPTCY COURT

__________ District of __________

In re ______________________________ Case No. ____________
Debtor (if known)

## EXHIBIT D - INDIVIDUAL DEBTOR'S STATEMENT OF COMPLIANCE WITH CREDIT COUNSELING REQUIREMENT

**Warning: You must be able to check truthfully one of the five statements regarding credit counseling listed below. If you cannot do so, you are not eligible to file a bankruptcy case, and the court can dismiss any case you do file. If that happens, you will lose whatever filing fee you paid, and your creditors will be able to resume collection activities against you. If your case is dismissed and you file another bankruptcy case later, you may be required to pay a second filing fee and you may have to take extra steps to stop creditors' collection activities.**

*Every individual debtor must file this Exhibit D. If a joint petition is filed, each spouse must complete and file a separate Exhibit D. Check one of the five statements below and attach any documents as directed.*

❒ 1. Within the 180 days **before the filing of my bankruptcy case,** I received a briefing from a credit counseling agency approved by the United States trustee or bankruptcy administrator that outlined the opportunities for available credit counseling and assisted me in performing a related budget analysis, and I have a certificate from the agency describing the services provided to me. *Attach a copy of the certificate and a copy of any debt repayment plan developed through the agency.*

❒ 2. Within the 180 days **before the filing of my bankruptcy case,** I received a briefing from a credit counseling agency approved by the United States trustee or bankruptcy administrator that outlined the opportunities for available credit counseling and assisted me in performing a related budget analysis, but I do not have a certificate from the agency describing the services provided to me. *You must file a copy of a certificate from the agency describing the services provided to you and a copy of any debt repayment plan developed through the agency no later than 14 days after your bankruptcy case is filed.*

❒ 3. I certify that I requested credit counseling services from an approved agency but was unable to obtain the services during the seven days from the time I made my request, and the following exigent circumstances merit a temporary waiver of the credit counseling requirement so I can file my bankruptcy case now. *[Summarize exigent circumstances here.]*

____________________________________________________________

____________________________________________________________

____________________________________________________________

____________________________________________________________

**If your certification is satisfactory to the court, you must still obtain the credit counseling briefing within the first 30 days after you file your bankruptcy petition and promptly file a certificate from the agency that provided the counseling, together with a copy of any debt management plan developed through the agency. Failure to fulfill these requirements may result in dismissal of your case. Any extension of the 30-day deadline can be granted only for cause and is limited to a maximum of 15 days. Your case may also be dismissed if the court is not satisfied with your reasons for filing your bankruptcy case without first receiving a credit counseling briefing.**

❒ 4. I am not required to receive a credit counseling briefing because of: *[Check the applicable statement.] [Must be accompanied by a motion for determination by the court.]*

❒ Incapacity. (Defined in 11 U.S.C. § 109(h)(4) as impaired by reason of mental illness or mental deficiency so as to be incapable of realizing and making rational decisions with respect to financial responsibilities.);

❒ Disability. (Defined in 11 U.S.C. § 109(h)(4) as physically impaired to the extent of being unable, after reasonable effort, to participate in a credit counseling briefing in person, by telephone, or through the Internet.);

❒ Active military duty in a military combat zone.

❒ 5. The United States trustee or bankruptcy administrator has determined that the credit counseling requirement of 11 U.S.C. § 109(h) does not apply in this district.

**I certify under penalty of perjury that the information provided above is true and correct.**

Signature of Debtor: ________________________

Date: ________________

(Added Aug. 1, 1991; amended Mar. 16, 1993; Mar. 14, 1995; Oct. 1, 1997; Dec. 1, 2001; Dec. 1, 2002; Dec. 1, 2003; Oct. 17, 2005; Oct. 1, 2006; Dec. 1, 2007; Jan. 1, 2008; Dec. 1, 2008; Dec. 1, 2009.)

NOTES OF ADVISORY COMMITTEE ON RULES—1991

Form 1, the Voluntary Petition, is to be used to commence a voluntary case under chapter 7, 11, 12, or 13 of the Bankruptcy Code. A chapter 9 petition requires other allegations, (see §109(c) of the Code), but this form may be adapted for such use. The form also may be adapted for use in filing a petition ancillary to a foreign proceeding under §304 of the Code.

The form departs from the traditional format of a captioned pleading. All of the elements of the caption prescribed in Rule 1005 have been retained. Their placement on the page, however, has been changed to make the form compatible with electronic data processing by the clerk. The form of the caption of the case for use in other documents, formerly incorporated in Official Form No. 1, has been made a separate Form 16A.

All names used by the debtor, including trade names, names used in doing business, married names, and maiden names should be furnished in the spaces provided. If there is not sufficient room for all such names on the form itself, the list should be continued on an additional sheet attached to the petition. A complete list will enable creditors to identify the debtor properly when they receive notices and orders.

Redesign of this form into a box format also is intended to provide the court, the United States trustee, and other interested parties with as much information as possible during the 15-day period provided by Rule 1007(c), when schedules and statements may not have been filed. The box format separates into categories the data provided by the debtor, and enables the form to be used by all voluntary debtors in all chapters.

For the first time, the form requires both a street address and any separate mailing address, as well as any separate addresses used by a joint debtor. Disclosure of prior bankruptcies is new to the petition but formerly was required in the statement of financial affairs; its inclusion in the petition is intended to alert the trustee to cases in which an objection to discharge pursuant to §727(a)(8) or (a)(9) or a motion to dismiss under §109(g) may be appropriate. The information about pending related cases, also new to the petition, signals the clerk to assign the case to the judge to whom any related case has been assigned.

Rule 1008 requires all petitions to be verified or contain an unsworn declaration as provided in 28 U.S.C. §1746. The unsworn declaration on page two of the petition conforms with 28 U.S.C. §1746, which permits the declaration to be made in the manner indicated with the same force and effect as a sworn statement. The form may be adapted for use outside the United States by adding the words "under the laws of the United States" after the word "perjury."

Exhibit "A," to be attached to the petition of a corporate debtor, is for the purpose of supplying the Securities and Exchange Commission with information it needs at the beginning stages of a chapter 11 case in order to determine how actively to monitor the proceedings. Exhibit "B" was added by §322 of Pub. L. No. 98-353, the Bankruptcy Amendments and Federal Judgeship Act of 1984. The references to chapters 11 and 12 of the Code found in Exhibit "B" and its related allegations were added by §283(aa) of the 1986 amendments, (Pub. L. No. 99-554). This exhibit has been included in the form of the petition.

The form effects a merger of the petition and the bankruptcy cover sheet to assist the clerk in providing the statistical information required by the Director of the Administrative Office of the United States Courts pursuant to the Congressional reporting mandates of 28 U.S.C. §604. The Director is authorized to change the particulars of the statistical portion of the form as needed in the performance of these statutory duties.

NOTES OF ADVISORY COMMITTEE ON RULES—1993 AMENDMENT

The form has been amended to require a debtor not represented by an attorney to provide a telephone number so that court personnel, the trustee, other parties in the case, and their attorneys can contact the debtor concerning matters in the case.

NOTES OF ADVISORY COMMITTEE ON RULES—1995 AMENDMENT

The form is amended to provide space for signing by a "bankruptcy petition preparer," as required under section 110 of the Code, which was added by the Bankruptcy Reform Act of 1994. In addition to signing, a bankruptcy petition preparer is required by section 110 to disclose the information requested. All signatories of Form 1 are requested to provide the clerk's office with a telephone number.

A chapter 11 debtor that qualifies as a "small business" under section 101 of the Code, as amended by the 1994 Act, may elect special, expedited treatment under amendments made to chapter 11 by the 1994 Act. The court may order that a creditors committee not be appointed in a small business case. Accordingly, the first page of the petition is amended to require a small business filing under chapter 11 to identify itself. The petition also is amended to offer a small business chapter 11 debtor an opportunity to exercise its right to elect to be considered a small business at the commencement of the case.

Several clarifying and technical amendments also have been made to indicate that a debtor is to check only one box with respect to "Type of Debtor" and "Nature of Debt," to clarify the intent that the individual signing on behalf of a corporation or partnership is authorized to file the petition, and to require a debtor to represent that it is eligible for relief under the chapter of title 11 specified in the petition.

NOTES OF ADVISORY COMMITTEE ON RULES—1997 AMENDMENT

The form has been substantially amended to simplify its format and make the form easier to complete correctly. The Latin phrase "In re" has been deleted as unnecessary. The amount of information requested in the boxes labeled "Type of Debtor" and "Nature of Debt" has been reduced, and the reporting by a corporation of whether it is a publicly held entity has been moved to Exhibit "A" of the petition. The box labeled "Representation by Attorney" has been deleted; the information it contained is requested in the signature boxes on the second page of the form.

In the statistical information section, the labels on the ranges of estimated assets and liabilities have been rewritten to improve the accuracy of reporting. The asset/liability range of $10 million to $100 million has been divided into two categories to promote better statistical reporting of business cases. Requests for information in chapter 11 and chapter 12 cases concerning the number of the debtor's employees and equity security holders have been deleted.

The second page of the form has been simplified so that a debtor need only sign the petition once. The request for information concerning the filing of a plan has been deleted.

Exhibit "A" has been simplified. In addition, the category of chapter 11 debtors required to file Exhibit "A" is modified to include a corporation, partnership, or other entity, but only if the debtor has issued publicly-traded equity securities or debt instruments. Most small corporations will not be required to file Exhibit "A."

COMMITTEE NOTES ON RULES—2001 AMENDMENT

The form has been amended to require the debtor to disclose whether the debtor owns or has possession of any property that poses or is alleged to pose a threat of imminent and identifiable harm to public health or safety. If any such property exists, the debtor must complete and attach Exhibit "C" describing the property, its location, and the potential danger it poses. Exhibit "C" will alert the United States trustee and any person selected as trustee that immediate precautionary action may be necessary.

COMMITTEE NOTES ON RULES—2002 AMENDMENT

The form has been amended to provide a checkbox for designating a clearing bank case filed under subchapter V of chapter 7 of the Code enacted by §112 of Pub. L. No. 106-554 (December 21, 2000).

COMMITTEE NOTES ON RULES—2003 AMENDMENT

The form is amended to require the debtor to disclose only the last four digits of the debtor's social security number to afford greater privacy to the individual debtor, whose bankruptcy case records may be available on the Internet. Pursuant to §110(c) of the Bankruptcy Code, the certification by a non-attorney bankruptcy petition preparer requires a petition preparer to provide the full social security number of the individual who actually prepares the document.

COMMITTEE NOTES ON RULES—2005 AMENDMENT

The form is amended to implement amendments to the Bankruptcy Code contained in the Bankruptcy Abuse Prevention and Consumer Protection Act of 2005, Pub. L. No. 109–8, 119 Stat. 23 (April 20, 2005). The period for which the debtor must provide all names used and information about any prior bankruptcy cases is now eight years to match the required time between the granting of discharges to the same debtor in §727(a)(8) of the Code as amended in 2005. The box indicating the debtor's selection of a chapter under which to file the case has been amended to delete "Sec. 304 - Case ancillary to foreign proceeding" and replace it with "Chapter 15 Petition for Recognition of a Foreign Main Proceeding" and "Chapter 15 Petition for Recognition of a Foreign Nonmain Proceeding" reflecting the 2005 repeal of §304 and enactment of chapter 15 of the Code. A statement of venue to be used in a chapter 15 case also has been added.

The section of the form labeled "Type of Debtor" has been revised and subtitled "Form of Organization." This section is revised to make it clear that a limited liability corporation ("LLC") and limited liability partnership ("LLP") should identify itself as a "corporation." A new section titled "Nature of Business" has been created that includes both existing check boxes that identify certain types of debtors for which the Bankruptcy Code provides special treatment, such as stockbrokers and railroads, and a new checkbox for a "health care business" for which the 2005 amendments to the Code include specific requirements. This section of the form also contains checkboxes for single asset real estate debtors and nonprofit organizations which will be used by trustees and creditors and by the Director of the Administrative Office of the United States Courts in preparing statistical reports and analyses. The statistical section of the form also is amended to provide more detail concerning the number of creditors in a case. A check box also has been added for a debtor to indicate that the debtor is applying for a waiver of the filing fee, to implement the 2005 enactment of 28 U.S.C. §1930(f) authorizing the bankruptcy court to waive the filing fee in certain circumstances.

Although the 2005 Act eliminated an eligible debtor's option to elect to be treated as a "small business" in a chapter 11 case, new provisions for such debtors added to the Code in 2005 make it desirable to identify eligible debtors at the outset of the case. Accordingly, the section of the form labeled "Chapter 11 Small Business" has been revised and renamed "Chapter 11 Debtors" for this purpose. Chapter 11 debtors that meet the definition of "small business debtor" in §101 of the Code are directed to identify themselves in this section of the form. In addition, chapter 11 debtors whose aggregate noncontingent debts owed to non-insiders or affiliates are less than $2 million are directed to identify themselves in this section.

A space is provided for individuals to certify that they have received budget and credit counseling prior to filing, as required by §109(h) which was added to the Code in 2005, or to request a waiver of the requirement. Space also is provided for a debtor who is a tenant of residential real property to state whether the debtor's landlord has a judgment against the debtor for possession of the premises, whether under applicable nonbankruptcy law the debtor would be permitted to cure the monetary default, and whether the debtor has made the appropriate deposit with the court. This addition to the form implements §362(l) which was added to the Code in 2005.

The signature sections and the declaration under penalty of perjury by an individual debtor concerning the notice received about bankruptcy relief, the declaration under penalty of perjury by a bankruptcy petition preparer, and the declaration and certification by an attorney all are amended to include new material mandated by the 2005 Act. A signature section also is provided for a representative of a foreign proceeding.

COMMITTEE NOTES ON RULES—2006 AMENDMENT

Page one of the form is amended in several ways to assist the courts in evaluating their workload and fulfilling the statistical reporting requirements of 28 U.S.C. §159. Section 159 was enacted as part of the Bankruptcy Abuse Prevention and Consumer Protection Act of 2005 (BAPCPA), Pub. L. No. 109–8 and takes effect October 17, 2006. Accordingly, in the section of the form labeled "Nature of Business," the instruction is amended to specify that only one box should be checked and only if the debtor is any of the entities listed. The "nonprofit" choice is separated into a discrete section and the language amended to the more precise "tax-exempt."

In addition, the section labeled "Type of Debtor" is amended to include, below the checkbox for "Individual or Joint," a direction to "See Exhibit D on page 2 of this form." Exhibit D replaces the certification concerning prepetition credit counseling and is described below. The section labeled "Nature of Debts" is amended to state the statutory definition of a "consumer debt" and to modify both the consumer and business categories by adding the word "primarily" to both make it clearer to individual debtors that "business" may be the more appropriate choice if personal debts have been incurred to finance a business venture.

In the section labeled "Chapter 11 Debtors," the language concerning whether the debtor owes less than $2 million is re-styled for clarity. This section also is augmented to provide the court with notice when a case if [sic] filed as a "pre-packaged" chapter 11 reorganization case. Two checkboxes are offered, using language adapted from §1126(b) of the Code. Lastly, the information requested concerning estimated assets and liabilities is abbreviated, with the number of ranges reduced and the scope of each range amended. Statistical reports now will be derived from actual dollar amounts of assets and liabilities as shown on the debtor's schedules. The information on the petition, accordingly, is for case management and public information purposes only.

Exhibit D replaces the section formerly labeled "Certification Concerning Debt Counseling by Individual/Joint Debtor(s)." Early cases decided under the 2005 amendments to the Bankruptcy Code indicate that individual debtors may not be aware of the requirement to obtain prepetition credit counseling, the few and very narrow exceptions to that requirement, or the potentially dire consequences to their efforts to obtain bankruptcy relief if they fail to complete the requirement. Accordingly, page 2 of the petition instructs individual debtors to attach a completed Exhibit D and makes it clear that each spouse in a joint case must complete and attach a separate Exhibit D. Exhibit D itself includes a warning about the requirement to obtain counseling and the consequences of failing to fulfill this requirement. It further provides checkboxes and instructions concerning the additional documents that are required in particular circumstances, in order to minimize the number of cases which the court must dismiss for ineligibility.

COMMITTEE NOTES ON RULES—2005–2007 AMENDMENT

[The 2005–2007 Committee Note incorporates Committee Notes previously published in 2005 and 2006.]

The form is amended to implement amendments to the Bankruptcy Code contained in the Bankruptcy Abuse Prevention and Consumer Protection Act of 2005, Pub. L. No. 109–8, 119 Stat. 23 (April 20, 2005) ("BAPCPA"). The period for which the debtor must provide all names used and information about any prior bankruptcy cases is now eight years to match the required time between the granting of discharges to the same debtor in §727(a)(8) of the Code as amended in 2005. In conformity with Rule 9037, the debtor is directed to provide only the last four digits of any individual's tax-identification number.

The box indicating the debtor's selection of a chapter under which to file the case is amended to delete "Sec. 304—Case ancillary to foreign proceeding" and replace it with "Chapter 15 Petition for Recognition of a Foreign Main Proceeding" and "Chapter 15 Petition for Recognition of a Foreign Nonmain Proceeding" reflecting the 2005 repeal of §304 and enactment of chapter 15 of the Code. A statement of venue to be used in a chapter 15 case also is added on page 2 of the form.

The section labeled "Type of Debtor" is amended to include, below the checkbox for "Individual or Joint," a direction to "See Exhibit D on page 2 of this form." This addition alerts individual debtors that Exhibit D on page 2 of the form applies to them. Exhibit D, more fully described below, addresses the prepetition credit counseling requirements added to the Code by BAPCPA. The subtitle, "Form of Organization," is added, and this section also is revised to make clear that a limited liability corporation ("LLC") or limited liability partnership ("LLP") should identify itself as a "corporation."

The form also is amended in several ways to assist the courts in evaluating their workload and fulfilling the statistical reporting requirements of 28 U.S.C. §159, enacted as part of BAPCPA. Accordingly, a new section of the form labeled "Nature of Business," is added that contains both existing checkboxes that identify certain types of debtors for which the Bankruptcy Code provides special treatment, such as stockbrokers and railroads, and a new checkbox for a "health care business" for which the 2005 amendments to the Code include specific requirements. This section of the form also contains a checkbox for single asset real estate debtors, so they can be identified at the time of filing. All other businesses will mark the checkbox labeled "Other." Another new section titled "Tax-Exempt Entity" contains a checkbox to be used by qualified organizations. The Judicial Conference of the United States and the Administrative Office of the United States Courts will use this information in preparing statistical reports and analyses for Congress.

A checkbox also is added for an individual debtor to indicate that the debtor is applying for a waiver of the filing fee, to implement the 2005 enactment of 28 U.S.C. §1930(f) authorizing the bankruptcy court to waive the filing fee in certain circumstances. The description directs the debtor to the Official Form for the application that must be filed for the court's consideration.

The section labeled "Nature of Debts" is amended to state the statutory definition of a "consumer debt" and to modify both the consumer and business categories by adding the word "primarily" to both choices to make it clearer to individual debtors that "business" may be the appropriate choice if personal debts have been incurred to finance a business venture.

Although the 2005 Act eliminated from the Code any option to elect to be treated as a "small business" in a chapter 11 case, new provisions for "small business" debtors added by BAPCPA make it desirable to identify eligible debtors at the outset of the case. Accordingly, the section of the form labeled "Chapter 11 Small Business" is revised and renamed "Chapter 11 Debtors" for this purpose. Chapter 11 debtors that meet the definition of "small business debtor" in §101 of the Code are directed to identify themselves in this section of the form. Chapter 11 debtors whose aggregate noncontingent debts owed to non-insiders or affiliates are less than $2,190,000 are directed to identify themselves in this section. A third part of this section attempts to identify chapter 11 cases that are filed as pre-packaged cases, using criteria taken from §1126(b) of the Code. Identifying "pre-packs" at filing will assist judges and court staff to manage these cases appropriately.

The statistical information concerning the number of creditors and estimated assets and liabilities is revised to provide more detail.

BAPCPA also added a new §109(h) to the Code. To implement this provision, a section labeled "Exhibit D" is inserted on page 2 of the form, and a separate Exhibit D is added. These additions will enable individual debtors to certify that they have received budget and credit counseling prior to filing, as required by §109(h), or request a temporary waiver of, or exemption from, the requirement, if they meet the statutory requirements for such relief. Exhibit D includes directions to attach required documentation or, if the debtor requests a temporary waiver or an exemption, a motion for a determination by the court. Exhibit D also states the requirement that all individual debtors must obtain a briefing from an approved credit counseling agency before filing a bankruptcy case, unless one of the very limited exceptions applies, and further states the consequences that may be faced by any debtor who fails to comply.

Space is provided on page 2 for a debtor who is a tenant of residential real property to certify whether the debtor's landlord has a judgment against the debtor for possession of the premises, whether under applicable nonbankruptcy law the debtor would be permitted to cure the monetary default, and whether the debtor has made the appropriate deposit with the court. This addition to the form implements §362(l) which was added to the Code in 2005. And a box is provided that allows the debtor to certify that s/he has served the landlord with the certification as required by §362(l)(1).

The signature sections and the declaration under penalty of perjury by an individual debtor concerning the notice received about bankruptcy relief, the declaration under penalty of perjury by a bankruptcy petition preparer, and the attorney signature box are amended to include new material mandated by the 2005 Act. The attorney signature box is also amended to remind the attorney that in a case in which §707(b)(4)(D) applies, that the signature constitutes a certification that the attorney has no knowledge after an inquiry that the information in the schedules filed with the petition is incorrect. A signature section is also provided for a representative of a foreign proceeding.

COMMITTEE NOTES ON RULES—2008 AMENDMENT

Paragraph 3 of Exhibit D is amended to delete any reference to a requirement that a debtor file a motion with the court to obtain an order approving a request for the postponement of the debtor's obligation to obtain a credit counseling briefing prior to the commencement of the case. The paragraph immediately following numbered paragraph 3 is also amended to reflect the deletion of the need for a separate motion beyond the completion of the certification itself. That paragraph continues to warn the debtor that the case may be dismissed if the court does not find that a postponement is warranted. It also advises the debtor that, even if the court concludes that postponement of the obligation is appropriate, the debtor still must complete the briefing within the time allowed under the Code.

Official Form 2
6/90

# DECLARATION UNDER PENALTY OF PERJURY ON BEHALF OF A CORPORATION OR PARTNERSHIP

I, [the president *or* other officer *or* an authorized agent of the corporation] [*or* a member *or* an authorized agent of the partnership] named as the debtor in this case, declare under penalty of perjury that I have read the foregoing [list *or* schedule *or* amendment *or* other document (describe)] and that it is true and correct to the best of my information and belief.

Date ______________________

Signature ______________________

______________________
(Print Name and Title)

(Added Aug. 1, 1991.)

NOTES OF ADVISORY COMMITTEE ON RULES—1991

This form is derived from former Official Form No. 4. Rule 1008 requires that all petitions, lists, schedules, statements, and amendments thereto be verified or contain an unsworn declaration conforming with 28 U.S.C. §1746. This form or adaptations of the form have been incorporated into the official forms of the petitions, schedules, and statement of financial affairs. See Official Forms 1, 5, 6, and 7. The form has been amended for use in connection with other papers required by these rules to be verified or contain an unsworn declaration.

B 3A (Official Form 3A) (12/07)

# UNITED STATES BANKRUPTCY COURT

In re ______________________________,
Debtor

Case No. ______________

Chapter __________

## APPLICATION TO PAY FILING FEE IN INSTALLMENTS

1. In accordance with Fed. R. Bankr. P. 1006, I apply for permission to pay the filing fee amounting to $__________ in installments.

2. I am unable to pay the filing fee except in installments.

3. Until the filing fee is paid in full, I will not make any additional payment or transfer any additional property to an attorney or any other person for services in connection with this case.

4. I propose the following terms for the payment of the Filing Fee.*

$ ______________ Check one ☐ With the filing of the petition, or ☐ On or before __________

$ ______________ on or before ______________________

$ ______________ on or before ______________________

$ ______________ on or before ______________________

* The number of installments proposed shall not exceed four (4), and the final installment shall be payable not later than 120 days after filing the petition. For cause shown, the court may extend the time of any installment, provided the last installment is paid not later than 180 days after filing the petition. Fed. R. Bankr. P. 1006(b)(2).

5. I understand that if I fail to pay any installment when due, my bankruptcy case may be dismissed and I may not receive a discharge of my debts.

______________________________
Signature of Attorney Date

______________________________
Name of Attorney

______________________________
Signature of Debtor Date
(In a joint case, both spouses must sign.)

______________________________
Signature of Joint Debtor (if any) Date

---

**DECLARATION AND SIGNATURE OF NON-ATTORNEY BANKRUPTCY PETITION PREPARER (See 11 U.S.C. § 110)**

I declare under penalty of perjury that: (1) I am a bankruptcy petition preparer as defined in 11 U.S.C. § 110; (2) I prepared this document for compensation and have provided the debtor with a copy of this document and the notices and information required under 11 U.S.C. §§ 110(b), 110(h), and 342(b); (3) if rules or guidelines have been promulgated pursuant to 11 U.S.C. § 110(h) setting a maximum fee for services chargeable by bankruptcy petition preparers, I have given the debtor notice of the maximum amount before preparing any document for filing for a debtor or accepting any fee from the debtor, as required under that section; and (4) I will not accept any additional money or other property from the debtor before the filing fee is paid in full.

______________________________
Printed or Typed Name and Title, if any, of Bankruptcy Petition Preparer

______________________________
Social-Security No. (Required by 11 U.S.C. § 110.)

*If the bankruptcy petition preparer is not an individual, state the name, title (if any), address, and social-security number of the officer, principal, responsible person, or partner who signs the document.*

______________________________

______________________________
Address

x______________________________
Signature of Bankruptcy Petition Preparer

______________________________
Date

Names and Social-Security numbers of all other individuals who prepared or assisted in preparing this document, unless the bankruptcy petition preparer is not an individual:

*If more than one person prepared this document, attach additional signed sheets conforming to the appropriate Official Form for each person.*
*A bankruptcy petition preparer's failure to comply with the provisions of title 11 and the Federal Rules of Bankruptcy Procedure may result in fines or imprisonment or both.* 11 U.S.C. § 110; 18 U.S.C. § 156.

B 3A (Official Form 3A) (12/07) - Cont.

# UNITED STATES BANKRUPTCY COURT

In re ______________________________, Case No. ______________
Debtor

Chapter __________

## ORDER APPROVING PAYMENT OF FILING FEE IN INSTALLMENTS

☐ IT IS ORDERED that the debtor(s) may pay the filing fee in installments on the terms proposed in the foregoing application.

☐ IT IS ORDERED that the debtor(s) shall pay the filing fee according to the following terms:

$ ________________ Check one ☐ With the filing of the petition, or
☐ On or before ____________

$ ________________ on or before ______________________

$ ________________ on or before ______________________

$ ________________ on or before ______________________

☐ IT IS FURTHER ORDERED that until the filing fee is paid in full the debtor(s) shall not make any additional payment or transfer any additional property to an attorney or any other person for services in connection with this case.

BY THE COURT

Date: ________________

______________________________
*United States Bankruptcy Judge*

(Added Aug. 1, 1991; amended Mar. 14, 1995; Oct. 1, 1997; Dec. 1, 2003; Oct. 17, 2005; Dec. 1, 2007.)

NOTES OF ADVISORY COMMITTEE ON RULES—1991

This form is derived from former Official Form No. 2. A statement that the applicant is unable to pay the filing fee except in installments has been added as required by Rule 1006(b).

NOTES OF ADVISORY COMMITTEE ON RULES—1995 AMENDMENT

This form is a "document for filing" that may be prepared by a "bankruptcy petition preparer" as defined in 11 U.S.C. §110, which was added to the Code by the Bankruptcy Reform Act of 1994; accordingly, a signature line is provided for such preparer. In addition to signing, a bankruptcy petition preparer is required by section 110 to disclose the information requested. A signature line for a debtor's attorney also is added, as required by Rule 9011.

NOTES OF ADVISORY COMMITTEE ON RULES—1997 AMENDMENT

The form has been reorganized and the paragraphs numbered. The debtor's certification concerning payment for services in the case has been placed ahead of the statement of proposed terms for installment payment of court fees. Acknowledgement by the debtor of the potential consequences of failure to pay any installment when due has been added. (See 11 U.S.C. §707(a)(2).) The language of the form also has been changed to conform to Rule 1006 and to clarify that a debtor is not disqualified from paying the filing fee in installments because the debtor has paid money to a bankruptcy petition preparer.

COMMITTEE NOTES ON RULES—2003 AMENDMENT

Pursuant to §110(c) of the Bankruptcy Code, the certification by a non-attorney bankruptcy petition preparer requires a petition preparer to provide the full social security number of the individual who actually prepares the document pursuant to §110(c) of the Code.

COMMITTEE NOTES ON RULES—2005 AMENDMENT

The form is amended to direct the debtor to state that, until the filing fee is paid in full, the debtor will not make any additional payment or transfer any additional property to an attorney or any other person for services in connection with the case. The declaration and certification by a non-attorney bankruptcy petition preparer in the form are amended to include material mandated by §110 of the Code as amended by the Bankruptcy Abuse Prevention and Consumer Protection Act of 2005, Pub. L. No. 109–8, 119 Stat. 23 (April 20, 2005). The certification by a non-attorney bankruptcy petition preparer is re-named a declaration and also is revised to include material mandated by §110 of the Code as amended in 2005. The order is amended to provide space for the court to set forth a payment schedule other than the one proposed by the debtor.

COMMITTEE NOTES ON RULES—2005–2007 AMENDMENT

[The 2005–2007 Committee Note incorporates the Committee Note previously published in 2005.]

The form is amended to direct the debtor to state that, until the filing fee is paid in full, the debtor will not make any additional payment or transfer any additional property to an attorney or any other person for services in connection with the case. The declaration and certification by a non-attorney bankruptcy petition preparer in the form are amended to include material mandated by §110 of the Code as amended by the Bankruptcy Abuse Prevention and Consumer Protection Act of 2005, Pub. L. No. 109–8, 119 Stat. 23 (April 20, 2005). The certification by a non-attorney bankruptcy petition preparer is re-named a declaration and also is revised to include material mandated by §110 of the Code as amended in 2005. The order is amended to provide space for the court to set forth a payment schedule other than the one proposed by the debtor.

B 3B (Official Form 3B) (12/07)

## APPLICATION FOR WAIVER OF THE CHAPTER 7 FILING FEE FOR INDIVIDUALS WHO CANNOT PAY THE FILING FEE IN FULL OR IN INSTALLMENTS

The court fee for filing a case under chapter 7 of the Bankruptcy Code is $299.

If you cannot afford to pay the full fee at the time of filing, you may apply to pay the fee in installments. A form, which is available from the bankruptcy clerk's office, must be completed to make that application. If your application to pay in installments is approved, you will be permitted to file your petition, generally completing payment of the fee over the course of four to six months.

If you cannot afford to pay the fee either in full at the time of filing or in installments, you may request a waiver of the filing fee by completing this application and filing it with the Clerk of Court. A judge will decide whether you have to pay the fee. By law, the judge may waive the fee only if your income is less than 150 percent of the official poverty line applicable to your family size and you are unable to pay the fee in installments. You may obtain information about the poverty guidelines at www.uscourts.gov or in the bankruptcy clerk's office.

**Required information**. Complete all items in the application, and attach requested schedules. Then sign the application on the last page. If you and your spouse are filing a joint bankruptcy petition, you both must provide information as requested and sign the application.

B 3B (Official Form 3B) (12/07) -- Cont.

# UNITED STATES BANKRUPTCY COURT

In re: ____________________ Case No. ____________________
Debtor(s) (if known)

## APPLICATION FOR WAIVER OF THE CHAPTER 7 FILING FEE FOR INDIVIDUALS WHO CANNOT PAY THE FILING FEE IN FULL OR IN INSTALLMENTS

**Part A. Family Size and Income**

1. Including yourself, your spouse, and dependents you have listed or will list on Schedule I (Current Income of Individual Debtors(s)), how many people are in your family? (Do not include your spouse if you are separated AND are not filing a joint petition.) ________

2. Restate the following information that you provided, or will provide, on Line 16 of Schedule I. Attach a completed copy of Schedule I, if it is available.

   Total Combined Monthly Income (Line 16 of Schedule I): $______________

3. State the monthly net income, if any, of dependents included in Question 1 above. Do not include any income already reported in Item 2. If none, enter $0.

   $______________

4. Add the "Total Combined Monthly Income" reported in Question 2 to your dependents' monthly net income from Question 3.

   $______________

5. Do you expect the amount in Question 4 to increase or decrease by more than 10% during the next 6 months? Yes ___ No ___

   If yes, explain.

**Part B. Monthly Expenses**

6. EITHER (a) attach a completed copy of Schedule J (Schedule of Monthly Expenses), and state your total monthly expenses reported on Line 18 of that Schedule, OR (b) if you have not yet completed Schedule J, provide an estimate of your total monthly expenses.

   $______________

7. Do you expect the amount in Question 6 to increase or decrease by more than 10% during the next 6 months? Yes ___ No ___
   If yes, explain.

**Part C. Real and Personal Property**

EITHER (1) attach completed copies of Schedule A (Real Property) and Schedule B (Personal Property), OR (2) if you have not yet completed those schedules, answer the following questions.

8. State the amount of cash you have on hand. $______________

9. State below any money you have in savings, checking, or other accounts in a bank or other financial institution.

| Bank or Other Financial Institution: | Type of Account such as savings, checking, CD: | Amount: |
|---|---|---|
| ____________________ | ____________________ | $______________ |
| ____________________ | ____________________ | $______________ |

B 3B (Official Form 3B) (12/07) -- Cont.

10. State below the assets owned by you. **Do not list ordinary household furnishings and clothing.**

| | | |
|---|---|---|
| Home | Address: ______________ ______________ | Value: $ ______________ Amount owed on mortgages and liens: $ ______________ |
| Other real estate | Address: ______________ ______________ | Value: $ ______________ Amount owed on mortgages and liens: $ ______________ |
| Motor vehicle | Model/Year: ______________ ______________ | Value: $ ______________ Amount owed: $ ______________ |
| Motor vehicle | Model/Year: ______________ ______________ | Value: $ ______________ Amount owed: $ ______________ |
| Other | Description______________ ______________ | Value: $ ______________ Amount owed: $ ______________ |

11. State below any person, business, organization, or governmental unit that owes you money and the amount that is owed.

| Name of Person, Business, or Organization that Owes You Money | Amount Owed |
|---|---|
| ______________ | $ ______________ |
| ______________ | $ ______________ |

**Part D. Additional Information.**

12. Have you paid an **attorney** any money for services in connection with this case, including the completion of this form, the bankruptcy petition, or schedules? Yes ___ No ___
If yes, how much have you paid? $ ______________

13. Have you promised to pay or do you anticipate paying an **attorney** in connection with your bankruptcy case? Yes ___ No ___
If yes, how much have you promised to pay or do you anticipate paying? $ ______________

14. Have you paid **anyone other than an attorney** (such as a bankruptcy petition preparer, paralegal, typing service, or another person) any money for services in connection with this case, including the completion of this form, the bankruptcy petition, or schedules? Yes ___ No ___
If yes, how much have you paid? $ ______________

15. Have you promised to pay or do you anticipate paying **anyone other than an attorney** (such as a bankruptcy petition preparer, paralegal, typing service, or another person) any money for services in connection with this case, including the completion of this form, the bankruptcy petition, or schedules? Yes ___ No ___
If yes, how much have you promised to pay or do you anticipate paying? $ ______________

16. Has anyone paid an attorney or other person or service in connection with this case, on your behalf? Yes ___ No ___

If yes, explain.

B 3B (Official Form 3B) (12/07) -- Cont.

17. Have you previously filed for bankruptcy relief during the past eight years? Yes ___ No ___

| Case Number (if known) | Year filed | Location of filing | Did you obtain a discharge? (if known) |
|---|---|---|---|
| ______________ | ______ | ___________ | Yes ___ No ___ Don't know ___ |
| ______________ | ______ | ___________ | Yes ___ No ___ Don't know ___ |

18. Please provide any other information that helps to explain why you are unable to pay the filing fee in installments.

19. I (we) declare under penalty of perjury that I (we) cannot currently afford to pay the filing fee in full or in installments and that the foregoing information is true and correct.

Executed on: ______________ ______________________
Date Signature of Debtor

______________ ______________________
Date Signature of Codebtor

---

**DECLARATION AND SIGNATURE OF BANKRUPTCY PETITION PREPARER (See 11 U.S.C. § 110)**

I declare under penalty of perjury that: (1) I am a bankruptcy petition preparer as defined in 11 U.S.C. § 110; (2) I prepared this document for compensation and have provided the debtor with a copy of this document and the notices and information required under 11 U.S.C. §§ 110(b), 110(h), and 342(b); and (3) if rules or guidelines have been promulgated pursuant to 11 U.S.C. § 110(h) setting a maximum fee for services chargeable by bankruptcy petition preparers, I have given the debtor notice of the maximum amount before preparing any document for filing for a debtor or accepting any fee from the debtor, as required under that section.

______________________________________
Printed or Typed Name and Title, if any, of Bankruptcy Petition Preparer Social-Security No. (Required by 11 U.S.C. §110.)

*If the bankruptcy petition preparer is not an individual, state the name, title (if any), address, and social-security number of the officer, principal, responsible person, or partner who signs the document.*

______________________

______________________
Address

x______________________________ ______________
Signature of Bankruptcy Petition Preparer Date

Names and Social-Security numbers of all other individuals who prepared or assisted in preparing this document, unless the bankruptcy petition preparer is not an individual:

*If more than one person prepared this document, attach additional signed sheets conforming to the appropriate Official Form for each person.*
*A bankruptcy petition preparer's failure to comply with the provisions of title 11 and the Federal Rules of Bankruptcy Procedure may result in fines or imprisonment or both.* 11 U.S.C. § 110; 18 U.S.C. § 156.

B 3B (Official Form 3B) (12/07) -- Cont.

# UNITED STATES BANKRUPTCY COURT

In re: ____________________ Case No. ____________________
Debtor(s)

**ORDER ON DEBTOR'S APPLICATION FOR WAIVER OF THE CHAPTER 7 FILING FEE**

Upon consideration of the debtor's "Application for Waiver of the Chapter 7 Filing Fee," the court orders that the application be:

[ ] GRANTED.

This order is subject to being vacated at a later time if developments in the administration of the bankruptcy case demonstrate that the waiver was unwarranted.

[ ] DENIED.

The debtor shall pay the chapter 7 filing fee according to the following terms:

$ __________ on or before __________

$ __________ on or before __________

$ __________ on or before __________

$ __________ on or before __________

Until the filing fee is paid in full, the debtor shall not make any additional payment or transfer any additional property to an attorney or any other person for services in connection with this case.

IF THE DEBTOR FAILS TO TIMELY PAY THE FILING FEE IN FULL OR TO TIMELY MAKE INSTALLMENT PAYMENTS, THE COURT MAY DISMISS THE DEBTOR'S CASE.

[ ] SCHEDULED FOR HEARING.

A hearing to consider the debtor's "Application for Waiver of the Chapter 7 Filing Fee" shall be held on __________________ at ________ am/pm at ______________________________________.
(address of courthouse)

IF THE DEBTOR FAILS TO APPEAR AT THE SCHEDULED HEARING, THE COURT MAY DEEM SUCH FAILURE TO BE THE DEBTOR'S CONSENT TO THE ENTRY OF AN ORDER DENYING THE FEE WAIVER APPLICATION BY DEFAULT.

BY THE COURT:

DATE: __________

______________________________
United States Bankruptcy Judge

(Added Oct. 17, 2005; amended Apr. 9, 2006; Dec. 1, 2007.)

COMMITTEE NOTES ON RULES—2005

This form is new. 28 U.S.C. §1930(f), enacted as part of the Bankruptcy Abuse [Prevention] and Consumer Protection Act of 2005, Pub. L. No. 109-8, 119 Stat. 23 (April 20, 2005), provides that "under procedures prescribed by the Judicial Conference of the United States, the district court or the bankruptcy court may waive the filing fee in a case under chapter 7 of title 11 for an individual if the court determines that such individual has income less than 150 percent of the income official poverty line . . . applicable to a family of the size involved and is unable to pay that fee in installments." To implement this provision, Interim Rule 1006 adds a new subdivision (c). Official Form 3B is the form referenced in that subdivision, and is to be used by individual chapter 7 debtors when applying for a waiver of the filing fee. A corresponding standard order also is included.

COMMITTEE NOTES ON RULES—2005-2007 AMENDMENT

[The 2005-2007 Committee Note incorporates the Committee Note previously published in 2005.]

This form is new. 28 U.S.C. §1930(f), enacted as part of the Bankruptcy Abuse and Consumer Protection Act of 2005, Pub. L. No. 109-8, 119 Stat. 23 (April 20, 2005), provides that "under procedures prescribed by the Judicial Conference of the United States, the district court or the bankruptcy court may waive the filing fee in a case under chapter 7 of title 11 for an individual if the court determines that such individual has income less than 150 percent of the income official poverty line . . . applicable to a family of the size involved and is unable to pay that fee in installments." To implement this provision, Fed. R. Bankr. P.1006 adds a new subdivision (c). Official Form 3B is the form referenced in that subdivision, and is to be used by individual chapter 7 debtors when applying for a waiver of the filing fee. A corresponding standard order also is included.

**B4 (Official Form 4) (12/07)**

# United States Bankruptcy Court

______________ District Of ______________

In re ______________________________,
Debtor

Case No. ______________

Chapter ______________

## LIST OF CREDITORS HOLDING 20 LARGEST UNSECURED CLAIMS

Following is the list of the debtor's creditors holding the 20 largest unsecured claims. The list is prepared in accordance with Fed. R. Bankr. P. 1007(d) for filing in this chapter 11 [*or* chapter 9] case. The list does not include (1) persons who come within the definition of "insider" set forth in 11 U.S.C. § 101, or (2) secured creditors unless the value of the collateral is such that the unsecured deficiency places the creditor among the holders of the 20 largest unsecured claims. If a minor child is one of the creditors holding the 20 largest unsecured claims, state the child's initials and the name and address of the child's parent or guardian, such as "A.B., a minor child, by John Doe, guardian." Do not disclose the child's name. See, 11 U.S.C. §112 and Fed. R. Bankr. P. 1007(m).

| (1) | (2) | (3) | (4) | (5) |
|---|---|---|---|---|
| *Name of creditor and complete mailing address, including zip code* | *Name, telephone number and complete mailing address, including zip code, of employee, agent, or department of creditor familiar with claim who may be contacted* | *Nature of claim (trade debt, bank loan, government contract, etc.)* | *Indicate if claim is contingent, unliquidated, disputed or subject to setoff* | *Amount of claim [if secured also state value of security]* |

Date: ______________

______________________
Debtor

*[Declaration as in Form 2]*

(Added Aug. 1, 1991; amended Mar. 16, 1993; Oct. 17, 2005; Dec. 1, 2007.)

NOTES OF ADVISORY COMMITTEE ON RULES—1991

This form is derived from former Official Form No. 9.

In conformity with Rule 1007(d) and in recognition of the notice function served by this list under Rule 4001, governmental units must be listed if they are among the creditors holding the 20 largest claims.

Rule 1008 requires all lists to be verified or contain an unsworn declaration conforming with 28 U.S.C. §1746.

NOTES OF ADVISORY COMMITTEE ON RULES—1993 AMENDMENT

The form has been amended to delete reference to the specific subsection of 11 U.S.C. §101 in connection with the definition of the term "insider." Section 101 of the Bankruptcy Code contains numerous definitions, and statutory amendments from time to time have resulted in the renumbering of many of its subsections. The more general reference will avoid the necessity to amend the form further in the event of future amendments to §101.

COMMITTEE NOTES ON RULES—2005 AMENDMENT

The form is amended to direct that the name of any minor child not be disclosed. The amendment implements §112 of the Code, which was added by the Bankruptcy Abuse Prevention and Consumer Protection Act of 2005, Pub. L. No. 109–8, 119 Stat. 23 (April 20, 2005).

COMMITTEE NOTES ON RULES—2005–2007 AMENDMENT

[The 2005–2007 Committee Note incorporates Committee Notes previously published in 2005 and 2006.]

The form is amended to direct that the name of any minor child not be disclosed. The amendment implements §112 of the Code, which was added by the Bankruptcy Abuse Prevention and Consumer Protection Act of 2005, Pub. L. No. 109–8, 119 Stat. 23 (April 20, 2005). In addition, the form is amended to add to the reference to Rule 1007(m) a direction to include for noticing purposes the name, address, and legal relationship to the child of "a person described" in that rule. Rule 1007(m) requires the person named to be someone on whom process would be served in an adversary proceeding against the child.

B 5 (Official Form 5) (12/07)

# UNITED STATES BANKRUPTCY COURT

## INVOLUNTARY PETITION

IN RE (Name of Debtor – If Individual. Last, First, Middle)

ALL OTHER NAMES used by debtor in the last 8 years (Include married, maiden, and trade names )

Last four digits of Social-Security or other Individual's Tax-I.D No /Complete EIN (If more than one, state all )

STREET ADDRESS OF DEBTOR (No. and street, city, state, and zip code)

COUNTY OF RESIDENCE OR PRINCIPAL PLACE OF BUSINESS

ZIP CODE

MAILING ADDRESS OF DEBTOR (If different from street address)

ZIP CODE

LOCATION OF PRINCIPAL ASSETS OF BUSINESS DEBTOR (If different from previously listed addresses)

CHAPTER OF BANKRUPTCY CODE UNDER WHICH PETITION IS FILED

☐ Chapter 7 ☐ Chapter 11

**INFORMATION REGARDING DEBTOR (Check applicable boxes)**

**Nature of Debts**
(Check **one** box )

Petitioners believe

☐ Debts are primarily consumer debts
☐ Debts are primarily business debts

**Type of Debtor**
(Form of Organization)

☐ Individual (Includes Joint Debtor)
☐ Corporation (Includes LLC and LLP)
☐ Partnership
☐ Other (If debtor is not one of the above entities, check this box and state type of entity below.)

______________________________

**Nature of Business**
(Check **one** box.)

☐ Health Care Business
☐ Single Asset Real Estate as defined in 11 U.S.C. § 101(51)(B)
☐ Railroad
☐ Stockbroker
☐ Commodity Broker
☐ Clearing Bank
☐ Other

**VENUE**

☐ Debtor has been domiciled or has had a residence, principal place of business, or principal assets in the District for 180 days immediately preceding the date of this petition or for a longer part of such 180 days than in any other District

☐ A bankruptcy case concerning debtor's affiliate, general partner or partnership is pending in this District

**FILING FEE** (Check one box)

☐ Full Filing Fee attached

☐ Petitioner is a child support creditor or its representative, and the form specified in § 304(g) of the Bankruptcy Reform Act of 1994 is attached
*[If a child support creditor or its representative is a petitioner, and if the petitioner files the form specified in § 304(g) of the Bankruptcy Reform Act of 1994, no fee is required ]*

**PENDING BANKRUPTCY CASE FILED BY OR AGAINST ANY PARTNER OR AFFILIATE OF THIS DEBTOR** (Report information for any additional cases on attached sheets )

| Name of Debtor | Case Number | Date |
|---|---|---|
| Relationship | District | Judge |

**ALLEGATIONS**
**(Check applicable boxes)**

1 ☐ Petitioner (s) are eligible to file this petition pursuant to 11 U S C § 303 (b)
2 ☐ The debtor is a person against whom an order for relief may be entered under title 11 of the United States Code
3 a ☐ The debtor is generally not paying such debtor's debts as they become due, unless such debts are the subject of a bona fide dispute as to liability or amount,
or
b ☐ Within 120 days preceding the filing of this petition, a custodian, other than a trustee receiver, or agent appointed or authorized to take charge of less than substantially all of the property of the debtor for the purpose of enforcing a lien against such property, was appointed or took possession.

COURT USE ONLY

B 5 (Official Form 5) (12/07) – Page 2

**Name of Debtor**____________________

**Case No.**____________________________

**TRANSFER OF CLAIM**

☐ Check this box if there has been a transfer of any claim against the debtor by or to any petitioner. Attach all documents that evidence the transfer and any statements that are required under Bankruptcy Rule 1003(a).

**REQUEST FOR RELIEF**

Petitioner(s) request that an order for relief be entered against the debtor under the chapter of title 11, United States Code, specified in this petition. If any petitioner is a foreign representative appointed in a foreign proceeding, a certified copy of the order of the court granting recognition is attached.

| | |
|---|---|
| Petitioner(s) declare under penalty of perjury that the foregoing is true and correct according to the best of their knowledge, information, and belief. | |
| x________________________ Signature of Petitioner or Representative (State title) | x________________________ Signature of Attorney Date |
| Name of Petitioner Date Signed | Name of Attorney Firm (If any) |
| Name & Mailing Address of Individual Signing in Representative Capacity ____________ ____________ | Address |
| | Telephone No. |
| x________________________ Signature of Petitioner or Representative (State title) | x________________________ Signature of Attorney Date |
| Name of Petitioner Date Signed | Name of Attorney Firm (If any) |
| Name & Mailing Address of Individual Signing in Representative Capacity ____________ ____________ | Address |
| | Telephone No. |
| x________________________ Signature of Petitioner or Representative (State title) | x________________________ Signature of Attorney Date |
| Name of Petitioner Date Signed | Name of Attorney Firm (If any) |
| Name & Mailing Address of Individual Signing in Representative Capacity ____________ ____________ | Address |
| | Telephone No. |

**PETITIONING CREDITORS**

| | | |
|---|---|---|
| Name and Address of Petitioner | Nature of Claim | Amount of Claim |
| Name and Address of Petitioner | Nature of Claim | Amount of Claim |
| Name and Address of Petitioner | Nature of Claim | Amount of Claim |
| Note: If there are more than three petitioners, attach additional sheets with the statement under penalty of perjury, each petitioner's signature under the statement and the name of attorney and petitioning creditor information in the format above. | | Total Amount of Petitioners' Claims |

______continuation sheets attached

(Added Aug. 1, 1991; amended Sept. 22, 1992; Dec. 1, 2002; Dec. 1, 2003; Oct. 17, 2005; Oct. 1, 2006; Dec. 1, 2007.)

NOTES OF ADVISORY COMMITTEE ON RULES—1991

This form has been redesigned in a box format similar to that of Form 1. See Advisory Committee Note to Form 1.

The allegations required under §303 are grouped together, and a separate section has been provided for additional allegations based upon the prohibitions and requirements set forth in Rule 1003(a) concerning transfer of claims by petitioning creditors. Petitioners may wish to supplement the allegations set forth in the form with a further statement of facts. Additional information concerning any allegation can be requested by the debtor as part of the discovery process.

Each petitioning creditor, by signing on the line provided, signs both the petition and the unsworn declaration which 28 U.S.C. §1746 permits instead of verification. The addresses as well as the names of individuals signing the petition in a representative capacity are required, together with disclosure of which petitioner is represented by each signatory.

This form is intended to be used in every involuntary case, including that of a partnership. The separate form for a petition by a partner has been abrogated. Pursuant to §303(b)(3)(A) of the Code, a petition by fewer than all of the general partners seeking an order for relief with respect to the partnership is treated as an involuntary petition. Such a petition is adversarial in character because not all of the partners are joining in the petition.

Section 303(b)(3)(B) permits a petition against the partnership if relief has been ordered under the Code with respect to all of the general partners. In that event, the petition may be filed by a general partner, a trustee of a general partner's estate, or a creditor of the partnership. This form may be adapted for use in that type of case.

28 U.S.C. §1408(1) specifies the proper venue alternatives for all persons, including partnerships, as domicile, residence, principal place of business, or location of principal assets. Venue also may be based on a pending case commenced by an affiliate, general partner, or partnership pursuant to 28 U.S.C. §1408(2). Both options are set forth in the block labeled "Venue."

28 U.S.C. §1746 permits the unsworn declaration instead of a verification. See Committee Note to Form 2.

NOTES OF ADVISORY COMMITTEE ON RULES—1992 AMENDMENT

The form has been amended to require the dating of signatures.

COMMITTEE NOTES ON RULES—2002 AMENDMENT

The form is amended to give notice that no filing fee is required if a child support creditor or its representative is a petitioner, and if the petitioner also files a form detailing the child support debt, its status, and other characteristics, as specified in §304(g) of the Bankruptcy Reform Act of 1994, Pub. L. No. 103–394, 108 Stat. 4106 (Oct. 22, 1994).

COMMITTEE NOTES ON RULES—2003 AMENDMENT

The form is amended to require the petitioner to disclose the debtor's employer identification number, if any, and only the last four digits of the debtor's social security number to afford greater privacy to the individual debtor, whose bankruptcy case records may be available on the Internet. The form also is amended to delete the request for information concerning the "Type of Business," as this data no longer is collected for statistical purposes.

COMMITTEE NOTES ON RULES—2005 AMENDMENT

The form has been amended to delete statistical information no longer required and to add "as to liability or amount" to the language concerning debts that are the subject of a bona fide dispute, in conformity with §303 of the Code as amended by the Bankruptcy Abuse Prevention and Consumer Protection Act of 2005, Pub. L. No. 109–8, 119 Stat. 23 (April 20, 2005). The petitioning creditors must now provide, to the extent known to them, all other names used by the debtor during the 8 years, rather than 6 years, before the filing of the petition. A new check box is provided for the petitioning creditors to identify the debtor that is a "health care business" as defined in §101 of the Code, thereby alerting the court and the United States trustee of the necessity under §333 to appoint an ombudsman to represent the interests of the patients of the health care business. These amendments also implement the 2005 amendments to the Code. A new checkbox also is provided for a "clearing bank," which may become a debtor upon the filing of a petition at the direction of the Board of Governors of the Federal Reserve System; this addition conforms to an amendment to §109(b)(2) of the Code which was enacted in 2000.

COMMITTEE NOTES ON RULES—2006 AMENDMENT

The section of the form labeled "Information Regarding Debtor" is amended to facilitate, to the extent available in an involuntary case, the collection of the same statistical information that is requested in a voluntary case. Accordingly, information about whether the debtor is an individual, a corporation, or some other type of entity is separated from the checklist of types of debtors, such as health care businesses and railroads, concerning which the Code provides for specialized treatment.

COMMITTEE NOTES ON RULES—2005-2007 AMENDMENT

[The 2005-2007 Committee Note incorporates Committee Notes previously published in 2005 and 2006.]

The form has been amended to delete statistical information about the debtor that no longer is required, and to substitute checkboxes similar to those on the voluntary petition form. The form also is amended to add "as to liability or amount" to the language concerning debts that are the subject of a bona fide dispute, in conformity with §303 of the Code as amended by the Bankruptcy Abuse Prevention and Consumer Protection Act of 2005, Pub. L. No. 109–8, 119 Stat. 23 (April 20, 2005). The petitioning creditors must now provide, to the extent known to them, all other names used by the debtor during the 8 years, rather than 6 years, before the filing of the petition. In conformity with Rule 9037, the petitioning creditors are directed to provide only the last four digits of any individual's tax-identification number. A new checkbox is provided for the petitioning creditors to identify the debtor that is a "health care business" as defined in §101 of the Code, thereby alerting the court and the United States trustee of the necessity under §333 of the Code to appoint an ombudsman to represent the interests of the patients of the health care business. These amendments also implement the 2005 amendments to the Code. A new checkbox also is provided for a "clearing bank," which may become a debtor upon the filing of a petition at the direction of the Board of Governors of the Federal Reserve System; this addition conforms to an amendment to §109(b)(2) of the Code, which was enacted in 2000.

**B6 Cover (Form 6 Cover) (12/07)**

## FORM 6. SCHEDULES

Summary of Schedules
Statistical Summary of Certain Liabilities and Related Data (28 U.S.C. § 159)

Schedule A - Real Property
Schedule B - Personal Property
Schedule C - Property Claimed as Exempt
Schedule D - Creditors Holding Secured Claims
Schedule E - Creditors Holding Unsecured Priority Claims
Schedule F - Creditors Holding Unsecured Nonpriority Claims
Schedule G - Executory Contracts and Unexpired Leases
Schedule H - Codebtors
Schedule I - Current Income of Individual Debtor(s)
Schedule J - Current Expenditures of Individual Debtors(s)

Unsworn Declaration Under Penalty of Perjury

GENERAL INSTRUCTIONS: The first page of the debtor's schedules and the first page of any amendments thereto must contain a caption as in Form 16B. Subsequent pages should be identified with the debtor's name and case number. If the schedules are filed with the petition, the case number should be left blank.

Schedules D, E, and F have been designed for the listing of each claim only once. Even when a claim is secured only in part or entitled to priority only in part, it still should be listed only once. A claim which is secured in whole or in part should be listed on Schedule D only, and a claim which is entitled to priority in whole or in part should be listed on Schedule E only. Do not list the same claim twice. If a creditor has more than one claim, such as claims arising from separate transactions, each claim should be scheduled separately.

Review the specific instructions for each schedule before completing the schedule.

B6 Summary (Official Form 6 - Summary) (12/07)

# United States Bankruptcy Court

In re ______________________________,
Debtor

Case No. ________________

Chapter __________

## SUMMARY OF SCHEDULES

Indicate as to each schedule whether that schedule is attached and state the number of pages in each. Report the totals from Schedules A, B, D, E, F, I, and J in the boxes provided. Add the amounts from Schedules A and B to determine the total amount of the debtor's assets. Add the amounts of all claims from Schedules D, E, and F to determine the total amount of the debtor's liabilities. Individual debtors also must complete the "Statistical Summary of Certain Liabilities and Related Data" if they file a case under chapter 7, 11, or 13.

| NAME OF SCHEDULE | ATTACHED (YES/NO) | NO. OF SHEETS | ASSETS | LIABILITIES | OTHER |
|---|---|---|---|---|---|
| A - Real Property | | | $ | | |
| B - Personal Property | | | $ | | |
| C - Property Claimed as Exempt | | | | | |
| D - Creditors Holding Secured Claims | | | | $ | |
| E - Creditors Holding Unsecured Priority Claims (Total of Claims on Schedule E) | | | | $ | |
| F - Creditors Holding Unsecured Nonpriority Claims | | | | $ | |
| G - Executory Contracts and Unexpired Leases | | | | | |
| H - Codebtors | | | | | |
| I - Current Income of Individual Debtor(s) | | | | | $ |
| J - Current Expenditures of Individual Debtors(s) | | | | | $ |
| TOTAL | | | $ | $ | |

B 6 Summary (Official Form 6 - Summary) (12/07)

# United States Bankruptcy Court

In re ______________________________, Case No. ________________
Debtor

Chapter ___________

## STATISTICAL SUMMARY OF CERTAIN LIABILITIES AND RELATED DATA (28 U.S.C. § 159)

If you are an individual debtor whose debts are primarily consumer debts, as defined in § 101(8) of the Bankruptcy Code (11 U.S.C. § 101(8)), filing a case under chapter 7, 11 or 13, you must report all information requested below.

☐ Check this box if you are an individual debtor whose debts are NOT primarily consumer debts. You are not required to report any information here.

**This information is for statistical purposes only under 28 U.S.C. § 159.**

**Summarize the following types of liabilities, as reported in the Schedules, and total them.**

| **Type of Liability** | **Amount** |
|---|---|
| Domestic Support Obligations (from Schedule E) | $ |
| Taxes and Certain Other Debts Owed to Governmental Units (from Schedule E) | $ |
| Claims for Death or Personal Injury While Debtor Was Intoxicated (from Schedule E) (whether disputed or undisputed) | $ |
| Student Loan Obligations (from Schedule F) | $ |
| Domestic Support, Separation Agreement, and Divorce Decree Obligations Not Reported on Schedule E | $ |
| Obligations to Pension or Profit-Sharing, and Other Similar Obligations (from Schedule F) | $ |
| TOTAL | $ |

**State the following:**

| | |
|---|---|
| Average Income (from Schedule I, Line 16) | $ |
| Average Expenses (from Schedule J, Line 18) | $ |
| Current Monthly Income (from Form 22A Line 12; **OR**, Form 22B Line 11; **OR**, Form 22C Line 20 ) | $ |

**State the following:**

| | | |
|---|---|---|
| 1. Total from Schedule D, "UNSECURED PORTION, IF ANY" column | | $ |
| 2. Total from Schedule E, "AMOUNT ENTITLED TO PRIORITY" column. | $ | |
| 3. Total from Schedule E, "AMOUNT NOT ENTITLED TO PRIORITY, IF ANY" column | | $ |
| 4. Total from Schedule F | | $ |
| 5. Total of non-priority unsecured debt (sum of 1, 3, and 4) | | $ |

B6A (Official Form 6A) (12/07)

**In re** ______________________________, **Case No.** ______________________
**Debtor** **(If known)**

# SCHEDULE A - REAL PROPERTY

Except as directed below, list all real property in which the debtor has any legal, equitable, or future interest, including all property owned as a co-tenant, community property, or in which the debtor has a life estate. Include any property in which the debtor holds rights and powers exercisable for the debtor's own benefit. If the debtor is married, state whether the husband, wife, both, or the marital community own the property by placing an "H," "W," "J," or "C" in the column labeled "Husband, Wife, Joint, or Community." If the debtor holds no interest in real property, write "None" under "Description and Location of Property."

**Do not include interests in executory contracts and unexpired leases on this schedule. List them in Schedule G - Executory Contracts and Unexpired Leases.**

If an entity claims to have a lien or hold a secured interest in any property, state the amount of the secured claim. See Schedule D. If no entity claims to hold a secured interest in the property, write "None" in the column labeled "Amount of Secured Claim."

If the debtor is an individual or if a joint petition is filed, state the amount of any exemption claimed in the property only in Schedule C - Property Claimed as Exempt.

| DESCRIPTION AND LOCATION OF PROPERTY | NATURE OF DEBTOR'S INTEREST IN PROPERTY | HUSBAND, WIFE, JOINT, OR COMMUNITY | CURRENT VALUE OF DEBTOR'S INTEREST IN PROPERTY, WITHOUT DEDUCTING ANY SECURED CLAIM OR EXEMPTION | AMOUNT OF SECURED CLAIM |
|---|---|---|---|---|
| | | | | |
| | | | | |
| | | | | |
| | | | | |
| | | | | |
| | | | | |
| | | | | |
| | | | | |
| | | Total➤ | | |

(Report also on Summary of Schedules.)

B 6B (Official Form 6B) (12/07)

**In re** ______________________________, **Case No.** ______________________
**Debtor** **(If known)**

# SCHEDULE B - PERSONAL PROPERTY

Except as directed below, list all personal property of the debtor of whatever kind. If the debtor has no property in one or more of the categories, place an "x" in the appropriate position in the column labeled "None." If additional space is needed in any category, attach a separate sheet properly identified with the case name, case number, and the number of the category. If the debtor is married, state whether the husband, wife, both, or the marital community own the property by placing an "H," "W," "J," or "C" in the column labeled "Husband, Wife, Joint, or Community." If the debtor is an individual or a joint petition is filed, state the amount of any exemptions claimed only in Schedule C - Property Claimed as Exempt.

**Do not list interests in executory contracts and unexpired leases on this schedule. List them in Schedule G - Executory Contracts and Unexpired Leases.**

If the property is being held for the debtor by someone else, state that person's name and address under "Description and Location of Property." If the property is being held for a minor child, simply state the child's initials and the name and address of the child's parent or guardian, such as "A.B., a minor child, by John Doe, guardian." Do not disclose the child's name. See, 11 U.S.C. §112 and Fed. R. Bankr. P. 1007(m).

| TYPE OF PROPERTY | NONE | DESCRIPTION AND LOCATION OF PROPERTY | HUSBAND, WIFE, JOINT, OR COMMUNITY | CURRENT VALUE OF DEBTOR'S INTEREST IN PROPERTY, WITHOUT DEDUCTING ANY SECURED CLAIM OR EXEMPTION |
|---|---|---|---|---|
| 1. Cash on hand. | | | | |
| 2. Checking, savings or other financial accounts, certificates of deposit or shares in banks, savings and loan, thrift, building and loan, and homestead associations, or credit unions, brokerage houses, or cooperatives. | | | | |
| 3. Security deposits with public utilities, telephone companies, landlords, and others. | | | | |
| 4. Household goods and furnishings, including audio, video, and computer equipment. | | | | |
| 5. Books; pictures and other art objects; antiques; stamp, coin, record, tape, compact disc, and other collections or collectibles. | | | | |
| 6. Wearing apparel. | | | | |
| 7. Furs and jewelry. | | | | |
| 8. Firearms and sports, photographic, and other hobby equipment. | | | | |
| 9. Interests in insurance policies. Name insurance company of each policy and itemize surrender or refund value of each. | | | | |
| 10. Annuities. Itemize and name each issuer. | | | | |
| 11. Interests in an education IRA as defined in 26 U.S.C. § 530(b)(1) or under a qualified State tuition plan as defined in 26 U.S.C. § 529(b)(1). Give particulars. (File separately the record(s) of any such interest(s). 11 U.S.C. § 521(c).) | | | | |

B 6B (Official Form 6B) (12/07) -- Cont.

In re ______________________________, Case No. ______________________
Debtor (If known)

# SCHEDULE B - PERSONAL PROPERTY

(Continuation Sheet)

| TYPE OF PROPERTY | NONE | DESCRIPTION AND LOCATION OF PROPERTY | HUSBAND, WIFE, JOINT, OR COMMUNITY | CURRENT VALUE OF DEBTOR'S INTEREST IN PROPERTY, WITH-OUT DEDUCTING ANY SECURED CLAIM OR EXEMPTION |
|---|---|---|---|---|
| 12. Interests in IRA, ERISA, Keogh, or other pension or profit sharing plans. Give particulars. | | | | |
| 13. Stock and interests in incorporated and unincorporated businesses. Itemize. | | | | |
| 14. Interests in partnerships or joint ventures. Itemize. | | | | |
| 15. Government and corporate bonds and other negotiable and non-negotiable instruments. | | | | |
| 16. Accounts receivable. | | | | |
| 17. Alimony, maintenance, support, and property settlements to which the debtor is or may be entitled. Give particulars. | | | | |
| 18. Other liquidated debts owed to debtor including tax refunds. Give particulars. | | | | |
| 19. Equitable or future interests, life estates, and rights or powers exercisable for the benefit of the debtor other than those listed in Schedule A – Real Property. | | | | |
| 20. Contingent and noncontingent interests in estate of a decedent, death benefit plan, life insurance policy, or trust. | | | | |
| 21. Other contingent and unliquidated claims of every nature, including tax refunds, counterclaims of the debtor, and rights to setoff claims. Give estimated value of each. | | | | |

B 6B (Official Form 6B) (12/07) -- Cont.

**In re** ______________________________________________, **Case No.** ______________________
**Debtor** **(If known)**

# SCHEDULE B - PERSONAL PROPERTY

(Continuation Sheet)

| TYPE OF PROPERTY | N O N E | DESCRIPTION AND LOCATION OF PROPERTY | HUSBAND, WIFE, JOINT, OR COMMUNITY | CURRENT VALUE OF DEBTOR'S INTEREST IN PROPERTY, WITH-OUT DEDUCTING ANY SECURED CLAIM OR EXEMPTION |
|---|---|---|---|---|
| 22. Patents, copyrights, and other intellectual property. Give particulars. | | | | |
| 23. Licenses, franchises, and other general intangibles. Give particulars. | | | | |
| 24. Customer lists or other compilations containing personally identifiable information (as defined in 11 U.S.C. § 101(41A)) provided to the debtor by individuals in connection with obtaining a product or service from the debtor primarily for personal, family, or household purposes. | | | | |
| 25. Automobiles, trucks, trailers, and other vehicles and accessories. | | | | |
| 26. Boats, motors, and accessories. | | | | |
| 27. Aircraft and accessories. | | | | |
| 28. Office equipment, furnishings, and supplies. | | | | |
| 29. Machinery, fixtures, equipment, and supplies used in business. | | | | |
| 30. Inventory. | | | | |
| 31. Animals. | | | | |
| 32. Crops - growing or harvested. Give particulars. | | | | |
| 33. Farming equipment and implements. | | | | |
| 34. Farm supplies, chemicals, and feed. | | | | |
| 35. Other personal property of any kind not already listed. Itemize. | | | | |

________continuation sheets attached Total➤ $

(Include amounts from any continuation sheets attached. Report total also on Summary of Schedules.)

B 6C (Official Form 6C) (12/07)

**In re ____________________________________,** **Case No. ____________________**
**Debtor** **(If known)**

# SCHEDULE C - PROPERTY CLAIMED AS EXEMPT

Debtor claims the exemptions to which debtor is entitled under:
(Check one box)
☐ 11 U.S.C. § 522(b)(2)
☐ 11 U.S.C. § 522(b)(3)

☐ Check if debtor claims a homestead exemption that exceeds $136,875.

| DESCRIPTION OF PROPERTY | SPECIFY LAW PROVIDING EACH EXEMPTION | VALUE OF CLAIMED EXEMPTION | CURRENT VALUE OF PROPERTY WITHOUT DEDUCTING EXEMPTION |
|---|---|---|---|
| | | | |

B 6D (Official Form 6D) (12/07)

**In re** ______________________________, **Case No.** ______________________________
**Debtor** **(If known)**

## SCHEDULE D - CREDITORS HOLDING SECURED CLAIMS

State the name, mailing address, including zip code, and last four digits of any account number of all entities holding claims secured by property of the debtor as of the date of filing of the petition. The complete account number of any account the debtor has with the creditor is useful to the trustee and the creditor and may be provided if the debtor chooses to do so. List creditors holding all types of secured interests such as judgment liens, garnishments, statutory liens, mortgages, deeds of trust, and other security interests.

List creditors in alphabetical order to the extent practicable. If a minor child is the creditor, state the child's initials and the name and address of the child's parent or guardian, such as "A.B., a minor child, by John Doe, guardian." Do not disclose the child's name. See, 11 U.S.C. §112 and Fed. R. Bankr. P. 1007(m). If all secured creditors will not fit on this page, use the continuation sheet provided.

If any entity other than a spouse in a joint case may be jointly liable on a claim, place an "X" in the column labeled "Codebtor," include the entity on the appropriate schedule of creditors, and complete Schedule H – Codebtors. If a joint petition is filed, state whether the husband, wife, both of them, or the marital community may be liable on each claim by placing an "H," "W," "J," or "C" in the column labeled "Husband, Wife, Joint, or Community."

If the claim is contingent, place an "X" in the column labeled "Contingent." If the claim is unliquidated, place an "X" in the column labeled "Unliquidated." If the claim is disputed, place an "X" in the column labeled "Disputed." (You may need to place an "X" in more than one of these three columns.)

Total the columns labeled "Amount of Claim Without Deducting Value of Collateral" and "Unsecured Portion, if Any" in the boxes labeled "Total(s)" on the last sheet of the completed schedule. Report the total from the column labeled "Amount of Claim Without Deducting Value of Collateral" also on the Summary of Schedules and, if the debtor is an individual with primarily consumer debts, report the total from the column labeled "Unsecured Portion, if Any" on the Statistical Summary of Certain Liabilities and Related Data.

☐ Check this box if debtor has no creditors holding secured claims to report on this Schedule D.

| CREDITOR'S NAME AND MAILING ADDRESS INCLUDING ZIP CODE AND AN ACCOUNT NUMBER (*See Instructions Above.*) | CODEBTOR | HUSBAND, WIFE, JOINT, OR COMMUNITY | DATE CLAIM WAS INCURRED, NATURE OF LIEN, AND DESCRIPTION AND VALUE OF PROPERTY SUBJECT TO LIEN | CONTINGENT | UNLIQUIDATED | DISPUTED | AMOUNT OF CLAIM WITHOUT DEDUCTING VALUE OF COLLATERAL | UNSECURED PORTION, IF ANY |
|---|---|---|---|---|---|---|---|---|
| ACCOUNT NO. | | | VALUE $ | | | | | |
| ACCOUNT NO. | | | VALUE $ | | | | | |
| ACCOUNT NO. | | | VALUE $ | | | | | |
| ____continuation sheets attached | | | Subtotal ► (Total of this page) | | | | $ | $ |
| | | | Total ► (Use only on last page) | | | | $ | $ |
| | | | | | | | (Report also on Summary of Schedules.) | (If applicable, report also on Statistical Summary of Certain Liabilities and Related Data.) |

B 6D (Official Form 6D) (12/07) – Cont 2

**In re** ______________________________, **Case No.** ______________________________
**Debtor** **(if known)**

# SCHEDULE D - CREDITORS HOLDING SECURED CLAIMS

(Continuation Sheet)

| CREDITOR'S NAME AND MAILING ADDRESS INCLUDING ZIP CODE AND AN ACCOUNT NUMBER (*See Instructions Above.*) | CODEBTOR | HUSBAND, WIFE, JOINT, OR COMMUNITY | DATE CLAIM WAS INCURRED, NATURE OF LIEN, AND DESCRIPTION AND VALUE OF PROPERTY SUBJECT TO LIEN | CONTINGENT | UNLIQUIDATED | DISPUTED | AMOUNT OF CLAIM WITHOUT DEDUCTING VALUE OF COLLATERAL | UNSECURED PORTION, IF ANY |
|---|---|---|---|---|---|---|---|---|
| ACCOUNT NO. | | | VALUE $ | | | | | |
| ACCOUNT NO. | | | VALUE $ | | | | | |
| ACCOUNT NO. | | | VALUE $ | | | | | |
| ACCOUNT NO. | | | VALUE $ | | | | | |
| ACCOUNT NO. | | | VALUE $ | | | | | |
| Sheet no._____of_____continuation sheets attached to Schedule of Creditors Holding Secured Claims | | | Subtotal (s)► (Total(s) of this page) | | | | $ | $ |
| | | | Total(s) ► (Use only on last page) | | | | $ | $ |
| | | | | | | | (Report also on Summary of Schedules.) | (If applicable, report also on Statistical Summary of Certain Liabilities and Related Data.) |

B 6E (Official Form 6E) (12/07)

**In re** ______________________________,
**Debtor**

**Case No.**______________________
**(if known)**

# SCHEDULE E - CREDITORS HOLDING UNSECURED PRIORITY CLAIMS

A complete list of claims entitled to priority, listed separately by type of priority, is to be set forth on the sheets provided. Only holders of unsecured claims entitled to priority should be listed in this schedule. In the boxes provided on the attached sheets, state the name, mailing address, including zip code, and last four digits of the account number, if any, of all entities holding priority claims against the debtor or the property of the debtor, as of the date of the filing of the petition. Use a separate continuation sheet for each type of priority and label each with the type of priority.

The complete account number of any account the debtor has with the creditor is useful to the trustee and the creditor and may be provided if the debtor chooses to do so. If a minor child is a creditor, state the child's initials and the name and address of the child's parent or guardian, such as "A.B., a minor child, by John Doe, guardian." Do not disclose the child's name. See, 11 U.S.C. §112 and Fed. R. Bankr. P. 1007(m).

If any entity other than a spouse in a joint case may be jointly liable on a claim, place an "X" in the column labeled "Codebtor," include the entity on the appropriate schedule of creditors, and complete Schedule H-Codebtors. If a joint petition is filed, state whether the husband, wife, both of them, or the marital community may be liable on each claim by placing an "H," "W," "J," or "C" in the column labeled "Husband, Wife, Joint, or Community." If the claim is contingent, place an "X" in the column labeled "Contingent." If the claim is unliquidated, place an "X" in the column labeled "Unliquidated." If the claim is disputed, place an "X" in the column labeled "Disputed." (You may need to place an "X" in more than one of these three columns.)

Report the total of claims listed on each sheet in the box labeled "Subtotals" on each sheet. Report the total of all claims listed on this Schedule E in the box labeled "Total" on the last sheet of the completed schedule. Report this total also on the Summary of Schedules.

Report the total of amounts entitled to priority listed on each sheet in the box labeled "Subtotals" on each sheet. Report the total of all amounts entitled to priority listed on this Schedule E in the box labeled "Totals" on the last sheet of the completed schedule. Individual debtors with primarily consumer debts report this total also on the Statistical Summary of Certain Liabilities and Related Data.

Report the total of amounts not entitled to priority listed on each sheet in the box labeled "Subtotals" on each sheet. Report the total of all amounts not entitled to priority listed on this Schedule E in the box labeled "Totals" on the last sheet of the completed schedule. Individual debtors with primarily consumer debts report this total also on the Statistical Summary of Certain Liabilities and Related Data.

☐ Check this box if debtor has no creditors holding unsecured priority claims to report on this Schedule E.

TYPES OF PRIORITY CLAIMS (Check the appropriate box(es) below if claims in that category are listed on the attached sheets.)

☐ **Domestic Support Obligations**

Claims for domestic support that are owed to or recoverable by a spouse, former spouse, or child of the debtor, or the parent, legal guardian, or responsible relative of such a child, or a governmental unit to whom such a domestic support claim has been assigned to the extent provided in 11 U.S.C. § 507(a)(1).

☐ **Extensions of credit in an involuntary case**

Claims arising in the ordinary course of the debtor's business or financial affairs after the commencement of the case but before the earlier of the appointment of a trustee or the order for relief. 11 U.S.C. § 507(a)(3).

☐ **Wages, salaries, and commissions**

Wages, salaries, and commissions, including vacation, severance, and sick leave pay owing to employees and commissions owing to qualifying independent sales representatives up to $10,950* per person earned within 180 days immediately preceding the filing of the original petition, or the cessation of business, whichever occurred first, to the extent provided in 11 U.S.C. § 507(a)(4).

☐ **Contributions to employee benefit plans**

Money owed to employee benefit plans for services rendered within 180 days immediately preceding the filing of the original petition, or the cessation of business, whichever occurred first, to the extent provided in 11 U.S.C. § 507(a)(5).

B 6E (Official Form 6E) (12/07) – Cont.

**In re** ______________________________,  **Case No.**____________________
**Debtor** **(if known)**

☐ **Certain farmers and fishermen**

Claims of certain farmers and fishermen, up to $5,400* per farmer or fisherman, against the debtor, as provided in 11 U.S.C. § 507(a)(6).

☐ **Deposits by individuals**

Claims of individuals up to $2,425* for deposits for the purchase, lease, or rental of property or services for personal, family, or household use, that were not delivered or provided. 11 U.S.C. § 507(a)(7).

☐ **Taxes and Certain Other Debts Owed to Governmental Units**

Taxes, customs duties, and penalties owing to federal, state, and local governmental units as set forth in 11 U.S.C. § 507(a)(8).

☐ **Commitments to Maintain the Capital of an Insured Depository Institution**

Claims based on commitments to the FDIC, RTC, Director of the Office of Thrift Supervision, Comptroller of the Currency, or Board of Governors of the Federal Reserve System, or their predecessors or successors, to maintain the capital of an insured depository institution. 11 U.S.C. § 507 (a)(9).

☐ **Claims for Death or Personal Injury While Debtor Was Intoxicated**

Claims for death or personal injury resulting from the operation of a motor vehicle or vessel while the debtor was intoxicated from using alcohol, a drug, or another substance. 11 U.S.C. § 507(a)(10).

* Amounts are subject to adjustment on April 1, 2010, and every three years thereafter with respect to cases commenced on or after the date of adjustment.

____ continuation sheets attached

B 6E (Official Form 6E) (12/07) – Cont.

**In re** ______________________________, **Case No.** ______________________
**Debtor** **(if known)**

# SCHEDULE E - CREDITORS HOLDING UNSECURED PRIORITY CLAIMS

(Continuation Sheet)

**Type of Priority for Claims Listed on This Sheet**

| CREDITOR'S NAME, MAILING ADDRESS INCLUDING ZIP CODE, AND ACCOUNT NUMBER *(See instructions above.)* | CODEBTOR | HUSBAND, WIFE, JOINT, OR COMMUNITY | DATE CLAIM WAS INCURRED AND CONSIDERATION FOR CLAIM | CONTINGENT | UNLIQUIDATED | DISPUTED | AMOUNT OF CLAIM | AMOUNT ENTITLED TO PRIORITY | AMOUNT NOT ENTITLED TO PRIORITY, IF ANY |
|---|---|---|---|---|---|---|---|---|---|
| Account No. | | | | | | | | | |
| Account No. | | | | | | | | | |
| Account No. | | | | | | | | | |
| Account No. | | | | | | | | | |
| Sheet no. ___ of ___ continuation sheets attached to Schedule of Creditors Holding Priority Claims | | | | | | Subtotals➤ (Totals of this page) | $ | $ | |
| | | | | | | Total➤ (Use only on last page of the completed Schedule E. Report also on the Summary of Schedules.) | $ | | |
| | | | | | | Totals➤ (Use only on last page of the completed Schedule E. If applicable, report also on the Statistical Summary of Certain Liabilities and Related Data.) | | $ | $ |

B 6F (Official Form 6F) (12/07)

In re ______________________, Case No. ______________________
Debtor (if known)

# SCHEDULE F - CREDITORS HOLDING UNSECURED NONPRIORITY CLAIMS

State the name, mailing address, including zip code, and last four digits of any account number, of all entities holding unsecured claims without priority against the debtor or the property of the debtor, as of the date of filing of the petition. The complete account number of any account the debtor has with the creditor is useful to the trustee and the creditor and may be provided if the debtor chooses to do so. If a minor child is a creditor, state the child's initials and the name and address of the child's parent or guardian, such as "A.B., a minor child, by John Doe, guardian." Do not disclose the child's name. See, 11 U.S.C. §112 and Fed. R. Bankr. P. 1007(m). Do not include claims listed in Schedules D and E. If all creditors will not fit on this page, use the continuation sheet provided.

If any entity other than a spouse in a joint case may be jointly liable on a claim, place an "X" in the column labeled "Codebtor," include the entity on the appropriate schedule of creditors, and complete Schedule H - Codebtors. If a joint petition is filed, state whether the husband, wife, both of them, or the marital community may be liable on each claim by placing an "H," "W," "J," or "C" in the column labeled "Husband, Wife, Joint, or Community."

If the claim is contingent, place an "X" in the column labeled "Contingent." If the claim is unliquidated, place an "X" in the column labeled "Unliquidated." If the claim is disputed, place an "X" in the column labeled "Disputed." (You may need to place an "X" in more than one of these three columns.)

Report the total of all claims listed on this schedule in the box labeled "Total" on the last sheet of the completed schedule. Report this total also on the Summary of Schedules and, if the debtor is an individual with primarily consumer debts, report this total also on the Statistical Summary of Certain Liabilities and Related Data..

☐ Check this box if debtor has no creditors holding unsecured claims to report on this Schedule F.

| CREDITOR'S NAME, MAILING ADDRESS INCLUDING ZIP CODE, AND ACCOUNT NUMBER *(See instructions above.)* | CODEBTOR | HUSBAND, WIFE, JOINT, OR COMMUNITY | DATE CLAIM WAS INCURRED AND CONSIDERATION FOR CLAIM. IF CLAIM IS SUBJECT TO SETOFF, SO STATE. | CONTINGENT | UNLIQUIDATED | DISPUTED | AMOUNT OF CLAIM |
|---|---|---|---|---|---|---|---|
| ACCOUNT NO. | | | | | | | |
| ACCOUNT NO. | | | | | | | |
| ACCOUNT NO. | | | | | | | |
| ACCOUNT NO. | | | | | | | |

Subtotal➤ $

____continuation sheets attached

Total➤ $
(Use only on last page of the completed Schedule F.)
(Report also on Summary of Schedules and, if applicable, on the Statistical Summary of Certain Liabilities and Related Data.)

B 6F (Official Form 6F) (12/07) - Cont.

**In re** ______________________________, **Case No.** ______________________
**Debtor** **(if known)**

# SCHEDULE F - CREDITORS HOLDING UNSECURED NONPRIORITY CLAIMS

(Continuation Sheet)

| CREDITOR'S NAME, MAILING ADDRESS INCLUDING ZIP CODE, AND ACCOUNT NUMBER (See instructions above.) | CODEBTOR | HUSBAND, WIFE, JOINT, OR COMMUNITY | DATE CLAIM WAS INCURRED AND CONSIDERATION FOR CLAIM. IF CLAIM IS SUBJECT TO SETOFF, SO STATE. | CONTINGENT | UNLIQUIDATED | DISPUTED | AMOUNT OF CLAIM |
|---|---|---|---|---|---|---|---|
| ACCOUNT NO. | | | | | | | |
| ACCOUNT NO. | | | | | | | |
| ACCOUNT NO. | | | | | | | |
| ACCOUNT NO. | | | | | | | |
| ACCOUNT NO. | | | | | | | |
| | | | | | | Subtotal➤ | $ |
| | | | | | | Total➤ (Use only on last page of the completed Schedule F.) (Report also on Summary of Schedules and, if applicable on the Statistical Summary of Certain Liabilities and Related Data.) | $ |

Sheet no.______ of______ continuation sheets attached to Schedule of Creditors Holding Unsecured Nonpriority Claims

B 6G (Official Form 6G) (12/07)

In re ______________________________, Case No.____________________
Debtor (if known)

# SCHEDULE G - EXECUTORY CONTRACTS AND UNEXPIRED LEASES

Describe all executory contracts of any nature and all unexpired leases of real or personal property. Include any timeshare interests. State nature of debtor's interest in contract, i.e., "Purchaser," "Agent," etc. State whether debtor is the lessor or lessee of a lease. Provide the names and complete mailing addresses of all other parties to each lease or contract described. If a minor child is a party to one of the leases or contracts, state the child's initials and the name and address of the child's parent or guardian, such as "A.B., a minor child, by John Doe, guardian." Do not disclose the child's name. See, 11 U.S.C. §112 and Fed. R. Bankr. P. 1007(m).

☐ Check this box if debtor has no executory contracts or unexpired leases.

| NAME AND MAILING ADDRESS, INCLUDING ZIP CODE, OF OTHER PARTIES TO LEASE OR CONTRACT. | DESCRIPTION OF CONTRACT OR LEASE AND NATURE OF DEBTOR'S INTEREST. STATE WHETHER LEASE IS FOR NONRESIDENTIAL REAL PROPERTY. STATE CONTRACT NUMBER OF ANY GOVERNMENT CONTRACT. |
|---|---|
| | |
| | |
| | |
| | |
| | |
| | |

B 6H (Official Form 6H) (12/07)

In re ______________________, Case No. ______________________
Debtor (if known)

# SCHEDULE H - CODEBTORS

Provide the information requested concerning any person or entity, other than a spouse in a joint case, that is also liable on any debts listed by the debtor in the schedules of creditors. Include all guarantors and co-signers. If the debtor resides or resided in a community property state, commonwealth, or territory (including Alaska, Arizona, California, Idaho, Louisiana, Nevada, New Mexico, Puerto Rico, Texas, Washington, or Wisconsin) within the eight-year period immediately preceding the commencement of the case, identify the name of the debtor's spouse and of any former spouse who resides or resided with the debtor in the community property state, commonwealth, or territory. Include all names used by the nondebtor spouse during the eight years immediately preceding the commencement of this case. If a minor child is a codebtor or a creditor, state the child's initials and the name and address of the child's parent or guardian, such as "A.B., a minor child, by John Doe, guardian." Do not disclose the child's name. See, 11 U.S.C. §112 and Fed. R. Bankr. P. 1007(m).

☐ Check this box if debtor has no codebtors.

| NAME AND ADDRESS OF CODEBTOR | NAME AND ADDRESS OF CREDITOR |
|---|---|
| | |
| | |
| | |
| | |
| | |
| | |
| | |
| | |

B6I (Official Form 6I) (12/07)

In re ______________________________, Case No. ______________________
Debtor (if known)

# SCHEDULE I - CURRENT INCOME OF INDIVIDUAL DEBTOR(S)

The column labeled "Spouse" must be completed in all cases filed by joint debtors and by every married debtor, whether or not a joint petition is filed, unless the spouses are separated and a joint petition is not filed. Do not state the name of any minor child. The average monthly income calculated on this form may differ from the current monthly income calculated on Form 22A, 22B, or 22C.

| Debtor's Marital Status: | DEPENDENTS OF DEBTOR AND SPOUSE | |
|---|---|---|
| | RELATIONSHIP(S): | AGE(S): |

| **Employment:** | DEBTOR | SPOUSE |
|---|---|---|
| Occupation | | |
| Name of Employer | | |
| How long employed | | |
| Address of Employer | | |

| INCOME: (Estimate of average or projected monthly income at time case filed) | DEBTOR | SPOUSE |
|---|---|---|
| 1. Monthly gross wages, salary, and commissions (Prorate if not paid monthly) | $ | $ |
| 2. Estimate monthly overtime | $ | $ |
| 3. SUBTOTAL | $ | $ |
| 4. LESS PAYROLL DEDUCTIONS | | |
| a. Payroll taxes and social security | $ | $ |
| b. Insurance | $ | $ |
| c. Union dues | $ | $ |
| d. Other (Specify): ______________ | $ | $ |
| 5. SUBTOTAL OF PAYROLL DEDUCTIONS | $ | $ |
| 6. TOTAL NET MONTHLY TAKE HOME PAY | $ | $ |
| 7. Regular income from operation of business or profession or farm (Attach detailed statement) | $ | $ |
| 8. Income from real property | $ | $ |
| 9. Interest and dividends | $ | $ |
| 10. Alimony, maintenance or support payments payable to the debtor for the debtor's use or that of dependents listed above | $ | $ |
| 11. Social security or government assistance (Specify): ______________ | $ | $ |
| 12. Pension or retirement income | $ | $ |
| 13. Other monthly income (Specify): ______________ | $ | $ |
| 14. SUBTOTAL OF LINES 7 THROUGH 13 | $ | $ |
| 15. AVERAGE MONTHLY INCOME (Add amounts on lines 6 and 14) | $ | $ |
| 16. COMBINED AVERAGE MONTHLY INCOME: (Combine column totals from line 15) | $ | |

(Report also on Summary of Schedules and, if applicable, on Statistical Summary of Certain Liabilities and Related Data)

17. Describe any increase or decrease in income reasonably anticipated to occur within the year following the filing of this document:

______________________________________________________________

**B6J (Official Form 6J) (12/07)**

**In re** ______________________________,
**Debtor**

**Case No.** ______________________
**(if known)**

# SCHEDULE J - CURRENT EXPENDITURES OF INDIVIDUAL DEBTOR(S)

Complete this schedule by estimating the average or projected monthly expenses of the debtor and the debtor's family at time case filed. Prorate any payments made bi-weekly, quarterly, semi-annually, or annually to show monthly rate. The average monthly expenses calculated on this form may differ from the deductions from income allowed on Form22A or 22C.

☐ Check this box if a joint petition is filed and debtor's spouse maintains a separate household. Complete a separate schedule of expenditures labeled "Spouse."

1. Rent or home mortgage payment (include lot rented for mobile home) $ ________
   a. Are real estate taxes included? Yes ______ No ______
   b. Is property insurance included? Yes ______ No ______
2. Utilities: a. Electricity and heating fuel $ ________
   b. Water and sewer $ ________
   c. Telephone $ ________
   d. Other ______________________________ $ ________
3. Home maintenance (repairs and upkeep) $ ________
4. Food $ ________
5. Clothing $ ________
6. Laundry and dry cleaning $ ________
7. Medical and dental expenses $ ________
8. Transportation (not including car payments) $ ________
9. Recreation, clubs and entertainment, newspapers, magazines, etc. $ ________
10.Charitable contributions $ ________
11.Insurance (not deducted from wages or included in home mortgage payments)
   a. Homeowner's or renter's $ ________
   b. Life $ ________
   c. Health $ ________
   d. Auto $ ________
   e. Other ______________________________ $ ________
12. Taxes (not deducted from wages or included in home mortgage payments)
(Specify) ______________________________ $ ________
13. Installment payments: (In chapter 11, 12, and 13 cases, do not list payments to be included in the plan)
   a. Auto $ ________
   b. Other ______________________________ $ ________
   c. Other ______________________________ $ ________
14. Alimony, maintenance, and support paid to others $ ________
15. Payments for support of additional dependents not living at your home $ ________
16. Regular expenses from operation of business, profession, or farm (attach detailed statement) $ ________
17. Other ______________________________ $ ________
18. AVERAGE MONTHLY EXPENSES (Total lines 1-17. Report also on Summary of Schedules and, if applicable, on the Statistical Summary of Certain Liabilities and Related Data.) $ ________
19. Describe any increase or decrease in expenditures reasonably anticipated to occur within the year following the filing of this document:

20. STATEMENT OF MONTHLY NET INCOME
   a. Average monthly income from Line 15 of Schedule I $ ________
   b. Average monthly expenses from Line 18 above $ ________
   c. Monthly net income (a. minus b.) $ ________

B6 Declaration (Official Form 6 - Declaration) (12/07)

In re ______________________________, Case No. ______________________
Debtor (if known)

# DECLARATION CONCERNING DEBTOR'S SCHEDULES

## DECLARATION UNDER PENALTY OF PERJURY BY INDIVIDUAL DEBTOR

I declare under penalty of perjury that I have read the foregoing summary and schedules, consisting of _____ sheets, and that they are true and correct to the best of my knowledge, information, and belief.

Date ______________________________ Signature: ______________________________
Debtor

Date ______________________________ Signature: ______________________________
(Joint Debtor, if any)

[If joint case, both spouses must sign.]

---

## DECLARATION AND SIGNATURE OF NON-ATTORNEY BANKRUPTCY PETITION PREPARER (See 11 U.S.C. § 110)

I declare under penalty of perjury that: (1) I am a bankruptcy petition preparer as defined in 11 U.S.C. § 110; (2) I prepared this document for compensation and have provided the debtor with a copy of this document and the notices and information required under 11 U.S.C. §§ 110(b), 110(h) and 342(b); and, (3) if rules or guidelines have been promulgated pursuant to 11 U.S.C § 110(h) setting a maximum fee for services chargeable by bankruptcy petition preparers, I have given the debtor notice of the maximum amount before preparing any document for filing for a debtor or accepting any fee from the debtor, as required by that section.

______________________________ ______________________
Printed or Typed Name and Title, if any, of Bankruptcy Petition Preparer Social Security No. *(Required by 11 U.S.C. § 110.)*

*If the bankruptcy petition preparer is not an individual, state the name, title (if any), address, and social security number of the officer, principal, responsible person, or partner who signs this document.*

______________________________

______________________________

______________________________
Address

X ______________________________ ______________________
Signature of Bankruptcy Petition Preparer Date

Names and Social Security numbers of all other individuals who prepared or assisted in preparing this document, unless the bankruptcy petition preparer is not an individual:

*If more than one person prepared this document, attach additional signed sheets conforming to the appropriate Official Form for each person.*

*A bankruptcy petition preparer's failure to comply with the provisions of title 11 and the Federal Rules of Bankruptcy Procedure may result in fines or imprisonment or both. 11 U.S.C. § 110; 18 U.S.C. § 156*

---

## DECLARATION UNDER PENALTY OF PERJURY ON BEHALF OF A CORPORATION OR PARTNERSHIP

I, the ______________________________ [the president or other officer or an authorized agent of the corporation or a member or an authorized agent of the partnership ] of the ______________________________ [corporation or partnership] named as debtor in this case, declare under penalty of perjury that I have read the foregoing summary and schedules, consisting of _____ sheets (*Total shown on summary page plus 1*), and that they are true and correct to the best of my knowledge, information, and belief.

Date ______________________________ Signature: ______________________________

______________________________
[Print or type name of individual signing on behalf of debtor.]

*[An individual signing on behalf of a partnership or corporation must indicate position or relationship to debtor.]*

---

*Penalty for making a false statement or concealing property:* Fine of up to $500,000 or imprisonment for up to 5 years or both. 18 U.S.C. §§ 152 and 3571.

(Added Aug. 1, 1991; amended Mar. 16, 1993; Mar. 14, 1995; Oct. 1, 1997; Dec. 1, 2003; Oct. 17, 2005; Oct. 1, 2006; Dec. 1, 2007.)

NOTES OF ADVISORY COMMITTEE ON RULES—1991

These schedules shall be used to comply with § 521(1) of the Code and Rule 1007(b). Schedules A, B, D, E, and F constitute the schedule of assets and liabilities. Schedules I and J constitute a schedule of current income and current expenditures for individual and joint debtors. Two new schedules have been created, Schedule G—Executory Contracts and Unexpired Leases, and Schedule H—Codebtors.

The order of the schedules has been arranged with the summary sheet in front and with the schedules of assets appearing first, followed by the schedules of liabilities. This structure corresponds to the customary pattern by which trustees and creditors review these documents and to the format of the accounting profession for balance sheets.

The schedules require a complete listing of assets and liabilities but leave many of the details to investigation by the trustee. Instructions in the former schedules to provide details concerning "written instruments" relating to the debtor's property or debts have been deleted. Section 521(3) of the Code requires the debtor to cooperate with the trustee, who can administer the estate more effectively by requesting any documents from the debtor rather than relying on descriptions in the schedules which may prove to be inaccurate.

Leasehold interests in both real and personal property are to be reported in Schedule G—Executory Contracts and Unexpired Leases. This information should not be repeated in the schedules of assets.

Generally in these schedules, a creditor's claim will be listed only once, even if the claim is secured only in part, or is entitled only in part to priority under § 507(a) of the Code, with the remainder of the claim to be treated as a general unsecured claim. For example, a partially secured creditor whose claim is reported in Schedule D—Creditors Holding Secured Claims will be listed together with the value of the property securing the claim and a notation of the amount of any unsecured portion of the claim. Information concerning the unsecured portion should not be repeated in Schedule F—Creditors Holding Nonpriority Unsecured Claims. Any resulting overstatement of the amounts owed on secured and priority claims as reported on the summary sheet is offset by a corresponding understatement of the amount owed on unsecured claims.

If a debtor has no property or no creditors in a particular category, an affirmative statement to that effect is required. Married debtors should indicate whether property is jointly or separately owned and whether spouses are jointly or separately liable for debts, using the columns provided in the schedules.

Former "Schedule B-3. Property not otherwise scheduled," has been deleted and its two questions moved. Schedule B—Personal Property now includes at item 33, "Other personal property of any kind not already listed." The only other question on former Schedule B-3 concerned assignments for the benefit of creditors; it has been moved to the Statement of Financial Affairs.

*Schedule A—Real Property.* Instructions at the top of the form indicate the scope of the interests in property to be reported on the schedule. Leasehold interests of the debtor are not reported here but on the Schedule of Executory Contracts and Unexpired Leases. The trustee will request copies of deeds or other instruments necessary to the administration of the estate.

*Schedule B—Personal Property.* This schedule is to be used for reporting all of the debtor's interests in personal property except leases and executory contracts, which are to be listed on the Schedule of Executory Contracts and Unexpired Leases. Several new categories of property have been added to the schedule, *i.e.*, aircraft, and interests in IRA, ERISA, Keogh, or other pension or profit-sharing plans. To minimize the potential for concealment of assets, the debtor must declare whether the debtor has any property in each category on the schedule. The trustee can request copies of any documents concerning the debtor's property necessary to the administration of the estate.

*Schedule C—Property Claimed as Exempt.* The form of the schedule has been modified to eliminate duplication of information provided elsewhere. The location of property, for example, which formerly was required here, is disclosed in the schedules of real and personal property. The requirement that the debtor state the present use of the property also has been eliminated as best left to inquiry by the trustee. Exemptions in some states are granted by constitutional provisions; accordingly, the requirement that the debtor state the "statute" creating an exemption has been changed to request a statement of the relevant "law."

This schedule adds a new requirement that the debtor state the market value of the property in addition to the amount claimed as exempt.

*Schedule D—Creditors Holding Secured Claims.* Schedules D, E, and F have been redesigned with address boxes sized to match the number of characters which can be accommodated on the computerized noticing systems used by the courts. The size also closely approximates that of standard mailing labels. Space is designated at the top of the box for the debtor's account number with the creditor. The design of the form is intended to reduce the volume of misdirected creditor mail.

The form requires the debtor to state affirmatively that a claim is disputed, unliquidated, or contingent. The existence of any type of codebtor is to be disclosed, but details are to be provided in Schedule H, as they are not needed here. Duplication of information also has been kept to a minimum by deleting requests that the debtor indicate on this schedule whether a debt has been reduced to judgment and the date on which a creditor repossessed any collateral. Requests for details concerning negotiable instruments and the consideration for a claim, formerly part of the schedule, are left to the trustee's inquiries.

*Schedule E—Creditors Holding Unsecured Priority Claims.* The schedule lists all of the types of claims entitled to priority and requires the debtor to indicate the existence of claims in each category. Continuation sheets are provided. The type of priority claim is to be noted at the top of the continuation sheet, and each type must be reported on a separate sheet. This schedule also requires the debtor to indicate the existence of any codebtors. As in Schedule D—Creditors Holding Secured Claims, requests for information concerning judgments and negotiable instruments have been deleted.

*Schedule F—Creditors Holding Unsecured Nonpriority Claims.* This schedule has been revised generally in conformity with the other schedules of creditors. If a claim is subject to setoff, the debtor is required to so state.

*Schedule G—Executory Contracts and Unexpired Leases* Rule 1007(b) requires the debtor to file a schedule of executory contracts and unexpired leases, unless the court orders otherwise. All unexpired leases of either real or personal property are to be reported on this schedule. The schedule also requires the debtor to disclose specific information to assist the trustee in identifying leases which must be assumed within 60 days after the order for relief or be deemed rejected under § 365(d) of the Code.

*Schedule H—Schedule of Codebtors.* This schedule is designed to provide the trustee and creditors with information about codebtors of all types other than spouses in joint cases. The completed schedule provides information concerning non-debtor parties, such as guarantors and non-debtor spouses having an interest in property as tenants by the entirety. In chapter 12 and chapter 13 cases, the completed schedule also indicates those persons who may be entitled to certain protections from creditor action under §§ 1201 and 1301 of the Code.

*Schedule I—Schedule of Current Income of Individual Debtor(s) and Schedule J—Schedule of Current Expenditures of Individual Debtor(s).* Former Official Form No. 6A has been divided into a schedule of current income and a separate schedule of current expenditures. The language is substantially the same as in former Official Form No. 6A. In light of the abrogation of Official Form No. 10, the Chapter 13 Statement, style changes have been made so that these schedules can be used by individual and joint debtors in all chapters.

NOTES OF ADVISORY COMMITTEE ON RULES—1993 AMENDMENT

Schedule E (Creditors Holding Unsecured Priority Claims) has been changed to conform to the statutory amendment that added subsection (a)(8) to §507 of the Code. Pub. L. No. 101–647, (Crime Control Act of 1990), added the new subsection, which had the effect of creating an eighth priority for claims of certain governmental units based on commitments to maintain the capital of an insured depository institution.

NOTES OF ADVISORY COMMITTEE ON RULES—1995 AMENDMENT

Schedule E—Creditors Holding Unsecured Priority Claims is amended to add the new seventh priority afforded to debts for alimony, maintenance, or support of a spouse, former spouse, or child of the debtor by the Bankruptcy Reform Act of 1994. Statutory references are amended to conform to the paragraph numbers of section 507(a) of the Code as renumbered by the 1994 Act. Schedule E also is amended to add commissions owed to certain independent sales representatives and to raise the maximum dollar amounts for certain priorities in accordance with amendments made by the 1994 Act to section 507(a) of the Code. The 1994 Act also amended section 104 of the Code to provide for future adjustment of the maximum dollar amounts specified in section 507(a) to be made by administrative action at three-year intervals to reflect changes in the consumer price index. Schedule E is amended to give notice that these dollar amounts are subject to change without formal amendment to the official form.

The Schedules are a "document for filing" that may be prepared by a "bankruptcy petition preparer" as defined in 11 U.S.C. §110, which was added to the Code by the 1994 Act; accordingly, a signature line for such preparer is added. In addition to signing, a bankruptcy petition preparer is required by section 110 to disclose the information requested.

NOTES OF ADVISORY COMMITTEE ON RULES—1997 AMENDMENT

The form is amended to add to the column labels a reference to community liability for claims. The amendment is technical and corrects an editorial oversight.

COMMITTEE NOTES ON RULES—2003 AMENDMENT

The instructions to Schedule D (Creditors Holding Secured Claims), Schedule E (Creditors Holding Unsecured Priority Claims), and Schedule F (Creditors Holding Unsecured Nonpriority Claims) are amended to inform the debtor that the debtor must list the last four digits of any account number with the listed creditor, and that the debtor may, in its discretion, include the entire account number in the schedules. Schedule I (Current Income of Individual Debtor(s)) is amended to provide greater privacy to minors and other dependents of the debtor by deleting the requirement that the debtor disclose their names. Pursuant to §110(c) of the Bankruptcy Code, the certification by a non-attorney bankruptcy petition preparer requires a petition preparer to provide the full social security number of the individual who actually prepares the document.

COMMITTEE NOTES ON RULES—2005 AMENDMENT

The forms of the Schedules of Assets and Liabilities are amended to implement the provisions of the Bankruptcy Abuse Prevention and Consumer Protection Act of 2005, Pub. L. No. 109–8, 119 Stat. 23, (April 20, 2005). An amendment that directs the debtor to avoid disclosing the name of any minor child occurs in several of the schedules in conformity with §112 which was added to the Code in 2005. Section 112 provides for the debtor to provide the name of any minor child confidentially to the court, should the trustee need the information to evaluate properly the information filed by the debtor.

The "Statistical Summary of Certain Liabilities" is added to collect information needed to prepare statistical reports required under 28 U.S.C. §159, which was enacted as part of the 2005 Act.

Schedules A, B, C, and D are amended to delete the word "market" from the columns in which the debtor reports the value of various kinds of property. Amendments to §506 of the Code enacted in 2005 specify that "replacement value" must be used in connection with certain property. The schedules no longer specify "market" value and permit the debtor to choose the appropriate one, whether that be replacement, market, or some other value. Valuation of property, generally, is the subject of extensive provisions in the Code, and the deletion of the word "market" from the determinations of value to be made by the debtor on the schedules is intended to remove any inference about choice of valuation standard. This deletion simply indicates that the form takes no position on which Code provision or valuation standard may be applicable in any instance.

The following paragraphs describe changes that are specific to each schedule.

Schedule B—Personal Property is amended to require the debtor to list any interests in an education IRA, as §541(b)(5), added to the Code in 2005, makes special provision for them. The schedule also is amended to require the debtor to disclose the existence of any customer lists or other compilations containing personally identifiable information provided by an individual to the debtor in connection with obtaining a product or service from the debtor for personal, family, or household purposes. This amendment implements §332, which was added to the Code in 2005.

Schedule C—Property Claimed as Exempt is amended to delete descriptive information concerning the length of domicile required for the debtor to qualify to claim certain exemptions. Any summary of the amendments enacted in 2005 to §522 of the Code concerning these requirements might inadvertently cause the debtor to lose important rights. Accordingly, the form now directs the debtor to indicate whether exemptions are being claimed under §522(b)(2) or §522(b)(3) and whether the debtor claims a homestead exemption that exceeds $125,000.

Schedule E—Creditors Holding Unsecured Priority Claims is amended to implement the changes in priority to which a claim may be entitled under 11 U.S.C. §507 as amended by the 2005 Act and to add the new priority included in the Reform Act for claims for death or personal injury while the debtor was intoxicated. "Subtotal" and "Total" boxes have been added to the column labeled "Amount Entitled to Priority" to assist the individual debtor to complete the Current Monthly Income ("CMI" or "Means Test") form.

Schedule G—Executory Contracts and Unexpired Leases is amended by deleting the note to the debtor advising that parties listed on this schedule may not receive notice of the filing of the bankruptcy case unless they also are listed on one of the schedules of liabilities. The better practice is for all parties to transactions with the debtor to receive notice of the filing of the case, and an amendment to Rule 1007 requiring the debtor to provide a mailing list that includes these parties is scheduled to take effect December 1, 2005.

Schedule H—Codebtors is amended to add specifics about community property jurisdictions in connection with the requirement to provide the name of any spouse of a debtor who resides or resided in a community property jurisdiction. This amendment also mirrors amendments made in 1997 to Official Form 7, the Statement of Financial Affairs, and will assure that these codebtors receive notice of the filing of the bankruptcy case. The form also is amended to extend from six years to eight years the time period for which this information is reported pursuant to the 2005 amendments to §727(a)(8) of the Code.

Schedule I—Current Income of Individual Debtor(s) is amended to require the income of a nondebtor spouse to be reported in cases filed under chapters 7 and 11. Line numbers have been added to assist the debtor in calculating and reporting totals. A new subtotal line for income from sources other than as an employee and a new "total monthly income" line provide for this form to be used in conjunction with Schedule J to satisfy the requirements of §521(a)(1)(B)(v), which was added to the Code in 2005. The form also has been revised to provide the statement concerning any anticipated increase or decrease in income required in §521(a)(1)(B)(vi), which also was added to the Code in 2005.

Schedule J—Current Expenditures of Individual Debtor(s). A direction has been added to require the debtor to report any increase or decrease in expenses anticipated to occur within the year following the filing of the document, as required by §521(a)(1)(B)(vi), which was added to the Code in 2005. The form also is amended to provide, in conjunction with Schedule I, a statement of monthly net income, itemized to show how the amount is calculated, as required by §522(a)(1)(B)(v), which was added to the Code in 2005.

Declaration Concerning Debtor's Schedules. The declaration by a non-attorney bankruptcy petition preparer is amended to include material mandated by §110 of the Code as amended in 2005.

COMMITTEE NOTES ON RULES—2006 AMENDMENT

In order to comply fully with the statistical reporting requirements of 28 U.S.C. §159, which was enacted as part of the 2005 Act [Bankruptcy Abuse Prevention and Consumer Protection Act of 2005, Pub. L. 109–8, Apr. 20, 2005, 119 Stat. 23] and takes effect in October 2006, the "Statistical Summary of Certain Liabilities" is renamed "Statistical Summary of Certain Liabilities and Related Data," and additional information is required to be stated there. Collecting in one place the bulk of the information to be used in the reports required under 28 U.S.C. §159 will assist the courts and the Director of the Administrative Office of the United States Courts to fulfill their statutory responsibilities.

Schedule D is amended to provide for creating a total of any unsecured amounts (amounts that exceed the value of the collateral) owed to creditors holding secured claims, and for stating this amount on the Statistical Summary of Certain Liabilities and Related Data. Schedule E is amended to provide for creating totals of the amounts entitled to priority and of any amounts that exceed the statutory limits on certain priorities and to direct the debtor to report these amounts on the Statistical Summary of Certain Liabilities and Related Data. Schedule F is amended to direct the debtor to report the total of this schedule both on the Summary of Schedules and on the Statistical Summary of Certain Liabilities.

The statistical reports required under 28 U.S.C. §159 must include "the current monthly income, average income, and average expenses" of individual debtors with primarily consumer debts as reported on the schedules filed by those debtors. Accordingly, Schedules I and J, on which debtors already are directed to report average income and average expenses are amended to label the totals arrived at by completing the schedules as "average monthly income" and "average monthly expenses." These amendments make no substantive changes, simply conforming the terminology on these schedules to that used in §159.

The amount of the debtor's current monthly income, which also is required by §159, is derived from Official Forms 22A, 22B, or 22C, depending on the chapter under which the debtor files. This amount is included on the Statistical Summary of Certain Liabilities and Related Data as a convenience to make reports under §159 easier to compile.

The Declaration Concerning Debtor's Schedules is amended in the section designated for signing and verifying by an individual or joint debtor. The amendment accommodates the requirement that individual debtors must complete both the Summary of Schedules and the Statistical Summary of Certain Liabilities and Related Data by directing the debtor to state number of pages being verified as the number of sheets in the completed schedules "plus 2."

COMMITTEE NOTES ON RULES—2005–2007 AMENDMENT

[The 2005–2007 Committee Note incorporates Committee Notes previously published in 2005 and 2006.]

The forms of the Schedules of Assets and Liabilities are amended to implement the provisions of the Bankruptcy Abuse Prevention and Consumer Protection Act of 2005, Pub. L. No. 109–8, 119 Stat. 23, (April 20, 2005) ("BAPCPA"). An amendment that directs the debtor to avoid disclosing the name and address of any minor child occurs in Schedules B, D, E, F, G, and H in conformity with §112 which was added to the Code in 2005. Section 112 provides for the debtor to furnish the name of any minor child confidentially to the court, should the trustee need the information to evaluate properly the information filed by the debtor. In addition, those schedules are amended to add to the reference to Rule 1007(m), with respect to a minor child, a direction to include for noticing purposes the name, address, and legal relationship to the child of "a person described" in that rule. Rule 1007(m) requires the person named to be someone on whom process would be served in an adversary proceeding against the child.

The "Statistical Summary of Certain Liabilities and Related Data" is added to collect from individual debtors with primarily consumer debts the information needed to prepare statistical reports required under 28 U.S.C. §159, which was enacted as part of BAPCPA. Collecting the bulk of the information to be used in these statistical reports in the Summary of Schedules and the statistical summary will assist the courts and the Director of the Administrative Office to fulfill their statutory responsibilities. Schedules D and E are amended to provide additional totals and, together with Schedule F, to direct debtors who must complete the statistical summary to report total amounts there. Similarly, Schedules I and J are amended to conform their terminology to that used in 28 U.S.C. §159 and direct debtors who must complete the statistical summary to report the specified amounts there.

Schedules A, B, C, and D are amended to delete the word "market" from the columns in which the debtor reports the value of various kinds of property. Amendments to §506 of the Code enacted in 2005 specify that "replacement value" must be used in connection with certain property. The schedules no longer specify "market" value and permit the debtor to choose the appropriate one, whether that be replacement, market, or some other value. Valuation of property, generally, is the subject of extensive provisions in the Code, and the deletion of the word "market" from the determinations of value to be made by the debtor on the schedules is intended to remove any inference about choice of valuation standard. This deletion simply indicates that the form takes no position on which Code provision or valuation standard may be applicable in any particular instance.

The following paragraphs describe changes that are specific to each schedule:

Schedule B—Personal Property is amended to require the debtor to list any interests in an education IRA, because §541(b)(5), added to the Code in 2005, makes special provision for them. The schedule is also amended to require the debtor to disclose the existence of any customer lists or other compilations containing personally identifiable information provided by an individual to the debtor in connection with obtaining a product or service from the debtor for personal, family, or household purposes. This amendment implements §332, which was added to the Code by BAPCPA in 2005.

Schedule C—Property Claimed as Exempt is amended to delete descriptive information concerning the length of domicile required for the debtor to qualify to claim certain exemptions. Any summary of the BAPCPA amendments to §522 of the Code concerning these requirements might inadvertently cause the debtor to lose important rights. Accordingly, the form now directs the debtor to indicate whether exemptions are being claimed under §522(b)(2) or §522(b)(3) and whether the debtor claims a homestead exemption that exceeds $136,875.

Schedule D—Creditors Holding Secured Claims is amended to provide for creating a total of any unsecured amounts (amounts that exceed the value of the collateral) owed to creditors holding secured claims. In addition to facilitating statistical reporting, providing a breakdown of the amounts owed to creditors listed on this schedule will assist the individual debtor in completing the means test calculation under §707(b)(2)(A)(i) of the Code.

Schedule E—Creditors Holding Unsecured Priority Claims is amended to implement the changes in priority to which a claim may be entitled under 11 U.S.C. §507 as amended by BAPCPA and to add the new priority included in the 2005 Act for claims for death or personal injury while the debtor was intoxicated. "Subtotal" and "Total" boxes have been added to the columns labeled "Amount Entitled to Priority" and "Amount Not Entitled to Priority" for statistical reporting purposes and to assist the individual debtor in completing the means test calculation under §707(b)(2)(A)(i) of the Code.

Schedule H—Codebtors is amended to add specifics about community property jurisdictions in connection with the requirement to provide the name of any spouse of a debtor who resides or resided in a community property jurisdiction. This amendment also mirrors amendments made in 1997 to Official Form 7, the Statement of Financial Affairs, and will assure that these codebtors receive notice of the filing of the bankruptcy case. The form also is amended to extend from six years to eight years the time period for which this information is reported pursuant to the 2005 amendments to §727(a)(8) of the Code.

Schedule I—Current Income of Individual Debtor(s) is amended to make it clear that "every" married debtor must provide income information for both spouses, unless the spouses are separated and a joint petition is not filed. The description of the income to be reported is revised to clarify that the purpose of this schedule is to obtain information about actual income on the date the bankruptcy case is filed and which a debtor reasonably expects in the future in contrast to the debtor's "current monthly income" as defined in §101(10A) and reported on Form 22A, 22B, or 22C. And a statement included at the top of the form also explains that the income calculated [sic] this form may be different than the current monthly income. Line numbers have been added to assist the debtor in calculating and reporting totals. A new subtotal line for income from sources other than as an employee and a new "average monthly income" line will enable this form to be used in conjunction with Schedule J to satisfy the requirements of §521(a)(1)(B)(v), which was added to the Code by BAPCPA. New statistical reporting requirements in 28 U.S.C. §159 also require "average monthly income." In addition, the form is revised to provide the statement concerning any anticipated increase or decrease in income required in §521(a)(1)(B)(vi), also added to the Code in 2005.

Schedule J—Current Expenditures of Individual Debtor(s). In conjunction with amendments to Schedule I, the form is amended to provide for reporting the debtor's actual "average monthly expenses," as required by 28 U.S.C. §159 and a statement of monthly net income, itemized to show how the amount is calculated, as required by §522(a)(1)(B)(v), which was added to the Code by BAPCPA in 2005. In addition, line numbers have been inserted and the description of expenses revised to make it clear than [sic] the purpose of this schedule is to obtain information about a debtor's actual and reasonably foreseeable expenses on the date the bankruptcy case is filed. And a statement similar to the statement at the top of Schedule I explains that the expenses calculated on the form may differ from the expenses calculated on Forms [sic] 22A or 22C. A direction has been added to require the debtor to report any increase or decrease in expenses anticipated to occur within the year following the filing of the document, as required by §521(a)(1)(B)(vi), which also was added to the Code in 2005.

Declaration Concerning Debtor's Schedules. The declaration by individual or joint debtors is amended to require the debtor to merely state the total number of pages being verified. The declaration and signature of any non-attorney bankruptcy petition preparer is amended to include material mandated by §110 of the Code as amended in 2005.

B 7 (Official Form 7) (12/07)

# UNITED STATES BANKRUPTCY COURT

In re:____________________________________________, Case No. ____________________________________
Debtor (if known)

## STATEMENT OF FINANCIAL AFFAIRS

This statement is to be completed by every debtor. Spouses filing a joint petition may file a single statement on which the information for both spouses is combined. If the case is filed under chapter 12 or chapter 13, a married debtor must furnish information for both spouses whether or not a joint petition is filed, unless the spouses are separated and a joint petition is not filed. An individual debtor engaged in business as a sole proprietor, partner, family farmer, or self-employed professional, should provide the information requested on this statement concerning all such activities as well as the individual's personal affairs. To indicate payments, transfers and the like to minor children, state the child's initials and the name and address of the child's parent or guardian, such as "A.B., a minor child, by John Doe, guardian." Do not disclose the child's name. See, 11 U.S.C. §112 and Fed. R. Bankr. P. 1007(m).

Questions 1 - 18 are to be completed by all debtors. Debtors that are or have been in business, as defined below, also must complete Questions 19 - 25. **If the answer to an applicable question is "None," mark the box labeled "None."** If additional space is needed for the answer to any question, use and attach a separate sheet properly identified with the case name, case number (if known), and the number of the question.

*DEFINITIONS*

*"In business."* A debtor is "in business" for the purpose of this form if the debtor is a corporation or partnership. An individual debtor is "in business" for the purpose of this form if the debtor is or has been, within six years immediately preceding the filing of this bankruptcy case, any of the following: an officer, director, managing executive, or owner of 5 percent or more of the voting or equity securities of a corporation; a partner, other than a limited partner, of a partnership; a sole proprietor or self-employed full-time or part-time. An individual debtor also may be "in business" for the purpose of this form if the debtor engages in a trade, business, or other activity, other than as an employee, to supplement income from the debtor's primary employment.

*"Insider."* The term "insider" includes but is not limited to: relatives of the debtor; general partners of the debtor and their relatives; corporations of which the debtor is an officer, director, or person in control; officers, directors, and any owner of 5 percent or more of the voting or equity securities of a corporate debtor and their relatives; affiliates of the debtor and insiders of such affiliates; any managing agent of the debtor. 11 U.S.C. § 101.

---

**1. Income from employment or operation of business**

None ☐

State the gross amount of income the debtor has received from employment, trade, or profession, or from operation of the debtor's business, including part-time activities either as an employee or in independent trade or business, from the beginning of this calendar year to the date this case was commenced. State also the gross amounts received during the **two years** immediately preceding this calendar year. (A debtor that maintains, or has maintained, financial records on the basis of a fiscal rather than a calendar year may report fiscal year income. Identify the beginning and ending dates of the debtor's fiscal year.) If a joint petition is filed, state income for each spouse separately. (Married debtors filing under chapter 12 or chapter 13 must state income of both spouses whether or not a joint petition is filed, unless the spouses are separated and a joint petition is not filed.)

AMOUNT SOURCE

**2. Income other than from employment or operation of business**

None ☐

State the amount of income received by the debtor other than from employment, trade, profession, operation of the debtor's business during the **two years** immediately preceding the commencement of this case. Give particulars. If a joint petition is filed, state income for each spouse separately. (Married debtors filing under chapter 12 or chapter 13 must state income for each spouse whether or not a joint petition is filed, unless the spouses are separated and a joint petition is not filed.)

| AMOUNT | SOURCE |
|---|---|

**3. Payments to creditors**

***Complete a. or b., as appropriate, and c.***

None ☐

a. *Individual or joint debtor(s) with primarily consumer debts:* List all payments on loans, installment purchases of goods or services, and other debts to any creditor made within **90 days** immediately preceding the commencement of this case unless the aggregate value of all property that constitutes or is affected by such transfer is less than $600. Indicate with an asterisk (*) any payments that were made to a creditor on account of a domestic support obligation or as part of an alternative repayment schedule under a plan by an approved nonprofit budgeting and credit counseling agency. (Married debtors filing under chapter 12 or chapter 13 must include payments by either or both spouses whether or not a joint petition is filed, unless the spouses are separated and a joint petition is not filed.)

| NAME AND ADDRESS OF CREDITOR | DATES OF PAYMENTS | AMOUNT PAID | AMOUNT STILL OWING |
|---|---|---|---|

None ☐

b. *Debtor whose debts are not primarily consumer debts: List each payment or other transfer to any creditor made* within **90 days** immediately preceding the commencement of the case unless the aggregate value of all property that constitutes or is affected by such transfer is less than $5,475. If the debtor is an individual, indicate with an asterisk (*) any payments that were made to a creditor on account of a domestic support obligation or as part of an alternative repayment schedule under a plan by an approved nonprofit budgeting and credit counseling agency. (Married debtors filing under chapter 12 or chapter 13 must include payments and other transfers by either or both spouses whether or not a joint petition is filed, unless the spouses are separated and a joint petition is not filed.)

| NAME AND ADDRESS OF CREDITOR | DATES OF PAYMENTS/ TRANSFERS | AMOUNT PAID OR VALUE OF TRANSFERS | AMOUNT STILL OWING |
|---|---|---|---|

None

☐ c. *All debtors:* List all payments made within **one year** immediately preceding the commencement of this case to or for the benefit of creditors who are or were insiders. (Married debtors filing under chapter 12 or chapter 13 must include payments by either or both spouses whether or not a joint petition is filed, unless the spouses are separated and a joint petition is not filed.)

| NAME AND ADDRESS OF CREDITOR AND RELATIONSHIP TO DEBTOR | DATE OF PAYMENT | AMOUNT PAID | AMOUNT STILL OWING |
|---|---|---|---|

---

**4. Suits and administrative proceedings, executions, garnishments and attachments**

None

☐ a. List all suits and administrative proceedings to which the debtor is or was a party within **one year** immediately preceding the filing of this bankruptcy case. (Married debtors filing under chapter 12 or chapter 13 must include information concerning either or both spouses whether or not a joint petition is filed, unless the spouses are separated and a joint petition is not filed.)

| CAPTION OF SUIT AND CASE NUMBER | NATURE OF PROCEEDING | COURT OR AGENCY AND LOCATION | STATUS OR DISPOSITION |
|---|---|---|---|

None

☐ b. Describe all property that has been attached, garnished or seized under any legal or equitable process within **one year** immediately preceding the commencement of this case. (Married debtors filing under chapter 12 or chapter 13 must include information concerning property of either or both spouses whether or not a joint petition is filed, unless the spouses are separated and a joint petition is not filed.)

| NAME AND ADDRESS OF PERSON FOR WHOSE BENEFIT PROPERTY WAS SEIZED | DATE OF SEIZURE | DESCRIPTION AND VALUE OF PROPERTY |
|---|---|---|

---

**5. Repossessions, foreclosures and returns**

None

☐ List all property that has been repossessed by a creditor, sold at a foreclosure sale, transferred through a deed in lieu of foreclosure or returned to the seller, within **one year** immediately preceding the commencement of this case. (Married debtors filing under chapter 12 or chapter 13 must include information concerning property of either or both spouses whether or not a joint petition is filed, unless the spouses are separated and a joint petition is not filed.)

| NAME AND ADDRESS OF CREDITOR OR SELLER | DATE OF REPOSSESSION, FORECLOSURE SALE, TRANSFER OR RETURN | DESCRIPTION AND VALUE OF PROPERTY |
|---|---|---|

---

**6. Assignments and receiverships**

None ☐ a. Describe any assignment of property for the benefit of creditors made within **120 days** immediately preceding the commencement of this case. (Married debtors filing under chapter 12 or chapter 13 must include any assignment by either or both spouses whether or not a joint petition is filed, unless the spouses are separated and a joint petition is not filed.)

| NAME AND ADDRESS OF ASSIGNEE | DATE OF ASSIGNMENT | TERMS OF ASSIGNMENT OR SETTLEMENT |
|---|---|---|

None ☐ b. List all property which has been in the hands of a custodian, receiver, or court-appointed official within **one year** immediately preceding the commencement of this case. (Married debtors filing under chapter 12 or chapter 13 must include information concerning property of either or both spouses whether or not a joint petition is filed, unless the spouses are separated and a joint petition is not filed.)

| NAME AND ADDRESS OF CUSTODIAN | NAME AND LOCATION OF COURT CASE TITLE & NUMBER | DATE OF ORDER | DESCRIPTION AND VALUE Of PROPERTY |
|---|---|---|---|

**7. Gifts**

None ☐ List all gifts or charitable contributions made within **one year** immediately preceding the commencement of this case except ordinary and usual gifts to family members aggregating less than $200 in value per individual family member and charitable contributions aggregating less than $100 per recipient. (Married debtors filing under chapter 12 or chapter 13 must include gifts or contributions by either or both spouses whether or not a joint petition is filed, unless the spouses are separated and a joint petition is not filed.)

| NAME AND ADDRESS OF PERSON OR ORGANIZATION | RELATIONSHIP TO DEBTOR, IF ANY | DATE OF GIFT | DESCRIPTION AND VALUE OF GIFT |
|---|---|---|---|

**8. Losses**

None ☐ List all losses from fire, theft, other casualty or gambling within **one year** immediately preceding the commencement of this case **or since the commencement of this case**. (Married debtors filing under chapter 12 or chapter 13 must include losses by either or both spouses whether or not a joint petition is filed, unless the spouses are separated and a joint petition is not filed.)

| DESCRIPTION AND VALUE OF PROPERTY | DESCRIPTION OF CIRCUMSTANCES AND, IF LOSS WAS COVERED IN WHOLE OR IN PART BY INSURANCE, GIVE PARTICULARS | DATE OF LOSS |
|---|---|---|

**9. Payments related to debt counseling or bankruptcy**

None ☐

List all payments made or property transferred by or on behalf of the debtor to any persons, including attorneys, for consultation concerning debt consolidation, relief under the bankruptcy law or preparation of a petition in bankruptcy within **one year** immediately preceding the commencement of this case.

| NAME AND ADDRESS OF PAYEE | DATE OF PAYMENT, NAME OF PAYER IF OTHER THAN DEBTOR | AMOUNT OF MONEY OR DESCRIPTION AND VALUE OF PROPERTY |
|---|---|---|

---

**10. Other transfers**

None ☐

a. List all other property, other than property transferred in the ordinary course of the business or financial affairs of the debtor, transferred either absolutely or as security within **two years** immediately preceding the commencement of this case. (Married debtors filing under chapter 12 or chapter 13 must include transfers by either or both spouses whether or not a joint petition is filed, unless the spouses are separated and a joint petition is not filed.)

| NAME AND ADDRESS OF TRANSFEREE, RELATIONSHIP TO DEBTOR | DATE | DESCRIBE PROPERTY TRANSFERRED AND VALUE RECEIVED |
|---|---|---|

None ☐

b. List all property transferred by the debtor within **ten years** immediately preceding the commencement of this case to a self-settled trust or similar device of which the debtor is a beneficiary.

| NAME OF TRUST OR OTHER DEVICE | DATE(S) OF TRANSFER(S) | AMOUNT OF MONEY OR DESCRIPTION AND VALUE OF PROPERTY OR DEBTOR'S INTEREST IN PROPERTY |
|---|---|---|

---

**11. Closed financial accounts**

None ☐

List all financial accounts and instruments held in the name of the debtor or for the benefit of the debtor which were closed, sold, or otherwise transferred within **one year** immediately preceding the commencement of this case. Include checking, savings, or other financial accounts, certificates of deposit, or other instruments; shares and share accounts held in banks, credit unions, pension funds, cooperatives, associations, brokerage houses and other financial institutions. (Married debtors filing under chapter 12 or chapter 13 must include information concerning accounts or instruments held by or for either or both spouses whether or not a joint petition is filed, unless the spouses are separated and a joint petition is not filed.)

| NAME AND ADDRESS OF INSTITUTION | TYPE OF ACCOUNT, LAST FOUR DIGITS OF ACCOUNT NUMBER, AND AMOUNT OF FINAL BALANCE | AMOUNT AND DATE OF SALE OR CLOSING |
|---|---|---|

---

**12. Safe deposit boxes**

None ☐ List each safe deposit or other box or depository in which the debtor has or had securities, cash, or other valuables within **one year** immediately preceding the commencement of this case. (Married debtors filing under chapter 12 or chapter 13 must include boxes or depositories of either or both spouses whether or not a joint petition is filed, unless the spouses are separated and a joint petition is not filed.)

| NAME AND ADDRESS OF BANK OR OTHER DEPOSITORY | NAMES AND ADDRESSES OF THOSE WITH ACCESS TO BOX OR DEPOSITORY | DESCRIPTION OF CONTENTS | DATE OF TRANSFER OR SURRENDER, IF ANY |
|---|---|---|---|

**13. Setoffs**

None ☐ List all setoffs made by any creditor, including a bank, against a debt or deposit of the debtor within **90 days** preceding the commencement of this case. (Married debtors filing under chapter 12 or chapter 13 must include information concerning either or both spouses whether or not a joint petition is filed, unless the spouses are separated and a joint petition is not filed.)

| NAME AND ADDRESS OF CREDITOR | DATE OF SETOFF | AMOUNT OF SETOFF |
|---|---|---|

**14. Property held for another person**

None ☐ List all property owned by another person that the debtor holds or controls.

| NAME AND ADDRESS OF OWNER | DESCRIPTION AND VALUE OF PROPERTY | LOCATION OF PROPERTY |
|---|---|---|

**15. Prior address of debtor**

None ☐ If debtor has moved within **three years** immediately preceding the commencement of this case, list all premises which the debtor occupied during that period and vacated prior to the commencement of this case. If a joint petition is filed, report also any separate address of either spouse.

| ADDRESS | NAME USED | DATES OF OCCUPANCY |
|---|---|---|

**16. Spouses and Former Spouses**

None ☐ If the debtor resides or resided in a community property state, commonwealth, or territory (including Alaska, Arizona, California, Idaho, Louisiana, Nevada, New Mexico, Puerto Rico, Texas, Washington, or Wisconsin) within **eight years** immediately preceding the commencement of the case, identify the name of the debtor's spouse and of any former spouse who resides or resided with the debtor in the community property state.

NAME

---

**17. Environmental Information.**

For the purpose of this question, the following definitions apply:

"Environmental Law" means any federal, state, or local statute or regulation regulating pollution, contamination, releases of hazardous or toxic substances, wastes or material into the air, land, soil, surface water, groundwater, or other medium, including, but not limited to, statutes or regulations regulating the cleanup of these substances, wastes, or material.

"Site" means any location, facility, or property as defined under any Environmental Law, whether or not presently or formerly owned or operated by the debtor, including, but not limited to, disposal sites.

"Hazardous Material" means anything defined as a hazardous waste, hazardous substance, toxic substance, hazardous material, pollutant, or contaminant or similar term under an Environmental Law.

None ☐ a. List the name and address of every site for which the debtor has received notice in writing by a governmental unit that it may be liable or potentially liable under or in violation of an Environmental Law. Indicate the governmental unit, the date of the notice, and, if known, the Environmental Law:

| SITE NAME AND ADDRESS | NAME AND ADDRESS OF GOVERNMENTAL UNIT | DATE OF NOTICE | ENVIRONMENTAL LAW |
|---|---|---|---|

None ☐ b. List the name and address of every site for which the debtor provided notice to a governmental unit of a release of Hazardous Material. Indicate the governmental unit to which the notice was sent and the date of the notice.

| SITE NAME AND ADDRESS | NAME AND ADDRESS OF GOVERNMENTAL UNIT | DATE OF NOTICE | ENVIRONMENTAL LAW |
|---|---|---|---|

None ☐ c. List all judicial or administrative proceedings, including settlements or orders, under any Environmental Law with respect to which the debtor is or was a party. Indicate the name and address of the governmental unit that is or was a party to the proceeding, and the docket number.

| NAME AND ADDRESS OF GOVERNMENTAL UNIT | DOCKET NUMBER | STATUS OR DISPOSITION |
|---|---|---|

---

**18. Nature, location and name of business**

None ☐ a. *If the debtor is an individual,* list the names, addresses, taxpayer-identification numbers, nature of the businesses, and beginning and ending dates of all businesses in which the debtor was an officer, director, partner, or managing executive of a corporation, partner in a partnership, sole proprietor, or was self-employed in a trade, profession, or other activity either full- or part-time within **six years** immediately preceding the commencement of this case, or in which the debtor owned 5 percent or more of the voting or equity securities within **six years** immediately preceding the commencement of this case.

*If the debtor is a partnership,* list the names, addresses, taxpayer-identification numbers, nature of the businesses, and beginning and ending dates of all businesses in which the debtor was a partner or owned 5 percent or more of the voting or equity securities, within **six years** immediately preceding the commencement of this case.

*If the debtor is a corporation,* list the names, addresses, taxpayer-identification numbers, nature of the businesses, and beginning and ending dates of all businesses in which the debtor was a partner or owned 5 percent or more of the voting or equity securities within **six years** immediately preceding the commencement of this case.

| NAME | LAST FOUR DIGITS OF SOCIAL-SECURITY OR OTHER INDIVIDUAL TAXPAYER-I.D. NO. (ITIN)/ COMPLETE EIN | ADDRESS | NATURE OF BUSINESS | BEGINNING AND ENDING DATES |
| --- | --- | --- | --- | --- |

None ☐ b. Identify any business listed in response to subdivision a., above, that is "single asset real estate" as defined in 11 U.S.C. § 101.

| NAME | ADDRESS |
| --- | --- |

---

The following questions are to be completed by every debtor that is a corporation or partnership and by any individual debtor who is or has been, within **six years** immediately preceding the commencement of this case, any of the following: an officer, director, managing executive, or owner of more than 5 percent of the voting or equity securities of a corporation; a partner, other than a limited partner, of a partnership, a sole proprietor, or self-employed in a trade, profession, or other activity, either full- or part-time.

*(An individual or joint debtor should complete this portion of the statement **only** if the debtor is or has been in business, as defined above, within six years immediately preceding the commencement of this case. A debtor who has not been in business within those six years should go directly to the signature page.)*

---

**19. Books, records and financial statements**

None ☐ a. List all bookkeepers and accountants who within **two years** immediately preceding the filing of this bankruptcy case kept or supervised the keeping of books of account and records of the debtor.

| NAME AND ADDRESS | DATES SERVICES RENDERED |
| --- | --- |

None ☐ b. List all firms or individuals who within **two years** immediately preceding the filing of this bankruptcy case have audited the books of account and records, or prepared a financial statement of the debtor.

| NAME | ADDRESS | DATES SERVICES RENDERED |
| --- | --- | --- |

None ☐ c. List all firms or individuals who at the time of the commencement of this case were in possession of the books of account and records of the debtor. If any of the books of account and records are not available, explain.

| NAME | ADDRESS |
|---|---|

None ☐ d. List all financial institutions, creditors and other parties, including mercantile and trade agencies, to whom a financial statement was issued by the debtor within **two years** immediately preceding the commencement of this case.

| NAME AND ADDRESS | DATE ISSUED |
|---|---|

---

**20. Inventories**

None ☐ a. List the dates of the last two inventories taken of your property, the name of the person who supervised the taking of each inventory, and the dollar amount and basis of each inventory.

| DATE OF INVENTORY | INVENTORY SUPERVISOR | DOLLAR AMOUNT OF INVENTORY (Specify cost, market or other basis) |
|---|---|---|

None ☐ b. List the name and address of the person having possession of the records of each of the inventories reported in a., above.

| DATE OF INVENTORY | NAME AND ADDRESSES OF CUSTODIAN OF INVENTORY RECORDS |
|---|---|

---

**21 . Current Partners, Officers, Directors and Shareholders**

None ☐ a. If the debtor is a partnership, list the nature and percentage of partnership interest of each member of the partnership.

| NAME AND ADDRESS | NATURE OF INTEREST | PERCENTAGE OF INTEREST |
|---|---|---|

None ☐ b. If the debtor is a corporation, list all officers and directors of the corporation, and each stockholder who directly or indirectly owns, controls, or holds 5 percent or more of the voting or equity securities of the corporation.

| NAME AND ADDRESS | TITLE | NATURE AND PERCENTAGE OF STOCK OWNERSHIP |
|---|---|---|

---

**22 . Former partners, officers, directors and shareholders**

None ☐ a. If the debtor is a partnership, list each member who withdrew from the partnership within **one year** immediately preceding the commencement of this case.

| NAME | ADDRESS | DATE OF WITHDRAWAL |
| --- | --- | --- |

None ☐ b. If the debtor is a corporation, list all officers or directors whose relationship with the corporation terminated within **one year** immediately preceding the commencement of this case.

| NAME AND ADDRESS | TITLE | DATE OF TERMINATION |
| --- | --- | --- |

---

**23 . Withdrawals from a partnership or distributions by a corporation**

None ☐ If the debtor is a partnership or corporation, list all withdrawals or distributions credited or given to an insider, including compensation in any form, bonuses, loans, stock redemptions, options exercised and any other perquisite during **one year** immediately preceding the commencement of this case.

| NAME & ADDRESS OF RECIPIENT, RELATIONSHIP TO DEBTOR | DATE AND PURPOSE OF WITHDRAWAL | AMOUNT OF MONEY OR DESCRIPTION AND VALUE OF PROPERTY |
| --- | --- | --- |

---

**24. Tax Consolidation Group.**

None ☐ If the debtor is a corporation, list the name and federal taxpayer-identification number of the parent corporation of any consolidated group for tax purposes of which the debtor has been a member at any time within **six years** immediately preceding the commencement of the case.

| NAME OF PARENT CORPORATION | TAXPAYER-IDENTIFICATION NUMBER (EIN) |
| --- | --- |

---

**25. Pension Funds.**

None ☐ If the debtor is not an individual, list the name and federal taxpayer-identification number of any pension fund to which the debtor, as an employer, has been responsible for contributing at any time within **six years** immediately preceding the commencement of the case.

| NAME OF PENSION FUND | TAXPAYER-IDENTIFICATION NUMBER (EIN) |
| --- | --- |

* * * * * *

11

*[If completed by an individual or individual and spouse]*

I declare under penalty of perjury that I have read the answers contained in the foregoing statement of financial affairs and any attachments thereto and that they are true and correct.

Date ______________________ Signature of Debtor ______________________

Date ______________________ Signature of Joint Debtor (if any) ______________________

---

*[If completed on behalf of a partnership or corporation]*

I declare under penalty of perjury that I have read the answers contained in the foregoing statement of financial affairs and any attachments thereto and that they are true and correct to the best of my knowledge, information and belief.

Date ______________________ Signature ______________________

Print Name and Title ______________________

[An individual signing on behalf of a partnership or corporation must indicate position or relationship to debtor.]

___continuation sheets attached

*Penalty for making a false statement Fine of up to $500,000 or imprisonment for up to 5 years, or both. 18 U.S.C. §§ 152 and 3571*

---

**DECLARATION AND SIGNATURE OF NON-ATTORNEY BANKRUPTCY PETITION PREPARER (See 11 U.S.C. § 110)**

I declare under penalty of perjury that: (1) I am a bankruptcy petition preparer as defined in 11 U.S.C. § 110; (2) I prepared this document for compensation and have provided the debtor with a copy of this document and the notices and information required under 11 U.S.C. §§ 110(b), 110(h), and 342(b); and, (3) if rules or guidelines have been promulgated pursuant to 11 U.S.C. § 110(h) setting a maximum fee for services chargeable by bankruptcy petition preparers, I have given the debtor notice of the maximum amount before preparing any document for filing for a debtor or accepting any fee from the debtor, as required by that section

______________________ ______________________

Printed or Typed Name and Title, if any, of Bankruptcy Petition Preparer Social-Security No. (Required by 11 U.S.C. § 110.)

*If the bankruptcy petition preparer is not an individual, state the name, title (if any), address, and social-security number of the officer, principal, responsible person, or partner who signs this document.*

______________________

Address

______________________ ______________________

Signature of Bankruptcy Petition Preparer Date

Names and Social-Security numbers of all other individuals who prepared or assisted in preparing this document unless the bankruptcy petition preparer is not an individual:

If more than one person prepared this document, attach additional signed sheets conforming to the appropriate Official Form for each person

***A bankruptcy petition preparer's failure to comply with the provisions of title 11 and the Federal Rules of Bankruptcy Procedure may result in fines or imprisonment or both. 18 U.S.C. § 156.***

(Added Aug. 1, 1991; amended Mar. 16, 1993; Mar. 14, 1995; Sept. 19, 2000; Dec. 1, 2003; Oct. 17, 2005; Dec. 1, 2007.)

NOTES OF ADVISORY COMMITTEE ON RULES—1991

This form consolidates questions from former Official Forms No. 7, No. 8, and No. 10. This form is to be completed by all debtors. An individual debtor engaged in business as a sole proprietor, partner, family farmer, or self-employed professional should provide the information requested on this statement concerning all such activities as well as the individual's personal affairs.

The Chapter 13 Statement, former Official Form No. 10, has been abrogated. Chapter 13 debtors are to complete this statement and the schedules prescribed in Official Form 6.

All questions have been converted to affirmative directions to furnish information, and each question must be answered. If the answer is "none," or the question is not applicable, the debtor is required to so state by marking the box labeled "None" provided at each question.

See Committee Note to Form 2 for a discussion of the unsworn declaration at the end of this form.

NOTES OF ADVISORY COMMITTEE ON RULES—1993 AMENDMENT

The form has been amended in two ways. In the second paragraph of the instructions, the third sentence has been deleted to clarify that only a debtor that is or has been in business as defined in the form should answer Questions 16–21. In addition, administrative proceedings have been added to the types of legal actions to be disclosed in Question 4.a.

NOTES OF ADVISORY COMMITTEE ON RULES—1995 AMENDMENT

This form is a "document for filing" that may be prepared by a "bankruptcy petition preparer" as defined in 11 U.S.C. §110, which was added to the Code by the Bankruptcy Reform Act of 1994; accordingly, a signature line for such preparer is added. In addition to signing, a bankruptcy petition preparer is required by section 110 to disclose the information requested.

NOTES OF ADVISORY COMMITTEE ON RULES—2000 AMENDMENT

The form has been amended to provide more information to taxing authorities, pension fund supervisors, and governmental units charged with environmental protection and regulation. Four new questions have been added to the form, covering community property owned by a debtor and the debtor's non-filing spouse or former spouse (Question 16), environmental information (Question 17), any consolidated tax group of a corporate debtor (Question 24), and the debtor's contributions to any employee pension fund (Question 25). In addition, every debtor will be required to state on the form whether the debtor has been in business within six years before filing the petition and, if so, must answer the remaining questions on the form (Questions 19–25). This is an enlargement of the two-year period previously specified. One reason for the longer "reach back" period is that business debtors often owe taxes that have been owed for more than two years. Another is that some of the questions already addressed to business debtors request information for the six-year period before the commencement of the case. Application of a six-year period to this section of the form will assure disclosure of all relevant information.

COMMITTEE NOTES ON RULES—2003 AMENDMENT

Pursuant to §110(c) of the Bankruptcy Code, the certification by a non-attorney bankruptcy petition preparer requires a petition preparer to provide the full social security number of the individual who actually prepares the document.

COMMITTEE NOTES ON RULES—2005 AMENDMENT

The form is amended in several ways to reflect changes in the Bankruptcy Code made by the Bankruptcy Abuse Prevention and Consumer Protection Act of 2005, Pub. L. No. 109–8, 119 Stat. 23 (April 20, 2005). A new sentence in the introduction advises the debtor not to disclose the name and address of any minor child.

The definition of "in business" is amended in the introductory section and in Question 1 and Question 18 to clarify that various part-time activities can result in the debtor being "in business" for purposes of the form.

Question 1 is amended to specify that, in addition to the income from the debtor's primary employment, the debtor must include income from part-time activities either as an employee or from self-employment. The debtor now also will report the source of all income from employment or operation of a business, even if there is only one source, in order to assist the trustee in reviewing the pay stubs, etc., filed by the debtor in the case.

Question 3 is amended to accommodate amendments to §547(c) of the Code enacted in 2005 which exempt from recovery by the trustee payments by a debtor for a domestic support obligation or as part of an alternative repayment schedule negotiated by an approved nonprofit budgeting and credit counseling agency. In addition, Question 3 now requires a debtor with primarily non-consumer debts to report only those transfers that aggregate more than $5,000 to any creditor in the 90-day period prior to the filing of the petition, as a result of the addition of §547(c)(9) to the Code in 2005.

In Question 10, the extension of the reachback period for transfers from one year to two years reflects the 2005 amendment to §548(a)(1) of the Code to permit a trustee to avoid a fraudulent transfer made by the debtor within two years of the date of the filing of the petition. Question 10 also is amended to implement new §548(e) added to the Code in 2005 to require the debtor to disclose all transfers to any self-settled asset protection trust within the ten years before the filing of the petition.

Question 15 is amended to extend from two years to three years the preterition time period for which the debtor must disclose the addresses of all premises occupied by the debtor. This information will assist the trustee, the United States trustee, and the court to ascertain whether any homestead exemption asserted by the debtor is properly claimed under §522(v)(3)(A) as amended, and §§522(p) and (q) as added to the Code in 2005.

The form also is amended to extend from six years to eight years the period before the filing of the petition concerning which the debtor is required to disclose the name of the debtor's spouse or of any former spouse who resides or resided with the debtor in a community property state. In addition, the certification by a non-attorney bankruptcy petition preparer is renamed a "declaration" and is amended to include material mandated by 11 U.S.C. §110 as amended by the 2005 Act.

COMMITTEE NOTES ON RULES—2005–2007 AMENDMENT

[The 2005–2007 Committee Note incorporates the Committee Note previously published in 2005.]

The form is amended in several ways to reflect changes in the Bankruptcy Code made by the Bankruptcy Abuse Prevention and Consumer Protection Act of 2005, Pub. L. No. 109–8, 119 Stat. 23 (April 20, 2005). A new sentence in the introduction advises the debtor not to disclose the name and address of any minor child in conformity with §112, which was added to the Code by the 2005 Act. In addition, the form is amended to add to the reference to Rule 1007(m) with respect to a minor child a direction to include for noticing purposes the name, address, and legal relationship to the child of "a person described" in that rule. Rule 1007(m) requires the person named to be someone on whom process would be served in an adversary proceeding against the child.

The definition of "in business" is amended in the introductory section and in Question 1 and Question 18 to clarify that various part-time activities can result in the debtor being "in business" for purposes of the form.

Question 1 is amended to specify that, in addition to the income from the debtor's primary employment, the debtor must include income from part-time activities either as an employee or from self-employment. The debtor now also will report the source of all income from employment or operation of a business, even if there is only one source, in order to assist the trustee in reviewing the pay stubs, etc., filed by the debtor in the case.

Question 3 is amended to accommodate amendments to § 547(c) of the Code enacted in 2005 which exempt from recovery by the trustee payments by a debtor for a domestic support obligation or as part of an alternative repayment schedule negotiated by an approved nonprofit budgeting and credit counseling agency. In addition, Question 3 now requires a debtor with primarily non-consumer debts to report only those transfers that aggregate more than $5,475 to any creditor in the 90-day period prior to the filing of the petition, as a result of the addition of § 547(c)(9) to the Code in 2005. In addition, the language of the question is revised for clarity.

In Question 10, the extension of the reach-back period for transfers from one year to two years reflects the 2005 amendment to § 548(a)(1) of the Code to permit a trustee to avoid a fraudulent transfer made by the debtor within two years before the date of the filing of the petition. Question 10 also is amended to implement new § 548(e) added to the Code in 2005 to require the debtor to disclose all transfers to any self-settled asset protection trust within the ten years before the filing of the petition.

Question 15 is amended to extend from two years to three years the prepetition time period for which the debtor must disclose the addresses of all premises occupied by the debtor. This information will assist the trustee, the United States trustee, and the court to ascertain whether any homestead exemption asserted by the debtor is properly claimed under § 522(b)(3)(A) as amended, and §§ 522(p) [sic] and (q) as added to the Code in 2005.

The form also is amended to extend from six years to eight years the period before the filing of the petition concerning which the debtor is required to disclose the name of the debtor's spouse or of any former spouse who resides or resided with the debtor in a community property state. In addition, the certification by a non-attorney bankruptcy petition preparer is renamed a "declaration" and is amended to include material mandated by 11 U.S.C. § 110 as amended by the 2005 Act.

B 8 (Official Form 8) (12/08)

# UNITED STATES BANKRUPTCY COURT

In re ______________________________,
Debtor

Case No. ______________
Chapter 7

## CHAPTER 7 INDIVIDUAL DEBTOR'S STATEMENT OF INTENTION

**PART A** – Debts secured by property of the estate. *(Part A must be fully completed for **EACH** debt which is secured by property of the estate. Attach additional pages if necessary.)*

| Property No. 1 | |
|---|---|
| **Creditor's Name:** | **Describe Property Securing Debt:** |

Property will be *(check one)*:
❒ Surrendered ❒ Retained

If retaining the property, I intend to *(check at least one)*:
❒ Redeem the property
❒ Reaffirm the debt
❒ Other. Explain ______________________________ (for example, avoid lien using 11 U.S.C. § 522(f)).

Property is *(check one)*:
❒ Claimed as exempt ❒ Not claimed as exempt

| Property No. 2 *(if necessary)* | |
|---|---|
| **Creditor's Name:** | **Describe Property Securing Debt:** |

Property will be *(check one)*:
❒ Surrendered ❒ Retained

If retaining the property, I intend to *(check at least one)*:
❒ Redeem the property
❒ Reaffirm the debt
❒ Other. Explain ______________________________ (for example, avoid lien using 11 U.S.C. § 522(f)).

Property is *(check one)*:
❒ Claimed as exempt ❒ Not claimed as exempt

B 8 (Official Form 8) (12/08) Page 2

**PART B** – Personal property subject to unexpired leases. *(All three columns of Part B must be completed for each unexpired lease. Attach additional pages if necessary.)*

| Property No. 1 | | |
|---|---|---|
| **Lessor's Name:** | **Describe Leased Property:** | Lease will be Assumed pursuant to 11 U.S.C. § 365(p)(2):<br>❒ YES ❒ NO |

| Property No. 2 *(if necessary)* | | |
|---|---|---|
| **Lessor's Name:** | **Describe Leased Property:** | Lease will be Assumed pursuant to 11 U.S.C. § 365(p)(2):<br>❒ YES ❒ NO |

| Property No. 3 *(if necessary)* | | |
|---|---|---|
| **Lessor's Name:** | **Describe Leased Property:** | Lease will be Assumed pursuant to 11 U.S.C. § 365(p)(2):<br>❒ YES ❒ NO |

_____ continuation sheets attached *(if any)*

**I declare under penalty of perjury that the above indicates my intention as to any property of my estate securing a debt and/or personal property subject to an unexpired lease.**

Date: ____________________

______________________________
Signature of Debtor

______________________________
Signature of Joint Debtor

# CHAPTER 7 INDIVIDUAL DEBTOR'S STATEMENT OF INTENTION

*(Continuation Sheet)*

**PART A** - Continuation

| Property No. | |
|---|---|
| **Creditor's Name:** | **Describe Property Securing Debt:** |

Property will be *(check one)*:
❒ Surrendered ❒ Retained

If retaining the property, I intend to *(check at least one)*:
❒ Redeem the property
❒ Reaffirm the debt
❒ Other. Explain ______________________ (for example, avoid lien using 11 U.S.C. § 522(f)).

Property is *(check one)*:
❒ Claimed as exempt ❒ Not claimed as exempt

**PART B** - Continuation

| Property No. | | |
|---|---|---|
| **Lessor's Name:** | **Describe Leased Property:** | Lease will be Assumed pursuant to 11 U.S.C. § 365(p)(2):<br>❒ YES ❒ NO |

| Property No. | | |
|---|---|---|
| **Lessor's Name:** | **Describe Leased Property:** | Lease will be Assumed pursuant to 11 U.S.C. § 365(p)(2):<br>❒ YES ❒ NO |

(Added Aug. 1, 1991; amended Mar. 14, 1995; Oct. 1, 1997; Dec. 1, 2003; Oct. 17, 2005; Dec. 1, 2008.)

NOTES OF ADVISORY COMMITTEE ON RULES—1991

This form is derived from former Official Form No. 8A. Rule 1007(b)(2) requires the debtor to serve a copy of this statement on the trustee and all creditors named in the statement. In a joint case, if the property and debts of both debtors are the same, the form may be adapted for joint use. If joint debtors have separate debts, however, each debtor must use a separate form.

NOTES OF ADVISORY COMMITTEE ON RULES—1995 AMENDMENT

This form is a "document for filing" that may be prepared by a "bankruptcy petition preparer" as defined in 11 U.S.C. §110, which was added to the Code by the Bankruptcy Reform Act of 1994; accordingly, a signature line for such preparer is added. In addition to signing, a bankruptcy petition preparer is required by section 110 to disclose the information requested.

NOTES OF ADVISORY COMMITTEE ON RULES—1997 AMENDMENT

The form is amended to conform more closely to the language of the Bankruptcy Code. The amendments also make clear that the form is not intended to take a position regarding whether the options stated on the form are the only choices available to the debtor. Compare *Lowry Federal Credit Union v. West*, 882 F.2d 1543 (10th Cir. 1989), with *In re Taylor*, 3 F.3d 1512 (11th Cir. 1993).

COMMITTEE NOTES ON RULES—2003 AMENDMENT

Pursuant to §110(c) of the Bankruptcy Code, the certification by a non-attorney bankruptcy petition preparer requires a petition preparer to provide the full social security number of the individual who actually prepares the document.

COMMITTEE NOTES ON RULES—2005 AMENDMENT

The form is amended to conform to §521(a)(6), which was added to the Code by the Bankruptcy Abuse Prevention and Consumer Protection Act of 2005, Pub. L. No. 109–8, 119 Stat. 23 (April 20, 2005), by adding a section covering personal property subject to an unexpired lease and an option labeled "lease will be assumed pursuant to 11 U.S.C. §362(h)(1)(A)" to the choices a debtor may make. The certification by a non-attorney bankruptcy petition preparer in the form is renamed a "declaration" and is amended to include material mandated by the 2005 amendments to §110 of the Code.

COMMITTEE NOTES ON RULES—2008 AMENDMENT

The form is amended to conform to §362(h), which was added to the Code, and §521(a)(2), which was amended, by the Bankruptcy Abuse Prevention and Consumer Protection Act of 2005, Pub. L. No. 109–8, 119 Stat. 23 (April 20, 2005), by expanding the questions directed to the debtor regarding leased personal property and property subject to security interests. The form is also amended and reformatted to require the debtor to complete a series of statements describing the property and setting out what actions the debtor intends to take for each listed asset. The amended form is intended to elicit more complete information about the debtor's intentions with regard to property subject to security interests and personal property leases than has been obtained under the current version of the form.

In addition, the form is amended to specify that the debtor's signature is a declaration under penalty of perjury, as required by Rule 1008, and to provide space for the co-debtor's signature. A continuation page has been provided for use if necessary. The Declaration of Non-Attorney Bankruptcy Petition Preparer has been deleted from the form as duplicative of Form 19, Declaration and Signature of Non-Attorney Bankruptcy Petition Preparer. Form 19 contains both the petition preparer's declaration and signature and the notice the petition preparer is required to give to the debtor under §110 of the Code.

Official Form 9
(9/97)

# FORM 9. NOTICE OF COMMENCEMENT OF CASE UNDER THE BANKRUPTCY CODE, MEETING OF CREDITORS, AND DEADLINES

| | |
|---|---|
| 9A..........Chapter | 7, Individual/Joint, No-Asset Case |
| 9B..........Chapter | 7, Corporation/Partnership, No-Asset Case |
| 9C..........Chapter | 7, Individual/Joint, Asset Case |
| 9D..........Chapter | 7, Corporation/Partnership, Asset Case |
| 9E..........Chapter | 11, Individual/Joint Case |
| 9E(Alt.)..Chapter | 11, Individual/Joint Case |
| 9F..........Chapter | 11, Corporation/Partnership Case |
| 9F(Alt.)..Chapter | 11, Corporation/Partnership Case |
| 9G..........Chapter | 12, Individual/Joint Case |
| 9H..........Chapter | 12, Corporation/Partnership Case |
| 9I..........Chapter | 13, Individual/Joint Case |

**B9A (Official Form 9A)** (Chapter 7 Individual or Joint Debtor No Asset Case) (12/07)

UNITED STATES BANKRUPTCY COURT______________ **District of** ________________________

## Notice of
## Chapter 7 Bankruptcy Case, Meeting of Creditors, & Deadlines

[A chapter 7 bankruptcy case concerning the debtor(s) listed below was filed on ________________(date).]
or [A bankruptcy case concerning the debtor(s) listed below was originally filed under chapter______________on
___________________(date) and was converted to a case under chapter 7 on_______________(date).]

You may be a creditor of the debtor. **This notice lists important deadlines.** You may want to consult an attorney to protect your Rights. All documents filed in the case may be inspected at the bankruptcy clerk's office at the address listed below. NOTE: The staff of the bankruptcy clerk's office cannot give legal advice.

See Reverse Side for Important Explanations

| | |
|---|---|
| Debtor(s) (name(s) and address): | Case Number: |
| | Last four digits of Social-Security or Individual Taxpayer-ID (ITIN) No(s)./Complete EIN: |
| All other names used by the Debtor(s) in the last 8 years (include married, maiden, and trade names): | Bankruptcy Trustee (name and address): |
| Attorney for Debtor(s) (name and address): Telephone number: | Telephone number: |

**Meeting of Creditors**

Date: / / Time: ( ) A. M. ( ) P. M. Location:

**Presumption of Abuse under 11 U.S.C. § 707(b)**

*See "Presumption of Abuse" on the reverse side.*

*Depending on the documents filed with the petition, one of the following statements will appear.*

The presumption of abuse does not arise.

*Or*

The presumption of abuse arises.

*Or*

Insufficient information has been filed to date to permit the clerk to make any determination concerning the presumption of abuse. If more complete information, when filed, shows that the presumption has arisen, creditors will be notified.

**Deadlines:**

Papers must be *received* by the bankruptcy clerk's office by the following deadlines:

**Deadline to File a Complaint Objecting to Discharge of the Debtor or to Determine Dischargeability of Certain Debts:**

**Deadline to Object to Exemptions:**

Thirty (30) days after the *conclusion* of the meeting of creditors.

**Creditors May Not Take Certain Actions:**

In most instances, the filing of the bankruptcy case automatically stays certain collection and other actions against the debtor and the debtor's property. Under certain circumstances, the stay may be limited to 30 days or not exist at all, although the debtor can request the court to extend or impose a stay. If you attempt to collect a debt or take other action in violation of the Bankruptcy Code, you may be penalized. Consult a lawyer to determine your rights in this case.

Please Do Not File A Proof of Claim Unless You Receive a Notice To Do So.

**Creditor with a Foreign Address:**

A creditor to whom this notice is sent at a foreign address should read the information under "Do Not File a Proof of Claim at This Time" on the reverse side.

| | |
|---|---|
| **Address of the Bankruptcy Clerk's Office:** | **For the Court:** |
| Telephone number: | Clerk of the Bankruptcy Court: |
| Hours Open: | Date: |

**EXPLANATIONS** **B9A (Official Form 9A) (12/07)**

| | |
|---|---|
| Filing of Chapter 7 Bankruptcy Case | A bankruptcy case under Chapter 7 of the Bankruptcy Code (title 11, United States Code) has been filed in this court by or against the debtor(s) listed on the front side, and an order for relief has been entered. |
| **Legal Advice** | The staff of the bankruptcy clerk's office cannot give legal advice. Consult a lawyer to determine your rights in this case. |
| Creditors Generally May Not Take Certain Actions | Prohibited collection actions are listed in Bankruptcy Code § 362. Common examples of prohibited actions include contacting the debtor by telephone, mail, or otherwise to demand repayment; taking actions to collect money or obtain property from the debtor; repossessing the debtor's property; starting or continuing lawsuits or foreclosures; and garnishing or deducting from the debtor's wages. Under certain circumstances, the stay may be limited to 30 days or not exist at all, although the debtor can request the court to extend or impose a stay. |
| Presumption of Abuse | If the presumption of abuse arises, creditors may have the right to file a motion to dismiss the case under § 707(b) of the Bankruptcy Code. The debtor may rebut the presumption by showing special circumstances. |
| Meeting of Creditors | A meeting of creditors is scheduled for the date, time, and location listed on the front side. *The debtor (both spouses in a joint case) must be present at the meeting to be questioned under oath by the trustee and by creditors.* Creditors are welcome to attend, but are not required to do so. The meeting may be continued and concluded at a later date without further notice. |
| Do Not File a Proof of Claim at This Time | There does not appear to be any property available to the trustee to pay creditors. *You therefore should not file a proof of claim at this time.* If it later appears that assets are available to pay creditors, you will be sent another notice telling you that you may file a proof of claim, and telling you the deadline for filing your proof of claim. If this notice is mailed to a creditor at a foreign address, the creditor may file a motion requesting the court to extend the deadline. |
| Discharge of Debts | The debtor is seeking a discharge of most debts, which may include your debt. A discharge means that you may never try to collect the debt from the debtor. If you believe that the debtor is not entitled to receive a discharge under Bankruptcy Code § 727 (a) *or* that a debt owed to you is not dischargeable under Bankruptcy Code § 523 (a) (2), (4), or (6), you must start a lawsuit by filing a complaint in the bankruptcy clerk's office by the "Deadline to File a Complaint Objecting to Discharge of the Debtor or to Determine Dischargeability of Certain Debts" listed on the front side. The bankruptcy clerk's office must receive the complaint and any required filing fee by that Deadline. |
| Exempt Property | The debtor is permitted by law to keep certain property as exempt. Exempt property will not be sold and distributed to creditors. The debtor must file a list of all property claimed as exempt. You may inspect that list at the bankruptcy clerk's office. If you believe that an exemption claimed by the debtor is not authorized by law, you may file an objection to that exemption. The bankruptcy clerk's office must receive the objections by the "Deadline to Object to Exemptions" listed on the front side. |
| Bankruptcy Clerk's Office | Any paper that you file in this bankruptcy case should be filed at the bankruptcy clerk's office at the address listed on the front side. You may inspect all papers filed, including the list of the debtor's property and debts and the list of the property claimed as exempt, at the bankruptcy clerk's office. |
| Creditor with a Foreign Address | Consult a lawyer familiar with United States bankruptcy law if you have any questions regarding your rights in this case. |

Refer To Other Side For Important Deadlines and Notices

**B9B (Official Form 9B)** (Chapter 7 Corporation/Partnership No Asset Case) (12/07)

UNITED STATES BANKRUPTCY COURT________________ **District of**________________________

**Notice of**
**Chapter 7 Bankruptcy Case, Meeting of Creditors, & Deadlines**

[A chapter 7 bankruptcy case concerning the debtor(s) listed below was filed on ____________________(date).]
or [A bankruptcy case concerning the debtor(s) listed below was originally filed under chapter_______________on ____________________(date) and was converted to a case under chapter 7 on________________(date).]

You may be a creditor of the debtor. **This notice lists important deadlines.** You may want to consult an attorney to protect your Rights. All documents filed in the case may be inspected at the bankruptcy clerk's office at the address listed below. NOTE: The staff of the bankruptcy clerk's office cannot give legal advice.

See Reverse Side for Important Explanations

| | |
|---|---|
| Debtor(s) (name(s) and address): | Case Number: |
| | Last four digits of Social-Security or Individual Taxpayer-ID (ITIN) No(s)./Complete EIN: |
| All other names used by the debtor(s) in the last 8 years (include trade names): | Bankruptcy Trustee (name and address): |
| Attorney for Debtor(s) (name and address):<br><br>Telephone number: | Telephone number: |

**Meeting of Creditors**

Date: / / Time: ( ) A. M. Location:
( ) P. M.

**Creditors May Not Take Certain Actions:**

In most instances, the filing of the bankruptcy case automatically stays certain collection and other actions against the debtor and the debtor's property. Under certain circumstances, the stay may be limited to 30 days or not exist at all, although the debtor can request the court to extend or impose a stay. If you attempt to collect a debt or take other action in violation of the Bankruptcy Code, you may be penalized. Consult a lawyer to determine your rights in this case.

Please Do Not File A Proof of Claim Unless You Receive a Notice To Do So.

**Creditor with a Foreign Address:**

A creditor to whom this notice is sent at a foreign address should read the information under "Do Not File a Proof of Claim at This Time" on the reverse side.

| | |
|---|---|
| **Address of the Bankruptcy Clerk's Office:**<br><br>Telephone number: | **For the Court:**<br>Clerk of the Bankruptcy Court: |
| Hours Open: | Date: |

**EXPLANATIONS** **B9B (Official Form 9B) (12/07)**

| | |
|---|---|
| Filing of Chapter 7 Bankruptcy Case | A bankruptcy case under Chapter 7 of the Bankruptcy Code (title 11, United States Code) has been filed in this court by or against the debtor(s) listed on the front side, and an order for relief has been entered. |
| **Legal Advice** | The staff of the bankruptcy clerk's office cannot give legal advice. Consult a lawyer to determine your rights in this case. |
| Creditors Generally May Not Take Certain Actions | Prohibited collection actions are listed in Bankruptcy Code § 362. Common examples of prohibited actions include contacting the debtor by telephone, mail, or otherwise to demand repayment; taking actions to collect money or obtain property from the debtor; repossessing the debtor's property; and starting or continuing lawsuits or foreclosures. Under certain circumstances, the stay may be limited to 30 days or not exist at all, although the debtor can request the court to extend or impose a stay. |
| Meeting of Creditors | A meeting of creditors is scheduled for the date, time, and location listed on the front side. *The debtor's representative must be present at the meeting to be questioned under oath by the trustee and by creditors.* Creditors are welcome to attend, but are not required to do so. The meeting may be continued and concluded at a later date without further notice. |
| Do Not File a Proof of Claim at This Time | There does not appear to be any property available to the trustee to pay creditors. *You therefore should not file a proof of claim at this time.* If it later appears that assets are available to pay creditors, you will be sent another notice telling you that you may file a proof of claim, and telling you the deadline for filing your proof of claim. If this notice is mailed to a creditor at a foreign address, the creditor may file a motion requesting the court to extend the deadline. |
| Bankruptcy Clerk's Office | Any paper that you file in this bankruptcy case should be filed at the bankruptcy clerk's office at the address listed on the front side. You may inspect all papers filed, including the list of the debtor's property and debts and the list of the property claimed as exempt, at the bankruptcy clerk's office. |
| Creditor with a Foreign Address | Consult a lawyer familiar with United States bankruptcy law if you have any questions regarding your rights in this case. |

Refer To Other Side For Important Deadlines and Notices

**B9C (Official Form 9C)** (Chapter 7 Individual or Joint Debtor Asset Case) (12/07)

UNITED STATES BANKRUPTCY COURT______________ **District of**______________________

**Notice of**
**Chapter 7 Bankruptcy Case, Meeting of Creditors, & Deadlines**

[A chapter 7 bankruptcy case concerning the debtor(s) listed below was filed on ____________________(date).]
or [A bankruptcy case concerning the debtor(s) listed below was originally filed under chapter______________on
____________________(date) and was converted to a case under chapter 7 on________________(date).]

You may be a creditor of the debtor. **This notice lists important deadlines.** You may want to consult an attorney to protect your Rights. All documents filed in the case may be inspected at the bankruptcy clerk's office at the address listed below. NOTE: The staff of the bankruptcy clerk's office cannot give legal advice.

See Reverse Side for Important Explanations

| | |
|---|---|
| Debtor(s) (name(s) and address): | Case Number: |
| | Last four digits of Social-Security or Individual Taxpayer-ID (ITIN) No(s)./Complete EIN: |
| All other names used by the Debtor(s) in the last 8 years (include married, maiden, and trade names): | Bankruptcy Trustee (name and address): |
| Attorney for Debtor(s) (name and address): Telephone number: | Telephone number: |

**Meeting of Creditors**

Date: / / Time: ( ) A. M. ( ) P. M. Location:

**Presumption of Abuse under 11 U.S.C. § 707(b)**
*See "Presumption of Abuse" on the reverse side.*

*Depending on the documents filed with the petition, one of the following statements will appear.*

The presumption of abuse does not arise.
*Or*
The presumption of abuse arises.
*Or*
Insufficient information has been filed to date to permit the clerk to make any determination concerning the presumption of abuse. If more complete information, when filed, shows that the presumption has arisen, creditors will be notified.

**Deadlines:**
Papers must be *received* by the bankruptcy clerk's office by the following deadlines:

**Deadline to File a Proof of Claim:**
For all creditors (except a governmental unit): For a governmental unit:

**Creditor with a Foreign Address:**
A creditor to whom this notice is sent at a foreign address should read the information under "Claims" on the reverse side.

**Deadline to File a Complaint Objecting to Discharge of the Debtor or to Determine Dischargeability of Certain Debts:**

**Deadline to Object to Exemptions:**
Thirty (30) days after the *conclusion* of the meeting of creditors.

**Creditors May Not Take Certain Actions:**
In most instances, the filing of the bankruptcy case automatically stays certain collection and other actions against the debtor and the debtor's property. Under certain circumstances, the stay may be limited to 30 days or not exist at all, although the debtor can request the court to extend or impose a stay. If you attempt to collect a debt or take other action in violation of the Bankruptcy Code, you may be penalized. Consult a lawyer to determine your rights in this case.

| | |
|---|---|
| **Address of the Bankruptcy Clerk's Office:** | **For the Court:** |
| | Clerk of the Bankruptcy Court: |
| Telephone number: | |
| Hours Open: | Date: |

**EXPLANATIONS** **B9C (Official Form 9C) (12/07)**

| | |
|---|---|
| Filing of Chapter 7 Bankruptcy Case | A bankruptcy case under Chapter 7 of the Bankruptcy Code (title 11, United States Code) has been filed in this court by or against the debtor(s) listed on the front side, and an order for relief has been entered. |
| **Legal Advice** | The staff of the bankruptcy clerk's office cannot give legal advice. Consult a lawyer to determine your rights in this case. |
| Creditors Generally May Not Take Certain Actions | Prohibited collection actions are listed in Bankruptcy Code § 362. Common examples of prohibited actions include contacting the debtor by telephone, mail, or otherwise to demand repayment; taking actions to collect money or obtain property from the debtor; repossessing the debtor's property; starting or continuing lawsuits or foreclosures; and garnishing or deducting from the debtor's wages. Under certain circumstances, the stay may be limited to 30 days or not exist at all, although the debtor can request the court to extend or impose a stay. |
| Meeting of Creditors | A meeting of creditors is scheduled for the date, time, and location listed on the front side. *The debtor (both spouses in a joint case) must be present at the meeting to be questioned under oath by the trustee and by creditors.* Creditors are welcome to attend, but are not required to do so. The meeting may be continued and concluded at a later date without further notice. |
| Claims | A Proof of Claim is a signed statement describing a creditor's claim. If a Proof of Claim form is not included with this notice, you can obtain one at any bankruptcy clerk's office. A secured creditor retains rights in its collateral regardless of whether that creditor files a Proof of Claim. If you do not file a Proof of Claim by the "Deadline to File a Proof of Claim" listed on the front side, you might not be paid any money on your claim from other assets in the bankruptcy case. To be paid you must file a Proof of Claim even if your claim is listed in the schedules filed by the debtor. Filing a Proof of Claim submits the creditor to the jurisdiction of the bankruptcy court, with consequences a lawyer can explain. For example, a secured creditor who files a Proof of Claim may surrender important nonmonetary rights, including the right to a jury trial. **Filing Deadline for a Creditor with a Foreign Address:** The deadlines for filing claims set forth on the front of this notice apply to all creditors. If this notice has been mailed to a creditor at a foreign address, the creditor may file a motion requesting the court to extend the deadline. |
| Discharge of Debts | The debtor is seeking a discharge of most debts, which may include your debt. A discharge means that you may never try to collect the debt from the debtor. If you believe that the debtor is not entitled to receive a discharge under Bankruptcy Code § 727 (a) *or* that a debt owed to you is not dischargeable under Bankruptcy Code § 523 (a) (2), (4), or (6), you must start a lawsuit by filing a complaint in the bankruptcy clerk's office by the "Deadline to File a Complaint Objecting to Discharge of the Debtor or to Determine Dischargeability of Certain Debts" listed on the front side. The bankruptcy clerk's office must receive the complaint and any required filing fee by that Deadline. |
| Exempt Property | The debtor is permitted by law to keep certain property as exempt. Exempt property will not be sold and distributed to creditors. The debtor must file a list of all property claimed as exempt. You may inspect that list at the bankruptcy clerk's office. If you believe that an exemption claimed by the debtor is not authorized by law, you may file an objection to that exemption. The bankruptcy clerk's office must receive the objections by the "Deadline to Object to Exemptions" listed on the front side. |
| Presumption of Abuse | If the presumption of abuse arises, creditors may have the right to file a motion to dismiss the case under § 707(b) of the Bankruptcy Code. The debtor may rebut the presumption by showing special circumstances. |
| Bankruptcy Clerk's Office | Any paper that you file in this bankruptcy case should be filed at the bankruptcy clerk's office at the address listed on the front side. You may inspect all papers filed, including the list of the debtor's property and debts and the list of the property claimed as exempt, at the bankruptcy clerk's office. |
| Liquidation of the Debtor's Property and Payment of Creditors' Claims | The bankruptcy trustee listed on the front of this notice will collect and sell the debtor's property that is not exempt. If the trustee can collect enough money, creditors may be paid some or all of the debts owed to them, in the order specified by the Bankruptcy Code. To make sure you receive any share of that money, you must file a Proof of Claim, as described above. |
| Creditor with a Foreign Address | Consult a lawyer familiar with United States bankruptcy law if you have any questions regarding your rights in this case. |

Refer To Other Side For Important Deadlines and Notices

**B9D (Official Form 9D)** (Chapter 7 Corporation/Partnership Asset Case) (12/07)

UNITED STATES BANKRUPTCY COURT______________ **District of**______________________

**Notice of**
**Chapter 7 Bankruptcy Case, Meeting of Creditors, & Deadlines**

[A chapter 7 bankruptcy case concerning the debtor(s) listed below was filed on __________________(date).]
or [A bankruptcy case concerning the debtor(s) listed below was originally filed under chapter______________on
____________________(date) and was converted to a case under chapter 7 on_______________(date).]

You may be a creditor of the debtor. **This notice lists important deadlines.** You may want to consult an attorney to protect your Rights. All documents filed in the case may be inspected at the bankruptcy clerk's office at the address listed below. NOTE: The staff of the bankruptcy clerk's office cannot give legal advice.

See Reverse Side for Important Explanations

| | |
|---|---|
| Debtor(s) (name(s) and address): | Case Number: |
| | Last four digits of Social-Security or Individual Taxpayer-ID (ITIN) No(s)./Complete EIN: |
| All other names used by the Debtor(s) in the last 8 years (include trade names): | Bankruptcy Trustee (name and address): |
| Attorney for Debtor(s) (name and address): Telephone number: | Telephone number: |

**Meeting of Creditors**

Date: / / Time: ( ) A. M. ( ) P. M. Location:

**Deadline to File a Proof of Claim**

Papers must be *received* by the bankruptcy clerk's office by the following deadlines:

For all creditors (except a governmental unit): For a governmental unit:

**Creditor with a Foreign Address:**
A creditor to whom this notice is sent at a foreign address should read the information under "Claims" on the reverse side.

**Creditors May Not Take Certain Actions:**

In most instances, the filing of the bankruptcy case automatically stays certain collection and other actions against the debtor and the debtor's property. Under certain circumstances, the stay may be limited to 30 days or not exist at all, although the debtor can request the court to extend or impose a stay. If you attempt to collect a debt or take other action in violation of the Bankruptcy Code, you may be penalized. Consult a lawyer to determine your rights in this case.

| | |
|---|---|
| **Address of the Bankruptcy Clerk's Office:** Telephone number: | **For the Court:** Clerk of the Bankruptcy Court: |
| Hours Open: | Date: |

**EXPLANATIONS** **B9D (Official Form 9D) (12/07)**

| | |
|---|---|
| Filing of Chapter 7 Bankruptcy Case | A bankruptcy case under Chapter 7 of the Bankruptcy Code (title 11, United States Code) has been filed in this court by or against the debtor(s) listed on the front side, and an order for relief has been entered. |
| **Legal Advice** | The staff of the bankruptcy clerk's office cannot give legal advice. Consult a lawyer to determine your rights in this case. |
| Creditors Generally May Not Take Certain Actions | Prohibited collection actions are listed in Bankruptcy Code § 362. Common examples of prohibited actions include contacting the debtor by telephone, mail, or otherwise to demand repayment; taking actions to collect money or obtain property from the debtor; repossessing the debtor's property; and starting or continuing lawsuits or foreclosures. Under certain circumstances, the stay may be limited to 30 days or not exist at all, although the debtor can request the court to extend or impose a stay. |
| Meeting of Creditors | A meeting of creditors is scheduled for the date, time, and location listed on the front side. *The debtor's representative must be present at the meeting to be questioned under oath by the trustee and by creditors.* Creditors are welcome to attend, but are not required to do so. The meeting may be continued and concluded at a later date without further notice. |
| Claims | A Proof of Claim is a signed statement describing a creditor's claim. If a Proof of Claim form is not included with this notice, you can obtain one at any bankruptcy clerk's office. A secured creditor retains rights in its collateral regardless of whether that creditor files a Proof of Claim. If you do not file a Proof of Claim by the "Deadline to File a Proof of Claim" listed on the front side, you might not be paid any money on your claim from other assets in the bankruptcy case. To be paid, you must file a Proof of Claim even if your claim is listed in the schedules filed by the debtor. Filing a Proof of Claim submits the creditor to the jurisdiction of the bankruptcy court, with consequences a lawyer can explain. For example, a secured creditor who files a Proof of Claim may surrender important nonmonetary rights, including the right to a jury trial. **Filing Deadline for a Creditor with a Foreign Address:** The deadlines for filing claims set forth on the front of this notice apply to all creditors. If this notice has been mailed to a creditor at a foreign address, the creditor may file a motion requesting the court to extend the deadline. |
| Liquidation of the Debtor's Property and Payment of Creditors' Claims | The bankruptcy trustee listed on the front of this notice will collect and sell the debtor's property that is not exempt. If the trustee can collect enough money, creditors may be paid some or all of the debts owed to them, in the order specified by the Bankruptcy Code. To make sure you receive any share of that money, you must file a Proof of Claim, as described above. |
| Bankruptcy Clerk's Office | Any paper that you file in this bankruptcy case should be filed at the bankruptcy clerk's office at the address listed on the front side. You may inspect all papers filed, including the list of the debtor's property and debts and the list of the property claimed as exempt, at the bankruptcy clerk's office. |
| Creditor with a Foreign Address | Consult a lawyer familiar with United States bankruptcy law if you have any questions regarding your rights in this case. |

Refer To Other Side For Important Deadlines and Notices

**B9E (Official Form 9E)** (Chapter 11 Individual or Joint Debtor Case) (12/07)

UNITED STATES BANKRUPTCY COURT______________ **District of**______________________

**Notice of**
**Chapter 11 Bankruptcy Case, Meeting of Creditors, & Deadlines**

[A chapter 11 bankruptcy case concerning the debtor(s) listed below was filed on ____________________ (date).]
or [A bankruptcy case concerning the debtor(s) listed below was originally filed under chapter________________ on ________________________ (date) and was converted to a case under chapter 11 on__________________(date).]

You may be a creditor of the debtor. **This notice lists important deadlines.** You may want to consult an attorney to protect your rights. All documents filed in the case may be inspected at the bankruptcy clerk's office at the address listed below.
NOTE: The staff of the bankruptcy clerk's office cannot give legal advice.

See Reverse Side for Important Explanations

| | |
|---|---|
| Debtor(s) (name(s) and address): | Case Number: |
| | Last four digits of Social-Security or Individual Taxpayer-ID (ITIN) No(s)./Complete EIN: |
| All other names used by the Debtor(s) in the last 8 years (include married, maiden, and trade names): | Attorney for Debtor(s) (name and address):<br><br>Telephone number: |

**Meeting of Creditors**

Date: / / Time: ( ) A. M. ( ) P. M. Location:

**Deadlines:**

Papers must be *received* by the bankruptcy clerk's office by the following deadlines:

**Deadline to File a Proof of Claim:**
Notice of deadline will be sent at a later time.

**Creditor with a Foreign Address:**
A creditor to whom this notice is sent at a foreign address should read the information under "Claims" on the reverse side.

**Deadline to File a Complaint to Determine Dischargeability of Certain Debts:**

**Deadline to File a Complaint Objecting to Discharge of the Debtor:**

*First date set for hearing on confirmation of plan*
Notice of that date will be sent at a later time.

**Deadline to Object to Exemptions:**

Thirty (30) days after the *conclusion* of the meeting of creditors.

**Creditors May Not Take Certain Actions:**

In most instances, the filing of the bankruptcy case automatically stays certain collection and other actions against the debtor and the debtor's property. Under certain circumstances, the stay may be limited to 30 days or not exist at all, although the debtor can request the court to extend or impose a stay. If you attempt to collect a debt or take other action in violation of the Bankruptcy Code, you may be penalized. Consult a lawyer to determine your rights in this case.

| | |
|---|---|
| **Address of the Bankruptcy Clerk's Office:**<br><br>**Telephone number:** | **For the Court:**<br>Clerk of the Bankruptcy Court: |
| Hours Open: | Date: |

**EXPLANATIONS** **B9E (Official Form 9E) (12/07)**

| | |
|---|---|
| Filing of Chapter 11 Bankruptcy Case | A bankruptcy case under Chapter 11 of the Bankruptcy Code (title 11, United States Code) has been filed in this court by or against the debtor(s) listed on the front side, and an order for relief has been entered. Chapter 11 allows a debtor to reorganize or liquidate pursuant to a plan. A plan is not effective unless confirmed by the court. You may be sent a copy of the plan and a disclosure statement telling you about the plan, and you might have the opportunity to vote on the plan. You will be sent notice of the date of the confirmation hearing, and you may object to confirmation of the plan and attend the confirmation hearing. Unless a trustee is serving, the debtor will remain in possession of the debtor's property and may continue to operate any business. |
| **Legal Advice** | The staff of the bankruptcy clerk's office cannot give legal advice. Consult a lawyer to determine your rights in this case. |
| Creditors Generally May Not Take Certain Actions | Prohibited collection actions are listed in Bankruptcy Code § 362. Common examples of prohibited actions include contacting the debtor by telephone, mail, or otherwise to demand repayment; taking actions to collect money or obtain property from the debtor; repossessing the debtor's property; starting or continuing lawsuits or foreclosures; and garnishing or deducting from the debtor's wages. Under certain circumstances, the stay may be limited to 30 days or not exist at all, although the debtor can request the court to extend or impose a stay. |
| Meeting of Creditors | A meeting of creditors is scheduled for the date, time, and location listed on the front side. *The debtor (both spouses in a joint case) must be present at the meeting to be questioned under oath by the trustee and by creditors.* Creditors are welcome to attend, but are not required to do so. The meeting may be continued and concluded at a later date without further notice. The court, after notice and a hearing, may order that the United States trustee not convene the meeting if the debtor has filed a plan for which the debtor solicited acceptances before filing the case. |
| Claims | A Proof of Claim is a signed statement describing a creditor's claim. If a Proof of Claim form is not included with this notice, you can obtain one at any bankruptcy clerk's office. You may look at the schedules that have been or will be filed at the bankruptcy clerk's office. If your claim is scheduled and is *not* listed as disputed, contingent, or unliquidated, it will be allowed in the amount scheduled unless you filed a Proof of Claim or you are sent further notice about the claim. Whether or not your claim is scheduled, you are permitted to file a Proof of Claim. If your claim is not listed at all *or* if your claim is listed as disputed, contingent, or unliquidated, then you must file a Proof of Claim or you might not be paid any money on your claim and may be unable to vote on a plan. The court has not yet set a deadline to file a Proof of Claim. If a deadline is set, you will be sent another notice. A secured creditor retains rights in its collateral regardless of whether that creditor files a Proof of Claim. Filing a Proof of Claim submits the creditor to the jurisdiction of the bankruptcy court, with consequences a lawyer can explain. For example, a secured creditor who files a Proof of Claim may surrender important nonmonetary rights, including the right to a jury trial. **Filing Deadline for a Creditor with a Foreign Address:** The deadline for filing claims will be set in a later court order and will apply to all creditors unless the order provides otherwise. If notice of the order setting the deadline is sent to a creditor at a foreign address, the creditor may file a motion requesting the court to extend the deadline. |
| Discharge of Debts | Confirmation of a chapter 11 plan may result in a discharge of debts, which may include all or part of your debt. *See* Bankruptcy Code § 1141 (d). Unless the court orders otherwise, however, the discharge will not be effective until completion of all payments under the plan. A discharge means that you may never try to collect the debt from the debtor except as provided in the plan. If you believe that a debt owed to you is not dischargeable under Bankruptcy Code § 523 (a) (2), (4), or (6), you must start a lawsuit by filing a complaint in the bankruptcy clerk's office by the "Deadline to File a Complaint to Determine Dischargeability of Certain Debts" listed on the front side. The bankruptcy clerk's office must receive the complaint and any required filing fee by that Deadline. If you believe that the debtor is not entitled to receive a discharge under Bankruptcy Code § 1141 (d) (3), you must file a complaint with the required filing fee in the bankruptcy clerk's office not later than the first date set for the hearing on confirmation of the plan. You will be sent another notice informing you of that date. |
| Exempt Property | The debtor is permitted by law to keep certain property as exempt. Exempt property will not be sold and distributed to creditors, even if the debtor's case is converted to chapter 7. The debtor must file a list of property claimed as exempt. You may inspect that list at the bankruptcy clerk's office. If you believe that an exemption claimed by the debtor is not authorized by law, you may file an objection to that exemption. The bankruptcy clerk's office must receive the objection by the "Deadline to Object to Exemptions" listed on the front side. |
| Bankruptcy Clerk's Office | Any paper that you file in this bankruptcy case should be filed at the bankruptcy clerk's office at the address listed on the front side. You may inspect all papers filed, including the list of the debtor's property and debts and the list of the property claimed as exempt, at the bankruptcy clerk's office. |
| Creditor with a Foreign Address | Consult a lawyer familiar with United States bankruptcy law if you have any questions regarding your rights in this case. |

Refer To Other Side For Important Deadlines and Notices

B9E ALT (Official Form 9E ALT) (Chapter 11 Individual or Joint Debtor Case) (12/07)

UNITED STATES BANKRUPTCY COURT_____________ **District of**______________________

**Notice of**
**Chapter 11 Bankruptcy Case, Meeting of Creditors, & Deadlines**

[A chapter 11 bankruptcy case concerning the debtor(s) listed below was filed on __________________ (date).]
or [A bankruptcy case concerning the debtor(s) listed below was originally filed under chapter_______________ on ___________________ (date) and was converted to a case under chapter 11 on________________ (date).]

You may be a creditor of the debtor. **This notice lists important deadlines.** You may want to consult an attorney to protect your rights. All documents filed in the case may be inspected at the bankruptcy clerk's office at the address listed below.
NOTE: The staff of the bankruptcy clerk's office cannot give legal advice.

See Reverse Side for Important Explanations

| | |
|---|---|
| Debtor(s) (name(s) and address): | Case Number: |
| | Last four digits of Social-Security or Individual Taxpayer-ID (ITIN) No(s)./Complete EIN: |
| All other names used by the Debtor(s) in the last 8 years (include married, maiden, and trade names): | Attorney for Debtor(s) (name and address):<br><br>Telephone number: |

**Meeting of Creditors**

Date: / / Time: ( ) A. M. ( ) P. M. Location:

**Deadlines:**

Papers must be *received* by the bankruptcy clerk's office by the following deadlines:

**Deadline to File a Proof of Claim:**

For all creditors (except a governmental unit): For a governmental unit:

**Creditor with a Foreign Address:**
A creditor to whom this notice is sent at a foreign address should read the information under "Claims" on the reverse side.

**Deadline to File a Complaint to Determine Dischargeability of Certain Debts:**

**Deadline to File a Complaint Objecting to Discharge of the Debtor:**

*First date set for hearing on confirmation of plan*
Notice of that date will be sent at a later time.

**Deadline to Object to Exemptions:**

Thirty (30) days after the *conclusion* of the meeting of creditors.

**Creditors May Not Take Certain Actions:**

In most instances, the filing of the bankruptcy case automatically stays certain collection and other actions against the debtor and the debtor's property. Under certain circumstances, the stay may be limited to 30 days or not exist at all, although the debtor can request the court to extend or impose a stay. If you attempt to collect a debt or take other action in violation of the Bankruptcy Code, you may be penalized. Consult a lawyer to determine your rights in this case.

| | |
|---|---|
| **Address of the Bankruptcy Clerk's Office:**<br><br>**Telephone number:** | **For the Court:**<br>Clerk of the Bankruptcy Court: |
| Hours Open: | Date: |

**EXPLANATIONS** **B9E ALT (Official Form 9E ALT) (12/07)**

| | |
|---|---|
| Filing of Chapter 11 Bankruptcy Case | A bankruptcy case under Chapter 11 of the Bankruptcy Code (title 11, United States Code) has been filed in this court by or against the debtor(s) listed on the front side, and an order for relief has been entered. Chapter 11 allows a debtor to reorganize or liquidate pursuant to a plan. A plan is not effective unless confirmed by the court. You may be sent a copy of the plan and a disclosure statement telling you about the plan, and you might have the opportunity to vote on the plan. You will be sent notice of the date of the confirmation hearing, and you may object to confirmation of the plan and attend the confirmation hearing. Unless a trustee is serving, the debtor will remain in possession of the debtor's property and may continue to operate any business. |
| **Legal Advice** | The staff of the bankruptcy clerk's office cannot give legal advice. Consult a lawyer to determine your rights in this case. |
| Creditors Generally May Not Take Certain Actions | Prohibited collection actions are listed in Bankruptcy Code § 362. Common examples of prohibited actions include contacting the debtor by telephone, mail, or otherwise to demand repayment; taking actions to collect money or obtain property from the debtor; repossessing the debtor's property; starting or continuing lawsuits or foreclosures; and garnishing or deducting from the debtor's wages. Under certain circumstances, the stay may be limited to 30 days or not exist at all, although the debtor can request the court to extend or impose a stay. |
| Meeting of Creditors | A meeting of creditors is scheduled for the date, time, and location listed on the front side. *The debtor (both spouses in a joint case) must be present at the meeting to be questioned under oath by the trustee and by creditors.* Creditors are welcome to attend, but are not required to do so. The meeting may be continued and concluded at a later date without further notice. The court, after notice and a hearing, may order that the United States trustee not convene the meeting if the debtor has filed a plan for which the debtor solicited acceptances before filing the case. |
| Claims | A Proof of Claim is a signed statement describing a creditor's claim. If a Proof of Claim form is not included with this notice, you can obtain one at any bankruptcy clerk's office. You may look at the schedules that have been or will be filed at the bankruptcy clerk's office. If your claim is scheduled and is *not* listed as disputed, contingent, or unliquidated, it will be allowed in the amount scheduled unless you filed a Proof of Claim or you are sent further notice about the claim. Whether or not your claim is scheduled, you are permitted to file a Proof of Claim. If your claim is not listed at all *or* if your claim is listed as disputed, contingent, or unliquidated, then you must file a Proof of Claim by the "Deadline to File a Proof of Claim" listed on the front side or you might not be paid any money on your claim and may be unable to vote on a plan. A secured creditor retains rights in its collateral regardless of whether that creditor files a Proof of Claim. Filing a Proof of Claim submits the creditor to the jurisdiction of the bankruptcy court, with consequences a lawyer can explain. For example, a secured creditor who files a Proof of Claim may surrender important nonmonetary rights, including the right to a jury trial. **Filing Deadline for a Creditor with a Foreign Address:** The deadlines for filing claims set forth on the front of this notice apply to all creditors. If this notice has been mailed to a creditor at a foreign address, the creditor may file a motion requesting the court to extend the deadline. |
| Discharge of Debts | Confirmation of a chapter 11 plan may result in a discharge of debts, which may include all or part of your debt. *See* Bankruptcy Code § 1141 (d). Unless the court orders otherwise, however, the discharge will not be effective until completion of all payments under the plan. A discharge means that you may never try to collect the debt from the debtor except as provided in the plan. If you believe that a debt owed to you is not dischargeable under Bankruptcy Code § 523 (a) (2), (4), or (6), you must start a lawsuit by filing a complaint in the bankruptcy clerk's office by the "Deadline to File a Complaint to Determine Dischargeability of Certain Debts" listed on the front side. The bankruptcy clerk's office must receive the complaint and any required filing fee by that Deadline. If you believe that the debtor is not entitled to receive a discharge under Bankruptcy Code § 1141 (d) (3), you must file a complaint with the required filing fee in the bankruptcy clerk's office not later than the first date set for the hearing on confirmation of the plan. You will be sent another notice informing you of that date. |
| Exempt Property | The debtor is permitted by law to keep certain property as exempt. Exempt property will not be sold and distributed to creditors, even if the debtor's case is converted to chapter 7. The debtor must file a list of property claimed as exempt. You may inspect that list at the bankruptcy clerk's office. If you believe that an exemption claimed by the debtor is not authorized by law, you may file an objection to that exemption. The bankruptcy clerk's office must receive the objection by the "Deadline to Object to Exemptions" listed on the front side. |
| Bankruptcy Clerk's Office | Any paper that you file in this bankruptcy case should be filed at the bankruptcy clerk's office at the address listed on the front side. You may inspect all papers filed, including the list of the debtor's property and debts and the list of the property claimed as exempt, at the bankruptcy clerk's office. |
| Creditor with a Foreign Address | Consult a lawyer familiar with United States bankruptcy law if you have any questions regarding your rights in this case. |

Refer To Other Side For Important Deadlines and Notices

**B9F (Official Form 9F)** (Chapter 11 Corporation/Partnership Case) (12/08)

UNITED STATES BANKRUPTCY COURT____________ **District of**________________

**Notice of**
**Chapter 11 Bankruptcy Case, Meeting of Creditors, & Deadlines**

[A chapter 11 bankruptcy case concerning the debtor(s) listed below was filed on __________________(date).]
or [A bankruptcy case concerning the debtor(s) listed below was originally filed under chapter______________on
____________________(date) and was converted to a case under chapter 11 on________________(date).]

You may be a creditor of the debtor. **This notice lists important deadlines.** You may want to consult an attorney to protect your rights. All documents filed in the case may be inspected at the bankruptcy clerk's office at the address listed below.
NOTE: The staff of the bankruptcy clerk's office cannot give legal advice.

See Reverse Side for Important Explanations

| | |
|---|---|
| Debtor(s) (name(s) and address): | Case Number: |
| | Last four digits of Social-Security or Individual Taxpayer-ID (ITIN) No(s)./Complete EIN: |
| All other names used by the Debtor(s) in the last 8 years (include trade names): | Attorney for Debtor(s) (name and address): <br><br> Telephone number: |

**Meeting of Creditors**

Date: / / Time: ( ) A. M. ( ) P. M. Location:

**Deadline to File a Proof of Claim**

Proof of Claim must be *received* by the bankruptcy clerk's office by the following deadline:

Notice of deadline will be sent at a later time.

**Creditor with a Foreign Address:**
A creditor to whom this notice is sent at a foreign address should read the information under "Claims" on the reverse side.

**Deadline to File a Complaint to Determine Dischargeability of Certain Debts:**

**Creditors May Not Take Certain Actions:**
In most instances, the filing of the bankruptcy case automatically stays certain collection and other actions against the debtor and the debtor's property. Under certain circumstances, the stay may be limited to 30 days or not exist at all, although the debtor can request the court to extend or impose a stay. If you attempt to collect a debt or take other action in violation of the Bankruptcy Code, you may be penalized. Consult a lawyer to determine your rights in this case.

| | |
|---|---|
| **Address of the Bankruptcy Clerk's Office:** <br><br> **Telephone number:** | **For the Court:** <br> Clerk of the Bankruptcy Court: |
| Hours Open: | Date: |

**EXPLANATIONS** **B9F (Official Form 9F ) (12/08)**

| | |
|---|---|
| Filing of Chapter 11 Bankruptcy Case | A bankruptcy case under Chapter 11 of the Bankruptcy Code (title 11, United States Code) has been filed in this court by or against the debtor(s) listed on the front side, and an order for relief has been entered. Chapter 11 allows a debtor to reorganize or liquidate pursuant to a plan. A plan is not effective unless confirmed by the court. You may be sent a copy of the plan and a disclosure statement telling you about the plan, and you might have the opportunity to vote on the plan. You will be sent notice of the date of the confirmation hearing, and you may object to confirmation of the plan and attend the confirmation hearing. Unless a trustee is serving, the debtor will remain in possession of the debtor's property and may continue to operate any business. |
| **Legal Advice** | The staff of the bankruptcy clerk's office cannot give legal advice. Consult a lawyer to determine your rights in this case. |
| Creditors Generally May Not Take Certain Actions | Prohibited collection actions are listed in Bankruptcy Code § 362. Common examples of prohibited actions include contacting the debtor by telephone, mail, or otherwise to demand repayment; taking actions to collect money or obtain property from the debtor; repossessing the debtor's property; and starting or continuing lawsuits or foreclosures. Under certain circumstances, the stay may be limited to 30 days or not exist at all, although the debtor can request the court to extend or impose a stay. |
| Meeting of Creditors | A meeting of creditors is scheduled for the date, time, and location listed on the front side. *The debtor's representative must be present at the meeting to be questioned under oath by the trustee and by creditors.* Creditors are welcome to attend, but are not required to do so. The meeting may be continued and concluded at a later date without further notice. The court, after notice and a hearing, may order that the United States trustee not convene the meeting if the debtor has filed a plan for which the debtor solicited acceptances before filing the case. |
| Claims | A Proof of Claim is a signed statement describing a creditor's claim. If a Proof of Claim form is not included with this notice, you can obtain one at any bankruptcy clerk's office. You may look at the schedules that have been or will be filed at the bankruptcy clerk's office. If your claim is scheduled and is *not* listed as disputed, contingent, or unliquidated, it will be allowed in the amount scheduled unless you filed a Proof of Claim or you are sent further notice about the claim. Whether or not your claim is scheduled, you are permitted to file a Proof of Claim. If your claim is not listed at all *or* if your claim is listed as disputed, contingent, or unliquidated, then you must file a Proof of Claim or you might not be paid any money on your claim and may be unable to vote on a plan. The court has not yet set a deadline to file a Proof of Claim. If a deadline is set, you will be sent another notice. A secured creditor retains rights in its collateral regardless of whether that creditor files a Proof of Claim. Filing a Proof of Claim submits the creditor to the jurisdiction of the bankruptcy court, with consequences a lawyer can explain. For example, a secured creditor who files a Proof of Claim may surrender important nonmonetary rights, including the right to a jury trial. **Filing Deadline for a Creditor with a Foreign Address:** The deadline for filing claims will be set in a later court order and will apply to all creditors unless the order provides otherwise. If notice of the order setting the deadline is sent to a creditor at a foreign address, the creditor may file a motion requesting the court to extend the deadline. |
| Discharge of Debts | Confirmation of a chapter 11 plan may result in a discharge of debts, which may include all or part of your debt. *See* Bankruptcy Code § 1141 (d). A discharge means that you may never try to collect the debt from the debtor, except as provided in the plan. If you believe that a debt owed to you is not dischargeable under Bankruptcy Code § 1141 (d) (6) (A), you must start a lawsuit by filing a complaint in the bankruptcy clerk's office by the "Deadline to File a Complaint to Determine Dischargeability of Certain Debts" listed on the front side. The bankruptcy clerk's office must receive the complaint and any required filing fee by that deadline. |
| Bankruptcy Clerk's Office | Any paper that you file in this bankruptcy case should be filed at the bankruptcy clerk's office at the address listed on the front side. You may inspect all papers filed, including the list of the debtor's property and debts and the list of the property claimed as exempt, at the bankruptcy clerk's office. |
| Creditor with a Foreign Address | Consult a lawyer familiar with United States bankruptcy law if you have any questions regarding your rights in this case. |
| Refer To Other Side For Important Deadlines and Notices | |

**B9F ALT (Official Form 9F ALT)** (Chapter 11 Corporation/Partnership Case) (12/07)

UNITED STATES BANKRUPTCY COURT______________ **District of**______________________

## Notice of
## Chapter 11 Bankruptcy Case, Meeting of Creditors, & Deadlines

[A chapter 11 bankruptcy case concerning the debtor(s) listed below was filed on ____________________(date).]
or [A bankruptcy case concerning the debtor(s) listed below was originally filed under chapter______________on ______________________(date) and was converted to a case under chapter 11 on_______________(date).]

You may be a creditor of the debtor. **This notice lists important deadlines.** You may want to consult an attorney to protect your rights. All documents filed in the case may be inspected at the bankruptcy clerk's office at the address listed below.
NOTE: The staff of the bankruptcy clerk's office cannot give legal advice.

See Reverse Side for Important Explanations

| Debtor(s) (name(s) and address): | Case Number: |
|---|---|
| | Last four digits of Social-Security or Individual Taxpayer-ID (ITIN) No(s)./Complete EIN: |
| All other names used by the Debtor(s) in the last 8 years (include trade names): | Attorney for Debtor(s) (name and address): <br> Telephone number: |

**Meeting of Creditors**

Date: / / Time: ( ) A. M. ( ) P. M. Location:

**Deadline to File a Proof of Claim**

Proof of Claim must be *received* by the bankruptcy clerk's office by the following deadline:

For all creditors (except a governmental unit): For a governmental unit:

**Creditor with a Foreign Address:**
A creditor to whom this notice is sent at a foreign address should read the information under "Claims" on the reverse side.

**Deadline to File a Complaint to Determine Dischargeability of Certain Debts:**

**Creditors May Not Take Certain Actions:**
In most instances, the filing of the bankruptcy case automatically stays certain collection and other actions against the debtor and the debtor's property. Under certain circumstances, the stay may be limited to 30 days or not exist at all, although the debtor can request the court to extend or impose a stay. If you attempt to collect a debt or take other action in violation of the Bankruptcy Code, you may be penalized. Consult a lawyer to determine your rights in this case.

| Address of the Bankruptcy Clerk's Office: | For the Court: |
|---|---|
| Telephone number: | Clerk of the Bankruptcy Court: |
| Hours Open: | Date: |

**EXPLANATIONS** **B9F ALT (Official Form 9F ALT) (12/07)**

| | |
|---|---|
| Filing of Chapter 11 Bankruptcy Case | A bankruptcy case under Chapter 11 of the Bankruptcy Code (title 11, United States Code) has been filed in this court by or against the debtor(s) listed on the front side, and an order for relief has been entered. Chapter 11 allows a debtor to reorganize or liquidate pursuant to a plan. A plan is not effective unless confirmed by the court. You may be sent a copy of the plan and a disclosure statement telling you about the plan, and you might have the opportunity to vote on the plan. You will be sent notice of the date of the confirmation hearing, and you may object to confirmation of the plan and attend the confirmation hearing. Unless a trustee is serving, the debtor will remain in possession of the debtor's property and may continue to operate any business. |
| **Legal Advice** | The staff of the bankruptcy clerk's office cannot give legal advice. Consult a lawyer to determine your rights in this case. |
| Creditors Generally May Not Take Certain Actions | Prohibited collection actions are listed in Bankruptcy Code § 362. Common examples of prohibited actions include contacting the debtor by telephone, mail, or otherwise to demand repayment; taking actions to collect money or obtain property from the debtor; repossessing the debtor's property; and starting or continuing lawsuits or foreclosures. Under certain circumstances, the stay may be limited to 30 days or not exist at all, although the debtor can request the court to extend or impose a stay. |
| Meeting of Creditors | A meeting of creditors is scheduled for the date, time, and location listed on the front side. *The debtor's representative must be present at the meeting to be questioned under oath by the trustee and by creditors.* Creditors are welcome to attend, but are not required to do so. The meeting may be continued and concluded at a later date without further notice. The court, after notice and a hearing, may order that the United States trustee not convene the meeting if the debtor has filed a plan for which the debtor solicited acceptances before filing the case. |
| Claims | A Proof of Claim is a signed statement describing a creditor's claim. If a Proof of Claim form is not included with this notice, you can obtain one at any bankruptcy clerk's office. You may look at the schedules that have been or will be filed at the bankruptcy clerk's office. If your claim is scheduled and is *not* listed as disputed, contingent, or unliquidated, it will be allowed in the amount scheduled unless you filed a Proof of Claim or you are sent further notice about the claim. Whether or not your claim is scheduled, you are permitted to file a Proof of Claim. If your claim is not listed at all *or* if your claim is listed as disputed, contingent, or unliquidated, then you must file a Proof of Claim by the "Deadline to File Proof of Claim" listed on the front side, or you might not be paid any money on your claim and may be unable to vote on a plan. A secured creditor retains rights in its collateral regardless of whether that creditor files a Proof of Claim. Filing a Proof of Claim submits the creditor to the jurisdiction of the bankruptcy court, with consequences a lawyer can explain. For example, a secured creditor who files a Proof of Claim may surrender important nonmonetary rights, including the right to a jury trial. **Filing Deadline for a Creditor with a Foreign Address:** The deadlines for filing claims set forth on the front of this notice apply to all creditors. If this notice has been mailed to a creditor at a foreign address, the creditor may file a motion requesting the court to extend the deadline. |
| Discharge of Debts | Confirmation of a chapter 11 plan may result in a discharge of debts, which may include all or part of your debt. *See* Bankruptcy Code § 1141 (d). A discharge means that you may never try to collect the debt from the debtor, except as provided in the plan. If you believe that a debt owed to you is not dischargeable under Bankruptcy Code § 1141 (d) (6) (A), you must start a lawsuit by filing a complaint in the bankruptcy clerk's office by the "Deadline to File a Complaint to Determine Dischargeability of Certain Debts" listed on the front side. The bankruptcy clerk's office must receive the complaint and any required filing fee by that deadline. |
| Bankruptcy Clerk's Office | Any paper that you file in this bankruptcy case should be filed at the bankruptcy clerk's office at the address listed on the front side. You may inspect all papers filed, including the list of the debtor's property and debts and the list of the property claimed as exempt, at the bankruptcy clerk's office. |
| Creditor with a Foreign Address | Consult a lawyer familiar with United States bankruptcy law if you have any questions regarding your rights in this case. |

Refer To Other Side For Important Deadlines and Notices

**B9G (Official Form 9G)** (Chapter 12 Individual or Joint Debtor Family Farmer or Family Fisherman) (12/07)

UNITED STATES BANKRUPTCY COURT______________ **District of**______________________

**Notice of**
**Chapter 12 Bankruptcy Case, Meeting of Creditors, & Deadlines**

[The debtor(s) listed below filed a chapter 12 bankruptcy case on ____________________(date).]
or [A bankruptcy case concerning the debtor(s) listed below was originally filed under chapter______________on
____________________ (date) and was converted to a case under chapter 12 on_______________(date).]

You may be a creditor of the debtor. **This notice lists important deadlines.** You may want to consult an attorney to protect your rights. All documents filed in the case may be inspected at the bankruptcy clerk's office at the address listed below.
NOTE: The staff of the bankruptcy clerk's office cannot give legal advice.

See Reverse Side for Important Explanations

| | |
|---|---|
| Debtor(s) (name(s) and address): | Case Number: |
| | Last four digits of Social-Security or Individual Taxpayer-ID (ITIN) No(s)./Complete EIN: |
| All other names used by the Debtor(s) in the last 8 years (include married, maiden, and trade names): | Bankruptcy Trustee (name and address): |
| Attorney for Debtor(s) (name and address): Telephone number: | Telephone number: |

**Meeting of Creditors**

Date: / / Time: ( ) A. M. ( ) P. M. Location:

**Deadlines:**

Papers must be *received* by the bankruptcy clerk's office by the following deadlines:

**Deadline to File a Proof of Claim:**

For all creditors(except a governmental unit): For a governmental unit:

**Creditor with a Foreign Address:**

A creditor to whom this notice is sent at a foreign address should read the information under "Claims" on the reverse side.

**Deadline to File a Complaint to Determine Dischargeability of Certain Debts:**

**Deadline to Object to Exemptions:**

Thirty (30) days after the *conclusion* of the meeting of creditors.

**Filing of Plan, Hearing on Confirmation of Plan**

[The debtor has filed a plan. The plan or a summary of the plan is enclosed. The hearing on confirmation will be held:
Date:____________________Time:____________________Location:______________________________]
*or* [The debtor has filed a plan. The plan or a summary of the plan and notice of confirmation hearing will be sent separately.]
*or* [The debtor has not filed a plan as of this date. You will be sent separate notice of the hearing on confirmation of the plan.]

**Creditors May Not Take Certain Actions:**

In most instances, the filing of the bankruptcy case automatically stays certain collection and other actions against the debtor, the debtor's property, and certain codebtors. Under certain circumstances, the stay may be limited to 30 days or not exist at all, although the debtor can request the court to extend or impose a stay. If you attempt to collect a debt or take other action in violation of the Bankruptcy Code, you may be penalized. Consult a lawyer to determine your rights in this case.

| | |
|---|---|
| **Address of the Bankruptcy Clerk's Office:** | **For the Court:** |
| | Clerk of the Bankruptcy Court: |
| **Telephone number:** | |
| Hours Open: | Date: |

**EXPLANATIONS** **B9G (Official Form 9G) (12/07)**

| | |
|---|---|
| Filing of Chapter 12 Bankruptcy Case | A bankruptcy case under Chapter 12 of the Bankruptcy Code (title 11, United States Code) has been filed in this court by the debtor(s) listed on the front side, and an order for relief has been entered. Chapter 12 allows family farmers and family fishermen to adjust their debts pursuant to a plan. A plan is not effective unless confirmed by the court. You may object to confirmation of the plan and appear at the confirmation hearing. A copy or summary of the plan [is included with this notice] *or* [will be sent to you later], and [the confirmation hearing will be held on the date indicated on the front of this notice] *or* [you will be sent notice of the confirmation hearing]. The debtor will remain in possession of the debtor's property and may continue to operate the debtor's business unless the court orders otherwise. |
| **Legal Advice** | The staff of the bankruptcy clerk's office cannot give legal advice. Consult a lawyer to determine your rights in this case. |
| Creditors Generally May Not Take Certain Actions | Prohibited collection actions against the debtor and certain codebtors are listed in Bankruptcy Code § 362 and § 1201. Common examples of prohibited actions include contacting the debtor by telephone, mail, or otherwise to demand repayment; taking actions to collect money or obtain property from the debtor; repossessing the debtor's property; starting or continuing lawsuits or foreclosures; and garnishing or deducting from the debtor's wages. Under certain circumstances, the stay may be limited in duration or not exist at all, although the debtor may have the right to request the court to extend or impose a stay. |
| Meeting of Creditors | A meeting of creditors is scheduled for the date, time, and location listed on the front side. *The debtor (both spouses in a joint case) must be present at the meeting to be questioned under oath by the trustee and by creditors.* Creditors are welcome to attend, but are not required to do so. The meeting may be continued and concluded at a later date without further notice. |
| Claims | A Proof of Claim is a signed statement describing a creditor's claim. If a Proof of Claim form is not included with this notice, you can obtain one at any bankruptcy clerk's office. A secured creditor retains rights in its collateral regardless of whether that creditor files a Proof of Claim. If you do not file a Proof of Claim by the "Deadline to File a Proof of Claim" listed on the front side, you might not be paid any money on your claim from other assets in the bankruptcy case. To be paid you must file a Proof of Claim even if your claim is listed in the schedules filed by the debtor. Filing a Proof of Claim submits the creditor to the jurisdiction of the bankruptcy court, with consequences a lawyer can explain. For example, a secured creditor who files a Proof of Claim may surrender important nonmonetary rights, including the right to a jury trial. **Filing Deadline for a Creditor with a Foreign Address:** The deadlines for filing claims set forth on the front of this notice apply to all creditors. If this notice has been mailed to a creditor at a foreign address, the creditor may file a motion requesting the court to extend the deadline. |
| Discharge of Debts | The debtor is seeking a discharge of most debts, which may include your debt. A discharge means that you may never try to collect the debt from the debtor. If you believe that a debt owed to you is not dischargeable under Bankruptcy Code § 523 (a) (2), (4), or (6), you must start a lawsuit by filing a complaint in the bankruptcy clerk's office by the "Deadline to File a Complaint to Determine Dischargeability of Certain Debts" listed on the front side. The bankruptcy clerk's office must receive the complaint and any required filing fee by that Deadline. |
| Exempt Property | The debtor is permitted by law to keep certain property as exempt. Exempt property will not be sold and distributed to creditors, even if the debtor's case is converted to chapter 7. The debtor must file a list of all property claimed as exempt. You may inspect that list at the bankruptcy clerk's office. If you believe that an exemption claimed by the debtor is not authorized by law, you may file an objection to that exemption. The bankruptcy clerk's office must receive the objection by the "Deadline to Object to Exemptions" listed on the front side. |
| Bankruptcy Clerk's Office | Any paper that you file in this bankruptcy case should be filed at the bankruptcy clerk's office at the address listed on the front side. You may inspect all papers filed, including the list of the debtor's property and debts and the list of the property claimed as exempt, at the bankruptcy clerk's office. |
| Creditor with a Foreign Address | Consult a lawyer familiar with United States bankruptcy law if you have any questions regarding your rights in this case. |

Refer To Other Side For Important Deadlines and Notices

**B9H (Official Form 9H)** (Chapter 12 Corporation/Partnership Family Farmer or Family Fisherman) (12/07)

UNITED STATES BANKRUPTCY COURT______________ **District of**______________________

**Notice of**
**Chapter 12 Bankruptcy Case, Meeting of Creditors, & Deadlines**

[The debtor [corporation] *or* [partnership] listed below filed a chapter 12 bankruptcy case on ________________ (date).]
or [A bankruptcy case concerning the debtor [corporation] *or* [partnership] listed below was originally filed under chapter______________ on ______________________ (date) and was converted to a case under chapter 12 on_____________(date).]

You may be a creditor of the debtor. **This notice lists important deadlines.** You may want to consult an attorney to protect your rights. All documents filed in the case may be inspected at the bankruptcy clerk's office at the address listed below.
NOTE: The staff of the bankruptcy clerk's office cannot give legal advice.

See Reverse Side for Important Explanations

| | |
|---|---|
| Debtor(s) (name(s) and address): | Case Number: |
| | Last four digits of Social-Security or Individual Taxpayer-ID (ITIN) No(s)./Complete EIN: |
| All other names used by the Debtor(s) in the last 8 years (include trade names): | Bankruptcy Trustee (name and address): |
| Attorney for Debtor(s) (name and address):<br><br>Telephone number: | Telephone number: |

**Meeting of Creditors**

Date: / / Time: ( ) A. M. ( ) P. M. Location:

**Deadlines:**
Papers must be *received* by the bankruptcy clerk's office by the following deadlines:

**Deadline to File a Proof of Claim:**

For all creditors(except a governmental unit): For a governmental unit:

**Creditor with a Foreign Address:**
A creditor to whom this notice is sent at a foreign address should read the information under "Claims" on the reverse side.

**Deadline to File a Complaint to Determine Dischargeability of Certain Debts:**

**Filing of Plan, Hearing on Confirmation of Plan**

[The debtor has filed a plan. The plan or a summary of the plan is enclosed. The hearing on confirmation will be held:
Date:____________________Time:__________________Location:________________________________]
*or* [The debtor has filed a plan. The plan or a summary of the plan and notice of confirmation hearing will be sent separately.]
*or* [The debtor has not filed a plan as of this date. You will be sent separate notice of the hearing on confirmation of the plan.]

**Creditors May Not Take Certain Actions:**
In most instances, the filing of the bankruptcy case automatically stays certain collection and other actions against the debtor and the debtor's property. Under certain circumstances, the stay may be limited to 30 days or not exist at all, although the debtor can request the court to extend or impose a stay. If you attempt to collect a debt or take other action in violation of the Bankruptcy Code, you may be penalized. Consult a lawyer to determine your rights in this case.

| | |
|---|---|
| **Address of the Bankruptcy Clerk's Office:**<br><br>**Telephone number:** | **For the Court:**<br>Clerk of the Bankruptcy Court: |
| Hours Open: | Date: |

**EXPLANATIONS** **B9H (Official Form 9H) (12/07)**

| | |
|---|---|
| Filing of Chapter 12 Bankruptcy Case | A bankruptcy case under Chapter 12 of the Bankruptcy Code (title 11, United States Code) has been filed in this court by the debtor listed on the front side, and an order for relief has been entered. Chapter 12 allows family farmers and family fishermen to adjust their debts pursuant to a plan. A plan is not effective unless confirmed by the court. You may object to confirmation of the plan and appear at the confirmation hearing. A copy or summary of the plan [is included with this notice] *or* [will be sent to you later], and [the confirmation hearing will be held on the date indicated on the front of this notice] *or* [you will be sent notice of the confirmation hearing]. The debtor will remain in possession of the debtor's property and may continue to operate the debtor's business unless the court orders otherwise. |
| **Legal Advice** | The staff of the bankruptcy clerk's office cannot give legal advice. Consult a lawyer to determine your rights in this case. |
| Creditors Generally May Not Take Certain Actions | Prohibited collection actions against the debtor and certain codebtors are listed in Bankruptcy Code § 362 and § 1201. Common examples of prohibited actions include contacting the debtor by telephone, mail, or otherwise to demand repayment; taking actions to collect money or obtain property from the debtor; repossessing the debtor's property; and starting or continuing lawsuits or foreclosures. Under certain circumstances, the stay may be limited in duration or not exist at all, although the debtor may have the right to request the court to extend or impose a stay. |
| Meeting of Creditors | A meeting of creditors is scheduled for the date, time, and location listed on the front side. *The debtor's representative must be present at the meeting to be questioned under oath by the trustee and by creditors.* Creditors are welcome to attend, but are not required to do so. The meeting may be continued and concluded at a later date without further notice. |
| Claims | A Proof of Claim is a signed statement describing a creditor's claim. If a Proof of Claim form is not included with this notice, you can obtain one at any bankruptcy clerk's office. A secured creditor retains rights in its collateral regardless of whether that creditor files a Proof of Claim. If you do not file a Proof of Claim by the "Deadline to File a Proof of Claim" listed on the front side, you might not be paid any money on your claim from other assets in the bankruptcy case. To be paid you must file a Proof of Claim even if your claim is listed in the schedules filed by the debtor. Filing a Proof of Claim submits the creditor to the jurisdiction of the bankruptcy court, with consequences a lawyer can explain. For example, a secured creditor who files a Proof of Claim may surrender important nonmonetary rights, including the right to a jury trial. **Filing Deadline for a Creditor with a Foreign Address:** The deadlines for filing claims set forth on the front of this notice apply to all creditors. If this notice has been mailed to a creditor at a foreign address, the creditor may file a motion requesting the court to extend the deadline. |
| Discharge of Debts | The debtor is seeking a discharge of most debts, which may include your debt. A discharge means that you may never try to collect the debt from the debtor. If you believe that a debt owed to you is not dischargeable under Bankruptcy Code § 523 (a) (2), (4), or (6), you must start a lawsuit by filing a complaint in the bankruptcy clerk's office by the "Deadline to File a Complaint to Determine Dischargeability of Certain Debts" listed on the front side. The bankruptcy clerk's office must receive the complaint and any required filing fee by that Deadline. |
| Bankruptcy Clerk's Office | Any paper that you file in this bankruptcy case should be filed at the bankruptcy clerk's office at the address listed on the front side. You may inspect all papers filed, including the list of the debtor's property and debts and the list of the property claimed as exempt, at the bankruptcy clerk's office. |
| Creditor with a Foreign Address | Consult a lawyer familiar with United States bankruptcy law if you have any questions regarding your rights in this case. |
| Refer To Other Side For Important Deadlines and Notices | |
| | |

**B9I (Official Form 9I)** (Chapter 13 Case) (12/07)

UNITED STATES BANKRUPTCY COURT______________ **District of**______________________

**Notice of**
**Chapter 13 Bankruptcy Case, Meeting of Creditors, & Deadlines**

[The debtor(s) listed below filed a chapter 13 bankruptcy case on ____________________ (date).]
or [A bankruptcy case concerning the debtor(s) listed below was originally filed under chapter______________
on ______________________ (date) and was converted to a case under chapter 13 on______________(date).]

You may be a creditor of the debtor. **This notice lists important deadlines.** You may want to consult an attorney to protect your rights. All documents filed in the case may be inspected at the bankruptcy clerk's office at the address listed below.
NOTE: The staff of the bankruptcy clerk's office cannot give legal advice.

See Reverse Side for Important Explanations

| | |
|---|---|
| Debtor(s) (name(s) and address): | Case Number: |
| | Last four digits of Social-Security or Individual Taxpayer-ID (ITIN) No(s)./Complete EIN: |
| All other names used by the Debtor(s) in the last 8 years (include married, maiden, and trade names): | Bankruptcy Trustee (name and address): |
| Attorney for Debtor(s) (name and address): Telephone number: | Telephone number: |

**Meeting of Creditors**

Date: / / Time: ( ) A. M. ( ) P. M. Location:

**Deadlines:**

Papers must be *received* by the bankruptcy clerk's office by the following deadlines:

**Deadline to File a Proof of Claim:**

For all creditors (except a governmental unit): For a governmental unit (except as otherwise provided in Fed . R. Bankr. P. 3002(c)(1)):

**Creditor with a Foreign Address:**

A creditor to whom this notice is sent at a foreign address should read the information under "Claims" on the reverse side.

**Deadline to File a Complaint to Determine Dischargeability of Certain Debts:**

**Deadline to Object to Exemptions:**

Thirty (30) days after the *conclusion* of the meeting of creditors.

**Filing of Plan, Hearing on Confirmation of Plan**

[The debtor has filed a plan. The plan or a summary of the plan is enclosed. The hearing on confirmation will be held:
Date:____________________Time:__________________Location:_______________________________]
*or* [The debtor has filed a plan. The plan or a summary of the plan and notice of confirmation hearing will be sent separately.]
*or* [The debtor has not filed a plan as of this date. You will be sent separate notice of the hearing on confirmation of the plan.]

**Creditors May Not Take Certain Actions:**

In most instances, the filing of the bankruptcy case automatically stays certain collection and other actions against the debtor, the debtor's property, and certain codebtors. Under certain circumstances, the stay may be limited to 30 days or not exist at all, although the debtor can request the court to extend or impose a stay. If you attempt to collect a debt or take other action in violation of the Bankruptcy Code, you may be penalized. Consult a lawyer to determine your rights in this case.

| | |
|---|---|
| **Address of the Bankruptcy Clerk's Office:** | **For the Court:** |
| **Telephone number:** | Clerk of the Bankruptcy Court: |
| Hours Open: | Date: |

**EXPLANATIONS** **B9I (Official Form 9I) (12/07)**

| | |
|---|---|
| Filing of Chapter 13 Bankruptcy Case | A bankruptcy case under Chapter 13 of the Bankruptcy Code (title 11, United States Code) has been filed in this court by the debtor(s) listed on the front side, and an order for relief has been entered. Chapter 13 allows an individual with regular income and debts below a specified amount to adjust debts pursuant to a plan. A plan is not effective unless confirmed by the bankruptcy court. You may object to confirmation of the plan and appear at the confirmation hearing. A copy or summary of the plan [is included with this notice] *or* [will be sent to you later], and [the confirmation hearing will be held on the date indicated on the front of this notice] *or* [you will be sent notice of the confirmation hearing]. The debtor will remain in possession of the debtor's property and may continue to operate the debtor's business, if any, unless the court orders otherwise. |
| **Legal Advice** | The staff of the bankruptcy clerk's office cannot give legal advice. Consult a lawyer to determine your rights in this case. |
| Creditors Generally May Not Take Certain Actions | Prohibited collection actions against the debtor and certain codebtors are listed in Bankruptcy Code § 362 and § 1301. Common examples of prohibited actions include contacting the debtor by telephone, mail, or otherwise to demand repayment; taking actions to collect money or obtain property from the debtor; repossessing the debtor's property; starting or continuing lawsuits or foreclosures; and garnishing or deducting from the debtor's wages. Under certain circumstances, the stay may be limited to 30 days or not exist at all, although the debtor can request the court to exceed or impose a stay. |
| Meeting of Creditors | A meeting of creditors is scheduled for the date, time, and location listed on the front side. *The debtor (both spouses in a joint case) must be present at the meeting to be questioned under oath by the trustee and by creditors.* Creditors are welcome to attend, but are not required to do so. The meeting may be continued and concluded at a later date without further notice |
| Claims | A Proof of Claim is a signed statement describing a creditor's claim. If a Proof of Claim form is not included with this notice, you can obtain one at any bankruptcy clerk's office. A secured creditor retains rights in its collateral regardless of whether that creditor files a Proof of Claim. If you do not file a Proof of Claim by the "Deadline to File a Proof of Claim" listed on the front side, you might not be paid any money on your claim from other assets in the bankruptcy case. To be paid you must file a Proof of Claim even if your claim is listed in the schedules filed by the debtor. Filing a Proof of Claim submits the creditor to the jurisdiction of the bankruptcy court, with consequences a lawyer can explain. For example, a secured creditor who files a Proof of Claim may surrender important nonmonetary rights, including the right to a jury trial. **Filing Deadline for a Creditor with a Foreign Address:** The deadlines for filing claims set forth on the front of this notice apply to all creditors. If this notice has been mailed to a creditor at a foreign address, the creditor may file a motion requesting the court to extend the deadline. |
| Discharge of Debts | The debtor is seeking a discharge of most debts, which may include your debt. A discharge means that you may never try to collect the debt from the debtor. If you believe that a debt owed to you is not dischargeable under Bankruptcy Code § 523 (a) (2) or (4), you must start a lawsuit by filing a complaint in the bankruptcy clerk's office by the "Deadline to File a Complaint to Determine Dischargeability of Certain Debts" listed on the front side. The bankruptcy clerk's office must receive the complaint and any required filing fee by that deadline. |
| Exempt Property | The debtor is permitted by law to keep certain property as exempt. Exempt property will not be sold and distributed to creditors, even if the debtor's case is converted to chapter 7. The debtor must file a list of all property claimed as exempt. You may inspect that list at the bankruptcy clerk's office. If you believe that an exemption claimed by the debtor is not authorized by law, you may file an objection to that exemption. The bankruptcy clerk's office must receive the objection by the "Deadline to Object to Exemptions" listed on the front side. |
| Bankruptcy Clerk's Office | Any paper that you file in this bankruptcy case should be filed at the bankruptcy clerk's office at the address listed on the front side. You may inspect all papers filed, including the list of the debtor's property and debts and the list of the property claimed as exempt, at the bankruptcy clerk's office. |
| Creditor with a Foreign Address | Consult a lawyer familiar with United States bankruptcy law if you have any questions regarding your rights in this case. |

Refer To Other Side For Important Deadlines and Notices

(Added Aug. 1, 1991; amended Sept. 22, 1992; Mar. 16, 1993; Mar. 14, 1995; Oct. 1, 1997; Dec. 1, 2003; Oct. 17, 2005; Oct. 1, 2006; Dec. 1, 2007; Dec. 1, 2008.)

NOTES OF ADVISORY COMMITTEE ON RULES—1991

The form has been redesigned to facilitate electronic generation of notice to creditors concerning the filing of the petition, the meeting of creditors, and important deadlines in the case. Adoption of a box format, with significant dates highlighted, is intended to assist creditors who may be unfamiliar with bankruptcy cases to understand the data provided. Nine variations of the form, designated 9A through 9I, have been created to meet the specialized notice requirements for chapters 7, 11, 12, and 13, asset and no-asset cases, and the various types of debtors.

NOTES OF ADVISORY COMMITTEE ON RULES—1992 AMENDMENT

Forms 9B, 9D, 9F, and 9H are amended to make a technical correction in the reference to Rule 9001(5). Form 9H also contains a technical correction deleting the reference to a complaint object to discharge of the debtor.

NOTES OF ADVISORY COMMITTEE ON RULES—1993 AMENDMENT

The title page of the form has been amended to conform to the headings used on Forms 9A–9I. Alternate versions of Form 9E and Form 9F have been added for the convenience of districts that routinely set a deadline for filing claims in a chapter 11 case. When a creditor receives the alternate form in a case, the box labeled "Filing Claims" will contain information about the bar date as follows: "Deadline for filing a claim: (date)." If no deadline is set in a particular case, either the court will use Form 9E or Form 9F, as appropriate, or the alternate form will be used with the following sentence appearing in the box labeled "Filing Claims": "When the court sets a deadline for filing claims, creditors will be notified."

NOTES OF ADVISORY COMMITTEE ON RULES—1995 AMENDMENT

The form is amended to provide notice of the claims filing period provided to "a governmental unit" by section 502(b)(9) of the Code as amended by the Bankruptcy Reform Act of 1994. A court that routinely sets a deadline for filing proofs of claim at the outset of chapter 11 cases and, accordingly, uses Form 9E(Alt.) or Form 9F(Alt.) retains the option in any case in which no deadlines actually are set to substitute a message stating that creditors will be notified if the court fixes a deadline.

The form also is amended to add, in the paragraph labeled "Discharge of Debts," a reference to dischargeability actions under section 523(a)(15) of the Code, which was added by the 1994 Act.

NOTES OF ADVISORY COMMITTEE ON RULES—1997 AMENDMENT

Forms 9A, 9I (and the alternate versions of Forms 9E and 9F) have been amended, redesigned, and rewritten. Minor conforming changes have been made to respond to amendments made in the Bankruptcy Reform Act of 1994: the longer claims filing period for governmental units in section 502(b)(9) of the Code (see Forms 9C, 9D, 9E(Alt.), 9F(Alt.), 9G, 9H, and 9I); and a reference to dischargeability actions under section 523(a)(15) (see Forms 9A, 9C, 9E, and 9E(Alt.), 9G, and 9H). All of the forms have been substantially revised to make them easier to read and understand. The titles have been simplified. Recipients are told why they are receiving the notice. Explanations are provided on the back of the form and are set in larger type. Plain English is used. Deadlines are highlighted on the front of the form. Recipients are told that papers must be received by the bankruptcy clerk's office by the applicable deadline. The box for the trustee has been deleted from the chapter 11 notices (Forms 9E and 9F and the alternates). Various alternatives are set out in brackets in many of the forms, permitting each bankruptcy clerk's office to tailor the forms even more precisely to fit the needs of a particular case. The court may use blank spaces on the form to include additional information applicable to the particular district.

COMMITTEE NOTES ON RULES—2003 AMENDMENT

The form is amended to add to the information provided to creditors, the trustee and the United States trustee, all the names used by the debtor during the six years prior to the filing of the petition. The form includes the debtor's full employer identification number, if any, as well as the last four digits of the debtor's social security number. Rule 2002(a)(1) also is amended to direct the clerk to include the debtor's full social security number and employer identification number on the notices served on the United States trustee, the trustee, and creditors. This will enable creditors to identify the debtor accurately. The copy of Official Form 9 included in the case file, however, will show only the last four digits of the debtor's social security number. This should afford greater privacy to the individual debtor, whose bankruptcy case records may be available on the Internet.

COMMITTEE NOTES ON RULES—2005 AMENDMENT

The form is amended in a variety of way [sic] to implement the provisions of the Bankruptcy Abuse Prevention and Consumer Protection Act of 2005, Pub. L. No. 109–8, 119 Stat. 23 (April 20, 2005). All versions of the form are amended to advise creditors to consult an attorney concerning what rights they may have in the specific case. All versions of the form are also amended to provide information about filing claims to creditors with foreign addresses and to advise those creditors to consult a lawyer familiar with United States bankruptcy law regarding any questions they may have about their rights in a particular case. These amendments implement § 1514, which was added to the Code in 2005.

Forms 9A and 9C are amended to include a box in which the clerk can notify creditors in a chapter 7 case filed by an individual with primarily consumer debts whether the presumption of abuse has arisen under § 707(b) of the Code as amended in 2005. Under § 342(d) of the Code, the clerk has a duty to notify creditors concerning the presumption within ten days of the filing of the petition. If [sic] cases in which the debtor does not file Official Form 22A with the petition, the forms provide for the clerk to state that insufficient information has been filed, and to inform creditors that if later-filed information indicates that the presumption arises, creditors will be sent another notice.

In cases involving serial filers (debtors who have filed more than one case within a specified period), the automatic stay provided by § 362(a) of the Code as amended in 2005 may not apply or may be limited in duration, unless the stay is extended or imposed by court order. The form contains a general statement alerting debtors to this possibility.

Section 1514, added to the Code in 2005, also requires that a secured creditor with a foreign address be advised whether the creditor is required to file a proof of claim, and Forms 9B, 9D, 9E, 9E (Alt.), 9F, 9F (Alt.), 9G, 9H, and 9I are amended to include general information addressing that question. Forms 9E, 9E (Alt.), 9F, and 9F (Alt.) also are amended to inform creditors that in a case in which the debtor has filed a plan for which it has solicited acceptances before filing the case, the court may, after notice and a hearing, order that the United States trustee not convene a meeting of creditors.

Forms 9E and 9E Alt. are amended to state that, unless the court orders otherwise, an individual chapter 11 debtor's discharge is not effective until completion of all payments under the plan, as provided in § 1141(d)(5) which was added to the Code in 2005. Forms 9F and 9F (Alt.) are amended to include a deadline to file a complaint to determine the discharge ability of a debt, in conformity with § 1141(d)(6) which was added to the Code in 2005.

Form 9I is amended to include a deadline to file a complaint to determine the discharge ability of certain debts. This amendment implements 2005 amendment [sic] to § 1328(a)(1) of the Code.

COMMITTEE NOTES ON RULES—2006 AMENDMENT

Forms 9G and 9H are amended to add "family fisherman" to the title and to the description of chapter 12. The 2005 amendments to the Code added a "family fisherman," as defined in § 101(19A), to the persons eligible to file a bankruptcy case under chapter 12. Form 9I is amended to provide general notice to parties in interest of the potential for a claim to be filed late in the case.

COMMITTEE NOTES ON RULES—2005-2007 AMENDMENT

[The 2005-2007 Committee Note incorporates Committee Notes previously published in 2005 and 2006.]

The form is amended in a variety of ways to implement the provisions of the Bankruptcy Abuse Prevention and Consumer Protection Act of 2005, Pub. L. No. 109-8, 119 Stat. 23 (April 20, 2005). All versions of the form are amended to advise creditors to consult an attorney concerning what rights they may have in the specific case. All versions of the form also are amended to provide to creditors with foreign addresses information about filing claims and to advise those creditors to consult a lawyer familiar with United States bankruptcy law regarding any questions they may have about their rights in a particular case. These amendments implement § 1514, which was added to the Code in 2005.

Forms 9A and 9C are amended to include a box in which the clerk can notify creditors in a chapter 7 case filed by an individual with primarily consumer debts if the presumption of abuse has arisen under § 707(b) of the Code as amended in 2005. Under § 342(d) of the Code, the clerk has a duty to notify creditors concerning the presumption within ten days of the filing of the petition. In cases in which the debtor does not file Official Form 22A with the petition, the forms provide for the clerk to state that insufficient information has been filed, and to inform creditors that if later-filed information indicates that the presumption arises, creditors will be sent another notice. Forms 9G and 9H are amended to add "family fishermen" to the notices used in chapter 12 cases, in conformity with the 2005 amendments to the Code extending the provisions of chapter 12 to family fishermen.

In cases involving serial filers (debtors who have filed more than one case within a specified period), the automatic stay provided by § 362(a) of the Code as amended in 2005 may not apply or may be limited in duration, unless the stay is extended or imposed by court order. The form contains a general statement alerting debtors to this possibility.

Section 1514, added to the Code in 2005, also requires that a secured creditor with a foreign address be advised whether the creditor is required to file a proof of claim, and Forms 9B, 9D, 9E, 9E (Alt.), 9F, 9F (Alt.), 9G, 9H, and 9I are amended to include general information addressing that question. Forms 9E, 9E (Alt.), 9F, and 9F (Alt.) also are amended to inform creditors that in a case in which the debtor has filed a plan for which it has solicited acceptances before filing the case, the court may, after notice and a hearing, order that the United States trustee not convene a meeting of creditors.

Forms 9E and 9E (Alt.) are amended to state that, unless the court orders otherwise, an individual chapter 11 debtor's discharge is not effective until completion of all payments under the plan, as provided in § 1141(d)(5) which was added to the Code in 2005. Forms 9F and 9F (Alt.) are amended to include a deadline to file a complaint to determine the dischargeability of a debt, in conformity with § 1141(d)(6), which also was added to the Code in 2005.

Form 9I is amended to include a deadline to file a complaint to determine the dischargeability of certain debts. This amendment implements a 2005 amendment to § 1328(a) of the Code.

In addition, all versions of the form are amended to provide to the public only the last four digits of any individual debtor's taxpayer-identification number. This amendment implements Rule 9037.

B 10 (Official Form 10) (12/08)

**UNITED STATES BANKRUPTCY COURT** — **PROOF OF CLAIM**

Name of Debtor: | Case Number:

NOTE: *This form should not be used to make a claim for an administrative expense arising after the commencement of the case. A request for payment of an administrative expense may be filed pursuant to 11 U.S.C. § 503.*

Name of Creditor (the person or other entity to whom the debtor owes money or property):

Name and address where notices should be sent:

Telephone number:

☐ Check this box to indicate that this claim amends a previously filed claim.

**Court Claim Number:**__________
(*If known*)

Filed on:________________

Name and address where payment should be sent (if different from above):

Telephone number:

☐ Check this box if you are aware that anyone else has filed a proof of claim relating to your claim. Attach copy of statement giving particulars.

☐ Check this box if you are the debtor or trustee in this case.

**1. Amount of Claim as of Date Case Filed:** $____________________

If all or part of your claim is secured, complete item 4 below; however, if all of your claim is unsecured, do not complete item 4.

If all or part of your claim is entitled to priority, complete item 5.

☐Check this box if claim includes interest or other charges in addition to the principal amount of claim. Attach itemized statement of interest or charges.

**2. Basis for Claim:** ____________________
(See instruction #2 on reverse side.)

**3. Last four digits of any number by which creditor identifies debtor:** ________________

**3a. Debtor may have scheduled account as:** ________________
(See instruction #3a on reverse side.)

**4. Secured Claim** (See instruction #4 on reverse side.)
Check the appropriate box if your claim is secured by a lien on property or a right of setoff and provide the requested information.

**Nature of property or right of setoff:** ☐Real Estate ☐Motor Vehicle ☐Other
**Describe:**

**Value of Property:$**____________ **Annual Interest Rate**_______**%**

**Amount of arrearage and other charges as of time case filed included in secured claim,**

**if any: $**____________ **Basis for perfection:** ________________

**Amount of Secured Claim: $**____________ **Amount Unsecured: $**____________

**5. Amount of Claim Entitled to Priority under 11 U.S.C. §507(a). If any portion of your claim falls in one of the following categories, check the box and state the amount.**

Specify the priority of the claim.

☐ Domestic support obligations under 11 U.S.C. §507(a)(1)(A) or (a)(1)(B).

☐ Wages, salaries, or commissions (up to $10,950*) earned within 180 days before filing of the bankruptcy petition or cessation of the debtor's business, whichever is earlier – 11 U.S.C. §507 (a)(4).

☐ Contributions to an employee benefit plan – 11 U.S.C. §507 (a)(5).

☐ Up to $2,425* of deposits toward purchase, lease, or rental of property or services for personal, family, or household use – 11 U.S.C. §507 (a)(7).

☐ Taxes or penalties owed to governmental units – 11 U.S.C. §507 (a)(8).

☐ Other – Specify applicable paragraph of 11 U.S.C. §507 (a)(__).

**Amount entitled to priority:**

$__________

**Amounts are subject to adjustment on 4/1/10 and every 3 years thereafter with respect to cases commenced on or after the date of adjustment.*

**6. Credits:** The amount of all payments on this claim has been credited for the purpose of making this proof of claim.

**7. Documents:** Attach redacted copies of any documents that support the claim, such as promissory notes, purchase orders, invoices, itemized statements of running accounts, contracts, judgments, mortgages, and security agreements. You may also attach a summary. Attach redacted copies of documents providing evidence of perfection of a security interest. You may also attach a summary. (*See instruction 7 and definition of "redacted" on reverse side.*)

DO NOT SEND ORIGINAL DOCUMENTS. ATTACHED DOCUMENTS MAY BE DESTROYED AFTER SCANNING.

If the documents are not available, please explain:

Date:

**Signature:** The person filing this claim must sign it. Sign and print name and title, if any, of the creditor or other person authorized to file this claim and state address and telephone number if different from the notice address above. Attach copy of power of attorney, if any.

**FOR COURT USE ONLY**

*Penalty for presenting fraudulent claim:* Fine of up to $500,000 or imprisonment for up to 5 years, or both. 18 U.S.C. §§ 152 and 3571.

B 10 (Official Form 10) (12/08) – Cont.

## INSTRUCTIONS FOR PROOF OF CLAIM FORM

*The instructions and definitions below are general explanations of the law. In certain circumstances, such as bankruptcy cases not filed voluntarily by the debtor, there may be exceptions to these general rules.*

**Items to be completed in Proof of Claim form**

**Court, Name of Debtor, and Case Number:**
Fill in the federal judicial district where the bankruptcy case was filed (for example, Central District of California), the bankruptcy debtor's name, and the bankruptcy case number. If the creditor received a notice of the case from the bankruptcy court, all of this information is located at the top of the notice.

**Creditor's Name and Address:**
Fill in the name of the person or entity asserting a claim and the name and address of the person who should receive notices issued during the bankruptcy case. A separate space is provided for the payment address if it differs from the notice address. The creditor has a continuing obligation to keep the court informed of its current address. See Federal Rule of Bankruptcy Procedure (FRBP) 2002(g).

**1. Amount of Claim as of Date Case Filed:**
State the total amount owed to the creditor on the date of the Bankruptcy filing. Follow the instructions concerning whether to complete items 4 and 5. Check the box if interest or other charges are included in the claim.

**2. Basis for Claim:**
State the type of debt or how it was incurred. Examples include goods sold, money loaned, services performed, personal injury/wrongful death, car loan, mortgage note, and credit card. If the claim is based on the delivery of health care goods or services, limit the disclosure of the goods or services so as to avoid embarrassment or the disclosure of confidential health care information. You may be required to provide additional disclosure if the trustee or another party in interest files an objection to your claim.

**3. Last Four Digits of Any Number by Which Creditor Identifies Debtor:**
State only the last four digits of the debtor's account or other number used by the creditor to identify the debtor.

**3a. Debtor May Have Scheduled Account As:**
Use this space to report a change in the creditor's name, a transferred claim, or any other information that clarifies a difference between this proof of claim and the claim as scheduled by the debtor.

**4. Secured Claim:**
Check the appropriate box and provide the requested information if the claim is fully or partially secured. Skip this section if the claim is entirely unsecured. (See DEFINITIONS, below.) State the type and the value of property that secures the claim, attach copies of lien documentation, and state annual interest rate and the amount past due on the claim as of the date of the bankruptcy filing.

**5. Amount of Claim Entitled to Priority Under 11 U.S.C. §507(a).**
If any portion of your claim falls in one or more of the listed categories, check the appropriate box(es) and state the amount entitled to priority. (See DEFINITIONS, below.) A claim may be partly priority and partly non-priority. For example, in some of the categories, the law limits the amount entitled to priority.

**6. Credits:**
An authorized signature on this proof of claim serves as an acknowledgment that when calculating the amount of the claim, the creditor gave the debtor credit for any payments received toward the debt.

**7. Documents:**
Attach to this proof of claim form redacted copies documenting the existence of the debt and of any lien securing the debt. You may also attach a summary. You must also attach copies of documents that evidence perfection of any security interest. You may also attach a summary. FRBP 3001(c) and (d). If the claim is based on the delivery of health care goods or services, see instruction 2. Do not send original documents, as attachments may be destroyed after scanning.

**Date and Signature:**
The person filing this proof of claim must sign and date it. FRBP 9011. If the claim is filed electronically, FRBP 5005(a)(2), authorizes courts to establish local rules specifying what constitutes a signature. Print the name and title, if any, of the creditor or other person authorized to file this claim. State the filer's address and telephone number if it differs from the address given on the top of the form for purposes of receiving notices. Attach a complete copy of any power of attorney. Criminal penalties apply for making a false statement on a proof of claim.

## DEFINITIONS

**Debtor**
A debtor is the person, corporation, or other entity that has filed a bankruptcy case.

**Creditor**
A creditor is a person, corporation, or other entity owed a debt by the debtor that arose on or before the date of the bankruptcy filing. See 11 U.S.C. §101 (10)

**Claim**
A claim is the creditor's right to receive payment on a debt owed by the debtor that arose on the date of the bankruptcy filing. See 11 U.S.C. §101 (5). A claim may be secured or unsecured.

**Proof of Claim**
A proof of claim is a form used by the creditor to indicate the amount of the debt owed by the debtor on the date of the bankruptcy filing. The creditor must file the form with the clerk of the same bankruptcy court in which the bankruptcy case was filed.

**Secured Claim Under 11 U.S.C. §506(a)**
A secured claim is one backed by a lien on property of the debtor. The claim is secured so long as the creditor has the right to be paid from the property prior to other creditors. The amount of the secured claim cannot exceed the value of the property. Any amount owed to the creditor in excess of the value of the property is an unsecured claim. Examples of liens on property include a mortgage on real estate or a security interest in a car. A lien may be voluntarily granted by a debtor or may be obtained through a court proceeding. In some states, a court judgment is a lien. A claim also may be secured if the creditor owes the debtor money (has a right to setoff).

**Unsecured Claim**
An unsecured claim is one that does not meet the requirements of a secured claim. A claim may be partly unsecured if the amount of the claim exceeds the value of the property on which the creditor has a lien.

**Claim Entitled to Priority Under 11 U.S.C. §507(a)**
Priority claims are certain categories of unsecured claims that are paid from the available money or property in a bankruptcy case before other unsecured claims.

**Redacted**
A document has been redacted when the person filing it has masked, edited out, or otherwise deleted, certain information. A creditor should redact and use only the last four digits of any social-security, individual's tax-identification, or financial-account number, all but the initials of a minor's name and only the year of any person's date of birth.

**Evidence of Perfection**
Evidence of perfection may include a mortgage, lien, certificate of title, financing statement, or other document showing that the lien has been filed or recorded.

## INFORMATION

**Acknowledgment of Filing of Claim**
To receive acknowledgment of your filing, you may either enclose a stamped self-addressed envelope and a copy of this proof of claim or you may access the court's PACER system (www.pacer.psc.uscourts.gov) for a small fee to view your filed proof of claim.

**Offers to Purchase a Claim**
Certain entities are in the business of purchasing claims for an amount less than the face value of the claims. One or more of these entities may contact the creditor and offer to purchase the claim. Some of the written communications from these entities may easily be confused with official court documentation or communications from the debtor. These entities do not represent the bankruptcy court or the debtor. The creditor has no obligation to sell its claim. However, if the creditor decides to sell its claim, any transfer of such claim is subject to FRBP 3001(e), any applicable provisions of the Bankruptcy Code (11 U.S.C. § 101 *et seq.*), and any applicable orders of the bankruptcy court.

(Added Aug. 1, 1991; amended Mar. 16, 1993; Mar. 14, 1995; Oct. 1, 1997; Dec. 1, 2003; Oct. 17, 2005; Dec. 1, 2007; Dec. 1, 2008.)

NOTES OF ADVISORY COMMITTEE ON RULES—1991

This form replaces former Official Forms No. 19, No. 20, and No. 21. The box format and simplified language are intended to facilitate completion of the form.

The form directs the claimant to attach documents to support the claim or, if voluminous, a summary of such documents. These include any security agreement (if not included in the writing on which the claim is founded), and evidence of perfection of any security interest. See Committee Note to Rule 3001(d) concerning satisfactory evidence of perfection. If the claim includes prepetition interest or other charges such as attorney fees, a statement giving a detailed breakdown of the elements of the claim is required.

Rule 2002(g) requires the clerk to update the mailing list in the case by substituting the address provided by a creditor on a proof of claim, if that address is different from the one supplied by the debtor. The form contains checkboxes to assist the clerk in performing this duty. The form also alerts the trustee when the claim is an amendment to or replacement for an earlier claim.

NOTES OF ADVISORY COMMITTEE ON RULES—1993 AMENDMENT

The form has been amended to accommodate inclusion of the priority afforded in §507(a)(8) of the Code, which was added by Pub. L. No. 101–647, (Crime Control Act of 1990), and to avoid the necessity of further amendment to the form if other priorities are added to §507(a) in the future. In addition, sections 4 and 5 of the form have been amended to clarify that only prepetition arrearages and charges are to be included in the amount of the claim.

NOTES OF ADVISORY COMMITTEE ON RULES—1995 AMENDMENT

The form is amended to add the seventh priority granted by the Bankruptcy Reform Act of 1994 to debts for alimony, maintenance, or support of a spouse, former spouse, or child of the debtor. The form also amends the Code reference to the priority afforded to tax debts and the dollar maximums for the priorities granted to wages and customer deposits in conformity with amendments made by the 1994 Act to section 507(a) of the Code. The 1994 Act also amended section 104 of the Code to provide for future adjustment of the dollar amounts specified in section 507(a) to be made by administrative action at three-year intervals to reflect changes in the consumer price index. The form is amended to include notice that these dollar amounts are subject to change without formal amendment to the official form.

NOTES OF ADVISORY COMMITTEE ON RULES—1997 AMENDMENT

Numbered sections 4. and 5. of the form have been reformatted to eliminate redundant information and make it easier to complete the form correctly. A creditor will report the total amount of the claim first, and will report only that amount unless the claim is secured by collateral or entitled to a priority under §507 of the Code.

Explanatory definitions and instructions for completing the form also have been added.

COMMITTEE NOTES ON RULES—2003 AMENDMENT

The form is amended to require a wage, salary, or other compensation creditor to disclose only the last four digits of the creditor's social security number to afford greater privacy to the creditor. A trustee can request the full information necessary for tax withholding and reporting at the time the trustee makes a distribution to creditors.

COMMITTEE NOTES ON RULES—2005 AMENDMENT

The form is amended to conform to changes in the priority afforded the claims of certain creditors in §507(a) of the Code as amended by the Bankruptcy Abuse Prevention and Consumer Protection Act of 2005, Pub. L. No. 109–8, 119 Stat. 23 (April 20, 2005).

COMMITTEE NOTES ON RULES—2005–2007 AMENDMENT

[The 2005–2007 Committee Note incorporates the Committee Note previously published in 2005.]

The form is amended to conform to changes in the priority afforded the claims of certain creditors in §507(a) of the Code as amended by the Bankruptcy Abuse Prevention and Consumer Protection Act of 2005, Pub. L. No. 109–8, 119 Stat. 23 (April 20, 2005).

In addition, the form and its instructions are amended in several respects based on the experiences of creditors and trustees in using it and on the technological changes that have occurred in the courts' processing of claims. A definition of the word "redacted" has been added in conformity with Rule 9037.

The creditor now has a space in which to provide a separate payment address if different from the creditor's address for receiving notices in the case. The checkboxes for indicating that the creditor's address provided on the proof of claim is a new address, and that the creditor never received any notices from the court in the case have been deleted. The computer systems now used by the courts make it unnecessary for a creditor to "flag" a new address or call attention to the fact that the creditor is making its first appearance in the case. In place of the deleted items is a new checkbox to be used when a debtor or a trustee files a proof of claim for a creditor; it will alert the clerk to send the notice required by Rule 3004. The box for indicating whether the claim replaces a previously filed claim also has been deleted as no longer necessary in light of the 2005 amendments to Rules 3004 and 3005. The creditor simply will amend the claim filed by the other party.

Requests for the creditor to state the date on which the debt was incurred and the date on which any court judgment concerning the debt was obtained have been deleted, based on reports from trustees that they rely on the documents supporting the claim for this information. The checkboxes for stating the basis for the creditor's claim have been replaced with a blank in which the creditor is to provide this information. Examples of the most common categories, based on the former checkboxes, can be found in the instructions on the form. The request to state the account number by which the creditor identifies the debtor has been moved to paragraph 3 of the form and has been revised to request only the last four digits of the number, in conformity with Rule 9037. In addition, a new paragraph 3a gives the creditor a place to notify the trustee and the court of any change in the creditor's name, or that the claim has been transferred, or to provide any other information to clarify a difference between the proof of claim and the creditor's claim as scheduled by the debtor.

The adjective "total" is deleted from the sections of the form where the creditor states the amount of the claim and the creditor now simply reports the amount of the claim. If the claim is a general unsecured claim, no further details are stated on the form, although a creditor still must attach a copy of any writing on which the claim is based, as required by Rule 3001(c), and must attach a statement itemizing any interest or other charges (in addition to the principal) that are included in the claim. If the claim or any part of it is secured or entitled to priority under §507(a) of the Code, the creditor is directed to provide details in the appropriate sections of the form. The creditor now states the amount to be afforded priority only once, in the section of the form designated for describing the specific priority being asserted. The introductory language in the section where the creditor describes any priority to which it is entitled has been revised for clarity. The word "collateral" has been replaced with the less colloquial and more accurate phrase "lien on property" throughout the form.

Information about obtaining acknowledgment from the court of the filing of the proof of claim is revised and moved to a new section on the reverse side called "Information." This new section also alerts a creditor to the possibility that it may be approached about selling its claim, advises that the court has no role in any such solicitations, and states that a creditor is under no obligation to accept any offer to purchase its claim. A new instruction is added about signing a proof of claim. This instruction includes citations to Rules 9011 and 5005(a)(2) concerning signature requirements in an electronic filing environment.

Finally, all of the definitions and instructions on the reverse side of the form are amended generally to reflect the deletions, additions, and other changes made on page 1. These include a reminder to the creditor to keep the court informed of any changes in its address. The instructions now appear at the top of the page, and the text is revised both to reflect the substantive changes to the form and to improve the clarity and style of this explanatory material.

COMMITTEE NOTES ON RULES—2008 AMENDMENT

The form is amended at box seven on page one, and instructions two and seven on page two, to instruct the claimant that the information contained in or attached to a claim based on the delivery of health care goods or services should be limited so as to avoid embarrassment or the unnecessary disclosure of confidential information. The claimant is informed that additional disclosure may be required if the trustee or another party in interest objects to the claim.

Page two of the form is also amended to revise slightly the definitions of "creditor" and "claim" to conform more closely to the definitions of those terms in the Code.

Official Form 11A
6/90

# United States Bankruptcy Court

_______________ District Of _______________

In re ____________________,
Debtor

Case No. __________

Chapter __________

## GENERAL POWER OF ATTORNEY

To ______________________________ of * ______________________________, and
______________________________ of * ______________________________.

The undersigned claimant hereby authorizes you, or any one of you, as attorney in fact for the undersigned and with full power of substitution, to vote on any question that may be lawfully submitted to creditors of the debtor in the above-entitled case; [*if appropriate*] to vote for a trustee of the estate of the debtor and for a committee of creditors; to receive dividends; and in general to perform any act not constituting the practice of law for the undersigned in all matters arising in this case.

Dated: ____________________

Signed: ______________________________

By ______________________________
as ______________________________

Address: ______________________________
______________________________

[*If executed by an individual*] Acknowledged before me on ______________________________.

[*If executed on behalf of a partnership*] Acknowledged before me on ______________________________, by ______________________________, who says that he [*or* she] is a member of the partnership named above and is authorized to execute this power of attorney in its behalf.

[*If executed on behalf of a corporation*] Acknowledged before me on ______________________________, by ____________________, who says that he [*or* she] is ____________________ of the corporation named above and is authorized to execute this power of attorney in its behalf.

______________________________

______________________________
*[Official character.]*

* State mailing address.

(Added Aug. 1, 1991.)

NOTES OF ADVISORY COMMITTEE ON RULES—1991

This form previously was numbered Official Form No. 17.

Official Form 11B
6/90

# United States Bankruptcy Court

_______________ District Of _______________

In re ____________________,
Debtor

Case No. ___________

Chapter _________

## SPECIAL POWER OF ATTORNEY

To ______________________________ of* ______________________________, and
______________________________ of* ______________________________.

The undersigned claimant hereby authorizes you, or any one of you, as attorney in fact for the undersigned [*if desired*: and with full power of substitution,] to attend the meeting of creditors of the debtor or any adjournment thereof, and to vote in my behalf on any question that may be lawfully submitted to creditors at such meeting or adjourned meeting, and for a trustee or trustees of the estate of the debtor.

Dated: ____________________

Signed: ______________________________

By ______________________________

as ______________________________

Address: ______________________________

______________________________

[*If executed by an individual*] Acknowledged before me on ____________________.

[*If executed on behalf of a partnership*] Acknowledged before me ______________________________, by ____________________, who says that he [*or* she] is a member of the partnership named above and is authorized to execute this power of attorney in its behalf.

[*If executed on behalf of a corporation*] Acknowledged before me on ______________________________, by ____________________, who says that he [*or* she] is ______________________________ of the corporation named above and is authorized to execute this power of attorney in its behalf.

______________________________

______________________________
[*Official character.*]

* State mailing address.

(Added Aug. 1, 1991.)

NOTES OF ADVISORY COMMITTEE ON RULES—1991

This form previously was numbered Official Form No. 18.

Official Form 12
(12/03)

## Form 12. ORDER AND NOTICE FOR HEARING ON DISCLOSURE STATEMENT

*[Caption as in Form 16A]*

## ORDER AND NOTICE FOR HEARING ON DISCLOSURE STATEMENT

To the debtor, its creditors, and other parties in interest:

A disclosure statement and a plan under chapter 11 [*or* chapter 9] of the Bankruptcy Code having been filed by ______________________________ on ______________________________,

IT IS ORDERED and notice is hereby given, that:

**1.** The hearing to consider the approval of the disclosure statement shall be held at: ____________________, on ____________________, at ____________ o'clock __.m.

**2.** ____________________ is fixed as the last day for filing and serving in accordance with Fed. R. Bankr. P. 3017(a) written objections to the disclosure statement.

**3.** Within __________ days after entry of this order, the disclosure statement and plan shall be distributed in accordance with Fed. R. Bankr. P. 3017(a).

**4.** Requests for copies of the disclosure statement and plan shall be mailed to the debtor in possession [*or* trustee *or* debtor *or* ____________________ ] at * ____________________.

Dated: ____________________

BY THE COURT

______________________________
*United States Bankruptcy Judge*

* State mailing address

(Added Aug. 1, 1991.)

NOTES OF ADVISORY COMMITTEE ON RULES—1991

This form previously was numbered Official Form No. 28. The form is related to Rule 3017(a). Section 1125 of the Code requires court approval of a disclosure statement before votes may be solicited for or against a plan in either chapter 11 reorganization or chapter 9 municipality cases.

Objections to the disclosure statement may be filed. Rule 3017(a) specifies that the court may fix a time for the filing of objections or they can be filed at any time prior to approval of the statement.

Rule 3017(a) also specifies the persons who are to receive copies of the statement and plan prior to the hearing. These documents will not be sent to all parties in interest because at this stage of the case it could be unnecessarily expensive and confusing. However, any party in interest may request copies. The request should be made in writing (Rule 3017(a)), and sent to the person mailing the statement and plan which, as the form indicates, would usually be the proponent of the plan.

This form may be adapted for use if more than one disclosure statement is to be considered by the court.

Official Form 13
(12/03)

# Form 13. ORDER APPROVING DISCLOSURE STATEMENT AND FIXING TIME FOR FILING ACCEPTANCES OR REJECTIONS OF PLAN, COMBINED WITH NOTICE THEREOF

*[Caption as in Form 16A]*

## ORDER APPROVING DISCLOSURE STATEMENT AND FIXING TIME FOR FILING ACCEPTANCES OR REJECTIONS OF PLAN, COMBINED WITH NOTICE THEREOF

A disclosure statement under chapter 11 of the Bankruptcy Code having been filed by ______________________________, on ________________ [*if appropriate*, and by ______________________________, on ________________ ], referring to a plan under chapter 11 of the Code filed by ______________________________, on ______________ [*if appropriate*, and by ______________________________, on ________________ respectively] [*if appropriate*, as modified by a modification filed on ________________]; and

It having been determined after hearing on notice that the disclosure statement [*or* statements] contain[s] adequate information:

IT IS ORDERED, and notice is hereby given, that:

A. The disclosure statement filed by ______________________________ dated ______________ [*if appropriate*, and by ______________________________, dated ______________ is [are] approved.

B. ______________________ is fixed as the last day for filing written acceptances or rejections of the plan [*or* plans] referred to above.

C. Within ____________ days after the entry of this order, the plan [*or* plans] *or* a summary *or* summaries thereof approved by the court, [and [*if appropriate*] a summary approved by the court of its opinion, if any, dated ______________, approving the disclosure statement [*or* statements]], the disclosure statement [*or* statements], and a ballot conforming to Official Form 14 shall be mailed to creditors, equity security holders, and other parties in interest, and shall be transmitted to the United States trustee, as provided in Fed. R. Bankr. P. 3017(d).

D. If acceptances are filed for more than one plan, preferences among the plans so accepted may be indicated.

E. *[If appropriate]* ______________ is fixed for the hearing on confirmation of the plan [*or* plans].

F. *[If appropriate]* ______________ is fixed as the last day for filing and serving pursuant to Fed. R. Bankr. P. 3020(b)(1) written objections to confirmation of the plan.

Dated: ________________

BY THE COURT

______________________________
*United States Bankruptcy Judge*

*[If the court directs that a copy of the opinion should be transmitted in lieu of or in addition to the summary thereof, the appropriate change should be made in paragraph C of this order.]*

(Added Aug. 1, 1991.)

NOTES OF ADVISORY COMMITTEE ON RULES—1991

This form is derived from former Official Form No. 29. The form may be adapted for use if more than one disclosure statement is approved by the court.

Official Form 14
(12/03)

# Form 14. CLASS [ ] BALLOT FOR ACCEPTING OR REJECTING PLAN OF REORGANIZATION

*[Caption as in Form 16A]*

## CLASS [ ] BALLOT FOR ACCEPTING OR REJECTING PLAN OF REORGANIZATION

*[Proponent]* filed a plan of reorganization dated *[Date]* (the "Plan") for the Debtor in this case. The Court has *[conditionally]* approved a disclosure statement with respect to the Plan (the "Disclosure Statement"). The Disclosure Statement provides information to assist you in deciding how to vote your ballot. If you do not have a Disclosure Statement, you may obtain a copy from *[name, address, telephone number and telecopy number of proponent/proponent's attorney.]* Court approval of the disclosure statement does not indicate approval of the Plan by the Court.

**You should review the Disclosure Statement and the Plan before you vote. You may wish to seek legal advice concerning the Plan and your classification and treatment under the Plan. Your *[claim] [equity interest]* has been placed in class [ ] under the Plan. If you hold claims or equity interests in more than one class, you will receive a ballot for each class in which you are entitled to vote.**

**If your ballot is not received by [*name and address of proponent's attorney or other appropriate address*] on or before *[date]*, and such deadline is not extended, your vote will not count as either an acceptance or rejection of the Plan.**

**If the Plan is confirmed by the Bankruptcy Court it will be binding on you whether or not you vote.**

### ACCEPTANCE OR REJECTION OF THE PLAN

*[At this point the ballot should provide for voting by the particular class of creditors or equity holders receiving the ballot using one of the following alternatives;]*

*[If the voter is the holder of a secured, priority, or unsecured nonpriority claim:]*

The undersigned, the holder of a Class [ ] claim against the Debtor in the unpaid amount of Dollars ($ )

*[or, if the voter is the holder of a bond, debenture, or other debt security:]*

The undersigned, the holder of a Class [ ] claim against the Debtor, consisting of Dollars ($ ) principal amount of *[describe bond, debenture, or other debt security]* of the Debtor (For purposes of this Ballot, it is not necessary and you should not adjust the principal amount for any accrued or unmatured interest.)

*[or, if the voter is the holder of an equity interest:]*

The undersigned, the holder of Class [ ] equity interest in the Debtor, consisting of ______ shares or other interests of *[describe equity interest]* in the Debtor

Official Form 14 continued
(12/03)

*[In each case, the following language should be included:]*

(Check one box only)

[ ] ACCEPTS THE PLAN [ ] REJECTS THE PLAN

Dated: ____________________

Print or type name: ____________________________

Signature: __________________________________

Title (if corporation or partnership) _____________

Address: ______________________________

______________________________

RETURN THIS BALLOT TO:

*[Name and address of proponent's attorney or other appropriate address]*

(Added Aug. 1, 1991; amended Oct. 1, 1997.)

NOTES OF ADVISORY COMMITTEE ON RULES—1991

This form is derived from former Official Form No. 30. The form has been amended to facilitate the voting of a debtor's shares held in "street name." The form may be adapted to designate the class in which each ballot is to be tabulated. It is intended that a separate ballot will be provided for each class in which a holder may vote.

NOTES OF ADVISORY COMMITTEE ON RULES—1997 AMENDMENT

The form has been substantially amended to simplify its format and make it easier to complete correctly.

Directions or blanks for proponent to complete the text of the ballot are in italics and enclosed within brackets. A ballot should include only the applicable language from the alternatives shown on this form and should be adapted to the particular requirements of the case.

If the plan provides for creditors in a class to have the right to reduce their claims so as to qualify for treatment given to creditors whose claims do not exceed a specified amount, the ballot should make provisions for the exercise of that right. See section 1122(b) of the Code.

If debt or equity securities are held in the name of a broker/dealer or nominee, the ballot should require the furnishing of sufficient information to assure that duplicate ballots are not submitted and counted and that ballots submitted by a broker/dealer or nominee reflect the votes of the beneficial holders of such securities. See Rule 3017(e).

In the event that more than one plan of reorganization is to be voted upon, the form of ballot will need to be adapted to permit holders of claims or equity interests (a) to accept or reject each plan being proposed, and (b) to indicate preferences among the competing plans. See section 1129(c) of the Code.

Form B15
(Rev. 12/01)

## Form 15. ORDER CONFIRMING PLAN

*[Caption as in Form 16A]*

## ORDER CONFIRMING PLAN

The plan under chapter 11 of the Bankruptcy Code filed by ______________________________, on ____________________ [*if applicable*, as modified by a modification filed on ____________________,] or a summary thereof, having been transmitted to creditors and equity security holders; and

It having been determined after hearing on notice that the requirements for confirmation set forth in 11 U.S.C. § 1129(a) [*or, if appropriate,* 11 U.S.C. § 1129(b)] have been satisfied;

IT IS ORDERED that:

The plan filed by ______________________________, on ____________________, *[If appropriate, include dates and any other pertinent details of modifications to the plan]* is confirmed. *[If the plan provides for an injunction against conduct not otherwise enjoined under the Code, include the information required by Rule 3020.]*

A copy of the confirmed plan is attached.

Dated: ____________________

BY THE COURT

______________________________
*United States Bankruptcy Judge.*

(Added Aug. 1, 1991; amended Dec. 1, 2001.)

NOTES OF ADVISORY COMMITTEE ON RULES—1991

This form is derived from former Official Form No. 31. The form has been simplified to avoid the necessity of repeating the statutory requirements of 11 U.S.C. §1129(a). In the case of an individual chapter 11 debtor, Form 18 may be adapted for use together with this form.

COMMITTEE NOTES ON RULES—2001 AMENDMENT

The form is amended to conform to the December 1, 2001, amendments to Rule 3020.

B16A (Official Form 16A) (12/07)

# Form 16A. CAPTION (FULL)

## United States Bankruptcy Court

_______________ District Of _______________

| | | |
|---|---|---|
| In re ________________________________________, | ) | |
| *[Set forth here all names including married, maiden, and trade names used by debtor within last 8 years.]* | ) | |
| Debtor | ) | Case No. ______________ |
| Address ________________________________________ | ) | |
| ________________________________________ | ) | Chapter __________ |
| Last four digits of Social-Security or Individual Tax-Payer-Identification (ITIN) No(s).,(if any): __________ | ) | |
| ________________________________________ | ) | |
| Employer Tax-Identification (EIN) No(s).(if any): _____ | ) | |
| ________________________________________ | ) | |

*[Designation of Character of Paper]*

(Added Aug. 1, 1991; amended Mar. 14, 1995; Dec. 1, 2003; Oct. 17, 2005; Dec. 1, 2007.)

NOTES OF ADVISORY COMMITTEE ON RULES—1991

This form has been transferred from former Official Form No. 1, which included the form of caption for the case. Rule 9004(b) requires a caption to set forth the title of the case. Rule 1005 provides that the title of the case shall include the debtor's name, all other names used by the debtor within six years before the commencement of the case, and the debtor's social security and tax identification numbers. This form of caption is prescribed for use on the petition, the notice of the meeting of creditors, the order of discharge, and the documents relating to a chapter 11 plan, (Official Forms 1, 9, 12, 13, 14, 15, and 18). See Rule 2002(m). In the petition (Official Form 1), and the notice of the meeting of creditors, (Official Form 9), the information required by Rule 1005 appears in a block format. A notation of the chapter of the Bankruptcy Code under which the case is proceeding has been added to the form.

NOTES OF ADVISORY COMMITTEE ON RULES—1995 AMENDMENT

The form is amended to provide for the debtor's address to appear in the caption in furtherance of the duty of the debtor to include this information on every notice given by the debtor. The Bankruptcy Reform Act of 1994 amended section 342 of the Code to add this requirement.

COMMITTEE NOTES ON RULES—2003 AMENDMENT

The form is amended to require disclosure of only the last four digits of the debtor's social security number to afford greater privacy to the individual debtor, whose bankruptcy case records may be available over the Internet.

COMMITTEE NOTES ON RULES—2005 AMENDMENT

The form is amended to require that the title of the case include all names used by the debtor within the last eight years in conformity with § 727(a)(8) as amended by the Bankruptcy Abuse Prevention and Consumer Protection Act of 2005, Pub. L. No. 109-8, 119 Stat. 23

(April 20, 2005), extending from six years to eight years the period during which a debtor is barred from receiving successive discharges.

COMMITTEE NOTES ON RULES—2005-2007 AMENDMENT

[The 2005-2007 Committee Note incorporates the Committee Note previously published in 2005.]

The form is amended to require that the title of the case include all names used by the debtor within the last eight years in conformity with § 727(a)(8) as amended by the Bankruptcy Abuse Prevention and Consumer Protection Act of 2005, Pub. L. No. 109-8, 119 Stat. 23 (April 20, 2005), extending from six years to eight years the period during which a debtor is barred from receiving successive discharges. In conformity with Rule 9037, the filer is directed to provide only the last four digits of any individual debtor's taxpayer-identification number.

Official Form 16B
12/94

## FORM 16B. CAPTION (SHORT TITLE)

*(May be used if 11 U.S.C. § 342(c) is not applicable)*

# United States Bankruptcy Court

_______________ District Of _______________

In re ________________________,
Debtor

Case No. ____________________

Chapter _____________

*[Designation of Character of Paper]*

(Added Aug. 1, 1991; amended Mar. 14, 1995.)

NOTES OF ADVISORY COMMITTEE ON RULES—1991

This form of caption is prescribed for general use in filing papers in a case under the Bankruptcy Code. Rule 9004(b) requires a caption to set forth the title of the case, and Rule 1005 specifies that the title must include all names used by the debtor within six years before the commencement of the case and the debtor's social security and tax identification numbers. This information is necessary in the petition, the notice of the meeting of creditors, the order of discharge, and the documents relating to the plan in a chapter 11 case. See Rule 2002(m) and Official Form 16A. In other notices, motions, applications, and papers filed in a case, however, a short title containing simply the names of the debtor or joint debtors may be used. Additional names, such as any under which the debtor has engaged in business, may be included in the short title as needed.

NOTES OF ADVISORY COMMITTEE ON RULES—1995 AMENDMENT

The title of this form is amended to specify that it can be used when section 342(c) of the Code, as added by the Bankruptcy Reform Act of 1994, is not applicable.

Official Form 16C
(12/03)

# FORM 16C. CAPTION OF COMPLAINT IN ADVERSARY PROCEEDING FILED BY A DEBTOR

[Abrogated]

(Added Aug. 1, 1991; amended Mar. 14, 1995; Dec. 1, 2003.)

NOTES OF ADVISORY COMMITTEE ON RULES—1991

This form previously was numbered Official Form No. 34. A notation of the chapter of the Bankruptcy Code under which the case is proceeding has been added to the form. Rule 7010 refers to this form as providing the caption of a pleading in an adversary proceeding.

NOTES OF ADVISORY COMMITTEE ON RULES—1995 AMENDMENT

The form is amended to conform to the amendments made to section 342 of the Code by the Bankruptcy Reform Act of 1994.

COMMITTEE NOTES ON RULES—2003 AMENDMENT

The form is abrogated. An amendment to Official Form 16A directs that only the last four digits of the debtor's social security number should appear in a caption. Section 342(c) of the Bankruptcy Code continues to require the debtor to provide a creditor with the debtor's name, address, and taxpayer identification number on any notice the debtor is required to give to the creditor. An individual debtor can fulfill this requirement by including the debtor's social security account number on only the creditor's copy of any notice or summons the debtor may serve on the creditor.

Official Form 16D
(12/04)

## Form 16D. CAPTION FOR USE IN ADVERSARY PROCEEDING

# United States Bankruptcy Court

______________ District Of ______________

| | | |
|---|---|---|
| In re ______________________, *Debtor* | ) | Case No. ______________ |
| | ) | Chapter ____________ |
| ______________________, *Plaintiff* | ) | |
| | ) | |
| ______________________, *Defendant* | ) | Adv. Proc. No. ______________ |

**COMPLAINT** [*or* other Designation]

[If in a Notice of Appeal (see Form 17) or other notice filed and served by a debtor, this caption must be altered to include the debtor's address and Employer's Tax Identification Number(s) or last four digits of Social Security Number(s) as in Form 16A.]

(Added Mar. 14, 1995; amended Dec. 1, 2004.)

NOTES OF ADVISORY COMMITTEE ON RULES—1995

This form of caption may be used in an adversary proceeding when section 342(c) of the Code, as added by the Bankruptcy Reform Act of 1994, is not applicable.

COMMITTEE NOTES ON RULES—2004 AMENDMENT

This form is amended to reflect the 2003 abrogation of Form 16C. As a complaint initiating an adversary proceeding serves as a notice to the defendant of the filing of an action, a debtor filing an adversary proceeding must follow the notice requirements of § 342(c) of the Code. To protect individual privacy a debtor should use the defendant's copy of the summons to be served with the complaint to provide the information required by § 342(c) to any creditor named as a defendant.

Official Form 17
(12/04)

# United States Bankruptcy Court

_______________ District Of _______________

In re ______________________,
Debtor

Case No. ______________

Chapter ___________

*[Caption as in Form 16A, 16B, or 16D, as appropriate]*

## NOTICE OF APPEAL

______________________, the plaintiff [*or* defendant *or* other party] appeals under 28 U.S.C. § 158(a) or (b) from the judgment, order, or decree of the bankruptcy judge (describe) entered in this adversary proceeding [*or other proceeding, describe type*] on the __________ day of ______________, ______.
(month) (year)

The names of all parties to the judgment, order, or decree appealed from and the names, addresses, and telephone numbers of their respective attorneys are as follows:

Dated: ______________________

Signed: ______________________________
Attorney for Appellant (or Appellant, if not represented by an Attorney)

Attorney Name: ______________________________

Address: ______________________________
______________________________

Telephone No: ______________________________

If a Bankruptcy Appellate Panel Service is authorized to hear this appeal, each party has a right to have the appeal heard by the district court. The appellant may exercise this right only by filing a separate statement of election at the time of the filing of this notice of appeal. Any other party may elect, within the time provided in 28 U.S.C. § 158(c), to have the appeal heard by the district court.

*If a child support creditor or its representative is the appellant, and if the child support creditor or its representative files the form specified in § 304(g) of the Bankruptcy Reform Act of 1994, no fee is required.*

(Added Aug. 1, 1991; amended Mar. 14, 1995; Oct. 1, 1997; Dec. 1, 2002; Dec. 1, 2004.)

NOTES OF ADVISORY COMMITTEE ON RULES—1991 AMENDMENT

This form is derived from former Official Form No. 35. The form has been amended to indicate that a final order may be entered other than in an adversary proceeding.

NOTES OF ADVISORY COMMITTEE ON RULES—1995 AMENDMENT

The form is amended to reflect the amendments to 28 U.S.C. §158 concerning bankruptcy appellate panels made by the Bankruptcy Reform Act of 1994. Section 158(d) requires an appellant who elects to appeal to a district court rather than a bankruptcy appellate panel to do so "at the time of filing the appeal."

The 1994 Act also amended 28 U.S.C. §158(a) to permit immediate appeal of interlocutory orders increasing or reducing a chapter 11 debtor's exclusive period to file a plan under section 1121 of the Code. The form is amended to provide appropriate flexibility.

NOTES OF ADVISORY COMMITTEE ON RULES—1997 AMENDMENT

The form has been amended to conform to Rule 8001(a), which requires the notice to contain the names of all parties to the judgment, order, or decree appealed from and the names, addresses, and telephone numbers of their respective attorneys. A party filing a notice of appeal pro se should provide equivalent information.

COMMITTEE NOTES ON RULES—2002 AMENDMENT

The form is amended to give notice that no filing fee is required if a child support creditor or its representative is the appellant, and if the child support creditor or its representative files a form detailing the child support debt, its status, and other characteristics, as specified in §304(g) of the Bankruptcy Reform Act of 1994, Pub. L. No. 103-396[394], 108 Stat. 4106 (Oct. 22, 1994).

COMMITTEE NOTES ON RULES—2004 AMENDMENT

The form is amended to reflect the 2003 abrogation of Form 16C.

**B18 (Official Form 18) (12/07)**

# United States Bankruptcy Court

________________ District Of ________________

In re ________________________________,
*[Set forth here all names including married, maiden, and trade names used by debtor within last 8 years.]*
Debtor

Case No. ______________

Address ______________________________
______________________________

Chapter 7

Last four digits of Social-Security or other Individual Taxpayer-Identification No(s)(if any).: ____________________
________________________________________
Employer Tax-Identification No(s).(EIN) [if any]:________________
________________________________________

## DISCHARGE OF DEBTOR

It appearing that the debtor is entitled to a discharge, **IT IS ORDERED:** The debtor is granted a discharge under section 727 of title 11, United States Code, (the Bankruptcy Code).

Dated: ____________________

BY THE COURT

______________________________
United States Bankruptcy Judge

**SEE THE BACK OF THIS ORDER FOR IMPORTANT INFORMATION.**

B18 (Official Form 18) (12/07) - Cont.

## EXPLANATION OF BANKRUPTCY DISCHARGE IN A CHAPTER 7 CASE

This court order grants a discharge to the person named as the debtor. It is not a dismissal of the case and it does not determine how much money, if any, the trustee will pay to creditors.

**Collection of Discharged Debts Prohibited**

The discharge prohibits any attempt to collect from the debtor a debt that has been discharged. For example, a creditor is not permitted to contact a debtor by mail, phone, or otherwise, to file or continue a lawsuit, to attach wages or other property, or to take any other action to collect a discharged debt from the debtor. *[In a case involving community property:* There are also special rules that protect certain community property owned by the debtor's spouse, even if that spouse did not file a bankruptcy case.] A creditor who violates this order can be required to pay damages and attorney's fees to the debtor.

However, a creditor may have the right to enforce a valid lien, such as a mortgage or security interest, against the debtor's property after the bankruptcy, if that lien was not avoided or eliminated in the bankruptcy case. Also, a debtor may voluntarily pay any debt that has been discharged.

**Debts that are Discharged**

The chapter 7 discharge order eliminates a debtor's legal obligation to pay a debt that is discharged. Most, but not all, types of debts are discharged if the debt existed on the date the bankruptcy case was filed. (If this case was begun under a different chapter of the Bankruptcy Code and converted to chapter 7, the discharge applies to debts owed when the bankruptcy case was converted.)

**Debts that are Not Discharged.**

Some of the common types of debts which are not discharged in a chapter 7 bankruptcy case are:

a. Debts for most taxes;

b. Debts incurred to pay nondischargeable taxes;

c. Debts that are domestic support obligations;

d. Debts for most student loans;

e. Debts for most fines, penalties, forfeitures, or criminal restitution obligations;

f. Debts for personal injuries or death caused by the debtor's operation of a motor vehicle, vessel, or aircraft while intoxicated;

g. Some debts which were not properly listed by the debtor;

h. Debts that the bankruptcy court specifically has decided or will decide in this bankruptcy case are not discharged;

i. Debts for which the debtor has given up the discharge protections by signing a reaffirmation agreement in compliance with the Bankruptcy Code requirements for reaffirmation of debts; and

j. Debts owed to certain pension, profit sharing, stock bonus, other retirement plans, or to the Thrift Savings Plan for federal employees for certain types of loans from these plans.

This information is only a general summary of the bankruptcy discharge. There are exceptions to these general rules. Because the law is complicated, you may want to consult an attorney to determine the exact effect of the discharge in this case.

(Added Aug. 1, 1991; amended Mar. 14, 1995; Oct. 1, 1997; Oct. 17, 2005; Dec. 1, 2007.)

NOTES OF ADVISORY COMMITTEE ON RULES—1991

This form previously was numbered Official Form No. 27. The form has been revised to accommodate cases commenced by the filing of either a voluntary or an involuntary petition.

NOTES OF ADVISORY COMMITTEE ON RULES—1995 AMENDMENT

The form is amended to include debts described in section 523(a)(15) of the Code, which was added by the Bankruptcy Reform Act of 1994, in the list of debts discharged unless determined by the court to be nondischargeable.

NOTES OF ADVISORY COMMITTEE ON RULES—1997 AMENDMENT

The discharge order has been simplified by deleting paragraphs which had detailed some, but not all, of the effects of the discharge. These paragraphs have been replaced with a plain English explanation of the discharge. This explanation is to be printed on the reverse of the order, to increase understanding of the bankruptcy discharge among creditors and debtors. The bracketed sentence in the second paragraph should be included when the case involves community property.

COMMITTEE NOTES ON RULES—2005 AMENDMENT

The form is amended to require that the title of the case include all names used by the debtor within the eight years prior to the filing of the petition in the case in conformity with § 727(a)(8) as amended by the Bankruptcy Abuse Prevention and Consumer Protection Act of 2005, Pub. L. No. 109–8, 119 Stat. 23 (April 20, 2005), extending from six years to eight years the period during which a debtor is barred from receiving successive discharges. The explanation part of the form is amended to include additional types of debts that are not discharged under § 523(a) as amended in 2005 and to revise certain terminology in conformity with provisions of the 2005 Act.

COMMITTEE NOTES ON RULES—2005-2007 AMENDMENT

[The 2005–2007 Committee Note incorporates the Committee Note previously published in 2005.]

The form is amended to require that the title of the case include all names used by the debtor within the eight years prior to the filing of the petition in the case in conformity with § 727(a)(8) as amended by the Bankruptcy Abuse Prevention and Consumer Protection Act of 2005, Pub. L. No. 109–8, 119 Stat. 23 (April 20, 2005), extending from six years to eight years the period during which a debtor is barred from receiving successive discharges. The explanation part of the form is amended to include additional types of debts that are not discharged under § 523(a), as amended in 2005, and to revise certain terminology in conformity with provisions of the 2005 Act. In conformity with Rule 9037 and Official Form 16A, the caption also is amended to provide only the last four digits of any individual debtor's taxpayer-identification number.

B19 (Official Form 19) (12/07)

# United States Bankruptcy Court

In re ______________________________,
Debtor

Case No. ________________

Chapter ______________

## DECLARATION AND SIGNATURE OF NON-ATTORNEY BANKRUPTCY PETITION PREPARER (*See* 11 U.S.C. § 110)

I declare under penalty of perjury that: (1) I am a bankruptcy petition preparer as defined in 11 U.S.C. § 110; (2) I prepared the accompanying document(s) listed below for compensation and have provided the debtor with a copy of the document(s) and the attached notice as required by 11 U.S.C. §§ 110(b), 110(h), and 342(b); and (3) if rules or guidelines have been promulgated pursuant to 11 U.S.C. § 110(h) setting a maximum fee for services chargeable by bankruptcy petition preparers, I have given the debtor notice of the maximum amount before preparing any document for filing for a debtor or accepting any fee from the debtor, as required by that section.

Accompanying documents:
______________________________
______________________________
______________________________
______________________________
______________________________

Printed or Typed Name and Title, if any, of Bankruptcy Petition Preparer:
______________________________

Social-Security No. of Bankruptcy Petition Preparer (Required by 11 U.S.C. § 110):
______________________________

*If the bankruptcy petition preparer is not an individual, state the name, title (if any), address, and social-security number of the officer, principal, responsible person, or partner who signs this document.*

______________________________

______________________________
Address

X______________________________
Signature of Bankruptcy Petition Preparer Date

Names and social-security numbers of all other individuals who prepared or assisted in preparing this document, unless the bankruptcy petition preparer is not an individual:

*If more than one person prepared this document, attach additional signed sheets conforming to the appropriate Official Form for each person.*

**A bankruptcy petition preparer's failure to comply with the provisions of title 11 and the Federal Rules of Bankruptcy Procedure may result in fines or imprisonment or both. 11 U.S.C. § 110; 18 U.S.C. § 156.**

B19 (Official Form 19) (12/07) - Cont. 2

## NOTICE TO DEBTOR BY NON-ATTORNEY BANKRUPTCY PETITION PREPARER

*[Must be filed with any document(s) prepared by a bankruptcy petition preparer.]*

I am a bankruptcy petition preparer. I am not an attorney and may not practice law or give legal advice. Before preparing any document for filing as defined in § 110(a)(2) of the Bankruptcy Code or accepting any fees, I am required by law to provide you with this notice concerning bankruptcy petition preparers. Under the law, § 110 of the Bankruptcy Code (11 U.S.C. § 110), I am forbidden to offer you any legal advice, including advice about any of the following:

- whether to file a petition under the Bankruptcy Code (11 U.S.C. § 101 et seq.);
- whether commencing a case under chapter 7, 11, 12, or 13 is appropriate;
- whether your debts will be eliminated or discharged in a case under the Bankruptcy Code;
- whether you will be able to retain your home, car, or other property after commencing a case under the Bankruptcy Code;
- the tax consequences of a case brought under the Bankruptcy Code;
- the dischargeability of tax claims;
- whether you may or should promise to repay debts to a creditor or enter into a reaffirmation agreement with a creditor to reaffirm a debt;
- how to characterize the nature of your interests in property or your debts; or
- bankruptcy procedures and rights.

*[The notice may provide additional examples of legal advice that a bankruptcy petition preparer is not authorized to give.]*

In addition, under 11 U.S.C. § 110(h), the Supreme Court or the Judicial Conference of the United States may promulgate rules or guidelines setting a maximum allowable fee chargeable by a bankruptcy petition preparer. As required by law, I have notified you of this maximum allowable fee, if any, before preparing any document for filing or accepting any fee from you.

____________________________ ____________________________

Signature of Debtor Date Joint Debtor (if any) Date

*[In a joint case, both spouses must sign.]*

(Added Dec. 1, 2007.)

COMMITTEE NOTES ON RULES—2005–2007

[The 2005–2007 Committee Note incorporates the Committee Notes to Forms 19A and 19B previously published in 2005.]

This form is new. It is derived from form 19B and replaces forms 19A and 19B (which forms are abrogated). The form contains the notice a bankruptcy petition preparer is required to give to a debtor under §110 of the Code as amended by the Bankruptcy Abuse Prevention and Consumer Protection Act of 2005, Pub. L. No. 109–8, 119 Stat. 23 (April 20, 2005), and the bankruptcy petition preparer's signed declaration (also required by §110 of the Code) that the notice was given to the debtor.

The notice states, in language mandated in the 2005 Act, that the bankruptcy petition preparer is not an attorney and must not give legal advice. The notice also includes examples of advice a bankruptcy petition preparer may not give that are taken from §110(e)(2) of the Code.

Although space is provided in the declaration to list multiple documents prepared for a single filing, a new form 19 must be completed and accompany subsequent filings. For example, one form 19 listing all forms prepared by the bankruptcy petition preparer would be filed with the debtor's petition package. Another form 19 would be required if the debtor files amended schedules later in the case that were prepared by the bankruptcy petition preparer.

The form must be signed by the debtor and the bankruptcy petition preparer where indicated, and must be filed with each document for filing prepared by the bankruptcy petition preparer.

**[Form 19A. Abrogated Dec. 1, 2007]**

(Added Mar. 14, 1995; amended Dec. 1, 2003; Oct. 17, 2005.)

NOTES OF ADVISORY COMMITTEE ON RULES—1995

This form is new. The Bankruptcy Reform Act of 1994 requires a "bankruptcy petition preparer," as defined in 11 U.S.C. § 110, to sign any "document for filing" that the bankruptcy petition preparer prepares for compensation on behalf of a debtor, to disclose on the document certain information, and to provide the debtor with a copy of the document. This form or adaptations of this form have been incorporated into the official forms of the voluntary petition, the schedules, the statement of financial affairs, and other official forms that typically would be prepared for a debtor by a bankruptcy petition preparer. This form is to be used in connection with any other document that a bankruptcy petition preparer prepares for filing by a debtor in a bankruptcy case.

COMMITTEE NOTES ON RULES—2003 AMENDMENT

Pursuant to § 110(c) of the Bankruptcy Code, the certification by a non-attorney bankruptcy petition preparer requires a petition preparer to provide the full social security number of the individual who actually prepares the document.

COMMITTEE NOTES ON RULES—2005 AMENDMENT

The certification by a non-attorney bankruptcy petition preparer in this form is renamed a "declaration" and is amended to include material mandated by amendments to § 110 of the Code in the Bankruptcy Abuse Prevention and Consumer Protection Act of 2005, Pub. L. No. 109–8, 119 Stat. 23 (April 20, 2005).

**[Form 19B. Abrogated Dec. 1, 2007]**

(Added Oct. 17, 2005.)

COMMITTEE NOTES ON RULES—2005

This form is new. It contains the notice a non-attorney bankruptcy petition preparer is required to give to a debtor under § 110 of the Code as amended by the Bankruptcy Abuse Prevention and Consumer Protection Act of 2005, Pub. L. No. 109–8, 119 Stat. 23 (April 20, 2005). The notice states, in language mandated in the 2005 Act, that the bankruptcy petition preparer is not an attorney and must not give legal advice. The form includes examples of advice a bankruptcy petition preparer may not give that are take [sic] from § 110(e)(2), which also was added to the Code in 2005. The notice must be signed by the debtor and by the bankruptcy petition preparer and filed with any document for filing prepared by the bankruptcy petition preparer.

Official Form 20A
(12/03)

# United States Bankruptcy Court

________________ District Of ________________

| | |
|---|---|
| In re ________________________________, *Set forth here all names including married, maiden, and trade names used by debtor within last 6 years.]* Debtor | ) Case No. ____________ |
| Address ________________________________ ________________________________ | ) Chapter __________ |
| Employer's Tax Identification (EIN) No(s). *[if any]:* ________ ________________________________________ | ) |
| Last four digits of Social Security No(s).: _____________ | ) |

**NOTICE OF [MOTION TO ] [OBJECTION TO ]**

________________has filed papers with the court to [relief sought in motion or objection].

**<u>Your rights may be affected.</u> You should read these papers carefully and discuss them with your attorney, if you have one in this bankruptcy case. (If you do not have an attorney, you may wish to consult one.)**

If you do not want the court to [relief sought in motion or objection], or if you want the court to consider your views on the [motion] [objection], then on or before <u>(date)</u>, you or your attorney must:

[File with the court a written request for a hearing {*or, if the court requires a written response*, an answer, explaining your position} at:

{address of the bankruptcy clerk's office}

If you mail your {request}{response} to the court for filing, you must mail it early enough so the court will **receive** it on or before the date stated above.

You must also mail a copy to:

{movant's attorney's name and address}

{names and addresses of others to be served}]

[Attend the hearing scheduled to be held on <u>(date)</u>, <u>(year)</u>, at ____a.m./p.m. in Courtroom ____, United States Bankruptcy Court, {address}.]

[Other steps required to oppose a motion or objection under local rule or court order.]

If you or your attorney do not take these steps, the court may decide that you do not oppose the relief sought in the motion or objection and may enter an order granting that relief.

Date: ____________________

Signature: ____________________
Name:
Address:

(Added Oct. 1, 1997.)

NOTES OF ADVISORY COMMITTEE ON RULES—1997

These forms [20A and 20B] are new. They are intended to provide uniform, plain English explanations to parties regarding what they must do to respond in certain contested matters which occur frequently in bankruptcy cases. Such explanations have been given better in some courts than in others. The forms are intended to make bankruptcy proceedings more fair, equitable, and efficient, by aiding parties, who sometimes do not have counsel, in understanding the applicable rules. It is hoped that use of these forms also will decrease the number of inquiries to bankruptcy clerks' offices.

These notices will be sent by the movant unless local rules provide for some other entity to give notice.

These forms are not intended to dictate the specific procedures to be used by different bankruptcy courts. The forms contain optional language that can be used or adapted, depending on local procedures. Similarly, the signature line will be adapted to identify the actual sender of the notice in each circumstance. All adaptations of the form should carry out the intent to give notice of applicable procedures in easily understood language.

Official Form 20B
(12/03)

# United States Bankruptcy Court

______________ District Of ______________

| | | |
|---|---|---|
| In re ______________________________, | ) | |
| *Set forth here all names including married, maiden, and trade names used by debtor within last 6 years.]* | ) | |
| Debtor | ) | Case No. ____________ |
| | ) | |
| Address ______________________________ | ) | |
| ______________________________ | ) | Chapter ________ |
| | ) | |
| Employer's Tax Identification (EIN) No(s). *[if any]*: _______ | ) | |
| ______________________________ | ) | |
| Last four digits of Social Security No(s).: ____________ | ) | |

**NOTICE OF OBJECTION TO CLAIM**

__________________ has filed an objection to your claim in this bankruptcy case.

**Your claim may be reduced, modified, or eliminated. You should read these papers carefully and discuss them with your attorney, if you have one.**

If you do not want the court to eliminate or change your claim, then on or before __(date)__, you or your lawyer must:

{If required by local rule or court order.}

[File with the court a written response to the objection, explaining your position, at:

{address of the bankruptcy clerk's office}

If you mail your response to the court for filing, you must mail it early enough so that the court will **receive** it on or before the date stated above.

You must also mail a copy to:

{objector's attorney's name and address}

{names and addresses of others to be served}]

Attend the hearing on the objection, scheduled to be held on (date), (year) , at _____a.m./p.m. in Courtroom ____, United States Bankruptcy Court, {address}.

If you or your attorney do not take these steps, the court may decide that you do not oppose the objection to your claim.

Date: ______________ Signature: ______________________
Name:
Address:

(Added Oct. 1, 1997.)

NOTES OF ADVISORY COMMITTEE ON RULES—1997

These forms [20A and 20B] are new. They are intended to provide uniform, plain English explanations to parties regarding what they must do to respond in certain contested matters which occur frequently in bankruptcy cases. Such explanations have been given better in some courts than in others. The forms are intended to make bankruptcy proceedings more fair, equitable, and efficient, by aiding parties, who sometimes do not have counsel, in understanding the applicable rules. It is hoped that use of these forms also will decrease the number of inquiries to bankruptcy clerks' offices.

These notices will be sent by the movant unless local rules provide for some other entity to give notice.

These forms are not intended to dictate the specific procedures to be used by different bankruptcy courts. The forms contain optional language that can be used or adapted, depending on local procedures. Similarly, the signature line will be adapted to identify the actual sender of the notice in each circumstance. All adaptations of the form should carry out the intent to give notice of applicable procedures in easily understood language.

B 21 (Official Form 21) (12/07)

# UNITED STATES BANKRUPTCY COURT

In re ______________________________,
[Set forth here all names including married, maiden, and trade names used by debtor within last 8 years]

Debtor

Address

Case No. ____________

Chapter ____________

Last four digits of Social-Security or Individual Taxpayer-Identification (ITIN) No(s).,(if any):

Employer Tax-Identification (EIN) No(s).(if any):

## STATEMENT OF SOCIAL-SECURITY NUMBER(S)

*(or other Individual Taxpayer-Identification Number(s) (ITIN(s)))**

1.Name of Debtor (Last, First, Middle):______________________________
*(Check the appropriate box and, if applicable, provide the required information.)*

☐ Debtor has a Social-Security Number and it is: ____________
*(If more than one, state all.)*

☐ Debtor does not have a Social-Security Number but has an Individual Taxpayer-Identification Number (ITIN), and it is: ____________
*(If more than one, state all.)*

☐ Debtor does not have either a Social-Security Number or an Individual Taxpayer-Identification Number (ITIN).

2.Name of Joint Debtor (Last, First, Middle):______________________________
*(Check the appropriate box and, if applicable, provide the required information.)*

☐ Joint Debtor has a Social-Security Number and it is: ____________
*(If more than one, state all.)*

☐ Joint Debtor does not have a Social-Security Number but has an Individual Taxpayer-Identification Number (ITIN) and it is: ____________
*(If more than one, state all.)*

☐ Joint Debtor does not have either a Social-Security Number or an Individual Taxpayer-Identification Number (ITIN).

I declare under penalty of perjury that the foregoing is true and correct.

X ______________________________________________
Signature of Debtor Date

X ______________________________________________
Signature of Joint Debtor Date

* *Joint debtors must provide information for both spouses.*

*Penalty for making a false statement: Fine of up to $250,000 or up to 5 years imprisonment or both. 18 U.S.C. §§ 152 and 3571.*

(Added Dec. 1, 2003; amended Dec. 1, 2007.)

COMMITTEE NOTES ON RULES—2003

The form implements Rule 1007(f), which requires a debtor to submit a statement under penalty of perjury setting out the debtor's Social Security number. The form is necessary because Rule 1005 provides that the caption of the petition includes only the final four digits of the debtor's Social Security number. The statement provides the information necessary for the clerk to include the debtor's full Social Security number on the notice of the meeting of creditors, as required under Rule 2002(a)(1). Creditors in a case, along with the trustee and United States trustee or bankruptcy administrator, will receive the full Social Security number on their copy of the notice of the meeting of creditors. The copy of that notice which goes into the court file will show only the last four digits of the number.

COMMITTEE NOTES ON RULES—2007 AMENDMENT

The form is amended to direct an individual debtor who does not have a social-security number but has another government-issued individual taxpayer-identification number to furnish that number to the court. In light of the new Rule 9037 which limits public disclosure to all but the last four digits of any individual taxpayer-identification number, the amendment to this form will ensure that the court and creditors can properly identify a debtor who does not have a social-security number.

B22A (Official Form 22A) (Chapter 7) (12/08)

| | |
|---|---|
| In re _______________________<br>Debtor(s)<br><br>Case Number: _______________<br>(If known) | According to the information required to be entered on this statement (check one box as directed in Part I, III, or VI of this statement):<br>☐ **The presumption arises.**<br>☐ **The presumption does not arise.**<br>☐ **The presumption is temporarily inapplicable.** |

## CHAPTER 7 STATEMENT OF CURRENT MONTHLY INCOME AND MEANS-TEST CALCULATION

In addition to Schedules I and J, this statement must be completed by every individual chapter 7 debtor, whether or not filing jointly. Unless the exclusion in Line 1C applies, joint debtors may complete a single statement. If the exclusion in Line 1C applies, each joint filer must complete a separate statement.

| Part I. MILITARY AND NON-CONSUMER DEBTORS | |
|---|---|
| 1A | **Disabled Veterans.** If you are a disabled veteran described in the Declaration in this Part IA, (1) check the box at the beginning of the Declaration, (2) check the box for "The presumption does not arise" at the top of this statement, and (3) complete the verification in Part VIII. Do not complete any of the remaining parts of this statement.<br><br>☐ **Declaration of Disabled Veteran.** By checking this box, I declare under penalty of perjury that I am a disabled veteran (as defined in 38 U.S.C. § 3741(1)) whose indebtedness occurred primarily during a period in which I was on active duty (as defined in 10 U.S.C. § 101(d)(1)) or while I was performing a homeland defense activity (as defined in 32 U.S.C. §901(1)). |
| 1B | **Non-consumer Debtors.** If your debts are not primarily consumer debts, check the box below and complete the verification in Part VIII. Do not complete any of the remaining parts of this statement.<br><br>☐ **Declaration of non-consumer debts.** By checking this box, I declare that my debts are not primarily consumer debts. |
| 1C | **Reservists and National Guard Members; active duty or homeland defense activity.** Members of a reserve component of the Armed Forces and members of the National Guard who were called to active duty (as defined in 10 U.S.C. § 101(d)(1)) after September 11, 2001, for a period of at least 90 days, or who have performed homeland defense activity (as defined in 32 U.S.C. § 901(1)) for a period of at least 90 days, are excluded from all forms of means testing during the time of active duty or homeland defense activity and for 540 days thereafter (the "exclusion period"). If you qualify for this temporary exclusion, (1) check the appropriate boxes and complete any required information in the Declaration of Reservists and National Guard Members below, (2) check the box for "The presumption is temporarily inapplicable" at the top of this statement, and (3) complete the verification in Part VIII. **During your exclusion period you are not required to complete the balance of this form, but you must complete the form no later than 14 days after the date on which your exclusion period ends, unless the time for filing a motion raising the means test presumption expires in your case before your exclusion period ends.**<br><br>☐ **Declaration of Reservists and National Guard Members.** By checking this box and making the appropriate entries below, I declare that I am eligible for a temporary exclusion from means testing because, as a member of a reserve component of the Armed Forces or the National Guard<br><br>a. ☐ I was called to active duty after September 11, 2001, for a period of at least 90 days and<br>☐ I remain on active duty /or/<br>☐ I was released from active duty on _______________, which is less than 540 days before this bankruptcy case was filed;<br><br>OR<br><br>b. ☐ I am performing homeland defense activity for a period of at least 90 days /or/<br>☐ I performed homeland defense activity for a period of at least 90 days, terminating on _______________, which is less than 540 days before this bankruptcy case was filed. |

| | Part II. CALCULATION OF MONTHLY INCOME FOR § 707(b)(7) EXCLUSION | | |
|---|---|---|---|
| 2 | **Marital/filing status.** Check the box that applies and complete the balance of this part of this statement as directed.<br>a. ☐ Unmarried. **Complete only Column A ("Debtor's Income") for Lines 3-11.**<br>b. ☐ Married, not filing jointly, with declaration of separate households. By checking this box, debtor declares under penalty of perjury: "My spouse and I are legally separated under applicable non-bankruptcy law or my spouse and I are living apart other than for the purpose of evading the requirements of § 707(b)(2)(A) of the Bankruptcy Code." **Complete only Column A ("Debtor's Income") for Lines 3-11.**<br>c. ☐ Married, not filing jointly, without the declaration of separate households set out in Line 2.b above. **Complete both Column A ("Debtor's Income") and Column B ("Spouse's Income") for Lines 3-11.**<br>d. ☐ Married, filing jointly. **Complete both Column A ("Debtor's Income") and Column B ("Spouse's Income") for Lines 3-11.** | | |
| | All figures must reflect average monthly income received from all sources, derived during the six calendar months prior to filing the bankruptcy case, ending on the last day of the month before the filing. If the amount of monthly income varied during the six months, you must divide the six-month total by six, and enter the result on the appropriate line. | **Column A Debtor's Income** | **Column B Spouse's Income** |
| 3 | **Gross wages, salary, tips, bonuses, overtime, commissions.** | $ | $ |
| 4 | **Income from the operation of a business, profession or farm.** Subtract Line b from Line a and enter the difference in the appropriate column(s) of Line 4. If you operate more than one business, profession or farm, enter aggregate numbers and provide details on an attachment. Do not enter a number less than zero. **Do not include any part of the business expenses entered on Line b as a deduction in Part V.**<br>a. Gross receipts — $<br>b. Ordinary and necessary business expenses — $<br>c. Business income — Subtract Line b from Line a | $ | $ |
| 5 | **Rent and other real property income.** Subtract Line b from Line a and enter the difference in the appropriate column(s) of Line 5. Do not enter a number less than zero. **Do not include any part of the operating expenses entered on Line b as a deduction in Part V.**<br>a. Gross receipts — $<br>b. Ordinary and necessary operating expenses — $<br>c. Rent and other real property income — Subtract Line b from Line a | $ | $ |
| 6 | **Interest, dividends and royalties.** | $ | $ |
| 7 | **Pension and retirement income.** | $ | $ |
| 8 | **Any amounts paid by another person or entity, on a regular basis, for the household expenses of the debtor or the debtor's dependents, including child support paid for that purpose.** Do not include alimony or separate maintenance payments or amounts paid by your spouse if Column B is completed. | $ | $ |
| 9 | **Unemployment compensation.** Enter the amount in the appropriate column(s) of Line 9. However, if you contend that unemployment compensation received by you or your spouse was a benefit under the Social Security Act, do not list the amount of such compensation in Column A or B, but instead state the amount in the space below:<br>Unemployment compensation claimed to be a benefit under the Social Security Act — Debtor $ ______ — Spouse $ ______ | $ | $ |

| | | | |
|---|---|---|---|
| 10 | **Income from all other sources.** Specify source and amount. If necessary, list additional sources on a separate page. **Do not include alimony or separate maintenance payments paid by your spouse if Column B is completed, but include all other payments of alimony or separate maintenance.** Do not include any benefits received under the Social Security Act or payments received as a victim of a war crime, crime against humanity, or as a victim of international or domestic terrorism.<br>a. ______ $<br>b. ______ $<br>Total and enter on Line 10 | $ | $ |
| 11 | **Subtotal of Current Monthly Income for § 707(b)(7).** Add Lines 3 thru 10 in Column A, and, if Column B is completed, add Lines 3 through 10 in Column B. Enter the total(s). | $ | $ |
| 12 | **Total Current Monthly Income for § 707(b)(7).** If Column B has been completed, add Line 11, Column A to Line 11, Column B, and enter the total. If Column B has not been completed, enter the amount from Line 11, Column A. | $ | |

| | | |
|---|---|---|
| | **Part III. APPLICATION OF § 707(b)(7) EXCLUSION** | |
| 13 | **Annualized Current Monthly Income for § 707(b)(7).** Multiply the amount from Line 12 by the number 12 and enter the result. | $ |
| 14 | **Applicable median family income.** Enter the median family income for the applicable state and household size. (This information is available by family size at www.usdoj.gov/ust/ or from the clerk of the bankruptcy court.)<br>a. Enter debtor's state of residence: ______ b. Enter debtor's household size: ______ | $ |
| 15 | **Application of Section 707(b)(7).** Check the applicable box and proceed as directed.<br>☐ **The amount on Line 13 is less than or equal to the amount on Line 14.** Check the box for "The presumption does not arise" at the top of page 1 of this statement, and complete Part VIII; do not complete Parts IV, V, VI or VII.<br>☐ **The amount on Line 13 is more than the amount on Line 14.** Complete the remaining parts of this statement. | |

**Complete Parts IV, V, VI, and VII of this statement only if required. (See Line 15.)**

| | | |
|---|---|---|
| | **Part IV. CALCULATION OF CURRENT MONTHLY INCOME FOR § 707(b)(2)** | |
| 16 | **Enter the amount from Line 12.** | $ |
| 17 | **Marital adjustment.** If you checked the box at Line 2.c, enter on Line 17 the total of any income listed in Line 11, Column B that was NOT paid on a regular basis for the household expenses of the debtor or the debtor's dependents. Specify in the lines below the basis for excluding the Column B income (such as payment of the spouse's tax liability or the spouse's support of persons other than the debtor or the debtor's dependents) and the amount of income devoted to each purpose. If necessary, list additional adjustments on a separate page. If you did not check box at Line 2.c, enter zero.<br>a. ______ $<br>b. ______ $<br>c. ______ $<br>Total and enter on Line 17. | $ |
| 18 | **Current monthly income for § 707(b)(2).** Subtract Line 17 from Line 16 and enter the result. | $ |
| | **Part V. CALCULATION OF DEDUCTIONS FROM INCOME** | |
| | **Subpart A: Deductions under Standards of the Internal Revenue Service (IRS)** | |
| 19A | **National Standards: food, clothing and other items.** Enter in Line 19A the "Total" amount from IRS National Standards for Food, Clothing and Other Items for the applicable household size. (This information is available at www.usdoj.gov/ust/ or from the clerk of the bankruptcy court.) | $ |

| | | |
|---|---|---|
| 19B | **National Standards: health care.** Enter in Line a1 below the amount from IRS National Standards for Out-of-Pocket Health Care for persons under 65 years of age, and in Line a2 the IRS National Standards for Out-of-Pocket Health Care for persons 65 years of age or older. (This information is available at www.usdoj.gov/ust/ or from the clerk of the bankruptcy court.) Enter in Line b1 the number of members of your household who are under 65 years of age, and enter in Line b2 the number of members of your household who are 65 years of age or older. (The total number of household members must be the same as the number stated in Line 14b.) Multiply Line a1 by Line b1 to obtain a total amount for household members under 65, and enter the result in Line c1. Multiply Line a2 by Line b2 to obtain a total amount for household members 65 and older, and enter the result in Line c2. Add Lines c1 and c2 to obtain a total health care amount, and enter the result in Line 19B. | $ |

| **Household members under 65 years of age** | | | **Household members 65 years of age or older** | | |
|---|---|---|---|---|---|
| a1. | Allowance per member | | a2. | Allowance per member | |
| b1. | Number of members | | b2. | Number of members | |
| c1. | Subtotal | | c2. | Subtotal | |

| | | |
|---|---|---|
| 20A | **Local Standards: housing and utilities; non-mortgage expenses.** Enter the amount of the IRS Housing and Utilities Standards; non-mortgage expenses for the applicable county and household size. (This information is available at www.usdoj.gov/ust/ or from the clerk of the bankruptcy court). | $ |
| 20B | **Local Standards: housing and utilities; mortgage/rent expense.** Enter, in Line a below, the amount of the IRS Housing and Utilities Standards; mortgage/rent expense for your county and household size (this information is available at www.usdoj.gov/ust/ or from the clerk of the bankruptcy court); enter on Line b the total of the Average Monthly Payments for any debts secured by your home, as stated in Line 42; subtract Line b from Line a and enter the result in Line 20B. **Do not enter an amount less than zero.** | $ |

| | | |
|---|---|---|
| a. | IRS Housing and Utilities Standards; mortgage/rental expense | $ |
| b. | Average Monthly Payment for any debts secured by your home, if any, as stated in Line 42 | $ |
| c. | Net mortgage/rental expense | Subtract Line b from Line a. |

| | | |
|---|---|---|
| 21 | **Local Standards: housing and utilities; adjustment.** If you contend that the process set out in Lines 20A and 20B does not accurately compute the allowance to which you are entitled under the IRS Housing and Utilities Standards, enter any additional amount to which you contend you are entitled, and state the basis for your contention in the space below: | $ |
| 22A | **Local Standards: transportation; vehicle operation/public transportation expense.** You are entitled to an expense allowance in this category regardless of whether you pay the expenses of operating a vehicle and regardless of whether you use public transportation.<br><br>Check the number of vehicles for which you pay the operating expenses or for which the operating expenses are included as a contribution to your household expenses in Line 8.<br>☐ 0 ☐ 1 ☐ 2 or more.<br><br>If you checked 0, enter on Line 22A the "Public Transportation" amount from IRS Local Standards: Transportation. If you checked 1 or 2 or more, enter on Line 22A the "Operating Costs" amount from IRS Local Standards: Transportation for the applicable number of vehicles in the applicable Metropolitan Statistical Area or Census Region. (These amounts are available at www.usdoj.gov/ust/ or from the clerk of the bankruptcy court.) | $ |
| 22B | **Local Standards: transportation; additional public transportation expense.** If you pay the operating expenses for a vehicle and also use public transportation, and you contend that you are entitled to an additional deduction for your public transportation expenses, enter on Line 22B the "Public Transportation" amount from IRS Local Standards: Transportation. (This amount is available at www.usdoj.gov/ust/ or from the clerk of the bankruptcy court.) | $ |

| | | |
|---|---|---|
| 23 | **Local Standards: transportation ownership/lease expense; Vehicle 1.** Check the number of vehicles for which you claim an ownership/lease expense. (You may not claim an ownership/lease expense for more than two vehicles.)<br>☐ 1 ☐ 2 or more.<br>Enter, in Line a below, the "Ownership Costs" for "One Car" from the IRS Local Standards: Transportation (available at www.usdoj.gov/ust/ or from the clerk of the bankruptcy court); enter in Line b the total of the Average Monthly Payments for any debts secured by Vehicle 1, as stated in Line 42; subtract Line b from Line a and enter the result in Line 23. **Do not enter an amount less than zero.**<br>a. IRS Transportation Standards, Ownership Costs — $<br>b. Average Monthly Payment for any debts secured by Vehicle 1, as stated in Line 42 — $<br>c. Net ownership/lease expense for Vehicle 1 — Subtract Line b from Line a. | $ |
| 24 | **Local Standards: transportation ownership/lease expense; Vehicle 2.** Complete this Line only if you checked the "2 or more" Box in Line 23.<br>Enter, in Line a below, the "Ownership Costs" for "One Car" from the IRS Local Standards: Transportation (available at www.usdoj.gov/ust/ or from the clerk of the bankruptcy court); enter in Line b the total of the Average Monthly Payments for any debts secured by Vehicle 2, as stated in Line 42; subtract Line b from Line a and enter the result in Line 24. **Do not enter an amount less than zero.**<br>a. IRS Transportation Standards, Ownership Costs — $<br>b. Average Monthly Payment for any debts secured by Vehicle 2, as stated in Line 42 — $<br>c. Net ownership/lease expense for Vehicle 2 — Subtract Line b from Line a. | $ |
| 25 | **Other Necessary Expenses: taxes.** Enter the total average monthly expense that you actually incur for all federal, state and local taxes, other than real estate and sales taxes, such as income taxes, self-employment taxes, social-security taxes, and Medicare taxes. **Do not include real estate or sales taxes.** | $ |
| 26 | **Other Necessary Expenses: involuntary deductions for employment.** Enter the total average monthly payroll deductions that are required for your employment, such as retirement contributions, union dues, and uniform costs. **Do not include discretionary amounts, such as voluntary 401(k) contributions.** | $ |
| 27 | **Other Necessary Expenses: life insurance.** Enter total average monthly premiums that you actually pay for term life insurance for yourself. **Do not include premiums for insurance on your dependents, for whole life or for any other form of insurance.** | $ |
| 28 | **Other Necessary Expenses: court-ordered payments.** Enter the total monthly amount that you are required to pay pursuant to the order of a court or administrative agency, such as spousal or child support payments. **Do not include payments on past due obligations included in Line 44.** | $ |
| 29 | **Other Necessary Expenses: education for employment or for a physically or mentally challenged child.** Enter the total average monthly amount that you actually expend for education that is a condition of employment and for education that is required for a physically or mentally challenged dependent child for whom no public education providing similar services is available. | $ |
| 30 | **Other Necessary Expenses: childcare.** Enter the total average monthly amount that you actually expend on childcare—such as baby-sitting, day care, nursery and preschool. **Do not include other educational payments.** | $ |
| 31 | **Other Necessary Expenses: health care.** Enter the total average monthly amount that you actually expend on health care that is required for the health and welfare of yourself or your dependents, that is not reimbursed by insurance or paid by a health savings account, and that is in excess of the amount entered in Line 19B. **Do not include payments for health insurance or health savings accounts listed in Line 34.** | $ |
| 32 | **Other Necessary Expenses: telecommunication services.** Enter the total average monthly amount that you actually pay for telecommunication services other than your basic home telephone and cell phone service—such as pagers, call waiting, caller id, special long distance, or internet service—to the extent necessary for your health and welfare or that of your dependents. **Do not include any amount previously deducted.** | $ |
| 33 | **Total Expenses Allowed under IRS Standards.** Enter the total of Lines 19 through 32. | $ |

## Subpart B: Additional Living Expense Deductions
## Note: Do not include any expenses that you have listed in Lines 19-32

| | | |
|---|---|---|
| 34 | **Health Insurance, Disability Insurance, and Health Savings Account Expenses.** List the monthly expenses in the categories set out in lines a-c below that are reasonably necessary for yourself, your spouse, or your dependents.<br>a. Health Insurance $<br>b. Disability Insurance $<br>c. Health Savings Account $<br>Total and enter on Line 34 | $ |
| | **If you do not actually expend this total amount,** state your actual total average monthly expenditures in the space below:<br>$ ____________ | |
| 35 | **Continued contributions to the care of household or family members.** Enter the total average actual monthly expenses that you will continue to pay for the reasonable and necessary care and support of an elderly, chronically ill, or disabled member of your household or member of your immediate family who is unable to pay for such expenses. | $ |
| 36 | **Protection against family violence.** Enter the total average reasonably necessary monthly expenses that you actually incurred to maintain the safety of your family under the Family Violence Prevention and Services Act or other applicable federal law. The nature of these expenses is required to be kept confidential by the court. | $ |
| 37 | **Home energy costs.** Enter the total average monthly amount, in excess of the allowance specified by IRS Local Standards for Housing and Utilities, that you actually expend for home energy costs. **You must provide your case trustee with documentation of your actual expenses, and you must demonstrate that the additional amount claimed is reasonable and necessary.** | $ |
| 38 | **Education expenses for dependent children less than 18.** Enter the total average monthly expenses that you actually incur, not to exceed $137.50 per child, for attendance at a private or public elementary or secondary school by your dependent children less than 18 years of age. **You must provide your case trustee with documentation of your actual expenses, and you must explain why the amount claimed is reasonable and necessary and not already accounted for in the IRS Standards.** | $ |
| 39 | **Additional food and clothing expense.** Enter the total average monthly amount by which your food and clothing expenses exceed the combined allowances for food and clothing (apparel and services) in the IRS National Standards, not to exceed 5% of those combined allowances. (This information is available at www.usdoj.gov/ust/ or from the clerk of the bankruptcy court.) **You must demonstrate that the additional amount claimed is reasonable and necessary.** | $ |
| 40 | **Continued charitable contributions.** Enter the amount that you will continue to contribute in the form of cash or financial instruments to a charitable organization as defined in 26 U.S.C. § 170(c)(1)-(2). | $ |
| 41 | **Total Additional Expense Deductions under § 707(b).** Enter the total of Lines 34 through 40 | $ |

## Subpart C: Deductions for Debt Payment

42 **Future payments on secured claims.** For each of your debts that is secured by an interest in property that you own, list the name of the creditor, identify the property securing the debt, state the Average Monthly Payment, and check whether the payment includes taxes or insurance. The Average Monthly Payment is the total of all amounts scheduled as contractually due to each Secured Creditor in the 60 months following the filing of the bankruptcy case, divided by 60. If necessary, list additional entries on a separate page. Enter the total of the Average Monthly Payments on Line 42.

| | Name of Creditor | Property Securing the Debt | Average Monthly Payment | Does payment include taxes or insurance? |
|---|---|---|---|---|
| a. | | | $ | ☐ yes ☐ no |
| b. | | | $ | ☐ yes ☐ no |
| c. | | | $ | ☐ yes ☐ no |
| | | | Total: Add Lines a, b and c. | |

$

43 **Other payments on secured claims.** If any of debts listed in Line 42 are secured by your primary residence, a motor vehicle, or other property necessary for your support or the support of your dependents, you may include in your deduction 1/60th of any amount (the "cure amount") that you must pay the creditor in addition to the payments listed in Line 42, in order to maintain possession of the property. The cure amount would include any sums in default that must be paid in order to avoid repossession or foreclosure. List and total any such amounts in the following chart. If necessary, list additional entries on a separate page.

| | Name of Creditor | Property Securing the Debt | 1/60th of the Cure Amount |
|---|---|---|---|
| a. | | | $ |
| b. | | | $ |
| c. | | | $ |
| | | | Total: Add Lines a, b and c |

$

44 **Payments on prepetition priority claims.** Enter the total amount, divided by 60, of all priority claims, such as priority tax, child support and alimony claims, for which you were liable at the time of your bankruptcy filing. **Do not include current obligations, such as those set out in Line 28.** $

45 **Chapter 13 administrative expenses.** If you are eligible to file a case under chapter 13, complete the following chart, multiply the amount in line a by the amount in line b, and enter the resulting administrative expense.

| | | |
|---|---|---|
| a. | Projected average monthly chapter 13 plan payment. | $ |
| b. | Current multiplier for your district as determined under schedules issued by the Executive Office for United States Trustees. (This information is available at www.usdoj.gov/ust/ or from the clerk of the bankruptcy court.) | x |
| c. | Average monthly administrative expense of chapter 13 case | Total: Multiply Lines a and b |

$

46 **Total Deductions for Debt Payment.** Enter the total of Lines 42 through 45. $

## Subpart D: Total Deductions from Income

47 **Total of all deductions allowed under § 707(b)(2).** Enter the total of Lines 33, 41, and 46. $

B22A (Official Form 22A) (Chapter 7) (12/08) 8

## Part VI. DETERMINATION OF § 707(b)(2) PRESUMPTION

| | | |
|---|---|---|
| 48 | **Enter the amount from Line 18 (Current monthly income for § 707(b)(2))** | $ |
| 49 | **Enter the amount from Line 47 (Total of all deductions allowed under § 707(b)(2))** | $ |
| 50 | **Monthly disposable income under § 707(b)(2).** Subtract Line 49 from Line 48 and enter the result | $ |
| 51 | **60-month disposable income under § 707(b)(2).** Multiply the amount in Line 50 by the number 60 and enter the result. | $ |
| 52 | **Initial presumption determination.** Check the applicable box and proceed as directed.<br>☐ **The amount on Line 51 is less than $6,575** Check the box for "The presumption does not arise" at the top of page 1 of this statement, and complete the verification in Part VIII. Do not complete the remainder of Part VI.<br>☐ **The amount set forth on Line 51 is more than $10,950.** Check the box for "The presumption arises" at the top of page 1 of this statement, and complete the verification in Part VIII. You may also complete Part VII. Do not complete the remainder of Part VI.<br>☐ **The amount on Line 51 is at least $6,575, but not more than $10,950.** Complete the remainder of Part VI (Lines 53 through 55). | |
| 53 | **Enter the amount of your total non-priority unsecured debt** | $ |
| 54 | **Threshold debt payment amount.** Multiply the amount in Line 53 by the number 0.25 and enter the result. | $ |
| 55 | **Secondary presumption determination.** Check the applicable box and proceed as directed.<br>☐ **The amount on Line 51 is less than the amount on Line 54.** Check the box for "The presumption does not arise" at the top of page 1 of this statement, and complete the verification in Part VIII.<br>☐ **The amount on Line 51 is equal to or greater than the amount on Line 54.** Check the box for "The presumption arises" at the top of page 1 of this statement, and complete the verification in Part VIII. You may also complete Part VII. | |

## Part VII: ADDITIONAL EXPENSE CLAIMS

56 **Other Expenses.** List and describe any monthly expenses, not otherwise stated in this form, that are required for the health and welfare of you and your family and that you contend should be an additional deduction from your current monthly income under § 707(b)(2)(A)(ii)(I). If necessary, list additional sources on a separate page. All figures should reflect your average monthly expense for each item. Total the expenses.

| | Expense Description | Monthly Amount |
|---|---|---|
| a. | | $ |
| b. | | $ |
| c. | | $ |
| | Total: Add Lines a, b and c | $ |

## Part VIII: VERIFICATION

57 I declare under penalty of perjury that the information provided in this statement is true and correct. *(If this is a joint case, both debtors must sign.)*

Date: ________________ Signature: ________________________
*(Debtor)*

Date: ________________ Signature: ________________________
*(Joint Debtor, if any)*

(Added Oct. 17, 2005; amended Oct. 1, 2006; Jan. 1, 2008; Dec. 19, 2008.)

### COMMITTEE NOTES ON RULES—2005

A. Overview

Among the changes introduced by the Bankruptcy Abuse Prevention and Consumer Protection Act of 2005 [Pub. L. 109–8, Apr. 20, 2005, 119 Stat. 23] are interlocking provisions defining "current monthly income" and establishing a means test to determine whether relief under Chapter 7 should be presumed abusive. Current monthly income ("CMI") is defined in §101(10A) of the Code, and the means test is set out in §707(b)(2). These provisions have a variety of applications. In Chapter 7, if the debtor's CMI exceeds a defined level the debtor is subject to the means test, and §707(b)(2)(C) specifically requires debtors to file a statement of CMI and calculations to determine the applicability of the means test presumption. In Chapters 11 and 13, CMI provides the starting point for determining the disposable income that must be contributed to payment of unsecured creditors. Moreover, Chapter 13 debtors with CMI above defined levels are required by §1325(b)(3) to complete the means test in order to determine the amount of their monthly disposable income, and pursuant to §1325(b)(4), the level of CMI determines the "applicable commitment period" over which projected disposable income must be paid to unsecured creditors.

To provide for the reporting and calculation of CMI and for the completion of the means test where required, three separate official forms have been created—one for Chapter 7, one for Chapter 11, and one for Chapter 13. This note first describes the calculation of CMI that is common to all three of the forms, next describes the means test as set out in the Chapter 7 and 13 forms, and finally addresses particular issues that are unique to each of the separate forms.

B. Calculation of CMI

Although Chapters 7, 11, and 13 use CMI for different purposes, the basic computation is the same in each. As defined in §101(10A), CMI is the monthly average of certain income that the debtor (and in a joint case, the debtor's spouse) received in the six calendar months before the bankruptcy filing. The definition includes in this average (1) income from all sources, whether or not taxable, and (2) any amount paid by an entity other than the debtor (or the debtor's spouse in a joint case) on a regular basis for the household expenses of the debtor, the debtor's dependents, and (in a joint case) the debtor's spouse if not otherwise a dependent. At the same time, the definition excludes from the averaged income "benefits received under the Social Security Act" and certain payments to victims of terrorism, war crimes, and crimes against humanity.

Each of the forms provides for reporting income items constituting CMI. The items are reported in a set of entry lines—Part II of the Chapter 7 form and Part I of the forms for Chapter 11 and Chapter 13—that include separate columns for reporting income of the debtor and of the debtor's spouse. The first of these entry lines includes a set of instructions and check boxes indicating when the "debtor's spouse" column must be completed. The instructions also direct the required averaging of reported income.

The subsequent entry lines specify several common types of income and are followed by a "catch-all" line for other income. The specific entry lines address (a) gross wages; (b) business income; (c) rental income; (d) interest, dividends, and royalties; (e) pension and retirement income; (f) regular contributions to the debtor's household expenses; and (g) unemployment compensation. Gross wages (before taxes) are required to be entered. Consistent with usage in the Internal Revenue Manual and the American Community Survey of the Census Bureau, business and rental income is defined as gross receipts less ordinary and necessary expenses. Unemployment compensation is given special treatment. Because the federal government provides funding for state unemployment compensation under the Social Security Act, there may be a dispute about whether unemployment compensation is a "benefit received under the Social Security Act." The forms take no position on the merits of this argument, but give debtors the option of reporting unemployment compensation separately from the CMI calculation. This separate reporting allows parties in interest to determine the materiality of an exclusion of unemployment compensation and to challenge it. The forms provide for totaling the income lines.

C. The means test: deductions from current monthly income (CMI)

The means test operates by deducting from CMI defined allowances for living expenses and payment of secured and priority debt, leaving disposable income presumptively available to pay unsecured non-priority debt. These deductions from CMI under are set out in the Code at §707(b)(2)(A)(ii)–(iv). The forms for Chapter 7 and Chapter 13 have identical sections (Parts V and III, respectively) for calculating these deductions. The calculations are divided into subparts reflecting three different kinds of allowed deductions.

1. Deductions under IRS standards

Subpart A deals with deductions from CMI, set out in §707(b)(2)(A)(ii), for "the debtor's applicable monthly expense amounts specified under the National Standards and Local Standards, and the debtor's actual monthly expenses for the categories specified as Other Necessary Expenses issued by the Internal Revenue Service for the area in which the debtor resides." The forms provide entry lines for each of the specified expense deductions under the IRS standards, and instructions on the entry lines identify the website of the U.S. Trustee Program, where the relevant IRS allowances can be found. As with all of the deductions in §707(b)(2)(A)(ii), deductions under the IRS standards are subject to the proviso that they not include "any payments for debts."

The IRS National Standards provide a single allowance for food, clothing, household supplies, personal care, and miscellany, depending on income and household size. The forms contain an entry line for the applicable allowance.

The IRS Local Standards provide one set of deductions for housing and utilities and another set for transportation expenses, with different amounts for different areas of the country, depending on the size of the debtor's family and the number of the debtor's vehicles. Each of the amounts specified in the Local Standards are treated by the IRS as a cap on actual expenses, but because §707(b)(2)(A)(ii) provides for deductions in the "amounts specified under the . . . Local Standards," the forms treat these amounts as allowed deductions. The forms again direct debtors to the website of the U.S. Trustee Program to obtain the appropriate allowances.

The Local Standards for housing and utilities, as published by the IRS for its internal purposes, present single amounts covering all housing expenses; however, for bankruptcy purposes, the IRS has separated these amounts into a non-mortgage component and a mortgage/rent component. The non-mortgage component covers a variety of expenses involved in maintaining a residence, such as utilities, repairs and maintenance. The mortgage/rent component covers the cost of acquiring the residence. For homeowners with mortgages, the mortgage/rent component involves debt payment, since the cost of a mortgage is part of the allowance. Accordingly, the forms require debtors to deduct from the mortgage/rent component their average monthly mortgage payment (including required payments for taxes and insurance), up to the full amount of the IRS mortgage/rent component, and instruct debtors that this average monthly payment is the one reported on the separate line of the forms for deductions of secured debt under §707(b)(2)(a)(iii). The forms allow debtors to challenge the appropriateness of this method of computing the Local Standards allowance for housing and utilities and to claim any additional housing allowance to which they contend they are entitled, but the forms require specification of the basis for such a contention.

The IRS issues Local Standards for transportation in two components for its internal purposes as well as for bankruptcy: one component covers vehicle operation/public transportation expense and the other ownership/lease expense. The amount of the vehicle operation/public transportation allowance depends on the number of vehicles the debtor operates, with debtors who do not operate vehicles being given a public transportation allowance. The instruction for this line item makes it clear that every debtor is thus entitled to some transportation expense allowance. No debt payment is involved in this allowance. The ownership/lease component, on the other hand, may involve debt payment. Accordingly, the forms require debtors to reduce the allowance for ownership/lease expense by the average monthly loan payment amount (principal and interest), up to the full amount of the IRS ownership/lease expense amount. This average payment is as reported on the separate line of the forms for deductions of secured debt under §707(b)(2)(a)(iii).

The IRS does not set out specific dollar allowances for "Other Necessary Expenses." Rather, it specifies a number of categories for such expenses, and describes the nature of the expenses that may be deducted in each of these categories. Section 707(b)(2)(a)(ii) allows a deduction for the debtor's actual expenses in these specified categories, subject to its requirement that payment of debt not be included. Several of the IRS categories deal with debt repayment and so are not included in the forms. Several other categories deal with expense items that are more expansively addressed by specific statutory allowances. Subpart A sets out the remaining categories of "Other Necessary Expenses" in individual entry lines. Instructions in these entry lines reflect limitations imposed by the IRS and the need to avoid inclusion of items deducted elsewhere on the forms.

Subpart A concludes with a subtotal of the deductions allowed under the IRS standards.

2. Additional statutory expense deductions

In addition to the expense deductions allowed under the IRS standards, the means test makes provision—in subclauses (I), (II), (IV), and (V) of § 707(b)(2)(A)(ii)—for six special expense deductions. Each of these additional expense items is set out on a separate entry line in Subpart B, introduced by an instruction that there should not be double counting of any expense already included in the IRS deductions. Contributions to tax-exempt charities provide another statutory expense deduction. Section 1325(b)(2)(A)(ii) expressly allows a deduction from CMI for such contributions (up to 15% of the debtor's gross income), and § 707(b)(1) provides that in considering whether a Chapter 7 filing is an abuse, the court may not take into consideration "whether a debtor . . . continues to make [tax-exempt] charitable contributions." Accordingly, Subpart B also includes an entry line for charitable contributions. The subpart concludes with a subtotal of the additional statutory expense deductions.

3. Deductions for payment of debt

Subpart C of the forms deals with the means test's deductions from CMI for payment of secured and priority debt, as well as a deduction for administrative fees that would be incurred if the debtor paid debts through a Chapter 13 plan. In accord with § 707(b)(2)(A)(iii), the deduction for secured debt is divided into two entry lines—one for payments that are contractually due during the 60 months following the bankruptcy filing, the other for amounts needed to retain necessary collateral securing debts in default. In each situation, the instructions for the entry lines require dividing the total payment amount by 60, as the statute directs. Priority debt, deductible pursuant to § 707(b)(2)(A)(iv), is treated on a single entry line, also requiring division by 60. The defined deduction for the expenses of administering a Chapter 13 plan is allowed by § 707(b)(2)(A)(ii)(III) only for debtors eligible for Chapter 13. The forms treat this deduction in an entry line requiring the eligible debtor to state the amount of the prospective Chapter 13 plan payment and multiply that payment amount by the percentage fee established for the debtor's district by the Executive Office for United States Trustees. The forms refer debtors to the website of the U.S. Trustee Program to obtain this percentage fee. The subpart concludes with a subtotal of debt payment deductions.

4. Total deductions

Finally, the forms direct that the subtotals from Subparts A, B, and C be added together to arrive at the total of allowed deductions from CMI under the means test.

5. Additional claimed deductions

The forms do not provide for means test deductions from CMI for expenses in categories that are not specifically identified as "Other Necessary Expenses" in the Internal Revenue Manual. However, debtors may wish to claim expenses that do not fall within the categories listed as "Other Necessary Expenses" in the forms. Part VII of the Chapter 7 form and Part VI of the Chapter 13 form provide for such expenses to be identified and totaled. Although expenses listed in these sections are not deducted from CMI for purposes of the means test calculation, the listing provides a basis for debtors to assert that these expenses should be deducted from CMI under § 707(b)(2)(A)(ii)(I), and that the results of the forms' calculation, therefore, should be modified.

D. The chapter-specific forms

1. Chapter 7

The Chapter 7 form has several unique aspects. The form includes, in the upper right corner of the first page, a check box directing the debtor to state whether or not the calculations required by the form result in a presumption of abuse. The debtor is not bound by this statement and may argue, in response to a motion brought under § 707(b)(1), that there should be no presumption despite the calculations required by the form. The check box is intended to give clerks of court a conspicuous indication of the cases for which they are required to provide notice of a presumption of abuse pursuant to § 342(d).

Part I of the form implements the provision of § 707(b)(2)(D) that excludes certain disabled veterans from all means testing, making it unnecessary to compute the CMI of such veterans. Debtors who declare under penalty of perjury that they are disabled veterans within the statutory definition are directed to verify their declaration in Part VII, to check the "no presumption" box at the beginning of the form, and to disregard the remaining parts of the form.

Part II of the form is the computation of CMI. Section 707(b)(7) eliminates standing to assert the means test's presumption of abuse if the debtor's annualized CMI does not exceed a defined median state income. For this purpose, the statute directs that CMI of the debtor's spouse be combined with the debtor's CMI even if the debtor's spouse is not a joint debtor, unless the debtor declares under penalty of perjury that the spouses are legally separated or living separately other than for purposes of evading the means test. Accordingly, the calculation of CMI in Part II directs a computation of the CMI of the debtor's spouse not only in joint cases, but also in cases of married debtors who do not make the specified declaration, and the CMI of both spouses in these cases is combined for purposes of determining standing under § 707(b)(7).

Part III of the form provides for the comparison of the debtor's CMI to the applicable state median income for purposes of § 707(b)(7). It then directs debtors whose income does not exceed the applicable median to verify the form, to check the "no presumption" box at the beginning of the form, and not to complete the remaining parts of the form. Debtors whose CMI does exceed the applicable state median are required to complete the remaining parts of the form.

Part IV of the form provides for an adjustment to the CMI of a married debtor, not filing jointly, whose spouse's CMI was combined with the debtor's for purposes of determining standing to assert the means test presumption. The means test itself does not charge a married debtor in a non-joint case with the income of the non-filing spouse, but rather only with contributions made by that spouse to the household expenses of the debtor or the debtor's dependents, as provided in the definition of CMI in § 101(10A). Accordingly, Part IV calls for the combined CMI of Part II to be reduced by the amount of the non-filing spouse's income that was not contributed to the household expenses of the debtor or the debtor's dependents.

Part V of the form provides for a calculation of the means test's deductions from the debtor's CMI, as described above.

Part VI provides for a determination of whether the debtor's CMI, less the allowed deductions, gives rise to a presumption of abuse under § 707(b)(2)(A). Depending on the outcome of this determination, the debtor is directed to check the appropriate box at the beginning of the form and to sign the verification in Part VIII. Part VII allows the debtor to claim additional deductions, as discussed above.

2. Chapter 11

The Chapter 11 form is the simplest of the three, since the means-test deductions of § 707(b)(2) are not employed in determining the extent of an individual Chapter 11 debtor's disposable income. Section 1129(a)(15) requires payments of disposable income "as defined in section 1325(b)(2)," and that paragraph allows calculation of disposable income under judicially-determined standards, rather than pursuant to the means test deductions, specified for higher income Chapter 13 debtors by § 1325(b)(3). However, § 1325(b)(2) does require that CMI be used as the starting point in the judicial determination of disposable income, and so the Chapter 11 form requires this calculation (in Part I of the form), as described above, together with a verification (in Part II).

3. Chapter 13

Like the Chapter 7 form, the form for Chapter 13 debtors contains a number of special provisions. The upper right corner of the first page includes check boxes requiring the debtor to state whether, under the calculations required by the statement, the applicable commitment period under § 1325(b)(4) is three years or five years and whether the means test deductions are required by § 1325(b)(3) to be used in determining the debtor's disposable income. The check box is intended to inform standing trustees and other interested parties about these items, but does not prevent the debtor from arguing that the calculations required by the form do not accurately reflect the debtor's disposable income.

Part I of the form is a report of income to be used for determining CMI. Section 1325(b)(4) imposes a five-year applicable commitment period—rather than a three-year period—if the debtor's annualized CMI is not less than a defined median state income. For this purpose, as under § 707(b)(4), the CMI of the debtor's spouse is required by the statute to be combined with the debtor's CMI, and there is no exception for spouses who are legally separated or living separately. Accordingly, the report of income in Part I directs a combined reporting of the income of both spouses in all cases of married debtors.

Part II of the form computes the applicable commitment period by annualizing the income calculated in Part I and comparing it to the applicable state median. The form allows debtors to contend that the income of a non-filing spouse should not be treated as CMI and permits debtors to claim a deduction for any income of a non-filing spouse to the extent that this income was not contributed to the household expenses of the debtor or the debtor's dependents. The debtor is directed to check the appropriate box at the beginning of the form, stating the applicable commitment period.

Part III of the form compares the debtor's CMI to the applicable state median, allowing a determination of whether the means-test deductions must be used, pursuant to § 1325(b)(3), in calculating disposable income. For this purpose, since § 1325(b)(3) does not provide for including the income of the debtor's spouse, the form directs a deduction of the income of a non-filing spouse that is not contributed to the household expenses of the debtor or the debtor's dependents. Again, the debtor is directed to check the appropriate box at the beginning of the form, indicating whether the means test deductions are applicable. If so, the debtor is directed to complete the remainder of the form. If not, the debtor is directed to complete the verification in Part VII but not complete the other parts of the form.

Part IV provides for calculation of the means-test deductions provided in § 707(b)(2), described above, as incorporated by § 1325(b)(3) for debtors with CMI above the applicable state median.

Part V provides for three adjustments required by special provisions affecting disposable income in Chapter 13. First, § 1325(b)(2) itself excludes from the CMI used in determining disposable income certain "child support payments, foster care payments, [and] disability payments for a dependent child." Because payments of this kind are included in the definition of CMI in § 101(10A), a line entry for deduction of these payments is provided. Second, a line entry is provided for deduction of contributions by the debtor to certain retirement plans, listed in § 541(b)(7)(B), since that provision states that such contributions "shall not constitute disposable income, as defined in section 1325(b)." Third, the same line entry also allows a deduction from disposable income for payments on loans from retirement accounts that are excepted from the automatic stay by § 362(b)(19), since § 1322(f) provides that for a "loan described in section 362(b)(19) . . . any amounts required to repay such loan shall not constitute 'disposable income' under section 1325."

The Chapter 13 form does not provide a deduction from disposable income for the Chapter 13 debtor's anticipated attorney fees. There is no specific statutory allowance for such a deduction, and none appears necessary. Section 1325(b)(1)(B) requires that disposable income contributed to a Chapter 13 plan be used to pay "unsecured creditors." A debtor's attorney who has not taken a security interest in the debtor's property is an unsecured creditor who may be paid from disposable income.

Part VI of the form allows the debtor to claim additional deductions, as described above, and Part VII is the verification.

COMMITTEE NOTES ON RULES—2006 AMENDMENT

Forms [sic] 22A, Line 43, and Form 22C, Line 48, are amended to delete the phrase "in default" with respect to "Other payments on secured claims." A debtor may be required to make other payments to the creditor even when the debt is not in default, such as to retain collateral. Form 22C, Line 17, also is amended to require all chapter 13 debtors, including those whose income falls below the applicable median income, to determine their disposable income under § 1325(b)(3) of the Code by completing Part III of the form. Both forms contain stylistic amendments to conform the wording more closely to that used in the 2005 Act [Bankruptcy Abuse Prevention and Consumer Protection Act of 2005, Pub. L. 109–8, Apr. 20, 2005, 119 Stat. 23].

COMMITTEE NOTES ON RULES—2005–2008 AMENDMENT

[The 2005–2007 [sic] Committee Note incorporates Committee Notes previously published in 2005 and 2006.]

A. Overview

Among the changes introduced by the Bankruptcy Abuse Prevention and Consumer Protection Act of 2005 was a set of interlocking provisions defining "current monthly income" and establishing a means test to determine whether relief under Chapter 7 should be presumed abusive. Current monthly income ("CMI") is defined in § 101(10A) of the Code, and the means test is set out in § 707(b)(2). These provisions have a variety of applications. In Chapter 7, if the debtor's CMI exceeds a defined level the debtor is subject to the means test, and § 707(b)(2)(C) specifically requires debtors to file a statement of CMI and calculations to determine the applicability of the means test presumption. In Chapters 11 and 13, CMI provides the starting point for determining the disposable income that debtors may be required to pay to unsecured creditors. Moreover, Chapter 13 debtors with CMI above defined median income levels are required by § 1325(b)(3) to use the deductions from income prescribed by the means test in order to determine what part of their income is "disposable," and pursuant to § 1325(b)(4), the level of CMI determines the "applicable commitment period" over which projected disposable income must be paid to unsecured creditors.

To provide for the reporting and calculation of CMI and for the completion of the means test where required, three separate official forms have been created—one for Chapter 7, one for Chapter 11, and one for Chapter 13. This note first describes the calculation of CMI that is common to all three of the forms, next describes the means test deductions set out in the Chapter 7 and 13 forms, and finally addresses particular issues that are unique to each of the separate forms.

B. Calculation of CMI

Although Chapters 7, 11, and 13 use CMI for different purposes, the basic computation is the same in each. As defined in § 101(10A), CMI is the monthly average of certain income that the debtor (and in a joint case, the debtor's spouse) received in the six calendar months before the bankruptcy filing. The definition includes in this average (1) income from all sources, whether or not taxable, and (2) any amount paid by an entity other than the debtor (or the debtor's spouse in a joint case) on a regular basis for the household expenses of the debtor, the debtor's dependents, and (in a joint case) the debtor's spouse if not otherwise a dependent. At the same time, the definition excludes from the averaged income "benefits received under the Social Security Act" and certain payments to victims of terrorism, war crimes, and crimes against humanity.

Each of the three forms provides for reporting income items constituting CMI. The items are reported in a set of entry lines—Part II of the form for Chapter 7 and Part I of the forms for Chapter 11 and Chapter 13—that include separate columns for reporting income of the debtor and of the debtor's spouse. The first of these entry lines includes a set of instructions and check boxes indicating when the "debtor's spouse" column must be completed. The instructions also direct the required averaging of reported income.

The subsequent entry lines for income reporting specify several common types of income and are followed by a "catch-all" line for other income. The entry lines address (a) gross wages; (b) business income; (c) rental income; (d) interest, dividends, and royalties; (e) pension and retirement income; (f) regular payments of the household expenses of the debtor or the debtor's dependents; (g) unemployment compensation, and (h) all other forms of income (the "catch-all" line).

Gross wages (before taxes) are required to be entered. However, consistent with usage in the Internal Revenue Manual and the American Community Survey of the Census Bureau, business and rental income are defined as gross receipts less ordinary and necessary expenses.

Unemployment compensation is given special treatment. Because the federal government provides funding for state unemployment compensation under the Social Security Act, there may be a dispute about whether unemployment compensation is a "benefit received under the Social Security Act." The forms take no position on the merits of this argument, but give debtors the option of reporting unemployment compensation separately from the CMI calculation. This separate reporting allows parties in interest to determine the materiality of an exclusion of unemployment compensation and to challenge it.

Alimony and child support are also given special treatment. Child support is not generally considered "income" to the recipient. See 26 U.S.C. §71(c). Thus, child support is only part of CMI if it is paid on a regular basis for the household expenses of the debtor or the debtor's dependents. On the other hand, alimony and other forms of spousal support are considered income to the recipient, and thus are within CMI regardless of the regularity and use of the payments. To address this distinction, the instruction in the entry line for regular payments of household expenses directs that the entry include regular child support payments used for household expenses of the debtor or the debtor's dependents, and the instruction for the "catch-all" line directs inclusion of all spousal support payments that are not otherwise reported as spousal income.

The forms provide for totaling the income reporting lines.

C. The means test: deductions from current monthly income

The means test operates by deducting from CMI defined allowances for living expenses and payment of secured and priority debt, leaving disposable income presumptively available to pay unsecured non-priority debt. These deductions from CMI are set out in the Code at §707(b)(2)(A)(ii)–(iv). The forms for Chapter 7 and Chapter 13 have similar sections (Parts V and IV, respectively) for calculating these deductions. The calculations are divided into subparts reflecting three different kinds of allowed deductions.

1. Deductions under IRS standards

Subpart A deals with deductions from CMI, set out in §707(b)(2)(A)(ii), for "the debtor's applicable monthly expense amounts specified under the National Standards and Local Standards, and the debtor's actual monthly expenses for the categories specified as Other Necessary Expenses issued by the Internal Revenue Service for the area in which the debtor resides." The forms provide entry lines for each of the specified expense deductions under the IRS standards, and instructions on the entry lines identify the website of the U.S. Trustee Program, where the relevant IRS allowances can be found. As with all of the deductions in §707(b)(2)(A)(ii), deductions under the IRS standards are subject to the proviso that they not include "any payments for debts."

*National Standards.* The IRS National Standards provide a single allowance for food, clothing, household supplies, personal care, and miscellany, depending on household size, which can be entered directly from a table supplied by the IRS. There is also a National Standard for out-of-pocket health care expenses, which provides two different per-person allowances, depending on age group: the allowance for persons 65 or older is greater than the allowance for those under 65. Accordingly, the forms direct debtors to compute the National Standard allowance for health care by first multiplying each of the two age-group allowances by the number of household members within that age group and then adding subtotals for the two age groups to obtain the total allowance.

*Local Standards.* The IRS Local Standards provide one set of deductions for housing and utilities and another set for transportation expenses, with different amounts for different areas of the country, depending on the size of the debtor's household and the number of the debtor's vehicles. Each of the amounts specified in the Local Standards are treated by the IRS as a cap on actual expenses, but because §707(b)(2)(A)(ii) provides for deductions in the "amounts specified under the . . . Local Standards," the forms treat these amounts as allowed deductions.

The Local Standards for housing and utilities, as published by the IRS for its internal purposes, present single amounts covering all housing expenses; however, for bankruptcy purposes, the IRS has provided the Executive Office for United States Trustees with information allowing a division of these amounts into a non-mortgage component and a mortgage/rent component. The non-mortgage component covers a variety of expenses involved in maintaining a residence, such as utilities, repairs and maintenance. The mortgage/rent component covers the cost of acquiring the residence. The forms take no position on the question of whether the debtor must actually be making payments on a home in order to claim a mortgage/rent allowance. For homeowners with mortgages, the mortgage/rent allowance involves debt payment, since the cost of a mortgage is the basis for the allowance. Accordingly, the forms require debtors to deduct from the mortgage/rent allowance their average monthly mortgage payment, up to the full amount of the IRS mortgage/rent allowance, and instruct debtors that this average monthly payment is the one reported on the separate line of the forms for deductions of secured debt under §707(b)(2)(a)(iii). The forms allow debtors to challenge the appropriateness of this method of computing the Local Standards allowance for housing and utilities and to claim any additional housing allowance to which they contend they are entitled, but the forms require specification of the basis for such a contention.

The IRS issues Local Standards for transportation in two components for its internal purposes as well as for bankruptcy: one component covers vehicle operation/public transportation expense and the other ownership/lease expense. The amount of the vehicle operation/public transportation allowance depends on the number of vehicles the debtor operates; debtors who do not operate vehicles are given a public transportation allowance, regardless of whether they actually use public transportation. It is not clear whether the public transportation allowance may also be claimed by debtors who do make use of public transportation but also operate vehicles. The forms permit debtors to claim both a public transportation and vehicle operating allowance, but take no position as to whether it is appropriate to claim both allowances. No debt payment is involved in the vehicle operation/public transportation component of the Local Standards for transportation.

The ownership/lease component, on the other hand, may involve debt payment. Accordingly, the forms require debtors to reduce the allowance for ownership/lease expense by the average monthly loan payment amount (principal and interest), up to the full amount of the IRS ownership/lease expense amount. This average payment is as reported on the separate line of the forms for deductions of secured debt under §707(b)(2)(a)(iii). The forms take no position on the question of whether the debtor must actually be making payments on a vehicle in order to claim the ownership/lease allowance.

*Other Necessary Expenses.* The IRS does not set out specific dollar allowances for "Other Necessary Expenses." Rather, it specifies a number of categories for such expenses, and describes the nature of the expenses that may be deducted in each of these categories. Section 707(b)(2)(a)(ii) allows a deduction for the debtor's actual expenses in these specified categories, subject to its requirement that payment of debt not be included. Several of the IRS categories deal with debt repayment and so are not included in the forms. Several other categories deal with expense items that are more expansively addressed by specific statutory allowances. Subpart A sets out the remaining categories of "Other Necessary Expenses" in individual entry lines. Instructions in these entry lines reflect limitations imposed by the IRS and the need to avoid inclusion of items deducted elsewhere on the forms.

Subpart A concludes with a subtotal of the deductions allowed under the IRS standards.

2. Additional statutory expense deductions

In addition to the expense deductions allowed under the IRS standards, the means test makes provision—in subclauses (I), (II), (IV), and (V) of §707(b)(2)(A)(ii)—for six special expense deductions. Each of these additional expense items is set out on a separate entry line in Subpart B, introduced by an instruction that tracks the statutory language and provides that there should not be double counting of any expense already included in the IRS deductions.

One of these special expense deductions presents a problem of statutory construction. Section 707(b)(2)A)(ii)(I) [sic], after directing the calculation of the debtor's monthly expenses under the IRS standards, states, "Such expenses shall include reasonably necessary health insurance, disability insurance, and health saving account expenses . . . ." There is no express statutory limitation to expenses actually incurred by the debtor, and so the provision appears to allow a reasonable "monthly expense" deduction for health and disability insurance or a health savings account even if the debtor does not make such payments, similar to the way in which the National Standards give an allowance for food, clothing and personal care expenses without regard to the debtor's actual expenditures. However, the statutory language might also be read as providing that the debtor's "Other Necessary Expenses" should include reasonable insurance and health savings account payments. Since "Other Necessary Expenses" are limited to actual expenditures, such a limitation could be implied here. The forms deal with this ambiguity by allowing the debtor to claim a deduction for reasonable insurance and health savings account expenses even if not made, but also require a statement of the amount actually expended in these categories, thus allowing a challenge by any party who believes that only actual expenditures are properly deductible.

Contributions to tax-exempt charities provide another statutory expense deduction. Section 707(b)(1) provides that in considering whether a Chapter 7 filing is an abuse, the court may not take into consideration "whether a debtor . . . continues to make [tax-exempt] charitable contributions." Section 1325(b)(2)(A)(ii) expressly allows a deduction from CMI for such contributions that are "reasonably necessary" (up to 15% of the debtor's gross income), and the Religious Liberty and Charitable Donation Clarification Act of 2005 [2006] added language to §1325(b)(3) to provide the same deduction for above-median income debtors whose disposable income is determined using means test deductions. Accordingly, Subpart B of both the Chapter 7 and Chapter 13 forms includes an entry line for charitable contributions, employing the different statutory deductions allowed in each context.

The Subpart B concludes with a subtotal of the additional statutory expense deductions.

3. Deductions for payment of debt

Subpart C deals with the means test's deductions from CMI for payment of secured and priority debt, as well as a deduction for administrative fees that would be incurred if the debtor paid debts through a Chapter 13 plan.

In accord with §707(b)(2)(A)(iii), the deduction for secured debt is divided into two entry lines—one for payments that are contractually due during the 60 months following the bankruptcy filing, the other for amounts needed to retain necessary collateral securing debts in default. In each situation, the instructions for the entry lines require dividing the total payment amount by 60, as the statute directs. The forms recognize another ambiguity in this connection: "payments contractually due" might either be understood as limited to payments of principal and interest (payable to secured creditor) or, in the context of a mortgage with an escrow, might be understood as including payments of property taxes and insurance (ultimately paid to taxing bodies and insurers, but initially payable to the mortgagee). The forms require the debtor to specify whether the amount deducted includes taxes and insurance, allowing a party in interest to inquire into the deduction and raise an objection.

Priority debt, deductible pursuant to §707(b)(2)(A)(iv), is treated on a single entry line, also requiring division by 60. The instruction for this line makes clear that only past due priority debt—not anticipated debts—should be included. Thus, future support or tax obligations, and future fees that might be payable to a Chapter 13 debtor's attorney, are not included.

The defined deduction for the expenses of administering a Chapter 13 plan is allowed by §707(b)(2)(A)(ii)(III) only for debtors eligible for Chapter 13. The forms treat this deduction in an entry line requiring the eligible debtor to state the amount of the prospective Chapter 13 plan payment and multiply that payment amount by the percentage fee established for the debtor's district by the Executive Office for United States Trustees. The forms refer debtors to the website of the U.S. Trustee Program to obtain this percentage fee.

The subpart concludes with a subtotal of debt payment deductions.

4. Total deductions

Finally, the forms direct that the subtotals from Subparts A, B, and C be added together to arrive at the total of allowed deductions from CMI under the means test.

5. Additional claimed deductions

The forms do not provide for means test deductions from CMI for expenses in categories that are not specifically identified as "Other Necessary Expenses" in the Internal Revenue Manual. However, debtors may wish to claim expenses that do not fall within the categories listed as "Other Necessary Expenses" in the forms. Part VII of the Chapter 7 form and Part VI of the Chapter 13 form provide for such expenses to be identified and totaled. Although expenses listed in these sections are not deducted from CMI for purposes of the means test calculation, the listing provides a basis for debtors to assert that these expenses should be deducted from CMI under §707(b)(2)(A)(ii)(I), and that the results of the forms' calculation should therefore be modified.

D. The chapter-specific forms

1. Chapter 7

The Chapter 7 form has several unique aspects. The form includes, in the upper right corner of the first page, a check box directing the debtor to state whether or not the calculations required by the form result in a presumption of abuse. The debtor is not bound by this statement and may argue, in response to a motion brought under §707(b)(1), that there should be no presumption despite the calculations required by the form. The check box is intended to give clerks of court a conspicuous indication of the cases for which they are required to provide notice of a presumption of abuse pursuant to §342(d).

Part I implements the provision of §707(b)(2)(D) that excludes certain disabled veterans from all means testing, making it unnecessary to compute the CMI of such veterans. Debtors who declare under penalty of perjury that they are disabled veterans within the statutory definition are directed to verify their declaration in Part VII, to check the "no presumption" box at the beginning of the form, and to disregard the remaining parts of the form.

Part I also provides an exclusion for debtors who do not have primarily consumer debts. These debtors are not subject to any of the provisions of §707(b)—including the requirement of §707(b)(2)(C) for filing a CMI statement—since §707(b) applies, by its terms, only to "an individual debtor . . . whose debts are primarily consumer debts." However, a debtor may be found to have asserted non-consumer status incorrectly. Unless such a debtor has filed the CMI form within the 45 days after filing the case, the case could be subject to automatic dismissal under §521(i). To avoid this possibility, debtors asserting principally non-consumer status may complete the appropriate portions of Part I, claim an exclusion from the balance of the form, and promptly file the form. If it is subsequently determined that the debtor does have primarily consumer debts, the form will have been filed within the deadline established by §521(i), and can be amended to include the necessary CMI and means test information.

Part II computes CMI for purposes of the safe harbor of §707(b)(7). Section 707(b)(7) prohibits a motion to dismiss based on the means test's presumption of abuse if the debtor's annualized CMI does not exceed a defined median state income. For this purpose, the statute directs that CMI of the debtor's spouse be combined with the debtor's CMI even if the debtor's spouse is not a joint debtor, unless the debtor declares under penalty of perjury that the spouses are legally separated or living separately other than for purposes of evading the means test.Accordingly, the calculation of CMI in Part II directs a computation of the CMI of the debtor's spouse not only in joint cases, but also in cases of married debtors who do not make the specified declaration, and the CMI of both spouses in these cases is combined for purposes of determining standing under §707(b)(7).

Part III compares the debtor's CMI to the applicable state median income for purposes of §707(b)(7). It then directs debtors whose income does not exceed the applicable median to verify the form, to check the "no presumption" box at the beginning of the form, and not to complete the remaining parts of the form. Debtors whose CMI does exceed the applicable state median are required to complete the remaining parts of the form.

Part IV adjusts the CMI of a married debtor, not filing jointly, whose spouse's CMI was combined with the debtor's in Part II. The means test itself does not charge a married debtor in a non-joint case with the income of the non-filing spouse, but only with payments regularly made by that spouse for the household expenses of the debtor or the debtor's dependents, as provided in the definition of CMI in §101(10A). Accordingly, Part IV calls for the combined CMI of Part II to be reduced by the amount of the non-filing spouse's income that was not regularly paid for the household expenses of the debtor or the debtor's dependents. The form requires that the alternative uses of the spouse's income be specified.

Part V of the form provides for a calculation of the means test's deductions from the debtor's CMI, as described above in §C.

Part VI provides for a determination of whether the debtor's CMI, less the allowed deductions, gives rise to a presumption of abuse under §707(b)(2)(A). Depending on the outcome of this determination, the debtor is directed to check the appropriate box at the beginning of the form and to sign the verification in Part VIII. Part VII allows the debtor to claim additional deductions, as discussed above in §C.5.

2. Chapter 11

The Chapter 11 form is the simplest of the three, since the means-test deductions of §707(b)(2) are not employed in determining the extent of an individual Chapter 11 debtor's disposable income. Section 1129(a)(15) requires payments of disposable income "as defined in section 1325(b)(2)," and that paragraph allows calculation of disposable income under judicially-determined standards, rather than pursuant to the means test deductions, specified for higher income Chapter 13 debtors by §1325(b)(3). However, §1325(b)(2) does require that CMI be used as the starting point in the judicial determination of disposable income, and so the Chapter 11 form requires this calculation (in Part I of the form), as described above, together with a verification (in Part II).

3. Chapter 13

Like the Chapter 7 form, the form for Chapter 13 debtors contains a number of special provisions. The upper right corner of the first page includes check boxes requiring the debtor to state whether, under the calculations required by the statement, the applicable commitment period under §1325(b)(4) is three years or five years and whether §1325(b)(3) requires the means-test deductions to be used in determining the debtor's disposable income. The check box is intended to inform standing trustees and other interested parties about these items, but does not prevent the debtor from arguing that the calculations required by the form do not accurately reflect the debtor's disposable income.

Part I is a report of income to be used for determining CMI. In the absence of full payment of allowed unsecured claims, §1325(b)(4) imposes a five-year applicable commitment period—rather than a three-year period—if the debtor's annualized CMI is not less than a defined median state income. For this purpose, as under §707(b)(7), §1325(b)(4) requires that the CMI of the debtor's spouse be combined with the debtor's CMI, but, unlike §707(b)(7), no exception is made for spouses who are legally separated or living separately. Accordingly, the report of income in Part I directs a combined reporting of the income of both spouses in all cases of married debtors.

Part II computes the applicable commitment period by annualizing the income calculated in Part I and comparing it to the applicable state median. The form allows debtors to contend that the income of a non-filing spouse should not be treated as CMI and permits debtors to claim a deduction for any income of a non-filing spouse to the extent that this income was not regularly paid for the household expenses of the debtor or the debtor's dependents (with the alternative uses specified). The debtor is directed to check the appropriate box at the beginning of the form, stating the applicable commitment period. The check box does not prevent a debtor from proposing an applicable commitment period of less than three or five years in conjunction with a plan that pays all allowed unsecured claims in full.

Part III compares the debtor's CMI to the applicable state median, allowing a determination of whether the means-test deductions must be used, pursuant to §1325(b)(3), in calculating disposable income. For this purpose, since §1325(b)(3) does not provide for including the income of the debtor's spouse, the form directs a deduction of the income of a nonfiling spouse that was not contributed to the household expenses of the debtor or the debtor's dependents. Again, the debtor is directed to check the appropriate box at the beginning of the form, indicating whether the means test deductions are applicable. If so, the debtor is directed to complete the remainder of the form. If not, the debtor is directed to complete the verification in Part VII but not complete the other parts of the form.

Part IV provides for calculation of the means-test deductions provided in §707(b)(2), described above in §C, as incorporated by §1325(b)(3) for debtors with CMI above the applicable state median.

Part V provides for four adjustments required by special provisions affecting disposable income in Chapter 13. First, §1325(b)(2) itself excludes from the CMI used in determining disposable income certain "child support payments, foster care payments, [and] disability payments for a dependent child." Because payments of this kind are included in the definition of CMI in §101(10A), a line entry for deduction of these payments is provided. Second, a line entry is provided for deduction of contributions by the debtor to certain retirement plans, listed in §541(b)(7)(B), since that provision states that such contributions "shall not constitute disposable income, as defined in section 1325(b)." Third, the same line entry also allows a deduction from disposable income for payments on loans from retirement accounts that are excepted from the automatic stay by §362(b)(19), since §1322(f) provides that for a "loan described in section 362(b)(19) . . . any amounts required to repay such loan shall not constitute 'disposable income' under section 1325." Finally, §1325(b)(3) requires that deductions from income for above-median income debtors be determined not only in accordance with the means test deductions, set out in subparagraph (A) of §707(b)(2), but also in accordance with subparagraph (B), which sets out the grounds for rebutting a presumption of abuse based on a demonstration of additional expenses justified by special circumstances. Part V includes an entry line for such additional expenses, with a warning that the debtor will be required (as provided by §707(b)(2)(B)) to document the expenses and provide a detailed explanation of the special circumstances that make them reasonable and necessary.

The Chapter 13 form does not provide a deduction from disposable income for the Chapter 13 debtor's anticipated attorney fees. No specific statutory allowance for such a deduction exists, and none appears necessary. Section 1325(b)(1)(B) requires that disposable income contributed to a Chapter 13 plan be used to pay "unsecured creditors." A debtor's attorney who has not taken a security interest in the debtor's property is an unsecured creditor who may be paid from disposable income.

Part VI allows the debtor to declare expenses not allowed under the form without deducting them from CMI, as described above in §C.5.

COMMITTEE NOTES ON RULES—2008 AMENDMENT

The chapter 7 form is amended to implement the temporary exclusion from means testing created by the National Guard and Reservists Debt Relief Act of 2008. That law amended §707(b)(2)(D) for a period of three years by adding a new subsection (ii) to provide a temporary exclusion from the application of the means test for certain members of the National Guard and reserve components of the Armed Forces. The new temporary exclusion would last for the period that the qualifying debtor is on active duty or is performing a homeland defense activity, and for 540 days thereafter.

Because the exclusion for Reservists and National Guard members applies only for a defined period of time, it may expire during the course of the chapter 7 case filed by a debtor initially entitled to the exclusion. For that reason, a new check box is added to the top of the form that states that the "presumption is temporarily inapplicable." A debtor who is entitled to claim the Reservists and National Guard exclusion at the commencement of the chapter 7 case may check that box.

The new exclusion applies only to a debtor who satisfies all of the requirements of §707(b)(2)(D)(ii), and its expiration date depends on facts specific to each debtor. Therefore, in a joint case in which the exclusion in part 1C is claimed by either or both filers, each joint filer must complete a separate statement. If only one joint debtor qualifies for the exclusion in part IC [sic], the other joint debtor must complete the form.

Part 1C is added to the form to allow qualifying debtors to claim the temporary exclusion under §707(b)(2)(D)(ii). Debtors who declare under penalty of perjury that they satisfy all of the requirements of that provision are directed to verify their declaration in Part VIII and to check the "temporary presumption" box at the beginning of the form. They are not required to complete the remaining parts of the form for so long as the exclusion remains applicable.

A debtor who is or has been a Reservist or a National Guard member may qualify for the exclusion described in part 1C by being called to active duty service after September 11, 2001, for a period of at least 90 days, or while performing homeland defense activity for a period of at least 90 days. After the debtor has been released from active duty or has ceased performing homeland defense activity, the exclusion applies for a period of 540 days after the release date or cessation of homeland defense activity. Under those circumstances the debtor must state the date of release from active duty or the date on which the performance of homeland defense activity terminated.

If the Reservist and National Guard exclusion terminates during the course of a chapter 7 case—because of the expiration of the 540 day period following the release from active duty or the cessation of homeland defense activity—then the debtor may be required to complete the remaining parts of the form that are applicable to the debtor. If the exclusion terminates while a timely motion to dismiss under §707(b)(2) may still be filed, Interim Rule 1007-I(n) requires that the debtor complete the remaining parts of the form no later than 14 days after the termination. If the obligation to complete the form arises in these circumstances and the debtor has not previously completed the form, the clerk is required to give the debtor notice of the obligation.

B 22B (Official Form 22B) (Chapter 11) (01/08)

In re ______________________
Debtor(s)

Case Number: ______________
(If known)

## CHAPTER 11 STATEMENT OF CURRENT MONTHLY INCOME

In addition to Schedules I and J, this statement must be completed by every individual chapter 11 debtor, whether or not filing jointly. Joint debtors may complete one statement only.

| Part I. CALCULATION OF CURRENT MONTHLY INCOME | | | |
|---|---|---|---|
| 1 | **Marital/filing status.** Check the box that applies and complete the balance of this part of this statement as directed.<br>a. ☐ Unmarried. **Complete only Column A ("Debtor's Income") for Lines 2-10.**<br>b. ☐ Married, not filing jointly. **Complete only Column A ("Debtor's Income") for Lines 2-10.**<br>c. ☐ Married, filing jointly. **Complete both Column A ("Debtor's Income") and Column B ("Spouse's Income") for Lines 2-10.** | | |
| | All figures must reflect average monthly income received from all sources, derived during the six calendar months prior to filing the bankruptcy case, ending on the last day of the month before the filing. If the amount of monthly income varied during the six months, you must divide the six-month total by six, and enter the result on the appropriate line. | **Column A Debtor's Income** | **Column B Spouse's Income** |
| 2 | **Gross wages, salary, tips, bonuses, overtime, commissions.** | $ | $ |
| 3 | **Net income from the operation of a business, profession, or farm.** Subtract Line b from Line a and enter the difference in the appropriate column(s) of Line 3. If more than one business, profession or farm, enter aggregate numbers and provide details on an attachment. Do not enter a number less than zero.<br>a. Gross receipts — $<br>b. Ordinary and necessary business expenses — $<br>c. Business income — Subtract Line b from Line a. | $ | $ |
| 4 | **Net rental and other real property income.** Subtract Line b from Line a and enter the difference in the appropriate column(s) of Line 4. Do not enter a number less than zero.<br>a. Gross receipts — $<br>b. Ordinary and necessary operating expenses — $<br>c. Rent and other real property income — Subtract Line b from Line a. | $ | $ |
| 5 | **Interest, dividends, and royalties.** | $ | $ |
| 6 | **Pension and retirement income.** | $ | $ |
| 7 | **Any amounts paid by another person or entity, on a regular basis, for the household expenses of the debtor or the debtor's dependents, including child support paid for that purpose.** Do not include alimony or separate maintenance payments or amounts paid by the debtor's spouse if Column B is completed. | $ | $ |
| 8 | **Unemployment compensation.** Enter the amount in the appropriate column(s) of Line 8. However, if you contend that unemployment compensation received by you or your spouse was a benefit under the Social Security Act, do not list the amount of such compensation in Column A or B, but instead state the amount in the space below:<br>Unemployment compensation claimed to be a benefit under the Social Security Act — Debtor $ ________ — Spouse $ ________ | $ | $ |

B 22B (Official Form 22B) (Chapter 11) (01/08) 2

| | | | |
|---|---|---|---|
| 9 | **Income from all other sources.** Specify source and amount. If necessary, list additional sources on a separate page. Total and enter on Line 9. **Do not include alimony or separate maintenance payments paid by your spouse if Column B is completed, but include all other payments of alimony or separate maintenance. Do not include** any benefits received under the Social Security Act or payments received as a victim of a war crime, crime against humanity, or as a victim of international or domestic terrorism.<br>a. ______ $<br>b. ______ $ | $ | $ |
| 10 | **Subtotal of current monthly income.** Add Lines 2 thru 9 in Column A, and, if Column B is completed, add Lines 2 through 9 in Column B. Enter the total(s). | $ | $ |
| 11 | **Total current monthly income.** If Column B has been completed, add Line 10, Column A to Line 10, Column B, and enter the total. If Column B has not been completed, enter the amount from Line 10, Column A. | $ | |

| | |
|---|---|
| | **Part II: VERIFICATION** |
| 12 | I declare under penalty of perjury that the information provided in this statement is true and correct. *(If this a joint case, both debtors must sign.)*<br>Date: ____________ Signature: ____________ (Debtor)<br>Date: ____________ Signature: ____________ (Joint Debtor, if any) |

(Added Oct. 17, 2005; amended Jan. 1, 2008.)

COMMITTEE NOTES ON RULES—2005

For Committee Notes on Rules—2005 for form 22B, see note set out under form 22A.

COMMITTEE NOTES ON RULES—2005-2008 AMENDMENT

For Committee Notes on Rules—2005-2008 for form 22B, see note set out under form 22A.

B 22C (Official Form 22C) (Chapter 13) (01/08)

In re ______________________
Debtor(s)

Case Number: ______________
(If known)

According to the calculations required by this statement:
☐ **The applicable commitment period is 3 years.**
☐ **The applicable commitment period is 5 years.**
☐ **Disposable income is determined under § 1325(b)(3).**
☐ **Disposable income is not determined under § 1325(b)(3).**
(Check the boxes as directed in Lines 17 and 23 of this statement.)

# CHAPTER 13 STATEMENT OF CURRENT MONTHLY INCOME AND CALCULATION OF COMMITMENT PERIOD AND DISPOSABLE INCOME

In addition to Schedules I and J, this statement must be completed by every individual chapter 13 debtor, whether or not filing jointly. Joint debtors may complete one statement only.

## Part I. REPORT OF INCOME

| | | | |
|---|---|---|---|
| 1 | **Marital/filing status.** Check the box that applies and complete the balance of this part of this statement as directed.<br>a. ☐ Unmarried. **Complete only Column A ("Debtor's Income") for Lines 2-10.**<br>b. ☐ Married. **Complete both Column A ("Debtor's Income") and Column B ("Spouse's Income") for Lines 2-10.** | | |
| | All figures must reflect average monthly income received from all sources, derived during the six calendar months prior to filing the bankruptcy case, ending on the last day of the month before the filing. If the amount of monthly income varied during the six months, you must divide the six-month total by six, and enter the result on the appropriate line. | **Column A Debtor's Income** | **Column B Spouse's Income** |
| 2 | **Gross wages, salary, tips, bonuses, overtime, commissions.** | $ | $ |
| 3 | **Income from the operation of a business, profession, or farm.** Subtract Line b from Line a and enter the difference in the appropriate column(s) of Line 3. If you operate more than one business, profession or farm, enter aggregate numbers and provide details on an attachment. Do not enter a number less than zero. **Do not include any part of the business expenses entered on Line b as a deduction in Part IV.**<br>a. Gross receipts — $<br>b. Ordinary and necessary business expenses — $<br>c. Business income — Subtract Line b from Line a | $ | $ |
| 4 | **Rent and other real property income.** Subtract Line b from Line a and enter the difference in the appropriate column(s) of Line 4. Do not enter a number less than zero. **Do not include any part of the operating expenses entered on Line b as a deduction in Part IV.**<br>a. Gross receipts — $<br>b. Ordinary and necessary operating expenses — $<br>c. Rent and other real property income — Subtract Line b from Line a | $ | $ |
| 5 | **Interest, dividends, and royalties.** | $ | $ |
| 6 | **Pension and retirement income.** | $ | $ |
| 7 | **Any amounts paid by another person or entity, on a regular basis, for the household expenses of the debtor or the debtor's dependents, including child support paid for that purpose.** Do not include alimony or separate maintenance payments or amounts paid by the debtor's spouse. | $ | $ |
| 8 | **Unemployment compensation.** Enter the amount in the appropriate column(s) of Line 8. However, if you contend that unemployment compensation received by you or your spouse was a benefit under the Social Security Act, do not list the amount of such compensation in Column A or B, but instead state the amount in the space below:<br>Unemployment compensation claimed to be a benefit under the Social Security Act — Debtor $ ________ — Spouse $ ________ | $ | $ |

B 22C (Official Form 22C) (Chapter 13) (01/08) 2

| | | | |
|---|---|---|---|
| 9 | **Income from all other sources.** Specify source and amount. If necessary, list additional sources on a separate page. Total and enter on Line 9. **Do not include alimony or separate maintenance payments paid by your spouse, but include all other payments of alimony or separate maintenance. Do not include** any benefits received under the Social Security Act or payments received as a victim of a war crime, crime against humanity, or as a victim of international or domestic terrorism.<br>a. ______ $<br>b. ______ $ | $ | $ |
| 10 | **Subtotal.** Add Lines 2 thru 9 in Column A, and, if Column B is completed, add Lines 2 through 9 in Column B. Enter the total(s). | $ | $ |
| 11 | **Total.** If Column B has been completed, add Line 10, Column A to Line 10, Column B, and enter the total. If Column B has not been completed, enter the amount from Line 10, Column A. | $ | |

| | | |
|---|---|---|
| | **Part II. CALCULATION OF § 1325(b)(4) COMMITMENT PERIOD** | |
| 12 | **Enter the amount from Line 11.** | $ |
| 13 | **Marital adjustment.** If you are married, but are not filing jointly with your spouse, AND if you contend that calculation of the commitment period under § 1325(b)(4) does not require inclusion of the income of your spouse, enter on Line 13 the amount of the income listed in Line 10, Column B that was NOT paid on a regular basis for the household expenses of you or your dependents and specify, in the lines below, the basis for excluding this income (such as payment of the spouse's tax liability or the spouse's support of persons other than the debtor or the debtor's dependents) and the amount of income devoted to each purpose. If necessary, list additional adjustments on a separate page. If the conditions for entering this adjustment do not apply, enter zero.<br>a. ______ $<br>b. ______ $<br>c. ______ $<br>Total and enter on Line 13. | $ |
| 14 | **Subtract Line 13 from Line 12 and enter the result.** | $ |
| 15 | **Annualized current monthly income for § 1325(b)(4).** Multiply the amount from Line 14 by the number 12 and enter the result. | $ |
| 16 | **Applicable median family income.** Enter the median family income for applicable state and household size. (This information is available by family size at www.usdoj.gov/ust/ or from the clerk of the bankruptcy court.)<br>a. Enter debtor's state of residence: __________ b. Enter debtor's household size: __________ | $ |
| 17 | **Application of § 1325(b)(4).** Check the applicable box and proceed as directed.<br>☐ **The amount on Line 15 is less than the amount on Line 16.** Check the box for "The applicable commitment period is 3 years" at the top of page 1 of this statement and continue with this statement.<br>☐ **The amount on Line 15 is not less than the amount on Line 16.** Check the box for "The applicable commitment period is 5 years" at the top of page 1 of this statement and continue with this statement. | |
| | **Part III. APPLICATION OF § 1325(b)(3) FOR DETERMINING DISPOSABLE INCOME** | |
| 18 | **Enter the amount from Line 11.** | $ |

| | | |
|---|---|---|
| 19 | **Marital adjustment.** If you are married, but are not filing jointly with your spouse, enter on Line 19 the total of any income listed in Line 10, Column B that was NOT paid on a regular basis for the household expenses of the debtor or the debtor's dependents. Specify in the lines below the basis for excluding the Column B income (such as payment of the spouse's tax liability or the spouse's support of persons other than the debtor or the debtor's dependents) and the amount of income devoted to each purpose. If necessary, list additional adjustments on a separate page. If the conditions for entering this adjustment do not apply, enter zero.<br>a. ______ $<br>b. ______ $<br>c. ______ $<br>Total and enter on Line 19. | $ |
| 20 | **Current monthly income for § 1325(b)(3).** Subtract Line 19 from Line 18 and enter the result. | |
| 21 | **Annualized current monthly income for § 1325(b)(3).** Multiply the amount from Line 20 by the number 12 and enter the result. | $ |
| 22 | **Applicable median family income.** Enter the amount from Line 16. | $ |
| 23 | **Application of § 1325(b)(3).** Check the applicable box and proceed as directed.<br>☐ **The amount on Line 21 is more than the amount on Line 22.** Check the box for "Disposable income is determined under § 1325(b)(3)" at the top of page 1 of this statement and complete the remaining parts of this statement.<br>☐ **The amount on Line 21 is not more than the amount on Line 22.** Check the box for "Disposable income is not determined under § 1325(b)(3)" at the top of page 1 of this statement and complete Part VII of this statement. **Do not complete Parts IV, V, or VI.** | |

## Part IV. CALCULATION OF DEDUCTIONS FROM INCOME

### Subpart A: Deductions under Standards of the Internal Revenue Service (IRS)

| | | |
|---|---|---|
| 24A | **National Standards: food, apparel and services, housekeeping supplies, personal care, and miscellaneous.** Enter in Line 24A the "Total" amount from IRS National Standards for Allowable Living Expenses for the applicable household size. (This information is available at www.usdoj.gov/ust/ or from the clerk of the bankruptcy court.) | $ |
| 24B | **National Standards: health care.** Enter in Line a1 below the amount from IRS National Standards for Out-of-Pocket Health Care for persons under 65 years of age, and in Line a2 the IRS National Standards for Out-of-Pocket Health Care for persons 65 years of age or older. (This information is available at www.usdoj.gov/ust/ or from the clerk of the bankruptcy court.) Enter in Line b1 the number of members of your household who are under 65 years of age, and enter in Line b2 the number of members of your household who are 65 years of age or older. (The total number of household members must be the same as the number stated in Line 16b.) Multiply Line a1 by Line b1 to obtain a total amount for household members under 65, and enter the result in Line c1. Multiply Line a2 by Line b2 to obtain a total amount for household members 65 and older, and enter the result in Line c2. Add Lines c1 and c2 to obtain a total health care amount, and enter the result in Line 24B. | $ |

| **Household members under 65 years of age** | | | **Household members 65 years of age or older** | | |
|---|---|---|---|---|---|
| a1. | Allowance per member | | a2. | Allowance per member | |
| b1. | Number of members | | b2. | Number of members | |
| c1. | Subtotal | | c2. | Subtotal | |

| | | |
|---|---|---|
| 25A | **Local Standards: housing and utilities; non-mortgage expenses.** Enter the amount of the IRS Housing and Utilities Standards; non-mortgage expenses for the applicable county and household size. (This information is available at www.usdoj.gov/ust/ or from the clerk of the bankruptcy court). | $ |

| | | |
|---|---|---|
| 25B | **Local Standards: housing and utilities; mortgage/rent expense.** Enter, in Line a below, the amount of the IRS Housing and Utilities Standards; mortgage/rent expense for your county and household size (this information is available at www.usdoj.gov/ust/ or from the clerk of the bankruptcy court); enter on Line b the total of the Average Monthly Payments for any debts secured by your home, as stated in Line 47; subtract Line b from Line a and enter the result in Line 25B. **Do not enter an amount less than zero.**<br>a. IRS Housing and Utilities Standards; mortgage/rent expense — $<br>b. Average Monthly Payment for any debts secured by your home, if any, as stated in Line 47 — $<br>c. Net mortgage/rental expense — Subtract Line b from Line a. | $ |
| 26 | **Local Standards: housing and utilities; adjustment.** If you contend that the process set out in Lines 25A and 25B does not accurately compute the allowance to which you are entitled under the IRS Housing and Utilities Standards, enter any additional amount to which you contend you are entitled, and state the basis for your contention in the space below:<br>________________________________________<br>________________________________________ | $ |
| 27A | **Local Standards: transportation; vehicle operation/public transportation expense.** You are entitled to an expense allowance in this category regardless of whether you pay the expenses of operating a vehicle and regardless of whether you use public transportation.<br>Check the number of vehicles for which you pay the operating expenses or for which the operating expenses are included as a contribution to your household expenses in Line 7. ☐ 0 ☐ 1 ☐ 2 or more.<br>If you checked 0, enter on Line 27A the "Public Transportation" amount from IRS Local Standards: Transportation. If you checked 1 or 2 or more, enter on Line 27A the "Operating Costs" amount from IRS Local Standards: Transportation for the applicable number of vehicles in the applicable Metropolitan Statistical Area or Census Region. (These amounts are available at www.usdoj.gov/ust/ or from the clerk of the bankruptcy court.) | $ |
| 27B | **Local Standards: transportation; additional public transportation expense.** If you pay the operating expenses for a vehicle and also use public transportation, and you contend that you are entitled to an additional deduction for your public transportation expenses, enter on Line 27B the "Public Transportation" amount from IRS Local Standards: Transportation. (This amount is available at www.usdoj.gov/ust/ or from the clerk of the bankruptcy court.) | $ |
| 28 | **Local Standards: transportation ownership/lease expense; Vehicle 1.** Check the number of vehicles for which you claim an ownership/lease expense. (You may not claim an ownership/lease expense for more than two vehicles.) ☐ 1 ☐ 2 or more.<br>Enter, in Line a below, the "Ownership Costs" for "One Car" from the IRS Local Standards: Transportation (available at www.usdoj.gov/ust/ or from the clerk of the bankruptcy court); enter in Line b the total of the Average Monthly Payments for any debts secured by Vehicle 1, as stated in Line 47; subtract Line b from Line a and enter the result in Line 28. **Do not enter an amount less than zero.**<br>a. IRS Transportation Standards, Ownership Costs — $<br>b. Average Monthly Payment for any debts secured by Vehicle 1, as stated in Line 47 — $<br>c. Net ownership/lease expense for Vehicle 1 — Subtract Line b from Line a. | $ |

| | | |
|---|---|---|
| 29 | **Local Standards: transportation ownership/lease expense; Vehicle 2.** Complete this Line only if you checked the "2 or more" Box in Line 28.<br>Enter, in Line a below, the "Ownership Costs" for "One Car" from the IRS Local Standards: Transportation (available at www.usdoj.gov/ust/ or from the clerk of the bankruptcy court); enter in Line b the total of the Average Monthly Payments for any debts secured by Vehicle 2, as stated in Line 47; subtract Line b from Line a and enter the result in Line 29. **Do not enter an amount less than zero.**<br>a. IRS Transportation Standards, Ownership Costs — $<br>b. Average Monthly Payment for any debts secured by Vehicle 2, as stated in Line 47 — $<br>c. Net ownership/lease expense for Vehicle 2 — Subtract Line b from Line a. | $ |
| 30 | **Other Necessary Expenses: taxes.** Enter the total average monthly expense that you actually incur for all federal, state, and local taxes, other than real estate and sales taxes, such as income taxes, self-employment taxes, social-security taxes, and Medicare taxes. **Do not include real estate or sales taxes.** | $ |
| 31 | **Other Necessary Expenses: involuntary deductions for employment.** Enter the total average monthly deductions that are required for your employment, such as mandatory retirement contributions, union dues, and uniform costs. **Do not include discretionary amounts, such as voluntary 401(k) contributions.** | $ |
| 32 | **Other Necessary Expenses: life insurance.** Enter total average monthly premiums that you actually pay for term life insurance for yourself. **Do not include premiums for insurance on your dependents, for whole life or for any other form of insurance.** | $ |
| 33 | **Other Necessary Expenses: court-ordered payments.** Enter the total monthly amount that you are required to pay pursuant to the order of a court or administrative agency, such as spousal or child support payments. **Do not include payments on past due obligations included in Line 49.** | $ |
| 34 | **Other Necessary Expenses: education for employment or for a physically or mentally challenged child.** Enter the total average monthly amount that you actually expend for education that is a condition of employment and for education that is required for a physically or mentally challenged dependent child for whom no public education providing similar services is available. | $ |
| 35 | **Other Necessary Expenses: childcare.** Enter the total average monthly amount that you actually expend on childcare—such as baby-sitting, day care, nursery and preschool. **Do not include other educational payments.** | $ |
| 36 | **Other Necessary Expenses: health care.** Enter the total average monthly amount that you actually expend on health care that is required for the health and welfare of yourself or your dependents, that is not reimbursed by insurance or paid by a health savings account, and that is in excess of the amount entered in Line 24B. **Do not include payments for health insurance or health savings accounts listed in Line 39.** | $ |
| 37 | **Other Necessary Expenses: telecommunication services.** Enter the total average monthly amount that you actually pay for telecommunication services other than your basic home telephone and cell phone service—such as pagers, call waiting, caller id, special long distance, or internet service—to the extent necessary for your health and welfare or that of your dependents. **Do not include any amount previously deducted.** | $ |
| 38 | **Total Expenses Allowed under IRS Standards.** Enter the total of Lines 24 through 37. | $ |

**Subpart B: Additional Living Expense Deductions**
**Note: Do not include any expenses that you have listed in Lines 24-37**

<table>
<tr><td>39</td><td>Health Insurance, Disability Insurance, and Health Savings Account Expenses. List the monthly expenses in the categories set out in lines a-c below that are reasonably necessary for yourself, your spouse, or your dependents.<br>a. Health Insurance $<br>b. Disability Insurance $<br>c. Health Savings Account $<br>Total and enter on Line 39<br><b>If you do not actually expend this total amount,</b> state your actual total average monthly expenditures in the space below:<br>$ ______</td><td>$</td></tr>
<tr><td>40</td><td>Continued contributions to the care of household or family members. Enter the total average actual monthly expenses that you will continue to pay for the reasonable and necessary care and support of an elderly, chronically ill, or disabled member of your household or member of your immediate family who is unable to pay for such expenses. Do not include payments listed in Line 34.</td><td>$</td></tr>
<tr><td>41</td><td>Protection against family violence. Enter the total average reasonably necessary monthly expenses that you actually incur to maintain the safety of your family under the Family Violence Prevention and Services Act or other applicable federal law. The nature of these expenses is required to be kept confidential by the court.</td><td>$</td></tr>
<tr><td>42</td><td>Home energy costs. Enter the total average monthly amount, in excess of the allowance specified by IRS Local Standards for Housing and Utilities, that you actually expend for home energy costs. You must provide your case trustee with documentation of your actual expenses, and you must demonstrate that the additional amount claimed is reasonable and necessary.</td><td>$</td></tr>
<tr><td>43</td><td>Education expenses for dependent children under 18. Enter the total average monthly expenses that you actually incur, not to exceed $137.50 per child, for attendance at a private or public elementary or secondary school by your dependent children less than 18 years of age. <b>You must provide your case trustee with documentation of your actual expenses, and you must explain why the amount claimed is reasonable and necessary and not already accounted for in the IRS Standards.</b></td><td>$</td></tr>
<tr><td>44</td><td>Additional food and clothing expense. Enter the total average monthly amount by which your food and clothing expenses exceed the combined allowances for food and clothing (apparel and services) in the IRS National Standards, not to exceed 5% of those combined allowances. (This information is available at www.usdoj.gov/ust/ or from the clerk of the bankruptcy court.) You must demonstrate that the additional amount claimed is reasonable and necessary.</td><td>$</td></tr>
<tr><td>45</td><td>Charitable contributions. Enter the amount reasonably necessary for you to expend each month on charitable contributions in the form of cash or financial instruments to a charitable organization as defined in 26 U.S.C. § 170(c)(1)-(2). Do not include any amount in excess of 15% of your gross monthly income.</td><td>$</td></tr>
<tr><td>46</td><td>Total Additional Expense Deductions under § 707(b). Enter the total of Lines 39 through 45.</td><td>$</td></tr>
<tr><td colspan="3">Subpart C: Deductions for Debt Payment</td></tr>
<tr><td>47</td><td>Future payments on secured claims. For each of your debts that is secured by an interest in property that you own, list the name of the creditor, identify the property securing the debt, state the Average Monthly Payment, and check whether the payment includes taxes or insurance. The Average Monthly Payment is the total of all amounts scheduled as contractually due to each Secured Creditor in the 60 months following the filing of the bankruptcy case, divided by 60. If necessary, list additional entries on a separate page. Enter the total of the Average Monthly Payments on Line 47.<br><table><tr><td></td><td>Name of Creditor</td><td>Property Securing the Debt</td><td>Average Monthly Payment</td><td>Does payment include taxes or insurance?</td></tr><tr><td>a.</td><td></td><td></td><td>$</td><td>☐ yes ☐ no</td></tr><tr><td>b.</td><td></td><td></td><td>$</td><td>☐ yes ☐ no</td></tr><tr><td>c.</td><td></td><td></td><td>$</td><td>☐ yes ☐ no</td></tr><tr><td></td><td></td><td></td><td>Total: Add Lines a, b, and c</td><td></td></tr></table></td><td>$</td></tr>
</table>

| | | |
|---|---|---|
| 48 | **Other payments on secured claims.** If any of debts listed in Line 47 are secured by your primary residence, a motor vehicle, or other property necessary for your support or the support of your dependents, you may include in your deduction 1/60th of any amount (the "cure amount") that you must pay the creditor in addition to the payments listed in Line 47, in order to maintain possession of the property. The cure amount would include any sums in default that must be paid in order to avoid repossession or foreclosure. List and total any such amounts in the following chart. If necessary, list additional entries on a separate page. | |

| | Name of Creditor | Property Securing the Debt | 1/60th of the Cure Amount |
|---|---|---|---|
| a. | | | $ |
| b. | | | $ |
| c. | | | $ |
| | | | Total: Add Lines a, b, and c |

| | | |
|---|---|---|
| 48 | (Total) | $ |
| 49 | **Payments on prepetition priority claims.** Enter the total amount, divided by 60, of all priority claims, such as priority tax, child support and alimony claims, for which you were liable at the time of your bankruptcy filing. **Do not include current obligations, such as those set out in Line 33.** | $ |
| 50 | **Chapter 13 administrative expenses.** Multiply the amount in Line a by the amount in Line b, and enter the resulting administrative expense. | |

| | | |
|---|---|---|
| a. | Projected average monthly chapter 13 plan payment. | $ |
| b. | Current multiplier for your district as determined under schedules issued by the Executive Office for United States Trustees. (This information is available at www.usdoj.gov/ust/ or from the clerk of the bankruptcy court.) | x |
| c. | Average monthly administrative expense of chapter 13 case | Total: Multiply Lines a and b |

| | | |
|---|---|---|
| 50 | (Total) | $ |
| 51 | **Total Deductions for Debt Payment.** Enter the total of Lines 47 through 50. | $ |
| | **Subpart D: Total Deductions from Income** | |
| 52 | **Total of all deductions from income.** Enter the total of Lines 38, 46, and 51. | $ |
| | **Part V. DETERMINATION OF DISPOSABLE INCOME UNDER § 1325(b)(2)** | |
| 53 | **Total current monthly income.** Enter the amount from Line 20. | $ |
| 54 | **Support income.** Enter the monthly average of any child support payments, foster care payments, or disability payments for a dependent child, reported in Part I, that you received in accordance with applicable nonbankruptcy law, to the extent reasonably necessary to be expended for such child. | $ |
| 55 | **Qualified retirement deductions.** Enter the monthly total of (a) all amounts withheld by your employer from wages as contributions for qualified retirement plans, as specified in § 541(b)(7) and (b) all required repayments of loans from retirement plans, as specified in § 362(b)(19). | $ |
| 56 | **Total of all deductions allowed under § 707(b)(2).** Enter the amount from Line 52. | $ |

| | | |
|---|---|---|
| 57 | **Deduction for special circumstances.** If there are special circumstances that justify additional expenses for which there is no reasonable alternative, describe the special circumstances and the resulting expenses in lines a-c below. If necessary, list additional entries on a separate page. Total the expenses and enter the total in Line 57. **You must provide your case trustee with documentation of these expenses and you must provide a detailed explanation of the special circumstances that make such expenses necessary and reasonable.**<br><br>\| \| Nature of special circumstances \| Amount of expense \|<br>\| a. \| \| $ \|<br>\| b. \| \| $ \|<br>\| c. \| \| $ \|<br>\| \| \| Total: Add Lines a, b, and c \| | $ |
| 58 | **Total adjustments to determine disposable income.** Add the amounts on Lines 54, 55, 56, and 57 and enter the result. | $ |
| 59 | **Monthly Disposable Income Under § 1325(b)(2).** Subtract Line 58 from Line 53 and enter the result. | $ |

## Part VI: ADDITIONAL EXPENSE CLAIMS

**60** **Other Expenses.** List and describe any monthly expenses, not otherwise stated in this form, that are required for the health and welfare of you and your family and that you contend should be an additional deduction from your current monthly income under § 707(b)(2)(A)(ii)(I). If necessary, list additional sources on a separate page. All figures should reflect your average monthly expense for each item. Total the expenses.

| | Expense Description | Monthly Amount |
|---|---|---|
| a. | | $ |
| b. | | $ |
| c. | | $ |
| | Total: Add Lines a, b, and c | $ |

## Part VII: VERIFICATION

**61** I declare under penalty of perjury that the information provided in this statement is true and correct. *(If this is a joint case, both debtors must sign.)*

Date: ____________________ Signature: ____________________
(Debtor)

Date: ____________________ Signature: ____________________
(Joint Debtor, if any)

(Added Oct. 17, 2005; amended Oct. 1, 2006; Jan. 1, 2008.)

COMMITTEE NOTES ON RULES—2005

For Committee Notes on Rules—2005 for form 22C, see note set out under form 22A.

COMMITTEE NOTES ON RULES—2006 AMENDMENT

For Committee Notes on Rules—2006 Amendment for form 22C, see note set out under form 22A.

COMMITTEE NOTES ON RULES—2005-2008 AMENDMENT

For Committee Notes on Rules—2005-2008 Amendment for form 22C, see note set out under form 22A.

B 23 (Official Form 23) (12/08)

# UNITED STATES BANKRUPTCY COURT

In re ______________________________________,
Debtor

Case No. ____________________

Chapter ___________

## DEBTOR'S CERTIFICATION OF COMPLETION OF POSTPETITION INSTRUCTIONAL COURSE CONCERNING PERSONAL FINANCIAL MANAGEMENT

*Every individual debtor in a chapter 7, chapter 11 in which § 1141(d)(3) applies, or chapter 13 case must file this certification. If a joint petition is filed, each spouse must complete and file a separate certification. Complete one of the following statements and file by the deadline stated below:*

☐ I, ______________________________________, the debtor in the above-styled case, hereby
*(Printed Name of Debtor)*
certify that on ____________________ *(Date)*, I completed an instructional course in personal financial management provided by ______________________________________, an approved personal financial
*(Name of Provider)*
management provider.

Certificate No. *(if any)*: ______________________________.

☐ I, ______________________________________, the debtor in the above-styled case, hereby
*(Printed Name of Debtor)*
certify that no personal financial management course is required because of *[Check the appropriate box.]*:

☐ Incapacity or disability, as defined in 11 U.S.C. § 109(h);

☐ Active military duty in a military combat zone; or

☐ Residence in a district in which the United States trustee *(or bankruptcy administrator)* has determined that the approved instructional courses are not adequate at this time to serve the additional individuals who would otherwise be required to complete such courses.

Signature of Debtor: ______________________________

Date: ____________

---

*Instructions:* Use this form only to certify whether you completed a course in personal financial management. (Fed. R. Bankr. P. 1007(b)(7).) Do NOT use this form to file the certificate given to you by your prepetition credit counseling provider and do NOT include with the petition when filing your case.

*Filing Deadlines:* In a chapter 7 case, file within 45 days of the first date set for the meeting of creditors under § 341 of the Bankruptcy Code. In a chapter 11 or 13 case, file no later than the last payment made by the debtor as required by the plan or the filing of a motion for a discharge under § 1141(d)(5)(B) or § 1328(b) of the Code. (See Fed. R. Bankr. P. 1007(c).)

(Added Oct. 17, 2005; amended Oct. 1, 2006; Dec. 1, 2007; Dec. 1, 2008.)

### COMMITTEE NOTES ON RULES—2005

The form is new. Sections 727(a)(11) and 1328(g)(1), which were added to the Code by the Bankruptcy Abuse Prevention and Consumer Protection Act of 2005, Pub. L. No. 109-8, 119 Stat. 23 (April 20, 2005), require the debtor to complete an instructional course concerning personal financial management as a condition for receiving a discharge. The completed form, when filed by the debtor, will signal the clerk that this condition has been satisfied.

### COMMITTEE NOTES ON RULES—2006 AMENDMENT

The form is amended to direct each individual debtor, including both spouses in a joint case, to file a separate certification and to provide the certificate number of the certificate of completion issued to the debtor by the approved personal financial management counselor. The form also is amended to include the deadlines for filing the certification in cases under chapters 7 and 13 and to instruct the debtor that the form is not to be used to file the certificate provided by the debtor's prepetition credit counselor.

COMMITTEE NOTES ON RULES—2005–2007 AMENDMENT

[The 2005–2007 Committee Note incorporates Committee Notes previously published in 2005 and 2006.]

The form was issued in 2005. Sections 727(a)(11), 1141(d)(3) and 1328(g)(1), which were added to the Code by the Bankruptcy Abuse Prevention and Consumer Protection Act of 2005, Pub. L. No. 109–8, 119 Stat. 23 (April 20, 2005), require individual debtors to complete an instructional course concerning personal financial management as a condition for receiving a discharge. The completed form will signal the clerk that this condition has been satisfied. Each individual debtor, including both spouses in a joint case, must file a separate certification and provide the certificate number of the certificate of completion issued to the debtor by the approved personal financial management counselor. Instructions are included that state the deadlines for filing the certification in chapter 7, chapter 11 in which §1141(d)(3) applies, and chapter 13 cases, and remind the debtor that the form is not to be used for filing a certification of prepetition credit counseling.

B 24 (Official Form 24) (12/07)

**[Caption as described in Fed. R. Bankr. P. 7010 or 9004(b), as applicable.]**

**CERTIFICATION TO COURT OF APPEALS**
**BY ALL PARTIES**

A notice of appeal having been filed in the above-styled matter on _________ *[Date]*, ____________________, ____________________, and ____________________, *[Names of all the appellants and all the appellees, if any]*, who are all the appellants [and all the appellees] hereby certify to the court under 28 U.S.C. § 158(d)(2)(A) that a circumstance specified in 28 U.S.C. § 158(d)(2) exists as stated below.

Leave to appeal in this matter ☐ is ☐ is not required under 28 U.S.C. § 158(a).

*[If from a final judgment, order, or decree]* This certification arises in an appeal from a final judgment, order, or decree of the United States Bankruptcy Court for the _________ District of ______________ entered on ____________ *[Date]*.

*[If from an interlocutory order or decree]* This certification arises in an appeal from an interlocutory order or decree, and the parties hereby request leave to appeal as required by 28 U.S.C. § 158(a).

*[The certification shall contain one or more of the following statements, as is appropriate to the circumstances.]*

The judgment, order, or decree involves a question of law as to which there is no controlling decision of the court of appeals for this circuit or of the Supreme Court of the United States, or involves a matter of public importance.

*Or*

The judgment, order, or decree involves a question of law requiring resolution of conflicting decisions.

*Or*

An immediate appeal from the judgment, order, or decree may materially advance the progress of the case or proceeding in which the appeal is taken.

B 24 (Official Form 24) (12/07) - Cont. Page 2

*[The parties may include or attach the information specified in Rule 8001(f)(3)(C).]*

Signed: *[If there are more than two signatories, all must sign and provide the information requested below. Attach additional signed sheets if needed.]*

____________________________
Attorney for Appellant (or Appellant, if not represented by an attorney)

____________________________
Printed Name of Signer

____________________________
____________________________
Address

____________________________
Telephone No.

____________________________
Date

____________________________
Attorney for Appellee (or Appellee if not represented by an attorney)

____________________________
Printed Name of Signer

____________________________
____________________________
Address

____________________________
Telephone No.

____________________________
Date

(Added Oct. 17, 2005; amended Dec. 1, 2007.)

COMMITTEE NOTES ON RULES—2005

This form is new. Rule 8001, as amended in 2005, requires that any certification of an appeal, bankruptcy court judgment, order, or decree directly to the United States Court of Appeals by all the appellants and appellees (if any) acting jointly be filed on this form.

COMMITTEE NOTES ON RULES—2005–2007 AMENDMENT

[The 2005–2007 Committee Note incorporates the Committee Note previously published in 2005.]

This form was issued in 2005. Rule 8001 requires that any certification of an appeal, bankruptcy court judgment, order, or decree directly to the United States Court of Appeals by all the appellants and appellees (if any) acting jointly be filed on this form.

B25A (Official Form 25A) (12/08)

# United States Bankruptcy Court

____________________ District of ______________

In re____________________, Case No. ____________________
Debtor

Small Business Case under Chapter 11

## [NAME OF PROPONENT]'S PLAN OF REORGANIZATION, DATED [INSERT DATE]

## ARTICLE I
## SUMMARY

This Plan of Reorganization (the "Plan") under chapter 11 of the Bankruptcy Code (the "Code") proposes to pay creditors of [insert the name of the debtor] (the "Debtor") from [specify sources of payment, such as an infusion of capital, loan proceeds, sale of assets, cash flow from operations, or future income].

This Plan provides for __________ classes of secured claims; _____ classes of unsecured claims; and ______ classes of equity security holders. Unsecured creditors holding allowed claims will receive distributions, which the proponent of this Plan has valued at approximately __ cents on the dollar. This Plan also provides for the payment of administrative and priority claims [if payment is not in full on the effective date of this Plan with respect to any such claim (to the extent permitted by the Code or the claimant's agreement), identify such claim and briefly summarize the proposed treatment.]

All creditors and equity security holders should refer to Articles III through VI of this Plan for information regarding the precise treatment of their claim. A disclosure statement that provides more detailed information regarding this Plan and the rights of creditors and equity security holders has been circulated with this Plan. **Your rights may be affected. You should read these papers carefully and discuss them with your attorney, if you have one. (If you do not have an attorney, you may wish to consult one.)**

## ARTICLE II
## CLASSIFICATION OF CLAIMS AND INTERESTS

2.01 Class 1. All allowed claims entitled to priority under § 507 of the Code (except administrative expense claims under § 507(a)(2), ["gap" period claims in an involuntary case under § 507(a)(3),] and priority tax claims under § 507(a)(8)).

2.02 Class 2. The claim of ________________________, to the extent allowed as a secured claim under § 506 of the Code.

**B25A (Official Form 25A) (12/08) - Cont.** 2

[Add other classes of secured creditors, if any. Note: Section 1129(a)(9)(D) of the Code provides that a secured tax claim which would otherwise meet the description of a priority tax claim under § 507(a)(8) of the Code is to be paid in the same manner and over the same period as prescribed in § 507(a)(8).]

2.03 Class 3. All unsecured claims allowed under § 502 of the Code.

[Add other classes of unsecured claims, if any.]

2.04 Class 4 . Equity interests of the Debtor. [If the Debtor is an individual, change this heading to "The interests of the individual Debtor in property of the estate."]

**ARTICLE III**
**TREATMENT OF ADMINISTRATIVE EXPENSE CLAIMS, U.S. TRUSTEES FEES, AND PRIORITY TAX CLAIMS**

3.01 Unclassified Claims. Under section §1123(a)(1), administrative expense claims, ["gap" period claims in an involuntary case allowed under § 502(f) of the Code,] and priority tax claims are not in classes.

3.02 Administrative Expense Claims. Each holder of an administrative expense claim allowed under § 503 of the Code [, and a "gap" claim in an involuntary case allowed under § 502(f) of the Code,] will be paid in full on the effective date of this Plan (as defined in Article VII), in cash, or upon such other terms as may be agreed upon by the holder of the claim and the Debtor.

3.03 Priority Tax Claims. Each holder of a priority tax claim will be paid [specify terms of treatment consistent with § 1129(a)(9)(C) of the Code].

3.04 United States Trustee Fees. All fees required to be paid by 28 U.S.C. §1930(a)(6) (U.S. Trustee Fees) will accrue and be timely paid until the case is closed, dismissed, or converted to another chapter of the Code. Any U.S. Trustee Fees owed on or before the effective date of this Plan will be paid on the effective date.

**ARTICLE IV**
**TREATMENT OF CLAIMS AND INTERESTS UNDER THE PLAN**

4.01 Claims and interests shall be treated as follows under this Plan:

**B25A (Official Form 25A) (12/08) - Cont.**



| Class | Impairment | Treatment |
|---|---|---|
| Class 1 - Priority Claims | [State whether impaired or unimpaired.] | [Insert treatment of priority claims in this Class, including the form, amount and timing of distribution, if any. For example: "Class 1 is unimpaired by this Plan, and each holder of a Class 1 Priority Claim will be paid in full, in cash, upon the later of the effective date of this Plan as defined in Article VII, or the date on which such claim is allowed by a final non-appealable order. Except: ________."] |
| Class 2 – Secured Claim of [Insert name of secured creditor.] | [State whether impaired or unimpaired.] | [Insert treatment of secured claim in this Class, including the form, amount and timing of distribution, if any.]<br>[Add class[es] of secured claims if applicable] |
| Class 3 - General Unsecured Creditors | [State whether impaired or unimpaired.] | [Insert treatment of unsecured creditors in this Class, including the form, amount and timing of distribution, if any.]<br>[Add administrative convenience class if applicable] |
| Class 4 - Equity Security Holders of the Debtor | [State whether impaired or unimpaired.] | [Insert treatment of equity security holders in this Class, including the form, amount and timing of distribution, if any.] |

## ARTICLE V
## ALLOWANCE AND DISALLOWANCE OF CLAIMS

5.01 Disputed Claim. A disputed claim is a claim that has not been allowed or disallowed [by a final non-appealable order], and as to which either: (i) a proof of claim has been filed or deemed filed, and the Debtor or another party in interest has filed an objection; or (ii) no proof of claim has been filed, and the Debtor has scheduled such claim as disputed, contingent, or unliquidated.

5.02 Delay of Distribution on a Disputed Claim. No distribution will be made on account of a disputed claim unless such claim is allowed [by a final non-appealable order].

5.03 Settlement of Disputed Claims. The Debtor will have the power and authority to settle and compromise a disputed claim with court approval and compliance with Rule 9019 of the Federal Rules of Bankruptcy Procedure.

**ARTICLE VI**
**PROVISIONS FOR EXECUTORY CONTRACTS AND UNEXPIRED LEASES**

6.01 Assumed Executory Contracts and Unexpired Leases.

(a) The Debtor assumes the following executory contracts and/or unexpired leases effective upon the [Insert "effective date of this Plan as provided in Article VII," "the date of the entry of the order confirming this Plan," or other applicable date]:

[List assumed executory contracts and/or unexpired leases.]

(b) The Debtor will be conclusively deemed to have rejected all executory contracts and/or unexpired leases not expressly assumed under section 6.01(a) above, or before the date of the order confirming this Plan, upon the [Insert "effective date of this Plan," "the date of the entry of the order confirming this Plan," or other applicable date]. A proof of a claim arising from the rejection of an executory contract or unexpired lease under this section must be filed no later than __________ (___) days after the date of the order confirming this Plan.

**ARTICLE VII**
**MEANS FOR IMPLEMENTATION OF THE PLAN**

[Insert here provisions regarding how the plan will be implemented as required under §1123(a)(5) of the Code. For example, provisions may include those that set out how the plan will be funded, as well as who will be serving as directors, officers or voting trustees of the reorganized debtor.]

**ARTICLE VIII**
**GENERAL PROVISIONS**

8.01 Definitions and Rules of Construction. The definitions and rules of construction set forth in §§ 101 and 102 of the Code shall apply when terms defined or construed in the Code are used in this Plan, and they are supplemented by the following definitions: [Insert additional definitions if necessary].

8.02 Effective Date of Plan. The effective date of this Plan is the eleventh business day following the date of the entry of the order of confirmation. But if a stay of the confirmation order is in effect on that date, the effective date will be the first business day after that date on which no stay of the confirmation order is in effect, provided that the confirmation order has not been vacated.

8.03 Severability. If any provision in this Plan is determined to be unenforceable, the determination will in no way limit or affect the enforceability and operative effect of any other provision of this Plan.

8.04 Binding Effect. The rights and obligations of any entity named or referred to in this Plan will be binding upon, and will inure to the benefit of the successors or assigns of such entity.

8.05 Captions. The headings contained in this Plan are for convenience of reference only and do not affect the meaning or interpretation of this Plan.

[8.06 Controlling Effect. Unless a rule of law or procedure is supplied by federal law (including the Code or the Federal Rules of Bankruptcy Procedure), the laws of the State of ___________ govern this Plan and any agreements, documents, and instruments executed in connection with this Plan, except as otherwise provided in this Plan.]

[8.07 Corporate Governance. [If the Debtor is a corporation include provisions required by § 1123(a)(6) of the Code.]]

## ARTICLE IX
## DISCHARGE

[If the Debtor is not entitled to discharge under 11 U.S.C. § 1141(d)(3) change this heading to **"NO DISCHARGE OF DEBTOR."**]

9.01. **[Option 1 – If Debtor is an individual and § 1141(d)(3) is not applicable]**
Discharge. Confirmation of this Plan does not discharge any debt provided for in this Plan until the court grants a discharge on completion of all payments under this Plan, or as otherwise provided in § 1141(d)(5) of the Code. The Debtor will not be discharged from any debt excepted from discharge under § 523 of the Code, except as provided in Rule 4007(c) of the Federal Rules of Bankruptcy Procedure.

**[Option 2 -- If the Debtor is a partnership and section 1141(d)(3) of the Code is not applicable]**
Discharge. On the confirmation date of this Plan, the debtor will be discharged from any debt that arose before confirmation of this Plan, subject to the occurrence of the effective date, to the extent specified in § 1141(d)(1)(A) of the Code. The Debtor will not be discharged from any debt imposed by this Plan.

**[Option 3 -- If the Debtor is a corporation and § 1141(d)(3) is not applicable]**

**B25A (Official Form 25A) (12/08) - Cont.** 6

Discharge. On the confirmation date of this Plan, the debtor will be discharged from any debt that arose before confirmation of this Plan, subject to the occurrence of the effective date, to the extent specified in § 1141(d)(1)(A) of the Code, except that the Debtor will not be discharged of any debt: (i) imposed by this Plan; (ii) of a kind specified in § 1141(d)(6)(A) if a timely complaint was filed in accordance with Rule 4007(c) of the Federal Rules of Bankruptcy Procedure; or (iii) of a kind specified in § 1141(d)(6)(B).

**[Option 4 – If § 1141(d)(3) is applicable]**

No Discharge. In accordance with § 1141(d)(3) of the Code, the Debtor will not receive any discharge of debt in this bankruptcy case.

**ARTICLE X**
**OTHER PROVISIONS**

**[Insert other provisions, as applicable.]**

Respectfully submitted,

By: ______________________________
The Plan Proponent

By: ______________________________
Attorney for the Plan Proponent

(Added Dec. 1, 2008.)

COMMITTEE NOTES ON RULES—2008

This form is new. It implements §433 of the Bankruptcy Abuse Prevention and Consumer Protection Act of 2005, Pub. L. No. 109-8, 119 Stat. 23 (April 20, 2005). This form for a small business chapter 11 plan of reorganization may be used in cases where the debtor (whether an individual or an artificial entity) is a small business debtor under §101(51D) of the Code. The form is intended to be used in conjunction with the small business chapter 11 disclosure statement form (Official Form 25B).

Because the type of debtor and the details of the proposed plan of reorganization may vary, the form is intended to provide an illustrative format, rather than a specific prescription for the language or content of a plan in any particular case. The form includes instructions and examples of the types of information needed to complete it.

B25B (Official Form 25B) (12/08)

# United States Bankruptcy Court

___________________ District of _______________

In re______________________, Case No. ____________________
Debtor

Small Business Case under Chapter 11

**[NAME OF PLAN PROPONENT]'S DISCLOSURE STATEMENT, DATED [INSERT DATE]**

*Table of Contents*

[Insert when text is finalized]

# I. INTRODUCTION

This is the disclosure statement (the "Disclosure Statement") in the small business chapter 11 case of ______________ (the "Debtor"). This Disclosure Statement contains information about the Debtor and describes the [insert name of plan] (the "Plan") filed by [the Debtor] on [insert date]. A full copy of the Plan is attached to this Disclosure Statement as Exhibit A. ***Your rights may be affected. You should read the Plan and this Disclosure Statement carefully and discuss them with your attorney. If you do not have an attorney, you may wish to consult one.***

The proposed distributions under the Plan are discussed at pages __-__ of this Disclosure Statement. [General unsecured creditors are classified in Class __, and will receive a distribution of ___% of their allowed claims, to be distributed as follows _________.]

## A. Purpose of This Document

This Disclosure Statement describes:

- The Debtor and significant events during the bankruptcy case,
- How the Plan proposes to treat claims or equity interests of the type you hold (*i.e.*, what you will receive on your claim or equity interest if the plan is confirmed),
- Who can vote on or object to the Plan,
- What factors the Bankruptcy Court (the "Court") will consider when deciding whether to confirm the Plan,
- Why [the Proponent] believes the Plan is feasible, and how the treatment of your claim or equity interest under the Plan compares to what you would receive on your claim or equity interest in liquidation, and
- The effect of confirmation of the Plan.

Be sure to read the Plan as well as the Disclosure Statement. This Disclosure Statement describes the Plan, but it is the Plan itself that will, if confirmed, establish your rights.

## B. Deadlines for Voting and Objecting; Date of Plan Confirmation Hearing

The Court has not yet confirmed the Plan described in this Disclosure Statement. This section describes the procedures pursuant to which the Plan will or will not be confirmed.

### 1. *Time and Place of the Hearing to [Finally Approve This Disclosure Statement and] Confirm the Plan*

The hearing at which the Court will determine whether to [finally approve this Disclosure Statement and] confirm the Plan will take place on [insert date], at [insert time], in Courtroom _____, at the [Insert Courthouse Name, and Full Court Address, City, State, Zip Code].

### 2. *Deadline For Voting to Accept or Reject the Plan*

If you are entitled to vote to accept or reject the plan, vote on the enclosed ballot and return the ballot in the enclosed envelope to [insert address]. See section IV.A. below for a discussion of voting eligibility requirements.

Your ballot must be received by [insert date] or it will not be counted.

3. *Deadline For Objecting to the [Adequacy of Disclosure and] Confirmation of the Plan*

Objections to [this Disclosure Statement or to] the confirmation of the Plan must be filed with the Court and served upon [insert entities] by [insert date].

4. *Identity of Person to Contact for More Information*

If you want additional information about the Plan, you should contact [insert name and address of representative of plan proponent].

C. **Disclaimer**

***The Court has [conditionally] approved this Disclosure Statement as containing adequate information to enable parties affected by the Plan to make an informed judgment about its terms. The Court has not yet determined whether the Plan meets the legal requirements for confirmation, and the fact that the Court has approved this Disclosure Statement does not constitute an endorsement of the Plan by the Court, or a recommendation that it be accepted. [The Court's approval of this Disclosure Statement is subject to final approval at the hearing on confirmation of the Plan. Objections to the adequacy of this Disclosure Statement may be filed until ______.]***

## II. BACKGROUND

### A. Description and History of the Debtor's Business

The Debtor is a [corporation, partnership, etc.]. Since [insert year operations commenced], the Debtor has been in the business of _________. [Describe the Debtor's business].

### B. Insiders of the Debtor

[Insert a detailed list of the names of Debtor's insiders as defined in §101(31) of the United States Bankruptcy Code (the "Code") and their relationship to the Debtor. For each insider, list all compensation paid by the Debtor or its affiliates to that person or entity during the two years prior to the commencement of the Debtor's bankruptcy case, as well as compensation paid during the pendency of this chapter 11 case.]

### C. Management of the Debtor Before and During the Bankruptcy

During the two years prior to the date on which the bankruptcy petition was filed, the officers, directors, managers or other persons in control of the Debtor (collectively the "Managers") were [List the Managers of the Debtor prior to the petition date].

The Managers of the Debtor during the Debtor's chapter 11 case have been: [List Managers of the Debtor during the Debtor's chapter 11 case.]

After the effective date of the order confirming the Plan, the directors, officers, and voting trustees of the Debtor, any affiliate of the Debtor participating in a joint Plan with the Debtor, or successor of the Debtor under the Plan (collectively the "Post Confirmation Managers"), will be: [List Post Confirmation Managers of the Debtor.] The responsibilities and compensation of these Post Confirmation Managers are described in section __ of this Disclosure Statement.

D. **Events Leading to Chapter 11 Filing**

[Describe the events that led to the commencement of the Debtor's bankruptcy case.]

E. **Significant Events During the Bankruptcy Case**

[Describe significant events during the Debtor's bankruptcy case:

- Describe any asset sales outside the ordinary course of business, debtor in possession financing, or cash collateral orders.
- Identify the professionals approved by the court.
- Describe any adversary proceedings that have been filed or other significant litigation that has occurred (including contested claim disallowance proceedings), and any other significant legal or administrative proceedings that are pending or have been pending during the case in a forum other than the Court.
- Describe any steps taken to improve operations and profitability of the Debtor.
- Describe other events as appropriate.]

F. **Projected Recovery of Avoidable Transfers [Choose the option that applies]**

**[Option 1 – If the Debtor does not intend to pursue avoidance actions]**

The Debtor does not intend to pursue preference, fraudulent conveyance, or other avoidance actions.

**[Option 2 – If the Debtor intends to pursue avoidance actions]**

The Debtor estimates that up to $____________ may be realized from the recovery of fraudulent, preferential or other avoidable transfers. While the results of litigation cannot be predicted with certainty and it is possible that other causes of action may be identified, the following is a summary of the preference, fraudulent conveyance and other avoidance actions filed or expected to be filed in this case:

| Transaction | Defendant | Amount Claimed |
|---|---|---|
| | | |
| | | |

**[Option 3 – If the Debtor does not yet know whether it intends to pursue avoidance actions]**

The Debtor has not yet completed its investigation with regard to prepetition transactions. If you received a payment or other transfer within 90 days of the bankruptcy, or other transfer avoidable under the Code, the Debtor may seek to avoid such transfer.

G. **Claims Objections**

Except to the extent that a claim is already allowed pursuant to a final non-appealable order, the Debtor reserves the right to object to claims. Therefore, even if your claim is allowed for voting purposes, you may not be entitled to a distribution if an objection to your claim is later upheld. The procedures for resolving disputed claims are set forth in Article V of the Plan.

H. **Current and Historical Financial Conditions**

The identity and fair market value of the estate's assets are listed in Exhibit B. [Identify source and basis of valuation.]

The Debtor's most recent financial statements [if any] issued before bankruptcy, each of which was filed with the Court, are set forth in Exhibit C.

[The most recent post-petition operating report filed since the commencement of the Debtor's bankruptcy case are set forth in Exhibit D.] [A summary of the Debtor's periodic operating reports filed since the commencement of the Debtor's bankruptcy case is set forth in Exhibit D.]

## III. SUMMARY OF THE PLAN OF REORGANIZATION AND TREATMENT OF CLAIMS AND EQUITY INTERESTS

A. **What is the Purpose of the Plan of Reorganization?**

As required by the Code, the Plan places claims and equity interests in various classes and describes the treatment each class will receive. The Plan also states whether each class of claims or equity interests is impaired or unimpaired. If the Plan is confirmed, your recovery will be limited to the amount provided by the Plan.

B. **Unclassified Claims**

Certain types of claims are automatically entitled to specific treatment under the Code. They are not considered impaired, and holders of such claims do not vote on the Plan. They may, however, object if, in their view, their treatment under the Plan does not comply with that required by the Code. As such, the Plan Proponent has *not* placed the following claims in any class:

1. *Administrative Expenses*

Administrative expenses are costs or expenses of administering the Debtor's chapter 11 case which are allowed under § 507(a)(2) of the Code. Administrative expenses also include the value of any goods sold to the Debtor in the ordinary course of business and received within 20 days before the date of the bankruptcy petition. The Code requires that all administrative expenses be paid on the effective date of the Plan, unless a particular claimant agrees to a different treatment.

The following chart lists the Debtor's estimated administrative expenses, and their proposed treatment under the Plan:

| Type | Estimated Amount Owed | Proposed Treatment |
|---|---|---|
| Expenses Arising in the Ordinary Course of Business After the Petition Date | | Paid in full on the effective date of the Plan, or according to terms of obligation if later |
| The Value of Goods Received in the Ordinary Course of Business Within 20 Days Before the Petition Date | | Paid in full on the effective date of the Plan, or according to terms of obligation if later |
| Professional Fees, as approved by the Court. | | Paid in full on the effective date of the Plan, or according to separate written agreement, or according to court order if such fees have not been approved by the Court on the effective date of the Plan |
| Clerk's Office Fees | | Paid in full on the effective date of the Plan |
| Other administrative expenses | | Paid in full on the effective date of the Plan or according to separate written agreement |
| Office of the U.S. Trustee Fees | | Paid in full on the effective date of the Plan |
| TOTAL | | |

2. *Priority Tax Claims*

Priority tax claims are unsecured income, employment, and other taxes described by § 507(a)(8) of the Code. Unless the holder of such a § 507(a)(8) priority tax claim agrees otherwise, it must receive the present value of such claim, in regular installments paid over a period not exceeding 5 years from the order of relief.

The following chart lists the Debtor's estimated § 507(a)(8) priority tax claims and their proposed treatment under the Plan:

| Description (name and type of tax) | Estimated Amount Owed | Date of Assessment | Treatment |
|---|---|---|---|
| | | | Pmt interval = <br>[Monthly] payment = <br>Begin date = <br>End date = <br>Interest Rate % = <br>Total Payout Amount = $ |
| | | | Pmt interval = <br>[Monthly] payment = <br>Begin date = <br>End date = <br>Interest Rate % = <br>Total Payout Amount = $ |

C. **Classes of Claims and Equity Interests**

The following are the classes set forth in the Plan, and the proposed treatment that they will receive under the Plan:

1. *Classes of Secured Claims*

Allowed Secured Claims are claims secured by property of the Debtor's bankruptcy estate (or that are subject to setoff) to the extent allowed as secured claims under § 506 of the Code. If the value of the collateral or setoffs securing the creditor's claim is less than the amount of the creditor's allowed claim, the deficiency will [be classified as a general unsecured claim].

**B25B (Official Form 25B) (12/08) – Cont.**



The following chart lists all classes containing Debtor's secured prepetition claims and their proposed treatment under the Plan:

| Class # | Description | Insider? (Yes or No) | Impairment | Treatment |
|---|---|---|---|---|
| | *Secured claim of:*<br>Name =<br><br>Collateral description =<br><br>Allowed Secured Amount =<br>$________<br><br>Priority of lien =<br><br>Principal owed =<br>$________<br>Pre-pet. arrearage =<br>$________<br><br>Total claim =<br>$________ | | [State whether impaired or unimpaired] | [Monthly] Pmt =<br><br>Pmts Begin =<br><br>Pmts End =<br><br>[Balloon pmt] =<br><br>Interest rate % =<br><br>Treatment of Lien =<br><br>[Additional payment required to cure defaults] = |
| | *Secured claim of:*<br>Name =<br><br>Collateral description =<br><br>Allowed Secured Amount =<br>$________<br>Priority of lien =<br><br>Principal owed =<br>$________<br>Pre-pet. arrearage =<br>$________<br><br>Total claim =<br>$________ | | [State whether impaired or unimpaired] | Monthly Pmt =<br><br>Pmts Begin =<br><br>Pmts End =<br><br>[Balloon pmt] =<br><br>Interest rate % =<br><br>Treatment of Lien =<br><br>[Additional payment required to cure defaults] = |

2. *Classes of Priority Unsecured Claims*

Certain priority claims that are referred to in §§ 507(a)(1), (4), (5), (6), and (7) of the Code are required to be placed in classes. The Code requires that each holder of such a claim receive cash on the effective date of the Plan equal to the allowed amount of such claim. However, a class of holders of such claims may vote to accept different treatment.

The following chart lists all classes containing claims under §§ 507(a)(1), (4), (5), (6), and (a)(7) of the Code and their proposed treatment under the Plan:

| Class # | Description | Impairment | Treatment |
|---|---|---|---|
| | Priority unsecured claim pursuant to Section [insert]<br><br>Total amt of claims =<br>$ | [State whether impaired or unimpaired] | |
| | Priority unsecured claim pursuant to Section [insert]<br><br>Total amt of claims =<br>$ | [State whether impaired or unimpaired] | |

3. *Class[es] of General Unsecured Claims*

General unsecured claims are not secured by property of the estate and are not entitled to priority under § 507(a) of the Code. [Insert description of §1122(b) convenience class if applicable.]

The following chart identifies the Plan's proposed treatment of Class[es] __ through __, which contain general unsecured claims against the Debtor:

| Class # | Description | Impairment | Treatment |
|---|---|---|---|
| | [1122(b) Convenience Class] | [State whether impaired or unimpaired] | [Insert proposed treatment, such as "Paid in full in cash on effective date of the Plan or when due under contract or applicable nonbankruptcy law"] |
| | General Unsecured Class | [State whether impaired or unimpaired] | Monthly Pmt =<br>Pmts Begin =<br>Pmts End =<br>[Balloon pmt] =<br>Interest rate % from [date] =<br>Estimated percent of claim paid = |

4. *Class[es] of Equity Interest Holders*

Equity interest holders are parties who hold an ownership interest (*i.e.*, equity interest) in the Debtor. In a corporation, entities holding preferred or common stock are equity interest holders. In a partnership, equity interest holders include both general and limited partners. In a limited liability company ("LLC"), the equity interest holders are the members. Finally, with respect to an individual who is a debtor, the Debtor is the equity interest holder.

The following chart sets forth the Plan's proposed treatment of the class[es] of equity interest holders: [There may be more than one class of equity interests in, for example, a partnership case, or a case where the prepetition debtor had issued multiple classes of stock.]

| Class # | Description | Impairment | Treatment |
|---|---|---|---|
| | Equity interest holders | [State whether impaired or unimpaired] | |

D. **Means of Implementing the Plan**

1. *Source of Payments*

Payments and distributions under the Plan will be funded by the following:

[Describe the source of funds for payments under the Plan.]

2. *Post-confirmation Management*

The Post-Confirmation Managers of the Debtor, and their compensation, shall be as follows:

| Name | Affiliations | Insider (yes or no)? | Position | Compensation |
|---|---|---|---|---|
| | | | | |
| | | | | |
| | | | | |

E. **Risk Factors**

The proposed Plan has the following risks:

[List all risk factors that might affect the Debtor's ability to make payments and other distributions required under the Plan.]

F. **Executory Contracts and Unexpired Leases**

The Plan, in Exhibit 5.1, lists all executory contracts and unexpired leases that the Debtor will assume under the Plan. Assumption means that the Debtor has elected to continue to perform the obligations under such contracts and unexpired leases, and to cure defaults of the type that must be cured under the Code, if any. Exhibit 5.1 also lists how the Debtor will cure and compensate the other party to such contract or lease for any such defaults.

If you object to the assumption of your unexpired lease or executory contract, the proposed cure of any defaults, or the adequacy of assurance of performance, you must file and serve your objection to the Plan within the deadline for objecting to the confirmation of the Plan, unless the Court has set an earlier time.

All executory contracts and unexpired leases that are not listed in Exhibit 5.1 will be rejected under the Plan. Consult your adviser or attorney for more specific information about particular contracts or leases.

If you object to the rejection of your contract or lease, you must file and serve your objection to the Plan within the deadline for objecting to the confirmation of the Plan.

[***The Deadline for Filing a Proof of Claim Based on a Claim Arising from the Rejection of a Lease or Contract Is*** _______. Any claim based on the rejection of a contract or lease will be barred if the proof of claim is not timely filed, unless the Court orders otherwise.]

G. **Tax Consequences of Plan**

***Creditors and Equity Interest Holders Concerned with How the Plan May Affect Their Tax Liability Should Consult with Their Own Accountants, Attorneys, And/Or Advisors.***

The following are the anticipated tax consequences of the Plan: [List the following general consequences as a minimum: (1)Tax consequences to the Debtor of the Plan; (2) General tax consequences on creditors of any discharge, and the general tax consequences of receipt of plan consideration after confirmation.]

## IV. CONFIRMATION REQUIREMENTS AND PROCEDURES

To be confirmable, the Plan must meet the requirements listed in §§ 1129(a) or (b) of the Code. These include the requirements that: the Plan must be proposed in good faith; at least one impaired class of claims must accept the plan, without counting votes of insiders; the Plan must distribute to each creditor and equity interest holder at least as much as the creditor or equity interest holder would receive in a chapter 7 liquidation case, unless the creditor or equity interest holder votes to accept the Plan; and the Plan must be feasible. These requirements are <u>not</u> the only requirements listed in § 1129, and they are not the only requirements for confirmation.

## A. Who May Vote or Object

Any party in interest may object to the confirmation of the Plan if the party believes that the requirements for confirmation are not met.

Many parties in interest, however, are not entitled to vote to accept or reject the Plan. A creditor or equity interest holder has a right to vote for or against the Plan only if that creditor or equity interest holder has a claim or equity interest that is both (1) allowed or allowed for voting purposes and (2) impaired.

In this case, the Plan Proponent believes that classes ______ are impaired and that holders of claims in each of these classes are therefore entitled to vote to accept or reject the Plan. The Plan Proponent believes that classes ______ are unimpaired and that holders of claims in each of these classes, therefore, do not have the right to vote to accept or reject the Plan.

### 1. *What Is an Allowed Claim or an Allowed Equity Interest?*

Only a creditor or equity interest holder with an allowed claim or an allowed equity interest has the right to vote on the Plan. Generally, a claim or equity interest is allowed if either (1) the Debtor has scheduled the claim on the Debtor's schedules, unless the claim has been scheduled as disputed, contingent, or unliquidated, or (2) the creditor has filed a proof of claim or equity interest, unless an objection has been filed to such proof of claim or equity interest. When a claim or equity interest is not allowed, the creditor or equity interest holder holding the claim or equity interest cannot vote unless the Court, after notice and hearing, either overrules the objection or allows the claim or equity interest for voting purposes pursuant to Rule 3018(a) of the Federal Rules of Bankruptcy Procedure.

***The deadline for filing a proof of claim in this case was ______.***
***[If applicable – The deadline for filing objections to claims is______.]***

### 2. *What Is an Impaired Claim or Impaired Equity Interest?*

As noted above, the holder of an allowed claim or equity interest has the right to vote only if it is in a class that is *impaired* under the Plan. As provided in § 1124 of the Code, a class is considered impaired if the Plan alters the legal, equitable, or contractual rights of the members of that class.

### 3. *Who is **Not** Entitled to Vote*

The holders of the following five types of claims and equity interests are *not* entitled to vote:

- holders of claims and equity interests that have been disallowed by an order of the Court;
- holders of other claims or equity interests that are not "allowed claims" or "allowed equity interests" (as discussed above), unless they have been "allowed" for voting purposes.
- holders of claims or equity interests in unimpaired classes;

- holders of claims entitled to priority pursuant to §§ 507(a)(2), (a)(3), and (a)(8) of the Code; and

- holders of claims or equity interests in classes that do not receive or retain any value under the Plan;

- administrative expenses.

***Even If You Are Not Entitled to Vote on the Plan, You Have a Right to Object to the Confirmation of the Plan [and to the Adequacy of the Disclosure Statement].***

4. *Who Can Vote in More Than One Class*

A creditor whose claim has been allowed in part as a secured claim and in part as an unsecured claim, or who otherwise hold claims in multiple classes, is entitled to accept or reject a Plan in each capacity, and should cast one ballot for each claim.

B. **Votes Necessary to Confirm the Plan**

If impaired classes exist, the Court cannot confirm the Plan unless (1) at least one impaired class of creditors has accepted the Plan without counting the votes of any insiders within that class, and (2) all impaired classes have voted to accept the Plan, unless the Plan is eligible to be confirmed by "cram down" on non-accepting classes, as discussed later in Section [B.2.].

1. *Votes Necessary for a Class to Accept the Plan*

A class of claims accepts the Plan if both of the following occur: (1) the holders of more than one-half (1/2) of the allowed claims in the class, who vote, cast their votes to accept the Plan, and (2) the holders of at least two-thirds (2/3) in dollar amount of the allowed claims in the class, who vote, cast their votes to accept the Plan.

A class of equity interests accepts the Plan if the holders of at least two-thirds (2/3) in amount of the allowed equity interests in the class, who vote, cast their votes to accept the Plan.

2. *Treatment of Nonaccepting Classes*

Even if one or more impaired classes reject the Plan, the Court may nonetheless confirm the Plan if the nonaccepting classes are treated in the manner prescribed by § 1129(b) of the Code. A plan that binds nonaccepting classes is commonly referred to as a "cram down" plan. The Code allows the Plan to bind nonaccepting classes of claims or equity interests if it meets all the requirements for consensual confirmation except the voting requirements of § 1129(a)(8) of the Code, does not "discriminate unfairly," and is "fair and equitable" toward each impaired class that has not voted to accept the Plan.

***You should consult your own attorney if a "cramdown" confirmation will affect your claim or equity interest, as the variations on this general rule are numerous and complex.***

C. **Liquidation Analysis**

To confirm the Plan, the Court must find that all creditors and equity interest holders who do not accept the Plan will receive at least as much under the Plan as such claim and equity interest holders would receive in a chapter 7 liquidation. A liquidation analysis is attached to this Disclosure Statement as Exhibit E.

D. **Feasibility**

The Court must find that confirmation of the Plan is not likely to be followed by the liquidation, or the need for further financial reorganization, of the Debtor or any successor to the Debtor, unless such liquidation or reorganization is proposed in the Plan.

1. *Ability to Initially Fund Plan*

The Plan Proponent believes that the Debtor will have enough cash on hand on the effective date of the Plan to pay all the claims and expenses that are entitled to be paid on that date. Tables showing the amount of cash on hand on the effective date of the Plan, and the sources of that cash are attached to this disclosure statement as Exhibit F.

2. *Ability to Make Future Plan Payments And Operate Without Further Reorganization*

The Plan Proponent must also show that it will have enough cash over the life of the Plan to make the required Plan payments.

The Plan Proponent has provided projected financial information. Those projections are listed in Exhibit G.

The Plan Proponent's financial projections show that the Debtor will have an aggregate annual average cash flow, after paying operating expenses and post-confirmation taxes, of $_-_. The final Plan payment is expected to be paid on _____.

[Summarize the numerical projections, and highlight any assumptions that are not in accord with past experience. Explain why such assumptions should now be made.]

***You Should Consult with Your Accountant or other Financial Advisor If You Have Any Questions Pertaining to These Projections.***

V. **EFFECT OF CONFIRMATION OF PLAN**

A. **DISCHARGE OF DEBTOR** [If the Debtor is not entitled to discharge pursuant to 11 U.S.C. § 1141(d)(3) change this heading to "**NO DISCHARGE OF DEBTOR.**"]

**[Option 1 – If Debtor is an individual and § 1141(d)(3) is not applicable]**

Discharge. Confirmation of the Plan does not discharge any debt provided for in the Plan until the court grants a discharge on completion of all payments under the Plan, or as otherwise provided in § 1141(d)(5) of the Code. Debtor will not be discharged from any debt excepted from discharge under § 523 of the Code, except as provided in Rule 4007(c) of the Federal Rules of Bankruptcy Procedure.

**[Option 2 -- If the Debtor is a partnership and § 1141(d)(3) of the Code is not applicable]**

Discharge. On the effective date of the Plan, the Debtor shall be discharged from any debt that arose before confirmation of the Plan, subject to the occurrence of the effective date, to the extent specified in § 1141(d)(1)(A) of the Code. However, the Debtor shall not be discharged from any debt imposed by the Plan. After the effective date of the Plan your claims against the Debtor will be limited to the debts imposed by the Plan.

**[Option 3 -- If the Debtor is a corporation and § 1141(d)(3) is not applicable]**

Discharge. On the effective date of the Plan, the Debtor shall be discharged from any debt that arose before confirmation of the Plan, subject to the occurrence of the effective date, to the extent specified in § 1141(d)(1)(A) of the Code, except that the Debtor shall not be discharged of any debt (i) imposed by the Plan, (ii) of a kind specified in § 1141(d)(6)(A) if a timely complaint was filed in accordance with Rule 4007(c) of the Federal Rules of Bankruptcy Procedure, or (iii) of a kind specified in § 1141(d)(6)(B). After the effective date of the Plan your claims against the Debtor will be limited to the debts described in clauses (i) through (iii) of the preceding sentence.

**[Option 4 – If § 1141(d)(3) is applicable]**

No Discharge. In accordance with § 1141(d)(3) of the Code, the Debtor will not receive any discharge of debt in this bankruptcy case.

## B. Modification of Plan

The Plan Proponent may modify the Plan at any time before confirmation of the Plan. However, the Court may require a new disclosure statement and/or revoting on the Plan.

[If the Debtor is not an individual, add the following: "The Plan Proponent may also seek to modify the Plan at any time after confirmation only if (1) the Plan has not been substantially consummated *and* (2) the Court authorizes the proposed modifications after notice and a hearing."]

[If the Debtor is an individual, add the following: "Upon request of the Debtor, the United States trustee, or the holder of an allowed unsecured claim, the Plan may be modified at any time after confirmation of the Plan but before the completion of payments under the Plan, to (1) increase or reduce the amount of payments under the Plan on claims of a particular class, (2) extend or reduce the time period for such payments, or (3) alter the amount of distribution to a creditor whose claim is provided for by the Plan to the extent necessary to take account of any payment of the claim made other than under the Plan."]

## C. Final Decree

Once the estate has been fully administered, as provided in Rule 3022 of the Federal Rules of Bankruptcy Procedure, the Plan Proponent, or such other party as the Court shall designate in the Plan Confirmation Order, shall file a motion with the Court to obtain a final decree to close the case. Alternatively, the Court may enter such a final decree on its own motion.

## VI. OTHER PLAN PROVISIONS

[Insert other provisions here, as necessary and appropriate.]

______________________________
[Signature of the Plan Proponent]

______________________________
[Signature of the Attorney for the Plan Proponent]



## EXHIBITS



**Exhibit A –** Copy of Proposed Plan of Reorganization



**Exhibit B –** Identity and Value of Material Assets of Debtor



**Exhibit C –** Prepetition Financial Statements
(to be taken from those filed with the court)



**Exhibit D –** [Most Recently Filed Postpetition Operating Report][Summary of Postpetition Operating Reports]

**Exhibit E** – Liquidation Analysis

***Plan Proponent's Estimated Liquidation Value of Assets***

| | |
|---|---|
| **Assets** | |
| a. Cash on hand | $ |
| b. Accounts receivable | $ |
| c. Inventory | $ |
| d. Office furniture & equipment | $ |
| e. Machinery & equipment | $ |
| f. Automobiles | $ |
| g. Building & Land | $ |
| h. Customer list | $ |
| i. Investment property (such as stocks, bonds or other financial assets) | $ |
| j. Lawsuits or other claims against third-parties | $ |
| k. Other intangibles (such as avoiding powers actions) | $ |
| ***Total Assets at Liquidation Value*** | $ |
| **Less:** Secured creditors' recoveries | $ |
| **Less:** Chapter 7 trustee fees and expenses | $ |
| **Less:** Chapter 11 administrative expenses | $ |
| **Less:** Priority claims, excluding administrative expense claims | $ |
| **[Less:** Debtor's claimed exemptions] | $ |
| (1) Balance for unsecured claims | $ |
| (2) Total dollar amount of unsecured claims | $ |
| ***Percentage of Claims Which Unsecured Creditors Would Receive Or Retain in a Chapter 7 Liquidation:*** | $ |
| ***Percentage of Claims Which Unsecured Creditors Will Receive or Retain under the Plan:*** | ____% [Divide (1) by (2)] |
| | ____% |

B25B (Official Form 25B) (12/08) – Cont. 23

**Exhibit F** – Cash on hand on the effective date of the Plan

| | |
|---|---|
| **Cash on hand on effective date of the Plan:** | $ |
| *Less* – | |
| Amount of administrative expenses payable on effective date of the Plan | - |
| Amount of statutory costs and charges | - |
| Amount of cure payments for executory contracts | - |
| Other Plan Payments due on effective date of the Plan | - |
| Balance after paying these amounts............... | $ |

The sources of the cash Debtor will have on hand by the effective date of the Plan are estimated as follows:

| | |
|---|---|
| $ | Cash in Debtor's bank account now |
| + | Additional cash Debtor will accumulate from net earnings between now and effective date of the Plan [state the basis for such projections] |
| + | Borrowing [separately state terms of repayment] |
| + | Capital Contributions |
| + | Other |
| $ | Total [This number should match "cash on hand" figure noted above |

B25B (Official Form 25B) (12/08) – Cont. 24

**Exhibit G** – Projections of Cash Flow and Earnings for Post-Confirmation Period

(Added Dec. 1, 2008.)

COMMITTEE NOTES ON RULES—2008

This form is new. It implements §433 of the Bankruptcy Abuse Prevention and Consumer Protection Act of 2005, Pub. L. No. 109-8, 119 Stat. 23 (April 20, 2005), which provides for an official form for a disclosure statement that may be used in cases where the debtor (whether an individual or an artificial entity) is a small business debtor under §101(51D) of the Code. The form provides a format for disseminating information to parties in interest about the plan of reorganization in a small business debtor's chapter 11 case, so that a party can make a reasonably informed judgment whether to accept, reject, or object to a proposed plan of reorganization or liquidation.

The form is intended to be used in conjunction with the form small business chapter 11 plan (Official Form 25A). As required by §433 of the 2005 Act, the form seeks to strike a practical balance between the reasonable needs of the courts, the United States trustee, creditors, and other parties in interest for reasonably complete information, on the one hand, and economy and simplicity for debtors, on the other. The form includes instructions and examples of the types of information needed to complete it.

Because the relevant legal requirements for, and effect of, a plan's confirmation may vary depending on the nature of the debtor and the details of the proposed plan, this form is intended to provide an illustrative format for disclosure, rather than a specific prescription for the language or content of a particular disclosure statement. The form highlights the factual and legal disclosures required for adequate disclosure under §1125 of the Code. The form is not intended to restrict a plan proponent from providing additional information where that would be useful. Plan proponents are encouraged to present material information in as clear a manner as possible, including, where feasible, by providing an accompanying executive summary, approved by the court, that highlights particular creditors' or interest holders' voting status and treatment under the plan.

Rule 3016 specifies the manner in which the disclosure statement is to be filed. Rule 3017 specifies the manner in which the court will consider it. Rule 3017.1 specifies special procedures for the court's conditional approval of a disclosure statement in a small business case.

B 25C (Official Form 25C) (12/08)

# UNITED STATES BANKRUPTCY COURT

In re ______________________________,
*Debtor*

Case No. ________________

Small Business Case under Chapter 11

## SMALL BUSINESS MONTHLY OPERATING REPORT

Month: ________________ Date filed: ____________________

Line of Business: ______________________________ NAISC Code: ____________________

IN ACCORDANCE WITH TITLE 28, SECTION 1746, OF THE UNITED STATES CODE, I DECLARE UNDER PENALTY OF PERJURY THAT I HAVE EXAMINED THE FOLLOWING SMALL BUSINESS MONTHLY OPERATING REPORT AND THE ACCOMPANYING ATTACHMENTS AND, TO THE BEST OF MY KNOWLEDGE, THESE DOCUMENTS ARE TRUE, CORRECT AND COMPLETE.

RESPONSIBLE PARTY:

______________________________________________
Original Signature of Responsible Party

______________________________________________
Printed Name of Responsible Party

| **Questionnaire:** *(All questions to be answered on behalf of the debtor.)* | **Yes** | **No** |
|---|---|---|
| 1. IS THE BUSINESS STILL OPERATING? | ❐ | ❐ |
| 2. HAVE YOU PAID ALL YOUR BILLS ON TIME THIS MONTH? | ❐ | ❐ |
| 3. DID YOU PAY YOUR EMPLOYEES ON TIME? | ❐ | ❐ |
| 4. HAVE YOU DEPOSITED ALL THE RECEIPTS FOR YOUR BUSINESS INTO THE DIP ACCOUNT THIS MONTH? | ❐ | ❐ |
| 5. HAVE YOU FILED ALL OF YOUR TAX RETURNS AND PAID ALL OF YOUR TAXES THIS MONTH | ❐ | ❐ |
| 6. HAVE YOU TIMELY FILED ALL OTHER REQUIRED GOVERNMENT FILINGS? | ❐ | ❐ |
| 7. HAVE YOU PAID ALL OF YOUR INSURANCE PREMIUMS THIS MONTH? | ❐ | ❐ |
| 8. DO YOU PLAN TO CONTINUE TO OPERATE THE BUSINESS NEXT MONTH? | ❐ | ❐ |
| 9. ARE YOU CURRENT ON YOUR QUARTERLY FEE PAYMENT TO THE U.S. TRUSTEE? | ❐ | ❐ |
| 10. HAVE YOU PAID ANYTHING TO YOUR ATTORNEY OR OTHER PROFESSIONALS THIS MONTH? | ❐ | ❐ |
| 11. DID YOU HAVE ANY UNUSUAL OR SIGNIFICANT UNANTICIPATED EXPENSES THIS MONTH? | ❐ | ❐ |
| 12. HAS THE BUSINESS SOLD ANY GOODS OR PROVIDED SERVICES OR TRANSFERRED ANY ASSETS TO ANY BUSINESS RELATED TO THE DIP IN ANY WAY? | ❐ | ❐ |
| 13. DO YOU HAVE ANY BANK ACCOUNTS OPEN OTHER THAN THE DIP ACCOUNT? | ❐ | ❐ |

| | | |
|---|---|---|
| 14. HAVE YOU SOLD ANY ASSETS OTHER THAN INVENTORY THIS MONTH? | ❒ | ❒ |
| 15. DID ANY INSURANCE COMPANY CANCEL YOUR POLICY THIS MONTH? | ❒ | ❒ |
| 16. HAVE YOU BORROWED MONEY FROM ANYONE THIS MONTH? | ❒ | ❒ |
| 17. HAS ANYONE MADE AN INVESTMENT IN YOUR BUSINESS THIS MONTH? | ❒ | ❒ |
| 18. HAVE YOU PAID ANY BILLS YOU OWED BEFORE YOU FILED BANKRUPTCY? | ❒ | ❒ |

**TAXES**

DO YOU HAVE ANY PAST DUE TAX RETURNS OR PAST DUE POST-PETITION TAX OBLIGATIONS? ❒ ❒

IF YES, PLEASE PROVIDE A WRITTEN EXPLANATION INCLUDING WHEN SUCH RETURNS WILL BE FILED, OR WHEN SUCH PAYMENTS WILL BE MADE AND THE SOURCE OF THE FUNDS FOR THE PAYMENT.

*(Exhibit A)*

**INCOME**

PLEASE SEPARATELY LIST ALL OF THE INCOME YOU RECEIVED FOR THE MONTH. THE LIST SHOULD INCLUDE ALL INCOME FROM CASH AND CREDIT TRANSACTIONS. *(THE U.S. TRUSTEE MAY WAIVE THIS REQUIREMENT.)*

**TOTAL INCOME** $ ______

**SUMMARY OF CASH ON HAND**

Cash on Hand at Start of Month $ ______

Cash on Hand at End of Month $ ______

PLEASE PROVIDE THE TOTAL AMOUNT OF CASH CURRENTLY AVAILABLE TO YOU **TOTAL** $ ______

*(Exhibit B)*

**EXPENSES**

PLEASE SEPARATELY LIST ALL EXPENSES PAID BY CASH OR BY CHECK FROM YOUR BANK ACCOUNTS THIS MONTH. INCLUDE THE DATE PAID, WHO WAS PAID THE MONEY, THE PURPOSE AND THE AMOUNT. *(THE U.S. TRUSTEE MAY WAIVE THIS REQUIREMENT.)*

**TOTAL EXPENSES** $ ______

*(Exhibit C)*

**CASH PROFIT**

INCOME FOR THE MONTH *(TOTAL FROM EXHIBIT B)* $ ______

EXPENSES FOR THE MONTH *(TOTAL FROM EXHIBIT C)* $ ______

*(Subtract Line C from Line B)* **CASH PROFIT FOR THE MONTH** $ ______

B 25C (Official Form 25C) (12/08)

**UNPAID BILLS**

PLEASE ATTACH A LIST OF ALL DEBTS (INCLUDING TAXES) WHICH YOU HAVE INCURRED SINCE THE DATE YOU FILED BANKRUPTCY BUT HAVE NOT PAID. THE LIST MUST INCLUDE THE DATE THE DEBT WAS INCURRED, WHO IS OWED THE MONEY, THE PURPOSE OF THE DEBT AND WHEN THE DEBT IS DUE. *(THE U.S. TRUSTEE MAY WAIVE THIS REQUIREMENT.)*

**TOTAL PAYABLES** $ ________

*(Exhibit D)*

**MONEY OWED TO YOU**

PLEASE ATTACH A LIST OF ALL AMOUNTS OWED TO YOU BY YOUR CUSTOMERS FOR WORK YOU HAVE DONE OR THE MERCHANDISE YOU HAVE SOLD. YOU SHOULD INCLUDE WHO OWES YOU MONEY, HOW MUCH IS OWED AND WHEN IS PAYMENT DUE. *(THE U.S. TRUSTEE MAY WAIVE THIS REQUIREMENT.)*

**TOTAL RECEIVABLES** $ ________

*(Exhibit E)*

**BANKING INFORMATION**

PLEASE ATTACH A COPY OF YOUR LATEST BANK STATEMENT FOR EVERY ACCOUNT YOU HAVE AS OF THE DATE OF THIS FINANCIAL REPORT OR HAD DURING THE PERIOD COVERED BY THIS REPORT.

*(Exhibit F)*

**EMPLOYEES**

NUMBER OF EMPLOYEES WHEN THE CASE WAS FILED? ________

NUMBER OF EMPLOYEES AS OF THE DATE OF THIS MONTHLY REPORT? ________

**PROFESSIONAL FEES**

*BANKRUPTCY RELATED:*

PROFESSIONAL FEES RELATING TO THE BANKRUPTCY CASE PAID DURING THIS REPORTING PERIOD? $ ________

TOTAL PROFESSIONAL FEES RELATING TO THE BANKRUPTCY CASE PAID SINCE THE FILING OF THE CASE? $ ________

*NON-BANKRUPTCY RELATED:*

PROFESSIONAL FEES NOT RELATING TO THE BANKRUPTCY CASE PAID DURING THIS REPORTING PERIOD? $ ________

TOTAL PROFESSIONAL FEES NOT RELATING TO THE BANKRUPTCY CASE PAID SINCE THE FILING OF THE CASE? $ ________

**PROJECTIONS**

COMPARE YOUR ACTUAL INCOME AND EXPENSES TO THE PROJECTIONS FOR THE FIRST 180 DAYS OF YOUR CASE PROVIDED AT THE INITIAL DEBTOR INTERVIEW.

| | Projected | Actual | Difference |
|---|---|---|---|
| INCOME | $ | $ | $ |
| EXPENSES | $ | $ | $ |
| CASH PROFIT | $ | $ | $ |

| | |
|---|---|
| TOTAL PROJECTED INCOME FOR THE NEXT MONTH: | $ |
| TOTAL PROJECTED EXPENSES FOR THE NEXT MONTH: | $ |
| TOTAL PROJECTED CASH PROFIT FOR THE NEXT MONTH: | $ |

**ADDITIONAL INFORMATION**

**PLEASE ATTACH ALL FINANCIAL REPORTS INCLUDING AN INCOME STATEMENT AND BALANCE SHEET WHICH YOU PREPARE INTERNALLY.**

(Added Dec. 1, 2008.)

COMMITTEE NOTES ON RULES—2008

This form is new. It implements §§434 and 435 of the Bankruptcy Abuse Prevention and Consumer Protection Act of 2005, Pub. L. No. 109-8, 119 Stat. 23 (April 20, 2005), which provided for rules and an official form to assist small business debtors in chapter 11 cases to fulfill their responsibilities under §308 of the Code, a provision added by the 2005 Act. The form directs the debtor to disclose the information required under §308 and resembles those developed earlier by the United States trustees for use in supervising debtors in possession in chapter 11 cases.

**Official Form 26 (12/08)**

# United States Bankruptcy Court

_________________ District of ____________

In re______________________, Case No. _______________

Debtor Chapter 11

## PERIODIC REPORT REGARDING VALUE, OPERATIONS AND PROFITABILITY OF ENTITIES IN WHICH THE ESTATE OF [NAME OF DEBTOR] HOLDS A SUBSTANTIAL OR CONTROLLING INTEREST

This is the report as of __________on the value, operations and profitability of those entities in which the estate holds a substantial or controlling interest, as required by Bankruptcy Rule 2015.3. The estate of [Name of Debtor] holds a substantial or controlling interest in the following entities:

| Name of Entity | Interest of the Estate | Tab # |
|---|---|---|
| | | |
| | | |
| | | |

This periodic report (the "Periodic Report") contains separate reports ("Entity Reports") on the value, operations, and profitability of each entity listed above.

Each Entity Report shall consist of three exhibits. Exhibit A contains a valuation estimate for the entity as of a date not more than two years prior to the date of this report. It also contains a description of the valuation method used. Exhibit B contains a balance sheet, a statement of income (loss), a statement of cash flows, and a statement of changes in shareholders' or partners' equity (deficit) for the period covered by the Entity Report, along with summarized footnotes. Exhibit C contains a description of the entity's business operations.

THIS REPORT MUST BE SIGNED BY A REPRESENTATIVE OF THE TRUSTEE OR DEBTOR IN POSSESSION.

The undersigned, having reviewed the above listing of entities in which the estate of [Debtor] holds a substantial or controlling interest, and being familiar with the Debtor's financial affairs, verifies under the penalty of perjury that the listing is complete, accurate and truthful to the best of his/her knowledge.

Official Form 26 (12/08) – Cont. 2

Date: ___________

_______________________________
Signature of Authorized Individual

_______________________________
Name of Authorized Individual

_______________________________
Title of Authorized Individual

[If the Debtor is an individual or in a joint case]

Signature(s) of Debtor(s) (Individual/Joint)

_______________________________
Signature of Debtor

_______________________________
Signature of Joint Debtor

Official Form 26 (12/08) – Cont. 3

**Exhibit A**
**Valuation Estimate for [Name of Entity]**

[Provide a statement of the entity's value and the value of the estate's interest in the entity, including a description of the basis for the valuation, the date of the valuation and the valuation method used. This valuation must be no more than two years old. Indicate the source of this information.]

Official Form 26 (12/08) – Cont. 4

**Exhibit B**
**Financial Statements for [Insert Name of Entity]**

Official Form 26 (12/08) – Cont. 5

**Exhibit B-1**
**Balance Sheet for [Name of Entity]**
As of [date]

[Provide a balance sheet dated as of the end of the most recent six-month period of the current fiscal year and as of the end of the preceding fiscal year. Indicate the source of this information.]

**Exhibit B-2**

**<u>Statement of Income (Loss) for [Name of Entity]</u>**

Period ending [date]

[Provide a statement of income (loss) for the following periods:

(i) For the initial report:
  a. the period between the end of the preceding fiscal year and the end of the most recent six-month period of the current fiscal year; and
  b. the prior fiscal year.
(ii) For subsequent reports, since the closing date of the last report.

Indicate the source of this information.]



**Exhibit B-3**

**<u>Statement of Cash Flows for [Name of Entity]</u>**

For the period ending [date]

[Provide a statement of changes in cash flows for the following periods:

(i) For the initial report:
  a. the period between the end of the preceding fiscal year and the end of the most recent six-month period of the current fiscal year; and
  b. the prior fiscal year.
(ii) For subsequent reports, since the closing date of the last report.

Indicate the source of this information.]



**Exhibit B-4**

**Statement of Changes in Shareholders'/Partners' Equity (Deficit) for [Name of Entity]**

period ending [date]

[Provide a statement of changes in shareholders'/partners equity (deficit) for the following periods:

(i) For the initial report:
  a. the period between the end of the preceding fiscal year and the end of the most recent six-month period of the current fiscal year; and
  b. the prior fiscal year.
(ii) For subsequent reports, since the closing date of the last report.

Indicate the source of this information.]

Official Form 26 (12/08) – Cont. 9

## Exhibit C
## Description of Operations for [name of entity]

[Describe the nature and extent of the estate's interest in the entity.

Describe the business conducted and intended to be conducted by the entity, focusing on the entity's dominant business segment(s). Indicate the source of this information.]

(Added Dec. 1, 2008.)

COMMITTEE NOTES ON RULES—2008

This form is new. It implements §419 of the Bankruptcy Abuse Prevention and Consumer Protection Act of 2005, Pub. L. No. 109-8, 119 Stat. 23 (April 20, 2005), which requires a chapter 11 debtor to file periodic reports on the profitability of any entities in which the estate holds a substantial or controlling interest. The form is to be used when required by Bankruptcy Rule 2015.3, with such variations as may be approved by the court pursuant to subdivisions (d) and (e) of that rule. The form includes instructions and examples of the types of information needed to complete it.

**B27 (Official Form27) (12/09)**

# United States Bankruptcy Court
## ______________ District Of ______________

In re ________________________,
Debtor

Case No. ______________
Chapter ____

## REAFFIRMATION AGREEMENT COVER SHEET

This form must be completed in its entirety and filed, with the reaffirmation agreement attached, within the time set under Rule 4008. It may be filed by any party to the reaffirmation agreement.

1. Creditor's Name:______________________________

2. Amount of the debt subject to this reaffirmation agreement:
$_____ on the date of bankruptcy $_____ to be paid under reaffirmation agreement

3. Annual percentage rate of interest: ______% prior to bankruptcy
______% under reaffirmation agreement ( ____ Fixed Rate ____ Adjustable Rate)

4. Repayment terms (if fixed rate): $_______ per month for _______ months

5. Collateral, if any, securing the debt: Current market value: $_________
Description: ______________________________________________

6. Does the creditor assert that the debt is nondischargeable? ___Yes ___ No
(If yes, attach a declaration setting forth the nature of the debt and basis for the contention that the debt is nondischargeable.)

| Debtor's Schedule I and J Entries | | Debtor's Income and Expenses as Stated on Reaffirmation Agreement | |
|---|---|---|---|
| 7A. Total monthly income from Schedule I, line 16 | $_______ | 7B. Monthly income from all sources after payroll deductions | $_______ |
| 8A. Total monthly expenses from Schedule J, line 18 | $_______ | 8B. Monthly expenses | $_______ |
| 9A. Total monthly payments on reaffirmed debts not listed on Schedule J | $_______ | 9B. Total monthly payments on reaffirmed debts not included in monthly expenses | $_______ |
| | | 10B. Net monthly income (Subtract sum of lines 8B and 9B from line 7B. If total is less than zero, put the number in brackets.) | $_______ |

11. Explain with specificity any difference between the income amounts (7A and 7B):

______________________________________________

______________________________________________

12. Explain with specificity any difference between the expense amounts (8A and 8B):

______________________________________________

______________________________________________

If line 11 or12 is completed, the undersigned debtor, and joint debtor if applicable, certifies that any explanation contained on those lines is true and correct.

| | |
|---|---|
| ______________________ | ______________________ |
| Signature of Debtor (only required if line 11 or 12 is completed) | Signature of Joint Debtor (if applicable, and only required if line 11 or 12 is completed) |

Other Information

☐ Check this box if the total on line 10B is less than zero. If that number is less than zero, a presumption of undue hardship arises (unless the creditor is a credit union) and you must explain with specificity the sources of funds available to the Debtor to make the monthly payments on the reaffirmed debt: ______________________________________________

______________________________________________

Was debtor represented by counsel during the course of negotiating this reaffirmation agreement?
_____Yes _______No

If debtor was represented by counsel during the course of negotiating this reaffirmation agreement, has counsel executed a certification (affidavit or declaration) in support of the reaffirmation agreement?
_____Yes _______No

## FILER'S CERTIFICATION

I hereby certify that the attached agreement is a true and correct copy of the reaffirmation agreement between the parties identified on this Reaffirmation Agreement Cover Sheet.

______________________
Signature

______________________
Print/Type Name & Signer's Relation to Case

(Added Dec. 1, 2009.)

COMMITTEE NOTES ON RULES—2009

This form is new. It gathers certain financial information, including information necessary for the court to determine whether a reaffirmation agreement creates a presumption of undue hardship under §524(m) of the Code, and it allows the debtor to provide additional information that may rebut such a presumption.

To implement the requirements of Bankruptcy Rule 4008(b), the form also provides for a disclosure of any differences between the income and expenses reported on schedules I and J and the income and expenses reported in the debtor's statement in support of the reaffirmation agreement, together with an explanation of any such differences.

Finally, the form requires a certification that the information supplied is true and correct.

Made in United States
North Haven, CT
04 November 2026

21774402R00183